D1871104

JOURNAL

OF

TRAVELS IN INDIA

Owing to the antiquity and rarity of this book, certain pages are regrettably absent, and readability is compromised due to the blurring of the original text. If you possess any insights regarding the availability of these missing sections, kindly inform us. Your assistance is crucial in ensuring the completion of this significant work for the benefit of future generations.

JOURNAL
OF
TRAVELS IN INDIA

ARDASEER FRAMJEE MOOS

GYAN

Published by

Gyan Publishing House
5, Ansari Road
Daryaganj, New Delhi-110002
Phone: 011-47034999, 9811692060
E-mail: books@gyanbooks.com

Distribution Network
gyanbooks.com
India, USA, Canada, UK, Australia

© Publisher

All rights reserved. No part of this work may be reproduced, stored, adapted, or transmitted in any form or by any means, electronic, mechanical, photocopying, micro-filming, recording or otherwise, or translated in any language, without the prior written permission of the copyright owner and the publisher.

ISBN: 978-93-7014-340-1 (PB)

First Published, 1871

2nd Impression 2025

Printed at: Gyan Press, Delhi.

The book is sold subject to the condition that it shall not, by way of trade or otherwise, be lent, resold, hired out, or otherwise circulated without the prior publisher's written consent.

JOURNAL OF TRAVELS IN INDIA
Author: ARDASEER FRAMJEE MOOS

H.R.H. THE DUKE OF EDINBURGH.

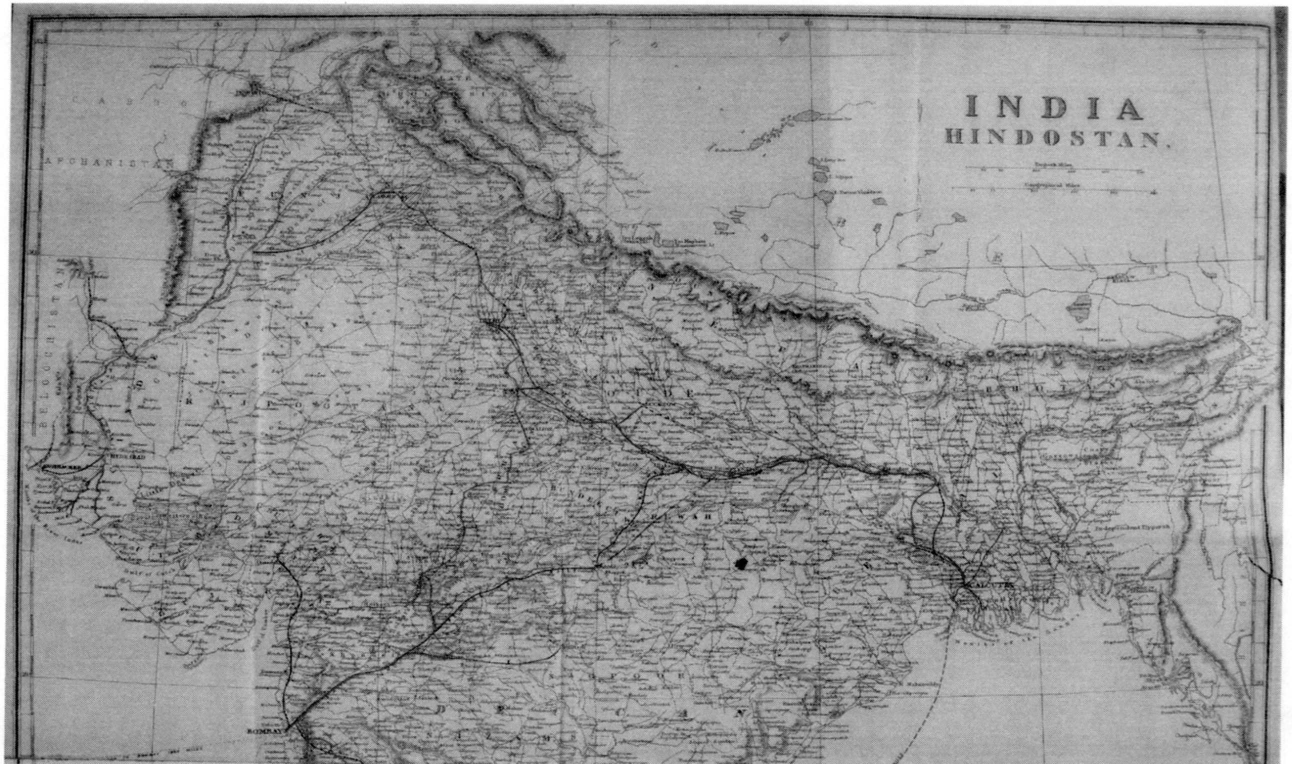
INDIA
HINDOSTAN.
AFGHANISTAN
BELOOCHISTAN
OUDE
BOMBAY

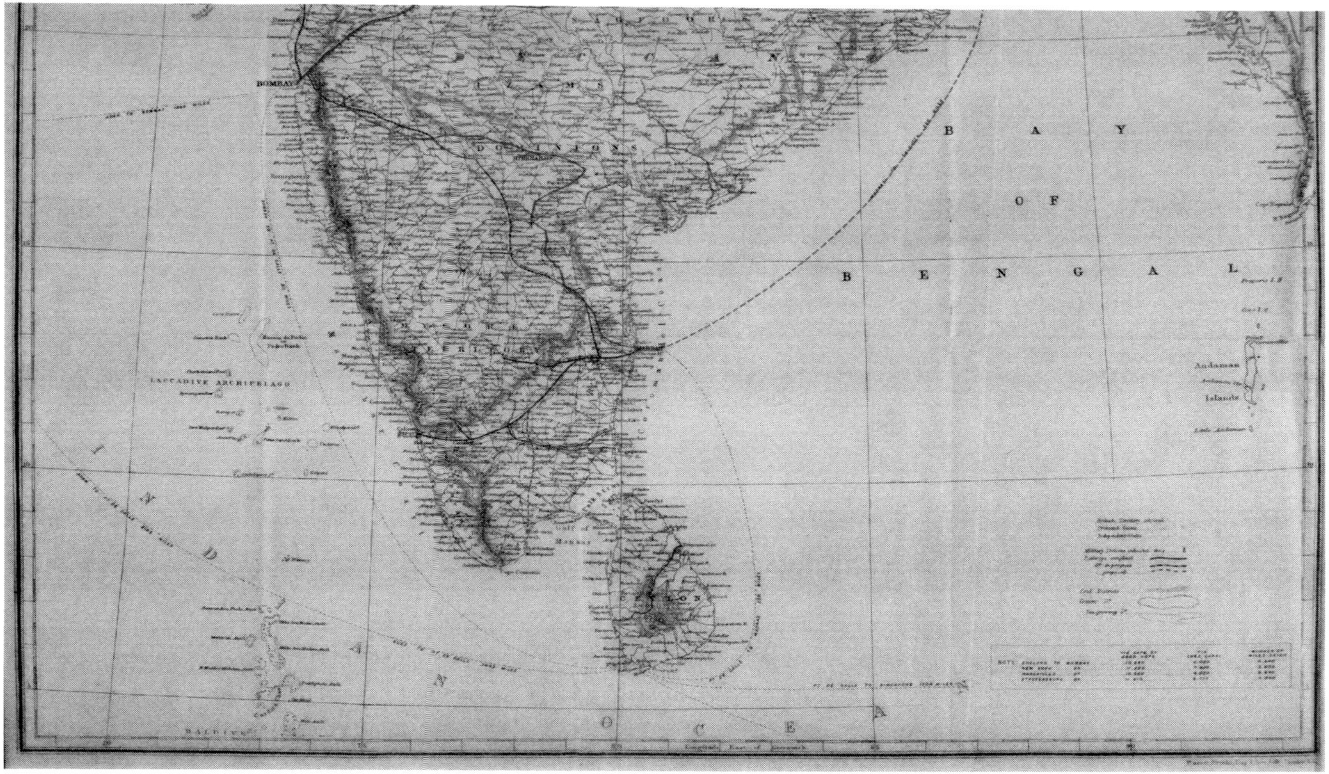
BOMBAY
BAY OF BENGAL
DOMINIONS
LACCADIVE ARCHIPELAGO
Andaman
Islands
INDIAN OCEAN

હિંદુસ્થાનમાં મુસાફરી.

બનાવનાર

અરદેસર ફરામજી મુસ,

વેપારી, રાણીના સુલેહનો અમલદાર, રાએલ એશીયાટીક સોસાઈટીની મુંબઈની
શાખાનો સભાસદ, આગલ એલફીનસ્ટન ઈનસ્ટીટયુશનની સેનત્રલ
સ્કુલના ઉતરતા ભાગનો ઉપરી અને ચઢતા ભાગનો રસાએણ
વીદ્યા અને સૃષ્ટિજ્ઞાન વીદ્યાનો આસીસટંટ પ્રોફેસર.

મુસાફરીના માર્ગનો નકશો તથા જે જે જગા અને મથકો જોવામાં આવીયાં
છે તેમના ફોટોગરાફ ઉપરથી ઇંગલંડમાં ક્રોમો-લીથોગરાફ પડાવી
આ પુસ્તકમાં ઘણા દાખલ કરેલા છે.

પુસ્તક પેહેલું.

મુંબઈ:
એડયુકેશન સોસાઇટીના છાપખાનાએ છાપી પ્રગટ કરીયું છે.

૧૮૭૧.

આએ પુસ્તક બાબદના સરવે હક્કો પોતે રાખેલા છે.

JOURNAL

OF

TRAVELS IN INDIA.

BY

ARDASEER FRAMJEE MOOS,

MERCHANT, JUSTICE OF THE PEACE, MEMBER OF THE BOMBAY BRANCH OF THE ROYAL ASIATIC SOCIETY, FORMERLY SUPERINTENDENT OF THE ELPHINSTONE INSTITUTION CENTRAL SCHOOL, LOWER DEPARTMENT, AND ASSISTANT PROFESSOR OF CHEMISTRY AND NATURAL PHILOSOPHY, UPPER DEPARTMENT, &c.

WITH MAP AND NUMEROUS ILLUSTRATIONS IN CHROMOLITHOGRAPHS,

copied from Photographs, collected by the Author, of places and sites visited by him during his travels in India.

VOLUME I.

Bombay:

PRINTED AND PUBLISHED BY THE

EDUCATION SOCIETY'S PRESS, BYCULLA.

1871.

અલિજાહાં જનાબેઅલી, શાહાજાદા

આલફ્રેડ અરનેસ્ટ આલબર્ટ

એડીનબરોનો અમીર, સાકસનીનો અમીર, કેંટનો અરલ તથા
અલસ્ટરનો અરલ, કોબર્ગ અને ગોથાનો શાહાજાદો,
કે. જી.; કે. ટી.; જી. સી. એમ. જી.;

તથા

ભારી બુલંદ મરતબાનો એકસ્ટ્રા નાઈટ ગ્રાંડ કમાનડર

આફ

ધી સ્ટાર આફ ઈનડીઆ,

પી. સી.; આર. એન.,

જેણે હિંદુસ્થાનની સર જમીનને અને તેની વીસ કરોડ વસ્તીને યાદ કીધી, જે
આપણી મોહોટી નવાજેશ ભરેલી મલીકા માઆઝમા વીકટોરીયા, હિંદુસ્થાનની
માહારાણીની ખલકતની હાલ હાલત પોતે પોતાની નજરે નજર
જોવાને અત્રે આવીયા અને આ ખલકતની વફાદારી અને
રાજસેવા જોઈ ખાત્રી ભરેલાં દીલથી પાછા રવાના થયા.

તેમને

આ પુસ્તક

તેમની મેહેરબાની ભરેલી મુંબઈની મુલાકાતની યાદગારી કાયમ
રાખવાને કૃતજ્ઞતા અને આદરમાન સાથે

પરવાનગીથી

અરપણ કરીયું છે.

અરદેસર ફરામજી મુસ.

મુંબઇ, તા. ૮ જુન ૧૮૭૧.

TO

His Royal Highness

Prince Alfred Ernest Albert,

THE DUKE OF EDINBURGH,

DUKE OF SAXONY, EARL OF KENT AND EARL OF ULSTER,
PRINCE OF COBURG AND GOTHA, K.T., K.G., G.C.M.G.,
EXTRA KNIGHT GRAND COMMANDER OF THE MOST EXALTED ORDER
OF THE STAR OF INDIA, P.C., R.N., &c. &c. &c.,

WHO THOUGHT OF INDIA AND ITS TWO HUNDRED MILLIONS OF INHABITANTS;
WHO CAME AND SAW FOR HIMSELF
THE CONDITION AND CIRCUMSTANCES OF THE SUBJECTS OF THIS VAST EMPIRE OF
HER MOST GRACIOUS MAJESTY QUEEN VICTORIA, EMPRESS OF INDIA,
AND WHO RETURNED CONVINCED OF THEIR LOYALTY AND FIDELITY TO THE QUEEN,

THIS WORK

IS GRATEFULLY AND RESPECTFULLY DEDICATED, BY PERMISSION,
TO PERPETUATE THE MEMORY OF THE GRACIOUS VISIT, OF

His Royal Highness,

BY HIS MOST FAITHFUL AND OBLIGED SERVANT,

ARDASEER FRAMJEE MOOS.

Bombay, 8th June 1871.

b

દીબાચો.

હિંદુસ્થાનમાં મુસાફરીનું પેહેલું પુસ્તક વાંચનારાઓની સેવામાં રજુ કરતી વેળા આ ગ્રંથ વીશે થોડા શબ્દો કહી જણાવાની ગ્રંથકર્તા રજા લીએછે.

ઈ. સ. ૧૮૬૪ ની આખરીમાં આ પુસ્તકનો મોટો ભાગ છપાવી જાહેર પાડવાને તઈયાર કરેલો હતો. પણ આ પુસ્તકમાં આપેલાં ચીત્રો તે વખતે તઈયાર નહી હોવાથી અને મી. વીનસેંટ બ્રુક્સ, ડે ઍંડ સન્સ નામના ઇંગલંડમાંના પ્રખ્યાત છાપનારાઓને આ કામ સોંપેલું હતું તેમને કોઈ તરેની અગતની ખાનગી રોકાણ થઈ પડ્યાથી ૧૮૬૬ ના સાલની સરૂઆત સુધી, તેઓ આ કામ હાતમાં નહી લઈ શક્યા હતા. આ સાલથી જે કઠણ દીવસો મુંબઈ શેહેર ઉપર ગુજરી ગયા છે, તે વખતમાં આ પુસ્તક બાહેર પાડવાને નાદુરૂસ્ત ધારીને, આ કામ થોડા વખત સુધી પડતું નાખીયું હતું, અને આ પુસ્તક જલદીથી બાહેર પડશે આવી કોઈબી તરેની ઉમેદ ગ્રંથકર્તાને મુદલ રેહી નહી હતી.

પણ, ઈ. સ. ૧૮૭૦ માં આપણી બખતાવર માહારાણીના શાહાજાદા આલફ્રેડનું આ દેશમાં ચોકસ આવવું થશે આવી ખબર સાંભળીયાથી, ગ્રંથકર્તાના દીલમાં ઉમેદનું એક કીરણ પાછું ઊતપન્ન થયું. આ પડતું નાખેલું કામ તુરત પાછૂં હાતમાં લીધું અને શાહાજાદા આલફ્રેડના આપણી મુંબઈ શેહેરમાં આવીજવાની એક યાદગારી રાખવાને, આ પુસ્તક તે નાગનારને પરવાનગીથી, અરપણ કરવાનો ઠરાવ કીધો. આ બાબદ વીશે શાહાજાદા ઉપર જે કાગજ લખીયું હતું અને તેનો જે જવાબ આવીયો હતો, તે આ પુસ્તકમાં જાહેર કરીયો છે. શાહાજાદાના જવાબથી, આ પુસ્તક પુરૂં કરવાને એક સારી ઉલટ મળી હતી.

મુસાફરીનો અહેવાલ જે આગળ લખી રાખેલો હતો, તેમાં ૧૮૬૪ થી તે ૧૮૭૦ સુધી જે છ વરશનો અંતર પડ્યો હતો, તેટલા વખતમાં આ પુસ્તકમાં લખાયલી કેટલીક બાબદોમાં ફેરફાર થઈ ગયો હતો, તે સઘળી પાછી તપાસીને ફેરવી હતી, અને બરોબર બોલીએ તો આ પુસ્તક ૧૮૭૦ ના સાલમાં જાણે પાછું નવું લખાયું હોય એવી રીતે તે ફરીને લખીયું છે.

ગ્રંથકર્તાએ, મુસાફરીનો અહેવાલ વાંચનારને એકવારતા મુઆફક પસંદ પડતો થઈ પડે, એવી રીતે લખીયો છે. મુસાફરીમાં જેબી કંઈ જોયું છે, તેનો અહેવાલ અમસથો લુખો અને કોરડો નથી લખીયો, પણ જેબી ચીજો અને બાબદો જોવામાં આવતી ગઈ છે, તે દરેકની ઉપર વીચાર કરીને, તેમનું બયાન વાંચનારનાં મન ઉપર અસર કરે એટલા સારૂ, તેમને, મુંબઈની તેવી ચીજો અને બાબદો સાથે સરખાવી છે, જેથી એવું પરીણામ નીપજવાની ઉમેદ છે કે વાંચનારોને પરદેશની જુદી જુદી હાલત સાથે પોતપોતાની હાલતની સરખામણી કરતાં કોણની હાલત બેહતર છે તે પીછાનવાને સારીપેઠે બની આવશે.

આ પુસ્તકમાંની કેટલીક બાબદનો ઇંગ્રેજી તરજુમો આપીયો છે તેનું કારણ એટલુંજ કે, જે શાહાજાદાને આ પુસ્તક અરપણ કરીયું છે, તે નામવરને તથા ઇંગ્રેજી વાંચનારાઓને જાણવાને બની આવે કે આ પુસ્તકમાં શું શું બાબદો આવી છે અને તે વીશે દેશી ભાશાની લઢણે કેવું લખાણ થયું છે.

આ પેહેલું પુસ્તક નજદીક ૪૦૦) સફા ઉપરનું થઇ ગયાથી, મુસાફરીનો બીજો વધારે અગતનો અને રસીલો ભાગ, આમાં સમાઈ શકાયો નથી તેથી ગ્રંથકર્તા બચીત દીલગીર છે. તેની સાથે આ બીજો ભાગ છાપી જાહેર પાડવાને ખરચની બાબદમાં ગ્રંથકર્તાની હીમત ચાલી નથી આ વાત છુપાવાની જરૂર નથી, પણ જો આ પેહેલાં પુસ્તકને સરકાર તરફથી તથા લોક તરફથી પુરતો આશરો મળીયો તો બીજું પુસ્તક થોડા વખતમાં તઇયાર થઈ બાહેર પાડી શકાશે.

છેલું ગ્રંથકર્તા સઘળી નમંતાઇથી ઉમેદ રાખેછે કે આ પુસ્તક જે નામવર શાહાજાદાને અરપણ કરીયું છે તેમને તથા સઘળાં વાંચનારાઓને પસંદ પડતું થશે અને તેમના બોહોળા આશરાને લાયકનું માલુમ પડશે.

અરદેસર ફરામજી મુસ.

મુંબઈ, તારીખ ૮ જુન ૧૮૭૧.

PREFACE.

In submitting the First Volume of "Travels in India" to the public, the Author wishes to make a few remarks in reference to the work.

A great portion of the Journal was ready for publication at the end of the year 1864. But the plates intended to illustrate the work, which were entrusted to Messrs. Vincent Brooks Day and Sons, photographers and printers in England, were then not ready, and, as the attention of these distinguished printers had then been very much occupied in some important private affairs of their own, they were not able to take the work in hand until the beginning of 1866. That year brought on Bombay such a fearful monetary crash that it was not considered advisable to bring out the work at such an unsuitable time. The Author, considering the prospects so unfavourable, set aside the publication of the work, as hopeless for some time.

In the year 1870, however, authentic news arrived in Bombay that one of the sons of our most beloved and gracious Queen, His Royal Highness Prince Alfred, was graciously allowed by Her Majesty to pay a visit to this country (India), and in this tour, His Royal Highness having condescended to come to Bombay, a ray of hope once more glimmered in the heart of the author. The work was at once resumed, and it was resolved to dedicate it, with permission, to His Royal Highness. A letter addressed to, and the reply received from, His Royal Highness on the subject of dedication, are herewith published. The favourable reply of His Royal Highness gave an additional stimulus to the early completion of the work.

The portion of the Journal which was ready for publication at the end of the year 1864 had to be revised, as an interval of nearly six years had elapsed, during which period many facts and circumstances narrated in the Journal had materially changed. In the revision, therefore, in the year 1870, the whole work, properly speaking, was re-written from the commencement.

The Journal has been written as a narrative. Descriptions of various places, events, objects, and habits of the people, which presented themselves in the tour, are related not merely in a dry manner, but have been maturely pondered over; and, with a view to make them interesting and impressive, comparisons are made between them and similar events, objects, and habits of the people of Bombay, in order that the readers may be able to know their respective positions by these comparisons, and decide on which side the elements of excellence preponderate.

It is needless to mention that the translation into English of some of the chief passages in the work, given herewith, is with the object of acquainting His Royal Highness the Duke, as well as the English-reading community, with the nature of the contents of the work, and the manner in which it has been written. The translation, though not very close, is nevertheless as faithful a version of the original as the idiom of the language permits, without aiming either at elegance of style or conforming it to the English mode of thinking.

The author sincerely regrets he is not able to insert the more interesting portion of the Travels in the first volume, as it already contains upwards of 400 pages. At the same time, he does not conceal his own pecuniary inability to publish the second volume together with this. But he hopes to do so early should the first receive liberal support from Government and the public.

In conclusion, the author humbly trusts that his efforts will meet the approbation of His Royal Highness the Duke and of the public, and prove worthy of their liberal support.

ARDASEER FRAMJEE MOOS.

Bombay, 8th June 1871.

To

His Royal Highness

PRINCE ALFRED ERNEST ALBERT,

The Duke of Edinburgh, Duke of Saxony, Earl of Kent and Earl of Ulster, Prince of Coburg and Gotha, K.G., K.T., G.C.M.G., G.C.S.I., P. C., R.N.

May it please your Royal Highness,

It is with deepest feelings of loyalty and respect towards our good and gracious Queen, your Royal Mother, as well as towards yourself, on the occasion of your visit to India, that I venture to approach to express my sense of respect I owe to your Royal Highness.

To show how Natives of this country appreciate your coming, I, as a member of the Native Community of this place, with the object of keeping amongst us a lasting remembrance of your gracious visit, humbly and respectfully beg that you would be pleased to confer on me the honour to permit me to dedicate my work entitled "Travels in India" to your Royal Highness.

I have written this work in the Gujarati language especially for the Natives of this country, its Princes, Chiefs, and others, with the object of creating among them a desire to travel abroad and improve their experience, holding before them the excellent example set by your Royal Highness and all your Royal Family.

The book will be illustrated by numerous chromolithographs, now being printed in England, copied from photographs of various places, sites, and buildings visited by the Author during his travels in India, and it is presumed that almost all these places may very probably have been visited by your Royal Highness.

A small collection of these lithographs is bound up in an Album which I beg most respectfully to submit for inspection and approval, and which, if agreeable to your Royal Highness, I would further beg you would do me the honour to accept as an humble tribute of loyalty and esteem from the Author.

I sincerely hope your Royal Highness will pardon the liberty I have taken in intruding thus upon your valuable time.

I have the honour to be,

You Royal Highness's most obedient Servant,

ARDASEER FRAMJEE MOOS,

Justice of the Peace.

Bombay, 15th March 1870.

PARELL, BOMBAY,

18*th March* 1870.

SIR,—I am directed by the Duke of Edinburgh to acknowledge the receipt of your letter of the 15th March, and also to inform you that His Royal Highness willingly consents to the request you have made, to be permitted to dedicate your work "Travels in India" to him.

His Royal Highness desires me further to thank you for the collection of lithographs that you have presented to him, and wishes me to say that he sincerely hopes that your book, which they are intended to illustrate, may realise the excellent object for which you have written it.

I have the honour to be,

Sir,

Your obedient Servant,

(Signed) ARTHUR P. HAIG,

Equerry in Waiting.

ARDASEER FRAMJEE MOOS, ESQ., J.P.

Forwarded by S. V. FITZGERALD,

Private Secretary, H. E. the Governor.

સાંકળિયું.

પાનું.

પાનું.

પાનું.

પાનું.

પાનું.

ચિત્રોનું સાંકળિયું.

પુસ્તક પેહેલું.

પુસ્તક બીજું.

CONTENTS.

f

PAGE

MADRAS.

LIST OF ILLUSTRATIONS.

Vol. I.

Vol. II.

TRAVELS IN INDIA

(WRITTEN IN GUJARATI).

ENGLISH TRANSLATION OF SOME OF THE CHIEF PASSAGES.

The Importance of Travelling—how it should be performed.

It is needless to show how travelling conduces to human improvement, and awakens a spirit of rational curiosity. As it is necessary for parents to send their children to school for their education, so is it incumbent on such as can afford it to send them to travel abroad before commencing life, that they may by that means gain in knowledge, and improve their powers of observation. The stock of knowledge acquired by travelling in the vast school of the world would be tenfold greater than that acquired from school education, and, coupled with the experience so obtained, would not fail to be valuable in after-life. The condition of the countries where this practice obtains is decidedly superior to that of others whose inhabitants confine themselves within their own borders. Our wealthy countrymen would therefore greatly benefit themselves, as well as their country, if they were to confer on their children the sort of education above indicated. They have an example set them by Her Most Gracious Majesty the Queen in the interests of her own children. The programme of the Princes' intended travels was drawn up by the late lamented Prince Consort himself previous to his decease, and it would have been carried out in its entirety had the life of that great and good man been spared; but Providence ruled otherwise. The Princes have, however, to a greater or less extent, effected the object intended, by making a tour over the more important parts of the globe, having thereby obtained vast experience, the good fruits of which we hope to enjoy hereafter. It is similarly imperative on the Princes and Chiefs of this country, as also their heirs and ministers, to follow this example; and it may be added here that our late Governor

Sir Bartle Frere never lost an opportunity to recommend to the Sirdars of the Deccan the adoption of so advantageous a course.

One of the Royal Princes of England, His Highness the Duke of Edinburgh, has travelled through many countries in the East. In his first cruise he visited Australia and the Cape. In his second voyage he reached China, proceeding as far as its capital, Pekin, whence he proceeded to Japan, Hongkong, and eventually landed on our shores, where he pushed his travels as far as Peshawur, the furthest north-western limit of the British possessions in India.

The recollection of Prince Alfred's visit to this city will be long cherished by its inhabitants. His reception was in every respect worthy of his exalted rank. Indeed, it may be safely affirmed that few cities could have accorded him a reception so cordial and honourable as that which he met with from the citizens of Bombay. Above all, His Royal Highness must have been particularly struck with the honours done him by the Parsee Ladies, in token of their loyalty and attachment to their beloved Sovereign the Queen. When his Royal Mother comes to know of this, it will no doubt speak much for them. We cannot help remarking, however, that, in their anxiety to outdo each other in such matters, the members of this community not unfrequently overstep the legitimate bounds of moderation and prudence, not only losing in that way the merit which would otherwise attach itself to their acts, but rendering them even liable to censure. Some such instances of indiscretion occurred on the occasion of the Duke's visit here, but, as they proceeded from misguided enthusiasm and simplicity of heart, it would be ungraceful to make any further allusion to them.

From the highly honourable character of the reception with which His Royal Highness was greeted everywhere in India, he could not but have been favourably impressed with the loyalty of the natives to the Throne. In the splendid welcome given to His Royal Highness by the munificent liberality of our Native Princes, Chiefs, and Gentry, the hosts were primarily actuated by a desire to evince their loyalty to his noble Mother. The Prince has himself given public utterance to his conviction of the evidences of loyalty and contentment on the part of the entire Native population, adding that, as education and enlightenment progressed among the people, they would become more and more contented, loyal, and obedient subjects. These words, few as they are, are pregnant with many salutary lessons.

There can be no other testimony so weighty in the estimation of the Queen, her Ministers, the Parliament—nay, of the whole British nation—to the loyalty and attachment which the people of India entertain towards their beloved Sovereign, as that which will be borne directly before herself by the lips of her own son, on his return home, in giving an account of his receptions. It cannot but strengthen the ties of amity and goodwill between the governors and the governed, and eventually lead to the establishment of a happy mutual relation, an event the consummation of which we shall anxiously await.

The author would here beg leave to state, for the information of his readers, that, availing himself of the Duke's visit to Bombay, he was induced to solicit His Royal Highness's permission to dedicate to him this account of his travels, with the object of commemorating the auspicious event among the reading public, more especially in view of its object being identical with that involved in the Duke's own undertaking. In doing so, the author begged leave to intimate to the Prince that his principal aim in preparing the work was to induce a desire for travelling among the Native Princes, Noblemen, Chiefs, and all other persons in independent circumstances, in which direction His Royal Highness had himself set a noble example before the world. The Prince was graciously pleased to grant the request, as also to accept, in a very kind manner, the collection of pictorial illustrations given in this work, which the author respectfully tendered to him, and moreover expressed his desire for the complete fulfilment of the object which the author proposed to himself in getting up his work. The author considers it his duty thus publicly to mark his sense of gratitude towards the Prince for the honour bestowed on him in acceding to his wishes.

While on this subject, the author deems it desirable to correct an utterly erroneous impression prevailing among some of his countrymen in respect to the conduct of Government towards Native Princes. He refers to the practice of the different Political Officers accompanying their respective Princes and Chiefs whenever they are invited to come and take a part in important political gatherings from time to time. This practice leads some to believe that it is introduced in order to watch and hamper the independent movements of the Rajas. Now the conversation which the author had with a high Political Officer of Government disclosed, on this point, the existence of the most benevolent intentions on the part of Government towards the Rajas. Far from the arrangement in question having had its rise in the object above referred to, it had been expressly made for the sole convenience and benefit of the Rajas themselves. The presence of the Political Officers is ordered specially with the view of precluding the possibility of any inconvenience occurring to the Princes in case they have to carry on correspondence with Government or others, and generally to look after their wants and desires, so as to make their stay in a strange land as comfortable as possible. Now these objects could not be gained in the absence of the above Officers. Those who perceive in this arrangement an intention on the part of Government to control and hamper the free movements of our Princes, Chiefs, &c., are therefore utterly mistaken in their view, which is simply groundless. Equally mistaken is the belief, again, which imputes to Government a disposition to thwart the desire of our Native Princes to travel abroad. It being the ardent wish of our rulers that our Princes, Chiefs, Sirdars, &c., should study the laws, manners, and institutions of different countries, and strive to remodel those of their own territories as may be suggested by the result of their comparison, such of them as may evince a desire for travel, whether in this country, in Europe or America, and for increasing their stock of knowledge and experience, will doubtless find it rather encouraged than thwarted. It is in order to give effect to this wish, indeed, though to a limited extent, and to bring them in contact with each other in happy ties of mutual friendship, that the Princes, Chiefs, &c., are invited on all important occasions to assemble at the Capital towns of the respective Presidencies.

Travelling should, as far as practicable, be performed in the company of men possessing experience, and habits of observation, as well as influence, inasmuch as the advantages derived therefrom are far greater than those of a solitary journey. By travelling with persons of this description, one is enabled to observe and make himself acquainted with a great many natural objects and phenomena, which he is not able to do to the same extent otherwise; for though a single man may overlook certain occurrences, yet they are not likely to escape the collective observation of many. Men of influence are also similarly very useful. Their presence contributes in a marked degree towards lessening the ordinary inconveniencies of travelling, particularly in a country like India, where, despite the construction of railways in several places one feels very keenly the want of many comforts and conveniences which are readily found in Europe on account of the facilities resulting from a complete network of locomotive communications. It is possible the lonely traveller may meet with undreamt-of difficulties and trials, which may oblige him to abandon his undertaking, and even place his life in jeopardy. The writer need hardly say, however, that his object in saying what he does is not to damp the traveller's heart; on the contrary, he states it as a matter of gratification and encouragement to his readers that the difficulties of Indian travelling are being perceptibly mitigated by the rapid extension of the line throughout the country. It is intended merely as a counsel not to venture, if it can be helped, on a lonely tour, but in the company of intelligent and influential men, with letters of introduction and other indispensable requisites. The accuracy of this view will be evident from the fact that though our party consisted of fourteen men, had furnished themselves with commendatory letters, and had free use of money at all times, we did not escape being occasionally subjected to serious inconveniences.

The journey had its origin in the desire of some gentlemen to make themselves acquainted by personal observation with the conditions and climates of the various cities and towns of India, as well as the ruins of their ancient architecture, and then to present the public with a brief account of their observations. The credit of initiating this undertaking is chiefly due to Mr. Cursetjee Nusserwanjee Cama. This worthy gentleman is always a warm encourager of all good works, and would strive to the last to bring his undertaking to a successful completion. He is, moreover, quite free from entertaining narrow ideas of his position, so much so that he would not think it beneath him even to carry a burden on his shoulders if it were necessary to do so by stress of circumstances. Finding, moreover, an accomplished scholar like Dr. Bhau Daji, and Mr. K. R. Cama, who had had experience of European travel, intending to accompany Mr. Cursetjee, the writer of this work was also induced to join the party. Mr. Mancherjee Merwanjee Naliarwalla had of his own accord undertaken the difficult and harassing duty of making all arrangements, and, being well experienced in worldly matters, and gifted with a genial and merry disposition, he proved himself a very useful and agreeable companion in our tour. Mr. Rustomjee Fakeerjee was engaged as an assistant to Mr. Mancherjee, but the poor fellow, having never moved beyond the suburbs, was, as will be seen further on, so far done up by working in the midst of the difficulties of his novel position, that, instead of being able to render assistance to others, he himself became, in a very amusing manner, an object thereof. Dr. Bhau Daji had also taken with him Mr. Edward Rehatsek, well known in Bombay for his linguistic attainments, for the purpose of making drawings of natural views, and generally to aid him in taking notes of passing occurrences.

Our original plan of travel was to go first to Kurrachee, thence to Mooltan, Lahore, and on to Cashmere; from Cashmere to Calcutta, visiting Delhi, Agra, Lucknow, Cawnpore, Allahabad, Benares, and other important cities; from Calcutta to Madras by steamer, visiting the different towns and cities of that presidency; and from Beypore to return to Bombay by steamer. We were, however, obliged to abandon this idea, having learnt from inquiries that there were many difficulties in the way, besides the fact that we had not sufficient time at our command for completing this tour. We next thought of going to Sholapore from Bombay, proceeding to the Nizam's Hydrabad, thence to Madras by any route that might be found suitable; then to Calcutta by steamer; and from Calcutta to Allahabad, Lucknow, Agra, and Delhi, and even up to Cashmere, should time permit, and eventually returning to Bombay through Lahore, Mooltan, Sind Hydrabad, and Kurrachee. But, as "Man proposes but God disposes," we were deterred from fully carrying out this resolution, in consequence of the occurrence of unforeseen difficulties on this route also. The weather became so hot and unbearable that we thought it prudent not to push our journey further up, and so retraced our steps. In returning we visited Gwalior and Indore, the chief cities of their Highnesses the Holkar and Sindhia respectively, descending thence *viá* Mhow, over the Sindhwa Ghaut, to Jalgam, whence we ultimately reached Bombay by rail.

The red circle marked in the annexed map shows the course and extent of our journey, which has been computed to extend to many hundreds of miles.

*Dawn at Manthal.**

Having got up at daybreak and washed and dressed, we fixed our attention on the aspect of the early morning until the breakfast was ready. Ah! what a serene and charming sight it was to behold! We have made an attempt in this place to depict the morning in words, in order to give our readers a faint idea of it, but we do not know how far we have succeeded in our efforts—we rely on their indulgence for its imperfections.

The angel Hoshen† had just completed her watch, and Hoshbami had begun to rule; the darkness of the night had now given place to the light of the dawn; the stars had merged under the rising light of the sun; man could discern the visage of man; "Rág Bhairao," the god of music of the dawn, had risen betimes and was chanting his melodious and melting song, "Arise, gentle sleepers!" Bewitched by his captivating tune, the sparrows, larks, peacocks, and cuckoos had commenced their morning strains; the nightingales, maddened by love, were engaged in kissing and re-kissing the blooming flowers and putting to them a host of questions; the beloved rose was being overwhelmed with a repetition of a very pert and puzzling question from them all—"O Rose, why (with all thy charming beauty) art thou surrounded with thorns concealed in

* A village with a travellers' bangalo about 72 miles from Sholapoor, on the way to Secundrabad.

† According to the Parsee religious belief, a day of twenty-four hours is divided into five parts, and an angel is appointed to rule over each part.

thy garments!" the busy bees, the merry-going butterflies and wasps, were enjoying happily their innocent pleasure in buzzing and wheeling round from one blooming blossom to another without stop or restraint. Among the merriment of all these creatures, creation's lord was also present to enjoy the pure pleasure of the morning dawn! His pleasure, however, was of a higher order! Diverting his thoughts from this transient world and its frail hopes, he was absorbed in the contemplation of his Creator. From his lips issued forth praise and supplication to Him, Who is the Life-giver to us all; in a slow and low voice he gave utterance to the following solemn words: "O great God! O Lord! O Protector! O Preserver! O merciful God!" Even in the wild solitude of Manthal we heard at this calm hour some such expressions from the lips of an aged devotee sitting in a lonely temple not far from our halting-place. All nature appeared to present an aspect of freshness, beauty and such spiritual and solemn pleasure, that we greatly wished it were possible to be absorbed into it! The mist was beginning gradually to disappear and recede from the hills, mountains, and from above the open plains; shining, pearl-like drops of dew were dripping from the leaves of trees; the buds and blossoms, unfolding, were spreading their fragrance all over the wilderness. Here and there clusters of flowers drooped their heads as if they longed to be plucked by man, that he might enjoy their fragrance, or adorn his head, or offer them as an oblation to some deity. We were fascinated by a scene that inspired in us thoughts of such pure and unmixed delight! It is difficult indeed to give anything like an adequate description of this glorious dawn; and as for the gratification resulting from thus holding communion with the Creator we have simply no words to express it. Indeed, how is it possible for the pen of impotent man to depict a divine happiness? We can only *feel* it inwardly, and he alone can appreciate its holiness and sublimity who has *felt* it! O man! thou hast only to leave aside for a moment all ideas of sublunary felicity to be able to realize to thyself the true and secret happiness of morning contemplation!

Soon our attention was again occupied by worldly affairs. We heard the voice of one of our party making inquiries, who turned out to be our erudite friend Dr. Bhau Daji. He had made it a point to institute inquiries at every halting-place respecting matters of antiquity connected with the Hindu religion, its temples, its idols, old inscriptions, coins, &c., with untiring industry and unflagging zeal. He was as diligent and regular in his inquiries regarding mental pabulum, therewith to feed his inquisitive mind, as our friend Mr. Mancherjee was at every resting-place regarding milk, butter, vegetables, and other articles of food, to satisfy the cravings of our animal appetite. The Doctor was accustomed to look upon every subject he met with that had reference to the antiquities of this country in the light of nutritious food. Our friend's carriage was sure to stop short on the road, even at midnight, if he received information of the existence of an old temple in the neighbourhood, when he would proceed to the spot and make his observations with the aid of torches. If, however, the object was found worthy of closer observation, he would pass the night there, and renew his inspection more carefully in the morning. Such was the intensity of ardour we remarked in our antiquarian friend.

The ignorance of Ryots respecting some of their rights under the British Government.

Feeling hungry on our way back to the village of Manthal, whence we had gone to look at the ruins of some old temples, we desired the cultivators working in the sugar-cane fields by the wayside to let us have some pieces of sugar-cane, which they refused, because many *Sáheb-lok*, on feeling hungry or thirsty on the road in the Moffussil, do not scruple to lay hold of anything they come across, without paying for it, as if they had a vested right so to do; and such is the impression under which many a poor ignorant cultivator labours even at the present day. Had we represented ourselves as such *Sáheb-lok*, or taken the sugar-cane by force, we too could have easily got it, though by no better right than that possessed by the man in the moon! Such unlawful exactions, however, being far from our intentions, we set the cultivators right on this point, and explained to them that no one had a right to take anything from anybody forcibly and without payment under the British *raj*. We paid for the sugar-cane, and they appeared to consider themselves very lucky that day.

An account of a Masjid at Kallianee :—gross ignorance of the natives respecting Government toleration of religious beliefs.*

On entering the masjid we noticed a marble tablet fixed on the gate, and inscribed in Persian characters, bearing date of the year 1028 of the Hijiri era, corresponding to the year 1619 of the Christian era, as that of its construction. The open space in front of the masjid is adorned with pretty gardens well laid out, promenades, tanks and fountains encircled by beautiful seats of marble. The domes are likewise of elegant construction, and under them is the place of worship.

Opposite to it is another magnificent edifice containing the tomb of Nawab Imtiaj Dowlah, with those of his son and daughter-in-law on each side of it. These three tombs are constructed of marble, and are of exquisite workmanship, and at them the Mohamadan residents offer flowers every Friday. Throughout the building the walls are so well polished that they appear as if they were made of marble and only finished yesterday. The pavement of the masjid is also entirely of marble, and serves to evince the well-known bigotry of the Mohamadans: the images of Hindu gods, as well as slabs bearing religious inscriptions, have been removed from temples and used for pavement, so that the Mohamadan may for ever trample them under foot in walking over the pavement. We saw two tablets of this kind placed among the steps leading to the tombs. Tracings from them were taken on cloth by Dr. Bhau, who, though he could not then decipher the inscription, believed it to be in Hala Kanari characters. While the Doctor was so engaged, we employed ourselves in conversing on various matters, with the so-called "fakeers" who had assembled there, in the course of which we had the opportunity of correcting some errors and misunderstandings into which they had fallen regarding the policy of the British Government in religious matters. They seemed strongly impressed with the belief that their rulers were now intent on making the people of this country converts to Christianity by all means in their power. Upon this we explained

* An ancient town west of Bedar, and on the borders of Karnáta and Maháráshtrá, now in possession of the Nizam, and formerly a capital of some of the Rájput kings of the Chalukya dynasty.

to them that there was no other government on earth which treated alien religions with so much consideration, and granted such entire toleration to the professors of each and all of them in their various practices in accordance with the dictates of their individual faith. When the British people had undergone so much persecution and made so many sacrifices for the express purpose of obtaining absolute religious freedom, and, through the Divine favour, had had their efforts finally crowned with success, could it be believed that the same people would use persecution against their own subjects? The Christian missionaries who are engaged in the work of proselytizing natives are entirely unconnected with Government. They come to this country of their own accord to expound and propagate their religion, without either encouragement or prohibition from the Government. In the same manner, there is no prohibition on the part of the latter to teachers of any Native religion preaching to Englishmen in their own country, or even to an Englishman joining it, if he were so disposed.

Hereupon one of them declared, in a vehement tone, "our information on this point is directly at variance with your story, for we have proofs to say that several clergymen are in the immediate service of Government." We at once perceived that they alluded to the clergymen attached to English regiments, and, thinking it necessary not to let this misapprehension pass uncorrected, we explained to them how the case really was. We pointed out that the only clergymen receiving pay from Government were those employed in the army for instructing the English officers and soldiers in matters connected with their religion, and for performing nuptial and funeral ceremonies among them; that they had nothing to do with anybody else; that the Native soldiers were as much at liberty to follow the dictates of their religion as the English soldiers; that the clergymen attached to English regiments had no official authority to instruct a Native soldier in the Christian religion, and that if they nevertheless did so they would be tried in a court of law, and, if convicted, dismissed from the service, or otherwise punished. All these stringent provisions are made by the English Government in order to protect their Native subjects in the free exercise of their various religions. The fact is, certain designing and riotous men, finding themselves unable otherwise to carry on their nefarious practices, resort to inciting the bigotry of fanatical and short-sighted persons by reviling the Government in every possible way their mendacious propensities can invent, and, driving them into rebellion, attempt to make the best they can of the favourable opportunity thus created to carry out their objects. The sensible portion of the people have by this time clearly seen through this dodge. It was the incendiarism of these unscrupulous malcontents which inflicted such terrible calamities on Delhi, and brought about its sack. It resulted in extinguishing the very name of its ruler, Bahadarsha, and of his dynasty; he became a prisoner of the British Government, was transported, and died a convict and in exile! Instead of remaining steadfast in his loyalty and allegiance, he became ungrateful, in consequence of the instigation of the base and faithless men around him, who turned his head, to his own cost. He certainly acted very improperly in attempting to measure swords with the English. Justice, however, ultimately prevailed, as it always does, and the English triumphed. It subsequently became apparent that the Mutiny was purely the doing of rebellious people, who drove the simple and credulous to the front by using all kinds of misrepresentations and deceptions, ostensibly in the name of religion, but really to gain their own private ends. These evil-doers, however, did not escape the stroke of Divine retribution. Some of them expiated their crimes on the gallows, others paid the penalty from the muzzles of guns, and some put an end to their lives by their own hands.

This rebellion has had the effect of sweeping away the names of some of the most illustrious families, of which not a vestige is now to be seen, any more than if they never had existed on the face of the earth! This explanation of ours produced, we observed, the desired effect on the minds of the fakeers, for on their having satisfied themselves as to the fact of our being independent Parsee gentlemen, pursuing travel on our own account, and quite unconnected with Government, they began to remark among themselves that under the circumstances, our statement could not but be regarded as true and disinterested, and admitted that, instead of reconquering Hindustan, the mutineers only perpetrated shocking atrocities, and, having eventually been worsted in fight, were blown away from guns.

They now thought differently of us from what they did on our first arrival, and began accordingly to treat us with courtesy. They even put themselves to some trouble on our account, and fetched water for us to wash our faces and hands with. Lastly, they became so obliging as to say that they would not object to our proceeding so far into the masjid with shoes on, if we liked. This, however, we declined to do, from motives of self-respect, saying that if they were forbidden to let people go into the masjid with their shoes on, we did not think it right to do so, notwithstanding their permission.

We then took leave of the masjid and returned to the bustle of Kallianee. The chief portion of the population appeared to consist of Lingayats and Mohamadans. We should not, by the way, omit to mention that our friends the usurious Marwadis were not absent from this place. These fleecing money-lenders are to be seen everywhere, for we do not remember having visited a single village in which there was not at least one Marwadi shop. In nooks and corners, and even in deserted villages, this grasping, greedy, usurer is sure to be seen, sitting up, like a poverty-stricken man, in his wretched shop.

Nawab Sir Salar Jung, Prime Minister of the Nizam.

We know of few Native Ministers who have maintained such cordial friendship with the British Government, as well as the British people, as Sir Salar Jung, the great nobleman and politician of the Deccan. Nor have the British Government been behindhand in reciprocating it, by holding him in high and sincere esteem. This happy relation has been the means of reflecting great honour on both sides, and of calling forth mutual assistance. Our countrymen may well be proud of the career of a Minister of the stamp of Sir Salar Jung.

An interview with the Nawab.

In company with Mr. Bapoojee Viccajee we drove to the Nawab's palace. As soon as we reached it, a crowd of spectators assembled to see us, and forthwith began to indulge in all sorts of conjectures respecting us. The idle Mohamadan spectators need no instruction in the art of conjecturing; their mind is prone to conjure up the wildest story, and to form opinions as may suit their whims and fancy. Hence some of them made us out to be members of Sir Jamsetjee Jejeebhoy Baronet's family, saying "*Mumbai ke Bátliwále ke amirzáde hae.*" It is not only in Hydrabad, but in many other parts of India, the name of this honoured and illustrious Parsee *Hatim* is widely known, and the extent of his fame reflects proportionally high honour on the Parsee community. Hence the natives in the interior, on seeing any wealthy Parsee among them, readily connect him with Sir Jamsetjee's family. Thus were the crowd busy in guessing who we were: some concluded we were *amirzade* of Sir Jamsetjee's family, others took us for the most wealthy bankers of Bombay, and some assigned to us corresponding high Indian titles of "Bánke Mirza," and many others too numerous to mention.

After seeing the palace, we proceeded to pay a visit to the Nawab. In doing this, we had to conform to the custom observed by all visitors of wearing small turbans and removing our shoes. In accordance with this form the Nawab himself entered the drawing-room barefooted, and, bidding us a courteous welcome, at once took his seat on a carpet spread on the ground—an act of condescension which we had not the remotest expectation of witnessing. Having taken his seat, he bade us take ours. Seeing it would be unbecoming in us to sit on chairs and sofas when the Nawab himself so humbly seated himself on the floor, we sat down cross-legged on the carpet opposite to him, after the fashion of our Iranian ancestors. A conversation then ensued on various subjects, with which His Excellency showed very creditable acquaintance. He expressed a highly favourable opinion of the power and merits of the British Government. He also thoroughly understood the benefits of education, but regretted his not being able to do much towards its diffusion in his country, owing to the prejudices and bigotry of his people. Notwithstanding these obstacles, he has not failed to direct his attention, by degrees, to all that admitted of being accomplished in that way.

After some desultory conversation, the Nawab desired to know our object in setting out to travel. We replied that it was to make ourselves acquainted, as far as practicable, by personal observation, with our native country and the condition of its inhabitants, and afterwards to communicate the result to our countrymen by means either of oral lectures or publications. He was much pleased with this, and said that great credit was due to us for our undertaking, at our own expense, a self-imposed journey necessarily involving much hardship and inconvenience, for the good of our fellow-men. But while thus approving the idea, he cautioned us to be careful not to fall into error in one important respect:—no traveller, he observed, could expect to acquire full and accurate knowledge of the condition of any people in the space of three or four days; that to effect his object it was necessary he should live among the people and carry on actual intercourse with them for a length of time; and then only would he be in a position to obtain trustworthy information. He then referred to Hydrabad, and declared that the opinion which we might have formed concerning that city and its inhabitants, from a flying visit extending over only two or three days, must necessarily be imperfect; and that it was therefore but right that, if it was our intention to publish an account of our travels, we should prolong our stay and make minute inquiries. Hereupon we informed His Excellency that it was not our intention to enter into minute details in the treatment of our subject—the work being intended merely to record a description of the various routes and places through which we passed, of their climate, and of the manners and customs of the inhabitants, with such account only of their condition as would be warranted by personal observation and by the trustworthiness of our informants. We further told the Nawab to rest assured that in speaking of his country and his subjects we would on no account give publicity to any statement which on inquiry would not be found to be true and reliable:—we could never bring ourselves to write anything which had no foundation in truth: if we had not sufficient time and leisure to observe any particular place or the state of its people, we would consider it more honourable to omit all mention of it, rather than write anything from imagination, or mislead people.

This reply was deemed satisfactory, and we held further conversation on other matters, until we perceived that the time of our taking leave had arrived, when each of us, in accordance with the custom of the Durbar—of which custom we had beforehand been informed, held five rupees on the fold of a white handkerchief laid on the palm of the right hand, and offered them to the Nawab as a small token of our respect. With a smiling face, he immediately took them from the hand of each with peculiar smartness, and laid them beside himself. So much good grace and courtesy were shown in the act of receiving these presents, that though he was only receiving his due by the custom of his court, yet we felt *pleasure* in tendering the "nazzar," and as if he were rather laying us under an obligation to himself by its acceptance. In short, his treatment of visitors is characterized by such a rare union of good sense, tact, and urbanity, that, notwithstanding their having rigidly to observe all the etiquette of his court, they depart well pleased with their visit. We do not know indeed what under the sun may not be done by the observance of a respectful and courteous deportment! On a nod from the Nawab, an officer came and removed the rupees, supplying their place with attar of roses, nosegays, and pan-supari. His Excellency then presented each of us with a gilt phial of attar of roses, rosewater, and a nosegay, with his own hands, and with the same smiling countenance and courtesy as he had shown in accepting our small presents.

This ceremony being over, we took our leave at about 6 P.M., the visit having lasted altogether an hour.

When parting, however, the Nawab informed us of a marriage in a nobleman's family on the same evening, and recommended us to witness the procession, which was to pass by his residence. Thinking that the marriage processions in the Native and Moglai States must be something worth observing, we promptly and gladly complied with his wishes, and took our seats in the special quarter of the palace which he graciously allotted to us for the purpose. The procession made its appearance at half-past six, and lasted till eight. The van was composed of men on foot, who were followed by others on horseback, and these latter by men on elephants, accompanied with torch-bearers, musicians, an exhibition of fireworks, &c., the whole forming an unbroken line. One remarkable and peculiar feature we noticed in connection with the procession was the practice prevalent in Hydrabad, in conformity with which every nobleman who attends a procession is accompanied by his own private retinue, composed as above, according to his means, and taking his place in the order of his rank and position. In this procession there were, we believe, ten noblemen present, each of whom was attended by his followers in the manner just mentioned. Their pomp and pageantry was really imposing, and, with the noise and shoutings from the crowd, imparted to the procession the pomp and glitter of a Native army in progress. We enjoyed the sight the whole time it lasted—an hour and a half—and so greatly delighted were we with its novelty and magnificence that we were far from being satisfied, and wished it had lasted longer.

Advantages of the English over the Moglai system of Land Revenue.

When the Jamabandi settlement of a country is made with fairness and due regard to the real welfare of its people, it cannot, we think, fail to be beneficial alike to its ryots and the government, besides insuring improvement of the soil. As an instance we shall refer to the system adopted by the British Government. The principles on which it is based, and the rules by which its operations are governed, are really most just and equitable, and well calculated to better the condition of both the cultivators and their lands. This fact is clearly observable in the case of all those districts in India where this system has been introduced,—the ryots and lands of those in which it has not, continue in the same wretched condition as before, and the government itself carries on its functions in embarrassment and disorder. Perhaps it will be said that even the English system would come under these remarks, in so far as famine, starvation, and other sufferings of a like nature are not unknown in the districts under its operation. This is true, but we must say that the defect does not lie in the system itself. These evils are to be attributed to the want of proper attention to the rules in some cases, and in others to dishonesty on the part of those intrusted with their execution. If these officers were all conscientious and fit for their work, the laws of the Jamabandi system are all that could be desired to raise the status of the agricultural classes. To perceive the contrast we have only to look at the condition of the lands in the territories under the Gaikawad and other Native Princes, and compare it with that of those which have come under the British system. We confidently assert that if our Native Princes and Chiefs would introduce the latter method into their dominions under the direction of properly qualified officers, a marked improvement would take place in the condition of all India in a few years.

But it is unnecessary to dwell on this subject at length. We have instances before our own eyes in which some of the Princes, discerning the benefits of the Ryotwari system, have already adopted it in their dominions, and their example is followed by others. Before all, the credit of adopting it is due to Sir Salar Jung, the able and far-sighted Minister of the Nizam, to whom we have already referred. Competent men, selected from among the members of the family of Messrs. Viccajee and Pestonjee Meherjee, well conversant with the affairs of the Nizam's Durbar, have been appointed to fill the onerous duties of carrying it into force. These officers perform their work in a manner which has amply fulfilled the expectations with which Sir Salar Jung had nominated them. Mr. Bapoojee Viccajee Meherjee carries on the duties of a Talookdar in the south of Hydrabad; Mr. Jewanjee Pestonjee is a member of Sir Salar's Durbar or Council; Mr. Rustomjee Viccajee, formerly Assistant Commissioner of the Raichoor District, conducts the duties of Talookdar in three large districts; and Mr. Jewanjee Ruttonjee, grandson to the late Mr. Viccajee, is intrusted with similar duties in "the Seven Districts." It will thus be seen that these able and meritorious officers are allowed a fair share in the administration of the Nizam's State, which they serve with a praiseworthy zeal and fidelity. Two or three members of this well-known family are also employed with credit in Bombay, in trade and under the British Government. This family is undoubtedly an honour to the Parsee community.

We close this subject of land revenue by citing one more instance to show the benefits derivable from the introduction of the English system. We allude to the Balaghát districts.

These districts came into the possession of the British Government on the 12th of October 1800, and were placed under the charge of Colonel T. Munro. The first thing he did was to effect considerable remissions in the amount of revenue previously exacted therefrom by the Hydrabad Government, increasing it only by degrees as the condition of the lands and the cultivators improved. Under the judicious management of this eminent officer, the revenue of these provinces rose in the course of seven years from 10,06,593 to 15,17,272 pagodas; and the ryots, who before lived like plunderers, had so far become peaceable that they came to be looked upon as the ryots of other zillas under the Madras Presidency. In 1817, *i.e.*, seventeen years after these districts came into the possession of the British Government, the revenue reached the enormous amount of 17,40,304 pagodas.*

The Soil of Karnul.

The soil of this city is fruitful, and, being composed of rich black clay, is well suited to the growth of cotton, but, owing to want of an ample supply of water, it is not tilled to a great extent. A private company has, however, undertaken the construction of a canal to apply the water of the river to the irrigation of the land. The work is already going on, and we saw the bridges being built for it. We noticed that the excavation was commenced from beside the city of Karnul.

There are many places in India whose lands would yield two crops a year if they were provided with a sufficient supply of water; and this can only be effected by the construction of canals, through whose agency water may be conveyed to the fields. Private enterprise, however, cannot be expected to prosecute such gigantic works. They must be undertaken by Government as an essential part of the public works of the State, and there is no doubt that their construction would alike benefit it and its subjects. It is unnecessary to point out the benefits arising from canals. The opening of a small portion of the "Ganges Canal" has not only had the effect of fertilizing the adjacent barren lands, but has given a sudden rise to population and cultivation all round it, in the same way as a village springs up on the banks of a river. The progress of a canal carries with it population and agriculture; but on this point we shall speak at some length in its proper place. We content ourselves here with merely remarking that the construction of canals and roads is the only sure way to unlock the extensive treasures whch lie hidden in several parts of India.

* Hamilton's Gazetteer, Second Edition, Vol. I, page 118.

Since the well-being of the rulers is necessarily dependent on their subjects, the adoption of this course would conduce alike to the interests of both—nay, the Government would be benefitted more largely than the other. Besides, the Indian subjects of the British Crown are so loyal and grateful that they would never be backward in requiting any measures which may tend to their advantage. If Government would, under these circumstances, bestow the necessary attention on works of this description, India would doubtless prove a never-failing source of wealth.

Madras Markets.

On the 23rd of January we went to see the markets. The best in the town is chiefly resorted to by Europeans and wealthy Natives, the poorer classes of the population making their purchases from others inferior, but at the same time more accessible. This fashionable market is situated in the "Black Town," and is an elegant fabric, constructed entirely of brickwork. The floor is built of granite flagstones. Separate stalls are appropriated to the sale of different articles, so that purchasers know at once where to look for any particular commodity. The right of opening stalls is let annually by public auction. Here we saw all sorts of things exposed for sale, and these, too, fresh and of excellent quality. The market and its stalls were in a state of thorough cleanliness : earthen pots were seen placed here and there to prevent the floor and walls from being befouled by the constant squirts of the juice of *pán supári*, of which the Madrasees are passionately fond. The sight of this building reminded us of the market of our own city, Bombay, as it then existed, and made us feel heartily sorry and ashamed of the contrast. We could not help envying the good fortune of the Madrasees in having such a fine clean market, and wishing to see one erected in Bombay on a similar model. Time has fulfilled our wish, and we observe with satisfaction the recent establishment of more elegant and cleanly markets in our town. The Crawford Markets excel those of Madras, Calcutta, and indeed those of the whole of Europe, with the exception of only one in Germany, said to have been built in that country by a benevolent lady at her own expense, and which stands unrivalled in Europe, both as regards its construction and convenience, as well as its beauty. Its only rival is the range of superb buildings which are justly named after our zealous, enterprising, and talented Municipal Commissioner, Mr. A. T. Crawford, to whom they owe their existence.

A decent market is, in our opinion, a great boon, for thither all classes of the people, rich and poor, male and female, find it equally inviting to resort in person, and make their own selections, instead of being obliged, as in the other case, to rely on the choice and honesty of servants as to the quality and price of food.

Another solid advantage of a cleanly market is that it keeps the articles also in a clean condition, so that it is gratifying to find that one can obtain pure and wholesome food, free from contaminating influences injurious to health.

The large Madras market under notice is thus daily thronged by respectable Native gentlemen and Europeans with their families, who leisurely walk about and inspect the various articles, purchasing through their servants what they choose. A similar practice obtains likewise in Calcutta. This was not the case in Bombay till very lately, owing chiefly to the want of proper accommodation and cleanliness. But, thanks to the Municipality, as already observed, this desideratum has lately been handsomely supplied. This is a matter of no small congratulation and advantage.

The smaller bazars of Madras, for the people in general, are known by the name of Kotwal bazars. They are in the busy and more populous parts of the city, and look not unlike those of some of our villages in the interior. During the monsoon they fall into a very dirty state, from the accumulation of water and mud.

Owing apparently to some time-honoured custom, it is more usual for women than men to sit in the shops in Madras and carry on the sales. There is evidently some philosophy in this practice, for the shop which is so graced by a woman, and especially one who is good-looking and a belle, will, in all probability, be able to attract a larger number of customers than one with a male vendor. In introducing this custom, therefore, the Madrasees appear to have consulted human nature to advantage.

This practice, it may be noticed, is followed in several European countries, to the positive benefit of the owners, consequent on the large sales thus effected.

Magdalen Asylum—Necessity of Foundling Hospitals in Bombay.

A charitable institution bearing the above name stands on the way to Kilpák. It is established with the noble and praiseworthy object of affording shelter and protection to such females of the European and Indo-British communities as have gone astray from the path of virtue, but are disposed to abandon their evil courses and return to the right way. The inmates are employed in work suited to their respective capacities, and the sale-proceeds of the articles are handed over to the inmates themselves, after reserving a portion for contingent expenses. With this exception, the asylum is entirely supported from funds raised by public subscription.

It is a pity that no institution of this kind has yet been opened in a city like Bombay, remarkable for its wealth and reputation for establishing charitable institutions. It is strange that while, through the munificence of our *Shettiás,* Bombay contains several benevolent institutions, not one of this character has been founded.

With it, the foundation of at least one foundling hospital is also urgently needed, to save the lives of innocent children who are destroyed to conceal the shame and guilt of illicit intercourse. Some persons are of opinion that the introduction of such an institution would be tantamount to offering a premium on unchastity; but patient consideration leads us to a different conclusion. As matters now stand, a double crime is committed—unchastity is followed by the murder of innocent infants so begotten; but if the suggested establishment were effectual in suppressing the latter heinous offence, and thereby in lessening the number of murders annually perpetrated, it could not but be placed in the foremost rank of humane institutions. If Government has passed a special legislative enactment for the purpose of preventing the spread of contagious diseases, and, from the taxes raised from the public, deemed it just even to maintain the Lock Hospital, established for the exclusive benefit of lewd and adulterous people,—is it right, we ask, that we should not take steps to prevent private individuals incurring the guilt of murder, which they do from motives of avoiding shame and exposure, and the poor infants from being so inhumanly destroyed? Though it may be found hard to support a foundling hospital at the commencement, it would not be the case after some time, as any one having experience of human nature can easily satisfy himself of. Though prostitutes at present submit to official supervision only through compulsion, we think they will not fail, ere long, to find out that it is for their own good, and to pay, moreover, without demur, any tax which Government may impose on them on this account. Such is the opinion which the author has formed in July 1870, when writing on this subject, and which, he believes, time will verify. And it would be regarded as an act of common justice to the pure and virtuous members of the community if some sort of tax were levied on the prostitutes, for it is hardly right to defray the expenses of this department from the taxes levied from people in general: it is palpably unjust to them to be laid under contribution to gratify the evil passions of the lascivious. We think, however, that the existing arrangement is only temporary, and that in due time this description of persons will be called upon to pay the entire expense out of their own pockets: the prostitutes who would pay the fixed tax would probably recover it with interest from the persons who visit them, and in this way the whole burden of supporting the department would fall upon the right class.

On the strength of the above reasoning, we similarly conclude that private individuals who are so frail as to fall into the crime of whoredom would similarly see the justice of maintaining at their own expense the department which might be opened for the protection of their illegitimate offspring. It is easy to see how they would do it. Every one secretly leaving such a child would naturally leave a larger or smaller sum of money, with the view of giving some aid towards its support: for, love of children being naturally implanted in every human breast, a lewd woman is as susceptible of maternal affection as any virtuous matron. There can be no doubt, therefore, regarding a foundling hospital becoming an asylum for the safety of innocent lives, which, in its absence, are now sacrificed, and of receiving support from the parents of such infants.

Thus far of prostitutes; but the same reasoning applies also in the case of private women of depraved morals. It is not in the nature of humanity to delight in depriving an innocent infant of its life: the wicked act is resorted to only with a view to conceal exposure and shame, and for this purpose thousands of rupees are paid to midwives and procuresses; but this act they would never think of perpetrating were such an institution as a foundling hospital in existence, as they would in that case at once send their children there with a purse of money. How many unoffending lives would then be annually saved from destruction! All honour to him, therefore, who takes the initiative in supplying this want in Bombay!

Foundling hospitals exist in England, as well as in the countries of continental Europe, and are supported by public subscriptions, endowments, and the large amounts which are sent with the children. Many of the inmates are now in society, and from their education are able to live respectably, though they have no knowledge of their parents.

St. Matthias's Cathedral.

This is designated by the name of "Vepery Church," from the locality in which it is situated. The internal arrangement at first glance seems plain, but as the spectator proceeds to view it minutely and leisurely, the first appearance of plainness changes into one of awe and solemnity. The marble-faced tombs among the seats attract the attention of the visitor, who is deeply moved by reading the maxims of wisdom inscribed thereon: the paintings depicted on the glass windows, and the carvings on the walls, inspire the observer with silent instruction as to the humility and meekness men should exercise in their social intercourse with each other, and cause him to say within himself "Alas, how often hitherto have I erred!" How instructive are these dumb pictures, reminding us of the errors of our ways! Are we to shut our eyes to these admonitions? How long shall we remain indifferent! Travellers should never lose sight of such buildings in any city they may visit, because a patient and attentive inspection of their exterior and interior serves to lead us to a fair insight into the manners, customs, religious feelings, and, to some extent, of the moral stamina, of the people of various countries.

The Madras Club.

It is situated on the Mount Road. The civil, military, and medical officers, and others occupying the position of gentlemen in society, are admitted as members or visitors, with certain privileges, under rules and regulations framed for its conduct. The building stands on a very airy and retired spot, surrounded by shrubberies, and affords conveniences which one cannot expect to enjoy even in a private establishment. Ample provision is here made for recreation, both for body and mind, by the establishment of billiard-rooms, a racket-court, a library, baths, ponds, &c., and is regarded as far superior to the "Byculla Club" of this place.

As for bathing, it has a special building set apart for it, containing a large tank of pure water. It is provided with a series of stages rising one above another from the bottom, so that each swimmer can find the depth of water he desires. The lowest stage is about twenty feet, a depth by no means small. This club was founded in 1832.

Public baths exist in almost every large city in India. We have given in their appropriate places a full description of those that have come under our observation in Benares, Delhi, Agra, Lucknow, and other towns, a perusal of which will show their construction and arrangement, as well as their connection with public health. In Europe and other civilized countries baths are to be met with everywhere, and are much resorted to by the inhabitants. Those especially who cannot obtain a sufficient supply of water, or other facilities for bathing in their houses, are greatly benefitted by them; for only at a trifling sum they can get as large a quantity of water as they wish. It is quite unnecessary to prove that human health is preserved in a great measure by personal cleanliness: every one will admit that the preservation or derangement of health is regulated by the cleanliness or filthiness of the body. It is consequently imperative on those attending to the health and conservancy of a city to make adequate arrangements for public bathing. It is remarkable that our city is devoid of a single establishment of this kind; but it is hoped that our energetic and intelligent Municipal Commissioner, who has given us such excellent markets, will supply this want also, which has already engaged his attention. He has seen the need of it, and is sure to carry out his purpose, in the interests of the poorer classes especially, as soon as his financial position becomes easier. If, however, some one of our public-spirited townsmen were to volunteer to share the expense with the municipality, there would then be no question as to the certainty of its accomplishment under their united efforts. The construction of public baths, we repeat, which have for their object the cleanliness, and therefore the preservation of health, of the lower classes of the population, is as noble and humane an act as the erection of hospitals for the relief and preservation of the diseased.

Necessity of a Native Society or Club in Bombay.

Speaking of the Madras Club, we are tempted to say a few words regarding the absence of a similar institution among the numerous body of educated natives of Bombay. There is no club where persons having the position of gentlemen can meet together, or which is conducted on principles and usages recognized in genteel society, and which has some sort of acknowledged status among the Native public. The absence of so important a thing as a club doubtless indicates the existence of some latent defect in the organization of Native society. Owing to there being no association of this description, its leaders and educated gentlemen remain isolated from each other. The consequence is that every one boldly shapes his deportment in accordance with his individual notions of propriety or otherwise, without caring in the least whether others regard it as proper or not. The laws and conventionalities of civilized societies, which every sensible man views in the light of restraints against any improper deviations on his part, are not at all observed in the present constitution of Native society. While such a club is not yet opened among our educated men, what can we say of their boasted enlightenment? It is a source of regret to us that in speaking of this subject we are touching on a most delicate point, in so far that we feel constrained to point out the faults of our friends, but in so doing, our readers may depend upon it, it is not our object to hurt the feelings of any one.

We ask with all respect, have not so many educated men of Bombay, Parsees and Hindoos, the ability or unanimity to open a club where all gentlemen of position can freely interchange their thoughts, where they can meet at stated times, converse freely, make inquiries regarding each other's welfare, and where those in a position to assist may hold out the right hand of fellowship to those needing it, and, in the event of any social or public question arising, they might be readily referred to if necessary, when they might all come forward with one voice, and command the respect and confidence of the public?

We ask once more whether it is possible to start such a club in our city, no matter if the members composing it belong to the middle class of the people? Since it is not yet established, it is necessary that we should point out what, in our humble opinion, are the deterrent causes, and these we regret are of such a character as to throw discredit on the sacred cause of education.

The "tall talk" in which we see Native journals and public meetings ever and anon indulging about reforms in Bombay, should not be thought an indication of solid and real reform, but merely fictitious and unreal, like hollow sounds proceeding from empty houses. We have hitherto been accustomed to hear the so-called reformers spout about it, as if talk were synonymous with action. There are many persons who take credit to themselves only for advising people, while they themselves remain utterly indifferent as to the necessity of suiting their practice to their preaching. They imagine that all improvement consists in putting their crudities in type, publishing them in journals, and exhibiting them as the banner of their vain-glory.

Solid and real improvement we find only in rare cases, and that too among men who have never uttered, nor are likely ever to utter, a single syllable in praise of themselves: in every other quarter it is, to use a Gujarati proverb, "dark notwithstanding the consumption of twelve *mans* of oil." For, reflect, sensible reader, to how small an extent unanimity and cordiality exist among our educated Native gentlemen. Is this state of things to be called "reform"? Would it be right for us to counsel others to the contrary while we continue in this state? They have indeed realized in their own case the truth of the Native proverb of a "sieve despising a water-pot." Should any one be inclined to ask, Is there unanimity among us or no? we would undertake to answer him. Though the answer is short, it is highly unpalatable, and will undoubtedly provoke a slap from the opposite party by way of rejoinder. It cannot, however, be helped; the correct answer must be given, even though it may subject us to a slap, as it inevitably will. Here it is:—We affirm that not only have they no unanimity, but, what is still worse, they look upon one another with an eye of jealousy. We are aware that this outspoken expression of our opinion will give offence to some of our associates, who will pronounce it unfounded. All we can say is that we think differently, though we would that we were in the wrong. We are rather inclined to believe that, while they may take offence at us on the one hand, their consciences will tell them that this charge against them is every whit true.

There are those among the educated who do not wish to see any one from their body rising to be their equal or superior, and who in consequence are ever ready to throw obstacles in the way of his advancement, with the view of retarding him. Then there are others who so selfishly and exclusively pursue their own interest, as not to allow any other of their rank and attainments to come within the pale of their pasture-ground. How many of the educated natives in well-to-dô circumstances have called before themselves the less fortunate members of their class and inquired respecting them, "Friends, tell us freely your condition; if we can in any way render you assistance, we will do so with great pleasure." We think there are few, if any, among us possessing such benevolence of heart. If the uneducated fail to discharge these humane duties, we cannot find much fault with them; but if the educated, who have read a great deal about this virtue of benevolence, manifest callousness or selfishness, they are deserving of heavy censure. Again, a few have learnt to be temporizing, adapting their course, like a ship trimming its sails, according to the direction of the wind: to-day speaking in behalf of the *Shettiás*, to-morrow speaking against them; again, for some reasons, veering round; and again, as soon, turning away. Some of them have not only lost their self-respect, and forfeited all claims to consideration from others by such vacillating conduct, but have caused the whole class of educated natives to become objects to be pointed at with the finger. Others have assumed an insolent, arbitrary, and defiant attitude towards their leaders. Such empty show has only produced dangerous thoughts in the minds of people, who are led to exclaim "God save us from the educated men!" When instead of humility, gravity, patience, foresight, and all possible obedience towards parents and other superiors (no matter how faulty their notions may be in some respects),—which ought to be the fruit of all right education, and the prominent traits in the character of all truly educated men,—pedantry, pride, obstinacy, and self-will are found, the uneducated portion pass a wholesale condemnation on all the educated as being wrong-headed. Though they have been hasty in forming this opinion, which admits of being altered on maturer consideration, yet it cannot be denied that repeated instances of such misconduct on the part of educated men have furnished grounds for this opinion. This circumstance has caused a serious estrangement between the educated few on the one hand, and the mass of the people and their leaders on the other. Though this censure is inapplicable to the whole class of educated men, yet it does apply to a few of them. This stigma it is now necessary to remove; and if the sensible and far-sighted portion of our educated men would think seriously on the subject, they would find that the duty of bridging over this social gulf devolves on themselves, and that they would be able to accomplish this by adopting in future a uniformly respectful deportment towards their elders, with a due regard to the preservation of self-respect.

It is now our duty to speak our mind with equal candour respecting the conduct of the professed leaders of Native society. We beg to point out, with all possible deference, that in keeping themselves aloof and isolated from the educated they commit a great mistake. Some of them have been heard to express an opinion that if the latter were suffered to advance in life, they would be inclined to slight them or treat them with disrespect! Now we want to know how many of the above class have behaved in this way. We assert without hesitation, and our *shettiás* may keep their hearts at ease on this score, that those who are possessed of true blood, and who have received genuine culture and breeding, are incapable of such conduct, which can only be possible with pedants of reverse nature, from whom it is vain to expect anything good or commendable. Men of this sort may acquire ever so high an education, yet if they lack genuine blood and breeding, their education can exercise but little influence on them, for "the young of a wolf," as is observed by Shaikh Saadi, "will only grow to be a wolf," no matter in how good company and with what care he is brought up. The case is, however, different with those in whom true blood is combined with sound education. However humble a stock they may have descended from, they may rise to occupy elevated positions and would yet never think of offending their elders or the leading members of their community, or of claiming superiority over them. The fact is, we humbly submit, that heretofore the *shettiás* have totally abstained from permitting anything like a long and well-tried and friendly intercourse to subsist between themselves and the truly educated and upright class; neither of them has as yet been placed in those positions in which prosperity and adversity try us; and hence the inability on both sides to arrive at a true discernment of each other's merits or demerits. If, through want of foresight or discernment, the *shettiás* mistook some bustling and pedantic fellows for highly-educated gentlemen, and treated them accordingly, and if they afterwards had to meet with insult or injury from them, or if they found them conceited and vainglorious, surely it would be an act of absolute injustice to the educated class if the *shettiás*, from a few solitary instances, pass a hasty and an indiscriminate condemnation on the entire body, and recommend others in their station to refrain from maintaining intercourse with them. This is a grave matter which we would commend to the attention of all the leading men of the community. In forming such a disparaging estimate of the worth or deserts of the whole educated class from the conduct of two or three men of hollow pretensions, our *shettiás* act like a man who having once been stung by a serpent, is apt at all times to take every piece of rope he may chance to meet with for a real snake. We all know how ill-founded this supposition is, and yet this is the way in which the *shettiás* act, which speaks poorly for their foresight and experience.

They are supposed to be aware of the fact that educated men are not all alike, any more than the five fingers of the hand. In the same manner ought the *shettiás* to be aware of the disparity that exists among their own body in point of virtue; all of them are not saints!

These gentlemen no doubt know, from their ripe experience, that the leading men of all civilized communities, being themselves possessed of high mental culture, generally keep the company of the enlightened; they render themselves accessible to their inferiors, inquiring of them from time to time concerning their welfare, and thus secure their love and regard, as also their own influence. It is, however, different with our *shettiás*, who, as is complained from several quarters, are so vain (we don't believe all to be so) as to imagine that they alone can accomplish everything, and that what is done by them should be implicitly acquiesced in by others; but a supposition, it may be stated, which is so obviously fallacious cannot be acted on in practice, as it has never hitherto been. History has made known to us numerous instances in which the representatives of the country were opposed and thrust overboard by the commoners in their attempt to exercise arbitrary powers over the latter. Our representative men are fully aware that if they desire to enjoy a dignified, influential, and an honourable pre-eminence over their compatriots, they should have none but dignified, influential, and honourable men for their associates. It is the men of rank and position—men of foresight and experience—men conversant with everything relative to the country—men well versed in law and politics—men of patience, circumspection, and calculation in matters of commerce—and, lastly, men of sound training and talents, as also of honesty and morals, who should compose the association. No association of men that does not possess these qualities can ever really command influence and respect; and our *shettiás* are well qualified to form a public association on this principle, if they choose.

Having referred to the description of persons who should be the companions of the *shettiás*, let us now proceed to examine what sort of men enjoy their company and confidence. It appears that, with very few exceptions, these associates and advisers are only men of limited education, apparently devoid of a capacity for sound judgment and counsel.

It is indeed a matter of both regret and surprise that there should be so much as it were studied isolation from the educated.

It puzzles one to discover what there can be in education which renders its possessors so disagreeable to the *shettiás*. This breach is, however, variously accounted for, according to individual opinion or fancy, which it is worth while noticing, as it leads to an important conclusion. Some impute it to a reluctance on the part of the educated men to truckle to the *shettiás*; others attribute it to an overbearing and disrespectful demeanour into which they are betrayed in the heat of their youthful blood on account of mere ordinary and excusable blunders; and some, again, ascribe it to a spirit of vanity, in consequence of which they arrogate to themselves the credit of a high enlightenment, and refuse it *in toto* to the other class, who they aver have nothing more than their ancestral wealth to rest their claims upon for exacting respect. Now if all these causes were weighed in the balance of judgment and the sins on both sides compared, the side on which vanity preponderates should be adjudged as deserving of particular censure, which those concerned should endeavour to adopt means to free themselves from. Courtesy, though it be combined with poverty, is better entitled to our esteem and approbation than the vanity of the opulent. Having thus dwelt at some length on the alienating causes, we may proceed to state briefly how a reunion can be effected. Letting bygones be bygones, it behoves our *shettiás* to establish a more friendly and familiar intercourse with the educated gentlemen, and receive them into a larger share of their confidence than heretofore. Similarly the latter should endeavour, by the observance of a respectful deportment, to satisfy their superiors that they are incapable of abusing the confidence reposed in them, and also regarding their proneness to overlook, at all times, any errors or shortcomings observable on the other side, as well as correcting their own. Once this relation is brought about between them, the bond of friendship and attachment will always continue to strengthen; once this bond is formed, the troubles and trials which we frequently encounter in the hard battle of life will be easily surmounted by the powerful weapon of their unanimity, and thus success uninterruptedly continue to attend both through life.

In conclusion, we sincerely regret the unpalatable nature of the observations which we have been thus led to make without reserve or partiality for either side; but we repudiate all intention of causing pain to any party. Bearing in mind the words of that master of human nature, Shakspeare, who, in the delineation of one of his subjects, observes, "Look on this picture and on that," we have likewise thought fit to show up both sides, and ask our readers to look at the conduct of the educated and reforming party, and also at that of the uneducated and conservative party, leaving each sensible reader to decide for himself on which side the shortcomings preponderate.

Charitable Military Asylums for Orphans in Madras.

Among the many institutions established in Madras for the protection of fatherless and destitute children, there are two, for the exclusive benefit of military orphans of both sexes, which require notice. The Male Asylum was opened in 1788, and the Female in 1786, and they are both conducted in a highly efficient manner. The former has up to this time turned out, it is said, about 3,300 well-educated boys, who are now engaged in different occupations, some being in the service of Government, a few in trade, and others labouring as Christian Missionaries. This establishment is likewise open to children whose parents are disabled, by accident or a like cause, from supporting them. Besides these, a limited number is also received on payment of charges for schooling and boarding, but in all cases orphans are allowed a preference.

In the Female Asylum,* which receives annual pecuniary aid from Government and the public, are taught household economy, sewing, washing, nursing the sick, and in the case of those girls who give early indications of intelligence and aptitude, they are instructed in the art of teaching. Its affairs are managed by a few philanthropic ladies, wives of public officials; and this circumstance has secured an efficient and highly beneficial watchfulness over the mental as well as moral training of the youthful inmates.

We devoutly wish our good countrywomen might be induced to copy such of their European sisters as those who labour so assiduously in the cause of charity and philanthropy. It is necessary, however, that the beginning should be made by the upper classes, who, by virtue of their position, are better qualified than others to do so.

This may probably give rise to a question as to how the upper class of women in our country can take the initiative in this matter, when they are themselves uneducated? The question admits of a simple answer, which is, that if influential ladies are joined in their efforts by the educated, there would then be no difficulty felt in making a beginning. The absence, in all kinds of movements, of the coöperation of the wealthy with the educated members of the community must be regarded as a great desideratum. The educated young Bombayites seem to have fallen into a curious blunder in this respect, which consists in a belief in their power to accomplish any arduous undertaking single-handed, without the help of their more influential countrymen. Our opinion, however, is diametrically opposed to this, in support of which the movement on behalf of female education may be referred to. Let us then ask, gentle readers, whether, although 'Young Bombay' originated and set on foot the movement in question, they were able to dispense with the assistance of the Shettiás in carrying it to a successful result? We ask, Did they not solicit and receive aid, either publicly or privately, from Messrs. Framjee Nusserwanjee Patell, Cursetjee Nusserwanjee Camajee, Dhunjeebhoy Nusserwanjee Camajee, and other leading townsmen? The answer is patent to everybody. We affirm that without the support and coöperation of these gentlemen, the cause of female education would perhaps never have succeeded. Similarly it may be asked if the legislative enactment regulating inheritance, marriage, and divorce among the Parsees, with which that community is provided, has not been obtained by the influence and with the coöperation of the Shettiás? It is therefore apparent, from these and other instances of a like nature, that the various measures of importance which we have been able to effect are not solely the result of the unassisted efforts of the educated; it is the result of the efforts of the educated aided by the prestige and position of their elders. It is only through such good understanding and harmonious working together of the upper and middle classes that we should expect to accomplish, in future, reforms like those we have been enabled to attain in the past.

An interview with His Highness the Raja of Peber.

Early in the morning we sent a message to His Highness, expressing our desire to pay him our respects; the messenger returned with a reply that His Highness would be very glad to see us. The Raja is named the Raja of "Vanpati," meaning the Raja of Forest, from the circumstance of his being the owner of an extensive forest round the village where he resides. He is known by the name and title of His Highness Raja Rameshwar Rao Behári Bahádhur. He was attired in the dress of an English Colonel when he received us. He conversed with us in English, which he spoke with marked ease and fluency. He talks equally well in Urdu, not to speak of Telugu, which is his native tongue. There is yet something more to be said in regard to his linguistic knowledge. The flow of melodious words which the Raja used in speaking the Urdu led our friend Mr. E. Rehatsek to conclude that he ought to be able to talk in Persian, and so under that impression he communicated his conjecture to the Raja in Persian itself. The Raja answered in the affirmative in the same language, adding that he had a great predilection for the aquisition of different languages, and that he could speak as many as ten, including Arabic, Kanaḍa, Sindhi, and Afghan. In order to keep up his practice, the Raja has employed different persons knowing these languages, as soldiers and officers in his army. Though a Hindu, he observes none of the prejudices peculiar to that religion, against the absurdities of which he openly expressed himself. His reception of us was marked by all the courtesy and etiquette of an English gentleman. After the usual civilities had been exchanged, he began to make many anxious inquiries on points connected with our tour, and seemed highly gratified on discovering that we were the gentlemen whom he had felt a desire to see on learning, from newspapers and other sources, the fact of our having set out from Bombay on a tour though the country. After some conversation he asked us to take a cup of tea or coffee, which we gladly did, except our friend Dr. Bhau, whose declining greatly surprised the Raja that such a sensible and erudite gentleman should cherish such puerile prejudices, adding that if gentlemen of Dr. Bhau's generally advanced ideas and liberal education displayed such narrowness of mind and lack of moral courage to shake off openly prejudices like this, we should never expect to see the people of Hindustan make any rapid strides in the onward march of civilization. As for himself, he further observed, mature reflection on the subject had led him completely to discard ill-founded bigotry, without involving his conversion from the Hindu faith. The Hindus of the present day, the Raja continued, are as superstitious, timid, and ignorant as those of former times were liberal, bold, warlike, and educated. The Raja has thus not only broken through prejudices of long standing, but has also fearlessly made known his views to his subjects, who, however, it may be stated to his credit, are allowed to continue in the free exercise of their choice to act as they may think proper according to individual belief. He entertains a very high opinion of the British Government, and has for the most part introduced British laws and regulations into the districts subject to his control. We were informed by him that he had received his early training, as well as his political and military education, at the hands of General Wahab V. C. Sinclair. The Raja is naturally of a brave and warlike disposition, having on several occasions drawn his sword against the Nizam (of whom he was at one time fairly considered a rival); however, except in some solitary cases, he had to sustain heavy defeats. After we had drunk the coffee, we were taken into the *Divan-khana*, where he showed increasing marks of familiarity. He made us presents of copies of his own photograph, and asked for ours, which we promised to send after our return to Bombay. We were next asked for our visiting cards, and, ascertaining our names and addresses, he entered them in his memorandum book. He next showed us the likenesses of his mother, sister, and other members of the family, on whose education, we observed, he bestowed much attention, in token of his avowed appreciation of the benefits accruing therefrom.

A visit to the "Bethune Female School" in Calcutta; Calcutta and Bombay female education compared.

On the 9th February we proceeded to see this institution, which took its rise under the following circumstances. The citizens of Calcutta had raised a public subscription with a view to perpetuate the memory of the Honourable Mr. Bethune, whose name is a household word in Calcutta, for the zeal evinced by him in the introduction of education, but more especially of female education, into India. To this fund a further sum was contributed by this true friend of the natives out of his own pocket, and the whole made over to a committee for the purpose of devoting it to the cause of female education. The result is the establishment of the present school, and the erection of a large and handsome building for its accommodation. There were 104 girls present in the school on the day of our visit, but the daily attendance, as we were informed by the European Governess and Superintendent, averaged 70. The girls are taught reading, writing, and the rudiments of arithmetic, sewing, and domestic economy; but neither instrumental nor vocal music is included in the course of studies. A gymnastic class is also opened in connection with the school, where girls from six to eight years of age are made to take exercise daily, in order to develope the tender powers of their body and mind. We were much pleased with some of their juvenile feats, and thought that if the Calcutta girls received proper education—or, to be more exact, if they received proper education at the proper time—they would turn out quite as smart as our Parsee girls, and in some cases even more so.

Though female education in Calcutta may appear to be more limited than in Bombay, we should not suffer ourselves to be misled by mere appearances, inasmuch as the reputation which the latter has acquired in this respect is owing exclusively to the outward show and bustle of her inhabitants, and not to any solid achievement. The Parsees have certainly manifested a greater degree of zeal than the Hindus in educating their daughters, but the result has been no better in the one case than in the other. Though a decade has elapsed since the introduction of education into this city, not a single girl has been found qualified for the office of governess of a school. The fact is, as soon as they reach their tenth or eleventh year, their parents and friends think it high time to remove them from school, and hence it is that not one of them has yet been able to write even a small book or pamphlet, or so much as even a passable *bonâ fide* production in the shape of an essay, of which we have any knowledge. Such being the present state of education among our females, it behoves us to reflect seriously on it, and strive earnestly to devise such means as may ensure solid and permanent results, instead of vainly flattering ourselves with the misleading supposition that it has arrived at perfection! Although Calcutta may appear behind Bombay in point of female education, such, we submit, is not the case in reality, for the system of private tuition among families, known as the "Zenana Education," obtains very largely in Calcutta, where European ladies are steadily but unostentatiously disseminating the blessings of knowledge and enlightenment. Ere long we shall see what fruits this Zenana education will bear, and the reforms it will introduce into Native society. Already the names of more than one Bengali woman have been before the public—one as an authoress, another as a proficient in Sanscrit, a third as a poetess, &c.; while all that has been heard and seen of the women (whether Parsi or Hindu) of our own city in this respect is the bold and open display, in imitation of European custom, of their coquetry as exhibited in their wearing English boots, stockings, and brocade caps; in accompanying their husbands in public and associating in the company of males. That so far they have surpassed their Bengali sisters no one, we think, will deny; but we would respectfully, and with the best intentions, impress upon our countrywomen that if they would endeavour to decorate their *minds* as they do their *persons*, by a sound secular and religious education, they would better consult their interests, and secure results of a more solid and permanent character. It is a grave mistake to suppose that education and reforms consist in the improvement of personal charms, and accordingly to make them the object of one's *exclusive* care and attention.

Our interview with Dr. Duff.

Leaving the Bethune School, we proceeded to pay a visit to the well-known missionary of the Free Church of Scotland—the

Rev. Dr. Duff—whose name is famous not only in Calcutta, but throughout all India, on account of his great learning, wide acquaintance with the customs and usages of the country, and for his benevolent intentions towards the people. In the course of a conversation extending to about an hour, we touched on various subjects, such as the Babus, the thoughts and tendencies of their rising youth, female education, the practices of the Hindus, &c., &c., and had the opportunity of making ourselves acquainted with the views of this eminent divine. He spoke hopefully of India's future, which, he said, mainly depended upon the spread of education, which, as it permeated more and more through the lower orders, would effect a corresponding change in their condition; and while it would not, of course, bring about a wholesale conversion of the people to Christianity, it would lead them, by degrees, to a renunciation of their idolatrous practices—a result which none can well prevent.

Talking of the intellectual qualities of the Babus, the Doctor expressed a very high opinion of them, giving them credit for possessing a marked capacity for the study of mathematical, legal, and medical sciences, as well as for powers of hard and systematic application as students in general.

Referring to the tendency of their religious views, the Doctor considered it to be in an unhealthy state—the free indulgence on the part of some of the Babus in eating, drinking, and other sensual pleasures, having given rise to feelings of deep sorrow in the heart of this well-wisher of theirs. Let us hope that such of the educated Hindus of our own island as have contracted a taste for the pleasures of the bottle will take this as a warning against the continuance of their habit: for their future, in the opinion of Dr. Duff, as well as of all right-thinking men, is most saddening to contemplate. Speaking of the Brahmo Samaj, he said that he had himself witnessed it to assume, one after another, three different phases since its birth, and that though he was far from agreeing with the views entertained by it, he liked the institution in so far that its fundamental object was to turn from the worship of idols to the adoration of one Supreme Being void of form or figure. The learned divine had a high conception of the worth of Babu Keshab Chundra Sen, who, if we are not mistaken, is his pupil, and who would appear to have always kept his veteran master before his eyes as a model for imitation in his eloquent and impassioned delivery.

Before leaving, we informed the Doctor of our intention to go and see the "Bália Ghaut" that evening, when at once he exhibited his emotions of compassion for the innocent victims of this custom, and deplored that although there were so many enlightened Babus in Calcutta, they had not bestirred themselves to put a stop to the continuance of the pernicious practice prevailing at that Ghaut even at the present day. This evil practice, and several other social and moral topics relating to the people of Calcutta and Bombay, are contrasted and discussed at length in the Gujarati portion of the work, but, from want of space in this volume, the author regrets he cannot give further translation of these subjects.

From a photograph

Vincent Brooks, Day & Son, Engrs

THE TRAVELLERS.

હિંદુસ્થાનમાં મુસાફરી.

TRAVELS IN INDIA.

મુસાફરીની અગત, તે કેમ કરવી.

મુસાફરી કીધાથી માણુસ જાતની અક્કલ અને હોશ ખરેખર વધેછે, એ વાત સાબેત કરવાની જરૂર નથી. જેમ બાળપણમાં છોકરાઓને કેળવણી લેવા નિશાળે મોકલવાની જરૂર છે, તેમજ છોકરાઓએ કેળવણી લીધા પછી, આ દુનીઆના સંસાર વેહેવારમાં નાખ્યા આગમચ, જે માબાપોની શક્તિ હોય તેઓએ તેમને મુસાફરી કરવા મોકલવાની જરૂર છે, જેથી તેમનાં ગ્નાન, હોશ અને હિંમતમાં વધારો થશે. નિશાળમાં કેળવણી લેઈ જેટલું ગ્નાન સંપાદન કરીયું હશે તેના કરતાં દશગણું વધારે ગ્નાન આ દુનીઆની મોહોટી નિશાળ તરફ મુસાફરી કરીઆથી મેળવી શકાશે. આ ગ્નાન તથા એથી મળતો અનુભવ, પછવાડેના દીવસમાં તેમને ઘણોજ ઉપયોગી થઈ પડવાનો. ટુંકાંમાં બોલીએ તો જે દેશના લોક મુસાફરી કરેછે અથવા વેપારને સારૂ દેશ પરદેશ ફરેછે તે દેશની તથા તીહાંના લોકની હાલત ખરેખર ચઢતીજ છે. જે દેશના લોક પોત પોતાની હદમાં અટકી અથવા ભરાઈ બંધ રહેલાં છે તેમની હાલત ખચીત ઉતરતીજ છે.

'ફરે તે ચરે, બાંધ્યો ભુખે મરે', આ કેહેવત મશહુર અને ખરી છે. જો આપણા દેશના માતબર લોક પોત પોતાના લાયક છોકરાઓને આવી તરેહની પુરી કેળવણી આપી ઉધારે તો તેઓ ખરેખર પોતાને તથા પોતાના દેશને ઘણોજ ફાયદો કરશે. આપણી નામદાર મહારાણીના રાજપુત્રોએ મુસાફરી કરી છે. એ મુસાફરી કરવાની ગોઠવણ રાણીના ભરથારે પોતાની હેયાતીમાંજ લખી મુકી હતી.

જો તે મહાપુરૂષ શાહાજાદો જીવ્યો હોત તો તેણે જે ગોઠવણ કરી હતી તે પ્રમાણે પુરતી મુસાફરી તેના કુંઅરોએ કરી હોત, પણ દૈવયોગે એવું નહીં બન્યું, તોપણ આપણી નામવર મહારાણીના રાજપુત્રો ઘણા અગતના દેશોમાં ફરી વળ્યા છે; એથી પુશ્કળ અનુભવ તેઓએ મેળવ્યો છે, જેના ફળ હવેપછી આપણ ચાખવાની ઉમેદ રાખીએ છૈએ. એજ પ્રમાણે હિંદુસ્થાનનાં જુદાં જુદાં પ્રાંતના સઘળા રાજવંશીઓએ પોતે અને તેમની ગાદીના વારસોએ મુસાફરી કરવી ઘણીજ અગતની છે. એ વીશે મુંબઈના નામદાર ગવરનર સર બારટલ ફ્રીઅરે એવી ભલામણ દક્ષણ પ્રાંતના સરદારોને અને તેમની ગાદીના વારસોને વારંવાર કરી છે.

આપણી મહારાણીના રાજકુંઅરોમાંના એક કુંઅરે તો પૂર્વદીશાના ઘણાક દેશો તરફ મુસાફરી કરી છે. આસ્ત્રેલીયા અને કેપ તરફ મુસાફરી કરી એકવાર પાછો પોતાની સ્વદેશભુમીમાં જઈ તીહાંથી ફરીને પાછો મુસાફરીએ નીકળ્યો તે છેક ચીનના પાયાતખ્ત સુધી જઈ પોહોંચી, જેપાન દેશમાં ફરી વળ્યો છે અને તીહાંથી હાંગકાંગ, સીંગાપોર તરફ જઈ આપણા દેશ હિંદુસ્થાનમાં મુસાફરી છેક પેશાવર સુધી કરી છે. આપણા શાહાજાદા આલફરેડના આપણા દેશમાં આવી જવાની યાદ તો દેશી લોકમાં ઘણીજ સારી પેઠે રેહેશે, અને હમો જણાવવાને જરાપણ અચકાતાં નથી કે મુંબઈ શેહેરમાં આ શાહાજાદા તરફ જે ખુલ્લું અને મોહોબત ભરેલું દીલ દેખાડવામાં આવીયું છે, એવું તેણે થોડેજ ઠેકાણે જોયું હશે. મુંબઈની પારસી કોમમાં તેમની સ્ત્રીઓ તરફથી તેને લાયકનું જે માન અને પાદશાહી ખાનદાન તરફ જે ઘટતો પીયાર સુધરેલી કોમવાળા તરફથી ખુદરતી રાહે દેખાવો જોઈએ તેવો તેણે જોયો છે, એથી અલબતાં પારસી કોમવીશે શાહાજાદો સારૂં મત લઈગયો છે, અને તે છેક તેની પીયારી માનવંતી માતાના કાન ઉપર જયા વગર નથીજ રેહેવાનું. આથી પારશી ટોલાને ભારી માન અને શાબાસી છે, તેમજ આટલું બોલીયા વગર પણ ચલાતું નથી કે પારશી ટોલામાં દેખાદેખીથી કોઈવાર હરેક સારૂં કામ કરતાં હદની બાહેર કેટલાકો જઈ લાગેછે, અને તેથી સારાં કામને કોઈવાર સાંભી ઝાંખ લાગે એવા કેટલાક દાખલા આ હીંગામે ભરઉલટમાં આવીયાથી બનીયા છે, પણ તે સાદાં દીલથી બનેલા સમજી તેપર આટલોજ ઈશારો કરેલો બસ છે.

શાહાજાદાને જે હુરમત ઈજ્જત મળી છે તેથી આપણી ભલી રઈઅતવીશે તેણે સારૂંજ મત બાંધીયું છે. આપણા દેશી રાજા અને અમીર ઉમરાઓએ અને દેશી રઈઅતે જબરી રકમબંધ પઈસો મોટાં દીલસાથે ખરચી, શાહાજાદાનો જે આદરસતકાર કરીયો છે, તેમાં ખોલ્લી રીતે એવું માલુમ પડીયું છે, કે જેબી આદરમાન આ રાજકુંઅરને આપીયામાં આવીયું છે તેમાં એ રાજકુંઅરની મહાસદગુણી અને ભલી પરોપકારી માતા આપણી માનવંતી મહારાણી તરફ તેઓ સઘળાઓએ અને દરેકે પેહેલી નજર રાખીને કરીયો છે. પણ પ્રમાણિક કુંઅરે તો એવીશે વિવેકી નજરથી જોઈ ખોલ્લું જાહેર કહી સંભળાવીયું છે કે, જે આદરમાન અને પીયાર આ દેશાની રઈઅતે દેખડાવીયો છે, તે ઉપરથી તેની ખાત્રી થઈ ચુકી છે કે, આ દેશાની રઈઅત મહારાણી તરફ સંતોષ અને વફાદારી ભરેલું દીલ ખરેખરજ ધરાવેછે, અને જેમ જેમ કેળવણીનો પ્રસારો રઈઅતમાં વધતો જશે તેમ તેમ લોક વધારે સંતોષ ભરેલા, કાયદાને માનભરેલી રીતે તાબેદાર અને વધારે વફાદાર થતાં જશે. શાહાજાદાના આ ટુંકાં વચનોમાં ઘણા લાંબા વિચારો સમાવેલા છે. પાદશાહી ખાનદાનના કેલવણી પામેલાઓ હંમેશ થોડુંજ બોલેછે, અને થોડાં બોલોમાં ઘણી મતલબ ધરાવેછે.

હવે ખરેખર આ નવજવાન શાહાજાદો જારે પોતાની વાહાલી માતા આપણી મહારાણી પાશે જઈ ઉભો રેહેશે અને હિંદુસ્થાનના દેશીઓ વીશે એવું જાહેર કરશે કે, જે જાહોજલાલી ભરેલી ઈજ્જત અને હુરમત તેને આ દેશમાં મળી છે તે સઘળી આ દેશાની રઈઅતની તે મહારાણી તરફ વફાદારી ભરેલાં દીલ હોવાના સબબથી મળી છે, તો આ જેવી મુખજુબાનીની અસર આપણી માનવંત રાણી ઉપર, તેના પ્રધાનો ઉપર, પારલમેંટની આખી સભા ઉપર, અને આખી ઇંગ્રેજી કોમ ઉપર એવી તો જબરદસ્ત થશે કે કોઈબી બીજી સાહેદી ગહવાઈથી એવી થઈ નથી શકનાર. આથી આપણ દેશીવચ્ચે અને આપણી ઉપર રાજકર્તા ઇંગ્રેજો વચ્ચે મીત્રાચારીનો ગાંઠ વધારે મજબુત બંધાવો જોઈએ, એમાં તો કંઈ શક છેજ નહીં. એના સારાં પરિણામો જોવાને ટંગાયલી નજરે ભવિષ્યકાળ ઉપર જોવાનું રહયું છે.

આ ઠેકાણે પુસ્તક બનાવનાર જણાવવાને રજા લીએછે કે જારે શાહાજાદા આલફરેડનું મુંબઈમાં આવવું થયું તે વખત જોગવાઈ હાત કરી, વાંચણ

રોખી મંડળીમાં એક નાહાની સરખી. પણ લાંબાં વખત સુધી ટકી શકે, એવી તેની પધરામણીની યાદગારી રાખવાની મતલબથી, ગ્રંથકર્તાએ હિંદુસ્થાનમાં કરેલી મુસાફરીનો એહવાલ જે લખી રાખીયો હતો તેનું પુસ્તક શાહાજાદાની મુસાફરીની મતલબને અનુકુળ હોવાથી, તેની પરવાનગી લઇ તેને અરપણ કરવાનું વાજબી ધારીયું, અને એવીરો શાહાજાદાને અરજ કરી, તેમાં એવું જણાવીયું કે, આ પુસ્તક લખવાની મુખીય મતલબ એજ છે કે, દેશીરાજા, અમીર ઉમરાઓ, અને બીજા શક્તિવાન સાહેબોમાં મુસાફરી કરવાનો તથા તેથી તેમનો અનુભવ વધારવાનો શેાખ ઉતપંન થાય, અને એવું કરવામાં શાહાજાદાએ તથા તેનાં આખાં પાદશાહી કુટંબે એક અછો કરી દેખડાવેલો દાખલો સઘળાંની નજર સાંમણે ધરીયો છે. એના જવાબમાં રાજકુંઅરે ખુશીસાથે આ પુસ્તક પોતાને અરપણ કરવાની પરવાનગી આપી તથા આ પુસ્તકમાં આપેલાં સઘળાં ચીત્રોનો એક સુંદર “ આલબમ ” બનાવીને ગ્રંથકર્તાએ તેની સાંમણે ભેટ દાખલ ધરીયો હતો, તે તેણે મોટી ખુસી અને ઉપકાર સાથે કબુલ રાખીયો અને કાગળના ઉત્તરમાં તેણે એવી ઇછા લખી જણાવી કે, આ પુસ્તક જે મતલબથી લખાયું છે તે મતલબ પારપડે. આ ભલા રાજકુંઅરે પુસ્તક લખનારની અરજ કબુલ રાખી તેથી તેને શેાભા થઈછે જે વીરો જાહેર રીતે આ ઠેકાણે શાહાજાદાનો ઉપકાર માનવાની ગ્રંથકર્તા એક પોતાની અગતની ફરજ સમજેછે.

આ ઠેકાણે એક બીજી અગતની બાબદ ઉપર ખુલાસો કરવાની પુસ્તક લખનારને એક સારી તક મળી છે. એ બાબદ વીરો ગ્રંથકર્તાને, સરકારી રાજદરબારી ખાતાંના એક મોટા અમલદાર સાથે વાતચીતમાં, ઇંગ્રેજ સરકારનું ઘણુંજ ભલું દીલ, આપણા દેશી રાજા અને મહારાજાઓ તરફ માલુમ પડીયું છે. જારેખી કોઈ એવા મોટા પ્રસંગો આવે કે જે વેળા રાજદરબારી મોટા મેલાવડા થાય તે વેળા અકસર કરીને ઇંગ્રેજ સરકારની એવીજ ઇછા છે કે આસપાસના દેશી રાજાઓ અને અમીર ઉમરાઓ તથા તેમના કુંઅરો અને પ્રધાનો તથા બીજા મોટી પદવીના દેશીઓ આવા મેલાવડામાં આવી બીરાજે અને સામેલ થાય. ઇંગ્રેજ સરકારની એવીજ ઇછા છે કે રાજા, મહારાજાઓ એક બીજામાં મળતા ભેટતા અને તેમની મીત્રાચારીમાં વધારો કરાતા રેહે, દેશો દેશાની રીત-

બાંત જોઈ તેમના પોતાના દેશમાં સું સું ફેરફાર કરવા તેવીશે કેટલાક નવા વીચારો તેમના મનમાં ઉત્પંન થાય. આવી શુભ ઇછા અને મતલબ-થીજ ઇંગ્રેજ સરકાર વારંવાર દેશી રાજાઓને આમંત્રણ કરેછે, અને આ રાજાઓને થોડા દીવસ પરકી જંગાપર આવી રેહેતાં, ઇંગ્રેજ સરકારસાથે અથવા કોઇ બીજાં કારણસર કોઈ કામકાજ અથવા મસલહત લેવી પડે અથવા કાગજ પત્રોનો સંદેશો ચલાવવો પડે તો તેજ વખતે જલદીથી કામ બજા લાવવાને દરેક દેશી રાજાની સાથે તેમના રેસીડિનટોને હાજર રેહેવાની ઇંગ્રેજ સરકાર જરૂર પાડેછે. આ સઘળી ગોઠવણ દેશી રાજાઓની સગવડ અને ફાયદાને સારૂ કરેલી છે, અને જેઓ આ ઉપરથી એવું સમજે અથવા વીચારેછે કે રેસીડિનટો દેશી રાજાઓ ઉપર અકસર કરીને દેખરેખ રાખવાને સાથે આવેછે, અને તેઓ રાજાને મનગમતી રીતે ફરવા દેતાં નથી, એ વીચાર તદન ખોટો અને એ વાત તદન પાયાવગરની છે. એજ મુજબ જેઓ એવું ધારેછે કે ઇંગ્રેજ સરકાર દેશી રાજાઓને બાહેર મુસાફરી કરવાની મનાઈ કરેછે, એ વાત પણ બીલકુલ ખોટી છે. આગળ ખુલાસો કીધો તે મુજબ જાણવું જોઈએછ કે કોઈબી દેશી રાજા અથવા રાજપુત્રો તેમનો પોતાનો અનુભવ વધારવાને આ દેશમાં અથવા ઇંગલંડ, યુરપ, અથવા અમેરીકા દેશોમાં મુસાફરી કરવાની ખાયશ બતલાવશે તો તેમને ઇંગ્રેજ સરકાર તરફથી જરાબી મનાઈ અથવા અટકાવ નથી થવાનો, બલકે ઓર સાંબું સરકાર તરફથી તેમને ઉત્તેજન મળવાની વકી થઈ પડશે.

મુસાફરી જો અનુભવવાળા તથા અવલોકનશક્તિ ધરાવનાર, તેમજ વગવાળા શખશોની સંગતમાં કરી હોય તો તેથી ઘણી એક તરેહનાં ફાયદા હાસિલ થાયછે, જે ફાયદા ખુદ પોતેજ એખલા મુસાફરી કરવાથી ઘણું કરીને નથી મળી શકવાના. પેહેલાં જણાવેલા ગુણોવાળા શખશોની સંગતમાં મુસાફરી કીધાથી આસપાસની ખુદરતી જોવાલાયક ચીજો તથા શાંભળવા લાયક બાબદો સારીપેઠે અને ચોકસાઈથી જોવાને અને જાણવાને બની શકેછે, તેવું અને તેટલું એકલાં જોયા અથવા પુછ-પરછ કીધાથી નથી બની શકતું. ઘણી એક જાણવા લાયક બાબતો અને ચીજો કોઈ વાર આપણી આંખ આગળથી પસાર થઈ જાયછે તે વીશે આપણ એક-લાને કશી ખબર પડતી નથી અથવા એકુ ખ્યાલ વટીક પણ આવતો નથી, પણ

જો સંગાતે ઉપલા ગુણવાળા શખશો હોય તો એક બીજાને અરસપરસ ઘણો ફાયદો થઈ શકેછે. તેમજ ત્રીજો ગુણ એટલે વગવાળાં માણસની સંગત મળ્યાથી મુસાફરીની રંજ અને અડચણો ઓછી થાયછે. તેમાં ઘણું કરીને હિંદુસ્થાનની હાલની હાલત પ્રમાણે મુસાફરીમાં એવી સંગતની અગત જો કે આગગાડી ચાલુ થઇ છે તોએપણ હજુ ઘણીજ છે. યુરોપખંડમાં ઘણુંકરીને સઘળી તરફ રેલવે હોયાથી મુસાફરોને જેવું સગવડ અને સુખતઈઆર મલી આવેછે તેવું હજુ હિંદુસ્થાનમાં હાલ ઘણેક ઠેકાણે નથી મળી આવતું. એ ઉપરથી જે કોઈ માણસ આ દેશમાં એકલું મુસાફરી કરવાને નીકળ્યું તો ખરેખર તે બીચારાનાં સ્વપનામાં પણ નહીં હશે એવી અડચણો તેને નડવાની અથવા મુસીબતો ખમવી પડવાની; જેથી તે મુસાફર સરૂઆતમાંજ હારખાઈ પાછો ફરે, અથવા કોઈવાર પોતાના જીવને ધાસ્તીમાં નાએ, એવું બનવાજોગ છે. હમારી મતલબ એવું જણાવીને કોઇને નાહીંમત કરવાની નથી. હમો સાંભી ઉલટ અને હીંમત આપી શકીએ છેએ કે જેમ જેમ આગગાડીનો રસ્તો વધતો જાયછે તેમ તેમ આપણા દેશમાં મંજલની રંજ અને અડચણો ટલતી જાયછે, તોએપણ એક ચેતવણી અથવા ઈસારો કરવાની અગત છે, કે મુસાફરે હિંદુસ્થાનમાં જેમ બની આવે તેમ એકલું અને ખાલી હાથે બાહેર નહીં નીકળવું. બની આવતાં તેવા હોશીઆર અને વગવાળાં આદમીની સંગત તથા ભલામણ મેળવવી તથા જરૂરની ચીજો સાથે રાખી બાહેર પડવું બેહેતર છે. હમારી મુસાફરીમાં ૧૪) ચૌદ પુરૂષોનો એક નાહાનો સરખો કાફલો થયલો હતો; વળી ઠેકાંણે ઠેકાંણેથી ઓળખાણ, ભલામણ અને સીફારસના કાગળ પત્રો સાથે લીધાં હતાં, તોએપણ જારે છતે વગે અને છતે છુટે હાથે પૈસો ખરચતાં કોઈ કોઈવાર હેરાનગતી જબરી ભોગવવી પડી હતી, ત્યારે વીચાર કરવો જોઇયે કે વગર વગવાળા અને એકલા મુસાફરને કેટલું સોસવું અને ખમવું પડે વારૂ ?

મુસાફરીની ઈછા ઉત્પંન થવાનું કારણ.

હિંદુસ્તાન દેશમાં ફરીને તેનાં શેહેરોની આબોહવા જાણવાની અને તાંહાંની વસ્તીની હાલત નજરે નજર જોઈ વાકેફ થવાની ઈચ્છા થયાથી, તથા આ દેશનાં પ્રાચીન કાળનાં કૃત્યો અને તેમનાં શેષની રહેલી નીશાનો જોવાની હોંસ થયાથી, અને એવું જોવાને જેઓથી નહી બની આવતું હોય તેઓની હજુરમાં એ

વીરોનું ટુંક બયાન ગુજારવાની ઉમેદ રાખીને આ દેશમાં મુસાફરી કરવાના કેટલાએક ગૃહસ્થોએ ઠરાવ કીધો. એ કામ ઉઠાવવામાં મુખ્ય આગેવાની કરવાનું માન શેઠ ખુરશેદજી નોશીરવાનજી કામાજીને ઘટેછે. એવાં કામમાં આ લાયકી ભરેલા ગૃહસ્થને અસલથીજ ઘણી ઉલટ છે. તે ઉલટ એટલે સુધી જોવામાં અને તપાસવામાં આવી છે કે કોઈ સારૂં કામ ઉઠાવી તેને પુરૂં થયલું જોવાને છેક છેલ્લી ઘડી સુધી બનતી કોશેશ કરવાને એ ગૃહસ્થ હઠનાર નથી; એટલુંજ નહીં, પણ કોઈવાર અડચણની વખતે કામ બજાવવાને પોતાને માથે બોજો પડે તેવી ચીજ ઉઠાવવી પડી તો તે પણ ઉઠાવવાને મોહોટી ખુશીથી શેઠનો દરજ્જો એકકોરે મુકવાને અચકાવાનાં નથી. એહેવા ગૃહસ્થની તથા એઓ-ની સાથે ડાકટર ભાઉ દાજી જેવા સકલગુણસંપંન વિદ્વાનની સંગત મળ્યાથી અને શેઠ ખુરશેદજી રૂસ્તમજી કામાજી જેઓએ યુરોપખંડમાં ઘણેક ઠેકાણે મુસાફરી કરી, સારૂં જ્ઞાન અને હોશીઆરી મેળવી છે તેમનાં આ મુસાફરીમાં સાથે જોડાવાથી, આ પુસ્તક લખનારને પણ એવી મંડળીમાં ભેગું થવાની ઉલટ થઈ. શેઠ મનચેરજી મેહેરવાંનજી નાજીએરવાળાએ પોતાની ખુશીથી આખી મુસાફરીને લગતી રસ્તાની સઘળી તજુમલ અને ગોઠવણ કરવાનું કઠણ કામ પોતાને માથે ઊંચકી લીધું હતું; અને એવાં કામમાં એમને સંસાર વેહેવારનો ઘણો અનુભવ હોયાથી તથા તેની સાથે ખુરા મીજાજની ખુદરતી બખશેશ ધરાવનાર શખસ એવણ હોયાથી એવણ એક ઘણાજ પસંત અને ઉપયોગી મીત્ર આખી મુસાફરીમાં થઈ પડ્યા હતા. એવણના હાત હેઠળ મદદગાર તરીકે, ભાઈ રૂસ્તમજી ફકીરજી કોપરને સાથે આપીયા હતા, પણ આગળ એહેવાલ વાંચતાં માલુમ પડશે કે આ જુવાન પેહેલવાન જેણે પોતાનો પગ કોઈ દાહાડે શેહરની ભાગળથી બાહેર નહીં કાહાડેલો, તેની ઉપર જારે અણજાણી જગા અને જંગલોમાં એકલું અવારસું કામ કરવાનું આવી પડતું, ત્યારે તે બીચારો મદદગાર થવાને બદલે "અરે મહને કોઈ લએઓરે" એવી મદદ લેવાજોગ હાલતમાં ઘણીવાર રમુજ પડે એવી રીતે આવી પડ્યો હતો. ડાકટર ભાઉ દાજીએ પોતાના એક જરમન મીત્ર નામે મીસ્તર "એડવર્ડ રીહીઆસ્ટિક" ને ખુદરતી દેખાવ જે જોવામાં આવે તેમના ચિત્રો પાડવાને તથા કેટલીએક બાબદોની નોંધ કરી લેવાને પોતાની સાથે મદદગાર લીધો, હતો.

પેહેલાં એવો વીચાર થયો કે મુંબઇથી કરાંચી જવું, અને તે માર્ગે મુલતાન થઈ લાહોર, અને તીહાંથી છેક કાશ્મીર સુધી ઉપર જવું. પછી તીહાંથી પાછું ફરી દિલ્લી, આગરા, લખ્નૌ, કાનપોર, અલાહબાદ, બનારસ વગેરે મુખ્ય સેહેરો જોતાં કલકત્તે પોહોંચવું; અને કલકત્તેથી આગબોટની મારફતે મદરાસ જવું. મદરાસની આસપાસની જગાઓ જોઈ તે વખતે ચાલુ થયલી રેલવેને રસ્તે બેપુર આવવું, અને બેપુરથી પાછા સ્ટીમરની મારફતે મુંબઈ આવવું. પુછપરછ કરતાં એ માર્ગે કેટલીએક અડચણો માલુમ પડી તથા એ માર્ગે ફરી વળવાને પુરતો વખત નથી મળી શકવાનો એવું જણાયાથી ઉપલો વીચાર ફેરવવાની જરૂર પડી. બીજો વીચાર પછી એવો કીધો કે મુંબઇથી પેહેલાં શોલાપુર જવું, અને તીહાંથી નીજામ હેદરાબાદ થઈ, જે રસ્તો ફાવતો માલુમ પડે તે રસ્તે મદરાસ જવું. તીહાંથી સ્ટીમરની મારફતે કલકત્તે જવું, અને કલકત્તેથી, અલાહબાદ, બનારસ, (કાશી) લખ્નૌ, આગરા, અને દિલ્લી જોઇને છેક કાશ્મીર સુધી જો વખત મળે તો પોહોંચવું, અને પછી તીહાંથી ઉતરતાં, લાહોર, મુલતાન, સિંધ હેદરાબાદ અને કરાંચી થઇને મુંબઈ આવવું. આ ઠરાવ પાકો તો કીધો, પણ "માણસનું તો બોલવું છે અને ખુદાનું તો કરવું છે." તે કેહેવત પ્રમાણે આ છેલ્લા ઠેરવેલા માર્ગની મુસાફરીમાં વગર ધારેલી અડચણો નડ્યાથી, માત્ર દિલ્લી સુધી પોહોંચતાં વખત એટલો તો ભરાઈ ગયો, ગરમી અને સખત તાપ એવો તો પડવા લાગ્યો કે આગળ જવું વાજબી નથી, એમ ધારીને દિલ્લીથીજ પાછું ફરવું બેહેતર જાણ્યું. પાછું ફરતાં, આગરાને માર્ગે સિંધીયા અને હોલકરની રાજધાનીના મુખ્ય સેહેરો, ગોવાલીઅર અને ઇંદોરની ભેટ લીધી હતી, અને તીહાંથી મહુને રસ્તે સીંધ્રવાઘાટ ઉપરથી જળગામ ઉતરયા હતા, જીહાંથી આગગાડીની મારફતે નાશીક થઇને પાછા મુંબઈ આવી પુગા હતા.

આ સાથે જોડેલા નકાશા ઉપરથી માલુમ પડશે કે જે ચક્કર આસમાની રેષાનું પાડેલું છે, તે અમારી મુસાફરીનો માર્ગ અને વલાણ બતલાવેછે. એ ચક્કરનો ઘેરાવો આસરે ૧૨૦૦) બારસેં માઈલનો ગણ્યામાં આવ્યો છે.

ઉપલી મુસાફરીમાંજો કેતરેવાર રંજ અને સંકટ પડ્યું હતું, જેવી કે ગાડીઓ ઉંધી વળી, તેમનાં પઈડાં નીકળી પડયાં, બળદો બેસી ગયા, કોઇવાર તેઓ ભર નદીનાં

પાણીમાં બેસી ગયાથી ગાડીમાં પાણી ભરાઈ ગયાં, કીચડમાં ગાડીનાં પઈડાં ખુતી રહયાં, તે કાહાડવાને જેમ ઇસપનીતીમાં કહેલા ગાડાંવાલાએ બુમો પાડી હતી તે પ્રમાણે નહીં, પણ બુમો પાડ્યા વગર હમોને ખેંચી કાહાડવાની ફરજ થઇ પડી હતી. દરીયાનાં તોફાનની યાદ રાખવા જોગ છકડ ખાધી હતી, અડીએલ ઘોડાંઓને લીધે ભર નદીના મછવાના પુલ ઉપર મધરાત્રે ધોધો વરસાત, અંધારૂં, પવન, ગાજવીજનું તોફાન, અને સખત થંડી, ભુખે પેટે, અને પેયાસે હોટે ખમવી પડી હતી, તોએપણ એ સઘળું દુઃખ મોહોટી ખુશીથી અને હોંસથી ખમી શકાયું હતું, અને તેમાં ખુદાની મેહેરબાનીથી એક્કે પણ શખસના શરીરને કોઇપણ તરેહેની ઇજા પોહોંચી નહીં હતી. જેમ સઘળા ખુશ દીલ, તનદરોસ્ત અને સંપ સાથે રવાના થયા હતા તેવાજ ખુશ દીલ, તનદરોસ્ત અને સંપ ભરેલા પાછા ફરયા હતા. એ કંઇજ નહીં પણ ખરેખર તે રેહેમી મેહેરબાન ખાદગરની હમો કમીના બંદાઓ ઉપર એક મોહોટી નવાજેશ થયલી સમજી, સઘળી નમનતાઇથી આ ઠેકાણે તેની નોંધ કરવાની એક આઇન ફરજ હમો સમજીએ છીએ.

એ મુસાફરીનો રસ્તાનો ખાધા પીધાનો અને ગાડી ભાડાં વીગેરે તમાંમ ખરચ રૂ ૧૨૦૦૦ થી ૧૩૦૦૦) તેર હજાર સુધી થયો હતો.

મુંબઈથી પુણા અને શોલાપોર.

તા૦ ૨૨ મી ડીસેંબર—આ દીને મુંબઈથી સહવારના આઠ કલાકે ભાએખલા સ્ટેશન ઉપરથી પુણા લાઇનની ગાડીમાં, દોસ્ત આસનાઓને મલીભેટીઆ પછી રવાને થયા હતા. બોરઘાટ ઉપર ટનલો (પાહાડો કોતરીને કરેલા રસ્તા) એ વરસમાં પુરા નહીં થયલા હતા તેથી ખપોલી આગળથી ઘાટ ઉપર ચઢવાને તટુ, ઘોડાં, પાલખી, ગાડીઓ વીગેરેનો ઉપયોગ થતો હતો. પાલખીમાં બેસીને ઘાટ ચઢવાની ગોઠવણ ઉતારૂઓ મુંબઇથી કરતા હતા અને તેનું દામ વટીક પણ આગળથી આપતા હતા, તોએપણ તેવા શખસોને રેલવેના બારભાયાના રાજકારભારથી એટલી ખાતરી નહીં મળતી હતી કે તેમનાં આપેલાં દામ પ્રમાણે તેમને પાલખી અથવા તેવી સારી ગાડી મળશેજ. પણ એ વાતની સાબેતી ખપોલી પોહોંચ્યા સીવાય મળી નહીં શકતી હતી; તેથી એટલી બાબત રેલવે-

વાળાઓનાં હકમાં ફાયદા ભરેલી હતી. એટલા સબબથી ખપોલી આગળ એ વખતમાં હંમેશ એક જોવા લાયક અને કોઈ કોઈવાર તો દીલગીરી ભરેલો બનાવ બનતો હતો. ખપોલી આગળ ટરેન (આગગાડી) આવી ઉભી એટલે પેહેલા અને બીજા વર્ગના ઉતારૂઓ જાણે ધાડ આવ્યાથી લોક નાહાસવા પડેલાં હોય તેમ દોડાદોડીમાં પડતાં હતાં. પછી "મારે તેની તલવાર" આ કેહેવત પ્રમાણે હરામીઓ અને લુચ્ચા લફંગા ઇંગરેજો અને કેટલાએક તેવા આપણા દેશીઓ પાલખી અને સારી ગાડીઓ જબરીથી પોતાને સારૂ લુટી લઈ જતા હતા, જેથી બીચારા રાંક ગૃથસ્થોને તેમની અસીલાઈ લીધે ઘણું દુઃખ અને હેરાનગતી ખમવી પડતી હતી. એ અંધેર કારભારમાં કનટરાકટરો અને તેઓનાં માણસો સારીપેઠે પોતાનું ભલું કરતા હતા, તેમ બીજા હાથ ઉપર ગરીબોને અને અસીલ ગૃહસ્થોને પૈસા ખરચી ઘાટ પગે ચાલી ચઢવો પડતો હતો, અથવા કોઈવાર "દમની" નામની બે પઇડાંની બળદની ગાડીમાં બેસીને જે ઉતારૂઓને ઘાટ ચઢવો પડતો હતો તેમનાં "દમની" સલામતી જોખમમાં આવી પડતી હતી.

હવડાં તો આવાં સઘળાં સંકટો ઘણાખરાં ટળી ગયાં છે. બોરઘાટની અંદરનાં સઘળા ટનલો અને પુલો તૈયાર અને પુરા થયા છે અને હાલ ગાડી ઘાટ ઉપરથી ઉતારૂ અને માલ સાથે થેઠ પસાર થઈ શકેછે. કમાઇ તો બહુ થાયછે પરંતુ ગ્રેટ ઇંડીયન પેનીનસુલર રેલવે કંપનીના ભાગીદારોને તેમની થાપણ લાયક વ્યાજ ઉતપંન નથી થતું, અને ખરચ ઘણી ખરી કમઇ ખેંચી જાયછે, આ વાત ખરેખર દીલગીરી ભરેલી છે. પણ ભાગીદારોએ આ એક મોહોટો સંતોષ માનવો જોઇયે કે તેમના પૈસાથી આજે બોરઘાટમાં જે જે ટનલો અને પુલો કોતરાયલા અને બંધાયલા છે, તથા નદીઓ ઉપર જે મોહોટાં બાંધકામો થયાં છે, એ ખરેખર જોવા લાયક અને યાદ રેહેવા જોગ એનજીનીઅરીંગ વિદ્યાની ફતેહની મહાભારત નીશાનો ઉભીથયલી છે. એ કામ પાર પાડવામાં જેટલી ઇંગરેજોએ મનશક્તિ વાપરી છે તેટલી શરીરશકિત વાપરીને આપણા દેશીઓએ એ શાહાશીક કામો ઉઠાવી લઇને પુરાં કરીયાં છે તે કાંઈ થોડી કીરતીના કામો નથી. મરનાર નામાંકીત જે. જે. બરકલી આ કંપનીના મુખ્ય એનજીનરે પોતાની અકલનાં બળે કરી બોરઘાટ ઉપરથી રેલવે લઈ જવાનો જે એક ઘણોજ કઠણ સવાલ હતો તેનો જેમ ફડચો કરી આપ્યો, તેથી જેવી તેની અકલની તારીફ તાજુબી સાથે આપણે

કરીએ છેએ, તેવીજ તાજુબી ભરેલી તારીફ, આપણે જે દેશી બેગારીઓ અને કારીગરોએ રાત દાહાડો પથર સાથે ટક્કર લડી તેને ફોડ્યો છે, તેમનાં ધીરજ અને હીંમતની કરવી જરૂર છે. શીરીન ઉપર ફરહાદ ફીદા થઈ પોતાની માશુકનાં ફકત મશ્કરીના માંગવા ઉપરથી પાહાડો ફોડીને તે વાટે નદીનું પાણી શીરીનના મેહેલ આગળ ખેંચી લાવ્યો હતો, એવું કિસ્સા કાહાંણીમાં લખેલું છે; પણ હાલના જમાનામાં તો અક્કલ, વિદ્યા, હુંનર, હીંમત, સબુરી ઈતીયાદીનાં બળે કરી ખરેખર પાહાડોને ખસેડ્યા છે, તેમની ઊપરથી, તેમનાં પેટમાંહેથી અને બાજુએથી અને કહો તાંહાંથી રસ્તા કાહાડ્યા છે; નદીઓ અને દરીઆ ઓળંગ્યા છે; આવાં મહાભારત કામોના મોજુદ જીવતા દાખલા આપણા દેશમાં આગગાડીના રસ્તા દેખડાવી આપેછે.

ખંડાળેથી નીકળેલા સાંજના ૬‌ા વાગે પુણાનાં સ્ટેશન ઉપર પોહોંતા હતા, તીહાં આપણી માનવંત સરકારથી માન પામેલા દસ્તુરજી શાહેબ ખાનબાહાદુર નોશેરવાનજી જામાસ્પજી પોતાની અને બીજી ગાડીઓ લઈ હમોને એસ્તેકબાલ લેવાને આવ્યા હતા, તેમની સાથે ભેટ થઈ. દસ્તુરજીએ હમારી મંડળીનો જે આદરસત્કાર કીધો હતો તે ઘણોજ લાયકી ભરેલો નજર આવ્યો હતો અને દસ્તુરજી પોતાના પરોણા તરફ હંમેશ મોહોબત ભરેલું દીલ રાખેછે, એવું ઘણીવાર હમારા સાંભળવામાં આવ્યું હતું તે આ વખતે નજરે પડ્યું હતું. એ વીશે આ વખતે હમોને આ દસ્તુરજીનાં આવા સદગુણોની એક નોંધ કરવાને મોહોટી ખુશી ઉતપંન થાયછે.

આ રાત્રે ભવાની પેંઠમાં શેઠ દીનશાહા માંણેકજી પેટીટનાં એક ઘણાજ ખુશનુમાં બાગવાળા બંગલામાં હમોએ ઉતારો કીધો હતો. રાત્રે ૧૦ વાગા પછી એટલી બધી તાહાડ લાગવા માંડી હતી કે વડા કામાજીને થંડીના લખલખાં ભરાઈ આવ્યાથી, તેવણને બેથી ચાર કલાક સુધી બીછાનામાં ઓઢીને સુઈ રેહેવું પડ્યું હતું. એ પ્રસંગે થંડી અટકાવાનાં ઉપાયો વીશે જે જે સાહેબો મળવા ભેટવાને આવ્યા હતા તેઓએ તરેહવાર અભિપ્રાય અને મતો આપીયાં હતાં. વધારે મત જલદ દારૂ ટાંકવા અને તીખું તમતમતું ખાવા વીશે પડ્યાં હતાં. પુણાની આબોહવા વીશે ઘણા જણનું એવું સાધારણ પણ ભુલ ભરેલું મત છે કે થંડીના દીવસમાં

બરાંડી દારૂ અને મરચાં અગત કરીને તે જગાએ ખાવાની જરૂરજ પડેછે. પણ આ વગરપાયાનું મત ફકત કલ્પનાથી બંધાયલું છે. દારૂનાં શોખી અને તએ-રાખનારને થંડી લાગ્યાથી દારૂજ પીવા ગમેછે, પણ જે દારૂનાં શોખી અને તએ-વાળા નથી તેમને થંડી લાગીયાથી દારૂ જરા પણ માફક આવતો નથી. અમોને લાગેલી થંડીને હમોએ થંડકથીજ મારી હતી; તેથી જેવા તંદરોસ્તી ભરેલા રાત્રે સુતા હતા તેવાજ સહવારનાં ઉઠયા હતા. હમારી સાથનાં સર સરંજામમાં હમા ચીજો રાખી હતી, પણ દારૂ માતરે દવા જેટલોજ વાપરવાને લીધો હતો. તાવના રોગમાં જરૂર પડતી ત્યારે જેમ હમારા મીત્ર ડાકટર ભાઉ દાજી તાવવાળાં માણુ-સને ત્રણથી છ ગ્રેન કુવીનીન આપતા હતા, તેવીજ તજુમલથી હમારા દારૂનો ઉપ-યોગ થતોહતો. પીવાની મજા તો હમોને સારૂં, સોજું, થંડું પાણી, અથવા લેહજત-દાર ચાહે અથવા કાફીનું એકું કપ (પ્યાલું) મળવાથી પડતી હતી, જે મજાદારી હમો ઠેકાણે ઠેકાણે જાણે એક ઘણીજ ઉકમાઈ હોય એવી સમજીને ભોગવતા હતા. લાંબી અને સખત મુસાફરીમાં જો તંદરોસ્તી સારી હાલતમાં રાખવી હોય તો જેમ બને તેમ દારૂનાં પીપણાથી પરેહજી રાખવી જરૂર છે; તેમજ ખાણું થોડું, સાદું પણ તરદુદનું અને વખતસર લયા કરવું જરૂર છે. એટલી બે બાબતની અગત કરીને મુસાફરોએ ચોકસી રાખી તો તેમને ફાયેદા થયા વગર રેહેરો નહીં.

તારીખ ૨૩ મી ડીસેંબર—સહવારના પોહોરમાં વેહેલા ઉઠી કાફી સાથે જરા હલકો નાસ્તો કીધો. દસ્તુરજી સાહેબ પોતાની મોહોબત ભરેલી રાહે ફરીને ગાડી-ઓ લઈ હમુને રવાના કરવાને બંગલાંમાં આવ્યા હતા, તેઓની સાથે રવાનગીની મુલાકત કીધા પછી, સઘળા જણ સાથે ગાડીમાં પુણાનાં સ્ટેશન ઉપર આવ્યા અને શોલાપુર જવાની તૈયારી કીધી.

પુણેથી શોલાપુર સુધી આગગાડીના રસ્તાની ડાબી અને જમણી બાજુએ ખેતરોમાં તે સાલની ખેતી સારી થયલી માલુમ પડી હતી. કોઠળમાં ઘણોખરો જુઆરનો પાક થયલો હતો, તેથી ઉતરતો ગહું, ચણા અને તુઅરનો હતો. જેવાં ખેતરો આબાદાન અને ખુશાનુમાં પુણેથી તે સોલાપુરના ટપ્પામાં નજરે પડયાં હતાં તેવાં ખંડાળા અને પુણા વચ્ચેના ટપ્પામાં દેખાયાં નહીં હતાં, તેનું કારણ એવું ધારવામાં આવેછે કે એ ટપ્પામાં કોઈ નદી નથી અને ખડકની જમીન છે. નાહાનાં નાડાનાં નાળાંઓ એણીગમ પેલીગમ આવેલાં છે પણ તેમનું પાણી

સઘળી તરફ ફરી નહીં વળી શકયાથી માતરે જે ખેતી થાયછે તે તે નાળાંઓની આસપાસની જગામાંજ થઈ શકેછે.

પુણા આગળથી "મુળામુઠા" નદી વેહેછે. તેનાં પાણીએ ઘણી જગાએ આબાદાની કરી છે. પુણેથી આગળ સોલાપુર તરફ જતાં બીજી નદીઓ "ભીમા" અને "સોન" આવેછે તેઓનું પાણી આસપાસનાં ખેતરોમાં કોળના પાકને ઘણુંજ ઉપયોગી પડેછે. એ નદીઓ કોઈ કોઈ ઠેકાણે રેલવેના રસ્તામાં આવી છે. તેથી તે ઉપર ઘણાજ જોવા લાયક પુલો બાંધેલા છે.

આગગાડીમાં બેસી જલદી દોડી જનાર મુસાફર એવી ઇચ્છા રાખે કે જે જગાએથી તે દોડતી ગાડીએ જતો હોય તે જગાએ રેહેનાર વસ્તીની હાલતનું જ્ઞાન મેળવે તથા તે જગાની આબાદાની કેવી છે તે વીશે વાકેફ થાય તો તેણે આટલી વાત સારીપેઠે ધ્યાનમાં રાખવી કે, જે કાંઈ જડફમાં તેની નજરે પડે તે ઉપરથી તેણે પોતાનું મત બાંધવું નહીં. આગગાડીના રસ્તાની ડાવી અને જમણી તરફ જોતાં તો ખેતરો ખરેખરાં લીલાં અને આબાદાન છેક દુર નજર પોંહોંચે તીહાંસુધી જોયામાં આવે છે, પણ તે તેટલાંજ. કોઈ જગાએ એક બે દીવશ ઉતરી તે ઠેકાણે રહી તીહાંની રૈયતની તથા જગાની હાલત આપણે નજરે નજર જોઈએ અને તે વીશે પોતાની જાતે પુછપરછ કરીએ તો દોડતી આગગાડીએ જે નજરે જોયામાં આવેછે તેમાં અને પુરતો વખત લઈ ધીરજથી જે એહેવાલ માલુમ પડશે એ બંધેમાં ઘણો ફરક પડી જવાનો. આ સાધારણ બાબતની ચોકસી હિંદુસ્થાનનાં પેહેલા ખજાનચી મરનાર મીસ્તર વીલસને ન રાખ્યાથી તેણે પોતાના વીચારમાં એક મોહોટું ગોતું ખાધું હતું. તે અંમલદાર જેવો હિંદુસ્થાનમાં આવ્યો તેવોજ આગગાડીએ હિંદુસ્થાનની જમીન અને લોકની હાલત તપાસવાને કલકત્તેથી મુસાફરી કરવા નીકળ્યો, અને જેટલું આગગાડીએ ફરાયું તેટલું ફરી વળી, દિલ્લી, આગરા અને ઉત્તર પ્રાંતોમાં બની આવતી સ્વારીએ મુસાફરી કરી વળ્યો, અને એક અથવા બે માસની દોડ દોડની મુસાફરીમાં તેણે જે જોયું, અથવા એણીગમ પેલીગમ, છુટાં છવાયાં માણસો સાથે તેણે જે વાતચીત કીધી તેટલા ઉપરથીજ આખાં હિંદુસ્થાન વીશે તેણે એકદમ મત એવું બાંધ્યું કે, આપણો હિંદુસ્થાન દેશ "યુરોપખંડનાં બેલજીઅમ દેશ જેવો ખેતીવાડીમાં આબાદાન છે, રૈયત સુખી છે, તેમને જે સુખ જોઇયે તે મળેછે, તેમને કોઈ વાતની વાણુતાણુ નથી

ઇત્યાદિ." એવું મત બાંધવામાં તે મરનારે જે ભુલ કીધી હતી તે ફકત ઉપલી બાબતમાં એક સાધારણ ચોકસાઈ રાખવી જોઈતી હતી તે નહીં રાખ્યાથી થઇ હતી. આ વાત તો ખરી હશે કે મીસ્તર વીલસનને તેની મુસાફરીમાં કસી વાતની વાણુતાણુતો નહજ પડી હશે. તેને સારૂ આગમચથી ઠેકાણે ઠેકાણે સઘળો સરસરંજામ અને જોઈતી ચીજોનો જુદા જુદા અંમલદારોએ બંદોબસ્ત કરી રાખીયો હશે. આવી જોઇતી ગોઠવણો કરવામાં શી શી મેહેનત પડી હશે, કેટલાં માણસોને અડચણો ભોગવવી પડી હશે, એનો વીચાર મીસ્તર વીલસનનાં મનમાં ઘણો થોડોજ આવ્યો હશે. યુરોપખંડમાં જેમ સઘળી વાતની મુસાફરોને સગવડ પડેછે તેવી સગવડ સરકારી પૈસે અને અંમલે આ દેશમાં મુસાફરી કરતાં એકવાર મીસ્તર વીલસને ભોગવી હોય તો તે ઉપરથી એવું નહીં સાબેત થતું કે તેથી આ દેશ સઘળી વાતે આબાદ અને હીયાંની રૈયત સુખી છે. રૈયતની હાલત જાણવા સારૂ ઠેકાણે ઠેકાણે અગત કરીને એક અથવા બે ત્રણ દીવસ રેહેવું જોઇયે. બીજું અગતનું એ છે કે, રૈયત પોતે ખુદ એટલી અણજાણી હાલતમાં છે કે તેમની હાલત વીશે વાકેફ થવાને આપણને તરેહવાર રીતે સવાલો પુછવાની જરૂર છે. એક બે સવાલમાંજ કાંઈ તેમના વીશે પકું જણાઈ શકાવાનું નથી. એક સવાલનો કોઈ કેમ જવાબ આપશે, અને કોઈ કેમ કેહેશે. તેમાં ઘણી વેળા એક જણનું બોલવું બીજાથી તદનજ ઉલટું હોયછે. શોલાપોરમાં હમોએ પુછપરછ કરી હતી, તેનો એક દાખલો હમોએ નોંધી લીધો છે. શોલાપોરમાં એક દીવસ સાંજના ફરવા નીકળ્યા હતા. હમારી સાથે ભોમીઆ દાખલ એક કારકુન આવ્યો હતો. વાતચીત કરતાં પુછવામાં આવ્યું કે તમો કોણની રૈયત છો? તમારી સરકાર તે કોણ છે? જવાબ મળ્યો કે, હમારી સરકાર સાહેબ લોક છે. હમોએ પુછ્યું કયા સાહેબ લોક? કલેકટર સાહેબ, રીજમીટના સાહેબ, અને બીજા ટોપીવાળા સાહેબો. તેઓ કેહેવા લોક છે? હમે શું જાણીએ. તેઓ સારાં માણસ હશે. - તમે કેમ જાણ્યું કે તેઓ સઘળાં સારાં માણસ છે? તેઓ સઘળાં સારાં માણસ છે, એમ જો હમે નહીં બોલીએ અને તેઓમાં કેટલાક ખરાબ લોક છે એમ બોલીએ તો હમુને વખતે તે લોકથી શીક્ષા થાય, હમુને પકડી લઈ જાય, અને હમે ખટપટમાં આવી પડીએ. તમારી ઉપર કાંઈ જુલમ થાયછે? જુલમ સાનો, સરકાર મોહોટા સાહેબો છે, તેઓ બધાનાં માબાપ છે. સરકાર

અને તેના કારભારીઓ જેમ લોકને કેહેછે તેમ લોક ચાલેછે. જે કહે તે હમુને કરવું જોઈયે. શું અણઘટતું કામ કરવા કેહેશે તો તે પણ તમે કરશો? અલબત, સરકાર જે કાંઈ કેહે તે કરવુંજ જોઇયે; પણ હમે ગરીબ કારકુનોને પેટ પુરતું ભાત અને દાળ મળી એટલે બસ છે; બીજી વાતની ખટપટમાં પડવાની હમારે શી જરૂર છે? હમો ગરીબોથી શું થઈ શકવાનું છે, કાંઈજ નહીં. તમો સઘળા સુખી છો અથવા દુખી છો? પેટ પુરતું ખાવાનું મળે તો હમે સુખી, જારે નહીં મળે ત્યારે દુખી. હમણા દાણાદુણી મોંઘો થયો છે તેથી ઈજા ભોગવવી પડેછે. વાણીઆ વગુ સાહુકારનાં હમે કરજદાર છેએ. આ ટુંક વાતચીત સાધારણ રૈયતનાં મનનો એક ચીતાર છે. લાંબી મુદત થઈ તેમની ઉપર આગલી સલતનતથી જે આફત અને મુફલસી ગુજરતી આવી છે, અને વગર કેળવણીએ જે અજ્ઞાની હાલતમાં તેઓ પડી રહેલા છે તેથી તેમને પોતાની હાલત કેવી છે તથા તેને બેહેતર કેમ કરવી અને એ બેહતર હાલત તે કેવી છે, એ વીશે તેઓને મુતલગ ખબરજ નથી. બેદરકારપણે તેઓ પોતાની જીંદગી જનાવરની પેઠે ગુજારેછે. માત્ર ફીકર ખાધા પીધાની અને તેમાંબી માત્ર દાળ અને ભાત સીવાય બીજી જુજ જીનસોની ગરજ તેમને લાગેછે. કેલળણીની હીયાં કેટલી અગત છે એ વીશે સરકારે સારીપેઠે ધીયાન આપવું જોઈએછ. એવી હાલતમાં પડેલી રૈયત વીશે ખરો એહેવાલ જલદીથી મેળવવો કંઈ સેહેલું કામ નથી.

તા૦ ૨૩ મી ડીસેંબર.—પુણાથી શનવારને દીને સહવારનાં ૭॥ વાગે નીકળેલા શોલાપોર સ્ટેશન ઉપર પાછલા પોહોરનાં ૪॥ કલાકે પોહોંતા હતા. મીસ્તર નવરોજજી બેહેરામજી આલપાઈવાળા શોલાપોરનાં ડેપ્યુટી કલેકટર હમને સઘળાને એસ્તેકબાલ લેવા આવ્યા હતા, અને પોતાને તીંહાં હમુને ઉતારો આપવાની ઈચ્છા દેખડાવી હતી. પણ રાજેશ્રી ગોવીંદ હરી વાલેકર શોલાપોરનાં એક હિંદુ વેપારીએ આગમચથી હમારે સારૂ એક એલાહેદો બંગલો તૈયાર રખાવ્યો હતો તીંહાં હમોએ ઉતારો કીધો. મુંબઈથી હમો નીકળ્યા તેની એક બે દાહાડા આગમચથી હમારો મુસાફરીમાં સાથે લઈ જવાનો સઘળો સરસરંજામ રેલવેની મારફતે શોલાપુર મોકલી દીધો હતો કે તે તીંહાં આગળથી ઈજ પુગે; પણ રેલવેનાં અંધેર કારભારને લીધે સામાનપોંહોંચ્યા પેહેલાં હમો જઈ પુગા, અને હમારો સામાન ખંડાળાનાં

સ્ટેશન ઉપર બારેવાટ પડેલા હમાએ જોયા હતા. એટલા ઉપરથી હમુને શેાલાપેા-રમાંતે સામાન આવી પુગે તાહાંસુધી એક બે દીવસ ખેાટી થઈ રેહેવું પડ્યું હતું.

શેાલાપેાર.

શેાલાપેાર મુંબઇથી રેલવેને રસ્તે ૨૮૨૩ માઈલ દુર, અને પુણા કરતાં નીચી જગાએ આવેલું એક શેહેર છે. શેાલાપેારમાં રેલવેનું એક મેાહેાટું સ્ટેશન છે, અને જે વખતે હમેા તીહાં પેાંહેાંતા હતા તે વખતે ગ્રેટ ઇનડીયન પેનીનસુલર રેલ-વેનેા દખણ તરફનેા છેડેા એ શેહેર આગળ આવી અટકેલેા હતેા. શેાલાપેાર રૂનું એક મેાહેાટું મથક થઈ પડ્યું છે. નીજામ હેદરાબાદના દખણ ભાગનેા રૂ તથા બારસી, કનારાનેા રૂ જે આગળ કેામટામાં એકઠેા થઈ બેાટેા અને પડાઉઓમાં ભરાઇને મુંબઈ આવતેા હતેા, તે સઘળેા રૂ શેાલાપેાર તરફ હવે આવતેા થયેા છે. બેલગામ, ધારવાડ તરફનેા રૂ પણ એજ તરફ આવવા લાગેા છે. એટલાં કારણેા ઉપરથી રૂના વેપારનું, શેાલાપેાર એક મેાહેાટું મથક થયું છે; અને જેમ રેલવે આગળ વધશે અને અંદરનાં પ્રાંતેા સાથે મળશે તેમ એ વધારે અગતનું મથક થતું જશે. આવી રીતે એ જગાએ વેપારની એક અગતની જીનસ આવતી થયાથી તથા સરાફેા મળી આવ્યાથી શેાલાપેારની વસ્તી ઘણી વધવા માંડી છે. કેાઈ ૪૦,૦૦૦ માણસની ગણેછે; અને કેાઈ ૫૦,૦૦૦ થી ૬૦,૦૦૦ માણસની ગણેછે. મુખ્ય વસ્તી લિંગાઇત લેાકની છે જેઓ કાનડી ભાષા બેાલછે. તેથી ઉતરતી વસ્તી મુસલમાન લેાકની છે.

શેાલાપેારની આસપાસની જમીનમાં ઘણું કરીને જુવાર પાકેછે. તેથી ઉતરતેા ઘઉ, બાજરી, ચણા, વટાણા, તુઅર અને એક બે બીજી જાતનાં કઠેાળનેા પાક થાયછે, દીવલી અને કરડી પાકેછે તેનું તેલ બાળવાનાં કામમાં ઘણું આવેછે.

શેાલાપેારમાં મુંબઇથી ઘણું કરીને સઘળી તહરાંનું કાપડ, સુતર, મીઠું તથા સઘળી જાતનું કરીઆણું જાયછે. નીજામ હેદરાબાદના જુદા જુદા તાલુકામાં વણાયલું કાપડ પણ એ શેહેરમાં ઉતરેછે. ખુદ શેાલાપેારમાં હાતથી કાપડ વણવાની આસરે ૧૫૦૦૦ થી ૧૭૦૦૦ સાર વણકર લેાક ચલાવેછે; તેમાં હિંદુ તથા મુસલમાન લેાકને પેહેરવાની સાડી, ધેાતીઆં, ચેાળખણ ઇત્યાદિ જાતનું કપડ થાયછે. હિંદુ જાતના વણકરેાને "સાગી કેાષ્ટી" અને મુસલમાન વણકરેાને "મેામીન" લેાક

કેકેછે. રેલવે થયાથી તથા નીજામ હૈદરાબાદ તાલુકામાં રોજગાર ધંધો બરોબર નહીં ચાલવાથી તથા તીહાં સરાફોની ખુટને લીધે અને ઘણી એક તરેહની બીજી બેદાદીના સબબથી એ ઠેકાણાના ઉપર રેહેનારા લોક શોલાપોર તરફ પુષ્કળ આવવા લાગ્યાં છે, તેથી થોડી મુદતમાં શોલાપોરની વસ્તી બમણી વધી પડેલી ગણાયછે, અને તેમાં દરરોજ વધારો થતો જાયછે.

શોલાપોર જે મુંબઈથી આટલું નજદીક છે તેની આખી વસ્તીમાં કેળવણીનો જોઇયે એટલો પ્રસારો કંઈજ થયો નથી. માત્ર એક સરકારી ઇંગ્રેજી નિશાળ છે, બાકી છ સાત પંતોજીઓની નિશાળો છે, તેમાં છોકરાઓ શું શીખતાં હશે તે લખી જણાવ્યા કરતાં મનમાંજ વાંચનાર વધારે સમજી શકશે. નિશાળનો અરધો ખરચ સરકાર આપેછે અને અરધો ખરચ છોકરાઓ પાસેથી દર માસે લવાજમ લઈ પુરો કરેછે. નિશાળની જગા તથા ઇમારત બાંધવાનો અરધો ખરચ સરકારે આપ્યો છે, અને અરધો ખરચ રૈયતે આપ્યો છે. રૈયતની હાલત પ્રમાણે જોતાં તો તીહાંની નિશાળ પોતાની મેળે પોતાનો ખરચ પુરો પાડી શકે એવી હોવી જોઇયે, પણ કેળવણી લેવાની જરૂર દેખડાવા વીશે તીહાંની રૈયતમાં કંઈ હીલચાલ થયલી હોય એવું નજર નહીં આવ્યું હતું. સ્ત્રી કેળવણીની નીશાન તવંગર અથવા ગરીબમાં જરા પણ પેડેલી જોયામાં નહીં આવી હતી. લોક અજ્ઞાની હાલતમાં અને તેવીજ હાલતમાં પડી રેહેવાને તેમને ગમતું હોય, તથા તેમજ જે શીખેલા વિદ્વાનો તેઓમાં વસેલા હતા તેઓએ પોતાના દેશી ભાઈબંધોને કેળવણી આપી તેમની હાલત સુધારવાની જરા પણ મેહેનત કરી હોય એવું જરા નજર નહીં આવ્યું હતું. તેઓ પોતે બેદરકાર, આપમતલબી રીતે પડેલા જણાયા હતા. કોઈ કાળે રૈયતનો અને તેમનો કોઈ ઠેકાણે મેળાવડો થયલો સાંભળ્યામાં આવ્યો નહીં હતો.

પારસીઓની તીહાં કેટલીએક દુકાનો છે. તેમાં તે વખતે, માત્ર તીહાં ઇંગ્રેજી સામાન તથા દારૂ વીગરે વેચાતો હમોએ જોયો હતો. કોઈ પારસી વેપારી તરીકે તે વખતે તીહાં નજર નહીં આવ્યો હતો. પારસી લોકની વસ્તી આસરે ૭૫) માણસની ગણત્રામાં આવી હતી. આ વસ્તીમાં એક આતશાદાદગાહની જગા મરહુમ શેઠ વીકાજી મેહેરજીએ આપેલાં એક મકાનમાં કરેલી છે અને તીહાં એકબે

મોબેદ બાજ, આફરીંગાનની ક્રિયા કરવાનાં કામસર હાજર રેહેછે. એ આતશાદાદગાહાનું કામ પુણાવાળા દસ્તુરજીના પંથક હેઠળ છે. આતશાદાદગાહનો ખરચ આ જગાના જરથોસ્તીઓ મળીને ચલાવે છે.

શોલાપોરનાં ઘરો ઘણુંકરીને અરધી કાદવની અને અરધી પથરની ભીતનાં બાંધેલાં છે. ઘરોની આસપાસ ફરતી પથરની ભીત બાંધી તેની ઉપર થોડીક મટોડાંની ભીત બાંધી એક ઉંચો કોટ જેવો કોટ કરી લીધેલો હોયછે. કોટની અંદર જવાને એક નાહાનું સાંકડું પણ મજબુત બારણું અથવા દરવાજો મુકેલો હોયછે. આ દરવાજો અંદરથી બંધ કીધો એટલે કિલ્લાનો દરવાજો બંધ કીધા બરોબર થાયછે; પછી જેટલાં અંદર ઘર આવેલાં હોય તેટલાં સઘળાંના દરવાજા જાણે બંધ થયા હોય એમ સમજવું. આવી રીતે ઘરોની આસપાશ ભીત બાંધવાનું કારણ સમજવાને સેહેલ છે. હિંદુ અને મુસલમાનોનાં રાજમાં દુશમનો ચઢી આવી રૈયતનાં ઘરબાર લુટતા હતા, તે લુટનો થોડોઘણો અટકાવ કરવાને આવી ભીતો કામ લાગતી હોય એવું સમજાયછે. પણ આ ભીતો હમણાનાં યુરોપીઅન લશ્કરની તોપના મારા આગળ એક મીનીટ પણ ટકી શકે તેવી નથી. શોલાપોરનાં ઘરોને ઘણુંખરાં છાપરાં નથી, પણ ઉપરથી અગાસી જેવાં મટોડાંનાં ધાબાં કરી લીધેલાં હોયછે. કેટલેક ઠેકાણે નળીયાં જોયામાં આવ્યાં છે પણ તે નળીયાં મુંબઈનાં નળીયાં જેવાં ઉપરથી ગોળ નથી, પણ ચપટાં છે. આ ઘાટ ઉપરથી એવું માલુમ પડેછે કે આ શેહેરમાં કુંભારના હુંનરમાં ઘણો સુધારો થયલો નથી. આ ચપટાં નળીયાં પણ સારાં પાકવેલાં નહી હતાં, પણ રંગ અને દેખાવ ઉપરથી કાચાં માલુમ પડતાં હતાં. લશ્કરની છાવણી અને ઇંગ્રેજ લોક રેહેછે તે લત્તા ઊપરનાજ રસ્તા પોહોળા છે અને તે ઊપર પાણી સીપાએછે; તે સીવાય શોલાપોર શેહેરના રસ્તા ઘણાજ સાંકડા અને ધુળવાળા છે, સામસામી બે ગાડી એક બીજાની આવેલી પસાર થઈ શકે તો ભાગ્ય જાણવાં. સઘળા રસ્તામાં ઘણી ધુળ અને કચરો પડેલો રેહે છે, જે સાફ રાખવાને શેહેરના લોકમાં કોઈ તરેહનો બંદોબસ્ત થયલો નહીં હતો. જે કોઈ રસ્તામાં માલ નાખે તેને થોડો ઘણો દંડ પડતો, એટલું માત્ર સાંભળવામાં આવ્યું હતું.

શોલાપોરના રેહેવાસીઓનો દેખાવ સારા ઘાટમનો છે. પુરૂષ તથા સ્ત્રીઓ દેખાવમાં શોહામણા અને સફાઈદાર નજરે પડેછે. સાંજની વખતે ઘણાખરી

સ્ત્રીઓ તેમના માથાંના બાલ ઉપર ફુલ ગુંથેછે તેથી તેઓ ઘણી સુંદર દેખાયછે. શોલાપોરમાં હિંદુઓનાં ત્રણ મોહોટાં દેહેરાં છે;—મલીકાઅરજુન નામનું શીવનું દેહેરૂં છે; સીદ્ધેશ્વર નામનું લીંગાએત લોકનું દેહેરૂં છે; અને બસ્તી નામનું જૈન લોકનું દેહેરૂં છે. આ છેલ્લાં દેહેરાંમાં પારસનાથની મુરતીની પુંજા થાયછે.

શોલાપોરથી આગળ મંજલપર જવા મુસાફરોને "નગર કાર્ટ" એટલે બળદની શીગરામો ભાડે મળેછે. એ શીગરામ ઘણુંકરીને એકજ જણને સારૂ મુસાફરી કરવાને ઘણીજ સગવડભરેલી છે, તોએપણ જો બે જણ બેસવા ચાહે તો પોતાની કપડાંની પેટીઓ સાથે લેતાં પણ જરા સગવડથી બેસી શકે એવી છે. મુસાફરીનો ખાવા પીવાનો અને ભારી સામાન બળદનાં સાધારણ ગાડાંઓમાં લઈ જાયછે. જુદા જુદા ધણીઓએ એવી "નગર કાર્ટ" ભાડે આપવાના કારખાના રાખ્યાં છે તેને "નગર કાર્ટ" નાં ટપાલ કરી કેહેછે. હમારે સારૂ એવી શીગરામો જે ભાડે કીધી હતી તે કોઈ તરેહની ગફલતીથી બે જુદા જુદા ધણીઓ પાસેથી લેવાઈ હતી, અને તેઓએ સંપ કીધાથી શોલાપોરથી નીજામ હેદરાબાદ સુધીનું દરએક શીગરામનું ગાડીભાડું રૂ ૬૦) સાઠ સુધી આપવાનું સાટું થયું હતું. આ રકમ ઘણીજ આકરી માલુમ પડી હતી, પણ એ વીશે એકાએક તકરાર નહીં ઉઠી હતી. રાત્રે જારે જવા નીકળ્યા ત્યારે શીગરામોનાં ફાનસો સલગાવવાનો હુકમ આપ્યો. એક બે ગાડીઓને ફાનસ નહીં હોવાથી એ વીશે ગાડીવાળાઓ વચ્ચે માંહોમાંહે ભાંજગડ ચાલવા લાગી. આ ભાંજગડ વધી પડ્યાથી શીગરામવાળા એક બીજાની ખોડ ખાપણ કાહાડવા લાગા કે તારી ગાડી તો આવી છે અને માહારી તો આવી છે. આ ઊપરથી માલુમ પડી આવ્યું કે બે જુદા જુદા ધણીઓની ગાડી આવી હતી. જારે તકરાર વધી પડી ત્યારે તેઓમાં માંહોમાંહે ફુટાફુટ થઈ પડી. ગાડીભાડું જે ૬૦) રૂપીઆ હતું તેમાં એકબીજા તરફથી ઘટાડો થવા માંડ્યો. અંત એવો આવ્યો કે શામસુંદર નામના ટપાલવાળાએ પોતાની દરએક શીગરામ ૪૦) રૂપીએ આપવા કહી જેથી એકદમ ૨૦) રૂપીઆનો ફેર પડી ગયો. તેણે વળી એવી સરતે ગાડીઓ આપવા કેહી કે ત્રણ ત્રણ કોશે એટલે છ છ માઈલે ગાડીને નવા બળદો પોતાની રાખેલી ચોકીઓ ઉપરથી જોડી આપવા, તથા રસ્તામાં ગાડીની રખેવાલી કરવાને પોતાના બે સીપાઇ આપવા. આ બે જણાની ભાંજગડ અને લડાઈમાં હમારૂં કામ નકી થઈ ગયું હતું.

તા૦ ૨૪ મી ડીસેંબર.—આ દીને રવીવારની રાત્રે ૮॥ વાગે શેાલાપોરથી કુચ કરી. હમારી સાથે ચાર શીગરામ અને સામાનનાં ચાર ગાડાં મળીને આઠ ગાડીઓનો કાફલો થયો હતો.

પેહેલે દાહાડે રાત્રે રસ્તામાં ત્રણ ત્રણ ગાઊએ જે જે ટપ્પા આવ્યા હતા તીહાં તાજા, મજબુત અને આશુદા બળદો મળ્યા, જેથી મંજલ ઘણીજ આસાનીથી અને ઝડપથી કપાઈ. પણ બીજે દીવસે રાત્રે ગાડીવાળાઓ બળદ બદલવાને વામાંટામાં અને માંહોમાંહે એક બીજા સાથે ગોલા લડાઈ કરવા લાગા, જેની સમજ ત્રીજે દીવસે બરોબર હમુને પડી હતી. જેમ જેમ આગળ મંજલ વધતી જતી હતી, તેમ તેમ બળદ બદલવાનાં ટપ્પા ત્રણ ગાઉને બદલે ચાર ગાઉને છેટે રાખેલા માલુમ પડતા ગીયા, અને તીહાં પણ નવા બળદોના વાંધા જણાવા લાગા. જો બળદો હેાયા તેા તે થાકેલા, અને કેટલાક ઠેકાંણે તેા બળદો બાંધવાનાં અમસથાં ખાલી છાપરાં નજર આવવા લાગાં. ગાડીવાળાઓ આ ઠેકાણે એક અછી નજર ચોરી કરતા હતા. પેહેલી ગાડીના બળદો છોડીને તેમને પેલાં ખાલી ઝુપડાં તરફ લઈ જઈ પાછલે રસ્તેથી પાછા તેજ બળદોને લાવી છેલ્લી ગાડીએ જોડતા હતા, અને છેલ્લી ગાડીના બળદોને એવીજ તરકટ ભરેલી રીતે પેહેલી ગાડી આગળ લાવી જોડતા, જેથી આપણને એકાએક જોતાં એવું નજર આવતું હતું કે બળદો બદલીને બીજા નવા આણ્યા છે, પણ એ ચોહાઈ તેમની પકડી કાહાડયાથી અને જરા ધમકી દેખડાવ્યાથી તેઓએ કબુલ કીધું કે ટપ્પે ટપ્પે બળદો પુરતા નહીં હેાવાથી એવી ઠગાઇ તેઓ હંમેશ કરતા આવ્યા છે.

તા૦ ૨૫ મી ડીસેંબર.—આ દીવસે સહવારના ૬ વાગે ખાનાપોરનાં નાળાં આગળ જઈ પોંહોંચ્યા. આ નાળાં આગળથી ઇંગ્રેજ સરકારની હકુમત તથા હદ બંધ થઈ નીજામ હેદરાબાદ સરકારની હકુમત અને હદ શીરૂ થાયછે. આ ઠેકાણેથી ગાડીવાળાઓએ હવે બળદો બદલવામાં વધારે બેપરવાઈ અને લુચ્ચાઈ કરવાં માંડી; જે ઉપરથી ઇંગરેજી રાજની હકુમતથી દેશીઓ કેટલા બીહીને ચોકસ ચાલવાની જરૂર જુએછે, અને નીજામનાં રાજની હકુમતમાં આવ્યા કે કેટલી બેપરવાઈથી ચાલવાને તેમને હીંમત આવેછે, તેનેા એક અછછેા દાખલો આ ગાડીવાળાઓની શેાખાઈ અને લુચ્ચાઈ ઊપરથી હમોને મળીયા હતા.

એજ દીને સહવારના ૧૧ વાગે "નલદુર્ગ" ના મુસાફરી બંગલામાં જઈ

પોહોંચ્યા. હીયાં ખાવા પીવા સારૂ ઊતારો કીધો. રોલાપોરથી નીકળેલા ધીમા ધીમી મંજલે ૧૩ થી ૧૪ કલાકે નલદ્રુગ જઈ પુગા હતા. જો સારા ઊતાવળી ચાલના બળદો હોયતો એથી પણ ઓછી વારમાં પોંહોંચી શકાયછે, કેમકે રોલાપોરથી "નલદ્રુગ" માત્ર ૨૭ માઈલ દુર છે, અને સારા બળદો કલાકના સરાસરી ૨ાા માઈલ આસાનીથી ચાલી શકેછે. નલદુગનો મુસાફરી બંગલો ટેકરીનાં શીખર ઊપર આવેલો છે તેથી તે સારી હવાની જગા છે, અને તીહાંનાં પાણી પણ ઘણાંજ સારાં છે, તથા ખાવા પીવાનો જે સામાન જોઈયે તે પણ તુરત ગામમાંથી મળી શકેછે. બંગલા ઊપરથી નલદ્રુગ ગામ નીચાણમાં ઓહ્લું દેખાયછે, તથા તીહાંનો કિલ્લો અને તેની ફરતી દેવાલ તથા કિલ્લાના ત્રણ બુરૂજો તોપ ગોઠવવા લાયક બાંધેલા નજરે પડેછે. બંગલામાં બે વખત સારી પેઠે જમ્યા, અને એ દાહાડો "ક્રિસ્તમસ" ના તેહેવારનો હતો તેથી તેની ખુશાલીમાં એકુ ગલાસ વાઈન તથા શામપેન લેવામાં આવીયા હતા, તેથી સઘળા ખુશ મીજાજી અને રંગીલા થઈ પડ્યા હતા. સાડાચાર વાગે જમીને કીલ્લો જોવા તે તરફ દોડી ગયા. જે વેળા જોવાને ગયા તે વેળાએ હમારામાંથી કોઈને ખબર નહી હતી કે તીહાં શું શું જોવાનુંછે. હમોએ ધાર્યું કે માત્ર સાધારણ કીલ્લો હશે, અને તેવું એકુ નાહાનું ગામડું હશે તે જોઈને હમો આગળ મંજલ જઈશું. પણ તીંહાં પોંહોંચ્યા પછી જે કાંઈ હમારી નજરે પડયું તે સાંજ પડી ગયાથી બરોબર જોવાયું નહી હતું, તોએપણ જે કાંઈ હમોએ જોયું તે જો દિવસનાં જોયું હોત તો ખચીત બેહેતર થાત એવું હમારા સઘળાઓના વીચારમાં પાછળથી આવ્યું હતું.

નલદ્રુગનો કિલ્લો.

નલદ્રુગ ગામમાં જે કિલ્લો છે તે હમણા ભાગી તુટી હાલતમાં આવી પડેલોછે. એ કિલ્લો નીજામ સરકારના તાબામાં છે. નલદ્રુગ ગામ તથા કિલ્લો શેઠ બરજોરજી વીકાજી મેહેરજી હસ્તકના તાલુકામાંતે વખતે હતો. જે વખતે હમે તે જોવા ગયા તે વખતમાં એ કિલ્લો નીજામના એક કેદખાનાં પ્રમાણે વપરાતો હતો. જુદા જુદા તાલુકામાં સપડાયલા, તકસીરવાનો જેવાકે ગાહામારૂ, ડાક લુટનાર, ચોરો વીગેરે નીજામના કેદીઓને, સખત બેડી સાતે આ ઠેકાણે બંદીમાં રાખેલા હતા. કિલ્લાના દરોગાનાં ઓહ્દા ઊપર બાઈ વીરાજી ડોસાભાઈ નાહાનપરાવાળા

નામના એક ચંચલ અને હુંશી જવાન પારસીને રાખેલા હતા. આ જવાન શખ્સ ઘણોજ મીલનસાર દીશીયો હતો અને કિલ્લો જોવાની હમારી ઈચ્છા થયા થી તેવણે તે મોહોટી ખુશી અને આરજુથી હમને દેખડાવ્યો હતો, તથા આ હુંશી અંમલદારે ઘણીજ મેહેનત લઇને જે કંઈ જોવા લાયક હતું તે સઘળું દેખડાવ્યું હતું, અને જોતાં જોતાં રાત પડી ગયાથી અંધારૂં થયું હતું તોએપણ એવી વખતે ફાનસો, મસાલો સલગાવીને આખો કીલ્લો દેખડાવવામાં હમારી ઘણીજ બરદાસ્ત અને તજુમલ કરી હતી જેથી હમો ઘણાજ ખુશી તથા તેમનાં ઉપકારી થયા હતા. નલદ્રુગના કીલ્લાનું બયાન જાણવા જોગ સમજી તે વીસ્તારીને આગળ કરેલું છે.

નલદ્રુગ ગામનાં ઘરો કોઈપણ રીતે જોવા લાયક નથી. થોડીક પથરની ભીત બાંધી, તે ઉપર વળી થોડીક પાતળા એાસારની મટોડાંની ભીત બાંધી, ઘરને મથાળે છાપરાંને ઠેકાણે મટેાડાંનાં ધાબાં અથવા અગાશી કરી લીધેલી છે. શોલાપોરનાં ઘરોનો ઘણોખરો નમુનો હીંયા નજર આવે છે. નલદ્રુગનાં ગામડાંનાં ઝુપડાં વટાવ્યા પછી કોટમાં જવાના ત્રણ દરવાજા એક પછી એક આવેછે, તે દરવાજાઓની પથરની બાંધણી તથા તે ઉપરનાં મેહેરાબો મુસલમાન લોકની એક ચોકસ રીતની બાંધણી જેને ઇંગરેજીમાં Byzantine Architecture ને નામે બોલેછે, એ તરીકાની છે. દરવાજા ઉપરના મેહેરાબોની ઉભરણી કંઈ નાહાની સરખી નથી. ઓછામાં ઓછા ૨૫ થી ૩૦ ફુટ ઊંચી છે અને તે મેહેરાબો ઘણી મુદ્દતના સબબથી ઘણા ખસ ભાગી તુટી અને ખીસમાર હાલતમાં પડેલાછે, તોએપણ કોઈ કોઈ ઠેકાણે હેવા તો મજબુત હજુ દેખાયછે કે જાણે હવડાંજ બાંધિયા હોય. ત્રણ દરવાજા વટાવ્યા પછી કોટમાંનાં ઘરોની હાર શીરૂ થાયછે. કોટમાં પેસતાંજ ત્રીજા દરવાજા આગળ એક લોઢાની તોપ પડેલી હમારી નજરે પડી હતી, જેની બનાવટ અને આકાર ઉપરથી એવું ધારવામાં આવ્યું હતું કે એ તોપને બનાવી હશે ત્યારથી તે હમોએ જોઈ ત્યાંહાંસુધી કોઈ દિવસેબી ફોડી નહી હશે. આ તોપ ૨૪ ફુટ લાંબી, અને તેમાં ગોળો મુકવાનો સુરાખ માત્ર સવાબે ઇંચનો નજર આવ્યો હતો, અને તોપની જાડાઈ અથવા ઘેરાવો તો માત્રે ૮ થી ૯ ઇંચ જણાયો હતો. થોડુંક આગળ ચાલતાં નલદ્રુગનો કિલ્લો આવેછે.

નલદ્રુગનો કિલ્લો ત્રણ કિલ્લા મળીને થયલોછે, અથવા બીજી રીતે બોલીએ તો એ કિલ્લામાં બીજા બે કિલ્લા છે. પેહેલા કિલ્લાનું નામ નલદ્રુગનો કિલ્લો, બીજાનું નામ શાહાદ્રુગનો કિલ્લો, અને ત્રીજાનું નામ રણમંડળનો કિલ્લો કરીને છે.

શાહાદ્રુગ અને રણમંડળનાં કિલ્લાઓ વચ્ચે આસરે ૩૦૦ ફુટ લાંબો અને ૪૦ થી ૪૫ ફુટ પોહોળો એક બંધ બાંધેલોછે, તે બંધ પોળો ગએલોછે. એ બંધની પોળાઈમાં ગરમીનાં દીવસે બેસવા ઉઠવા અને આરામથી રેહેવા સારૂ એક છુપો બેમાલુમ પણ દીલપસંદ મેહેલ, તીહાં હકુમત ચલાવી ગયલા કોઈ નવાબે બનાવ્યોછે. આ મેહેલ હાલ સઘળી તરફથી બીસમાર હાલતમાંછે, તોએ પણ તેવી હાલતમાં તેની આગલી જાહોજલાલી અને રચનાની ઘણીક નીશાનો હજુ રહેલીછે અને તે હજુર જોવા લાયક છે. આ મેહેલનું નામ પાણી મેહેલછે; કેમકે આસપાસ બંધનું પાણી ફરી વળેલું છે, અને ખરૂં કહીએ તો પાણીની અંદરજ જાણે તે મેહેલ બનાવેલો નજરે દેખાય છે. આ મેહેલની રચના વીશે વાંચનારના ધ્યાનમાં નથી આવી શકવાનું કે કેવી સમતલકથી તે બાંધેલો હશે. પણ એ વીશે એટલુંજ કેહેવાનું છે કે તેનું બયાન વાંચ્યા કરતાં એકવાર તે મકાનેં નજરે જોતાં તુરત ધ્યાનમાં આવી શકશે, કે ખરેખરજ તે પાણી મેહેલ છે. આ મેહેલની બારી, આગાશી અથવા હરકોઈ બીજી ઉઘાડી જગાએથી બાહાર જુઓ તો બધી ગમથી પાણીજ પાણી, ધમધોકાર દોડતું અને ધપધપનાં આકારમાં પડતું, નજર આવેછે. એક તરફ જરૂખાની બારી આગળ એવી તો આરામ ભોગવવા લાયકની જગા બનાવીછે કે પા કલાક તીહાં બેઠા અથવા ઉભા રહ્યા તો ગમે તેવી થાકથી અથવા દીલગીરીથી મંદ થઈ ગયલો જીવ સુખ અને શાંતી પામેછે, અને તીહાંથી જે એક પાણીનો ધોધ પડતો દેખાય છે, તે ધોધનો આવાજ અને દેખાવ થોડીવારમાંજ દીલને ચમન જેવો ખીલાવી નાખેછે. જે વખતે હમે એ મેહેલની અંદરથી આસપાસ બાહેરનો દેખાવ જોતા હતા તે વખતે છેક સાંજ પડેલી હતી, તોએપણ જે રળીયામણો દેખાવ તથા આસપાસની વનસ્પતીની સુગંધ હમો ભોગવતા હતા, તેથી હમારો જીવ બાગબાગ થતો હતો. જે વખતે આ મેહેલ પોતાની આબાદે આબાદ હાલતમાં હશે તે વખતે તીહાં કેવી મજાહાદારી લાગી હશે તથા કેટલું સુખ અંદરના લોકે

ભોગવ્યું હશે, તેનો થોડો ઘણો વીચાર હમારામાં આ વખતે આવી શકયો હતો. આવી હાલતે તીંહાં રેહેનારા નવાબોનો જીવ, રૂઢી પ્રમાણે બોલતાં, ખરેખર સુખેજ ગયો હોય એમાં નવાઈ નથી.

આ મેહેલ કેવી રીતે બાંધેલો છે, એનો વીચાર થોડોઘણો પણ વાંચનારનાં મનમાં આવે એટલા સારૂ હમો તેનું બયાન કરવાની કોશેશ કરીએ છે.

તુળજાપુરગામ, નળદુર્ગથી ૮ થી ૧૦ ગાઉને છેટે છે. તીહાં "બોરી" નામનું એક ગામડું છે. આ ગામડાંની પડોસમાં એજ ગામડાંનાં નામ વાળી "બોરી" નદી વેહેછે. આ નદીનું પાણી, નળદુર્ગ કિલ્લામાં ખેંચી લીધુંછે અને ઉપર જણાવેલો બંધ બાંધીને તે પાણી અટકાવેલું છે જેથી કિલ્લામાં એક ઘણોજ સુંદર વેહેતાં પાણીનો તળાવ અથવા સાગર બનેલો છે. આ સાગર અને તેની આસપાસની લીલોત્રી, કીલ્લા ઉપરથી અને તીહાંના જુદાં જુદાં મકાનો ઉપરથી જોતાં ઘણી દીલપસંદ અને ચમન જેવી ખુશનુમાહા લાગેછે. બંધની લંબાઈ પૂર્વથી પશ્ચિમ દિશાએ છે અને તેને બંને છેડે એકેક બુરૂજ બાંધેલો છે. તેનાં નામ "નર બુરૂજ" અને "માદી બુરૂજ" એવાં પાડેલાં છે. "નર બુરૂજ" ની સપાટી "માદી બુરૂજ" ની સપાટી કરતાં દોહોડ ફુટ ઉંચી રાખી છે; તે એટલા સારૂ કે જારે તલાવમાં જોઇયે તે કરતાં પાણી વધારે ઉંચે ચઢે ત્યારે "નર બુરૂજ" નો દરવાજો ઉઘાડો મુકયાથી તે વાટે પાણી બાહેર નીકળી જાય, જેથી કિલ્લામાં રેલ નહી આવે. સાધારણ વખતે "નર બુરૂજ" નો દરવાજો બંધ રાખેછે તેથી પાણી માત્ર "માદી બુરૂજ" વાટે ચાલ્યું જાયછે. ઉપલે બંધે રસ્તે જતું પાણી અમસથું સાધારણ રીતે વેહેતું કીધું નથી; પણ તે પાણીને એક ધોધનાં આકારમાં છેક ૩૦ થી ૪૦ ફુટની ઉંચાઇથી અને આસરે ૧૬ ફુટ પોહોળાઈમાં પડતું કીધુંછે. આ ધોધ દેખાવમાં ઘણોજ રળીયામણો છે અને "પાણી મેહેલ" નાં જરૂખા ઉપરથી તે જોવા લાયક દેખાવ દેછે. ઉપલા બંને બુરૂજો એક બીજાથી આસરે ૨૫૦) ફુટ દૂર છે અને બંધની પોહોળાઈ ૪૦ થી ૪૫ ફુટ છે તેથી એ બંધે બુરૂજો વચ્ચે ફરવા હરવાનો એક ઘણોજ અચ્છો પુલ અથવા પાણી વચેનો રસ્તો બની રહેલોછે, તેની ઉપર સઘળી તરફથી અચ્છી બનાવટની ફરસબંદી કરી લીધેલી છે. પૂર્વ તરફના બુરૂજ આગળથી બંધની અંદર ઉતરવાનો દરવાજો કરેલો છે. એ દરવાજો કોઈ સાધારણ જોનારને એકાએક માલુમ પડી આવે એવો

નથી. બંધની ફરસબંધીની એક મોહોટી લાદીથી તે ઢાંકી રાખેલો છે. આ લાદી ઉંચકી તો બંધની અંદર ભોયરામાં ઉતરવાની પગથીઓ દેખાયછે, અગર લાદી પાછી તેની જગા ઉપર મુકી તો જાણે સાફ રસ્તો હોય તે પ્રમાણે બંધ ખોલ્લો સપાટ નજરે આવેછે, અને તે ઉપરના બે બુરૂજ અને વચમાંથી પડતા ધપધપ (ધોધ) સીવાય બીજું કંઈ નજરે પડતું નથી. આ બંધનાં પેટાંમાં મેહેલછે એવું કોઈનાં સ્વપનાંમાં પણ નથી આવવાનું. એવું કેહેછે કે સન ૧૮૫૮ નાં સાલમાં તા૦ ૯ મી માહે જુનને દીને તુળજાપુર ગામમાં ઘણો વરસાદ પડ્યાથી, બોરી નદીએ ભારી મોહોટી રેલ આવી હતી તેથી કિલ્લામાં બનાવેલા સાગરમાં એટલું તો પાણી ચઢી ગયું હતું કે બંને બુરૂજોના દરવાજા ઉઘાડા મુક્યા છતાં, બંધ ઉપર પાણી ફરી વળ્યૂં હતું, જેથી પાણી મેહેલ તે ખરેખર પાણીથી ભરાઇને પાણીજ મેહેલ બની રહ્યો હતો. કિલ્લાના કેટલાક ભાગમાં રેલના પાણીએ જબરો ધસારો કરયો હતો, તથા રેલથી બુરૂજોનો કેટલોએક ભાગ તુટી પડ્યો હતો. પાણી મેહેલમાં ભરાયલાં પાણીને બાહાર કાહાડતાં કેટલાએક દિવસ લાગા હતા. જે વખતે હમો આ ઠેકાણે હતા તે વખતે હમારા જોવામાં આવ્યું હતું કે નર તથા માદી બુરૂજો ૧૦ થી ૧૨ ફુટ ઉંચાઇમાં ભાંગી પડ્યાથી તેઓની ઉંચાઈ કોતા થઈ પડેલી દેખાતી હતી. આ પ્રમાણે આવું મજબુત બાંધકામ ભાંગી જવાનાં કારણો વીશે પુછપરછ કરતાં માલુમ પડ્યું કે રેલના પાણી સાથે જંગલોમાંનાં ઝાડ અને લાકડાં વગેરે જે જીનસો ધસડાઈ આવી હતી તે આ બુરૂજો સાથે અથડીને તેમને ભાંગી ફોડી નાખીયા હતા. આ કિલ્લો નીજામ સરકારનાં હસ્તકમાં છે. એની સંભાળ વીશે નીજામ સરકાર તજવીજ રાખતી નથી તેથી થોડી મુદ્દતમાં આ કિલ્લા તથા બંધ બંનેની આખેરી જલદી આવે એમાં કંઈ નવાઈ નથી. આવી રચનાં ભરેલા અને જોવા લાયક તથા એક નવાઈ જેવા બંધને તથા તેની અંદરનાં પાણી મેહેલને બનાવતાં પુષ્કલ ખરચ અને અતિશય કારીગરી તથા મેહેનત લાગી હશે, તો તેવાં માહાભારત કામને હાલના વખતમાં મુસલમાન રાજની એક જુની અને નવાઈ જેવી બાંધણી તરીકે જાળવી રાખવાને બદલે નીજામ સરકારે તેને આવી બેદાદી ભરેલી અને બીસમાર હાલતમાં પડી રેહેવા દીધું છે, એ જણા-વાને હમને ઘણીજ દીલગીરી લાગેછે.

આગળ જણાવ્યું છે કે બંધના પૂર્વ તરફનાં છેડા આગળથી પાણી મેહેલમાં

ઉતરવાનો બેમાલુમ દરવાજો એક મોહોટી પોહોળી લાદીથી ઢાંકી રાખેલો છે. આ લાદી ઉચકતાં અંદર ઉતરવાને એકજ માણસ ઉતરી શકે એવી સાંકડી પથરની સેહેડી બાંધેલી છે. તેનાં પગથીયાંની ઉંચાઈ સાધારણ પગથીયાંની ઉંચાઈ કરતાં ઘણીજ વધારે છે, તેથી ઉતરનાર ચઢનારથી તે ઉપર એકદમ જલદી ઉતરાઈ અથવા ચઢાઈ શકાય એવું નથી. પેહેલાં પાંચ અથવા છ પગથીયાં અંદર સીધું ઉતરવાના છે, તે પછી ઉતરનારને બે વખત ડાવી બાજુએ વલાણ લઈ ઉતરવું પડે છે. બીજા શબ્દોમાં બોલીએ તો આખી સેહેડી ત્રણ રમણાની ગોલ ફરતી બાંધેલી છે. એવી રીતે આસરે ૧૫ ફુટ નીચે ઉતરયા પછી, એક મોહોટો ઓરડો આવે છે. આ ઓરડા અંદર આવ્યા કે આસપાસની હવા થંડી, અને શરીરને ઘણીજ ગમતી લાગે છે. હમારી પાસે જે પારાની શીશી હતી તે જોતાં માલુમ પડ્યું કે બાહાર ખુલ્લી હવામાં અને આ જગાની હવામાં નજદીક ૩ થી ૪ ડીગરી (એટલે અંશ) નો ફેર પડયો હતો. જે થંડો પવન આવતો હતો તે આસપાસનાં પાણી ઉપર થઇને દીવાનખાનામાં, ઘણીજ તજવીજથી મુકેલી બારીઓ વાટે આવતો હતો. આ ઓરડાની રચના ઉપરથી માલૂમ પડયું કે ત પાણી મેહેલનું દીવાનખાનું હશે. આસપાસની દેવાલ સઘળી નરદમ પથરની બાંધેલી છે, અને તેનાં એક ખુણામાં એક તખતી ફારશી ભાષામાં કોતરી મુકેલી છે. એ તખતી હમારી સાથનાં જરમન મિત્રે વાંચી તે ઉપરથી આ પાણી મેહેલનો સને માલુમ પડયો હતો. આ સને આંકડામાં કોતરેલો નથી પણ ફારશી સાહેરો, બેહેત બનાવી બેહેતમાં લખી જણાવે છે તેવી રીતે તે સને વાંચતાં, હીજરી સને ૧૦૨૩ જણાયો હતો, અને હમારી અગાઉ કોઈ બીજા મુસાફરો તીહાં આવી ગયા હશે તેઓએ પણ અક્ષરોની ગણતરી ઉપરથી જે આંકડા એ તખતીની પાસે દેવાલ ઉપર માંડેલા હતા તે આંકડા ઉપરથી પણ એજ સને ગણાયલો હતો.

આ ઠેકાણેથી આગળ ચાલતાં બીજા બે ત્રણ ઓરડા આવે છે તેમાં પવન આવવાને દેવાલમાં દક્ષણ તરફથી એકક બગાડું રાખેલું છે. આ ઓરડા એલવત ગાહાના ઓરડા હોય એવા માલુમ પડયા હતા. હીંયાંથી વળી નીચે થોડીક પગથીઓ ઉતરયા પછી મેહેલના બીજા તબકા અથવા માળ ઉપર અવાય છે. વાંચનારે આટલું હીંયાં વીચારવું જોઈએ કે ઘરના પેહેલા માળ ઉપરથી બીજા માળ ઉપર જવાને વધારે ઉપર ચઢવું પડે છે, પણ આ પાણી મેહેલ જે ભોયરાંમાં બના-

વેલો છે તેના પેહેલા માળ ઉપરથી બીજા માળ ઉપર જવાને નીચે ઉતરવું પડે છે. આ બીજા માળ ઉપરની રચના પેહેલાના કરતાં વધારે જોવા લાયક છે. એક જરૂખો બાહાર ઝોંકવેલો છે તીહાંથી પેલો ૫૦) ફુટ ઉંચેથી પડતો ધપધપ (ધોધ) દેખાય છે. ઝરૂખો શષ્ટ કોણ આકારની બાંધણીનો છે, તેની બારીઓ ઉપરથી હેઠળ નદી વેહેતી દેખાય છે. પાણીનો ધોધ પડેછે તે ઉપર જ્યારે સૂર્યનાં કિરણો પડતાં હશે ત્યારે તીહાં તરેવાર રંગની વરસાદી કમાનના દેખાવો થતાહશે; તથા ઉંચેથી જે ધોધ પડેછે તેના પાણીમાંથી ઝરમર ઝરમર વરસાતની પેઠે પાણીના બારીક બુંદનીયાં પડતાં હશે અને તે બુંદનીયાં પવનની લેહેરથી ઝરૂખાની બારી ઉપર આવતાં હશે ત્યારે તે જગા ઉપર બેસીને આસપાસની લીલાતરી અને આવી મનોરંજક રચના જોનારને કેવી મજા લાગતી હશે તેનો ખ્યાલ ભોગવનાર સીવાય અમસ્થી કલ્પના કરનારને રૂપીઆની એક આની જેટલો પણ આવવાનો નથી. તો એપણ કલ્પનાથી તેમોજ વીશે જે વીચાર ઉત્પન્ન થઈ શકે તે ઉપજાવવાની કોશેશ હમોએ કરી છે. વીચાર કરો કે એક ગમથી પાણીનો ધોધ ધમ ધોકાર ધોધો કરતો છેક ૨૫) અથવા ૩૦) ફુટ ઉપરથી, અને ઝરૂખાની બારી આગળથી વલી બીજી ૨૫) ફુટની ઉંડાઇએ પડતો દેખાય છે. બીજી ગમથી વમળદાર પાણી ફીણફીણ થઈ સફેદ દુધ જેવું બની સીલ સીલાટ ઝરૂખાની બારી આગળથી વેહેતું ચાલ્યું જાય છે. ત્રીજી ગમથી બારીક બુંદનીયાં નીચે શીતળગાર જેવાં વરસી રહ્યાં છે. ચોથી ગમથી તમામ આસપાસની વનસ્પતીમાંથી જે મધુર સુગંધની લપટ પસરી રહીછે, તે પેલાં બુંદનીયાં સાથે મીશરિત થઈ ઝરૂખાની બારી ઉપર ફેલાઈ આખા મેહેલને મીઠાસ ભરેલી લપટથી ભરી મધમધાવી નાખ્યો છે. પાંચમી ગમથી દમામી અને તોજાર નવાબ ઝરૂખા ઉપર નીશામાં ચકચુર થઈ પોતાની માશુકો સાથે એશકમાં આરામ ભોગવતો પડેલો છે. છઠ્ઠી ગમથી તેના હુકેબરદારો જરરીન હુક્કાની સાપ જેવી પેચદાર નળીનો છેડો ૨૦ થી ૨૫ ફુટ છેટેથી નવાબના હાથમાં આપી થર થર ધ્રુજતા ઉભેલાછે. સાતમી મેરથી નવાબે નળીમાંથી એકદમ ખેંચી ધુમાડો પોતાના ભરેલા ફરબેહગાલના ફુકાઓમાંથી બાહાર કાહાડેલોછે, અને એવી રીતે બે ચાર દંમ ખેચીને અરધી વીંચેલી આંખે, નવાબે પાણી મેહેલની એરો આફીએત વીશે પુછપરછ ચલાવીછે. "ધપધપકા પાની કોન બુરૂજસેં ચલતા રહાહે?" આ સવાલનો જવાબ આસપાસના

હાલીમવાલીઓ સુખનો પડતાનેવાર આપેછે, "બંદે નવાજ, નરબુરૂજસેં ચલરહા હે." તે ઉપરથી નવાબે જાણે કેહેવી એક મોહોટી ગણત્રી અથવા અગમચેતી કરી હોય, એમ ફુલાઇને બોલેછે, "તબતો પાનીકા બોહોતહી ઝોર હો રેહા હોઇંગા." ચાપલુસી અને ખુશામતખોર ખાનસામાનોને સહરાઈથી બોલતાં શીખવવું પડતું નથી, તેથી તેઓ નવાબના ભારી કઠણ મન શકતીથી કરેલા કયાસ-ને છેક આસમાને ચઢાવી જવાબમાં બોલે છે. "હાંજી ખુદાવંદ, હાંજી ગરીબ પરવર, પાનીકા બહોત હી ઝોર હો રેહયાહે. ઝીહાં પનાહને બીન દેખે કૈસી પઇછાન કરી હે! તેહેકીક; પાની બોહોત ઝોરસે વાહા રહાહે." નવાબ મનમાં ફુલાઇને બોલે છે, "હાં, મેરી નજરમેં તો પાની મેહેલકી કરામત સબ એક ખેલ બરોબર બન રહીહે." જારે નવાબે પોતાના ખીદમતગારોથી સાંભળ્યું કે નરબુરૂજ વાટેથી પાણી ચાલીયું જાયછે, તારે અલબતાં પાણીનો વધારે જોર હોયાથીજ એવું બનવું જોઇએ, એમાં ગણત્રી શાની અને પઇછાન શાની!

આ પાણીમેહલની કરાંમત પીછાનવા મનશકતી કેટલી કઠણ હોવી જોઇએ એ વાંચનાર સેહેલાઇથી વીચારી શકશે. પણ જીહાં "હાજી ખુદાવંદ, બંદેનવા-જની લપલપી ચાલતી હોય તીહાં કીડી ને વાઘ, અથવા રાઇનો પરવત બનાવી દેવાની કસીબી પાંતીની કસર થઈ શકાતીજ નથી. પણ આપણ આપણી વાત ઉપર આગળ ચાલીએ. નવાબની પુછપરછ ઉપરથી જાણે એવું માલુમ પડયું કે પાણીનું જોર વધી ગયું છે. આ વાતની મેહલમાં ખબર પડી. નવાબની માશુકોના પેટમાં જાણે ધાસ્તીથી ધરકો પડયો. પાણી વધીને છેક ઝરૂખાની નજદીક આવ્યું. આ વખતથી તેમની મકર ભરેલી હીલચાલ થવા માંડી, કોઈ કીહા ઓરડામાં અને કોઈ કહી ખોલીમાં ભરાવાં અને દોડી જવા લાગાં, ભોલો નવાબ પોતાની માશુકોની દોડધામ અને હીચકારાપણું જોઈ હસવા પડ્યો; તીયાર પછી મેહેલમાં જે દોડાદોડ અને તરેવાર પ્રપંચ ગોંધળ થયું હશે તેનો તો ખરો ચીતાર આપવાને આ ઠેકાણે કલ્પના વધારે ચલાવી શકતા નથી. જે ખ્યાલ દોડેછે તે સાંભળેલી અસલ વાત સાથે સરખાવતાં આપણી મનશકિતની માત્ર મશકરી કરેછે, અને ઉપર જે કલ્પિત ચીત્ર આપીયું છે તે અસલ બનાવની અધુરી નકલ પણ દેખાડી શકતું નથી. નવાબે ભોગવેલી મોજની વાતો પાણીમેહેલનાં પાણીમાં વહી ગઇછે, અને આપણે તો માત્ર હવાઈ વીચાર કરતાં રેહેલા છઇએ.

બીજા તબ્બકા અથવા માલ ઉપરથી ત્રીજા તબ્બકા અથવા માલમાં ઉતરવાને વળી બીજી સેહેડીઓછે તેનાં પગથીઆં ઘણાજ ઊંચાં છે. એ પગથીયાં ઉપરથી ઉતરતાં છેક નદીનાં પાણી આગળ જવાઈ શકાય છે. આ માર્ગ મેહેલમાં વાપરવાનું પાણી લાવવાને કરેલો હોય એવું નજર આવ્યું હતું, અંધારૂં ઘણું થયલું હતું, હમારી સાથે બળતી મસાલો રાખેલી હતી તોએપણ એ માર્ગે ઉતરવાનું ઘણું કઠણ નજર આવ્યું હતું તથા હમારી સાથનાં માણસોમાંથી કોઈનું તે માર્ગે ઉતરવાનું મન થયું નહી હતું. સેહેડી ઊંચી હતી, વળી પાણી અંદર ફુટી આવ્યાથી ભીનાઈ સરકણી થઈ ગયલી હતી, અને જીહાં જોઇયે તીહાં વાંગળાંઓની અધાર એટલી તો જમાવ થઈ પડેલી હતી કે તેની દુરગંધી ખમાઈ નહી શકાતી હતી, જેથી વધારે વાર તીહાં ઉભા નહી રહી શકયા હતા. ઈહાંથી પાછા ફરતા બીજાં બે ત્રણ નાહાનાં દીવાનખાનાં જોયામાં આવ્યાં હતાં, તેમાં એકનું નામ ગંદી મેહેલ રાખેલું સંભળાયું હતું. આ વીશે ખુલાસો એવો થયો હતો કે તરેવાર જાતની ખુશબોથી આ ઓરડાને ભરવામાં આવતો હતો, અને તેમાંથી તરેવાર સુગંધ જે નીકળતી હતી તે પાણીમેહેલનાં સઘળા જુદા જુદા ઓરડામાં પસરતી હતી. આવી રચના કરી હોય તેમાં નવાઈ નથી; પણ જે વખતે હમો તીહાં હાજર હતા તે વખતે ગંદી મેહેલમાંથી સુગંધને બદલે સઘળી તરેહની દુરગંધો એવી તો નીકળતી હતી કે હમારી સાથના સઘળાં માણસોએ રૂમાલો પોતાના નાક ઉપર દીધા હતા, તથા મસાલો પણ ઘણીજ ઝાંખી બળવા લાગી હતી, તેથી સાફ માલુમ પડયું હતું કે પાણી મેહેલની તે વખતની હાલત ઘણીજ વેરાન અને પડી ભાગતી હતી, ભીતમાં તડ પડેલી હતી તેમાંથી કોઈ કોઈ ઠેકાણેથી નદીનું પાણી પેવસ થયલું હતું, અને તેથી ઠેકાણે ઠેકાણે કાદવ અને કોચડ થઈ પડેલો હતો.

નહી કેહેવા જોગ એક ઓરાડાની હમોને આ ઠેકાણે નોંધ કરવાની જરૂર થઈ પડીછે, અને તે કરવાનું કારણ માત્ર એટલાજ ઉપરથી છે કે તે ઓરડાની બાંધણી ઉપરથી મુસલમાન નવાબોમાં સફાઈ તથા સુઘડાઈનાં વીચાર કેટલા થોડા હશે તે ઓલું માલુમ પડી આવેછ. નવાબો અને હાકમો અત્તર તથા ચંપેલી અને તરેવાર ખુશબોનાં ઘણા શોખી હોય છે, પણ જેઓનાં દરબારી મેહેલમાં મોહોડાં પાસેજ જાય જરૂરનાં મકાનો બનાવેલાં હોય તીહાં આવી ખુશબોની જરૂર હોવીજ જોઈએ. એ ઓરડાનું નામ "બાયખાના" બોલે છે. ગરીબ માણસોનાં ઘરમાં બોએ ઉપર

બેઠા ચુહુલા બાંધેલા હોય છે તેવી આ ઠેકાણે જમીનની સપાટી ઉપરથી આસરે દોઢેક ફુટ ઊંચી ચુહુલા જેવી પથરની બેઠક નજર આવી અને એ બંધેની વચ્ચે જરા પણ પડદા જેવું કંઈજ નહીં હતું. કોઈ પણ સાધારણ જોનારને આ બાંધણીના આકાર ઉપરથી રાંધવાની જગા શીવાય કદી પણ એવો ખ્યાલ નથી આવવાનો કે આ આટલી જેટલી ઊંચી બેઠક તે જાયજરૂર એટલે ઝાડે ફરવાની જગો છે. આ સાંકડી બેઠકમાં જાયજરૂરની સઘળી ગોઠવણો કીધેલી હતી તેની ગલીચી, ગંધારો કેટલો હશે તે ખ્યાલમાં આવ્યાથી ખરેખર કંટાળો ઊપજ્યા વગર રેહેતો નથી. હમોએ આગળ કહ્યું તેમ આ બાબતની અત્રે નોંધ કરવાની જરૂર એટલીજ કે મેહેલ જેવા આરાસ્તગી ભરેલાં મકાનમાં આવી ખામીઓ જેઓ તપાસિને જુએછે તેમની નજરે પડેછે, અને આથી વીચારવાને બની આવેછે કે મુસલમાન લોકોએ, પછી શું ગરીબ કે તવંગર, અદનાથી આલા તુલીક સફાઈ, સોજાઈ, સુઘડાઈ અને તંદરોસ્તીની જાળવણી કરવાનાં જે કુદરતી કાયદાછે તે જાણવાને જરાએ પણ ધ્યાન પોહોંચાડ્યું હોય એવું લાગતું નથી. તેઓ આજ સુધી એ વીશે કમનસીબ રહી ગયા છે. આ સઘળું અંધારૂં અજ્ઞાનપણાથી તેઓમાં ચાલેછે. કેળવણીની ખુબી તો તેઓ જાણુતાજ નથી.

પાણીમેહેલની તારીફ હમારા ભોમીયાએ ઘણી અચ્છી રીતે કરી સંભળાવી હતી અને જણાવ્યું હતું કે ગરમીની રૂતુમાં ઘણોખરો વખત નવાબ સાહેબ આ મેહેલમાંજ ગુજારતા હતા. આ મેહેલ ગરમીની રૂતુમાં આસાએશ લેવાને બનાવ્યો હોય એ એકવાર માનવા જોગ છે; પણ તેની સાથે એક બીજો વીચાર પણ ઉત્પન્ન થાયછે, કે દુશમનની નજરથી છુપાઈ સંતાઈ રેહેવાને અથવા સંકટની વેલાએ નાહાસભાગ કરવાને આ છુપો મકાન ઘણોજ કામજોગ થઈ પડે, એટલા સારૂ પણ તે બનાવી રાખ્યો હોય. આ મેહલમાં ભરાઈ સંતાઈ રેહવાના ઓરડા, તેમની બાંધણીની રીત, સેહેડીઓના ટપ્પાની કઢોરી ઉંચાઈ, સંકડાસ, તથા ઓરડા ઓરડીઓની પેચ ભરેલી રચના, નાહાની નાહાની ગલી, અને વલાણદાર જવા આવવાના મારગો જે હીયાં જોવામાં આવેછે તે સઘળા ઉપરથી ઉપલો વીચાર મનમાં ઉત્પન્ન થયા વગર રેહેતો નથી. પુછપરછ કરતાં એવું પણ માલુમ પડ્યું કે આ મેહેલમાંથી બાહારો બાર છેક દુરવેર નીકલી જવાનો ભોંયરાંમાંથી રસ્તો

કોતરી કાહાડેલા છે, અને હમારી સાથે દેખાડાવા આવેલા મુસલમીનોની બોલવાની લઢણ પ્રમાણે હમોએ સાંભળ્યું કે ૧૨ ગાઉ દુર નીકળી જવાય એટલો રસ્તો ભોંયરાંમાં બનાવેલાછે, પણ આવી તોપ મારનારોના બોલવામાંથી ઘટતા ટકા બાદ કરી માનીએ તો અલબતાં પા કે અરધો માઈલ સુધી નાહાસી જવાનો રસ્તો બનાવ્યો હોય એ માનવા જોગ છે. એવી એક ગલીમાં, મસાલ સલગાવીને અંદર જવાનો ઈરાદો હમોએ કીધો હતો, પણ અંધીયાર હવાના સબબથી મસાલ તેમાં બલી નહી શકી, અને ૩૦ ફુટ ચાલ્યા એટલાં તો તે હોલવાઈ ગઈ હતી.

છેલ્લું, પાણીમેહેલ વીશે એક ત્રીજો વીચાર આવીયા વગર રેહેતો નથી. મુસલમાન નવાબ, અમીર, ઉમરાવો એશઆરામમાં મશહુર થયલાછે. તેઓ પોતાના નીચ હવસો પુરા પાડવાને, તેમનો પ્રજાનો ઉડાવવાને કશી વાતે પાછળ પડયા નથી; તેવા કોઈએ એવી મતલબથી આ મેહેલ બંધાવ્યો હોય જેમાં રૈયતની પારકી સ્ત્રીઓને ચોરી લાવી છુપાવી રાખે અથવા એવી જગાએથી છુપે રસ્તે રાત્રે નવાબ પોતે અને તેના જેવા અમલદારો જેમ જેને વગ ફાવે તેમ પોશાક બદલીને શેહેરમાં નીરલજ કામ કરવાને બાહાર નીકળતા હોય, અને તેજ છુપે રસ્તે પાછા આવી કીલ્લામાં હાજર રેહેતા હોય, જાણે કિલ્લામાંથી કોઈપણ શખ્સ બાહાર નીકળ્યોજ નથી. કિલ્લાનો દરબાન બીચારો જાણતોબી નથી કે કોઈપણ દરબારી માણસ કિલ્લાના દરવાજા વાટે રાત્રે બાહાર જતો હોય.

પાણીમેહેલ જોઈ રહયા પછી જે માર્ગે અંદર દાખલ થયા હતા તેજ માર્ગે પાછા બંધ ઉપર બાહેર આવ્યા, અને તીંહાંથી "ઉપલી બુરૂજ" નામના કિલ્લા ઉપર ગયા. આ કિલ્લો આસરે ૭૦ ફુટ ઉંચો છે, અને તે ઉપર ચઢવાને પથરની સેહેડી બનાવેલીછે. આ સેહેડીઓ જેમ જેમ ઉપર જઈએ છઈએ તેમ તેમ તેનાં પગથીયાં એટલાં બધાં ઉંચાં માલુમ પડાં જાય છે કે તે ઉપર જલદીથી તો ચઢાયજ નહી, અને ચઢતાં ઘણાજ મેહનત કરવી પડેછે. એવું કરવાની મતલબ એવી ધારવામાં આવેછે કે દુશમન કિલ્લા ઉપર ચઢી આવે તેને ચઢી આવવાને જેટલું પેહેલાં સેહેલું લાગે તેટલું છેક ઉપર ચઢયા પછી કઠણ પડે, અને ઉંચાં પગથીયાં ઉપરથી ચઢતાં તેમની ઉપ્પર તોપનો અથવા તેવો કોઈ બીજો મારો સારીપેઠે ચાલુ થઈ શકે.

એ બુરૂજને મથાળે બે તોપ જોવામાં આવીછે. એકનું નામ "મગરધ્વજ, બીજીનું નામ "નવગજી" કરીને છે. બંધે તોપો બેદાદ હાલતમાં પડેલી હતી, અને તેઓ ફોડવા લાયક હાલતમાં હોય એવું લાગતું નહી હતું. ઉપલા બુરૂજને મથાળેથી બુરૂજનાં પેટાંમાં ઉતારવાનો એક બાજુએથી પથરની સેહેડીનો રસ્તો છે. એ માર્ગે અંદર ઉતરયાથી એક નાહાનો સરખો ઓરડો આવેછે, તેની આગળ એક ઝરૂખો આવેલોછે, તેની ઉપરથી આસરે ૬૦ થી ૭૦ ફુટ નીચે, કિલ્લાનું મેદાન દેખાયછે. એ ઝરૂખાની જગા ઘણી સાંકડી છે તેથી ભાએગે બેથી ચાર માણસ સગવડે બેસી શકે. એ ઉપરથી વાઘ, હાથી, ગેંડા અને એવાં બીજાં જનાવરોની લડાઇનો તમાસો જોવાને એ ઝરૂખો કામે લાગ્યો હોય એવું ધારવામાં આવે છે.

ઉપલા બુરૂજ ઉપરથી ઉતરીને શેઠ બરજોરજી વીકાજી મેહેરજીનો રેહેવાનો બંગલો જોવાને ગયા. આ બંગલો કિલ્લાની અંદર લાવેલી નદીનાં કિનારા ઉપર બાંધેલોછે તેથી તે ઘણો ખુશનુમાં મકાન બનેલોછે, અને તીહાંની આબોહવા પણ સારી છે. બંગલાની બાંધણી સાધારણ તરીકાની છે, માત્ર તીહાંના કીસબી કારીગરોએ જે જે ભાગોને રૈનકદાર કીધાછે, તે કરવામાં મગર, સુસવાટ અને એવાં જનાવરોનાં આકારની નકલ ઘણે ઠેકાણે કીધેલી જણાઇછે. એજ નદીનાં કિનારા ઉપર બારાદારી મેહેલ એટલે બાર દરવાજાનો મેહેલ, તથા બેગમનો મેહેલ, કચેરી, જમવાનું દીવાનખાનું, એવાં કેટલાંએક અચ્છાં મકાનો બાંધેલાછે.

એ જોયા પછી ઓરતો તથા મરદોનું બંધીખાનું જોયું. જે હાલતમાં આ બંને જાતીનાં કેદીઓ બંધીખાનામાં રાખેલાં જોયા, તે ઉપરથી આટલું જણાવ્યા વગર ચાલતું નથી કે સુધરેલા દેશોનાં કેદખાનાંમાં જેવી તરબીએત અને માવજત થાય છે તેવી આ કેદખાનામાં મુતલક જોયામાં આવી નહી હતી. તોએપણ હીયાંના બંધીવાનોનાં ભાગ્ય, સારાં કે પેલા ચંચલ ધુંધી પારસી ભાઈ વીરાજી જેવા દરોગાનાં ઉપરીપણા તળે તેઓ પડેલા હતા. કેદખાનાંના કેદીઓની તરબીઅત અને માવજત કેમ કરવી એ વીરો ભાઈ વીરાજી અંજાણ્યા હતા તોએપણ એ ધુંધી શખસમાં એ બાબતનું કેટલુંએક ખુદરતી જ્ઞાન સારૂં દેખાતું હતું. તેવણે કેટલાએક પોતાની તરફનાં સારા ઉપાય કામે લગાડયા હતા. તોએપણ બંધીવાનો પાસે સહવારનાં સખત મજુરી કરાવવી અને હલકાં

જનાવરની પેઠે તેમને રાત્રે સખત બંધીમાં કેદ રાખી, ખાવા પીવાની વેહેલા પાડવી અને જેમ બને તેમ બંધવાને શરીર ઈજા ઘણી પોહોંચાડવી, એટલાજ કાયદા નીજામ સરકારનાં બંધીખાનાંની તરબીએત વીશે અમલમાં આવેલા માલુમ પડયા હતા. મુસલમાની હકુમત તળે આવી બેકદર અને બેદાદી ચાલેલી સાંભળી આપણને ઘણું તાજુબ થવા જેવું કાંઈ નથી, માત્રે તાજુબી એટલાજ ઉપરથી લાગેછે, કે નીજામની હાલની હકુમત જે ચાલાક અને બાહોશ વજીરને હસ્તકછે, જે ચંચલ નવાબ ઇંગરેજી હકુમતની રીતભાંતથી સારી રીતે વાકેફછે, તેવા અકલ-વાળાની અને પુરતું રાજદરબારી જ્ઞાન ધરાવનારાની કારકીરદીમાં તેના બંધીવાને આવી બેદાદ હાલતમાં રેહે, એ અતિશય દીલગીરી ભરેલું તેમજ સખુન નાખવા જોગછે. આ વિશય ઉપર ધ્યાન પોહોંચાડવાની ઘણીજ અગતછે. નીજામ હૈદરાબાદની નજદીક સીકંદરાબાદમાં ઇંગરેજની જે છાવણી છે તીંહાં ત્રીમલગીરી આગળ ઇંગરેજનાં તાબા તળે જે કેદખાનું બનાવેલુંછે, તે એક નમુના દાખલ જોયલું બસછે. આ ઠેકાણાનાં કેદખાનાં વીશે લંબાણથી ઘટતી જગાએ બયાન કરેલું છે; અત્રે એટલું કેહેવું બસછે કે કેદખાનું કેટલી સફાઈ ભરેલું, કેવું રળીયામણું, અને તેમાં પડેલા બંધવાઓને ઈમાનદાર અને મેહેનતુ બનાવવાને તેમને ધંધો પેશે, સીખાડવા અને ઉદ્યોગી કરવા કેવી તરેહની તરબીઅત આપવી, એનો એક અછો નમુનો હમારા જોવામાં તીંહાં આવ્યોછે. મુંબઈનાં કેદખાનાં અને બીજાં જે કાંઈ આ દેશમાં હમોએ જોયાંછે તે સઘળાં ત્રીમલ-ગિરીનાં કેદખાનાં આગલ પોઇસ છે.

નલદ્રુગના કિલ્લામાંથી નીકળીને કોટની બાહાર આવ્યા ત્યારે રાત્રે ૮॥ વાગાનો અમલ થયલો હતો. બાહાર પડતાં આ ગામને લગતી એક મોહોટી મસજીદ જોવામાં આવી, જેના દરવાજા ઉપર મુકેલી તકતી ઉપર ૯૬૮ હીજરી સને વાંચવામાં આવ્યો, તે ઉપરથી ગણતાં નજદીક ૨૫૦) વરસની જુની તે ઈમારત જણાઈ હતી. જેમ હિંદુઓએ પોતાનાં વખતમાં દેવળો, દેહેરાં અને પાહાડી કોતરકામો કીધાંછે તેમ મુસલમાનોએ પોતાની કારકીરદીમાં શેહેરે શેહેર અને ઠામે ઠામ મસજીદો બાંધીછે. મસજીદ સાથે ઓટલા બાંધવામાં આવ્યાછે, જે મુસલમાન જાતના મુસાફરો ઉતારો કરવાની જગા તરીકે વાપરેછે. આ મસ-જીદો, વીશે અત્રે નોંધ કરવાની જરૂર એટલીજ છે કે એવી જાતની કેટલીક ઈમારતો હિંદુસ્થાનમાં ઘણીજ સુંદર, જોવાજેવી અને યાદગારીના નમુના લાયક

બંધાયલી છે; તેમાંની એક મસજીદ "મોતી મસજીદ" જે આગરાના કિલ્લામાં છે, જેનું ચીત્ર હીયાં આપેલું છે, તેની બાંધણી, ખુબસુરતી, અને સફાઈમાં મીસત્રીઓએ જે મનરાકતી અને ઉચે દરજેનો શોખ દેખડાવેલો છે, તે યુરોપખંડની કેટલીએક ઉંચા તરીકાંની બાંધણીઓ અથવા મોહોટ મોહોટી ઇમારતોની બરોબરી કરી શકેછે, એટલુંજ નહીં પણ તેમાંની કેટલીકોને ટકર મારે એવાછે.

નલદ્રુગથી નીજામ હેદરાબાદ જતાં રસ્તામાં આવતાં જુદાં જુદાં મથકો, મુસાફરી બંગલા, ટપાલની આફીસો તથા બળદ બદલવાનાં ઠેકાંણાં અને એક ઠેકાંણું બીજાથી કેટલું દુર છે તેના માઇલોની ટીપ.

નલદ્રુગ સેકંદરાબાદથી	૧૫૮ માઇલ.
હાલીયાબાદ.. ,, ..	૧૫૪ ,,
જલકોટ.... ,, ..	૧૫૧ ,,
દસ્તાપોર*... ,, ..	૧૪૮ ,,
ઇયાનાગુર*.. ,, ..	૧૪૪ ,,
દાલીમ.... ,, ..	૧૪૧ ,,
એલી .... ,, ..	૧૩૭ ,,
જકાપુર.... ,, ..	૧૩૫ ,,
ઉમરગામ*.. ,, ..	૧૩૧ ,,
થરૂરી†.... ,, ..	૧૨૭ ,,
નલમોર*.. ,, ..	૧૨૧ ,,
મનકાપોર*.. ,, ..	૧૧૬ ,,
હલી...... ,, ..	૧૧૪ ,,
મનથાલ†.. ,, ..	૧૧૩ ,,
હસ્તાપોર*.. ,, ..	૧૧૦ ,,
દોલદત્તી*.. ,, ..	૧૦૭ ,,
થરૂલ્લા .... ,, ..	૧૦૪ ,,
રાજસર* .. ,, ..	૧૦૨ ,,
મલીયારી .. ,, ..	૧૦૦ ,,
હોમનાબાદ† . ,, ..	૯૬ ,,
કાપરગામ*.. ,, ..	૯૦ ,,
તાલમરગી.. ,, ..	૮૬ ,,
મંગલગીઈ*.. ,, ..	૮૪ ,,
છોટાએકલી+ . ,, ..	૭૯ ,,
મરકુનડા ... ,, ..	૭૬ ,,

બનગુર સેકંદરાબાદથી	૭૪ માઇલ.
ચીમકપટી† .. ,, ..	૭૧ ,,
સતવા* .... ,, ..	૬૯ ,,
બડાએકેલી†.. ,, ..	૬૨ ,,
રંમજોલી .... ,, ..	૫૯ ,,
હુગાલી ..... ,, ..	૫૮ ,,
દીગવાલ* ... ,, ..	૫૬ ,,
ગુનદમકોડુર.. ,, ..	૫૨ ,,
કમકોલી† ... ,, ..	૪૯ ,,
અકુર...... ,, ..	૪૪ ,,
સદાશીવપટ†.... ,, ..	૩૮ ,,
નંદીકંદી .... ,, ..	૩૬ ,,
પેદાપુર ..... ,, ..	૩૫ ,,
પોથલીપટી* .. ,, ..	૩૦ ,,
કંદી†....... ,, ..	૨૮ ,,
કોમલપંદ .... ,, ..	૨૬ ,,
રૂદરારાંમ*.... ,, ..	૨૪ ,,
ઓથાનગીઈ .. ,, ..	૨૦ ,,
પટનચેરૂ† ... ,, ..	૧૭ ,,
રામચંદર પોર . ,, ..	૧૫ ,,
ગંગારામ*.... ,, ..	૧૨ ,,
મીયાપોર .... ,, ..	૧૦ ,,
કુકરપટી..... ,, ..	૬ ,,
બાલાનગર*.. ,, ..	૩ ,,
સેકંદરાબાદ .. ,, ..	૦ ,,

સેકંદરાબાદ જે ઇંગરેજી હદમાં છે. તીહાંથી હેદરાબાદ શેહેર જે નીજામ હદમાં આવેલું છે તેમની વચે સાત માઇલનો અંતર છે.

---

* બળદ બદલવાની ચોકી તથા પોસ્ટ આફીસ.

† મુસાફરી બંગલા.

તા૦ ૨૬ મી ડીસેંબર—આ દીને નલદુગથી રાત્રે ૯ વાગે ગાડીમાં બેઠા તે સહવારના ઉમરગામ આગળ ૬) વાગે જરાવાર વીસામો લીધો કેમકે આ જગાનું પાણી ઘણું સારૂંછે. આ ઠેકાણે રસ્તાની ડાબી બાજુએ હિંદુના શીવનું એક દેહેરૂં હમારી નજરે પડયું. હિંદુ ધર્મ પ્રમાણે તેમનાં કેટલાંએક દેહેરાંઓમાં તેમના દેવ તથા દેવીઓની અને તેમના સેવક તથા સેવકીઓની મુરતીઓ અને ચાત્રો નિરલજ આકૃતીમાં અને અનીતી ભરેલાં આસનમાં ભીતો ઉપર અને એવી બીજી જગાએ ચીત્રેલાં અથવા કોતરેલાં હોય છે એ સરવ કોઈ જાણેછે. પણ એવી મુરતીઓ હીંયાં મુંબઈમાં હિંદુ શીવાએ કોઈ બીજી ગ્નાતના લોકની નજરે પડતી હોય એવું જાણ્યામાં આવ્યું નથી, જેનાં કારણો ઘણા હશે. એક તો અત્રેનાં હિંદુઓ ઇંગરેજી ધારા અને કાયદાથી વાકેફ છે કે આવી નાગી મુરતીઓ તેઓથી ખુલ્લી મુકાઈ નથી રાકાવાની તેથી તેઓ છુપી જગાએ તેમને મેલતા હશે; બીજું કારણ એ કે મુંબઈનાં કેટલાક સમજુ અને અનુભવિક હિંદુઓ તેમનાં ધરમનાં એવાં નીરલજ તત્વો લોકમાં હોહો થઈ પડે હેવી રીતે જાહેર નહી પાડવા ઇછિતા હોય, તેથી આવી મુરતીઓ દેહેરાંઓમાં છુપી રાખી મેળતા હોય. ગમે એ કારણ હોય, પણ ઘણા હિંદુઓ તેમની પુજા કરે છે આ વાત કોઇથી ના પાડી નથી શકાવાની. આવી મુરતીઓ હિંદુસ્થાનના મધ્ય પ્રાંતોનાં દેહેરાંઓમાં ઠેકાણે ઠેકાણે જોયામાં આવીછે. તેનું વીગતવાર બયાન આગળ જણાવેલું છે. પણ આ નાહાનાં સરખાં ગામડાંમાં થોડાંક ઝુપડાં જોયામાં આવ્યાં હતાં તીહાં હમારી નજરે એવી નાગી અને નિરલજ આસને ઉભેલી મુરતીઓ પેહેલ વેહેલી પડી હતી. આ મુરતીઓ દેહેરાંની બાહારની ફરતી બાજુએ ભીત ઉપર તથા પથરની સેહેડીઓની બાજુએ જોયામાં આવી હતી. એક મુરતી એવી હતી કે દેવનો લીંગ તેનાં પુજારીઓ ચુમતા હતાં, બીજી તરફ પુજારીઓ લિંગ હાથમાં ઝાલીને નમસ્કાર કરતા પાડેલા હતાં. હમો એવી અસભ્ય બાબત આ પુસ્તકમાં વિગતવાર દાખલ કરવા અને તેનું બયાન કરવાને મુતલગ ચાહાતા નથી. પણ હિંદુ ધર્મમાં આવી વાત છે જે વાજબી છે અથવા ગેરવાજબી છે એ વીશે આ ઠેકાણે મુજાહેમત અથવા તકરાર કરવાનું પડતું મેલી, તે બીજાઓને જણાવા સારૂજ માત્ર અત્રે એક ઈશારા તરીકે દાખલ કરવાની જરૂર સમજીએ છીએ. એ મુરતીઓની બેહાઈ ભરેલી રચનામાં આટલું પણ જણાવવું જોઇએ છ કે એવી મૂરતીઓમાં ફકત પુરૂશોનીજ મુરતીઓ

એવી રીતે દેખાડાવેલીછે એટલુંજ નથી, પણ મદરાસ ઇલાકામાં "ઉન્ટામીટ" નામનાં ગામમાં શીવનાં એક મોહોટાં દેહેરાંમાં તો દેવદેવીઓનો એવો તો નઠારો, ભેળભાળ કરી નાખ્યો છે કે તે જોયાથી આપણને ખરેખર લજવાઈ જવું પડેછે. આ વીશે આગળ વાંચવામાં આવશે.

બપોરના ૧૨ વાગે થરૂરી ગામના મુસાફરી બંગલામાં જઈ પોહોંચ્યા. આ ઠાણે જઈ પોહોંચતાં છેક બપોરનાં ૧૨ વાગા હતા. ભુખ એવી તો કડકડતી લાગી હતી કે તેથી હમારા સઘળાના પણ બાર વાગી ગયા હતા. પેહેલાં હમારી ભુખને શાંત કરવાનાં ઉપાય લેવાની હમોએ એકદમ ઘણીજ અગત જોઈ, તોએ પણ તે કરતાં બપોરનાં બે વાગાનો સુમાર થયો હતો. આ ઠેકાણે જોવા જેવું કાંઇ નહીં હોવાથી બપોરના ત્રણ વાગે આગળ કુચ કીધી. હીયાંથી નીકળેલા પાછલી રાત્રે બે વાગે મંથાલગામના મુસાફરી બંગલે જઈ પુગા; થંડી ઘણી હતી, તેથી ગાડીમાંથી ઉતરીને બંગલામાં ખાલી કોચ ઉપર સુઈ તાહાડે થરથરવાને બદલે ગાડીમાં બીછાંનાની હુંફમાંજ પડી રેહેવું હમને તથા હમારા કેટલાક મીત્રોને વધારે ગમીયું હતું.

તા૦ ૨૭ મી ડીસેંબર— આ દીને પરોઢીયામાં ઉઠી જે કંઈ કરવું ઘટતું હતું તે કરી બાહેર નીકલવા આગમચ કાફી તથા દુધ, મંથાલનું ફરમાસું માખણ તથા બેદાં અને રોટીનો નાસ્તો જલદી બનાવવાનો હુકમ હમારા મીત્ર શેઠ મંચેરજી તરફથી થયલો સંભળાયો હતો. આ નાસ્તો તઈયાર થાય તીહાંસુધી મંથાલનાં પરોઢીયાનાં દેખાવ ઉપર ચીત લગાડયું. આહા કેવો ગંભીર ! તેની સાથે કેવો ખુશનુમાં અને દીલ બાગબાગ થાય એવો દેખાવ દેખાઇ રહ્યો હતો ! વાંચનારના મનમાં આ પરોઢીયાંના દેખાવનું થોડુંક પણ જ્ઞાન આવવાને અત્રે શબ્દોમાં તેનું ચિત્ર આપવાની કોશેશ કરી છે, પછી તે કેટલે દરજે અધુરી થઈ હોય, આ વીશે હમો વાંચનારની મેહરબાની ઉપર આધાર રાખીએછ.

ઓરોહેનગેહની આ બેરી થઈ હોશબાંમીનો અમલ શરૂ થઈ રહો હતો. રાત્રની સીહાઇ દફે થઈ બામદાદની રોશની નીકલી રહી હતી; ખુરશેદની તેજીથી સેતારાઓ બેમાલુમ થઈ ગયા હતા; આદમ જાત આદમ જાતનું નુર ચશ્મો ચશ્મથી જોઈ શકતું હતું; રાગ ભૈરવ પોતાનાં વખતે પોંહોંચી "ઉઠો પ્યારે ભોર" આ રાગની ધુણીમાં મલસ્કાનું મધુર ગાયણ ગાતો રહેલો હતો; તેના મનોહારી રાગથી ચકિત થઈ, ચલીયાં, મઈના, મોર, કાક અને કોકીલા પક્ષી લાલ અને કલ્લોર કરી રહેલાં

હતાં; મોહબ્બતથી દેવાના થયલાં બુલબુલો, ખીલતાં ગુલોને ચાંચે ચાંચે ચુમતાં તરેવાર સવાલો પુછતાં રેહેલાં હતાં; માસુક ગોલાબને એક સખત સવાલ પુછાઈ રેહેલો હતો કે આવી ખુબસુરતી સાથે તારા દામાનમાં કાંટા કેમ લપટાઈ રેહેલાછે! ચંચલ મધુમાંખી, પોપટી, પતંગીયાં અને ભમરા પ્રફુલ્લિત પુષ્પો ઉપર એક છોડી બીજાં અને બીજું છોડી ત્રીજાં ઊપર વગર અટકવે ભમતા અને ચક્કર મારતાં પોતાનાં સ્વતંત્ર અને નીરદોષપણાનાં સુખમાં આનંદ પામતાં, ભણુભણી રેહેલાં હતાં. આ સઘળાં પ્રાણીઓની પરોઢીયાંની લીલામાં તેમનાં સઘળાં કરતાં જે શ્રેષ્ઠ મનુષ્ય તે પણ સામેલ હતો. પણ તેની લીલા ઊંચે દરજજેની મનશાકતીની મોજ ભોગવવામાં હતી. આ પૃથ્વી ઉપરથી તથા તેને લગતી સઘળી મીઆ બાબદો ઉપરથી તેનું મન વેગળું થઈ, તેને જીવતર આપનાર, જે ઇશ્વર તેની ઉપર લાગેલું હતું. તેના હોટમાંથી ખુશ આવાજે, પણ હળવે, હળવે હર! હર! હર! રામ! રામ! રામ! ઓ પરવર! પરવર! પરવર!— ઓ સાહેબ! ઓ દાદગર! આવા ગંભીર શબ્દો, ઇશ્વરસ્તુતી અને પ્રાર્થનાનાં નીકળતા રેહેલા હતા. મંથાલના જંગલમાં પણ આવા સમએ આવો આવાજ હમોએ એક એકાંત દેહેરામાંથી તીહાંનાં એક બુઢા જોગીનાં મોહોડામાંથી નીકળતો શાંભળીયો હતો. કુદરતનો સઘળો દેખાવ તાજો, રળીઆમણો, પવિત્ર અનેતેની સાથે ગંભીર લીલા ભરેલો દેખાઈ રહો હતો; તેમાં તો જાણે ગર્ક થઈ જવા ગમતું હતું! ડુંગર, ટેકરીઓ અને કેટલેક સુધી ખોલી સપાટ જમીન ઉપરથી ધુમસ હજુ હજુ દુર થતો જતો હતો; ઝાડોનાં પાત્રાં ઉપર મોતી જેવાં દવનાં ટીપાં ઝલકી અને ટપકી રેહેલાં હતાં; ફુલો અને મોહોરોના મોહોડાં ઉઘડીને તેમાંથી લપટ અને પમરાટ છુટી સઘળાં જંગલમાં પસરી રહો હતો. કેટલેક ઠેકાણે ફુલોનાં ઝુમખા વિચિત્ર આસને ઑંક ખાઈ એટલાતો નીચા લટકી રહેલા હતા કે જાણે તેઓ ઇચ્છતા હોય કે કીયારે "હમને તોડી લઇ માનવી તેના નાખ આગલ લઈ જાય, તેનાં મસ્તક ઉપર ધરે, અથવા ઇશ્વર આગળ હમને અરપણ કરે." આવાં ખરાં અને પવિત્ર સુખ આપનાર દેખાવમાં હમારૂં મન છક થઈ ગયું હતું! આહા! આ પરોઢીયાનું પુરતું બયાન કેમ થઈ શકે! વલી આ વખતે ઇશ્વર સાથે દીલ મળી ગયાથી આત્માને જે સુખ અને આનંદ થતો હતો તે જણાવાને તો હમને શબ્દોજ મલી આવી શકતા નથી. ખરેખર ઇશ્વરી સુખનું બયાન તે આ તકલીદાં કાગજ ઊપર, કમલ, સીહાઈ

અને ચામડાની જબાનથી નીકળતા શબ્દોથી કેમ થઈ શકે? આ છુપું સુખ આપણા મનમાં છુપુંજ ભોગવી શકશું! જેણે આ ભોગવીયું હશે તેજ એનું ખરાપણું, પવીત્રપણું, અને મોહોટપણું જાણી શકશે! ઓ માનવી! આ પૃથ્વીનાં મિથ્યા તકલીદી સુખનો વીચાર થોડોવાર એક કોરે રાખી, પરોઢીયાંની બંદગીમાં કેવું ખરૂં સુખ છે, તેની જરા તપાસતો કરી જો!

થોડા વારમાં હમારૂં મન પાછું આ દુનીયાની બાબદો ઉપર લાગું. હમારા એક મીત્રની પુછપરછનો આવાજ હમારે કાને પડયો. આ પુછપરછ હમારા પ્રવીણ મીત્ર ડાકટર ભાઉ સાહેબ કરતા હતા. આ વીદ્વાન મીત્ર, વગર થાકવે અને કંટાળવે, સઘળાં દીલ અને ઉલટથી જીહાં જીહાં ઉભા રેહેતા અથવા ઉતારો કરતા તીહાં પેહેલી પુછપરછ હીંદુ ધરમની પ્રાચીન બાબદો વીશે, તેના દેવલ, દેહેરાં, અને મુરતીઓ વીશે, અથવા તેના જુનામાં જુના પુરાણા લેખો, તખતી, સીક્કા ઇતીઆદી વીશે કરતા હતા. જેમ હમારા મીત્ર ભાઈ મંચેરજી દરેક જગાએ ઉતારો કરતાં સઘળાનાં ભોજનને સરૂં પેહેલી પુછપરછ અને શોધ તે ઠેકાણાનાં દુધ, દહી, માખણ, તરકારી અને બીજી ખાવાની જીનસોને સારૂં કરતા હતા, તેમ બીજી તરફથી આ હમારા ધુંધી મીત્ર ડાકટર સાહેબ પોતાના શોધ કર્તા મનનાં ભોજન વીશે તલાસ અને ચોકાશી કરતા હતા. પ્રાચીન કાલની આ દેશને લગતી કોઇબી બાબદ મળી તો તે તેમના મનને એક ઉત્તમ અને પુષ્ટીકારક ખોરાક મલીઆ બરોબર હતું. રાત્રે ૧૨) વાગે ચાલુ મંજલમાં પણ કોઈ એવું કેહે કે આ ઠેકાણે પુરાણાં દેહેરાં છે, તો ડાકટરની ગાડી પેહેલી ઉભેલી જાણવી. મસાલો સલગાવીને રાત્રે તે ઠેકાણા ઉપર ઉતરીને તે જોઈ લેવું, અગર જો તે જગા વધારે ધીયાન પોહોંચાડવા જોગ માલુમ પડી તો રાત્રે તે ઠેકાણા ઉપર અટકી સહવારે તે ચોકસાઇથી ફરીને જોવી. આટલી ઇંતેજારી આ વીદ્વાન મીત્રમાં હમોએ જોઈ હતી. મંથાલના મુસાફરી બંગલામાં ડાકટરને ખબર મલી કે તે ઠેકાણે હીંદુઓનાં જુના દેહેરાં પડી ભાગેલાંછે, તેથી તે જોવાને સઘળા મીત્રોએ એકદમ ઠરાવ કીધો. જલદીથી નાસ્તો કરી લીધો. દુધ અને માખણનીતો તારીફજ નહી થાય; ગામડાંના ગાય ઢોરને મંથાલમાં એવો તો સારો ચારો મલી શકતો હતો કે હીયાંનાં માંખણ, દુધ, દહી અને છાસની વખાણ થતી સાંભળી હતી. ઠંડી પણ સારીપડતી હતી તેથી નાસ્તો સારી રૂચાથી કર્યો હતો, "મંથાલનું માખણ અને દુધ."

એટલા શબ્દોની નોંધ હમારાં સ્મરણ પુસ્તકમાં જેવી કરી લીધી હતી તેવીજ નોંધ આ જીનસોની સઘળા મીત્રોએ તેમની જઠરાગનીમાં પણ કરી લીધી હતી. નાસ્તો લઈ ઉલટ ભરીયા ચાલતા બાહેર નીકળ્યા. પણ જેવી ઉલટથી જોવાને બાહેર પડયા હતા તેવા સંતોષ પામી પાછા નહીં ફર્યા હતાં, કેમકે જે કાંઈ જોયામાં આવ્યું તે માત્ર ૫૦) વરસથી વધારે જુનું નહીં હતું, અને વલી તે સઘળું નજીવું હતું. બંગલાથી આસરે ૨॥ અઢી માઈલ દુર "અંબીલકુંડ" નામનું શીવનું દેહેરૂં જોયું. પરોઢીયાંની લેહેકી અને જંગલની ખુશબોથી જેટલું મન ખુશી થયું હતું તેટલું તે દેહેરૂં જોયાથી નહીં થયું હતું. અત્રે થોડીક ભાગેલી મુરતીઓ એણીગમ પેલીગમ રખડતી વેરાયલી પડેલી જોઈ હતી. આમાંથી ડાકટરે પ્રાચીન કાલની બાબદો વીશે શોધ કરનાર તરીકે પોતાના હક દાખલ કેટલીએક નાહાની નાહાની મુરતીઓ વગર હુકમે ઉપાડી લીધી હતી. આ નજીવી મુરતી ઉપર જેટલું ડાકટરનું મન અને ચીત્ત લાગેલું હતું તેના કરતાં વધારે ઇનતેજારીથી હમારૂં અચકચારૂં મન સફેદ બદનના તથા કાળાં મોહોડાનાં, દાહાડી અને લાંબી પુછડીવાળા વાંદરો, દુર ઝાડ ઉપર બેસીને હમુને ટીકી ટીકી જોતા હતા, તેમની સાથે ચેશ્ટા કરવા લાગું હતું. હમારા મનમાં ધારતી પડી કે રખેને આ હનુમાનનું લસ્કર જેમ રાવણની ઉપર સીતાને છોડાવવા ઉલટયું હતું, તેમ પેલી ઉપાડી લીધેલી મુરતીઓ છોડવી લેવાને ડાકટર અને હમારી ઉપર તુટી પડે. પણ દાહાડી સાથે અકલ હંમેશા ભેળાએલી રેહેછે, તે પ્રમાણે આ હનુમાની ટોલાંએ પોતાના ખુદરતી ચાળા અને ચેશ્ટા કરવાની ચાલ છોડીને, ઘણાંજ ડાહાપણથી સેતાન ડાવો કરીને ઝાડની છેક ટોંચ ઉપર ચઢી બેસવું વાજબી જાણીયું હતું, અને તીહાંથીજ ઘણા ગંભીર દેખાવે હમુને જોયા કીધું હતું; જેમાં હમને એવું લાગ્યું હતું કે પ્રાચીન કાળના હિંદુ ધરમનો નાશ થયાથી હવડાં આગ્નાનપણે હિંદુઓ હનુમાન (વાંદર) ની પુજા કરેછે, આ ઘણુંજ ખોટું અને તિરસ્કારિક કર્મ છે, એથી ઇશ્વર બારે કોપાયમાન થાયછે, અને હાલ વાંદરો ઘણું કરીને માણસને જોઇ છેક ઉંચે ઝાડ ઉપર અથવા કોઈ બીજી જગા ઉપર તિરસ્કારથી નાહાસ ભાગ કરી જાયછે તેનું એજ કારણ છે. આ ગંભીર અને ચાનક આપે એવા દેખાવ જોઈ હમારાં મન ઉપર ઘણી મજબુત અસર થઈ હતી. પણ સઉથી મજબુત અસર ડાકટર બાઉનાં બે હિંદુ ચાકરો ઉપર થઈ હતી, અને તેઓએ ડાહાપણથી તેજ વેળા નિશ્ચય કીધો

હતો કે હવે પછી હનુમાનની પુજા કરવી નહી! અને તેમને કેટલાંએક વેહેમી હિંદુઓ લાડુ વીગરે ખવડાવેછે, તથા કેટલાએક હિંદુઓ તો જેમ ગોકળ અને બીંદ-રાબીન તથા મથુરામાં વાંદરાની નીયાત જમાડેછે તેમ કદાપી કરવું નહીં! વાંદરો પછવાડે હિંદુઓ ધરમની ગેરસમજણથી કેટલા પૈસા ખરચેછે, અને તેઓ એવા ખરચ કરવાને કેવા ફીદા ફીદા થઈ ગયલાછે તેનું બયાન, મથુરા, બીંદરાબીન અને ગોકળ તરફનો અહેવાલ વાંચ્યાથી માલુમ પડશે.

અંબીલકુંડથી ઉત્તર તરફ આસરે ત્રણ માઇલ દુર "ઉમનાપુર" કરીને એક બીજું ગામડું છે તીંહાં માત્ર એક મોહોટી આસરે ૮ ફુટ ઉંચી, ૪ાા ફુટ પોહોળી અને ૨) ઇંચ જાડી ગણપતીની પથરની મુરતી જોયામાં આવી હતી. તે સઘળી સીંદુરથી ભરેલી હતી, અને તેની આસપાસ બે ચાર નાગી મુરતીઓ હતી તેઉપર પણ સિંદુર ચોળેલું હતું. હીયાં કંઈ પણ નવું, અથવા નવાઈ જેવું જોવાનું નહીં હતું, તેથી બપોરનાં ૧૧ વાગે મંથાલનાં મુસાફરી બંગલામાં પાછાં આવ્યા, અને જોકે માખણ સારીપેઠે ખાધેલું હતું તોએપણ ભુખે પાછો હુમલો કીધો હતો. રસ્તાની બાજુએ સેરડીનાં ખેતરો હતાં, તીહાંનાં કામ કરતા ખેડુતો પાસે હમો-એ સેરડી માંગી, પણ તેઓએ તે આપી નહીં, કેમકે જીલ્લાઓમાં રસ્તે જનારા ઘણાક સાહેબ લોકને જારે ભુખ અથવા તરસ લાગેછે તારે આસપાસની હરેક ચીજ મુફ્ત લઈ લેવાનો તેમને સરકારથી જાણે હક મળેલો હોય, એવું આ દેશનાં બીચારા કેટલાક અજ્ઞાની ખેડુતો સમજેછે. હમોએબી સેરડી મુફ્ત અને જબરીથી સાહેબ લોકની કાણી લીધી હતેતો હમને પણ ઉપર જણાવેલા સરકારી તો નહી પણ આકાશના ચંદ્રમાંથી મળેલા હક પ્રમાણે મળી શકતે. પણ એવું હમોએ કરવું વાજબી નહીં ગણી ખેડુતોને આ વીશે ખુલાસાથી સમજણ આપી હતી, તથા ઉપર જણાવેલો હક તદન ખોટો હતો એ વીશે તેમને સમજાવીયું હતું અને સેરડીનું દામ આપીયું, તેથી તેઓ પોતાને તે દીવસે ભાગ્યશાલી સમજીયા હોય એવું હમને લાગું હતું.

બપોરનાં ૧૧ વાગે મુસાફરી બંગલામાં આવીને ખોદાની આપેલી બખશીસો ઉપર સારીપેઠે નેયામત ગુજારી કીધી અને તેથી તનદરોસ્ત થયા. પાછી કુચ કરવાની તેયારી થઈહતી, એવામાં હમારા મીત્ર ડાકટર સાહેબ જેવણનાં મનમાં પેલી શોધોનો ખ્યાલતો રમીજ રહેલો હતો, તેઓએ આવીને ખબર આપી કે

"મારા વાંચવા તથા સાંભળવામાં એવું આવ્યુંછે કે "કલ્યાંણી" કરીને આગલા વખતમાં હિંદુઓનું એક મોહોટું શેહેર હતું, તે હવડાં બીસ્માર હાલતમાં આવી પડેલુંછે; પણ એક વખત હિંદુ રાજાઓની આ એક મોટી રાજધાની હતી, વીહાં આપણે જઈશું તો અલબતાં જાણવાજોગ કાંઈ જુની નીશાણો, લેખો, વીગરે કંઈપણ કદાચ જોવામાં આવી શકશે." એટલા સારૂ તે શેહેર તરફના રસ્તાની પુછપરછ ડાકટરે કરી રાખી હતી. એ વીશે એવું જાણવામાં આવ્યું હતું કે મંથાલથી હેદરાબાદ જતાં એક આડ રસ્તો આવેછે, તે રસ્તે કલ્યાણી જવાઈ શકાયછે, અને મંથાલથી કલ્યાણી જવાને માત્ર ૪ કલાકનો રસ્તો છે. ડાકટરની ઉલટને સઘળા મીત્રો હંમેશ ઉત્તેજન આપતાજ હતા, તેથી તુરત તેમની વાત કબુલ રાખી કલ્યાણી જવાનો ઠરાવ કીધો.

ઉપર જણવેલાં કલ્યાણી શેહેર વીશે થોડી ઓળખ અને બયાન વાંચનારને આપવાની જરૂર છે, આ ઉપરથી માલુમ પડી આવશે કે પાધરો રસ્તો મુકી આડ ગયા હતા તે વગર કારણે નહીં ગયા હતા.

કરનાટક અને માહારાષ્ટ્રની સરહદ ઉપર બેદર નામનું શેહેર છે. તેની પશ્ચીમે કલ્યાંણી શેહેર આવેલુંછે. કલ્યાણી શેહેરમાં "ચાલુકય" જાતના રજપુત વંશના રાજાઓ ઈસવી સનના ૧૦ માં શૈકાની આખેરીથી ૧૨ માં શૈકડાની આખેરી સુધી રાજ ચલાવી ગયાછે, એવું લેખો ઉપરથી માલુમ પડેલુંછે. આ રાજાઓએ ચોળ અને ગુજરાત લઈ લીધાં હતાં, એવું પણ એક લેખ ઉપરથી માલુમ પડયુંછે. આખા માહારાષ્ટ્ર દેશ ઉપર અને તેલંગણનાં પશ્ચીમ ભાગ ઉપર તથા છેક નર્મદા નદી સુધી આ રાજાઓની હકુમત ચાલતી હતી. આ વંશમાંના એકની સાથે ચૌરે વંશની વારસ છોકરીનાં લગ્ન થયાથી ગુજરાત તેને મલ્યું હોય એવું લાગેછે. છેલ્લે ચાલુકય રાજાને તેનાં વજીરે ઉઠાડી મેલી તેની ગાદી છીનવી લીધી. આ વખતે "લીંગાયત" જાતનો એક ધરમ જનુની ટોળો પગજોર થયલો હતો, તેમાંના કેટલાએકોએ પેલા વજીરને કતલ કીધો અને અંતે આવું બનીયું કે આ રાજ દેવગીરીનાં યાદવોનાં હાથમાં જઈ પડયું. આજે કલ્યાંણી ફકત નાહાનું સરખું ગામ થઈ ગએલુંછે જે નીજામ હેદરાબાદનાં તાલુકામાંછે, અને નાંહાં એક નવાબ હાકમી ચલાવેછે. રૈયતનો ઘણોખરો ભાગ મુસલમાનોછે

અને બાકીનાં હિંદુઓછે.* એ શેહેર અથવા ગામની બીજી વીગત આગળ વાંચવામાં આવશે.

મંથાલથી બપોરના ૧ વાગે જમીને નીકળ્યા તે ત્રણ વાગે પેલા આડ રસ્તા આગળ આવી પુગા તીહાંથી આડ રસ્તો ડુંગરની બીણમાંથી ચાલેલોછે. આ બીણમાનો રસ્તો ઘણોજ વાંકો ટીકો અને ઢેકાંઢલીયાં વાળો છે, તેથી હીયાંથી ગાડીમાં બેસી ધક્કા આચકા ખાતાં જવાને બદલે ચાલતાં જવું અથવા ઘોડા ઉપર બેસીને જવું બેહેતર છે. હમારામાંના કેટલાંએકનાં હાડકાં સારીપેઠે દોદરાં થયાંપછી તેઓ મુંગા મુંગા ઉતરી ચાલવા લાગા હતા. પણ ભારી શરીરથી વાંકી ચુકી જગાએ ચાલી હાથ પગ ભાગવાની ધાસ્તી હમારા એક દોસ્તને લાગાથી તેવણે ગાડીમાંજ બેસી રહી તેની અંદરજ સારીપેઠે દોદરા થવું વધારે સલામતી ભરેલું ધારયું હતું. તેવણે પોતાનાં શરીરને ઇજા નહી પોંહોંચવા દેવા સારૂ થઇ તેટલી તરેહવાર યુક્તીઓ કીધી હતી; ગોદડાં તળે કમાનને ઠેકાણે સારીપેઠે દાબી ચાંપીને ઘાસ ભરયું હતું જે કમાન કરતાં વધારે ઉપયોગી થઇ પડયું હતું; ગાડીમાં આસપાસ તકીયાતો ચાંપ્યા હતા, અને થઇ તેટલી સઘળી ગોઠવણ શરીરના સંભાળ સારૂ કીધી હતી; તોએપણ કુદરતની અડચણો આગળ માણસની યુક્તીની ઠઠ્ઠા મશકરી થઇ હતી. બે કે ચાર આંચકા બીણની એક ઉતરણમાં એવાતો લાગા હતા કે હમારા મીત્રનું ગોદડું કીહાં અને તકીયા કીહાં, અને ગાડીની અંદર જેમ એક ડરો વાંકી ચુંકી જગો ઉપર ગગડે તેમ અંદર એણીગમથી પેલીગમ સઘળું ગડગડવા લાગ્યું, અને હમારા મીત્રે પોતાની સામે જે માણસને મજબુત પકડીને બેસવા કહ્યું હતું તેની સાથે રખેને એક ટક્કર લાગીને માથું ફુટે તેથી તે માણસને જલદી ઉતારી પાડી ચલાવ્યો હતો અને ત્યારપછી પોતે કંમર ઉપર રૂમાલ બાંધી બંને હાથે ગાડીની બે બાજુ મજબુત પકડીને અકડુ કુડે બેસી જે આપદા તેમની ઉપર પડતી હતી તેને શરણ થઇ એહેવા તો જબરદસ્ત આંચકા સોસતા હતા, કે કોઇવાર ગાડીવાળાનાં દીલ ઉપર ધસી આવતા અને કોઇવાર ગાડીના પાછલા ભાગ ઉપર ગગડી જતા હતા. આ રમુજી દેખાવ જોઇને જેવી હમોને મજાહ પડતી હતી તેવી તો વાંચનારને નથી પડવાની. ગાડીના દરેક ગડ-

* એલફિન્સ્ટન ઇંડિયા વાલમ ૧ લું પાનુ ૪૨૪ મું.

ગડ્તા આંચકા સાથે તેમની એકેક બુમ તરેવાર સંબોધનના રૂપમાં સંભળાતી હતી, અને તે વખતે હિંદુસ્થાનની પ્રાચીન બાબદોની શોધ ઉપર જે જે જખરી પણ ખુરા ટીકા આ હમારા આંચકા ખાતા મીત્રે કરી હતી, તે નીરદોષ ભાષણનું વર્ણન હમારા પ્રવીણ મીત્ર ડાકટરથી અથવા હમારાથી થઇ શકતું નથી. હમુને તેની યાદ આવેછે ત્યારે એવી ઉલટ છુટેછે કે ફરીને પાછી આવી મુસાફરી બચીત તેમની સાથે કરવી પ્રમાણછે. દુખની પછવાડે સુખ હંમેશ તૈયારજ હોયછે, તેમ અમારા ભલા મીત્રના શરીરની ખીણમાં સારીપેઠ ચંપી થયાથી તેવણને એક ફાએદો એ થયો હતો કે જારે કલ્યાણી પોંહોચ્યા પછી રાત્રે નવાબી ખાણાના સુફરા ઉપર બેઠા હતા (કલ્યાંણીમાં ટેબલ ખુરશીના વાખા હતા) તે વખતે હમારા મીત્રે થોડીવારમાં સુફરા ઉપરની સઘળી નીયામતો ઉપર એવો તો હાથ, પેટ પસવારી પસવારીને લંબાવ્યો હતો અને એવીતો જબરી ભુખે સઘળી વાનીઓ સેરવી હતી કે તે એક જોવા જેવો દેખાવ બની રહયો હતો અને કલ્યાણી તરફની મુસાફરી સઘળાના કરતાં તેમને વધારે ફળી હતી.

પાછલા પોહોરના ૪॥ વાગે કલ્યાણી સેહરને પાદરે જઈ પુગા તીહાં એક મોહોટું ખુદરતી સરોવર લાલ રંગના પાણીનું નજરે પડયું. ગામના લોક તેમના વાપરવાને સારૂ આ સરોવરમાંથી પાણી લઈ જતાં હતાં. પાણી હાથમાં લઈ જોતાં તે સાફ કાચજેવું નીર્મળ માલુમ પડતું હતું, સ્વાદમાં તે જરા મોરચું હતું. હમારી સાથના એક મીત્રે "રેડસી" (લાલ સમુદ્ર) જોયો હતો તેવણે હમને જણાવ્યું કે આ સરોવરનાં પાણી ઘણાખરાં તે સમુદ્રના જેવાં દેખાતાં હતાં. આસપાસ જોતાં માલુમ પડયું કે એક નદીનું પાણી આ સરોવરમાં ઉતરતું હતું. સરોવરના તલીયાંમાં લાલ મટોડી છે, તથા નદીનાં પાણીમાં ડુંગર અને ટેકરીઓ ઉપરની લાલ મટોડી ખેંચાઈ આવેયાથી, પાણીનો રંગ લાલ દેખાતો હતો. કલ્યાણીમાં બે ત્રણ ઠેકાણે આવાં સરોવર હમારા જોયામાં આવીયાંછે.

સેહેરને પાદરે હિંદુઓનાં ભાંગી પડેલાં દેહેરાં તથા મુરતીઓ ઘણીછે. એમને ભાંગી પડવાને આસરે ૫૦૦ થી ૬૦૦ વરસ કેહેવાયછે, તોપણ કેટલીક મુરતીઓ આખી ને આખી અને જાણે આજે નવીજ બનાવી હોય એવી જોઇ હતી. તેમાં શીવની મુરતી તાનડેવના રૂપમાં એક મોહોટા કાળા પથરમાં એવીતો સુંદર અને વલી નકસીકામ સાથે બનાવેલી હમોએ જોઈ કે તેને યુરોપખંડનાં અથવા કોઈ પણ ઠેકાણાં

ઊપરનાં સંગ્રહસ્થાનમાં મુકી હોય તો તે તીહાં ભારી શોભા આપનારી એક વસ્તુ થઈ પડે. તેને ઉઠાવી સાથે લઈ જવા સઘળાની ઇચ્છા થઈ, અને તે જો નાહની હતે તો ખચીત તેને ઉઠાવી લઈ જવા હમો પછાત નહી પડતે. પણ આ મુરતી ઘણીજ મોહોટી અને ભારી હોવાથી, આવા ભારી દેવને હમારી નાહાની નબળી ગાડીમાં બેસાડતાં કદાચ ગાડી ભાંગી પડે એટલા ઉપરથી તેને તેજ ઠેકાણાં ઉપર રાખવાને તેને સારૂ વધારે માન ભરેલું હમોએ જાણીયું હતું.

આ ઠેકાણા ઉપર આગળા વખતમાં મોહોટ મોહટાં દેવલો, દેહરાં હશે એવું તીહાં બેસુમાર ભાંગી પડેલી મુરતીઓ ઉપરથી ધારીયામાં આવેછે. જોકે ઘણા હીંદુઓ પોતાના ધરમ ઉપર ચુસ્તછે, અને તેમના દેવ તથા દેવીઓની મુરતીઓને બહુ માન આપેછે, તોઓપણ આ ઠેકાણે એટલીતો મુરતીઓનો જમાવ થયલો હતો કે તીહાંના રેહેવાશી હીંદુઓએ આ મુરતીઓનો એક ઘણોજ સારો અને બરોબર ઉપીયોગ કરીયો હતો. તે એ પ્રમાણે કે તેમના ઝુંપડાંઓની આસપાસ બચાવ સારૂ પથરના જે ગડકા ભરી લીધા હતા તેમાં આ મુરતીઓનાજ પથરો કામે લગાડી દીધા હતા; તેમના મનમાં એવો વીચાર હોય કે હમારાં દેવો અમસ્થા જમીન ઉપર વીખરાએલા પડેલા ઠોકર ખાય તેના કરતાં બેહતર કે ગડકામાં આદરમાનથી બેસીને હમારા ઘરની જાલવણી કરે અને દીવસના, બપોરે, રાત્રે અને હર વખતે તેમના દરશણ વારંવાર થયાજ કરે, તો આથી મોટું પુન બીજી કહી મુકતીથી થઈ શકવાનું. ગમે હેવો વીચાર તીહાંના લોકનો હોય, પણ આટલી વાત તો સાચી હતી કે આવું કીધાથી બીચારા ગરીબ લોકને ગડકા બાંધવાને પથર લાવવાનો ખરચ નહીં લાગો હતો, અને વીખરાએલી મુરતીઓને જાલવી રાખવાનો આ એક સારો ઉપાય તેઓએ કામે લગાડીયો હતો. આ ભાગી પડેલાં ગામડાંને "હલી" નામથી તીહાંના લોક બોલતા હતા; અને આ ગામડાંનું પાણી સેહરના સઘળા કુવાના પાણી કરતાં ઘણુંજ સરસ હતું.

હીંયાંથી પાંચ વાગે સાંજના કલ્યાણી સેહર જઈ પુગા. તેનો દેખાવ અંદર જતાં આપણા કોઈ નાહાના ગાંમડાં જેવો દીસ્તો હતો. ખબર કાહાડતાં માલુમ પડયું કે આ ઠેકાણેનો હાકમ તો કોઈ જીંહાંપનાહ તાડની ઉંચાઈ ઉપર ચઢી બેસવા લાયક દરજાવાલો નવાબ હતો. તોએ પણ આ અશરીફની મુલાકાત લેવાનો વીચાર કીધો. ગાંમડાની પાદરથી એક માઈલ છેટે કીલ્લો છે, તીહાંસુધી હમો એક દોસ્ત

સાથે આગળથી જઈ, નવાબ સાહેબ ઉપર પેગામ મોકલીયો કે તેમની મોલાકાત લેવાને હમારા મીત્રો પાછળથી આવેછે. કિલ્લાના દરવાજા આગળ જઈ પોંહોંચ્યા પછી ઉપર જણાવીયા પ્રમાણે અંદર ખબર મોકલી કે મુંબઈ શેહેરથી કેટલાએક ગ્રહસ્થ મુસાફરો કલ્યાણી ગામ જોવાની ઇચ્છાથી અત્રે આવ્યાછે, અને નવાબ સાહેબની મુલાકાત લેવાની ઘણી આરજુ રાખેછે; અને અત્રેથી જલદી પાછા કુચ કરી જનારછે, માટે જો મુલાકાત હવડાં થાય તો મોહોટી મેહેરબાની અને નવાજેશ થયલી ગણાશે. પણ આ સઘળી સલુકાઈ અને આપેલું આદરમાન કોણને આપ્યું હતું, એ વીશે હમને તે વખતે કાંઈ ખબર હતી નહીં. પણ હમારા પેગામનો જવાબ જારે હમુને મળ્યો તારે હમુને માલુમ પડ્યું, કે કાંદા ઉપર કસ્તુરી લગાડીયામાં આવી હતી. હમુને જવાબ મળ્યો કે જીહાંપનાહ નવાબ સાહેબ એક કલાક થયો જનાનખાનામાં ગયા છે અને તીંહાંથી પાછા નીકળવાની વકી બીજે દાહાડે સુરજ ઉગે તીહાંસુધી નહી હતી. હમો નહી કહી શકતા કે આવો જવાબ નવાબે પોતે મોકલાવ્યો કે તેની આસપાસવાળાઓએ આપીયો હતો, એનો જોખમ હમો હમારે સર લેતા નથી. બેવાર હમોએ અરજ મોકલી હતી અને બેવાર માણસ પાછું આવ્યું હતું કે હવે રાત્ર થઇછે તેથી નવાબ સાહેબ આગળ કોઇથી સંદેસો લઈ જવાય નહી. કેટલાકોથી વળી એવું પણ સાંભળ્યું કે નવાબ સાહેબ રાત્રે પોતાની કચેરી ભરેછે, એટલા ઉપરથી તે વખતે મુલાકાત નહી થઈ શકે એવું હતું. કચેરી ભરી નવાબ સાહેબ શું શું માહાભારત રાજદરબારી મસલહત અને તકરાર કરતા હશે એ વીશે તો હમારીથી કંઈ કેહેવાઈ શકાતુંજ નથી, કારણ જીહાં હમારી મોલાકાતજ નહી થઈ શકી તારે હમો વધારે આ નવાબ વીશે શું બોલી શકીએ. થોડીવાર કિલ્લાના દરવાજા આગળ ખોટી થઈ પાછા ફરયા હતા, તેવાંમાં હમારી પછવાડે એક સીપાઈ કિલ્લામાંથી આવ્યો, અને હમને કહ્યું કે ઉતારો કરવાની જગા છે તીંહાં ઉતારો કરો, તમારી સંભાળ રાખ્યામાં આવશે. આ ઠેકાણે હમો આટલું બોલું કરીને જણાવવા માગીએ છેએ કે કલ્યાણીજેવાં નાહાનાં શેહેરમાં અર્ધા કલાકમાં ખબર પડી ચુકી હતી કે કોઈ આબરૂદાર દુરદેશી ગ્રહસ્થ મુસાફરો આવ્યાછે; ગામના લોક બાહાર નીકલીને જોવા આવ્યાં; ફોજદારને પણ ખબર પડી, અને એ ખબર શું નવાબના કાન ઉપર છેક રાત્રના ૯ વાગા સુધી પણ નહી ગઈહોય એ હમો માની શકતા નથી. હમો

હીંમતથી બોલીએ છેએ કે નવાબને સારીપેઠે ખબર પડી હશે કે કોઈ ગ્રહસ્થ મુસાફરો તેના ગામમાં આવ્યાછે પણ હમારી સાથ મોલાકાત કરવાને તેને ગમીયું હોય એવું હમુને મુતલગ નજર નહી આવીયું હતું જો મોલાકાત લેવાની મરજી હતે તો સહવારે મળવા ભેટવા વીશે હમુને પાછો જવાબ કેહેવાડીયો હતે, પણ આ સઘળી ચુપકીદી ઉપરથી એવું માલુમ પડયુંછે કે જે હાલતમાં કેટલાએક નવાબો પોતાની હાકમી કરેછે અને વખત ગુજારેછે તેઓ તે કેવી રીતે ગુજારેછે આ વાત પારકાને જણાવા તેઓ લજવાયછે. માટે એ વીશે તેઓ ઉપર તેમના ધણી અથવા માલિકોએ અચ્છી ચોકાસી રાખવી જરૂર છે. સારા કામદાર અને કારભારીઓથી પાદશાહાઓને શોભા અને માન મળેછે; નઠારા અને આળસુ કામદારોથી નેક પાદશાહાઓને બદ બોલાયછે.

આગળ કહ્યું તેમ, ઉતારાની જગો ઉપર હમને એક ભોમીઓ લાવ્યો. આ ઉતારાની જગો એક ઉજડ પડેલી મસજીદ હતી, તીહાં રાત્રે ૭ વાગે હમે સઘળાઓએ ઉતારો કીધો. શેહરનાં કોટવાલ તરફથી જુજવી મદદ ઘાસ લાકડાંની મળી હતી, તેમાં બાર મણ તેલ અંધારાં જેવું હતું. ઘાસનાં પૈસા હમારી પાસેથી લીધા હતા, તે કોણે લીધા હતા? કોટવાલનાં સીપાઈએ કે ઘાસવાળાએ તે ચોકસ કહી સકાતું નથી. લાકડાં મળ્યાં હતાં તેખી હાલહવાલ હતાં; મુંબઈનાં મછીમારો અથવા નવઘણીઓ ઉજાણી કરવાને એથી વધારે મોહોટી અને સારાં લાકડાંની ભારી લઈ જતા હશે. પૈસા આપતાં પણ મરઘી, બેદાં પુરાં મળી શકયાં નહી હતાં; ગોશ્ત બીજે દાને મળયું હતું, તે પણ કઈ વખાણવા જોગ નહી હતું; ઘી, મોહોડામાં લાગે એવું હતું. પાણીતો છેક એક માઈલ દુર હલી ગામડાંથી મંગાવવું પડયું હતું. સારામાં સારી ચીજ માત્ર પાણી સીવાએ બીજી કોઈ નહી હતી. રૈયત મુફલીસ હાલતમાં, અને ઘણોખરો ભાગ મુસલમાનનો હતો, બાકીનો ભાગ હિંદુઓનો હતો. ઘરોની બાંધણી ઘાણુંકરીને શોલાપોરના ઘરો જેવી, છાપરાંને ઠેકાણે ધાબાંવાલી હતી. હિંદુ રૈયતની હાલત ઘણુંકરીને મુસલમાનોની હકુમત તળે દબાયલી રેહેછે તેવી જણાઈ હતી, અને તેઓ સ્વતંત્રપણે તીહાં રહેલા હોય એવું નહી દેખાયું હતું.

રાત્રે ા વાગે હમે સઘળા જમવા બેઠા, જે કંઈ તે વખતસર મળી આવ્યું તે

ભર ઉલટ અને પુર શુકરથી નેયામત કરી તંદરોસ્ત થયા. જમી રહ્યા બાદ રાત્રે સારીપેઠે આરામ કરવાની તજવીજ કરવામાં હમો સઘળાનો કેટલોક વખ્ત રોકાયો. ઠેકાણે ઠેકાણે મુસાફરી' બંગલે મુકામ કરતા હતા તીંહાંતો એક બે કોચ, ખુરશીઓ વીગેરે આસાએરા કરવાનો સરસરંજામ મળી આવતો હતો, તેને બદલે આ કલ્યાણી શેહેરમાં જીહાં નવાબ સાહેબે હમને ઉતારો કરવાનો મકાન આપીયો હતો, વીડાં એક બાંક અથવા પાટલો વટીક પણ નહી હતો, તેથી હવે આરામથી રાત ગુજારવાને થાય તેટલી સઘળી યુકતી કરવાની હમને ફરજ થઈ પડી હતી. રાત્રે ઘણી થંડી લાગી હતી, અને પારાની શીશી ૬૫ ડીગરી (અંસ) ઉપર ઉતરેલી હતી, તે ઉપરથી ઊઘાડા ઓટલા ઉપર આરામ કરવાનું જરા વીચાર જેવું થઈ પડયું હતું; પણ માણસની ઊલટ આગળ સખ્ત ગરમી અથવા સખ્ત થંડીની અસર તસું ભાર ગણી શકાવાના! આ વખ્તે દરેક શખ્સે પોતપોતાની અકલ પ્રમાણે પોતાને સુખ કરવાને તજવીજો કીધી તે એવીતો હતી કે એથી જેટલી રમુજ અને આનંદ મળી તેટલો વખ્ત પણ જલદીથી કપાઈ ગયો હતો. કોઈએ એવો વીચાર કીધો કે ગાડીમાં આરામ કરવું બેહેતરછે, પણ જરા લાંબો વીચાર કરયા વગર જલદી અંદર જઈને લાંબો થઈ સુતાં તેની ગાડી ઊલારી ગઈ હતી; બીજો શખ્સ ગાડીનાં ઢાલ તરફ માથું કરી સુતાં હેઠળ સરી પડયો હતો. આ બે શખ્સોએ આ વખ્તે મેળવેલા અનુભવ ઉપરથી જાણીયું હતું કે મુસાફરી કરવાનાં ગાડાંમાં આરામ કેવી સંભાળથી કરવો જોઈએ. જોતર આગળ ઘોડી મુકીને, તેમજ ગાડાંની આગળ પાછળ ટેકો ગોઠવીયા સીવાએ ગાડું બરોબર ઉભું રેહેવાનું નથી. ગાડામાં સુતી વેળા બીજી બાબત ધ્યાનમાં રાખવા જોગ આ છે કે સઘળા ગાડીવાળા ઘણુંકરીને ગાડીની હેઠળજ બીચારા જમીન ઉપર સુઈ જાયછે, તેથી અંધારામાં ગાડી ઉપર ચઢતી અથવા ઉતરતી વેળા તે બીચારાઓ ઘણી વખ્ત આપણા પગતળે ચંપાયછે, અથવા તો, તેઓ ચઢવા ઉતરવાનાં જાણે પગથીયાં થઈ પડેછે. તેઓ એટલા તો અસાવધ હુંગાએછે કે અજાણતાં તેમનાં શરીર ઉપર આપણ પગ મુકીને ગાડી ઉપર ચઢયા કે ઉતરયા હોઈયે તોએપણ તેઓ કદી જાગીને ઉઠતા નથી; ઘણું થાય તો તેઓ ઉં કરીને એક કેડ ફરીને બીજી કોરે પાછા જેવાને તેવા હુંગમાં પડી રેહેછે. સુવાનાં બીછાનાની કરેલી તરેવાર યુકતીઓમાં હમારા જરમન

મીત્રની ગોઠવણ સઘળા કરતાં સરસ થઈ હતી. પોતાની કોથળીમાંથી કંતાનની એક ઝોળી કાહાડી તેના બંધે છેડા મસજીદનાં ગોલ થાંભલા સાથે બાંધ્યા અને તેમાં હીંચકા આવે એવું ખરેખર નરમ બીછાંનું કીધું. એ જોઇને હમે સઘળાએ તેની અક્કલ અને સમયયુક્તિની વખાણ કરી હતી, અને એક ચેતવણી લીધી હતી કે મુસાફરીમાં આવી એક ઝોળી સાથે રાખવી ખરેખર અગતની ચીજ છે. હમણાનાં વખતમાં એવી ઝોળી કરતાં સરસ સગવડ ભરેલાં હવાનાં બીછાંના, તથા લોહોડાંનાં બગલમાં મારીને ઉચકી ચાલી શકીએ એવાં નાહાનાં કોચો તથા પલંગો મળી શકેછે, તોએપણ તે વખતે હમારા મીત્રે પોતાને સારૂ કીધેલી સગવડ બીજાઓ કરતાં ખરેખર સરસ ઠરી હતી. પણ જેવો લાયક સરંજામ તેને મળી આવ્યો હતો તેવી લાયક રીતે તે મીત્રે તેનો ઉપયોગ કરવામાં ગફલત કરી હતી તેથી જેમ પેલા બે મીત્રોનો ગાડીમાં સુતી વખતે જે રમુજી દેખાવ થયો હતો તેનાં કરતાં સરસ અમારા આં જરમન મીત્રનો દેખાવ જોયામાં આવ્યો હતો. થાંભળા સાથે પોતાની ઝોળી બાંધીને મનમાં મધન થઈ તે મીત્રે હમને કહ્યું કે "મારૂ બીછાનું બીજાઓનાં બીછાનાં કરતાં કેટલું આરામ ભરેલુંછે! જેઓ ભોય ઉપર સુતાછે તેમને કદાચ સરદી લાગે, તેમના હાડકાં દુખે, જેઓ ગાડીમાં સુતાછે તેમને કેટલી અડચણ ભોગવવી પડીછે, પણ આ ઝોળીનું બીછાનું કેવું જમીનથી અતરંગ તથા રૂ જેવું નરમ! અને જેમ નીરદોષ બાળકને હજુ હજુ હીંચકો નાખી સુવાડીએછ તેમ મહને એ હવડાં હુંગમાં મુકસે એવું થયલુંછે! હમે એકમતથી આ બાબદમાં હમારા મીત્રને ખરેખર સઘળાના કરતાં વધારે ભાયગસાળી કહયો હતો. આ બોલવું સાંભળીને હમારો મીત્ર ઘણોજ ખુશી થયો, અને પોતાની જુની પુરાણી ઝોળીની ઘણી તારીફ કીધી, તથા તેનાં આવરદા લાંબા રેહે એવી દુઆ કીધી! ખુશાળ થઈ હમે સઘળા એક-બીજાને સુવા જતી વખતની સલામ અલેકુમ કરી ફારેગ થયા અને દરેક મીત્રે પોતપોતે બનાવેલી આરામ કરવાની જગા પકડી, તેવામાં ધંમ દઇને એક આવાજ થયો, જેની પછવાડે ઓ! ઓ! ઓ! એવો બીજો અવાજ હમારા સાંભળવામાં આવ્યો. તુરત સઘળા જણ ઉઠીને જુએછે, તો હમારો મીત્ર ઝોળી સાથે પથરની જમીન ઉપર જમીનદોસ્ત થઈ ગયલો હતો, અને એવું થયા પછી તે બીચારો ઉઠીને પોતાનાં નરમ તકીયા, ઓઢવાની ચાદર વીગેરે બીછાનાનો સામાન વીખરાઈ

પડેલા વીણીને બગલમાં એકઠો કરતો હતો. તુરત સઘળાનાં મોહોડાંમાંથી સવાલ નીકળ્યો કે અરે પ્યાર મીત્ર એ શુ થયું? ધીરજથી જવાબ મળ્યો કે ઝોળીનું પુરાણું દોરડું થાંબલાં ઉપરથી સરી પડયું અને વળી તુટી પણ ગયું, તેથી ખુદરતી કાયદા પ્રમાણે વગર આધારની જીનસો આકરશણ શકતીનાં કાયદાને તાબે થઈ જમીન ઉપર તુટી પડેછે તે પ્રમાણે જે ઝોળીમાં હું નીરંનજ બચ્ચાંની પેઠ હીંચકા ખાતો હતો તે મારી વાહાલી ઝોળી સમેત જમીનદોસ્ત થઈ પડયોછું અને તેમાં વળી જરા મહને વાગું પણ છે, પણ હું ધારૂંછું કે મારા જેવો સબુરી અને ધીરજવાળો તથા ખુસમીજાજી જમીનદોસ્ત જમીનને વારંવાર મળી નથીં આવવાનો. અંતે રાત્રે બાર અથવા એક વાગે સઘળાઓ સુતા હતા. ઘણો થાક લાગેલો હતો તેથી ઊંગ એવી તો સારી આવી હતી કે જો કે છેક મોડી રાત્રે ઊંગાયા હતા તોએપણ પાછા મળસ્કામાં હમો સઘળા તંદરોસ્ત થઈ ઊઠીયા હતા.

તા૦ ૨૮ મી ડીસેંબર—આ દીને સહવારનાં એક કપ કાફીનું પીને કલ્યાંણી શેહેર જોવા નીકળ્યા. શેહેરમાં ગાડી, ઘોડા અને કોઈ પણ તરેની એવી બીજી સગવડ ફરવા જવાની નહી મળી આવ્યાથી પગે ચાલતાજ શેહેરમાં ફરવા ગયા.

કલ્યાંણી શેહેરનો પરોઢીયાંનો દેખાવ ઘણોજ મુફલીસ નજર આવ્યો હતો, અને આ દેખાવ જેવો મુફલીસ હતો તેવીજ તે શેહેરની હાલત પણ દેખાતી હતી. ઉદ્યોગ ભરેલાં શેહેર અથવા ગામ ગામડાંમાં મનુષ્ય જાત પરોઢીયામાંથીજ પોતપોતાનાં તરેહવાર ઉદ્યમમાં લાગેલું જોઈએછ. સહવારનાં પોહોરથીજ તીહાં ઘોગાટ અને ધામધુમ થઈ પડેછે. દુધ વેચવાનો આવાજ, કોઈ દહી અથવા છાસ, કોઈ તાજી બાજી તરકારી, કોઈ ફુલ અથવા ફળ વેચતું સંભળાયછે. તેમજ વેચનાર સ્ત્રી અથવા પુરૂષોનાં ઉદયોગી, તાજા ખુબસુરત ચેહેરા જોઈ આપણને આનંદ ઉપજેછે. પણ આવી એકુ નીશાન હીંયાં હમારા જોવા અથવા સાંભળવામાં આવી નહી હતી. જે કોઈ હમારી સાંમે મળ્યાં હતાં તેઓ સુગા, શરીર ઉપર એકુ ફાટેલી ચાદર, પીછોડી અથવા ધાબળી નાખીને નહી બોલવા જોગ ખુદરતી હાજતે જતાં માલુમ પડયાં હતાં. થોડુંએક આગળ ચાલ્યા પછી ગામના લોકને ખબર પડી કે રાત્રે આવેલા મુસાફરો ફરવા નીકળ્યાછે, તેથી અનાડી

માણસોનાં ટોળાં હમારી પછવાડે થવા લાગાં, અને મુસલમાન તથા હિંદુના જુવાન છોકરાઓ હમોને રસ્તો દેખડાવા આગળ પડ્યા. થોડી વારમાં મોટી ભીડ થઈ પડી. આ ટોલાંમાંથી એક ચંચલ હિંદુનો છોકરો આસરે ૧૫ વરસનો હમારી નજરે પડ્યો. તેને આપણા મીત્ર ડાક્ટરે પુછ્યું કે આ શેહેરમાં પાહાડની અંદર કાંઈ ગુફા કોતરેલાછે? અથવા કાંઈ જુનાં પુરાનાં દેહેરાં અથવા લેખો કોઈ ઠેકાણેછે? તેણે તુરત હા કહી. હમને કહ્યું કે "માહારી સાથે ચાલો, હું તમને તે દેખાડું," આમ કહી તે હમને એક ટેકરી તરફ લઇ ગયો, તીહાં દુરથી કેટલાએક ગુફા હમારી નજરે પડીયા. એ ગુફાઓ જોઇ હમારા મીત્ર ડાકટરને ઘણો હર્ષ ઉત્પન્ન થયો. પણ તે લાંબા વખત સુધી ટકી નહી શક્યો. ગુફાની પાસે ગયા એટલે માલુમ પડ્યું કે (બુધ્ધ) ધરમનાં જોગીઓને સારૂ રેહેવાનાં જેવી કેટલીક નાહાની ઓલીયો એક ટેકરીમાં ખણેલી હતી, જેમાં જોગીઓને બદલે તે વખતે જાણે કેટલાક જોગીઓ ઊંધે મસ્તકે ટંગાઈ તપ કરતા હોય તેમ વાગુળો ઉંધા લટકી રેહેલાં હતાં; એ ઉપરથી હમુને એક કવીતા યાદ આવી હતી.

જો ન ઉઠાવે તનએકા ભાર,
ઓતા ગયા બયકા માર;
સુક્કી સમલી લટકે હાર,
ઓર મેડક ખાય ટાળ ટાળ;
બેઉ ગોસૈયાં હારે દોર,
ઔર નગરી ખાય ફોડફોડ.

પણ વાગુળ પ્રાણીઓની તો પુજા થાય છે, તેઓ સહવારના લટકતાં રેહેછે અને રાત્રે ચોરની પેઠે લોકનાં બાગબગીચાઓમાં જઈ તીહાંની ફળ ફુલાદીક ખાઈ નાશ કરેછે, અથવા તલાવોમાં પડીને દેડકાં, માછલીઓ વીગરે જીવતાંને જીવતાં ટાળી ટાળીને ગટ્ટ કરી જાએછે, તેમજ કેટલાક ઢોંગી જોગીઓ પણ દીવસના ઉંધે મસ્તકે લટકી તપ કરતા દેખાયછે, અને રાત્ર પડી એટલે તેઓ લોકના ઘર ફાડવા અને ચોરી તથા લુટ કરવાને બાહેર પડેછે. આ એક જાણવાલાયક નકલ છે.

આ ટેકરીના મથાલે હમો જઈ પોંહેચીયા તીહાંથી આખાં કલ્યાંણી ગામનો

દેખાવ જેમ ઉડતાં પક્ષીઓ એક સપાટે જુએછે તેમ હમારી નજરે પડયો. આંબા, આમલી, પીપલા, બીંડી, વડ અને કરંજ તથા આવાં બીજાં મોહોટ મોહોટાં ઝાડોનાં ઝુંખડાનો અછો પ્રસારો થયલો દેખાયો હતો, અને ઝુંખડાની ઝાડી વચે ઠેકાણે ઠેકાણે જે ખુલા ગાલા પડેલા હતા તેમાંથી ગામની મસજીદોનાં ઘુમટો તથા તેમની ઉપરનાં સોનેરી, રૂપેરી પંજા, તથા કળસો દેખાતા, તેમની ઉપર ઉગતા સુર્યનાં તેજસ્વી કીરણો પડયાથી તેઓ ચલકી રહેલા હતા. શેહર તો અસલ હિંદુઓનું હતું, તોએપણ મુસલમાનોનાં દોર હેઠળ હિંદુઓનાં દેહેરાં નાબુદ થઈ, દેહેરાંઓની જગા ઉપર મસજીદો ઉઠી ઉભી થઇ હતી, જેથી આખાં કલ્યાણી શેહેરનો દેખાવ ટેકરી ઉપરથી ખરેજ મુસલમાની રૌનક ભરેલો દેખાતો હતો.

પૂર્વ તરફ નીગાહ કરતાં ત્રણ ચાર મોહોટા ગુમબજો ઘણીજ ઝલેથી દીપતા નજરે પડયા અને પુછતાં માલુમ પડયું કે આખાં સેહરમાં તે સઉથી મોહોટી મસજીદ હતી. જેનું નામ મદીના મસજીદ હતું. હમારી પાસે દુરબીન અને આપેરા ગ્લાસો હતાં તેનો ઉપયોગ સારી રીતે સઘળી તરફ ફરી ફરીને હમો કરતા હતા, એવામાં હમારા મીત્ર મીસ્તર એડવર્ડે શેહેરના કિલ્લાનું એક ચીત્ર પોતાના પુસ્તકમાં પેનસીલથી ચીતરવાનું શરૂ કીધું. પણ આ હમારી નીરદોશ રમત વીશે આસપાસ ભમતા અગ્નાની લોકે જુદીજ મતલબનો વીચાર બાંધીયો અને તુરત અફવા ઉરાડી કે સાહેબ લોક આવ્યાછે તે કલ્યાણીનો કીલ્લો કેમ જીતી લેવો અને કહી જગાએથી તોપનો મારો ચલાવવો, આ સઘળું ટેકરી ઉપરથી જોઇને ચોપડીમાં નોંધી લીએછે. આ અફવા છેક કિલ્લાસુધી તુરત ફેલાઈ હતી, અને હમને જોવાને લોકની ભીડ થોડી વારમાં વધી ગઈ હતી. લોકની ચાલ ચલગતમાં ફેર પડતો જણાવા લાગો. આગળ જે સવાલો પુછતા તેનો જવાબ જલદી અને ખુલાસાથી મળતો હતો, તેને ઠેકાણે હવે લોક બરોબર જવાબ આપવાને અચકાવા લાગા. કંઇપણ પુછેલાંનો જવાબ સસ્સાના ત્રણ પગ જેવો મળવા લાગો, કોઈ વખતે તો છેકજ જાણે જાણતાજ નહી હોય તેમ લોક અખાડા કરીને ચાલતા થવા લાગા, જે ભીડ હમારી આસપાસ થયલી હતી તેમાંથી લોક દાંએબાં થતાં ગયાં; આથી હમને તો ફાયદો એ થયો હતો કે આસપાસ જોવાને વધારે સારીપેઠે બની આવ્યું હતું.

મદીના મસજીદ જોવાની ખાયસથી હમો ટેકરી ઉપરથી હેઠળ ઉતરીયા. પેલા ૧૫ વરસના હિંદુ છોકરાની રાહાનુમાઈ તળે આખા શેહેરના રસ્તા અને ગલી ગુચીમાં ફરી વળયા. ઘણેક ઠેકાણે રસ્તા ઉપર ગલીચી અને બદબો હતી, અને તીહાંથી પસાર થતાં નાકે રૂમાલ દેવો પડયો હતો. તેમ વલી કોઈ કોઈ ગલીઓ અને રસ્તા ઘણાજ સાફ નજરે આવીયા હતા, અને જો હમો ભુલતા નહી હોઇયે તો હિંદુઓનાં ઘર અને ચોક આગળ માત્રે સફાઈ જોઇ હતી, જેથી આટલું સાબેત થઇ શકેછે કે મુસલમાનોની વાપરવાસ જીહાં જોઇએ તીહાં વધારે ગલીચી ભરેલી ઘણુંકરીને હોય છે.

આગળ ચાલતાં એક ઠેકાણે એક દરવાજો હમારી નજરે પડયો જેની ઉપર જેમ આપણે કોઈવાર વાઘો અથવા સીંહના પુતલાં જોઇએછ, તેવીજ રીતે આ દરવાજા ઉપર ગધેડાંનાં બે પુતલાં મુકેલાં જોયાં અને તેમનાં શરીર ઉપર ધોળા અને આસમાની રંગના પટા પાડયા હતા, જેથી આ મુરતી નહી ખચરમાં કે નહી રોઝ, કે નહી ગધેડામાં જણાતી હતી. માત્ર મોહોડાંનો આકાર ખરો ગધેડાંના જેવો બનાવેલો હતો. આ જોઈ હમને જરા નવાઈ જેવું લાગું. તે વીશે હમોએ પુછ પરછ કીધી કે આ દરવાજા ઉપર ગધેડાંના પુતલાં બેસાડવાનું શું કારણ હશે. તુરત જવાબ મળ્યો કે ઘરની અંદરના રેહેવાસીએ પોતાના ધંધા રોજગારની આ એક નીશાન લોકને દેખડાવાને મુકીછે. વાંચનાર વીચારશે કે જેનાં ઘરના દરવાજા ઉપર ગધેડાને બેસાડેલા હોય તે કહ્યો ધંધાદારી હશે વારૂ? કોઈ ગધેબાનતો નહી હોય? નહી, આ ઠેકાણે તો કોઈ ચંચલ કુંભાર રેહેતો હતો, જેણે પોતાના ધંધા રોજગારમાં કામે લાગતો એક ઘણોજ ઉપયોગી અને પોતાનો વાહાલો મીત્ર હતો તેનું પુતલું દરવાજા ઉપર મુકવું તેણે માન ભરેલું જાણીયું હતું. દરેક કળા જાણનારો કારીગર પોતાની દુકાન ઉપર પોતાની કળાની બઢાઈ દેખાડવાને તરેહવાર ચીત્ર વીચીત્ર નીશાણો અને નામો સુનેરી અને રૂપેરી અક્ષરોમાં પાડી લોકને પોતાની તરફ ખેંચવાને મુકેછે અને લલચાવેછે, પણ આ ઠેકાણે તો કોઈ ફીલસુફી મગજવાલા કુંભારે ઉપલી રીત નાપસંદ કરી પોતાના ધંધામાં કેટલી મેહેનત, રંજ તથા સબુરીની જરૂર છે તેની ખરી હકીકત જણાવવાને ગધેડાનું પુતલું પોતાના દરવાજા ઉપર ખીરાજતું કરીયું હતું. આ દરવાજા આગળથી જતાં આવતાં લોકની આ કુંભાર અછી

પરીક્ષા લેતો હોય એવું હમને લાગ્યું હતું. વીચારવાળા શખ્સો આ પુતલાંને જોઈતે વીશે પુછ પરછ કરયા વગર ચાલી નથી જવાના, પણ જે અવિચારીઓ તેને જોઇ હસીને ચાલી જાએ તેમને પેલો કુંભાર પોતાનાં પુતલાંના નામ લાયક ગણતો હોય તો તેમાં કોણની તકસીર વારૂ? આગળ ચાલતાં પેલા હિંદુ છોકરાએ હમને કહ્યું કે હવે હું તમારી સાથે વધારે આગળ આવી શકતો નથી કેમકે પેલી મસજીદ છેક નજદીક આવીછે, અને તીહાંના મુસલમાનો મને જોરો તો મારી ઉપર જુલમ ગુજારશે કે પારકા લોકને મસજીદમાં શું કરવાને લઈ આવ્યો. હમો સઘળાને તેઓ ઇંગરેજ લોક સમજયા હતા. હમોએ તે છોકરાને હીમત આપી કે કંઈ ફીકર કરવી નહી, તોએપણ તે બીચારાએ ઘણા કાલાવાલા કીધા અને કહ્યું કે "તમે જોઇયે તો મસજીદ અંદર જાઓ, પણ હું તમારી સાથે અંદર આવનાર નથી, અને આવ્યો તો મારી કમબખતી પુરી આવેલી જાણવી." તેને બહાર દુર ઊભો રાખીને હમે મસજીદમાં ગયા. અંદરના લોકોએ હમને દાખલ થયલા જોઈ પેહેલો સવાલ આ કીધો હતો કે હમને એ મસજીદ તરફ કોણ ભોમીઓ લાવ્યો, જેથી પેલા છોકરાના બોલવાને ખરો ટેકો મળીયો હતો! હમોએ તેનો જવાબ નહી આપીયો.

મસજીદમાં પેસતાંજ દરવાજા ઉપર ફારસી અક્ષરે કોતરેલી એક સંગેમરમરની તખતી જડેલી જોઈ તેમાં તે મસજીદ બાંધવાનો હિજરી સને ૧૦૨૮ નો લખેલો હતો. મસજીદના ચોકમાં ખુશનુમા બાગ, ફરવા હરવાના કીયારા, પાણીની હોજો, ફુઆંરા અને તેની આસપાસ સંગેમરમરની બેઠકની ઘણીજ અચ્છી રચના કરેલીછે. ગુંબજો પણ હારેદોર ઘણીજ ખુબસુરત રચનાથી બાંધેલાછે. ગુંબજોની હેઠળ એબાદત કરવાની જગા કરેલીછે. એબાદતગાહની સાંમે એક બીજી ઘણીજ સુંદર બાંધણીછે, તે કબરગાહ છે. એમાં નવાબ ઇમતીઆજ દોલાની ઘોર છે; જેની પાસે એક બોરદુએ પોતાની વહુની અને બીજા હાથ ઉપર પોતાના છોકરાની ઘોર છે. બાપ, દીકરો અને દીકરાની બાયડી મળીને ત્રણ જણની ઘોર ઘણીજ નાદર બાંધણીની સંગેમરમરની બનાવીછે, અને શેહરનાં મુસલમાન લોક તેની ઉપર જાથુક ફૂલ ચહડાવે છે. સઘળી ઇમારતની દેવાલો એવી તો ઘુંટેલીછે કે જાણે તેઓ સંગેમરમરની બનાવી હોય એવી ચલકેછે, અને આજેજ નવી બનાવી હોય એવી નજર આવેછે. એ મસજીદની

ફરસબંધી પણ સઘળી સંગેમરમરની કરેલીછે; અને તેમાં એક બાબદ જાણવાજોગ એ છે કે મુસલમાન લોકની મશહુર થયલી ધરમની જનુની આ ઠેકાણા ઉપર સારીપેઠે દેખાડેલી છે. હિંદુઓનાં દેવોની મુરતીઓ તથા તેમનાં ધરમને લગતા શીલાલેખો દેહેરાંઓમાંથી ઉખેડી લાવીને આ મસજીદની ફરસબંધીમાં ચીણી લીધેલાંછે, એ મતલબથી કે હિંદુઓનાં દેવો અને તેમનાં પવિત્ર લેખો મસજીદમાં આવતા અને જતા દરેક ઇસલામી મજહબવાલાના પગતળે ચંપાઇને અપમાન પાંમે. આવી તહરાની બે તખ્તીયો કબરગાહ તરફ જવાના પગથીયામાં મુકેલી હમારી નજરે પડી હતી. આ તખ્તીઓની નકલ ડાકટર ભાઉએ કપડાં ઉપર છાપી લીધી હતી. એ તખ્તી હાલા કાનડી અક્ષરમાં કોતરેલી હતી એવું ડાકટરનું તે વખ્તે મત હતું, પણ તેની અંદર શું લખેલું હતું તે તેજ વખ્તે જાણી નહી શકયા હતા.

મસજીદમાં હમને વધારે વાર ખોટી થવું પડ્યું હતું, કારણ ડાકટર પેલી તખ્તીઓની નકલ લેવામાં ગુતાયા હતા. એટલા વખતમાં મસજીદ અંદરનાં ઘણાં માણસો સાથે તથા તીહાં પડીને ખીચડો ખાનારા નામના ફકીરો સાથે કેટલીએક બાબદોની તકરાર કરવાની તક હમોને મળી, જે તકરારમાં ઇંગરેજી રાજ વીશે તેમની કેટલીક ભુલ અને ગેરસમજુતીવીશેનો હમોએ ખુલાસો કીધો હતો, જેથી તેમની ખાત્રી થઈ હતી. આ ગેરસમજુતી ધરમ સંબંધી બાબદો વીશે હતી. તેઓનાં મનમાં એવો વીચાર ઠસી ગયલો માલુમ પડ્યો હતો કે ઇંગરેજ સરકાર હવે હિંદુસ્તાનની રૈયતને પોતાનાં ધરમમાં વટલાવવા માંગેછે અને એવું કરવાને તરેહવાર યુકતીઓ કરેછે. એનો ખુલાસો જારે હમોએ એવો કીધો કે પારકા ધરમવાળાઓનાં ઇમાનને ઇંગરેજ સરકાર જેવું માન આપેછે, અને દરેક ધરમવાળાને પોતપોતાનાં યકીન અથવા ઇતેકાદ પ્રમાણે ચાલવા દેછે તેવી અદલ સરકાર આજે પૃથ્વી ઉપર કોઈ ઠેકાણે બીજી નથી. સરવેને પોતપોતાનો ધરમ પાળવાની પુરતી છુટ આપવા સારૂ તો આ ઇંગ્રેજી સરકારે મોહોટ મોહોટી લડાઇઓ કરીછે, અને તેમાં પરમેશ્વરે ઇંગરેજને ફતેહ આપીછે. એવી સરકાર એવો જુલમ પોતાની રૈયત ઉપર કરે એ બીલકુલ ખોટી વાતછે. જે યુરોપીઅન પાદરીઓ દેશીઓને પોતાના ધરમથી વટલાવવાની કોશેશ કરેછે તે પાદરીઓને અને સરકારને કસો ઇલાકો અથવા સંબંધ નથી. પાદરીઓ પોતાની ખુશીથી પોતાનું

વતન છોડી પોતાનો ધરમ સમજાવવાને અને તેનો ફેલાવો કરવાને આ દેશમાં આવેછે. પણ તેમજ અગર દેશી ધર્મ ગુરૂઓ ઇંગરેજ લોકનાં દેશમાં જઈ તીહાંના લોકને ધર્મ સંબંધી ઉપદેશ કરે તો એ વીશે સરકારની બીલકુલ મનાઈ નથી. અગર તેવું કરતાં કોઈ ઇંગરેજ આપણા દેશી ધરમમાં વટલવા અથવા આવવા માંગે તો તેને કોઈ વાતનો અટકાવ નથી. આવું સાંભળીને એક જણ જોશમાં આવી બોલ્યો કે "હમોએ જે વાતો સાંભળી છે તે વાતો તમો કહોછો તેથી તદન ઉલટી છે. ઇંગ્રેજ સરકારે પોતે કેટલાક પાદરીઓને પગાર આપી રાખેલા છે, અને તે વીશે હમારી પાસે સાબેતી છે." હમો તુરત સમજી ગયા કે પગાર આપીને રાખેલા પાદરીઓ તે ઇંગરેજી લસકર ખાતાંનાં હશે અને એ વીશે બરોબર ખુલાસો થવોજ જોઇએછ, તેથી હમોએ પુરતો ખુલાસો કહી સંભળાવ્યો. ઇંગ્રેજી લશ્કરના ઇંગ્રેજ અમલદાર તથા સીપાઈઓને ધર્મ સંબંધી બાબદો સમજાવવાને તથા ઉપદેશ કરવાને અને તેમનાં લગન, મરણની ક્રીયા કરવાને સરકારે પાદરીઓ રાખેલા છે તેટલાજ પાદરીઓને સરકાર તરફથી મુસારો મળેછે. તેમનું કામ માત્ર લશ્કરના ઇંગ્રેજી સીપાઇઓ સીવાએ બીજા કોઈ સાથે નથી. જેમ દરેક ઇંગ્રેજ સીપાઇને તેના ધર્મનાં હુકમો પ્રમાણે ચાલવાની છુટ છે, તેમજ દરેક દેશી સીપાઇને પણ છુટ છે. ઇંગ્રેજી લશ્કર સાથનાં કોઈપણ પાદરીને હુકમ નથી કે દેશી સીપાઇને ઇંગ્રેજી ધર્મ વીશે ઉપદેશ કરે, બલકે અગર એવું કીધું તો તે પાદરીને ઇનસાફની દરબાર સાંમે ઉભો કરી જો તકસીર સાબેત થઈ તો ચાકરી ઉપરથી બરતરફ કરે છે, અથવા બીજી શીક્ષાને તે લાયક થાય છે. આવા પુરતા બંદોબસ્તો ઇંગ્રેજ સરકારે દેશી પ્રજાના ધરમ જાળવવા વીશે કરેલા છે. પણ કેટલાક મતલબી માણસો જેઓ ફીતુરી છે તેમને ચોરી, લુચ્ચાઈ, લુટફાંટ કરવા ઘણું ગમે છે, તેવા લુચ્ચાઓથી ચોરી અથવા લુટ જારે થઇ શકતી નથી તારે પોતાની તરફથી જેટલું જુઠું અને વાંકું બોલાય તેટલું ઇંગ્રેજી રાજ વિરૂધ બોલી કમ અકલ અને જનુની લોકની જનુન ઉશકેરી, બંડો અને ફીસાદ ઉઠાવે છે, અને તેવી ગડબડમાં લુટફાંટ કરી પોતાનું કામ કાહાડી લેછે. આ વાત શાહાણા લોક સારી પેઠે હવે સમજી ચુકાછે. દીલ્હી ઉપર જે આફત પડી હતી, અને તે શેહેર જેવું પાયામાલ અને મુલકે મેદાન થઈ ગયું તે આવા લુચ્ચા બંડખોર લોકની ઉશકેરણીથી થયું છે. વળી તેના અંતનો

ફેજ શું નીપજ્યો ! દીલ્હીના પાદશાહા બાહાદરશાહાનું નામ અને ખાનદાન ગુમ થઈ ગયું, ઇંગ્રેજી રાજનો તે એક બંધવો થઈ પડ્યો, તે તરીપાર થઈ મરણ પામ્યો, આ સઘળી ઉશ્કેરણી તેની આસપાસ બેસનાર નીચ અને નીમકહરામ લોકોએ કીધી તેથી પાદશાહાની અકલ ગુમરાહા થઈ ગઈ, અને ઇંગ્રેજી રાજ તરફ વફાદારી બતલાવવાને ઠેકાણે તેણે નીમકહરામી કીધી. ઇંગ્રેજી રાજ સાંમણે એ પાદશાહે લડાઈ કરવાને કંમર બાંધી એ ઘણુંજ અઘટીત કામ થયું. પણ રાસ્તીની હમેશ ફતેહે છે તેથી અંતે ઇંગ્રેજોનીજ ફતે થઈ. પછવાડેથી સઘળું માલુમ પડી આવ્યું કે હિંદુસ્થાનમાં જે સન ૧૮૫૭ નાં સાલમાં દેશી બળવો થયો તે માત્ર ફીતુરી લોકે પોતાની ખાનગી મતલબો પાર પાડવાને, ધરમનું બાહાનું આગળ કરી, બીચારા ગરીબ ભોલા લોકને ઉલટ પુલટ સમજાવી આગળ હોમીયા હતા. પણ તેમાં પરમેશ્વરે આવા દુષ્ટ લોકને સારીપેઠે શીક્ષા કીધી અને તેમની નીચ મતલબ મેળવવામાં એટલા તો તેમને હારમાર કિધા કે તેમાના કેટલા જણને સુલીઉપર, કેટલા જણને તોપને મોહડે પોતાનો જીવ આપવો પડ્યો અને કેટલાકોએ આપઘાત કીધો. આ બંડથી મોહટ મોહટાં ખાનદાનનાં નામ નીશાણ આજે ગુમ અને નાબુદ થઈ ગયાંછે, તેમની આજે જરાપણ એક રજ અથવા નીશાણ જોવામાં આવતી નથી. તેઓ જાણે આ દુનીયા ઉપર હસ્તી પામ્યાજ નહી હતા એવું બન્યુછે. આવું હમારૂં બોલેલું સાંભલી તેઓનાં મન ઉપર સારી અસર થએલી જણાઈ હતી. હમે પારસી લોક છેએ, અને ઇંગ્રેજ સરકારના મુસારાદાર અંમલદાર અથવા નોકર નથી પણ હમો સ્વતંત્ર ગૃહસ્થો માત્ર મુસાફરી કરવાને નીકલ્યા છેએ, એવી જારે તેમની પુરી ખાત્રી થઇ તારે હમારૂં સઘલું બોલેલું તેઓનાં મનમાં ઘણુંજ વજનદાર થઇ પડ્યું. તેઓ માહોમાહે બોલ્યા કે આ સેઠલોકો બીન તમાછે, એઓને મોહોડેથી જે વાત નીકળે તે સ્વાર્થ વગરની જાણવી, વાસ્તે એ લોકનું કેહેવું ખરૂંજ સમજવું; અને આતો ખરીજ વાતછે કે બંડખોરોએ હીંદ પાછું હાત કરી લેવાને ઠેકાણેતો તેઓએ ભારે લુચ્ચાઇ અને દંગો કરયો હતો, અને અંતે માર ખાઇ ચોર લોકની મુઆફક સુલીએ ચઢીને અથવા તોપને મોહોડે પોતાનો જીવ ખોયો હતો. આવી હમારી સાથે વાતચીત થયાથી મસજીદમાંના લોકનો વીચાર પેહેલ વેહેલાં હમો દાખલ થતાં જે હમારે વીશે થયો હતો તે હવે ફરી ગયો અને પછવાડેથી તેઓએ સારી સલુકાઈ દેખડાવી; તથા હમારી

કેટલીએક તજુમલ તથા ખાતરદારી પણ કરી, તે હીયાં સુધી કે હાત મોહોડું ધોવાને પાણી લાવીયા, અને સેવટે હમોને એવું પણ કહ્યું કે અગર બુટ સાથે મસજીદમાં કેટલેક સુધી હમો જઇએતો તેમાં તેઓને કંઈ અડચણ નહી હતી. પણ હમોએ હમારો મભો જાળવવા એં વીશે નાજ પાડી કે જો તેમને એ વીશે મનાઈ હોયતો, હમો કોઈબી પવીત્ર જગા ઉપર જોડા સાથે જવાનું વાજબી નથી સમજતા. તીહાંથી હમોએ રૂખસદ લીધી અને પાછા કલ્યાણી શેહેરની વસ્તીમાં આવ્યા. વસ્તીમાં ઘણુંકરીને લીંગાઈટ અને મુસલમાન લોક નજર પડયા હતા, તેમાં આટલું જણાવ્યા વગર હમુને ચાલતું નથી કે પ્રખ્યાત વ્યાજખોર મારવાડીઓ આ ઠેકાણે ગેરહાજર નહી હતા. જગે જગે આ કલેજાંફ્રોરા સાહુકારો હાજર છે; કોઈપણ ગામડાંમાં એ લોકની એકુ દુકાન નહી હોય એવું હમારી આખી મુસાફરીમાં હમોએ કેથે જોયું નથી. ખુણે ખચોલે, ઉજડ ગામડે પણ એકુ આ સર્વ વ્યાપક વ્યાજવટુક ગરીબ મુફલીસની પેઠે પોતાની કંગાલ દુકાન ઘાલીને બેઠેલો આપણને દેખાયા વગર નથી રેહેવાનો!

કલ્યાણી શેહેર જોયા પછી ડાકટર ભાઉએ એવી ઇચ્છા જણાવી કે કલ્યાણી શેહેરની પશ્ચીમ દીશાએ ઉજડ પડેલાં દેહેરાં, દેવળો અને ઈમારતો છે તે તરફ એક લટાર મારીએ. તુરત ઉલટભરતે ગામડાં તરફ પગ ઉપરજ કુચ કીધી. એ ગામડાંનું નામ "નારણપુરી" કરીને લોક બોલે છે. ગામડાંના ગરીબ લોકનાં જુફડાંની આસપાસ પથરનાં ગડકા બાંધેલાં છે. એક ગાંમડામાં એક ઠેકાણે મહાદેવનું એક મોહોટું દેહરૂં છે જે ૭૦ ફુટ લાંબું અને ૪૫ ફુટ પોહોળું છે, અને તે જગાએ બપોરના ૧૨ વાગે સુરીયનો સખત તાપ પડતો હતો તે વખતે હમો જઈ લાગા હતા તો પણ દેહેરાં અંદર જતાંવાર થંડક એવી તો લાગી હતી કે થાકેલાં શરીરને બહુ આરામએશ અને આનંદઉપજયો હતો. આ ઠેકાણે ઘણીજ સુંદર, પથરમાં કોતરેલી, મોહોટ મોહોટી મુરતીઓ વીખરાઇને બારેવાટ પડેલી હતી; તે મુંબઈમાં હોય તો લોક મોટી ખુશીથી જુએ, પણ તેમને ઉંચકી લાવે કોણ? માહાદેવ પોતે કે! આ ઠેકાણે પણ એક બીજું કુદરતી તળાવ જોયામાં આવ્યું, તેનાં પાણીનો રંગ કલ્યાની શેહેરને પાદરે જે લાલ પાણીનું તળાવ જોવામાં આવ્યું હતું તેવોજ લાલ હતો. આ ઠેકાણે જરા વીસામો લીધો અને બપોર થયા હતા તેથી ભુખ જબરી લાગી હતી તેને

નરમ પાડવાને ગાંમમાંથી દુધ મંગાવીને પીધું, જેથી જરા ટેકાવ થયો. થાક લાગાથી સઘળાનાં પગોએ સંપ કીધો કે હવે વધારે ચાલવું નહી, તેથી ઘાસ ભરવાની બલદની બે ગાડીઓ ખાલી જતી મળી તે ભાડે કરીને તેમાં બેઠા. "નારણપુરી" ગામડું છોડી "શીવપુરી" ગાંમડામાં આવ્યા. તીહાં ત્રીજું તળાવ લાલ રંગના પાણીનું જોયું. એ ઉપરથી અનુમાન થાય છે કે આખ્ખાં કલ્યાંણી શેહેરની આસપાસ લાલ મટોડીનો ખડક જેને ઇંગ્રેજીમાં (Laterite rock) કરીને કહેછે તે પુષ્કળ લાગેલા છે. રસ્તાની ધુળ વટીક લાલ ગુલાલ જેવી છે. ભુખ જબરી લાગાથી હમારા ગાડીવાળાને હમોએ ચાંપીને હાંકવાને કહ્યું, પણ તીહાં મુદલ રસ્તા જેવી ચીજ તો હતીજ નહી અને ઢેકાંઢળીયાંની ઘદેરમાંથી ગાડી દોડાવવી એતો બનવું કઠણ, તોઅપણ પઈસાના લાભથી ગાડીવાને બળદનાં પુછડાં મરડી એક પદકડી એવીતો મરાવી કે ગાડીમાં બેઠેલા શખસોનાં પેટમાંનાં ભુખ્યાં આંતરડાં આંચકાથી તળે ઉપર થવા લાગ્યાં. ગાડીમાં ગાદી અથવા બીછાંનાં જેવી કોઈ પણ નરમ બેઠક નહી તેથી બેસનારાઓનાં શરીરનાં હાડકાં ગાડીનાં લાકડાં સાથે સારીપેઠે ટક્કર લડ્યાં: જે ટક્કર બેસનારાઓથી જારે વધારે નહી ખમાઈ તારે તેઓ ગાડીમાં અકડું કુડે બેઠા, અને ગાડીની બંધે બાજુ મજબુત પકડી કે રખેને આંચકાથી તેઓ ઉડી પડે. આવી હાલતમાં જેમ એકગમથી શરીરને બચાવવું પડતું હતું તેમ બીજીગમથી જે હસવું બેઅખતીયાર આવતું હતું તેને શરણ થતાં હમારી ઉપર જબરી થઈ હતી. ગાડીનાં બળદોને જે ચોંક એક ત્રપત મળી હતી તેથી તેઓ એવાતો ઉછળીને દોડ્યા હતા કે તેમને રોકવાને બહુ મેહનત પડી. એવામાં એક ઠેકાણે એવો તો એક આંચકો લાગો કે હમારા એક મીત્રનો બંધ કરેલો ચામડાંનો "કેસ" પોતાની મેળે ઉઘડી ગયો. તેમાંની દુરબીન ઉડી પડી, તેના કાચ ઉખડીને છુટા પડ્યા; તેમની પાગડી ઉડી ગઈ, જેની પાછળ ચસ્મો ખેંચાઈ ગયો; તેમજ હમારા એક બીજા મીત્રનું તેજ આંચકા સમેત પાટલુન બેઠક આગળથી ફાટી ચીરાઈ ગયું, અને છેલે ગાડીની બેઠકનાં આડાં લાકડાંના ખીલા છુટા થઈ પડ્યાથી ગાડી વચમાંથી ભાંગી ગઈ. આ સઘળો બનાવ એકજ આંચકાથી અને થોડીએક પલમાં બની ગયો હતો, અને ગાડી તો દોડતીજ રહી હતી તેથી હસવા સાથે અરે રાખો? અરે રાખો? કરીને જે પોકાર નીકળ્યા કરતા હતા તે ગોંધાટથી બળદો

ઉલટા ગભરાઈ વધારે ભડકીને દોડતા હતા, તેમને ઉભા રખ્ખવાને ગાડીવાન પોતાનાં સઘળાં જોરથી પાછળ તણાઈ તણાઇને અને હોટ પીસી પીસીને બે હાથે બળદોને જે ખેંચતો હતો, તે સઘળો વીચીત્ર દેખાવ ચીત્ર પાડવા લાયક થઈ પડયો હતો. અંતે બળદો જારે ઉભા રહ્યા અને તેમાંથી ઉતારૂઓ નીચે કુદી પડયા ત્યારે તેમનાં સંકટનો અંત આવ્યો, અને નજદીક ૨૦ થી ૩૦ વાર સુધીમાં જે જે ચીજો ગાડીમાંથી ઉડીને વીખરાઈ પડી હતી તે પાછી વીણી લઈ, બાકી રહેલી બીજી ગાડીમાં વારા ફરતા કેટલાએક બેસતા અને કેટલાએક ચાલતા હળવે હળવે કલ્યાણી શેહેરની મસજીદમાં જીહાં ઉતારો કીધો હતો તીહાં બપોરનાં ૧॥ વાગે આવી પુગા. જુના પુરાણા લેખોતો આ ઠેકાણે નહી મળ્યા, પણ તેમની શોધમાં પગની પનોતી એટલીતો ઉતરી હતી કે "કલ્યાણી" સેહેરની યાદ પુરાણા લેખો પ્રમાણે હમારા સઘળાના મગજમાં લાંબા વખ્ત સુધી લખાયલી રહેશે. ખુદાના હુકમથી આ પડતી ખડતી સંકટમાં એકપણ મીત્રનાં શરીરને જરાપણ અલવાર પોહોંચી નહી હતી અથવા તે સાથે સખ્ત તડકાંનો તાપ પણ કોઇને લાગો નહી હતો. જરા વાર વીસામો લઈ બપોરના બે વાગે જમ્યા.

હમારાં નામ સાંભળીને કલ્યાણી શેહેરના ઉમદા! ગવૈયા હમોને ગાયન સંભળાવવાને આવ્યા હતા, તેઓએ કલાકેક સુધી સારંગી તબલા ઉપર ગાનતાન કીધું હતું. કલ્યાણીનું ગાયન સઘળું તાડીખાનાને લાયકનું હતું તોએપણ હમારા થાકેલા જીવને તેથી સારી આરામએશ મલી હતી. ગામડીયાની રૂઢી પ્રમાણે બોલતાં, હમારા એક મીત્રે કહ્યું તેમ આ ગાયન "ખાટી તાડી સાથનું ગજખ" જેવું ઠીકજ મળીઉં હતું.

જે ખીણને રસ્તે કલ્યાણી આવ્યા હતા તેજ ખીણને માર્ગે કલ્યાણીથી સાંજે ૫) વાગે રવાના થયા; ઘણો થાક લાગ્યો હતો તેથી એવીતો હુંગ ગાડીમાં આવી ગઈ હતી કે રસ્તામાં કેવા આંચકા લાગા હશે અને શું શું થયું હશે તેની નોંધ મુતલગ કરી શકાઈજ નથી, તે વીશેની ક્ષમા વાંચનાર પાસે માગી એટલુંજ જણાવીએ છેએ કે કલ્યાણીથી ૫) વાગે બેઠેલા,

તા૦ ૨૯ મી ડીસેંબર—સહવારનાં ૬॥ વાગે મંગળગીઈ નામનાં ગાંમડાં આગળ આવી પુગા એટલીજ યાદ માત્ર લખાઇછે. થંડી જબરી પડતી હતી. પારાની શીશીમાં ૫૮ ડીગરી ઉપર પારો ઉતરેલો હતો. થંડી જબરી લાગતી

હતી તોપણ તે હાડ કળાવે એવી નહી હતી. ખરી સુખકારક થંડીની ખુબી એવીજ હોયછે કે એથી હાડ નહી કળે. હમને સઘળાને ઉઠીને પગે ચાલવાને તે વખતે ઘણુંજ ગમ્યું હતું, તેમજ શરીરમાં જોર પણ આવ્યું હતું. અરધો દીવસ મુસાફરી બંગલામાંજ ગુજારયો. આ જગાનાં પાણી ઘણાંજ લેહેજતદાર અને હજમીયત છે. આ દીવસમાં નોંધ કરવા જેવું કાંઈ અગતનું જોયામાં નહી આવ્યું તેથી બપોરનાં ત્રણ વાગે હીયાંથી પાછી કુચ કીધી તે ખાજે દીને,

તા૦ ૩૦ મી ડીસેંબર—સહવારે ૮ વાગે કુમકુલ્લી ગામડાં આગળ જઈ પુગા. આ ઠેકાણે જમીનનો દેખાવ ફરી ગયલો માલુમ પડ્યો "મંથાલ" થી તે હીયાં સુધી લાલ મેટીડીનો ખડક લાગેલો છે, પણ હીંયાંથી "ગ્રાનાઈટ" (Granite) નામનો વધારે કઠણ પથર લાગેલો છે. ટેકરીઓ અને ડુંગરનો દેખાવ ચીત્ર વીચીત્ર દેખાયછે, જે દેખાવ ઘણું કરીને "ગ્રાનાઈટ" પથરવાળી ટેકરીઓનો સાધારણ જોયામાં આવેછે. નીજામ હેદરાબાદથી ૪૫ માઇલ દુર હશરગામ આગળથી "ગ્રાનાઈટ" ખડક લાગુ પડેલોછે, તેમજ બે માઈલ આગળ જતાં, એટલે હેદરાબાદથી ૪૩ માઈલ દુર "ગંગાકટવા" નામની નદી આવેલીછે, જેથી આ જગાની આસપાસના ખેતરો આબાદાન અને સારાં પાકવાળાં થાયછે. હીયાંસુધી હમોએ ઘણીક જગોએ જંગલ અને ઉજડ જમીન જોઈ હતી, પણ આ ઠેકાણેથી લીલાતરી, ખેડણી અને પુરાકળ વનસ્પતી જોવામાં આવી હતી. ડુંગર ઉપરથી ઉતરતાં નદીનાં પાણીને બંધથી અટકાવી તળાઓમાં એકઠું કરી, આ પાણીથી વર્ષના ધાન્યના બે પાક હીયાના ખેડુતો ઉતારેછે. રસ્તાની બંને બાજુએ ખજુરાંનું જંગલ ને જંગલ લાગેલુંછે. કોઇબી આપણા પારશી ભાઈઓ આ ઠેકાણેથી પસાર થતાં, આવા ખજુરાંની ખબર લેયા વગર અથવા ગાડી છોડી તેમની હાલતની સારીપેઠે પુછપરછ કરયા વગર આગળ નથી જઈ શકવાનાં. આ ઠેકાણે બે વાતથી હમને તાજુબી ઉપજી હતી. એક એજે ખજુરાંનાં હાવાં જબરાં વનમાં એકે તાડની નીસાણ દેખાઈ નહી હતી; બીજી એજે કેટલાંક જબરાં ખજુરાં છેજીયાવગર નકામા પડેલાં હતાં, કારણ તેઓ ઘણાંજ ઉંચાં હતાં. ઘણુંકરીને તાડ અને ખજુરાં પાસેપાસે અથવા થોડે થોડે છેટે એક બીજાની પડોસમાં હોયછે; પણ હીયાંતો માઈલનાં માઈલ સુધી ખજુરાંનુંજ વંન લાગેલુંછે. તેમાંથી

તાડી પુષ્કળ નીકળેછે, અને લોકમાં તાડીનો જખરો ખપ છે. દારૂને બદલે તાડીનોજ મારો આ જગાએ ચાલેછે, અને આખા દીવસમાં ભાગ્યેજ થોડાએક કલાક કોઈ તાડીની કેફથી ખાલી રેહેતું હશે. સહવારના ૧૧ વાગે સદાશીવ પેંટના મુસાફરી બંગલામાં જઈ પુગા. હીયાં પોસ્ટ આફીસનું મથકછે. આ ઠેકાણે મુંબઈ તરફ કાગળ પત્રો લખવાની પેહેલી જોગવાઈ લીધી. બંગલામાં બેસી વીસામો લઇએછ એટલામાં થોડેક વાર દુર, ગરીબ ખેડુતોની ઝુપડીઓ આગળ આગ લાગેલી દેખાઈ. આ આગ જુવારની એક ખળીમાં લાગી હતી, અને તે ખેડુતોની તદન બેપરવાઈ અને ગફલતથી લાગી હતી. સુકાયલી જુવારની ખળી સુકાં ઘાસની પેઠે સળગી ઉઠે એવી હોયછે, તેમાં કોઈ બેધ્યાન શખ્સે બીડી નાખીયાથી તે ખળી સળગી ઉઠી હતી. હમો કેટલાક મીત્રો તુરત ખેડુતોની મદદે દોડી પોંહોંચ્યા અને તજવીજથી ઓરતો અને મરદો પાસે ઘડે ઘડે પાણી રેડાવી જુવારની અરધી ખળી બળતાં બચાવી તથા હમો સઘળા મીત્રોએ મળી પેલા ગરીબ ખેડુતને જે નુકસાન થયું હતું તેનાં બદલામાં કાંઈ નાણું આપ્યું જેથી ખેડુતોને ઘણો આનંદ થયો હતો. ખળીમાં આગ લાગાથી બીચારા ગરીબ ખેડુતોની હોશ એટલીતો ઉડી ગઈ હતી કે મેહનત કરીયાથી તેમનાં માલનો બચાવ થશે, આ વીચાર તેમનાં મનમાં એકાએક ઉતરી શકયો નહી હતો. તેમના વીચાર-શકતીની ફીલસુફીતો અજાએબ જેવી હતી. તેઓ સાથે વાત કરતાં જાણીયું કે ઇશ્વરનો કોપ તેમના ઉપર થનાર હતો તે થયો; તેમનું નસીબ ફુટવાનું હતું તે ફુટું હતું. તેઓમાંના ઘણા જણ મોહોટેથી રડવા લાગા હતા કે જુવા-રનો ઢગલો હવે સઘળો બળી જવાનો; તે કેમ બચી શકશે? જો બચાવાનોજ હતેતો તેમાં આગ શા માટે લાગતે? તેને હોલવવા સારૂ ધુળ તથા જુજ પાણી નાખીને એણીગમથી પેલીગમ જુઆરને ખેંચી કાહાડવાનાં ફાંફાં માત્ર મારતા હતા, અને તેખી પારકાઓ. જુઆરનાં ધણીતો બીચારા ઘભરાઈ ગયલા ઉભા રહી આગનાં ભડકાં જોઈ રડતા હતા, અને જારે હમોએ ઘાગર ઘાગરે પાણી નાખવાને કહ્યું ત્યારે તેઓ બોલીયા કે પાણી નાખ્યાથી આગ કાંઈ હોલવાવાની નથી, આતો હમારા નસીબ ફુટ્યાથી આવું બનીયુંછે. આખરે જરા ધમકી આપીને હમોએ દોડધામ કીધી, તેથી કેટલાએકો પાણી લાવવાને ઉઠયા, અને

પાણી જબરૂં લાગટ પડયાથી જુવાર ભીનાઇને ભડકો નરમ પડેા, ત્યારે વધારે ઉલટથી તેઓએ પાણીનો મારો ચલાવ્યો. ભડકો નરમ પડીયાથી જુવારનાં ધણીઓ ઉપર ઇશ્વરે પાછી કૃપા કીધી હોય એવી વધામણી ભરેલી ખબર જાણે કોઈએ આવીને તેમને કહી હોય એવી રીતે તેઓ પોતે તુરત ઉઠીને દોડધામમાં પડયા અને પાણી નાખવાની તાકીદ કરવામાં પોતે જાતે મેહનત કરવા લાગ્યા. હમારામાંથી એક બે મીત્રનાં કપડાં આગ હોલવવામાં થોડાં બળ્યાં હતાં તે જોઇને, જ્યારે સઘલું સમાધાન થઇ ચુકું એટલે ખેડુતોએ તથા તેમનાં કુટંબ વીગરે બીજાઓએ વાંકા વળી બે હાથે હમો સઘળાને નમસ્કાર કીધો અને બોલ્યાં કે "મહારાજ, તમો જો નહી હોત તો આ જુવારનો સઘળો ઢગળો ખચીત બળીને રાખ થઈ જાત, હમો ગરીબ ખેડુતોને રૂપીઆ ૪૦૦) સુધીનું મોહોટું નુકસાન થાત, જે રકમ હમારી આખાં વરસની કમાઈ હતી, અને તે ગયાથી હમો બચ્ચાં છોકરાં સાથે જનમ સુધીનાં કરજદાર અને હેરાન થઈ પડત." આ સાંભળીયાથી હમારા મનમાં ધણી દયા છુટી હતી, અને એક ગંભીર વીચાર આવ્યો હતો કે ખુદાતાલાની મેહરબાંનીથી હમારા જેવા કમીનાઓને હાથે એક ગરીબ કુટુંબની ઉપર જનમ સુધી પડવાં આવેલાં દુખનું સેહેજ વારમાં અને થોડી મેહેનતથી નીવારણ થઈ શકયુ હતું! આ ઠેકાણેથી પાછલા પોહોરનાં ચાર વાગે નીકળ્યા. નંદીકંદી ગામડાં આગળ એક ઘણુંજ મોહોટું તળાવછે, જેમાં નંદીકંદી નામનાં નાળાનું પુશકળ પાણી ઉતરેછે. આ પાણીથી સઘળી તરફ ખેતી ધણીજ સારી થાયછે, અને ડુંગરની જમીન વટીક ઉપર સેહેડી જેવા તબક્કા બનાવી તીહાં પણ ખેડણી કરેલીછે. આવાં ખુદરતી તળાવોની રચના જેવી દીવસનાં રળીયામણી લાગેછે તેવીજ રાત્રે એક ઓર તરેનાં દેખાવથી જોવા લાયક થઈ પડેછે. રાત્રે બાર વાગે હમો આવા એક તળાવ આગળથી જતા હતા. તે વેળા હમારા એક મીત્રે મોહોટે આવાજે હમુને કહ્યું કે જુઓ, જુઓ રસ્તાની ડાવી અને જમણી તરફ શું દેખાયછે? હમોએ જોયું તો જાણે જમીન ઉપર આસમાન અને સઘળા સીતારા ઉતરી, આબેહુબ એક નવું આસમાન જમીન ઉપર બની રેહેલું હતું. તળાવનું પાણી એવું તો કાચ જેવું નીર્મળ અને સ્થીર હતું કે તેમાં આકાશનું પ્રતિબિંબ ઘણુંજ સુંદર રીતે અને સઘળી બારીકી સાથે દેખાતું હતું, જેમાં ઝાંખા તથા ચળકતા સઘળી જાતનાં તારા ખુલા

બરોબર નજરે પડતા હતા. આવો જોવા લાયક દેખાવ કોઈ ઠેકાણે હમારા જો-યામાં નથી આવ્યો. ઉપર, હેઠળ અને સઘળી તરફ આકાશ ફરી વળેલોછે અને તે વચે આપણી પૃથ્વી નીરાધાર લટકાઈ રહેલીછે. આ ખુદરતી દેખાવનુ ચીત્ર કોઈએ જોવું હોયતો નંદીકંદી ગામડા આગળનાં તળાઓની રચના રાત્રે અંધારામાં જઈ જોવી.

આ ઠેકાણે પણ ખજુરાંનું મોહોટું વનનું વન લાગેલુંછે, અને હીયાંતો કેટલાંક ખજુરાં એટલાં તો ઊંચાઈમાંછે કે તે ઊપર કોઈથી સેહેલાઈથી ચઢી નહી શકાય. કેટલાંક ૫૦) ફુટની ઊંચાઈ સુધીનાં હમોએ જોયાંછે. આ લત્તા તરફના લોક ખ-જુરાં ઊપર ચઢેછે તે જેમ આપણી તરફનાં તરવાડા ચાંમડાંના પટાના આધારથી ચઢેછે તેમ ચઢતા નથી. હીયાંતો બાંબુની હલકી નીસરણીથી ખજુરાં ઊપર ચઢેછે. ખજુરાં છેદવાવીશે ઊપર જણાવેલી બે રીતમાં મુંબઈ તથા ગુજરાત પ્રાંત તરફના તરવાડાઓની હીમત વધારે માલુમ પડેછે, કારણ તેમા ચાલાકી સાથે જો-ખમ વધારેછે. નીસરણી મુકીને ચઢવાનું જેટલું સલામતી ભરેલુંછે તેટલું ચાંમડાંના પટા અને પગનાં ટેકાવથી ચઢવું વધારે ધાસ્તી ભરેલું છે ; પણ હમારા જોવામાં આવ્યું કે નીસરણી મુકીને તેની મારફતે થોડીજ ઉંચાઈનાં ખજુરાં છેજાતાં હતાં, અને મોહોટી ઉંચાઈવાળાં ઝાડો છેદવા વગર પડી રહેલાં હતાં, સબબ નીસરણી ધણી લાંબી થયાથી એણીગમ પેલીગમ ઉંચકમુક કરવાને ધણીજ અગવડ ભરેલી લાગતી હતી. આગળ જણાવ્યું તેમ આ લત્તા ઉપરના લોક જબરદસ્ત તાડી પીનારા છે, અને વળી તાડીની તથા તેના દારૂની કેફને વધારે તેજ કરવા, તેમાં ભાંગ, ગાંજો, ધતુરો અને અફીણ વીગેરે તરેવાર કેફી વસ્તુઓ ભેળેછે. કેહેછે કે આ લોક આખો દીવસ પીપણાથી ભીનેલાં અને ભીનેલાં રેહેછે, અને જરાજરામાં મારામારી ઉપર આવી જાયછે. તાડીના ખપવીશે હેદરાબાદમાં હમોએ પુછપરછ કરી હતી તીહાં એવું માલુમ પડયું હતું કે નીજામ હેદરાબાદના તાલુકાઓમાં મહુડાંની ઝાઝી ઊતપત્તી છેજ નહી. ખુદરતે તાડીનુંજ વન તીહાં પેદા કરેલુંછે, અને એવું કરવામાં હમે ધારીએછે કે ઇશ્વર તરફથી આ લોક ઉપર એક મોહોટી કૃપા થઇછે; કેમકે જે લોક તાડી પીઈ આવા કજીઆખોર અને ફીસાદી બને છે, તેઓ પાસે જો જલદ જાતનો દારૂ બનાવાની બીજી ખુદરતી જીનસ મળી હતેતો રેયતનાં કેવા બુરા હાલ થતે, એ કેહેવાઈ

શકાતું નથી. ક્રિષ્ણા નદી આગળ હમોએ થોડીવાર વીસામો લીધો હતો તે વખતે આ તાડીનાં ખપ વીશે જે વધારે ખબર મેળવી છે તેની વીગત તે ઠેકાણુંના અહેવાલમાં જણાવીછે.

તા૦ ૩૧ મી ડીસેંબર—આ દીને સહવારનાં ૭ વાગે પટનચેરૂ નામનું ગામ જે હેદરાબાદથી આસરે ૧૭ માઇલ દુરછે તીહાં જઈ પુગા અને આ ઠેકાણે સીકંદરાબાદની શેઠ મંચેરજી બહમનજી પંથકીવાળાઓની પેહેડી તરફનાં કેટલાએક ભાઇયો હમને એસ્તેકબાલ લેવાને આવ્યા હતા તેમની સાથે મોલાકાત થઈ. મુંબઇથી કેટલાંક કાગજો અમારી ઉપર હેદરાબાદ આવી પોહોંચેલાં હતાં, તે પણ આ સાહેબો મેહરબાંનીની રાહે પોતાની સાથે લાવ્યા હતા, તથા સીકંદરાબાદ જે ઇંગ્રેજની સરહદમાં છે, તીહાં એક ગૃહસ્થનો સારી હવા પાણી અને બાગ વાલો બંગલો પણ હમારા ઉતારાને સારૂ તૈયાર કરી રાખ્યો હતો. ખરેખર આપણા જરથોસ્તીઓ જેવા પરદેશામાં અરસપરસ પોતાના હમજાતીઓની બરદાસ્ત કરવાની ઉલટ અને ખરૂં દીલ રાખેછે તેવું મુંબઈમાં એકબીજા તરફ મુતલક જોવામાં આવતું નથી. કોણ જાણે આ બાબદમાં મુબઈ શેહેરનાં પાણીનો વાંકછે, અથવા એવું થવાના કોઈ બીજાં જુદાંજ કારણોછે? હીયાનાં પારસીઓનાં સંપ અને એકબીજા તરફની અદેખાઈ વીશે શું બોલીએ! એ વીશે ખામોશી પકડેલી બેહતર જાણીએછ. પટનચેરૂ આગળ ગ્રાનાઇટનો ખડક જબરો લાગેલોછે, અને જેમ જેમ સીકંદરાબાદની નજદીક જઇએછ તેમ તેમ આ ખડક વધારે નજરે પડતો જાયછે. હીયાંથી તાડનાં ઝાડોનું વન લાગેલુંછે, જેમાં તાડોની સાથે ખજુરાંનાં ઝાડો પણ છુટાં છવાયાં નજરે આવેછે. સહવારનાં ૮॥ વાગે ઉપર જણાવેલા બંગલામાં જઈ ઉતર્યા અને ઉતરીને જરા હાથ મોહોડું ધોઈ આરાએસ લઇએછ એટલામાં હેદરાબાદનાં દસ્તુરજી સાહેબ દસ્તુર હોરમજજી જામાસ્પજી જામાસ્પ આશાના જેવણ આપણા પ્રખ્યાત કાબેલ દસ્તુર હોરાંગજી જામાસ્પજીનાં તથા પુણાવાલા ખાન બાહાદુર દસ્તુર નુશરવાનજી જામાસ્પજીનાં ભાઈ થાયછે, તેવણ મુંબઇથી આવેલાં થોડાંક બીજાં કાગજો લઈ હમોને એસ્તેકબાલ લેવાને આવ્યા હતા. એવણે આવીને શેઠ બાપુજી વીકાજી મેહેરજી તરફથી એવી ખાયરા જણાવી કે હમોએ હેદરાબાદમાં શેઠ બાપુજી વીકાજીનાં મકાન ઉપર સીધારવું, અને તે ઠેકાણે એક એલાહેદો મકાન શેઠ

બાપુજીએ હમારા ઉતારાને સારૂ તૈયાર કરી રખાવ્યોછે તીહાં ઉતારો કરવો. સીકંદરાબાદ, હેદરાબાદથી છેક ૭ માઈલ દુર પડયાથી અને જે બંગલામાં હમોએ ઉતારો લીધો હતો તે વસ્તીથી ઘણોજ દુર હોયાથી, તથા હેદરાબાદ સેહેરમાં ફરી વલી તે બરોબર જોવાને બની આવે એટલા સારૂ શેહેરની નજદીક જઈ રેહેવું હમો સઘળાઓએ બેહેતર વીચારીયું. શેઠ પંથકીની દુકાનનાં સાહેબો પાસે તેમની મેહેરબાંનીનો ઉપકાર માની, માંગી લીધું કે જે મતલબથી હમો મુસાફરી કરવા નીકળ્યા હતા તે મતલબ પુરી પાડવાને હેદરાબાદ શેહેરમાં જઈ અગર હમોએ ઉતારો કીધો તો તે વધારે ફાયદા ભરેલું થાઈ પડશે. આ હમારૂં માંગવું તે સાહેબોએ નાખુશ થઇને પણ વાજબી કારણોનાં સબબથી કબુલ રાખીયું હતું. હમારી બરદાસ્ત કરવાની ઘણીજ આરજુ તે સાહેબોમાં દેખાઈ હતી, તોએપણ જે બાબદથી હમને વધારે ફાયદો થતો હતો તે વાત તેઓનાં ધ્યાનમાં આવ્યાથી સઘળા જણ પાછળથી રાજી થયા હતા.

આ ઠેકાણેથી દસ્તુરજીની ગાડીમાં બેસીને હેદરાબાદ તરફ કુચ કીધી. હેદરાબાદમાં ઠેકાણે ઠેકાણે મોહટ મોહોટાં તળાવો છે, અને તે તળાવોને લગતી જુદી જુદી કાહાણીઓ પણ બોલાતી આવેલીછે. મીર આલમનું તલાવ પાહાડોની વચમાં આવેલુંછે અને તીહાંની રચના ઘણીજ સુંદર તથા રલીયામણી છે. આસપાસ કબરો અને રેહેવાનાં મકાનો આવેલાં છે. સીકંદરાબાદથી હેદરાબાદ જતાં પેહેલાં સદર-બજાર આવેછે; તે ઠેકાણેથી મોહોટ મોહોટી હવેલીઓ, બંગલા અને બાગો સરૂ થાય છે. હુશાન સાગરનાં મોહોટાં તળાવનું પાણી જુદા જુદા તબકાએ બાંધેલા દરવાજા વાટે આખાં હેદરાબાદ શેહેરમાં ફરી વળેલું અને વપરાતું છે.

હુશાન સાગરને "મુસી" નદી સાથે જોડવા નીજામના દીવાન સર સાલારજંગે ઠરાવ કીધો છે હેવું તેવખતે હમે સાંભળ્યું હતું. એ બંધેને જોડી નાખવાને નજદીક ૩૯ માઈલ લાંબી ચર એટલે ખાહી ખોદવાનો ખરચ રૂ ૨૫૦૦૦૦) હડી લાખનો ગણવામાં આવ્યો છે. એ તળાવની લંબાઈ પોહોળાઈ મલીને આસરે ૧૪૦૦) એકર જમીન ગણવામાં આવી છે; જેમાં પાણી ભરાતાં ૧૫૦૦૦૦૦૦) દોહોડ કરોડ કયુબીક ફીટ (એટલે આસરે નવકરોડ સાડત્રીસ લાખ ગ્યાલન) પાણી એકઠું થઈ શકશે. એ પાણી ફકત આખાં હેદરાબાદ શેહેરને પુરૂં પડશે એટલુંજ નહી પણ સીકંદરાબાદમાં પણ જઈ પુગશે. જે જે જમીન પાણી

વગર ઊજડ પડી હતી તે જમીન એ પાણીથી પાકવાલી થઈ પડવાની, અને એ કામ જો બરોબર નીભયું તો હેદરાબાદમાં દુકાલની મોસમમાં પડતાં દુખો એથી ટલી શકવાનાં. હુશાન સાગરની આસપાસનાં શેહેરનું નામ હુશંગાબાદ કરીને આગળ બોલાતું હતું તે ઇંગ્રેજના તાબામાં ગયા પછી સીકંદરાબાદ બોલાવા લાગ્યું છે.*

મહવારના ૧ાા વાગે હેદરાબાદમાં શેઠ બાપુજી વીકાજી મેહેરજીનાં રેહેવાનાં મકાનમાં જઈ પોંહોંચ્યા તે ઠેકાણે હમારી ઓળખાણના કેટલાએક સાહેબો મુંબઈથી આવેલા હતા તેમની સાથે મુલાકાત થઈ. શેઠ બાપુજીનો રેહેવાનો મકાન હેદરાબાદની ઇંગ્રેજી રેસીડિનસીની સરહદમાં છે. કેટલાંએક કારણો અને ફાયદા સારૂ હેદરાબાદમાં આપણા જરથોસ્તી તેમજ બીજા કેટલાક શેઠ સાહુકારોએ રેસીડેનસીની સરહદમાં રેહેવું બેહેતર જાણીયું છે. એ દીને પાછલા પોહોરના ૩ાા વાગે ઇંગ્રેજી સરહદની બજારમાં ફરીને સાંજના ૬ાા વાગે જલદી પાછા ફરયા. આઠ દીવસની લાગટ મુસાફરીથી અને ગાડીમાં ખાધેલા આંચકાથી શરીર ઓખરૂં થઈ ગયું હતું તેથી હવે જારે બે ચાર દીવસ એકજ ઠેકાણે થોભી આસાએશ લેવાનો પ્રસંગ મલ્યો તેનો લાભ લઈ પેહેલે દીવસે જલદી બીછાના ઉપર જઈ નીરાંતે હુંગાવાનો ઠરાવ કીધો હતો.

જે દીવસે હેદરાબાદ પુગા તે દીવસે દોસ્ત આશનાઓ સાથે મળવા ભેટવાથી હમને સઘળાને ઘણી ખુશી ઉત્પન્ન થઈ હતી, અને જે મીલનસારી અને મોહોબત ભરેલી મેહમાનદારીથી શેઠ બાપુજી વીકાજીએ હમારી મુલાકાત લીધી હતી અને બરદાસ્ત કીધી હતી, તેની યાદ હમારા મનમાંથી કદી ભીસરવાની નથી. ખરૂં મોહોટું દીલ, મીલનસારી, ઘરહસ્થપણું અને રાજદરબારી બાબદો ઉઠાવી લેવામાં બાહોશી, પુછપરછ, અને ખબરનો અછો બંડોળ આ સેઠ ધરાવેછે, એટલુંજ નહી પણ સેઠ વીકાજી મેહરજીના પ્રખ્યાત ખાનદાનના સાહેબો, સેઠ બાપુજી વીકાજી, સેઠ રૂસ્તમજી, સેઠ જીવણજી, સેઠ બરજોરજી વીગેરે બીજા સાહેબો રાજ દરબારી કામમાં બચગીથીજ પરોટાયલા છે તેથી તેઓ એવાં કામમાં ઘણા લાયક અમલદારો થઈ પડેયા છે, આથી આપણા પારસી ટોલાને મોટું માન છે.

---

*બ્રીગ્સ નિઝામ, વાલમ ૨) જો. પાનું ૨૪૯.

નીજામના રાજકારોબાર સાથે આ લાયકીવાળાં ખાનદાનને લાંબી મુદત થઈ સંબંધ થયલો છે, તેથી જેમ નીજામ સરકારને તેમજ આ ખાનદાનને અરસપરસ ઘણા ફાયદા થયલા છે. આજે પણ નીજામના જેટલા તાલુકા આ ખાનદાનવાલા સખસોના હાત તળેછે તેટલા સઘળાની જમાબંદી અને મેહસુલ વસુલ કરવામાં ઘણુંજ સારા બંદોબસ્તો તેઓએ કરેલાં સંભળાયા છે, જેથી જેમ નીજામ સરકારના રાજને ફાયદો થાયછે તેમ તેની રઈઅતની હાલત પણ બેહતર થતી જાયછે. આ વીશે વધારે આગળ લખવામાં આવીયું છે.

ખુશાલીની પાછળ દીલગીરી હંમેશ હોયજછે, તે પ્રમાણે મુંબઈમાં બનેલી એક એવીતો કફોરી વાત હેદરાબાદ પોંહોંચ્યા પછી તીહાં સાંભળવામાં આવી કે તેથી હમારો તથા હમારી સાથના એક બે મીત્રોનો જીવ જરા દીલગીરીમાં પડયો હતો. કોઈ તરેહની ભુલ થયાથી અને તે ભુલ ઉપર મશકરી કરવાની મતલબે એક બે મુંબઈના વર્તમાનપત્રમાં એવું છપાઈ જાહેર થયું કે આ પુસ્તક લખનાર કલકત્તામાં મરણ પામ્યો છે. આ અફવા ફેલાયાથી હમારાં કુટુંબમાં ઘણોજ ઘભરાટ અને દુઃખ ઉત્પન્ન થયું હતું. આ બનાવથી હમો હેદરાબાદ આવી પુગા આગમચ હમારે સારૂં ઘણાં કાગજ પત્રો કુટુંબ અને મીત્રો તરફનાં આવી એકઠાં થઈ પડી રેહેલાં હતાં. તે વાંચતાં હમારાં કુટુંબમાં થયલા ઘભરાટ અને દુખ વીશેનો વીચાર ધ્યાનમાં આવ્યાથી હમારૂં દીલ ઘણું ઉચાટ થયું; અને આઠ દાહાડાની મુસાફરીથી તથા ખુદરતની રચનાં મંજલે મંજલ જોયાથી દીલને જે ખુશી અને ચંગી ઉત્પન થઈ હતી તેના રંગમાં ભંગ થઈ ગયો હતો. જીવતાં જીવત કોઈએ પોતાનું મરણ સાંભળવું આ વાત અલબતાં ઘણા જણને નાપસંદ અને દીલગીરી ભરેલી લાગે એમાં અજાએબ જેવું નથી; પણ હમો પોતે જીવતાં છતાં મરણ પાંમેલા સાંભળીને જેટલા દીલગીર નહી થયા હતા તે કરતાં વધારે દીલગીર હમારાં કુટુંબમાં આ ખોટી ખબરથી જે ઘભરાટ અને દુઃખ ઉપજીયું હતું તે વાંચીને થયા હતા. આવા કફોરા બનાવની યાદ આખી મુસાફરીમાં હમારા મનમાંથી નીકળી નહી શકી હતી, અને કોઈ વાર તો ભર મઝામાં તેની એકાએક યાદ આવ્યાથી મનમાં ને મનમાં છુપીછાની ભારી બેચેની સોસવી પડી હતી.

તારીખ ૧ લી જાનેવારી ૧૮૬૩ ને રોજે બપોરનાં ૧॥ વાગે હેદરાબાદનાં ઇંગ્રેજી રેસીડેનટનો રેહેવાનો મકાન જોવાને ગયા હતા. આ મકાન એક મોહોટા

મેહેલ જેવો મેહેલ છે. મુંબઈના ગવરનરનો પરેલનો મકાન તેની આગલ કુચ્ચ ગણતરીમાં નથી. દેશી રાજોમાં ઇંગ્રેજ અમલદારો રાજવંશી લોકની પદવીની મોહોટાઇ અને જાહોજલાલી ભોગવતા રેહેછે, આ બીનાં જે કોઈ અંદરના પ્રાંતોમાં જઈ નજરે નજર જુએ તેમનેજ ખબર પડેછે. મુંબઈમાં જે હાલ તે ઇંગ્રેજો આપણી સાથે વસેછે તેઓની રેહેવાની રીતભાત અને ચાલ ચલગત અંદરનાં પ્રાંતોમાં રહેનારા લશ્કરી અને દીવાની ખાતાંના અમલદારોની રેહેવાની રીત-ભાત અને તેમનાં દોર દમામ સાથે સરખાવી શકાતીજ નથી. અત્રેતો ઇંગ-રેજ એક ફકત પ્રજાનાં જેવો રેહેવાસી જણાયછે, પણ અંદરનાં પ્રાંતમાં તો તે જાણે તે પ્રાંતનો પોતેજ રાજા હોય તેવાં ડોલ અને ભપકાથી રેહેછે, અને એવુંજ સમજેછે કે રાણીની તરફથી તેનેજ આ પ્રાંતો ઊપર રાજ કરવાને નેમેલોછે. અલબતાં આ બીનાં સઘળા અમલદારોને લાગુ પડતી નથી, તોપણ ઘણાખરા અમલદારોને તે લાગુ પડતીછે, તેમાં જાણવાની મોહોટી વાતતો એછે કે જેમ અમલદાર જેટલો ઊતરતી પદવીનો તેટલી વત્તી દમામી તેના મગજમાં હોયછે, આ ઊપરથી જેટલો તોર ગવરનર જનરલ પોતે રાખતો નહી હશે તેથી સો ઘણો તોર અને દમામ કોઈ કલેકટર અથવા લશ્કરી અથવા ઇનજીનીઅરીંગ ખાતાંનો સાધારણ અમલદાર રાખેછે. માહેલા દેશી લોક સાહેબલોકથી એટલા બધા બીહેછે કે કોઈ ત્રીજા વર્ગનો રસ્તાની શારવાઇ કરનાર ટોપસું જો મુસાફરી બંગલામાં આવીને ઊતરયો હોયતો ગામઠીઓને (જો તેઓ બીચારા નરમ હોયાતો) તે બંગ-લામાં ઉતારાની જગા મળવી મુશકેલ પડેછે. પેલા ટોપસું સરવેઅર મોહોટા સાહેબમાં ખપેછે, પોતાના એકુ બે સીપાઈઓથી તે તરેહવાર સાહેબી કરી શકેછે, અને આ ટોપસું જારે બબો ઠાંસીને ટેબલ ઉપરજ ચકચુર થઈ પડેલો હોય-છે, તારેતો તેની ઊંઘને હરકત નહી થવા બંગલાની આસપાસ દુરવેરથી ચોકી પેહેરો તેના આદમીઓ પાસે રખાવેછે કે રખેને કોઈનાં મોહોટા આવાજથી અથવા ઠોંસ-વાથી અથવા મુશાફરોની ગાડીનાં ખખડાટથી સાહેબની ઊંઘમાં ખલલ થાય અથવા કાચી હુંઘમાંથી તે જાગી ઊઠે! આવી કીસમની સઘળી મુસ્તાકી હલકી પદવીનાં અમલદારો અંદરનાં પ્રાંતોમાં બેધડક કરયા જાયછે, પણ એમાં જેટલો આપણા દેશીઓનો તેમનાં અજ્ઞાનપણાથી વાંક દેખાયછે તેટલો તે મુસ્તાકી કરનાર અમલદારનો નથી જણાતો. આપણા દેશી લોક આવી હલકી પદવીવાલા ઇંગ્રેજોની

અતીશય ચાપલુસી કરેછે, તેમની આગળ એક ગુલામની પેઠે હાથ જોડી ઉભા રેહેછે, અને નહી કરવા ઘટે તેવાં કાંમો બજાવા તઈયાર રેહેછે, ત્યારે પેલા હલકી પદવીવાળા ઇંગ્રેજો એમજ સમજેછે કે દેશી લોકે આવી ગોલામગીરીની ચાકરી કરવીજ જોઈએ; અને એવો વીચાર એકવાર તેમનાં મનમાં ઠસ્યો તો પછી જીહાં જાય તીહાંના લોક પાસે તે પોતાના હક દાખલ ચાકરી કરાવવાની ઉમેદ રાખેછે, અને તે પ્રમાણે થવામાં જરા કસુર થઈતો તે હલકો અમલદાર એમ સમજેછે કે તેનો હક લુટાયો, તેથી જબરદસ્તીથી તે પોતાનો હક પાછો મેળવવાને પોતાના હાથ તળેના માણસો ઉપર "થોબડ ફલાગ" ની અને તરેહવાર બીજી સખત શીક્ષા અથવા જુલમ કરેછે; અને તેમાં દીલગીરી ભરેલું એટલુંજછે કે આવી ગેરસમજુતી હલકા અંમલદારો અને રૈયત વચ્ચે થયાથી એક ઘણીજ માનવંત અને દયાલુ દીલની માહારાણીનાં રાજને હલકું બોલાય અથવા અપમાન પોહોંચે એમાં તકસીર કોણની? પણ આસ્તે આસ્તે એવા હલકા પીંજાડા અમલદારોની નેમણુક જેમ ઓછી થતી જશે અને તેમની જગા દેશીઓને અથવા ખરેખરા મોહોટાં દીલવાલા લાયક ઇંગ્રેજી અમલદારોને સરકારની તરફથી મલતી જશે તેમ તેમ આવી ગેરસમજુતીનો નીવેડો આવતો જશે.

જે વખતે હમો રેસીડેનસીનો મેહેલ જોવા ગયા તે વખતે તેની મરામત થતી હતી, અને એટલા માટે મેજર થારનહીલ તે વખતનો કામચલાઉ રેસીડેનટ એક બીજા નાહાના મકાનમાં જઈ રહેલો હતો. રેસીડેનસીના મેહેલનો દેખાવ બાહારથી મુંબઈના ટૌનહાલ જેવોછે, માત્ર તેને ટાઉનહાલનાં જેટલી પાયરી અથવા પગથીઓ નથી. પોરટીકોનાં થાંભલાંની બનાવટ ટાઉનહાલનાં થાંભલા જેવીછે; ફરક એટલોજ કે તે લોહોડાંને બદલે પથર તથા ચુનાનાં બનાવેલાછે. તે શંગેમરમરના જેવા ચલકતા દેખાયછે; તથા તેમની ઉપર કરેલું નકસીકામ કેટલેક દરજે આબેહુબ અને કેટલેક ઠેકાણે મુંબઈનાં ટાઉનહાલનાં થાંભલા ઉપરના નકસીકામ કરતાં સરસછે. આ લત્તા તરફનો ચુનો એવીતો સારી જાતનોછે કે તેની સફાઈ, ચીકાસ અને ચળકાટતો સંગેમરમરને એક કોરે બેસાડેછે. સાધારણ જોનારને ધુટેલી દેવાલો ઉપરની ચળકતી કફલાત અને તેવુંજ બીજું તારીજ કામ જાણે સંગેમરમરનુંજ બનાવેલું હોય એવું દેખાય છે, અને હમે પોતે પણ કેટલેક ઠેકાણે જોવામાં એવી ભુલ કરી હતી. રેસીડેનસીના મેહેલ ઉપરની છેક

ઉચાંમાં ઉંચી અગાસી ઉપરથી આખું હેદરાબાદ શેહેર નજરે પડી શકેછે, અને દુરબીનની મદદથી કેટલાંક જાહેર અમેવાન અને મેહેલો ઓળખી શકાયછે. મક્કા મસજીદ અને તેના ચાર સોનેરી ગુંબજો, ગોલકંડાના મકબરા, અને નીજામના હજુરનો મેહેલ હીંયાંથી ખુલા નજરે દેખાયછે. વળી દુર સેકંદરાબાદ સેહર દેખાયછે અને તીહાં ત્રીમલગીરીમાં જે ઇંગ્રેજી છાવણી સારૂ સુંદર બરાકો, હીસપીતાલ વીગરે ઈમારતો બાંધેલીછે તેપણ દેખાયછે. ટુકાંમાં બોલીએતો રેસીડિનસીનો મકાન જોનારને આખું હેદરાબાદ શેહેર નજરના એક લેહેકામાં દેખાડાવી શકેછે. રાજદરબારી બખેડા અથવા હુલડના વખતમાં આ ઠેકાણેથી આખાં શેહેરની દીદબાની કરવાને આ એક લાયક મકાન હમારી નજરમાં આવ્યોછે.

રેસીડિનસીના મેહેલના પેહેલા માળ ઉપર ચઢતાં સેહેડીનાં મથાળાં આગળ ડાવી અને જમણી બંધે બાજુએ પુરૂશના ભર કદ જેટલાં સંગેમરમરનાં બે નાગાં બાવલાં મુકેલાં જોયામાં આવ્યાં. આ ઉપરથી કદાચ એક સવાલ ઉઠશેકે શું આવા દરજાભરેલાં મકાનમાં ઉઘાડાં નાગાં બાવલાં મુકવાં વાજબીછે? મુંબઇમાં તો આવાં બાવલાં આપણા.જોયામાં ઘણાં નથી આવતાં. પણ એ સવાલનો ખુલાસો એટલોજ છે કે યુરોપખંડમાં પુતળઘડણીની બાબદ વીશે આવો વિચાર રાખવામાં આવતોજ નથી. બાવલું બનાવનાર કીસબી પોતાના હાથની કારીગીરીની સફાઈ બતલાવવાને આવાં નાગાં બાવલાં, બદનનો ગમે તે ભાગ ઊઘાડો રાખી બનાવેછે. પુતળઘડણીની કારીગરી પીછાનનાર માત્ર બનાવનારના હાથની કળા, સફાઈ અને તે સાથે ખુદરતની કેટલી આબેહુબ અને નજદીકીભરેલી નકલ થઈ શકીછે તેજ માત્ર જોવાની આરજુ રાખે છે: પણ હલકા વીચારવાલા, નીચહવસના શોખીઓ, જેઓ ફકત માણસનાં જાનવરી ગુણનાજ તાબેદાર છે, તેઓથી ખરી ઊંચા દરજાની ખુબી નહી બુજી શકાયાથી, માણસનાં શરીરનાં કેટલાક અવયવો ઊપર નેગાહ કરી તે વીશે હલકી અને અનીતી ભરેલી ટીકા કરેછે. મુંબઈ શેહેરમાં આજે પુતળઘડણીની કળા જાણનારો એકુ પણ દેશી નથી. તેમજ પુતળઘડણીની કળાથી ખુબસુરત ખુદરતની નકલનાં જે જે નમુનાં માહભારત,કીસબીઓનાં હાથથી બનેલાછે તેવાં બાવલાંની રકમની એક આની ભારનો પણ અત્રે કોઈપણ ઠેકાણે જમાવ કરેલો જોયામાં અવીયો નથી. આથી એટલુંજ સાબેત થઇ શકેછે કે પૂતલાં અથવા ચીત્રો કેવી સીફત અથવા ગુણ

ધરાવતાં રાખવાં એ વીશે મુંબઈના ઘણા દેશી શેઠીઆઓને થોડોજ શોખ છે અથવા તો તેની પુરી ખુબીથી તેમાના ઘણાજણ બેખબર હોય. એકુ બે શીવાએ મોહોટ મોહોટા શેઠીઆઓનાં ઘરો અથવા બાગોમાં રાખેલાં ચિત્રો અને પુતળાંઓમાં ખરા ઊમદા શોખની નીશાણો થોડીજ જોવામાં આવશે. આ બાબતમાં કલકત્તાના બાબુઓમાં મલીકનું ખાનદાન પ્રખ્યાત થયલું છે. તેઓ તો એવી ચીજનાં જાણે ખુદરતીજ શોખી શેઠીઆઓ છે, જેઓએ એક આખો મેહેલ ભરીને એવી સુંદર ચીજોનો સંગ્રહ કરેલોછે અને તે દેશી પરદેશીઓને જોવા સારૂ ખુલો મુકયોછે. બરદવાનના મહા રાજાના મેહેલમાં તો એવી ચીજોનું ખરેખર એક નવાઈ જેવું સંગ્રસ્થાન કરી રાખેલુંછે. એ વીશે વીગતવાર હકીકત કલકત્તા તરફના અહેવાલમાં જણાવેલીછે.

રેસીડન્સીનો મેહેલ એક મોહોટા બાગની વચોવચ્ચ બાંધેલોછે. આગલા વખતમાં એવો કાયદો હતો કે ઇંગરેજનાં રેસીડેનટને નીજામનો તે વખતનો જે કોઈ વજીર હોય તેના બાગમાં એક મકાન રેહેવાને મળતો હતો. થોડુંકપછી રેસીડેનટે પોતે પોતાનો મકાન એલાહેદો બાંધવાને સારૂ થોડીક જગા નીજામ સરકાર પાસેથી માંગી. આ માંગણીમાં રેસીડેનટે માત્ર બે ત્રણ ખેતરની જમીન માંગી હતી. આ બાબદમાં એક રમુજી બનાવ બન્યો હતો, તે જાણવા જોગ ધારી નીચે જાહેર કીધોછે. આ બનાવ ઉપરથી હિંદુસ્થાનનાં રાજા અને શાહા-જાદાઓ જે જે મુલકો ઉપર રાજ કરેછે તેઓ પોતાના મુલકની લંબાઈ, પોહોળાઈ અને મોહોટાઈ વીશે કેટલું ગ્નાન ધરાવેછે તેનો એક અછો નમુનો જાહેર થાયછે. કેહેછે કે આ ખેતરોની બરોબર માપણી કરાવીને મોહોટા ખુલા આકારનો નકશો બનાવી રેસીડેનટ પોતે નીજામની દરબારમાં સાથે લઈ ગયો હતો, અને તે વીશે વાત થતાં તે નકશો નીજામની સાંમે મુકયો. નીજામે ઘણીજ ગંભીરાઇથી તે નકશા ઊપર નજર કીધી, અને રેસીડેનટને જવાબ આપ્યો કે "હું દીલગીર છઊં કે તમારી માંગણી મારાથી કબુલ રાખી નથી શકાતી." આ શબ્દો સાંભળી રેસીડેનટ ઘણોજ તાજુબી સાથે નાઊમેદ થઈ પાછો ફરયો, અને વધારે તાજુબ થવાનું કારણ એટલા સબબથી થયું કે ફક્ત બે ત્રણ ખેતર જેટલી જમીન આપવા નીજામે રેસીડેનટ જેવા અમલદારની અરજ કબુલ નહી રાખી. એવાંમાં નીજામના તે વખતના વજીર મીર આલમે રેસીડેનટને

હસીને કહ્યું કે, તમને કચવાવાનું કાંઈ કારણ નથી, જે પ્લાન (નકશો) નીજામને દેખાડયામાં આવ્યોછે તે જોઇને તે બીધોછે. નકશામાં પાડેલાં અંતરો એટલાંતો મોહોટાં કદના પાડેલાંછે કે નીજામે પોતાનાં આખા મુલકનો જે નકશો જોયોછે તેનાં જેટલાં તે મોહોટાં તેની નજરમાં લાગાંછે, તેથી તાજુબ થવા જેવું કાંઈ નથી કે આટલી સઘલી જમીન તે તમુને આપવાને ના નહી કાં પાડે? વાસ્તે તમારો પ્લાન નાહાના આકારમાં કરીને લાવો એટલે સઘલી અડચણો મટી જશે. રેશીડનટે આ વાત એકાએક નહી માની, તોપણ બીજી વખતે નીજામની મુલાકાત લીધી ત્યારે પોતાની સાથે પેલી જગાનો પ્લાન છેક નાહાના આકારમાં બનાવી એક રમવાનાં પાનાં ઊપર પડાવીને લઈ ગયો અને તે નીજામને દેખાડયો અને અરજ કીધી કે આટલી થોડી જગા મને મળેતો બસછે. પેલો નાહાનો નકસો જોતાંવાર નીજામે મોટી ખુશીથી આ માગણી એકદમ કબુલ રાખી અને તેથી રેસીડિનટની ખાતરી થઇકે પેહેલી માંગણી નીષ્ફલ થઈ તેનું કારણ ખરેખર મીર આલમે ધારયું તેજ હતું. થોડી મુદતમાં એ જગા ઊપર આ ઈમારતની બાંધણી શીરૂ થઈ,અને મદ્રાસ ઈલાકાના ઈનજીનીઅરો માંહેના લેફટેનેનટ સામ્યુએલ રસલના ઉપરીપણાં હેઠળ તે પુરી કરવામાં આવી.

મુંબઇનો રીકારડર સર જેમસ મેકીનટાસ સન ૧૮૦૮ માં પોતાનાં દોસ્ત કપતાન સીનડનહામને હેદરાબાદ મળવા ગયો હતો તેણે પોતાના રોજના સ્મરણ પુસ્તકમાં એવી નોંધ કરી લીધી હતી કે હિંદુસ્થાનની ઇમારતોની બાંધણીઓમાં સઉથી સરસ બાંધણી હેદરાબાદનાં રેસીડિનટનો મેહેલછે. "કોરીનથીઅન" તરીકાની બાંધણીનાં થાંભલાં મેહેલનાં મુખડા આગળ ઉઠાવેલાછે તેની ઉપર એક સારો શોભાયમાન "પોરટીકો" બાંધેલોછે, જે લંબાઇમાં ૬૦ સાઠ ફુટ છે, અને ઉંચાઈમાં મેહેલની ઉભરણી જેટલોછે. હીંયાંથી આગળ ચાલ્યા એટલે મેહેલના દીવાનખાનામાં જવાયછે. તે દીવાનખાનું પણ સાઠ ફુટ લાંબું છે, અને પેહેલાં બાંધ્યું ત્યારે તેટલુંજ ઉંચું હતું, પણ કપતાન સીનડનહામે તેનાં બે તબક્કા અથવા માળ બનાવ્યાછે. ઉપરનાં માળને ટેકાવવા સારૂ હારબંધ થાંભલાં એટલાંતો ઉભાં કીધાંછે કે પેહેલો માળ થાંભલાંઓની હારથી ભરાઇ ગયલો દેખાયછે, પણ તે થાંભલાં એવીતો સુંદર રીતે રચેલાં અને બનાવેલાંછે કે તેની રચનાથી પેહેલા માળનો દેખાવ ઘણોજ ભપકાદાર બની રહેલોછે. તેના દરેક નાકે છતરીસ ફુટ

લાંબા અને ચોવીસ ફુટ પોહોલા બેવડાં રોકી ઓરડા છે. તેમાંનો એક જમવાનો ઓરડો, અને બીજો પુસ્તકખાનું અને ત્રીજો બચ્ચાં છોકરાંઓને બેસવા ઉઠવાનો ઓરડોછે. દર ખુણે ચાર નાહાના સમચોરસ ઓરડાછે. માળ ઉપર પણ ઓરડાઓની એવીજ રચના કરેલીછે, અને બંધે માળ ઉપર ફરસબંધી કરી લઇ તે ઉપર ગાલીચા અને નરમ ગાદીઓ ઘણાજ સારા શોખથી બીછાવેલીછે તથા સહુથી સુંદર ભાંતના મેહલ સીણગારનો ઇંગ્રેજી બનાવટનો સામાન એવોતો ચુંટી પસંદ કરીને ગોઠવેલોછે જેથી ટુંકાંમા બોલીએતો આખો મેહેલ જેવો ઉગમણુ તરફના રાજોના દમામ અને ભભકા લાયક થયલોછે તેવોજ સગવડ અને સુખવારામાં પુરો ઇંગ્રેજી રૌનક અને દમામ ભરેલો પણ બની રહેલોછે.

સન ૧૮૧૭ નાં સાલમાં તા૦ ૨૪ મી જુલાઇને રોજે સર જાન માલકમનું રાજદરબારી કામસર ફરતું ફરતું હેદરાબાદ તરફ આવવું થયું હતું. પોતાની બાયડી ઉપર દરરોજનો જે અહેવાલ લખી મોકલતો હતો તે રોજની યાદીમાં સર જાને એ મેહેલ વીશે એવું લખી જણાવ્યું કે પંદર વરસની વાત ઉપર હું જારે હેદરાબાદ આવ્યો હતો ત્યારે ઇંગ્રેજ સરકારનો અત્રેનો રેસીડિનટ એક દેશી ઉમરાવના બંગલામાં રેહેતો હતો. બંગલાની આસપાસ એક નાહાનો સરખો બાગ તથા કેટલાક ફુઆરા હતા, તેમાં કેટલોક ફેરફાર, ઇંગ્રેજની સગવડ અને સુખવાસને લાયક, જેમતેમ કરીને તે મકાનને આરાસ્તગી આપી હતી; પણ હવડાંની વાત શું લખું! હાલતો રેસીડિનટનો મકાન એક મેહેલ બની ગયલોછે, તેની નજદીક જતાંજ તેનો દમામ જોઈ ભય લાગેછે. કલકત્તા ગવરમેંટ હાઉસ માત્ર એનાથી દમામમાં સરસ કેહવાઈ શકાશે, પણ બીજી કોઈબી ઈમારત એની બરોબરી કરી નથી શકવાની. મદ્રાસના ગવરનરનો મકાન એની આગળ પોઇસ અથવા વટાવમાંછે. ઈમારતની બાંધણી અને અંદરનાં ઓરડાઓની રચનાનું ઉપર જણાવ્યા પ્રમાણે બયાન કરચા પછી સર જાને તીહાંની ખુરસી, કોચ, ઝુંમર એવી એવી ચીજોનું તાજુબ થઈ બયાન કર્યુંછે. આ આખો મેહેલ નીજામે પોતે પોતાને ખરચે બંધાવ્યો તથા સીણગારયોછે, તથા એની મરામત અને જાલવણી પણ નીજામનાંજ ખરચથી થાયછે. કેહેવતછે કે "મુફતકા ચંદન લગાદે લાલજી," તેમ નીજામના ખરચે એવો મેહેલ નહી કોણને બંધાવા અને વાપરવા ગમે વારુ!

હેદરાબાદની રેસીડિન્સીનો મેહેલ એક જોવા લાયક મકાનછે, અને કોઈ પણ

શાખસ એક ફેરો મારી તે જોઈ આવેતો તેની મેહેનતનો બદલો તે જોયાથી ખચીત વળી શકે એવુંછે. હવડાં એ મકાનની આરાસ્તગીમાં ઘણો સુધારો અને વધારો થયેલાછે, અને આસપાસ ગુલચમન અને તરેવાર મેવા તથા તરકારીનાં બગીચા અચ્છા બનાવેલાછે; તેની સાથે કેટલાંક જાનવરો પણ તીહાં પાળેલાંછે.

રેસીડન્સીનો મકાનજોયા પછી તેવખને તીહાં રેહેલા કામચલાઉ રેસીડનટ મેજર થારનહીલને મલવા ગયા. આ અમલદારે ઘણીજ મીલનસારીથી હમારી મોલાકાત લીધી હતી. થોડીએક વાર વાતચીત કીધા પછી હમો તીહાંથી બપોરના હડી વાગે રવાના થયા અને તીહાંથી ત્રીમલગીરી તરફ ઇંગરેજી લશ્કરને સારૂં જે નવી બરાકો, જેલ અને હાસપીટલ બાંધ્યામાં આવીછે તે જોવાને ગયા.

થોડા વખતસુધીતો હમો સઘળાની ગાડીઓ લગોલગ સાથે ચાલી, પણ કોચમેનોની બેવકુફાઈ અને હુલડાઈથી તેઓ એક બીજા સાથે વધારે વાર રહી નહીં શક્યા. થોડાવારમાં હમો એક બીજાથી બે ત્રણ માઈલને છીટે વેગળા પડી ગયા. વીચારો કે એક શીગરામ જાણે બે જણને લઈ મજગામ જવાને ઠેકાને પરેલ નીકલી ગઈ, બીજી ગાડી બે જણને લઈ જાણે મોટ તરફ ચાલી ગઈ; તે ગાડીઓને પાછી એકજ ઠેકાણે ભેગી થતાં નજદીક એક કલાક અમસ્થો નીકળીગયો, અને આ સઘળું થવાનું કારણ કોચમેનોની બેપરવાહી વગર બીજું કાંઈ નહી હતું. તેઓ એટલાતો કમઅકલ હતા કે આપણે કહીએ તે બરોબર સાંભળેજ નહી, અને વગર વીચારે હાંકયાજ કરે, જીહાંસુધી આપણે કંટાલીને પુછીએ નહીં કે "તું કીએ ઠેકાણે હાંકેછે." તારે ગાડી ઉભી રાખી તે કેહેછેકે "તમે કહો તીહાં હાંકુ" આ શું થોડું સતાવા જેવુંછે! પણ ખબર કાહાડતાં માલુમ પડયું કે તે ઠેકાણેના એકેએક કોચમેન આથી બેહેતર નહીં હતા, આતો તેમની એક ખુબીજ હતી! પણ વળી કલકત્તામાં આથી સરસ કોચમેનો હમોને મળ્યા હતા અને તેમનો અનુભવ જે હમોએ મેળવીયો છે તેનુ બયાંન ઘટતી જગોએ કરવામા આવ્યું છે. ટુંકાંમાં અત્રે કેહેવાનું એટલુંજછે કે મુંબઈના કોચમેન તથા ઘોડાવાળા ખરેખર પોતાનાં કામમાં વધારે હોશીયાર અને ચોકસ રોકડે ૭૫ મલી આવેતો મદ્રાસ, કલકત્તા અને ઉપરના પ્રાંતોમાં રોકડે ૧૫ મળવા મુશકેલ જાણવા. જારે હમો સઘળા પાછા મળ્યા ત્યારે એક બીજાને ઠપકો દેવા લાગા કે હેદરાબાદથી સાથે નીકળેલા કેમ આવી રીતે છુટા પડી ગયા? ત્યારે સઘળાના

જવાબનો સાર એટલોજ નીકળ્યો કે જે કોચમેને પેહેલાં ગાડી હાંકી તેણે એટલુંજ સાંભળવાની તસદી લીધી હતી કે "ત્રીમલગીરી" જવુંછે. પણ ત્રીમલગીરીમાં કહી જગાએ અથવા કહે ઠેકાણે અટકવું તે પુછવાની અથવા જાણવાની તેણે કંઇજ દરકાર નહીં રાખી અને ઠેઠ હાંકતો હાંકતો ત્રીમલગીરીનો છેક છેડો આવીયો તીહાં સુધી હાંકયાજ કીધું હતું. બીજા ગાડીવાળાને જારે પુછવામાં આવ્યું કે તારી સાથની બીજી ગાડીઓ કીહાં ગઇછે? ત્યારે તેણે થોડેવાર એવો જવાબ આપ્યા કીધો કે તે પછવાડે આવેછે, તે દુરછે; અને છેલ્લે સરવાળે કહ્યું કે કોણ જાણે તે કીહાં ગઇછે! ત્રીજા ગાડીવાલાને પુછીઉં કે તું કીહાં હાંકેછે, તારે તેણે જવાબ દીધો કે ત્રીમલગીરી તરફ તમે ફરવા નીકલેલા છેઓ તેથી જીહાં તીહાં હાંકુંછું, પણ હવે તમે કેહો તીહાં હાંકું! એટલા બેફામ અને બેદરકાર તેઓ માલુમ પડયા હતા. હમારી ગાડીતો છેક ત્રીમલગીરીની છેલ્લી હદ સુધી જઈ પુગી હતી, અને જો હમો કોચમેનને નહીં પુછતે કે તું હમને કહી જગાએ લઈ જાયછે, તો હમો ધારીએછેએ કે રાત્રે સાત વાગા સુધી તે ગાડી હાંકયાજ કરતે અને જેટલું દુર ઘોડાથી ચાલી શકાતે તેટલે દુર તે હમને લઇ ગયો હતે. એ વીશે હમને પછવાડેથી કઈ શક જેવું નહી લાગું, કેમકે તે જગાએ રેહેનારા અને રોજની ખબર રાખનારા પારસી ગ્રહસ્થોએ ખોલાસો કરી કહી જણાવીયું કે આવા બનાવ તીહાં કાંઇ નવાઇ જેવા બનતા હોય એવું નથી. બલકે કોઈ અજાણ્યો શખ્સ એખલો કોઈ દુર ઠેકાણે જઈ પાછો પોતાને ઘર બરોબર સીધોને સીધો આવ્યોતો તે જરા નવાઈ જેવું લાગતું હતું, અને તેની સાબાસી કોચમેનને ખરી મળવા જોગ હતી. એવી ગફલત થયાથી ત્રીમલગીરીમાં બાંધેલી જેલ જોવાની હમને તક મળી નહીં હતી, તોપણ હમારા બીજા ભાઈબંધુઓએ તે જોઈ હતી, તેમનાં કહેલા અહેવાલ પ્રમાણે તે ઈમારત ઘણીજ સગવડ અને આરાસ્તગી ભરેલી હતી. આરાસ્તગી આ શબ્દ સાંભલીને કેટલાક વાંચનારાઓનાં મનમાં અચંબો લાગશે કે વલી બંદીખાનાંમાં આરાસ્તગી શા માટે જોઈએ? પણ બંદીખાનાંની ખરી ખુબી ફકત ઇંગ્રેજ સરકાર પુરેપુરી અને બરોબર સમજેછે. હમો સહરાવીને નથી બોલતા, પણ આજે ઇંગ્લંડનું રાજ આખા યુરોપખંડમાં અને આખી પૃથ્વી ઉપર બંદીખાનાંની તરબીઅત, તરતીબ, તજુમલ અને બંધીવાનોની બરદાસ્ત અને તેમને બેહેતર કરવાનીજ મતલબે જે કાયદા કાનુ-

નથી આવાં ખાતાં ચલાવેછે, તેવું બીજું કોઈ રાજ ચલાવતું હોય એવું હમો જાણતા નથી. કોઈબી સરકાર આ વીશયમાં ઇંગ્રેજની અરધી બરોબરી નથી કરી શકવાની. ત્રીમલગીરીની જેલમાં જગાપણ દુરગંધ અથવા બંધીવાનોની તનદરોસતી બીગડે એવું કોઈબી કારણ અથવા કફોરી ગોઠવણ જોયામાં આવી નહીં હતી. બંધીવાનોને એક સારો દીલપસંદ બાગ બનાવવાનાં કાંમ ઉપર લાગાડેલા હતા; તથા કેટલાકોને ટોપલી, સાદડી, કાથાનાં બીછાંનાં બનાવવા વીગરે બીજી કીસમનો ધંધો પેશો શીખવતા હતા. બંધવાઓને તે ધંધા શીખાડીયાથી આ ફાયદો થઈ શકતો હતો કે બંધીખાનામાંથી બંધવાનો છુટકો થયા પછી તે પોતે ચાહેતો પોતાનું ગુજરાણ કરવાને પોતે સ્વતંત્ર થઈ શકતો હતો. હમારા મીત્રોએ હમને કહ્યું હતું કે જે જગા તેઓએ બંધીખાનાને નામે જોઈ તે જો તેમને આગળથી જણાવવામાં નહીં આવતેતો તેઓ તે મકાનને એક આરામથી રેહેવાની અને ઉદ્યોગ શીખવાની એક શાળા દાખલ સંજમતે. વાંચનારે એમ નહીં સમજવું કે સખત શીક્ષા કરવાનાં ઠેકાણાં આ બંદીખાનાંમાં કરયાં નહીં હતાં. કઠણ શીક્ષા સારૂ જુદી કોઠડીઓ એલાહેદી જગાએ કરી રાખેલી હતી; પણ સાધારણ રીતે જોતાં આ મકાન કંટાળો ઉપજાવનારૂં અથવા બંધીવાનોને રીબાવીને તેમનાં શરીરને ઇજા પોહોંચાડવાનું મકાન નહીં હતું, પણ ગુનેગાર માણસો પાસે તેમનાથી જાણી બુજીને થતી ભુલ, ચુક, શોખાઈ, દાંડપણું, મસ્તી અને ફેસાદ ભરેલી ચાલ ચલગત છોડાવી તેમને ઇનિસાનીઅત, સલુખાઈ, સુલેહસંપજ અને ઉદીયોગ શીખાડવાની તથા તેમને ભલા માણસ બનાવાને આ બંધીખાનું એક લાયક નીશાળ હતી.

આ મકાનથી આગળ વધીને ઇંગ્રેજી લશ્કરના સીપાઈઓએ પોતાના ફાયદા તથા વધારા સારૂ એક પુસ્તકખાનું સ્થાપ્યું હતું તે જોવા ગયા. આ મકાનનું નામ (Soldiers' Club) "સોલજર્સ કલબ" કરીને આપવામાં આવ્યુંછે અને તે દીલપસંદછે. આ ઠેકાણા ઉપર વાંચવા સારૂં એક પુસ્તકખાનું, અને ગમતને ખાતર નાટક કરવાનો એક મોહોટો ઓરડો બનાવેલો છે અને તેની આરાસ્તગી મોહોટ મોહોટી લડાઈ અને કીલ્લાઓનાં ચીત્રો અને તરવાર નકશા દેવાલો ઉપર ટાંગીને કરેલીછે. તેમાં કેટલાએક ઘણાજ જોવા લાયક અને સુશોભીત ચિત્રો જેવાં કે શીબાસ્ટેપોલ, ત્રાફાળગર, અને નાઈલની લડાઇઓના તથા જીબરાલ-

ટરના કિલ્લાના આઈલિકલાથ ઉપર પાડેલાં મોહોટા ચીતારો હમોએ જોયા હતા. આ મકાનનો સઘળો કારભાર માત્ર ઇંગ્રેજી લશ્કરના સીપાઈ અને અમલદારોથીજ ચાલેછે. એ મકાન દેખાડવાને હમારી સાથે તેનો ચંચલ સેક્રેટરી એક ઇંગ્રેજ સાર્જંટ હતો તેણે હમને જણાવ્યું કે સોલજરોને વાંચવા સારૂ ઇંગ્રેજી વર્તમાન પત્રો તથા ચોપાંનીઆં ખરીદ કરવામાં આવેછે, અને આ નાહાનાં પુસ્તકખાનાનો સારો ઉપયોગ આ જગા ઉપરનું ઇંગ્રેજી લશ્કર કરેછે. એક એલાહેદો ઓરડો તરેવાર રમતો બેસીને રમવાનો પણ કીધો હતો, તેમાં સેતરંજ, ડાંમ, પાનાં તથા તેવી બીજી રમતો મુકેલી હતી. આ પુસ્તકખાનાને ઇંગ્રેજી લશ્કરનાં અમલદારો તથા બીજા ગ્રહસ્થો વખતે વખત મદત કરેછે; અને સેક્રેટરીએ આવી ઇચ્છા જણાવ્યાથી હમારામાંથી બે ચાર જણે મળીને એક શારી રકમ બખશેશ તરીકે ભરી આપી હતી.

હીયાંથી નીકલીને નવી બાંધેલી ઇસપીટાલ જોવા ગયા; તે એક જોવાલાયક અને આંખમાંથી ખીસે નહી એવી ખુબસુરત બાંધણી થયલીછે. ત્રીમલગીરીમાં ઇંગ્રેજી લશ્કરની છાવણીછે, અને તેમને સારૂ જેટલી ઇમારતો બાંધ્યામાં આવીછે તે દરએક ઇમારત મુંબઇને શરમમાં નાખે એવીછે. આ ઇમારતોની શોભા તથા તેમની ઉપરની કફલાતનો ચળકાટ એવોતો સુંદરછે કે ઇમારતો જાણે સંગેમરમરની બનાવી હોય એવી લાગેછે. સઘળી ઇમારતોમાં "ગ્રાનાઇટ" પથર વાપરેલોછે અને ચુનો એવોતો ચીકણોછે કે એક ચીજને બીજી સાથે પંકડી રાખી પથર જેવી મજબુત કરેછે. હેદરાબાદમાં ઘણેક ઠેકાણે હમોએ ઇંટોનું ગુલમારીને બનાવેલું બાંધકામ જોયુંછે, અને તે જોકે ઘણી લાંબી મુદતનુંછે તોપણ આજે તેમાંથી એક કગરસભાર ચુનો છુટો પડ્યો નથી. સીકંદરાબાદના ચુનાના પથરની ખુબી પ્રખ્યાત થયલીછે. ત્રીમલગીરીમાં ઇંગ્રેજી લશ્કરની છાવણીને સારૂ બાંધેલી ઇમારતોમાં પરણેલા અને છડા સીપાઇઓના રેહેવાના જુદાં જુદાં મકાન કરીયાંછે. ઇસ્પીટાલમાં બીમાર માણસોને સારૂ જે ઓરડા બનાવેલાછે તેમાં રોશની અને હવા આવવા જવાના માર્ગો ઓલા અને કોશાદ રાખેલાછે તથા આસપાસ કાચનાં બારીબારણાંની જે ગોઠવણો કરેલીછે તેવી આજે મુંબઇમાં કેટલાએક મોહોટા શેઠીઆઓનાં સીણગારેલા મકાનોમાં નહીં કરેલી હશે. સઘળી ઇમારતો બાંધતાં ૧૧) અગીઆર લાખ

રૂપીઆ ખરચ થયલા કેહેવાયછે, અને તે સઘળો નીજામ સરકારે આપ્યોછે. ત્રીમલગીરીની આ ઈમારતોનાં ફોટોગ્રાફ વીશે હમોએ ઘણી ખોળ તે વખતે કીધી, કે તેમાંથી થોડાક આ ઠેકાણે આપીને વાંચનારને આ સુંદર બાંધણીનો દેખાવ નજરે પાડીએ; પણ તે વખતે તે નહીં મળી આવ્યાથી હમોને આ વીચાર છોડી દેવો પડયો હતો. તે બંધાયાપછી કોઈપણ ફોટોગ્રાફરે આ ઈમારતોનાં ચીત્રો લેવાને લાંબી મુદત જવા નહીં દીધી હશે, કારણ ફોટોગરાફીની પુરી ખુબી દેખાડવાને આ બાંધણીઓ ઘણીજ લાયક બનાવેલીછે.

ઈસપીટાલ જોયા પછી પાછા ફરતાં, સીકંદરાબાદનાં ફ્રીમેસનોની લાડ્જ નામે સેંટ જાન, નંબર ૬૨૮ વાળી ઇંગ્રેજી ગ્રાંડ લાડ્જનાં તાલુકા હેઠળની જોઈ. આ લાડ્જને સારૂ એક નાહાનો મકાન સીકંદરાબાદનાં લશ્કરી અમલદારોએ અને બીજા તીહાંના રેહેવાસીઓએ મલીને પોતાને ખરચે બાંધ્યોછે. આ મકાન છાવણીમાંજછે અને તેનો ઉપયોગ તથા લાભ જુજ બીજા સીવાએ ઘણુંકરીને લશ્કરીજ અમલદારો ભોગવેછે. તીહાંની છાવણીનાં સ્કુલ માસ્તર સાથ હમારી મોલાકાત અકસ્માત થઈ હતી અને તે પોતે ફ્રીમેસન ઓળખાયાથી તેની મારફતે લાડ્જનું મકાન અંદરથી હમને જોવાને બની આવ્યું હતું. રાત્રે ળ્ા વાગે શેઠ પંથકીની દુકાન ઉપર પાછા ફેરો મારીને ૮ા વાગે સેઠ વીકાજીનાં મકાન ઉપર જઈ પુગા હતા. રાત્રે જમતાં જમતાં ટેબલ ઉપર એવો ઠરાવ કીધો કે બીજે દીને એટલે (તારીખ ૨ જી જાનેવારીએ) ગોલકંડાનાં મકબરા એટલે કબરો જોવા જવું. આ મકબરા ઘણાજ ઉંચા અને જોવા લાયકછે. તેમનાં ઉપર ઘણાં ઉંચા મીનારા અથવા ગુંબજો બાંધેલાછે. તેમાંના ઘણાક હવડાં ખીસ્માર અને પાયમાલ થઈ ગયલી હાલતમાં પડેલાછે, તોપણ પોતાનો અસલી દબદબો તેઓએ હજુ ખોયા નથી, અને તેમની હાલની વેરાનીમાં હજુ તેમની અસલી શોભા અને રોનક દીપેછે અને તે વીશે જોનારનાં મન ઉપર સારી અસર થઈ શકેછે. શેઠ બાપુજીએ એવી મસલહત આપી કે તડકો નહીં લાગે એટલા અરસામાં હેદરાબાદથી ગોલ-કંડા પોહોંચવું બેહેતરછે, અને મંજલ માત્ર બે કલાકનીછે તેથી સહવારનાં પરો-ઢીયામાં ઉઠીને જવાની સઘળી તૈયારી કરાવી રાખશે એવું તેવણે હમને કેહ્યું હતું. પણ તે રાત્રે હમને તે વીશે કશી ખબર નહીં હતી કે તે તઈયારી તે કેહેવી કીસમ-ની હશે. પાછલી રાત્રે માલુમ પડીયું કે હમારે સારૂ એવીતો માહાભારત અને

જાણે કોઈ રાજવંશીઓને સારૂં તઈઆરી કીધી હોય એવી જાહોજલાલી અને દબદબા ભરેલી રચના કરી મેલી હતી. આવી હમારી માવજત ઉપરથી શેઠ બાપુજીનું ખઈ મોહોટું દીલ તથા પોતાનાં મીત્રોની મોહોબતથી કેમ મેહમાનદારી અને બરદાસત કરવી તે ખુલી માલુમ પડી આવી હતી.

તા૦ ૨ જી જાનેવારી—પાછલી રાત્રે ૪ાા વાગે હમો સઘળા ખાબથી બેદાર થયા. હુકમ આપી રાખેલો હતો તે મુજબ કાફી તૈયાર હતી, જે હાથ મોહોડું પાક કરી, નોરા કીધી અને થંડીની મોસમનાં કપડાં પેહેરી માલ ઉપરથી હેઠળ ઉતરી ઓ-ટલા ઉપર આવી ગાડીમાં બેસવાની ઉમેદથી જોઈએ છીએ તો ગાડીને ઠેકાણે છ મોહોટા બુલંદ હાથીઓ ઓટલાની પાયરી આગળ પોતાની લાંબી સુંડ ઝુલાવતા હારબંધ ઉભેલા જોયા. કેટલાએક ઉપર અંબાડી બાંધી હતી તેમાં માતર બેજ સવારને બેસવાની જગા કરેલી હતી; અને કેટલાએકો ઉપર બે બે જણા એક એકની પીઠ મેળવીને બેસે તેવી કોચ જેવી ખુલી બેઠક કરેલી હતી. જો સંકડા-ઇને બેસવા ચાહીએતો ત્રણ ત્રણ માણસ એક એકની પીઠ મેળવીને છ જણ પણ એક હાથી ઉપર બેસી શકેછે. પણ તેવી રીતે ભચડાઇને બેસવું દરબારી રવૈયામાં હલકું ગણાયછે, અને તે જાણે મુંબઈમાં જેમ રાત્રે વાડીથી જમી ખાઈ છાંટો પાણી લઇને આપણા કેટલાક સાહેબો એકબીજાનાં દોસ્ત આશનાઓને મોહોબતથી લઇ, એક બીજાને ઘેર પોંહોંચાડવા, એક શીગરામમાં બે જણ કોચ-બાકસ ઉપર, ત્રણ દુ છ જણ અંદર, અને રમુજી કોઈ શોખી દોસ્ત એક જણ પછવાડે બેસીને ધીમે ધીમે ઘેર પોંહોંચેછે, તેમનો જેવો રકાસ થાયછે, તેવો છ જણ હાથી ઉપર બેઠેલાનો હેદરાબાદમાં રકાસ થાયછે. આ સ્વારીમાં એક બે હાથીઓ ફકત સાદી ખુલી ઓધાવાળી બેઠકનાં પણ હતા. આવો દીગાંમ જોઇને હમને જેવી એક તરફથી ખુશી ઉપજી હતી તેવીજ બીજી તરફથી હાથી ઉપર કોઈ દીન બેઠેલા નહીં હતા અને બેસવાનો વખત એકાએક આવી પુગો તેથી દીલમાં જરા તાજુબી સાથે ધકધક પણ ઉતપન થઈ હતી. હાથી ઉપર બેસવાની અંબાડી ઘણી ઉંચી હોયછે, તેથી તે ઉપર બેસવા આગમચ હાથીને બેસાડવો પડેછે, અને બેસાડયા પછી પણ વળી તે ઉપર છ સાત ફાંગીયાની નાહાંની શિડી મુકેછે તેઉપર ચઢીને અંબાડીમા બેસાયછે. બેઠા પછી હાથીને પાછો જારે ઉઠાડેછે તે વખતે આ જનાવર પોતાના બે આગલે પગે પેહેલાં ઉભો થઈ પછી પાછલે પગે ઉઠેછે,

જેથી ઉપર બેસનારને પેહેલી ઉઠકમાં પછવાડે જાણે તે ગગડી જતો હોય એટલું નીચે ઢળાઈ જવું પડેછે. આ વખતે જો તેણે સાઉચેતી નહીં રાખીતો ખરેખરજ હાથી ઉપરથી તે ગગડીને નીચે જમીનદોસ્ત દશ બાર ફુટની ઉંચાઈ ઉપરથી કદાચ થયા વગર નહીં રેહે. પણ એકબે વાર આસરમ પડી એટલે એ વીરોની ધાસ્તી નીકલી જાયછે, અને જારે હાથી ઉઠવાનો હોય ત્યારે બેસનારે પોતાનાં શરીરને આગળથી ઝોકાવ્યુંતો ઉપર જણાવેલી રીતે પડી જવાની જરાપણ ધાસ્તી અથવા દીલને ખણુસા લાગતી નથી. હમો કેટલાએક જણ સવાર થઈ આગળ ચાલ્યા, અને હમારી પછવાડે કેટલાએક આવતા થયા. આ પુસ્તકની સીરૂઆતમાં ઈસારો કરેલા એક જુવાન પેહેલવાન મદદગારનો આ વખતે જેવો રમુજી તેવોજ દયા ઉપજાવનાર દેખાવ હાથી ઉપર બેશતાં થયો હતો. બેસવા આગમચથી તે જુઆન શખસ બીહીને તાટ થઈ ગયો હતો. તેના મનમાં વીચાર આવીયો કે આ શી આપદા આવી પડીછે; કેટલે ઉંચે ચઢીને બેસવું, એથી તેના મનમાં તુરત દેહેશત પેઠી. તેણે બેસવાની જરા આનાકાની પેહેલાં જણાવી પણ તુરત તેની રખેને મશકરી થાય એટલા ઉપરથી જેટલી હીંમત કરી શકાઈ તેટલી હીંમત તેણે કીધી અને હાથી ઉપર શિડીની મારફતે તે ચઢીતો બેઠો. જીવ તેનો સટોસટ થઈ ગયલો હતો; તોએપણ તેને જે ખુબ હીંમત આપ્યામાં આવી હતી તેથી તેણે દાંત પીસીને હીંમત પકડી રાખી હતી. પણ જેવો હાથી આગલ પગે ઉઠયો કે તેને પછવાડેથી ગગડી પડવા જેવું લાગાથી એકદમ બુમ પાડી કે, અરરર પડયો રે પડયો, અરે મને કોઈ પકડો, અરરર હું મરી ગયો, એવું બોલતાં તેની હોશ એટલીતો ઉડી ગઈ કે તે થંડોગાર થઈ ગયો. તેની પાસે બેઠેલા બીજા શખસે તેને સારી પેઠે સાઉચેતીથી પકડી રાખીયો હતો તોએપણ તેના હાથ પગ ધ્રુજવા લાગા, અને પસીનાંથી ગરકાવ થઈ તેની તબીયત છેક નાબુરા થઈ ગઈ. તુરત તેને નીચેઉતારયો, પડવાની ધાસ્તીએ તેનીઉપર એવીતો અસર કીધી કે તે બીચારાને તુરત બેત્રણ વખત ઝાડાની હાજત થઈ પડી હતી. થોડીક ગરમ ચાહે બનાવી તુરત પાયા પછી સઘળું સમાધાન થતામાં જે વખત ગયો તેટલાંમાં સહવારનો પોહોર થયો. હમારા મીત્રોમાનાં કેટલાએકજણ જેઓ પેહેલાં આગળ નીકલી ગયા હતા તેમને એ વીરોનીતો કાંઈજ ખબર નહીં હતી, તેઓ એવુંજ સમજતા હતા કે તેમના બીજા સાથીઓ પછવાડે હળવે હળવે આવેછે.

હવે એણી તરફ પેલા જુવાન શખ્સને હાથી ઉપર પાછી સવારી કરાવાને ઘણી હીમત ફરી આપીયામાં આવી હતી. અંતે, રાત્રે અંધારામાં જે ધાસ્તી ભરેલું લાગતું હતું અને બરોબર દેખાતું નહી હતું તે સહવારની રોશનીથી બરોબર તેને દેખાયું હતું. હાથી પેહેલાં ઊઠેછે ત્યારે પાછળથી તે કેટલો નીચે ઢળતો થાયછે તે નજરે દીઠાથી પેલા જુવાન શખ્સની હીમતે જરા મજબુતી પકડી. જેમ તેમ કરીને એકવાર ફરીથી અજમાએશ કીધી, તેમાં આસપાસના ભાઈઓની હીમતથી આખેરે તે લોકડી પેહેલવાને હાથી ઊપર સ્વારી કરવામાં ફતેહ મેળવી હતી. જે હાથી ઊપર આ શખ્સને પેહેલાં બેસાડીયો હતો તે હાથી ઉપર કોચ રોકી બેઠક બાંધેલી હતી, જે બેઠક ખુલી હોવાના સબબથી કાચા બેશનારને તે વધારે ધાસ્તી ભરેલી લાગે એમાં નવાઈ નથી. એટલા ઉપરથી આ શખ્સને બીજીવાર અંબાડીની બેઠક જે ચોતરફથી બંધીયાર હોયછે તેવી બેઠકમાં બેસાડીને છેક સહવારના ૭ વાગે ડોલતા ડોલતા ગોલકુંડાના મકબરા આગળ લાવીયા હતા.

ગોલકંડામાં જે પેહેલી કબર હમારા જોવામાં આવી તેની ઉપર જેવો મોહોટો ઉઠાવદાર અને દબદબા ભરેલો ગુંબજ બાંધેલો છે તેવો બીજી કબરો ઉપર હમારા જોવામાં નથી આવીયો. ૫૨) પાયરી ચઢયા પછી પેહેલો બેસવા ઉઠવાનો તબક્કો આવેછે, અને એટલા ઊંચા તબક્કા ઉપર પોંહોંચ્યા પછી ગુંબજનો ઘેર તથા ગોલ-વાટો શીરૂ થાયછે. આ ગોલવાટાનો કળસ ઉપલા તબક્કાથી આસરે બીજા ૬૦ ફુટ ઊંચો છે, તેથી આખો મકબરો જમીનની સપાટીથી તે ગુંબજની મથાળેની અણી શુધી નજદીક ૧૦૦થી ૧૧૨ ફુટ ઉંચો છે. આ ઉંચાઈ આપણા મુંબઈનાં સેંટ થામસ દેવળની ઊંચાઈથી માત્ર ૨૫) ફુટ ઓછી જાણવી. ગુંબજની ઊપર તરેવાર નકશીકામ કરેલું છે. તે હવડાં ભાંગી તુટી અને પરાગંદે હાલતમાં નજરે પડેછે. નકસીકામમાં તરેવાર જીનસોની નકલ કરેલી છે. નાગની ફેણો, અનેનાસ, કમ-રખ, સીતાફળ, અને નાળીએર વીગરે અનેક જીનસોનાં આબેહુબ આકાર અચ્છી કારીગીરી ભરેલા ચુનાંકામના બનાવેલા છે. ગુંબજનો ઘેર અષ્ટકોણ એટલે આઠ ખુણાનો બનાવ્યો છે, અને તેની આસપાસ ચોમેરથી દશ ફુટ પોહોળી ફરતી અગાસી બનાવી છે. ગુંબજ અંદર જવાનો માર્ગ એકજ છે, અને તે હેવણ પડયાથી તેમાં વાગુલોઆની અપાર પુશ્કળ એકઠી થયલી છે જેથી દર-વાજામાં પેસતાંજ અંદરથી અતીશય બદબો મારેછે. ગુંબજમાંથી પડસાદ

નીકળેછે પણ તેની પોકળાઈ અને કદ પ્રમાણે જેવો પડસાદ મોટો નીકળવો જોઇયે તેટલો નીકળતો નથી. એનું કારણ કદાચને અંદર જે અધારનો ઢગ પડેલો છે તેથી હોય. તોપણ તપાસ કરતાં એટલું માલુમ પડ્યું હતું કે જો કોઈ શખસ ગુંબજ અંદર જઈ દેવાલ આગળ નજદીક મોહોડું કરી ધીમે આવાજે બોલે તો તે છેક ૫૦) ફુટ દુર ગુંબજનાં દરવાજાની દેવાલ આગળ કાન મુકીને સાંભળનારને ખુલું અને પલગડું સંભળાતું હતું. મકબરામાં ગુંબજ સુધી ચઢવાને જે પાયરીઓ બનાવી છે તે પથરની ગોલ ચક્રાકારે બાંધેલી છે. સઘળું કામ પથરનું છે, અને આખા મકબરાની બાંધણીનો ખરચ રાજદરબારી કારભાર પ્રમાણે ગણતાં, પાંચથી છ લાખ સુધીનો થયો હોય એવું માનવામાં આવી શકેછે.

ઉપર જણાવેલું બયાન તો કબર ઉપર જે માહાભારત અને ઉંચો ગુંબજ બાંધીયો છે તેનું કીધું. હવે જે જગાએ ઘોર છે અથવા બીજા શબ્દોમાં બોલીએ તો જે ઠેકાણે મરનાર પાદશાહની લાશને ગાડી છે તે જગાનું બયાન કરીએછ. ખુલા એક દીવાનખાનાં જેવા ઓરડામાં (અરધી ફુટની ઊંચાઇનાં) ચાર નાહાનાં નાહાનાં તબક્કાવાલી એક કબર છે જે કાળા સગેમરમરનાં પથરની બનાવેલી છે. આ પથરને તીહાંના લોક "સંગેમુસા" કરીને કેહેછે. કબરની રચના એવી રીતે કરેલી છે કે છેક હેઠળ એક આખો પથર મુકેલો છે. આ પથરની ચોમેરથી ચાર અથવા પાંચ ઇંચ જગા છોડી એક બીજો પથર ઉપર ગોઠવીયો છે જેથી એક પાયરી અથવા તબક્કો થયો છે. વળી ત્રણ ચાર ઇંચ જગા છોડી બીજો તબક્કો ઉપર જણાવીયા પ્રમાણે બનાવીયો છે, અને તેમજ ત્રીજો અને ચોથો પણ કરીયો છે. આ પ્રમાણેની બાંધણીનો આકાર નીચે જણાવ્યા મુજબ થયો છેઃ—

સઉથી હેઠળનાં પથરની જાડાઈ તેની ઊપરનાં પથર કરતાં વધારે છે, અને એ પ્રમાણે છેક ઊપરનો પથર સઉથી ઓછી જાડાઇનો છે. એ કબરના સઉથી ઊપરના પથર ઉપર અરબી અક્ષરે પાદશાહનું નામ તથા તેના મરણની તારીખ, વાર, તથા સને લખેલો છે. મરદ અને ઓરતની કબર ઓળખવાનો ખુલાસો

એ છે કે જો છેક મથાલેના પથરની ઊપરની સપાટી સાફ સરખી હોયતો તે કબર મરદની જાણવી; પણ જો તે સપાટીમાં ખાંભણુ અથવા ખાડો કોતરેલો હોયતો તે કબર ઓરતની જાણવી.

ઊપલા મીનારાની પશ્ચીમ દીશાએ એક બીજો મીનારો છે, તેના ગુંબજ ઊપર મીનાકામ ઘણુંજ સુંદર આગલા વખતમાં કરેલું હશે તેની નીશાનો આજે હજુસુધી દેખાયછે. હવડાં તો તે ભાંગીને સઘળું બીસમાર હાલતમાં પડેલું છે, તોએપણ આગલી ખુબસુરતી અને રોનક હજુર ઠેકાણે ઠેકાણે વળગી રેહેલા મીના અને કોડીકામના કેટલાક આખાને આખા કકડાઓમાં હજુર આપણે જોઈ શકીએછ. જે મીનાકામ કરેલું છે તે ગુંબજ ઉપર અને આખી ઈમારતની દેવાલો ઉપર કરેલું છે જેમાં તરેહવાર રંગબેરંગીન સમચોરસ અને બીજી અનેક આકૃતીવાળા કોડીના કકડા ખીલાથી જડી લીધેલા છે. હાલ કેટલેક ઠેકાણે ખીલા મોજુદ દેખાયછે, અને બીજી જગાએ ખીલાના સુરાખો ખુલા નજરે પડેછે. જારે આ સઘળું મીનાકામ બરાબર હાલતમાં હશે ત્યારે આ ઈમારતનો દેખાવ કેટલો જેબદાર હશે એ વીશે વીચાર આ બાંધણીઓની હાલની હાલત જોનારને સેહેજમાં આવશે. આ કીસમની કારીગરીનો એક નમુનો આગળ આપેલો છે. હમો એવું નથી જણાવા માંગતા કે તે ચીત્રમાં જણાવેલો ગુંબજ જેવો રંગબેરંગી અને મીના અને નકસીકામથી ભરપુર ચીત્રેલો છે, તેવોજ ગોલકંડાનો ગુંબજ છે, પણ હમારી કેહેવાની મકસદ એજ છે કે જારે ગોલકંડાવાળો ગુંબજ આખો હશે તારે તેની શેાભાનો દેખાવ આવી તરેના ચીત્ર જેવો દેખાતો હશે એમાં કંઈ શખ નથી. જે ચીત્ર આગળ દેખડાવીયું છે તે પાદશાહા અકબરની કબરઘા ઊપર બાંધેલી ઈમારતના અંદરના ભાગમાં કરેલાં નકસી અને મીનાકામનું છે, જે વીશે ઠેકાણાસર વીસ્તારીને લખેલું છે. ગોલકંડામાં ૧૮ થી ૨૦ ગુંબજો એકેકની પાસે બાંધેલા છે, અને તેઓ સઘળા કબરઘા ઉપર બાંધેલા છે, આ ઊપરથી માલુમ પડેછે કે ગોલકંડામાં ઘણાખરા કુતબશાહી ખાનદાનના પાદશાહ, શાહાજાદા અને અમીરોની કબરઘા થયલી છે. ગોલકંડા, આગલા વખતમાં અને હેદરાબાદ શેહેર મસ્યાની આગમજ, કુતબશાહી પાદશાહોનું એક મુખ્ય મથક હતું.

એક મીનારો એવી સમતલતથી બાંધ્યામાં આવ્યો છે કે બાર તથા પંદર ફુટને

છેટે હારબંધ પથરના થાંભા બાંધી લઈ હેઠળની સઘળી જગા પોકળ અથવા ખુલી રાખી છે અને આ થાંભા ઊપર મીનારાનો ટેકાવ અથવા પાયો કરીયો છે. હેઠળની પોલાણમાં મુસાફરોને અથવા ફકીરોને ઊતારો કરવાની જગા છે અને તે સઘળી મળીને આસરે ૩૦૦૦) ત્રણ હજાર માણસો સેહેલાઇથી ઊતારો કરી રહી શકે એટલા મોહોટા વીસ્તારની છે. આ મુકામની આસપાસ સઘળી તરફ અચ્છી અમરાઈ અને લેહેજતદાર પાણી જેટલું જોઇયે તેટલું છે. હમારી સાથે હેદરાબાદથી હલકો જેવો જે નાસ્તો લઈ આવ્યા હતા તે હાવી અમરાઈની જગા ઉપર સારીપેઠે ખાવો હતો. સવાનવ વાગે તનદરોસ્ત થઈ પાછા હાથી ઉપર સ્વાર થયા અને હેદરાબાદ તરફ પાછા ફરતી વેળા, આ શેહેરનો કેટલોક ભાગ જોવાને બની આવવા સારૂ શેહેરમાં થઇને જવાનો હુકમ હાથીના માહવતને સેઠ બાપુજીએ આગમનથી આપી રાખેલો હતો, તે મુજબ હમો ગોલકંડાથી શેહેરને રસ્તે રવાના થયા. હરકોઈ શેહેર પગે ચાલીને જોવું અને હાથી ઉપર બેસીને જોવું એમાં ફેર છે. હાથી ઉપર બેસી સેહેલગાહા કરનારને ઊચી બેઠક મળ્યાથી જેમ આસપાસની જમીન ઉપરની રચના ખુલી દેખાયછે, તેમજ ઘરોનાં પેહેલા માળ ઉપરની રચના અને તીહાં બેઠેલાં લોક પણ નજરે પડી શકેછે, જે પગે ચાલનારને અથવા ગાડીમાં બેસી ફરનારને નજરે નથી પડી શકવાનાં. હાથી ઉપર બેસનારને આસપાસની રચના કેવી રીતે નજરે પડતી હશે આ વીશે જો કોઈ જાણવાં માગે તો "આમનીબસો" ની ઉપરની બેઠક પરથી જેમ મોહોલ્લા અથવા રસ્તા ઉપરનાં ઘરોનો દેખાવ નજરે પડેછે તે મુઆફક હાથી ઉપરથી પણ દેખાયછે, ફરક એટલોજ પડશે કે હાથી ધીમી ચાલ ચાલેછે તેથી જોનારને જોવાની તક અચ્છી મળી શકેછે. તેમજ બીજો ફરક એ છે કે મુંબઈમાંનાં ઘરોની ઉભરણી ઘણુંકરીને ઉંચી હોયાથી જેટલી સેહેલાઈથી હેદરાબાદનાં ઘરોનાં માળ ઉપરની રચના હાથી ઊપરથી જોવાઈ શકાયછે તેટલી અત્રેનાં ઘરોની નહી જોવાઈ શકાશે. હેદરાબાદનાં ઘરો ઘણાખરાં ઘણી ઊચી ઉભરણીનાં નથી તેથી હાથી ઉપર બેસી ફરનાર જો ચાહે તો કોઈ ઘરની બારીમાં બેઠેલા હરકોઈ માણસને હાથી ઉપર સેહેજ ખેંચી અથવા ઊચકી લેઈ શકે એવું છે, અથવા ચાહે તો હાથીને બારી આગળ લઈ જઈ આસાનીથી ફલાંગ મારી બારી વાટે ઘરનાં માળમાં ઘુસી શકે એવું છે, અને આવી રીતે ઘણીવાર કોઈ કોઈ શેહેરના લોકનાં ઘરમાંથી તેમનાં છોકરાં છૈયાંને જબરીથી

ઊંચકી લઈ જવાની અથવા જબરીથી ઘરોમાં પેસી જવાની ફરિઆદ, કેટલાક છંદી અમીર ઉમરાવો અને એવાજ વીલક્ષણીત માતબરો વીરો થયલી સાંભળ્યામાં આવી હતી તે ખરેખર બનવા જોગ છે. આવીશે, જારે હમો હાથી ઊપર બેસી રોહેરમાંથી પસાર થતા હતા તારે જે કંઈ હમોએ જોયું તેથી હમારી ખાતરી સારી પેઠે થઈ હતી.

રોહેરમાંથી પસાર થતાં ઘણાજ સાંકડા રસ્તા અને ગલી ગુંચીઓમાંથી હાથીઓને ચલાવવા પડયા હતા, પણ આવી સાંકડી જગામાં ચાલવાને હાથીઓને કંઈ પણ અડચણ લાગી હોય એવું હમારા જોયામાં આવ્યું નહી હતું. ભાજી તરકારી વીગરે બીજો ખાધ ખોરકીનો સામાન જેમ અત્રે ઘણુંકરીને ઉંચી દુકાનો અથવા બેઠકો ઉપર વેચવાને મુકેછે તેમ હેદરાબાદમાં નથી મુકતા. સહવારસાંજનું તરકારી બજાર ઘણુંકરીને રસ્તાની બંધે બાજુએ ભોંય ઊપર પીછોડી પાંથરી તે ઉપર માલ ગોઠવેલું ભરાયછે. આ પાંથરેલી દુકાંનો વચ્ચેથી હાથીઓ એવી તો સફાઈ અને સંભાળથી ચાલી જાયછે કે કોઈ પણ જીનસ તેમનાં પગતળે ચંપાતી નથી: આસપાસ વેરાએલી જીનસો રખેને તેમના ભારી પગતળે છુંદાઈ અથવા કચડાઈ જાય તેનો અટકાવ કરવાને આ જાનવરો તેમની પ્રેરણા બુદ્ધિથી સંભાળ રાખીને પોતાના કદમો મુકેછે, તે ઘણું જોવાલાયક છે.

હાથી ઉપર બેસનારને એક વાતની સંભાળ રાખવાની ઘણીજ જરૂર છે, તે એ છે જે જારે હાથી જંગલોમાંથી અથવા ઝાડોની હેઠળથી ચાલી જતો હોય ત્યારે ઘણીવાર એવું બનેછે કે સામા આવતાં ઝાડોની ડાળીઓ ગફલતીમાં બેસી રેહેનારને માથાંમાં વાગીયા અથવા અથડયા સીવાએ નથી રેહેતી, માટે એ વીરો બેસનારે પોતે સાઉચેતી રાખી દુરથી જોવું જોઇએછ. માર્ગમાં ઝાડો નમેલાં દેખાય અને માથાં સાથે અથડવાની ધાસ્તી હોયતો ઘણી વખતતો માહાવત પોતે હાથીને વટાવી બાજુએથી ચલાવેછે, પણ કોઈવાર તેમ નથી થઈ શકતું, તારે બેહતર એ છે કે તેવી જગા ઉપરથી જતાં વાંકા વળવું અથવા અંબાડી અંદર અકડુ બેસી જવું, પણ હાથી ઉપર અંબાડી બાંધેલી નહી હોય અને હોદો બાંધેલો હોય તો તે ઓલી બેઠક ઉપર બેસનારોએ એવી ઝાડ ઝાંખડની કફોરી જગાએથી કુચ કરતી વેળા સંભાળ રાખવી અગત્ય છે. હાથી ઉપર બેસવામાં અંબાડી જેવી સલામત બેઠક બીજી કોઈ નથી. હોદાની બેઠક બેસનારોને માત્ર દમામ અને દેખાવ

કરવાને તથા રોહેરના લોકને અને તેની રચના જોવા તથા ધુરવા ઘણીજ લાયક અને પસંદ છે. અંબાડી શીકાર કરવાને અને એવી બીજી સખત મુસાફરી કરવાને અથવા મંજલ મારવાને લાયકની બેઠક છે. સારી ચાલવાળા હાથીઓ ઉપર, બેસનારને કંઈજ આંચકો લાગતો નથી, પણ ભાર અથવા બોજો ઉંચકનાર એવાં જનાવરો ઉપર, બેસનારને આગળ પાછળ જબરો આંચકો લાગ્યાજ કરેછે, જેથી તેની કંમર ઘણી વખત દોદરી થઈ જાયછે. ગોલકંડાથી સહવારના ૯ વાગે નીકળેલા બપોરના ૧૨ વાગે પાછા રોઠ બાપુજી વીકાજીના મુકામ ઉપર આવી પોંહોંચ્યા.

એજ દીને પાછલા પોહોરના ૩। સવા ત્રણ વાગે નીજામના વજીર નવાબ સર સાલારજંગ, મુખતીયાર-ઉલ-મુલ્કની ભેટ લેવાને ગયા. આ ભેટ નીજામ દરબારનાં કાયદા કાનુનો મુજબ કેમ લેવી આ વીશે આગમચથી ગોઠવણ કરવાને રોઠ બાપુજી વીકાજી તથા નવાબના તે વખતના એક વીશ્વાસુ કારભારી, અને ખાસ દોસ્ત સેઠ જમરોદજી ખુરરોદજી સુરતી, જેવણને હેદરાબાદમાં મુનશીના એલકાબથી બોલતા હતા, તેવણ સાથે વાતચીત થઈ હતી, તે ઉપરથી હમને એવું જણાવામાં આવ્યું કે નીજામ દરબારમાં મોહોટી પાગડી બાંધીને જવું નાપસંદ છે. આ નાપસંદગીનું શું કારણ હશે એ વીશે કોઇથી પણ મનમાનતો અથવા ખરો ખુલાસો નહી મળ્યો હતો. કોઇથી એવું સાંભળ્યું હતું કે સર સાલારજંગ પોતાનાં માથાંઉપર નાહાનો સરપોશ અથવા પાગડી પેહેરેછે તે કર્તાં કોઇ બીજાએ વધારે મોહોટી પાગડી પેહેરીને તેની સાંમે જવું નહી, પણ આ બીના ખરી હોય એવું હમે માનતા નથી, તથા એનો જોખમ હમારે માથે લેતા નથી. હમોએ આવો પોશાક પેહેરવો અથવા નહી એ વીશે લાંબો વીચાર કીધો, તેનું પરીણામ એટલુંજ નીકળ્યું કે કોઈ રાજદરબારનો રવૈયો કેવો છે, એ જો જોવાની ઇચ્છા થઈ હોય તો તે ઇચ્છા પુરી પાડવા સારૂ તે રાજદરબારના રવૈયા તથા કાયદા કાનુનો પ્રમાણે ચાલવું તો જોઇયે. અગર તે પ્રમાણે નહી ચાલીયા તો તેવીરો આપણી ઉપર કોઇની જબરદસ્તી નથી, પણ એટલુંજ કે જે આપણે જોવા માગીએછ તે મળી નથી શકવાનું. સર સાલારજંગને મળવાની ઇચ્છા હમારી થઈ હતી તેથી તેને મળવા જતાં જેમ તેની દરબારના કાનુનો હોય તે મુજબ ચાલવાની હમારી ઉપર એક ફરજ થઇ. તે કબુલ રાખવી કે નહી તે હમારે સ્વાધીન હતું.

કબુલ રાખતાં તે વજીરની મુલાકાત લેવાઈ શકાતી હતી અને તેની દરબારનો ઠાહાથાટ જોવાની તક મળી શકતી હતી. નહી કબુલ રાખવાથી સર સાલારજંગ કેવો વજીર છે, નીજામની દરબારનો ઠાહાથાટ કેવો છે, તેની દરબારનો રવૈયો અને બીજો આદરસતકાર કેવી રીતે તીહાં ચાલેછે, તે જોવાની અથવા જાણવાની તક નહી મળી શકે એવું નકી હતું. નાહાની પાગડી બાંધવી આ એક નિર્દોષ રેવાજ છે, એમાં કાંઇ પણ અનીતી અથવા અઘટીત રવૈયાને તાબે થયલું નથી બોલાવાનું, માટે નાહાની પાગડી બાંધીને મોહોટી ખુશીથી તે વજીરની મુલાકાત લેવાનો હમોએ નિશ્ચય કીધો. શેઠ બાપુજીને તીહાંથી તુરત હમારે સારૂ એવી નાહાની પાગડીઓ બાંધેલી તૈયાર મળી આવી. આ નાહાની પાગડીનું કદ વાંચનાર જાણવાને આતુર હશે. હમો તે તુરત કહી દઇએ છેએ કે તે પાગડીનું કદ આપણા પારસીઓના અસલી ખરા શેઠીઆઓની નાહાની બચુકલી ઠુમકી પાગડીઓના જેટલું હતું. વાંચનારોમાં ઘણા સાહેબોએ મરહુમ દાદી સેઠ, હોરમજી સેઠ, સેઠ જીહાંગીર વાહાડીયા, સેઠ ફરામજી કાવસજી, સેઠ જીજીભાઇ દાદાભાઇ જેવા નામવર સેઠીઆઓને જોયા હશે, તે સાહેબોનાં માથાં ઉપર જે અરધી વેહેંત જેટલી ઉંચાઇમાં અને ઘેરાવામાં પણ તેટલીજ, પાગડી નજર આવતી હતી અને જેને વીરો હવડાં ઇશકી ઓખ્ખાં પેહેરનારો અને ઉભા પેચની જીહીણાદાર ઘપની પાગડી બાંધનારો ટીકા કરેછે, તેવા કદની પાગડી હમોને પેહેરવી પડી હતી અને તે હમોએ મોટી ખુશીથી પેહેરી હતી. એવી પાગડી અને તેની સાથે જામો પેહેરવાથી હમારો દેખાવ હસવા જેવો થઇ પડયો હતો, અને હમો એક બીજાને જોઇને ખુબ હસીયા હતા. હમારી એવી મરજી થઇ હતી કે એવા પોશાક સાથે હમારો સઘળાનો ફોટોગ્રાફ તે વખતે ઉતરાવીએ, પણ તે જગાએ એ વિદ્યાનો કોઈ હુંનરી નહી હતો માટે હમારાથી એ કામ થઇ શક્યું નહી હતું. ટુકમાં બોલીએ તો ખરેખર હમારો આ દેખાવ ચીત્રવીચીત્ર થઈ પડયો હતો, તેના મુખ્ય કારણો એ હતાં કે જામાના ઘેરાવાથી હમારા શરીરનું કદ જેટલું બીહલું હતું તેટલું કદ હમારા ચેહેરાનું પેલી બેઠી, બચુકલી, ઠુમકી પાગડીથી નાહાનું થઈ ગયલું દેખાતું હતું. હમારા મીત્ર ડાકતર ભાઉ દાજીની પાગડી પણ ઘેરાવમાં નાહાની કરવી પડી હતી. હિંદુ રાજવંશીઓની મોહોટાઇ તેમની પાગડીના મોહોટા ઘેરાવથી માલુમ પડેછે. બેથી ત્રણ અથવા ચાર ફુટના ઘેરાવની પાગડીઓ તેઓ માથે

પેહેરેછે, તડકામાં તેઓને છતરીની તો ત્યારે જરૂર નહી, એવી મોહોટી પાગડીને ઠેકાણે ડાકતર સાહેબને માત્ર બે ત્રણ વેહેંતના ઘેરાવાની પાગડી પેહેરવી પડી હતી, તેથી તેમનાં શરીરના કદ સાથે સરખાવતાં માથે એક ઘણીજ નાહાની સરખી ટોપી જેટલી તે દેખાતી હતી.

માથાંઉપર આવો બેડોલ શીણગાર પેહેરીને પાછલા પોહોરના ૪ા વાગે ગાડીમાં બેસી શેઠ બાપુજી વીકાજીની સાથે હમારી સ્વારી નવાબના મેહેલ તરફ ચાલી. મેહેલમાં દાખલ થતાંજ હમને જોવાસારૂ તમાસગીરોની ઠઠ મળી. મુસલમીન જાતના આળસુ તમાસો જોનારાઓને કલ્પના કરવા શીખાડવાની કંઇ જરૂર નથી. ગમે એવી ડંફાસ મારવાના વીચાર ઘણીજ સેહેલાઇથી તેમના મગજમાં ઉત્પન્ન થઈ શકેછે, તે મુજબ હમારે વીશે જોનાર લોકમાં તુરત તરેવાર વાતો ચાલી. મરાહુર સર જમશેદજી જીજીભાઈ બારોનેટનું બુલંદ નામ જેવું આશકાર થયલું છે તેવુંજ એ નામથી આપણા પારશી ટોલાને ખરેખર એક મોટું માન થયલું છે. હીંદુસ્થાનનાં અંદરનાં પ્રાંતોમાં ઘણે ઠેકાણે આ હાતમ નામવરનું નામ આશકારાં છે તેથી કોઈબી તવંગર પારશીને તીહાંના લોક વગર અચકવે સર જમશેદજીના ખાનદાન સાથે જોડી નાખેછે. એજ કારણ ઉપરથી હમો જારે સર સાલારજંગને મળવા ગયા, તારે હમો સઘળાને નામદાર સર જમશેદજીના ખાનદાનનાં અમીરજાદા ગોઠવી બેસાડીયા હતા, અને કેટલાકો બોલવા લાગા કે "મુંબઈકે બાટલીવાલે સેઠકે અમીરજાદે હએ." કેટલાકોએ હમને મુંબઇના કરોડપતી સેઠ સાહુકારો ગણીયા હતા, અને આવી રીતિ આખી ભીડમાં હમારે વીશે ઘણાએક કલ્પીત વીચારો ચાલીયા હતા તથા બાંકે મીરજાંના જેવા તરેવાર એલકાબો હમને મળ્યા હતા, તેનું તો દાસ્તાન થઇ શકતું નથી.

મેહેલમાં જતાં પેહેલી મોલાકાત મીરજાં અલીમોહામદ શુસતરી જેવણ સર સાલારજંગના એક માનીતા દોસ્ત છે, તેવણ સાથે થઇ. મીરજાં અલીમોહામદ તે મુંબઇમાં થોડાંક વરસ ઉપર મજગાંમમાં જે પ્રખ્યાત નવાબ રેહેતા હતા તેવણના છોકરા થાયછે, અને જારે મુંબઇમાં આ જુવાન ગૃહસ્થ રેહેતા હતા ત્યારે ઇંગ્રેજોમાં અને પારસીઓમાં તેમને સારી મીત્રાચારી અને ઘરોબો હતો. મીરજાં સાથે થોડીઘણી વાત કર્યા પછી હમારી મુલાકાત થવા વીશે સર સાલારજંગને પુછવા ગયા, અને તીહાંથી આવીને હમને એવો જબાબ કહયો કે નવાબ

બીમાજમાં મશગુલ છે તેમાંથી ફારગ થાય તેની આગમચ નવાબે પોતાની ખુશી એવી જણાવી છે કે તેનો બારાદારીનો (એટલે બાર દરવાજાનો મેહેલ) તથા બીજા તેવણના જોવાલાયક મકાનો છે તે હમને દેખડાવવાં. એવું કહી મીરજાં હમને નવાબનો મેહેલ દેખાડવા લઇ ગયા. પેહેલા મકાનનું નામ આઇના મેહેલ એટલે આરસીનો મેહેલ હતો. આ મેહેલની તે વખતની રચના તેનાં નાંમને શોભા આપનારી અથવા લાયક નહી હતી. નામ મોહોટું છે પણ તેનું બયાન તેના નામને ઝાંખ લગાડે એવું છે. એક મોહોટું દીવાનખાનું છે તેમાં સઘળી તરફ દેવાલ ઉપર, થાંમલાઓ ઉપર, સીલીંગ ઉપર અને દરખુણે ખાંચે આરસીઓના નાહાના મોહોટા તખતા જડી લીધેલા છે. જીહાં જોઇયે તીહાં આરસીજ આરશી ; અને વળી તે એક તરેહની નહી. જેમ અને જેવી ડોલ બેડોલ મળી આવી હોય તેમ અને તેવીજ આ ઠેકાણે જડી લીધેલી છે. તેમાં કોઇની કલાઈ નીકળી ગયલી, કેટલીએકોની ફ્રેમ ભાગેલી, તેમની ઉપરનો સોનેરી ઢોળ નીકળી ગયલો, નકસી કામ ભાગી ગયલું, અને કેટલેએક ઠેકાણે આરસીનાં કાચોમાં તડ પડેલી; એવી હાલતમાં આ આઈના મેહેલ હમારા જોવામાં આવીયો હતો. તેમાં વળી જગો જગોએ ઝુંમર ટાંગેલાં તથા વાલરોડ જડેલાં હતાં. તે ઝુંમરો પણ અસલી તરેહનાં હતાં, ધાતુકામ ઉપર કાટ ચઢેલો, કોઈનાં શેડ ભાગેલાં, કોઇના લોલકો ગેપ થઇ ગયલાં, એવી વગર સંભાળ ભરેલી હાલતમાં આઇના મેહેલ જાણે ઘરમીનગારનાં સામાનનું સંગ્રહસ્થાન હતું. આઇના મેહેલનો ખેયાલ કદાચ વાંચનાર પોતાના મનમાં લાવવા માંગે તો તેણે દીવાલીનાં તેહેવાર ઉપર મુંબઇમાં કેટલીક દુકાનો ઉપર પરચુરણ હાંડી, આરસી અને ઝુંમરોનો, કચુંબર જેવો જમાવ થાયછે તે વીચારીયાથી થોડોક ખેયાલ આવી શકશે. આઇના મેહેલ વીશે હમારા સાંભલવામાં આવીયું છે કે સર સાલરજંગે હવડાં તેની શોભા અને રચનામાં ઘણોજ સારો વધારો કીધો છે, જે હાલ ખરેખર તારીફ લાયક થઈ પડીયો છે.

આઈનાં મેહેલમાંથી નીકળી બીજા ઓરડામાં ગયા, તે મકાનનું નામ "પીયાલી મેહેલ" એટલે પીયાલાંનો મેહેલ હતું. આ મેહેલની રચનામાં એવું જોવામાં આવ્યું કે ભીત ઉપર અને બારણાં ઉપર, અને બારી ઉપર અને સઘળે ઠેકાણે સેંકડો ચીનાઈ પીયાલાં જડી લીધેલાં છે. પીયાલાં તરેવાર જાતનાં સુનેરી રૂપેરી

ધોરવાળાં રંગબેરંગી છે, જેથી રચના ઘણીજ સુંદર દેખાયછે. કેટલાંએક પ્યાલાં લાખથી વળગાવેલાં હતાં, કેટલાંએકને તળીએ સુરાખ પાડી મેખથી જડી લીધેલાં હતાં. નાહાનામાં નાહાની પીયાલી આગા લોક કાશી પીએછે એટલા કદની હતી. મોહોટામાં મોહોટાં પીયાલાં ચાહાનાં કપ જેટલાં અથવા ચપુ જેટલાં કદનાં હતાં, તેની સાથે ગાળે ગાળે નાહાની નાહાની કોડીની રકાબીઓ પણ જડી લીધેલી હતી. આ રચનાં એક નવીજ જોયામાં આવી હતી અને તે જોવા લાયક હતી. એમાં ઘણું નવાઈ જેવું કંઈ નહી હતું, તોપણ જે શખ્સે એ રચના વીશે પેહેલો વીચાર કીધો હશે તે શખ્સની મનરાકતી, રોનક અને શોભાયમાન રચના વીશે ઘણી ઉંચે દરજ્જેની કઉઅત ધરાવતી હશે. હીયાંથી નીકળીને ગાડીમાં બેસી થોડેક દુર સીરનગર જીહાં નવાબનો બાગદારીનો મેહેલ તથા એક નવુંજ સંગ્રહસ્થાન અને શીકારગાહ બનાવી છે તે જોવા ગયા. આ સંગ્રહસ્થાન તે વખતે આમ લોકને જોવા સારૂ ખોલ્લું મુકયું નહી હતું, માત્ર પરવાનગી મલ્યાથીજ આ મકાન જોવા જવાનું બની શકતું હતું. જે વખતે હમો જોવા ગયા તે વખતે ખુદરતી પદાર્થોને તેમના જુદા જુદા વર્ગોમાં વેહેંચીને કબાટોમાં ગોઠવવાનું કામ ચાલતું હતું. હીયાં એક "મ્યુઝીઅમ" બનાવવાની શીરૂઆત થયલી હતી, પણ તેની ગોઠવણનું કામ કોઈ પણ વીદ્વાન શખ્સને સોંપેલું નહી હતું. માત્ર એક બે ઇંડોબ્રિટન ટોપીવાળાને હસ્તક એ કામ ચાલતું હતું. તેઓ ઉજડ ગામમાં એરંડા પ્રધાનની પદવી ભોગવતા હતા. સર સાલારજંગ પોતે એવાં ખુદરતી સંગ્રહસ્થાનો કરવાને ઘણો શોખી અને ખંતી છે, અને એના ફાયદા ઇંગ્રેજી રેસિડેંટોની સંગતમાં રહયાથી તે સારીપેઠે સમજવા લાગ્યો છે, તોપણ એવાં કામો સંપૂર્ણ રીતે બજાવાને કેવા પુરૂશોને તે સોંપવું જોઇએ, એ બાબદમાં નવાબે દુરંદેશી કીધો હોય એવું હમે નથી જાણતા. જેવા શખ્સોને તે સોંપીયામાં આવ્યું હતું, તેઓ તે પુરૂં અને જેવું જોઇયે એવું કરશે અને તેનો ફાયદો રૈયત ભોગવી શકશે એવું હમારા વીચારમાં બરોબર નહી આવીયું હતું. એવાં કામો દેશી શીખેલા વિદ્યાર્થીઓને સોંપવાં જોઈતાં હતાં. તેઓ જેવી ઈમાનદારી, સંપુર્ણતા અને મનમાનતી રીતે એવાં કામો કરી શકશે તેટલા વગર ભણેલા, અને ઇંગ્રેજોમાં ફકત નામ ચલાવનારા લેભાગુ પોરટુગીસો, અને યુરેશીઅનોથી કદી નથી થઈ શકવાનું. ખરચ કેમ કરાવવો, અને

પોતે સાહેબી અને.સુખ કેમ ભોગવવું એટલુંજ તેઓ જાણેછે. હા, જો કોઈ ખરેાજ ખુંચી ઇંગ્રેજ વિદ્યાર્થી એવાં કામ ઉપર રાખ્યો હોય તો તેના જેવો બીજો લાયક અમલદાર મળવો મુશકેલ છે, પણ અમસ્થા સાહેબની જાતમાં ખપનારા ટોપસાંઓને રાખી જે પૈસો તેમના ઉપર ખરચાએ તે વીશે સઘળા દેશી રાજા અને નવાબોએ ખુબ સારીપેઠે વીચાર કરવો જોઇયેછ.

આ સંગ્રહસ્થાન જોઈ ઇંગરેજોને જાફત આપવાનો મેહેલ તથા બાગ જોયો. આ મકાનની રચના પણ ઘણી અચ્છી બનેલી જોયામાં આવી છે. નવાઇ જેવા ફુલપાનનાં કયારા ઘણીજ સારી માવજત અને શોખ ભરેલા બનાવેલા છે, અને બાગમાં ફરવા હરવાની ગોઠવણ ઘણી સારી કરેલી છે. બાગ અંદર નદીનો એક ભાગ ખેંચી, પાણીનો જે પ્રવાહ ચાલુ કીધો છે તે મેહેલની બારી ઉપરથી જોવાને ઘણોજ દીલપસંદ છે. શીકાર કરવાની જગા ઘણી અચ્છી બનાવેલી છે. એ લત્તા તરફ શીકારીઓનાં શોખ લાયક ઘણી તરેહનાં જાનવરો મળી શકેછે. તેમાં ઘણું કરીને આ દેશનો જંગલી ગોધો, વાઘ, ચીતો, રીછ, વરૂ, તરસ અને રાની ડુકર, નીલગાવ અને ચાર શીગડાંવાળા સાંબરો, કસતુરી બીલાડી, કોહોલાં, ફાલુ, સાહુડી, સસા, અને ઉડતી મોહોટી ખલેડી પૃષ્કળ મળેછે. રાની મુરગો પણ ઘણી જાતનાં મળી આવેછે, અને વાંદરા પણ તેટલાજ છે. કેહેછે કે હેદરાબાદ તરફ જેટલો શીકાર છે તેટલો તે જણાયલો નથી.* અને હિંદુસ્થાનમાં મઇસોર મુલક સીવાય બીજે કોઈ ઠેકાણે એટલો બધો શીકાર નથી.* એ બાગમાં કેટલાંક જંગલી જાનવરોનો સંગ્રહ કીધેલો હમારા જોયામાં આવ્યો હતો. સર સાલારજંગ જેવા દેશી દીવાને ઇંગ્રેજી રાજા તથા ઇંગ્રેજોની સાથે જેવી મીત્રાચારી, અને ખરૂં દીલ રાખીયું છે એવું થોડાજ દેશી દીવાનોએ રાખેલું હમો જાણીએછ, તેમજ આપણી ઇંગ્રેજ સરકારે આ બાહોશ અને જબરી મનશકતી ધરાવનાર દેશી રાજ-દરબારી ઉમરાવ સાથે જે લાયકી ભરેલી ચાલચલગત, મોહોબત અને માન રાખીયું છે, આથી બંધે બાજુવાળાઓની કીર્તિને અરસપરસ મોહોટું માન અને એક બીજાને અચ્છી મદદ થઈ પડેલી છે. સર સાલારજંગ જેવા દેશી રાજ દરબારી અમીરની રાજ કારકિર્દી વીશે આપણા સઘળા દેશીઓએ મગરૂબ રેહેવું જોઇએછ.

---

*બ્રીગ્સ નિઝામ, વાલમ બીજું, પાનું ૨૫૦.

હીયાંથી રૂખસદ લઈ પાછા નવાબનાં મેહેલમાં ગયા, જે વખતે નવાબ પોતાની સાંજની નીમાજથી ફારેગ થયલો હતો. નવાબની મુલાકાત લેવામાં નાહાની પાગડી પેહેરી જવાનો રવૈયો જેવો હમોને અખત્યાર કરવો પડયો હતો, તેમજ જોડા કાહાડીને તેની હજુરમાં જવાનો બીજો રવૈયો હતો તે પ્રમાણે પણ ચાલવાની હમોને જરૂર થઈ પડી હતી; અને એ રવઈયા મુજબ નવાબ પોતે એવી તો બાહોશીથી ચાલીયો હતો કે તે પોતે પણ દીવાનખાનામાં જોડો કાહાડીને આવ્યો હતો, એટલે બંધે બાજુવાળાને એકસરખી પદવી ઉપર તેણે લાવી મુકયા હતા. બીજી ઝડફ તે અમીરે વળી એવી તો બતલાવી દીધી હતી કે જેવો તે દીવાનખાનામાં આવ્યો અને હમારી મુલાકાત સલામ અલેકુમથી લીધી કે લાગલોજ પોતે જમીન ઉપર ગાલીચો પાંથરેલો હતો તે ઉપર બેસી ગયો, અને જારે હમને બેસવાને ફરમાવ્યું ત્યારે આસપાસ ખુરશી, કોચ વગેરે બેઠકનો બીજો સરસરંજામ હોયા છતાં નવાબ જારે પોતે નમનતાઈ ભરેલી તાજીમથી જમીન ઉપર બેઠો તારે હમને ખુરશી અથવા કોચ ઉપર બેસવું નાસજાવાર લાગાથી હમને પણ તેની સાંમે પગ વાળી મોગલાઈ દરબારનાં કાનુન પ્રમાણે અથવા આપણા વડીલ ઇરાનીઓ જે ઢપથી બેસતા હતા તે ઢપે જમીન ઉપર બેસવું પડયું હતું. આવો બનાવ બનશે એ હમારા કોઈનાં સ્વપ્નામાં પણ નહીં હતું, પણ આવા બાહોશ નવાબ, જેની ચાલાકી, હીમત અને મનશક્તીની વખાણ થયલી છે, અને જેનામાં સમયસુચકતા અતીશય છે, તેની સામે એવા બનાવો બને એ વીશે હવે પછી હમને નવાઈ જેવું નથી લાગવાનું. એની મુલાકાત કરવા જનાર ગૃહસ્થોને આ ચંચલ નવાબ પોતાની મુલાકાતમાં એવી તો તાજીમ તવાજો દેખડાવેછે કે તેઓ સઘળાને મોગલાઈ દરબારનાં કાયદા કાનુનો અને રેવાજો પ્રમાણે ચાલવાની ફરજ પાડતાં, સંભા તેમને રાજી ખુશીથી પાછા રવાનાં કરેછે.

બેઠા પછી તરેહવાર બાબતોની વાતચીત થઈ જેમાં નવાબે ઘણી સારી વાકેફગારી બતલાવી હતી. તેણે ઇંગ્રેજી રાજ વીશે તથા તેનાં બળ વીશે ઘણુંજ સારૂં મત જણાવ્યું હતું, અને કેળવણીનાં ફાયદા વીશે તે સારીપેઠે જાણીતો થયલો હતો, એટલું છતાં પોતાનાં રાજમાં કેળવણીનાં પ્રસાર વીશે તે કંઈ ઘણું કરી શકયો નહી હતો તેથી તેણે પોતાની દીલગીરી જણાવી હતી; અને એ બાબદ ઉપર જે ગફલતી જણાઈ હતી તેનું કારણ તેની રૈયતની જનુની અને ધરમની તાસુબી ઉપર લાગુ

પાડ્યું હતું. તોએપણ કેળવણીનો ફેલાવો કરવા વીશે તેનાથી જે કંઈ હળવે હળવે થઈ શકવા જોગ હતું તે ઉપર તેણે પોતાનું ધ્યાન પોંહોંચાડેલું હતું, અને તેને આગળ વધારવાને તે કોશેસમાંજ હતો. હીયાં તીહાંની થોડી ઘણી વાત કીધા પછી નવાબે હમને મુસાફરી કરવાની મકસદ પુછી જેનો ઉત્તર હમોએ એટલોજ આપ્યો કે હમારો સ્વદેશ કેવો છે અને દેશીઓ કેવી હાલતમાં છે, તે વીશે થોડું ઘણું નજરે નજર જોઈ વાકેફ થવું, અને તેથી જે જ્ઞાનસંપાદન થાય તે હમારા મીત્રો અને દેશીઓને કહી સંભળાવવું અથવા પુસ્તકની મારફતે જાહેર કરવું. આ સાંભળીને તે હમારી મતલબથી ઘણો ખુશી થયો હતો, અને હમારી રૂડી મતલબે તેનાં મન ઉપર સારી અસર કીધી હતી. તે બોલ્યો કે, તમારા ભાઈબેહેનોનાં ફાયદાને સારૂ તમોએ ગીરોનાં પૈસા ખરચી મુસાફરી જેવી સખત મેહનત અને રંજ તમે તમારી ઉપર ખેંચી લીધી છે તેથી તમને ઘણી સાબાસી ઘટેછે; અને હેવી તરેહની મુસાફરી કરવાની તરફેણમાં તેણે પોતાનું મત આપ્યું હતું, પણ એક વાતની તેણે હમને ચેતવણી આપી હતી. તે બોલીયો કે, હરેક જગાની વસ્તીની હાલત વીશે કોઈ પણ મુસાફરને એક બે અથવા ચાર દિવસમાં પુરતી અને ખરી વાકેફગારી નથી મળી શકનાર અને જો બરોબર અને પુરતીજ વાકેફગારી મેળવવી હોય તો લાંબા વખત સુધી તે રૈયત સાથે અને તેઓમાંજ વસવું તથા રેહેવું જોઇયેછ, લેવડ દેવડ કરવી જોઇયેછ, તોજ ખરો એહવાલ રૈયતની હાલત વીશેનો મેળવી શકાશે, અને એટલા ઉપરથી તેણે વધારે વીચાર જણાવ્યો કે તેના હૈદરાબાદ શેહેર વીશે અને તેની રૈયત વીશે હમોએ બેચાર દીવસની સેહેલગા ઉપરથી જે વીચારો બાંધ્યા હશે તે ખરેખર અધુરા હોવા જોઇયે, માટે જો પુસ્તક લખવું હોય તો સારીપેઠે તલાસ કરીને અને વધારે દીવસ હીયાં રહીને પુરતી રીતે ખોળ કરવી વાજબી છે. એ ઉપરથી હમોએ નવાબને જણાવ્યું કે હમારી મતલબ એવી બારીકી ભરેલી બાબદનું પુસ્તક લખવાની નથી. ફકત હમો કહે રસ્તેથી અને કેહેવી કેહેવી જગાઓપરથી કુચ કરીએછ તેનું બયાન તથા જે જે જગાઓ રસ્તામાં આવે તેની આબોહવા અને લોકની રેહેવાની રીતભાત તથા તેમની હાલત વીશે જેટલું નજરે પડે તથા પુછપરછ કરતાં વિશ્વાસુ માણસોને મોહોડેથી જેટલી ખબરઅંતર મળે તેટલીજ બાબદ માત્ર જણાવવાની હમારી મતલબ છે, અને તે ઉપરથી નવાબે બેશીકર રેહેવું કે તેનાં પ્રાંત વિશે અથવા તેની

રૈયતની હાલત વીશે અથવા કોઈબી બીજા શખ્સો વીશે જે કાંઈ હમારા જાણ-વામાં આવશે અને તે ખરેખરૂં હશે તેટલુંજ હમો જાહેર કરશું. કાંઈપણ ઓઠી અને વગર આધારની બાબદ લોકને ભુલાવામાં નાખવાની મતલબે કદી પણ હમારાથી લખાવાની નથી. કોઈ જગા અથવા વસ્તીની હાલત જોવાની જો હમને બરોબર ફુરસદ નહી મલી હશે, તો તેમને વીશે અમસ્થી કલ્પનાથી લખવા કરતાં હમો તદન મુંગા રેહેવું વધારે માન ભરેલું જાણશું. આ જવાબથી નવાબ સંતોશ પામીયો હતો. બીજી કેટલીએક વાતચીત થયા પછી રૂખશદ લેવાનો વખત નજદીક આવ્યો, તેથી જેમ હમને આગળથી જણાવી રાખ્યું હતું તેમ દર-બારી રવૈયા મુજબ હમો દરેક જણે સફેત ઘડીબંધ એક રૂમાલ ઉપર રૂ ૫) પાંચ મુકીને જમણે હાથે તે રૂમાલ હથેલી ઉપર ધરીને નવાબ આગળ એક નાહાના સરખાં નજરાણાં દાખલ ધરેયો, તે ધરતાંજ નવાબે હસતે મોહોડે દરેક જણના હાથમાંથી તડોતડ તે રૂપીઆ ઉઠાવી લઈ પોતાની પાસે બેઠક ઉપર એકઠા કીધા, અને એવું કરતી વખતે તેણે હેવી તો તાજીમ તવાજો હમને દેખડાવ્યો હતો કે જો કે તે હમારી પાસે પોતાના રવૈયા પ્રમાણે સાંભો એક પોતાનો હક લેતો હતો, તો એ-પણ જે તવાજો અને ખુશરોએ તેણે તે લીધો હતો તેથી સાંભું હમને આપવાને ગમ્યું હતું, અને એવું લાગતું હતું કે જાણે તે લીધાથી નવાબનો હમારી ઉપર સાંભો ઉપકાર થયો હોય. માન અને આદરસતકાર જો બરોબર રીતે થયો હોય તો તેથી કહયું કામ નહી બની શકે એ કેહેવાઈ શકતું નથી. નવાબની તરફથી એક ઈશારત થતાં, પેલા રૂપીઆની ઢગલી એક અમલદાર આવી ઉંચકી લઈ ગયો અને તેને ઠેકાણે ફુલના તોરા, પાન અને અત્તર લાવી મુકયું. જેવા હસતા ચેહે-રાથી અને આદરસતકારથી હમારૂં નાહાનું સરખું નજરાણું નવાબે લઈ લીધું હતું તેવેજ હસતે ચેહેરે અને આદરસતકારે હમને દરેક જણને અત્તરની એકેક સોનામાં મઢેલી સીસી, તથા અત્તરની સળી અને તુરા તથા ગુલાબ, નવાબે પોતાને હાથે આપ્યા હતા; આ સઘળી બીના બનતાં એક કલાકનો વખત મુલાકાતમાં ગયો હતો. સાંજે, છને અમલે હમોએ નવાબથી રૂખસદ ચાહી હતી.

છુટા પડતી વખતે નવાબે પોતાની ખુશી બતલાવી કે હીયાંના એક ઉમરાવને તીહાં તે રાત્રે શાદી હતી અને સાંજના છ વાગતે શાદીનું સાજન નવાબનાં મેહેલ ઉપર થઈ પસાર થવાનું હતું. આ રચના નવાબે જોવા લાયક જાણીને હમને જો-

વાને ભલાંમણ કીધી; અને તે સારીપેઠે જોવાને બની આવવા સારૂ પોતાના મેહેલનાં એક દીવાનખાનામાં બારી આગળ હમને બેઠક કરાવી આપી. રજવાડામાં અને નવાબી હાકમીમાં શાદીનાં સાજન અથવા સરઘસો તથા તેવાજ મેલાવડા કેવા થાયછે, આ જોવા લાયક જાણીને નવાબની ઇચ્છા હમોએ એકદમ ખુશીથી કબુલ રાખી, અને દીવાનખાનામાં જઈ બેઠા. શાદીનાં સરઘસનો પેહલો દેખાવ સાડાછ વાગે શીરૂ થયો તે છેક રાત્રે આઠ વાગે પુરો થયો હતો. એટલા લાંબા વખતમાં પેદલ માણસો, તેમની પછવાડે ઘોડસ્વારો, તેમની પછવાડે હાથીસ્વારોની અલગાર લાગટ ચાલુ રહેલી હતી. આ સરઘસમાં એક નોંધવા જોગ દેખાવ આ જાણીયામાં આવીયો કે જે જે અમીર ઉમરાવને સાજનમાં ખીરાજવાને નોતરૂં દેછે તે દરેક અમીર ઉમરાવ તેનાં હાલી મવાલીઓ સાથે પોતપોતાના દરજ્જાસર એકબીજાની પછવાડે, છુટા છુટા હાથી, ઘોડા અને ઉંટ સ્વારો તથા પેદલો સાથે ખીરાજેછે. એ મુજબ જો ફકત પાંચ અમીરનું એવાં સાજનમાં ખીરાજવું થયું તો જેવી જેની મવસર મુજબ દીવા, મસાલો, આતશબાજી, ઢોલ, તાસા, કરનાય, નગારા, ઇંગ્રેજી વાજાં અને એવી બીજી ભપકા, દમામ અને ધાંધલ ભરેલી રચના સાથે પાંચ જુદાં જુદાં સરઘસ એકબીજાની પાછલ પસાર થાયછે. હમોએ જે સાજન જોયું હતું તેમાં હમો ચુકતા નહી હોઇયે તો ૧૦ એવા મોહોટી પદવી ધરાવનારા ઉમરાવો ખીરાજ્યા હતા. તેમના દેખાવ અને દમદમામનું સું બયાન કરીએ! કોઈ ઘોડા ઉપર, કોઈ હાથી ઉપર સ્વાર થઈ પસાર થયા હતા, તેમાં તેમની આગળ પાછળ ઢોલ, તાસા, ઉંટ ઉપર ચઢાવેલા નગારાં, મૃદંગ, છમછમીયાં, ધુધારી, રણશીંગડાં, કરનાએ, ઇંગ્રેજી વાજાં વાગતાં હતાં, તેમની જોડે ઘોડા અને હાથી, પેદલ લસ્કર, અને તેમની વચ્ચે ગાલે ગાલે બાંડ, બપોરીયા, પેટીને પેટીઓ બંધ ફટાકા, અને એવીજ બીજી ગડબડાટ ભરેલી આતશબાજી છુટતી હતી. આ તમાસો જોવાને, સાથે ચાલતા તમાસગીરોની ભીડમાં જે કલોર અને ઘોંગાટ તથા ધુમ મચી રહી હતી તેથી એ સરઘસનો દેખાવ જેવા લઢાઈની ધામધુમ અને ધભરાટ બરેલો તેવાજ દીલપસંદ રચના ભરેલો, થઈ રહેલો હતો. આ સરઘસની આખી સ્વારી નવાબનાં મેહેલ ઉપર રહીને પસાર થઈ હતી, અને જો કે તેનો છેડો રાત્રે આઠ વાગે આવીયો તોએપણ હમને એવું ગમીયું કે તે હજુર વધારે લાંબો વાર ટકીયો હતે તો ઠીક.

હીયાંથી રૂખસત લઈ નીકળ્યા તે રાત્રે સવા આઠ કલાકે પાછા શેઠ બાપુજી પીકાજીનાં મુકામ ઉપર આવી પોંહોંચ્યા. એજ રાત્રે હમને શેઠ ખરશેદજી બહમજી પંથકીની પેહેડીવાળા સાહેબોએ જીયાફત આપી હતી માટે નવાબની દરબારમાં બીરાજવાને હમોએ પેહેરેલો હસવા જેવો બેડોલ પોશાક તુરત ઉતારી પાછો હમારો મુંબઇનો રોઆબદાર પાઘડી અને ડગલીનો પોશાક પેહેરી તેમને તીહાં ગયા. અવારૂં થઈ ગયું હતું અને વળી છેક ૪ થી ૫ માઈલ સીકંદરાબાદ સુધી દુર જવું હતું તે સબબથી તીહાં પોંહોંચતાં છેક રાત્રનાં નવ અથવા સવા નવ વાગાનો સુમાર થઈ ગયો હતો. આ ઠેકાણે હમારી મેહેમાનદારી ઘણીજ દીલભર રીતે કરીયામાં આવી હતી તથા સઘળી વાતે ખાણાં પીણાની અને બીજી બાબદની તે સાહેબોએ ઘણીજ તજુમલ કરી હતી તેથી તેમનો મોટો ઉપરકાર હમારી ઉપર થયો હતો, જે વીશે ઘટતું જાણી તેની હમો આ ઠેકાણે એક નોંધ કરીએછ. આ મેલાવડામાં સીકંદરાબાદ અને હેદરાબાદના ઘણાખરા જરથોસ્તી રેહેવાસીઓની મુલાકાત કરવાનો અને સાથે બેસી જમવાનો આ એક સારો સંજોગ હમને મળી આવીયો હતો તેથી હમો ઘણા ખુશી થયા હતા. મીજલસમાં આવેલા ઘણાખરા સાહેબો ઉલટ અને તંદરોસ્તી ભરેલા નજર આવ્યા હતા, અને સઘળાનાં મોહોડાં ઉપર સખત ઉદ્યોગ તથા મેહેનતની અને પરદેશ રેહેવાથી મળતી હીંમત અને આપઅખતીયારીની નીશાનો સારીપેઠે દેખાતી હતી. એ ઉપરથી હમો આ બીજીવાર નોંધ કરીએછ કે મુંબઈમાં ઘણોખરો પારસી જેટલો એક-બીજાના પંજામાં દબાએલો, ઓશીયાલો, નાહીમત, તેનીસાથે એકલપેટો અને આળસુ, બની આવે તીહાંસુધી બેઠા ખાવાની હોંસ ધરાવનાર જેવો નજરે પડેછે, તેટલો તે બાહાર ગામ અથવા પરદેશમાં આપઅખતીયાર, સુર ભરેલો, ઉદ્યોગી અને એક બીજાને મદદ કરનારો થઈ પડેછે. હમારૂં મત એઉપરથી એવું બંધાયલું છે કે પારસીઓએ એકજ ઠેકાણે અને એકજ ખુણે પડી રહી એકનાં એકજ ધંધામાં રોકાયલા નહી રેહેવું જોઇયે, પણ જેમ જેની મનશાકતી તેને અંદરખાનેથી ઉલટ આપે અને સુજ પાડે તેવો ધંધો આપઅખતીયારીથી, પછી હરકોઈ જગાએ અથવા દેશમાં ફાવે તીહાં ચલાવી, તીહાંના રેહેવાસી થઈ પડવું જોઈએછ અને તે જગા ઉપર પગભર થવાની કોશેશ કરવી જોઇએછ. આથી આપણાં ટોલાની હાલત ખચીતજ બેહેતર થવાની, અને આ જેવો માર્ગ મોકળો, સેહેલો

અને ખરો બીજો કોઈ નથી. અગર એથી ઉલટું થયું તો આપણી હાલત હળવે હળવે પડતી જયા વગર નથી રેહેનાર.

આ મેજબાનીમાં એક બનાવ જાણવા જોગ બનેલો જાણી તે વીશે અત્રે બે સુખન લખી જણાવવાની જરૂર જોઇ છે. મેજબાનીની મીજલસમાં હેદરાબાદનાં વડા દસ્તુરજી સાહેબ હોરમજજી જામાસ્પજી બીરાજયા હતા. દસ્તુરજી જેવા મોહોટી પદવીવાળા ગૃહસ્થનાં બીરાજવાથી આખી મીજલસને મોહોટું માન થયલું આપણને સમજવું જોઇયેછે. પણ જેવું માન બેહેદીનોએ દસ્તુરજીને આપ્યું હતું તેવું પ્રતિમાન મીજલસના તમામ બેહેદીનોને દસ્તુરજીની તરફથી હમારા વીચાર પ્રમાણે નહી મળ્યું હતું. તે એ સબબથી કે દસ્તુરજી સાહેબે પોતાના બેહદીનો સાથે એક ટેબલ ઉપર બેસી જમવું ના રવા ગણ્યું હતું, અને એ માટે તેમને સારૂ એલાહેદી જુદી એક ટેબલ માંડી હતી. આ જુદી માંડેલી ટેબલ ઉપર જારે હમારી પેહેલ વેહેલી નજર પડી ત્યારે હમો એમ સમજ્યા કે હમારી સાથે મી૦ એડવર્ડ રીડીઆસટીક નામનો જે યુરોપિયન ગૃહસ્થ હતો તેને જુદદીનનો ગણીને છુટો જમાડવાની ગોઠવણ કરી હશે; પણ થોડીવારમાં એ વીશે ખુલાસો થઇ ગયો હતો. તે ગૃહસ્થને સારૂ તો વળી એક ત્રીજી ટેબલ જુદી માંડેલી હતી. દસ્તુરજીને એવો ફરક પોતાના બેહેદીનો સાથે રાખવાનું સું કારણ હશે તે કાંઈ સમજ પડે એવું નહી હતું. પેલો યુરોપિયન જુદદીનનો હોવાથી એકવાર તેને સાથે નહી જમાડવાની કોઈએ અડચણ લીધી હોય અથવા એ વીશે કોઇનો જીવ કચવાયો હોય તો એકવાર તેને જુદો બેસાડવા આપણે કબુલ રાખીએ, પણ દસ્તુરજી અને તેઓના બેહેદીનો એકજ જરથોસ્તી દીનના થઈ જુદા બેસીને જમે એનું કારણ ધ્યાનમાં આવી શકતું નથી. નોહોણવાલા મોબેદો જુદા બેસી જમવાનો જે રવઇયો ચલાવેછે તે ધરમનાં ફરમાન મુજબ ચાલેછે કે ફકત એક રેવાજ પડી ગયાથી તેમ તેઓ ચાલેછે, એ વીશે કોઈ તરફથી મનપતીજ ભરેલો ખુલાસો થયો નથી. ખેર, પણ વળી હમોએ તાજુબીથી જોયું કે દસ્તુરજી સાહેબ જોકે જમવાને જુદા બેઠા હતા ખરા પણ જે જે ગળ્યાં ગળ્યાં પકવાનો અને લેહેજતદાર દારૂ બેહેદીનો જમતા અને નોશ કરતા હતા, તેજ પકવાનો અને દારૂ વીગરે બીજી જીનસો તેવણ પણ શુકરાંના કરીને જમતા હતા. ફરક માત્રે એટલોજ હતો કે બેહેદીનો બળાં માણસો ટેબલ ઉપર જમતાં જમતાં બોલતા અને વાતચીત અને કોઈવાર ગડબડ

કરતા હતા, પણ દસ્તુરજી સાહેબ આ મેજબાનીનાં સઘળાં પકવાન અને રચનાની મજા ઠંડે પેટે અને મુંગે મોહોડે બાજ ધરીને ખુશ મીજાજથી લેતા અને ભોગવતા હતા. હમને આ બાબદની અગત કરીને નોંધ કરવાની જરૂર એટલાજ ઉપરથી થઇ છે કે એજ દસ્તુરજી સાહેબનાં ભાઈ દસ્તુરજી હુશંગજી જામાસપજી જેઓ મહુ શેહરનાં પંથકનાં વડા દસ્તુર છે, તેઓ પોતે પોતાના બેહેદીનો સાથે બેસીને જમવું રવા ગણેછે અને જારે હમો થોડા દીવસ મહુ શેહરમાં રહેલા હતા તારે હમારી સાથે એકજ ટેબલ ઉપર બેસીને સઘળી મીલનસારી સાથે જમવાનું આ લાયકીભરેલા અને વીદ્યામાં પ્રવીણ થયલા દસ્તુરે વાજબી જાણ્યું હતું.

શેઠ પંથકીને તીહાંથી સઘળાઓને મળી ભેટીને મોડી રાત્રે રૂખસદ લેતી વખતે આ ઠેકાણે ભેગા થયલા સઘળા ભાઇઓની ઇચ્છા ઉપરથી બીજે દીને સહવારનાં ધંબારની ચાસણી કરવા સારૂ શેઠ નુશરવાંનજી શોરાબજી ચીનાઇનાં મકાન ઉપર સામેલ થવાની હમોએ કબુલાત આપી હતી.

તા૦ ૩ જી જાનેવારી—એ દીને સહવારનાં ૧૧ વાગે શેઠ નુશરવાનજી શોરાબજી ચીનાઇનાં બાગમાં ધંબારની ચાસણી કરવાને હેદરાબાદનાં જરથોસ્તી રેહેવાસીઓ સાથે હમો સઘળા સામેલ થયા હતા. ખાણું લેહેજતદાર હતું, અને જમીન ઉપર પાત્રાં માંડવાંને બદલે સફાઈથી ખાવાને બની આવવા સારૂ ટેબલ ઉપર પાત્રાં માંડેલાં હતાં. આ રેવાજ તીહાંના સઘળા સાહેબોને પસંદ પડેલા અને ચાલુ હતો. આ રેવાજ સાથે મુંબઈ શેહેરના પારસીઓ જેઓ સુધરાઈમાં પેહેલા ગણાવા માંગેછે, તેઓનાં ધંબારનાં જમણો જે ખરડાયલી ભોંય અને મેલાં ગલીચ પાથરણાં ઉપર થાયછે તે સાથે સરખાવીએ તો શું મુંબઈના લોકને એ વીશે કાંઈ અંદેશો નહીં ઉત્પન્ન થશે? અને ઉપર જણાવેલીજ રીતે સફાઈથી જમાડવાની શું અત્રે ગોઠવણ નહી કરી શકશે.

ઉપલાં ઠેકાણેથી નીકળી હેદરાબાદનાં આદરીઆનનું મકાન જોવા ગયા તીહાં સેજદો કરીને દસ્તુરજી સાહેબની મુલાકાત લીધી. દસ્તુરજી સાહેબ હમને પોતાના પુસ્તકખાતામાં લઈ ગયા હતા, તીહાં તેમની સાથે કેટલીક વાતચીત થઈ હતી. સેતારા અને આકાશનાં ગ્રહોની ચાલથી આપણી પૃથ્વિના રેહેવાસીઓ ઉપર અને અગત કરીને બીમાર માણસો ઉપર જે કેટલીક અસરો થાયછે, તે વિશયનાં અભ્યાસ ઉપર દસ્તુરજી સાહેબનું ધીયાન વધારે લાગેલું તેમની વાતચીત

ઉપરથી જણાયું હતું. બીમાર હાલતમાં દવાદારૂ લેવાની જરૂર અલબતાં તેઓ જાણતા હતા, તોપણ ગ્રહોની ચાલની અસર વીશે તેઓનાં મનમાં દવાદારૂ કરતાં વધારે કાળજી હોય, એવો સાર તેમના બોલવા ઉપરથી હમોએ ઉપજાવીયો હતો. એવી તરેહનાં મત ધરાવનારા આજે સઘળે ઠેકાણે મળી આવશે, જેવા આપણા દેશમાં તેવાજ યુરોપ અને બીજા ખંડોમાં પણ છે; પણ એવીશે એટલુંજ જણાવવાનું છે કે હાલનાં વૈદક શાસ્ત્રીઓના વિચારો પ્રમાણે સેતારા અને ગ્રહોની ચાલથી માણસ જાતની તંદરોસ્તી ઉપર જેટલી થોડી અસરો થતી માલુમ પડી છે, તેના કરતાં વધારે અસરો, માણસ જાતની રેહેવાની હાલતની સફાઈ તથા તેને લગતી બીજી તજુમલ અથવા તેના ફુઆડપણાથી નીપજતી જણાયલી છે. માણસનાં ખાવા પીવાની ચીજો કેહેવી હોવી જોઈએ, તે ઉપર, તેમની ખાવાપીવાની રીતભાત ઉપર, તેમની શરીર તથા મન કેળવણી ઉપર, તથા જે ઠેકાણે તેઓ રેહેતા હોય તે ઠેકાણાની આબોહવા ઉપર, અને છેલ્લું તેમનાં ધંધા રોજગાર અને પેશા ઉપર, તેમની તંદરોસ્તીનો જેટલો ઘણેએક દરજે આધાર રહેલો છે તેટલો ઓછે દરજે સીતારા અને ગ્રહોની ચાલની અસર ઉપર રહેલો છે. હાલ જમાનાનાં વૈદકશાસ્ત્રથી આ હકીકત સાબેત થયલી છે.

હેદરાબાદના આદરીઆન સાહેબના એબાદતખાનાંમાં હમને બંદગી કરવાને મુંબઈનાં એબાદતખાનાં કરતાં વધારે ગમ્યું હતું. તેના કારણો વીશે એકદમ વીચાર આપી શકતા નથી, પણ આટલું ખુલ્લે ખુલ્લું કેહેવાઈ શકાયછે કે બંદગી કરતી વખતે જે મુજબ મુંબઈમાં અને બીજે કેટલેએક ઠેકાણે જેમ બંદગી કરનારની આસપાસ મોબેદોની ભીડ થાયછે અને તેમની શોખાઈથી બંદગી કરનારને કંટાળો ઉપજેછે તેમ આ એબાદતગાહમાં હમને નહીં માલુમ પડયું હતું. એબાદતની વખતે ગંભીરાઈ અને એકાંતપણાની જેવી જરૂર છે તેવી આ ઠેકાણે જોવામાં આવી હતી. મોબેદો અંદર આવ્યા હતા પણ પોતપોતાને ઠેકાણે અને દરજાસર ઉભા હતા, અને તેમની તે વખતની સઘળી ચાલચલગત અને સલુકાઈ, વખત અને ઠેકાણાંસરની ગંભીરાઇને સજાવાર હતી, તેથી તીહાંનો દેખાવ દીલપસંદ થઈ પડયો હતો. આવી સારી તરબીએત અને મોબેદી દરજાની જાલવણી કરવાની તબે હેદરાબાદના મોબેદોમાં જોયામાં આવી હતી, આ ખુશાલીની વાત છે. એ તરબીએત તીહાંનાં દસ્તુરજી શાહેબ તરફથી

આપીયામાં આવી હતી જે વીરો દસ્તુરજીને ઘણુંજ માન ઘટેછે, અને તેની આ ઠેકાણે મોટી ખુશી સાથે હમો નોંધ કરીએછ.

તા૦ ૪ થી જાનેવારી—આ દીને હેદરાબાદથી આગળ કુચ કરવાનો ઠરાવ કરેલો હતો અને તે પ્રમાણે નીકળવાની સઘળી તૈયારી પણ થઈ હતી. પણ હેદરાબાદથી મદ્રાઝ જવાને નજદીકનો અને સેહેલો રસ્તો કહ્યો લેવા આ વીરો ભરોસો રાખવા જોગ અને ચોકસાઈ ભરેલી ખબર કોઈ આપી નહી શકયું હતું. કેટલાએકોથી એવી ભલામણ થઈ હતી કે હેદરાબાદથી મછલીપટણ જવું, અને તીહાંથી તરીને માર્ગે મદ્રાઝ જવું. પણ એ રસ્તો ઘણોજ લાંબો, બીકટ અને પુષ્કળ દિવસ હેજગારી ભોગવવી પડે એવો હતો, માટે તે રસ્તે જવાનું નહી વાજબી ધારીને બીજા ટુંકા રસ્તાની ખબર કહડાવી. આ બીજો રસ્તો "કરનુલ" અને "કડાપા" થઇને જવાનો હતો, અને તે ટુંકો હતો ખરો તોએપણ તે આડ રસ્તો હતો, અને મુસાફરીનો સાધારણ જવા આવવાનો તે ધોરી માર્ગ નહી હતો, તથા વળી તેનો કેટલાએક ભાગ ઘણોજ બીકટ જણાવ્યામાં આવ્યો હતો. આવો આડ રસ્તો, તે સાથે વળી શકતી ભરેલો છતાં પણ તે માર્ગ ટુંકો હતો એવું સાંભળ્યાથી અને મદ્રાઝ જલદી જઈ પોહોંચવાની ઉમેદથી, એજ રસ્તે થઇ જવાનો હમો સઘળાએ નિશ્ચય કીધો. તેની સાથે કડાપાથી બે ત્રણ દિવસના રસ્તા પછી, નજદીકીમાં ત્રીપટી આગળથી મદ્રાઝના મોહોટા રેલવેની એક શાખાનું મથક આવેલુંછે, એવું હમારા જાણીયામાં આવેયાથી, આગગાડી હમારી મુસાફરીમાં કામ લાગશે એવું વીચારીને, આ રસ્તે જવાની હમને વધારે હીંમત થઈ હતી.

સોલાપુરથી જે બળદની શીગરામ ભાડે લીધેલી હતી તેની મુસાફરીનો ટપ્પો હેદરાબાદમાં પુરો થયો હતો, અને હેદરાબાદથી તેવી ગાડીનો ડાક આગળની મંજલ કાપવાને નહી હોયાથી, હમારી હવે પછીની રસ્તાની હેજગારીનું ભવિષ્ય હમને થયું હતું. કોશાદ અને સગવડથી બેસાએ આવી ગાડીઓની ઘણી તલાસ કરાવી પણ હેદરાબાદમાં એકુ પણ ગાડી તેવી મળી શકી નહી હતી. અંતે સાંકડાં ગાડાં કરવાની ફરજ પડી. તે ગાડીઓ જારે બંગલાના ચોકમાં આવી ઉભી ત્યારે તે જોઇને હમને સઘળાને ઘણુંજ હસવું આવ્યું, તે એ વીચારથી કે બે દિવસની વાત ઉપર હમો જે હાથીના હોદા ઉપર બેસીને હેદરાબાદમાં તોજારની મીસાલે ફર્યા હતા, તેને ઠેકાણે હવે હમારો વખત, સાંકડી ગાડીમાં બેશી અકળાવા ઝીખાવા અને હાડકાં

દોદરાં કરવાનો આવ્યો. આ ગાડીઓની હાલત જોઇને હમારો યુરોપીયન મિત્ર કેહેવા લાગો કે આવી જોખમ ભરેલી ગાડીમાં જાણી જોઇને બેસી મદ્રાસ પોંહોંચવાની આગમચ અફળાયા કીખાયાથી મારૂં શરીર છુંદાઇને વગર હાડકાંનું કરી નાખવા કરતાં, હું મુંબઈ પાછો જેવો છઉં તેવો જાઉં તો તે બેહેતર છે. હમારો એક બીજો મિત્ર બોલ્યો કે, અરે, હું તો આ ગાડાંમાં માઈ શકતોજ નથી, અને જીહાં ફરૂંછું, હીલું છઉં, તીહાં ગાડાં સાથે મારૂં શરીર ઘસાયછે. આવું સંકટ કેમ ખમારો! આ વીરો ખુશ મસ્કરી ચાલેછે તેવામાં એક બીજી નવી મુશ્કેલી નજર સામણે આવી ઉભી. જેટલા ગાડીવાનો હતા તેટલા સઘળા તેલંગી અથવા મદ્રાસી ભાષા સિવાય બીજી કોઈપણ ભાષા સમજી અથવા બોલી શકતા નહી હતા. હિંદુસ્થાની જબાન થોડી ઘણી તો ગમે હેવો હેદરાબાદી હોય તે સમજી અથવા બોલી શકેછે, પણ હમારી પાંતીએ જે ૧૨) ગાડીવાનો મળ્યા તેઓ પોતાની મદ્રાસી તેપણ કોઈ ચોકસ પ્રગણાની બોલી સિવાય બીજી કોઈપણ ભાષા જાણતા નહી હતા તેથી તેમની સાથે રસ્તાની મજલ કાપતાં શી શી અડચણો ખમવી પડશે તેનો એક મોહોટો વિચાર ઉત્પન્ન થયો હતો. ઈશારતથી વાત કરવાની ફરજ થઈ અને તે થોડીવાર અજમાવી જોવાથી જે ગડબડાટ અને સમજણમાં ફેર પડતો હતો તેથી એક ઘણીજ રમુજ થઈ પડી હતી.

શેઠ બાપુજી વીકાજીએ પેહલાંથી હમો સઘળાની જેવી રીતે બરદાસ્ત કીધી તેવી છેક છેલ્લી ઘડી સુધી હમને સગવડ અને સુખ કરી આપવા પાછળ તેવણે તસદી લીધી હતી. તેવણે કેટલાએક પેદલ સીપાઈઓ હમારી સાથે કેટલીએક મંજલ સુધી આપ્યા હતા. તેઓ ગાડીવાનોને સમજાવવાને દુભાસીયા પ્રમાણે કામે લાગા હતા. નવાબ સર સાલારજંગે પણ હમારી રખેવાલી કરવાને અને નીજામની હદ સુધી સહી સલામત પોંહોંચાડવાને તથા રસ્તામાં કોઈ તરેહનો અટકાવ, હરકત, અડચણ નહી પડવા તથા તેનો આગળથી બંદોબસ્ત કરી રાખવાને પોતાના લશ્કરનાં ૧૨) ઘોડસ્વારો હમારી સાથે આપ્યા હતા. તેઓ એક બે દીવસ તો ઠીક ચાલ્યા પણ પછવાડેથી તેઓ એક પછી એક દાંયાબાંયાં થવા લગા અને તેઓ બીન કવાયદ તથા બીન તરબીએતવાળા હોયાથી, હમને કામજોગ થઈ પડવાને બદલે, ઉલટા કંટાળો આપનારા અને અડચણ ભરેલા થઈ પડયા હતા, તે એટલા સુધી કે તેમની

હદ પુરી થાય તેની આગમચ, બાર સ્વારોમાંથી હમોને બરોબર યાદ નથી, પણ ભાયેગે ત્રણ સ્વાર ઠેઠ સુધી હમારી સાથે રહ્યા હોય.

પેલા અનાડી ગાડીવાનોની ગડબડાટ અને ગોંદળથી તથા તેમની ગાડીઓમાં ઘાંસ પંથરાવવાની, અને તરેહવાર બીજી બનતી સગવડો કરતાં તથા જે કહીયે તે દુભાસીયાની મારફતે સમજાવતાં તથા કેટલીએક અગતની બાબદો વીશે તેમની સાથે વાતચીત કેમ કરવી, તે સારૂ કેટલાએક શબ્દો અને વાકયો દુભાસીયાની મારફતે અમારામાંથી કેટલાએક જણને લખી લેતાં પુષ્કળ વખત નીકળી ગયો હતો. જારે જમી બાઈ હેદરાબાદથી કુચ કીધી તારે રાત્રે ૧૨ા વાગાનો અમલ થયો હતો. બાર ગાડી હારબંધ, એકક પાછળ ચાલતી, અમારી સ્વારી નીકળી હતી, તથા તેની સાથે ઘોડસ્વાર અને પેદલ સીપાઈઓ, આગળ પાછળ સઘળા દબદબા સાથે ચાલતા હતા, પણ રાત્રે ૧૨ા વાગે હેદરાબાદમાં કોઈ જાગતું નહી હતું કે તેઓ આ સ્વારીનો દેખાવ જુએ. હમારો આ સુકો દમામ, માત્ર ચંદ્રમાં જે તેજ વખતે નીકળેલો હતો, તે જોઇને એક તરફથી હસતો હતો, અને બીજી તરફથી હમો ગાડીમાં આંચકા ઉચકી ખમતા હસતા હતા.

હેદરાબાદ શેહરની વસ્તી બરોબર કાયદાસર ગણાઈ નથી, તોએપણ તે આસરે ૨,૫૦,૦૦૦ અઢીલાખ માણસોની ધારીયામાં આવેછે, જેમાં ૧,૫૦,૦૦૦ દોડલાખ લોક શેહરની અંદર વસેછે અને બાકીના લાખ માણસો શેહર બાહેર વશેછે. વસ્તીનો મોટો ભાગ મુસલમાન લોકનો છે; શેહરમાં આસરે ૪૦,૦૦૦ ચાળીસ હજાર હિંદુઓ વશેછે, પણ શેહર બાહેર નજદીક ૬૦,૦૦૦ સાઠ હજાર હિંદુઓની વસ્તી છે. નીઝામ સરકારની આખી વસ્તી ૨૫,૦૦,૦૦૦ પચીસ લાખ માણસની ગણતાં, તેના મુખ્ય શેહેરની વસ્તી આખી વસ્તીનો દસમો ભાગ માત્રે ગણાયછે; આ વસ્તીમાં જમીન ખેડનારા મુખ્ય કરીને મરાઠા લોક, તેલંગી, કાનડી અને બીજી જાતનાં હિંદુઓ છે.

જમીન ઘણીજ ઉત્તમ, ફળવંત, અને રસાળ છે, અને ઘણે ઠેકાણે જીહાં પુરતું પાણી મળી શકેછે, તીહાં વરશમાં બે પાક થઈ શકેછે.

નીઝામના દેશમાં વેપાર ઘણોજ થોડો ચાલેછે, અને જેબી થોડો ઘણો ચાલેછે તેથી દેશને સાંભી ખોટ થાયછે. આસપાસના શેહેરોમાંથી નીઝામના લોક જોઈતી જીનસો લાવેછે, જેવું કે ત્રાંબું, સકલાત, મખમલ, રેસમ, છીટ અને

સણનું તથા તરેવાર રંગબેરંગી કપડ; તેની સાથે ખાંડ, કરીયાણું, મસાલાની જીનસો, સુપ્પડ, કારામીરથી શાળ, માલવાથી અફીમ, મારવાડથી બનદુસ અને ઉંટ, અને કોકણ ઝીલામાંથી નીમક, આવતું છે. હીયાંથી નીકાસની જીનસોમાં ઘહું, રૂ, ઉંચી કીસમનું સાગલી લાકડું, જે ગોદાવરી નદીના કીનારા ઉપરથી લાવે-છે, અને તીખું લોહોડું છે. હેદરાબદમાં નાણાનું વીયાજ દર માસે સેંકડે બેથી ત્રણ ટકાનું છે. ઓછામાં ઓછું વીયાજ જે સરકાર આપેછે તે વરસ દાહાડે સેંકડે ૧૨) ટકાનું છે.*

તા૦ ૫ મી જાનેવારી—હેદરાબાદથી રાત્રનાં ૧૨॥ વાગે નીકળેલા આખી રાત્ર મંજલ કીધા પછી એ દીને સહવારનાં સાડાસાત વાગે "રામરાબાદ" નાં મુસાફરી બંગલાંમાં જઇ પોહોંચ્યા. નીજામ તાલુકામાં ઇંગ્રેજી મુસાફરોને સારૂ એ સરકારે ટપે ટપે મુસાફરી બંગલાં રાખેલા છે, તેમાંના કેટલાએક સારી હાલત-માં છે; પણ જે લત્તા ઉપર યુરોપીઅન મુસાફરનું જવું આવવું ઘણું થતું નથી, તેવા લત્તા ઉપરનાં મુસાફરી બંગલાંની હાલત નીજામ તાલુકામાં ઘણીજ હાલહવાલ જણાઈ હતી. નીજામનાં આ લત્તા તરફનું જંગલ ઘણુંજ ખુરાનુમાં અને રળી-યાંમણું અને પક્ષીનાં શીકારીઓનો શોખ પુરો પાડે એવું છે. તળાવોનાં પાણીથી ખેતી ઠેકાણે ઠેકાણે ઘણીજ સારી કરવામાં આવેછે, અને ખાવા પીવાની જીનસો પૈસા ખરચતાં સારીપેઠે મળી શકેછે. આ ઠેકાણેથી બપોરનાં ૫॥ વાગે કુચ કીધી, તે છેક રાત્રે સાડાદસ વાગે "ફરક્કાપોર" નાં મુસાફરી બંગલાંમાં જઈ પોહોં-ચ્યા. જમીને રાત્રે ગાડાંમાંજ સુતા, કેમકે એ લત્તા ઉપરના બંગલાઓમાં કોઈ પણ તરેહની સુવા બેસાવાની સારી ગોઠવણ નહી હતી. કેટલએક ઠેકાણે તો સાધારણ ખુરશી, ટેબલ, અથવા એકુ કોચ પણ નથી. રાત્રે થડે પોહોરે બે વાગે, આ ઠેકાણેથી આગળ ચાલ્યા, તે બીજે દીને,

તા૦ ૬ ઠી જાનેવારીએ બપોરનાં સાડાબાર વાગે "કારૂમપેટા" નાં બંગલામાં જઈ પોહોંચ્યા. એ જગાનું બીજું નામ "જરતોલા" કરીને પણ કેહેછે. હીયાંથી જમીને સાંજના ૭ વાગે નીકળ્યા. આ ઠેકાણે કાંઈ પણ જાણવા અથવા નોંધ કરવા લાયકનું માલુમ પડ્યું નહી હતું.

---

* બ્રીગ્સ નિઝામ, વાલમ ૨ જો, પાનું ૨૩૯.

તા૦ ૭ મી જાનેવારીને દીને સહવારનાં ૯ ને ૨૦ મીનીટે શીયાપુરનું નાળું વટાવ્યું. નદીનાં પાણીથી આસપાસની જગા મધે ખેતી સારી કીધેલી હતી. નીજામ તાલુકામાં જીહાં જીહાં હમારી નજર પડી છે તીહાં રૈયત જોકે મુફલીસ હાલતમાં નજરે પડતી હતી તોએપણ જમીનની ખેતી તો સારી થતી માલુમ પડી છે, અને અગત કરીને જે તાલુકો શેઠ રૂસ્તમજી વીકાજીનાં જમાબંધીનાં અમલ હેઠળ નીજામ તરફથી આવેલો છે તે તાલુકાની ખેતીની આબાદી તો ઘણીજ સારી જોવામાં આવી હતી, અને તીહાંના લોકને પુછતાં તેમનાં અમલ વીશે લોકનું ઘણુંજ સારૂં મત આ શેઠ વીશે સંભળાયું હતું. બપોરનાં ૧૨ાા વાગે "કોટાકોટા" નાં મુસાફરી બંગલામાં જઈ પોંહોંચ્યા. એ બંગલામાં બેસવા ઉઠવાનું કંઈજ નહી હતું તેથી ભોંયચટાઈની બેઠક કરીયા વગર છુટકો નહી હતો, અને બંગલો પણ એટલી ભાગી તુટી અને ગેરસાલ હાલતમાં હતો કે રાત્રે તીહાં રેહેવું સલામતી ભરેલું નહી જાણીને રાત્રેજ નવ વાગામાં હીયાંથી આગળ કુચ કીધી. આ ઠેકાણેથી ઇંગ્રેજ સરકારના સીક્કા (દોહોડીયાં તથા અરધી એટલે પૈ) નું ચલણ જારી થાયછે. હીયાં સુધી નીજામ સરકારનાં સેવરાઈ કરીને ત્રાંબાનાં જાડા પાતળા ઢબુ જેવા પૈસાજ માત્ર ચાલેછે, અને ઇંગ્રેજી સીક્કાવાળાં દોહોડીયાં અથવા અરધીને કોઈ લેવડદેવડમાં વાપરતા નથી. આ ઠેકાણે ખાવા પીવાની અડચણને લીધે તથા ખોરાકની જીનસો જલદી નહી મળ્યાથી હીયાંથી પાછી કુચ કરતાં છેક રાત્ર થઈગઈ હતી. હીયાંથી નીકળતી વેળા એવું સાંભળવામાં આવ્યું હતું કે આગળ જતાં "પેબેર" નામનું એક ગામડું આવશે, તીહાંનો રાજા એક ઘણોજ ચાલાક, હોશીયાર, અને સુધરેલા ખુલ્લા વિચારવાળો તથા ઇંગ્રેજી જબાન સારીપેઠે જાણનારો છે; તેની સાથે તે ઘણોજ મીલનસાર છે, અને રૈયત ઉપર દયાલુપણે અને તેમને પસંદ પડતી રીતે તે હકુમત ચલાવેછે. આવા ચંચલ અને વખાણવાળા રાજાનું આવાં દુરદેશી ગામડામાં રેહેવું સાંભળીને હમને તેની મુલાકાત કરવાની ઘણીજ ઇછા થઇ હતી, અને ખરેખર તેની મુલાકાત થયાથી ઉપર જણાવેલા સગળા સદગુણો હમોએ આ રાજામાં જોયા હતા, જેથી હમને ઘણોજ આનંદ ઉપજીયો હતો.

તા૦ ૮ મી જાનેવારી—એ દીને સહવારના ૬ાા વાગે "પેબેર" ગામ આગળ હમો જઇ પોંહોંચ્યા તીહાં આગળથી ગોઠવણ કરી રાખેલી હતી તે પ્રમાણે ઉતરી

હાથ મોહોડું ધોઇ કપડાં પેહેરી રાજાની મુલાકાત લેવાનો સંદેસો મોકલ્યો, અને તે સદેસાનો જવાબ આવ્યો કે રાજા મોહોટી ખુશીથી હમને મળશે, એવું સાંભળીને હમો તેના મકાન ઉપર ગયા. આ રાજા વનપતીનો રાજા પણ કેહેવાયછે. વનપતી આ શબ્દનો અર્થ સંસ્કૃત ભાષામાં જંગલનો પતી એટલે ધણી અથવા રાજા એવો થાયછે, અને ખરેખર જે ગામમાંતે રાજા રેહેતો હતો તે ગામની આસપાસ મોહોટું જંગલ લાગેલું છે અને તે સઘળી જગાનો ધણી તેજ હતો. આ રાજાનું નામ તથા એલકાબ HIS HIGHNESS RAJA RAMESHWAR RAO BEHARY BAHADHUR એટલે અલીજાહા રાજા રામેશ્વર રાવ બેહારી બાહદુર છે. જારે હમારી મુલાકત થઇ તારે તેણે ઇંગ્રેજી લશ્કરના કલનલની પદવીનો પોશાક પેહેરેલો હતો. તેણે હમારી સાથે ઇંગ્રેજીમાં ઘણીજ સેહેલાઇથી અને સારી પેઠે વાતચીત કીધી હતી. હિંદુસ્થાની ભાષા પણ ઘણીજ સારી અલફાજથી બોલતો સંભળાયો હતો અને તેલંગી ભાષાં તો તેની પોતાનીજ ભાષા હતી. પણ હજી કેહેવાનું વધારે છે. હિંદુસ્થાની જબાંનના જે શીરીન લફજો તેના મોહોડામાંથી નીકલતા હતા તે ઉપરથી હમારા યુરોપિયન મિત્ર મી૦ એડવર્ડે તુરત પીછાન્યું કે રાજા ફારસી જબાન બોલી શકતો હોવો જોઇએ, અને એ વીચાર ઉપરથી ફારસી જબાનમાં રાજાને કેહેવામાં આવ્યું કે તમે સાહેબ ફારસી જબાન જાણોછો, એવું માલુમ પડેછે. તે સાંભળીને રાજાએ ફારસી જબાનમાંજ કહી જણાવ્યું કે હા, હું ફારસી જાણુંછું, અને તેની સાથે મહને જુદી જુદી જબાનો જાણવાનો ઘણોજ શોખ છે, તેથી તે વખતે પોતાના અભ્યાસનાં જોરથી તે સઘળી મલીને ૧૦ જબાન બોલી શકતો હતો. ફારસી ભાષા સાથે અરબી ભાષા પણ બોલી શકતો હતો અને તે વળી હમારા મીત્ર મી૦ એડવર્ડનાં મત પ્રમાણે ઘણીજ સારી રીતે બોલી શકતો હતો. બીજી ભાશામાં તેલંગી, કાનડી, સીંધી, અફગાની, વીગરે ભાષાની પણ તેને માહીતગારી હતી. આ સઘળી ભાષા બોલવાનો સારીપેઠે માહાવેરો રાખવાને, આ જુદી જુદી ભાષા બોલનારાં માણસોને આ રાજાએ પોતાની પાસે લશ્કરી સીપાઇઓ અને અંમલદારોની પદવી ઉપર રાખેલાં હતાં. તે પોતે હિદુ છે, તોપણ હિંદુ ન્યાત જાતની છીત તેનામાં બીલકુલ જોયામાં આવી નહી હતી, અને એ વીશે તેણે પોતાનું મત ખુલ્લું આ છીતની વીરૂદ્ધ કહી સંભળાવ્યું હતું. મુલાકાત થતાં, તેણે હમારી ભેટ એક ઇંગ્રેજ ગૃહસ્થની રીતભાત અને તાજીમ તવાજા

સાથે લીધી હતી. એકબીજાની ખેરોઆફીએત પુછયા પછી તેણે ઘણીજ ઇંતેજારીથી હમારી મુસાફરી વીશે પુછપરછ કીધી, અને હમારી ઈયાદદાસ્ત જો ભુલાવો દેતી નહી હોય તો, હમે ધારીએ છેએ કે વર્તમાનપત્રો અને પોતાની ખાનગી જોસ્તેજોથી, તેણે ખબર મેળવી રાખેલી હતી કે કેટલાએક દેશી ગૃહસ્થો મુંબઈથી મુસાફરી કરવાને નીકળેલા છે, તે કોણ હશે એ જાણવાને તે ઘણોજ ઉમેદવાર હતો, અને હમારી મોલાકાત થયાથી તેની ઇચ્છા એકાએક પુરી પડી હતી તેથી તેને વધારે ખુશાલી ઉત્પન્ન થઇ હતી. થોડીવાર વાતચીત થયા પછી, તેણે સઘળા આદરમાન સાથે હમો સઘળાને એક કપ કાફી અથવા ચાહે પીવાને પુછીઉં. આવી તેની ઇચ્છા જણાયાથી હમોએ તે મોહોટી ખુશીથી કબુલ રાખી હતી, પણ હમારા મીત્ર ડાકતર ભાઉ દાજીએ જારે એ વીશે ના પાડી ત્યારે રાજા ઘણોજ અજબ થઈ બોલવા લાગો કે અરે! આ સું અજાએબ વાત છે કે ડાકતર ભાઉ જેવા પ્રખ્યાત ડાકતર અને વિદ્વાને, હિંદુઓની આવી નજીવી છીત હજુર સુધી પોતાના વીચારમાં રાખી મુકી છે! રાજાએ કહ્યું કે જારે તમારા જેવા સુધરેલા વીચાર અને મતવાળા ગૃહસ્થો જો પોતાની તરફથી આવું સાંકડું મન દેખડાવે અને હીંમત રાખીને આવી નજીવી છીતોને ખુલ્લી રીતે છોડી નહી દે, તો હિંદુસ્થાનના લોકનું સુધારામાં જલદી આગળ વધવું કદી પણ આપણે નથી જોઈ શકવાનાં. તેણે લાંબો વીચાર કરીને પોતાની છીતો એકદમ છોડી દીધી હતી, પણ એવું કરીને તે હિંદુપણામાંથી વટલી નહી ગયો હતો. રાજા એવું બોલીયો કે જેટલા પ્રાચીનકાળના હિંદુઓ એવી છીત વગરનાં હતા, જેટલા તેઓ ખરા લઢાએક અને બાહદુર તથા વિદ્વાન હતા, તેટલા હાલના વખતના હિંદુઓ છીત ભરેલા, બીહીકણ અને અગ્નાની થઈ પડયા છે. રાજાએ હીંમત રાખીને સઘળી છીતો છોડી દીધી છે, તોએપણ પોતાની રૈયતને એ વીશે જેમ જેની નજરમાં નેક આવે તેમ ચાલવાની છુટ આપી છે. રાજાએ પોતાના વિચાર, વગર ભય રાખવે રૈયતને ખુલ્લા જણાવીયા છે. ઇંગ્રેજી રાજ વીશે તેનું મત ઘણુંજ સારૂં છે, અને પોતાનાં રાજમાં ઘણુંકરીને ઇંગ્રેજી રાજનાં કાયદા કાનુનો તેણે દાખલ કીધા છે. રાજાએ હમને કહ્યું કે તેણે બાળપણથી સઘળી કેળવણી તથા લશ્કરી અને રાજદરબારી તાલીમ જનરલ વાહાબ. વી. સી. સીંકલેરના હાથ તળે લીધી છે. રાજા પોતે જાતે હીંમતવાન અને લડાએક મરદ છે; અને નીજામ હેદરાબાદનાં રાજ સાથે એને કંઈ એકવાર

ગેરસમજુતી થતાં, નીજામ સાથે એણે પોતે ખુદ તલવાર ખેંચી છે, જેમાં ઘણીવાર એને શીકસ્ત ખમવી પડી છે, તેમ કોઈવાર રાજાએ પણ સારી ફતેહ નીજામ ઉપર મેળવી છે. નીજામ હેદરાબાદનો, આ રાજા એક અચ્છો હમનબરદ એક વાર ગણાયો હતો. કાફી પીધા પછી, રાજા હમને પોતાનાં દીવાનખાનામાં તેડી લઈ ગયો, અને થોડી વારમાં હમારી સાથે ઘણોજ મીલનસાર થઈ ગયો હતો. તેણે પોતાના ફોટોગ્રાફ હમને આપ્યા, અને હમારી પાસે તેણે હમારા ફોટોગ્રાફ માંગ્યા, પણ હમારી પાસે તે વખતે હમારા ફોટોગ્રાફ હાજર નહીં હતા તેથી હમોએ તે વીશે દીલગીરી જણાવી, પણ રાજાએ કહ્યું કે કંઈ ફીકર નહીં, મુંબઈ જઇને તે મોકલી દેવા. ત્યાર પછી હમારી પાસથી હમારા નામનાં કાર્ડ માંગી લીધા. હમારા નામ નીશાન સઘળાં વીગતવાર પુછી લીધાં ને તે પોતાની યાદદાસ્ત ચોપડીમાં નોંધી લીધાં. ત્યાર પછી તેણે પોતાની મા બેહેન તથા કુટુંબનાં બીજા માણસોની સબી હમને દેખડાવી. આ રાજા પોતાની બેહેન તથા કુટુંબના છોકરાંઓને સારી કેળવણી આપતો હતો, તથા સારી કેળવણી આપવાની જરૂર તે સારીપેઠે જાણતો હતો અને તે પ્રમાણે તે કરતો પણ હતો એવું તેણે હમને કહી જણાવ્યું હતું.

આસરે ૧ાા કલાક સુધી રાજા સાથે, જાણે કેટલાક વરશની મીત્રાચારી હોય એવી રીતે વાતચીત થઈ હતી, તેમાં તેણે મુસાફરી કરવાની અગત વીશેના ફાયદા કહી જણાવ્યા અને યુરોપ ખંડની મુસાફરી અગત કરીને હીંદુસ્થાનનાં રાજવંશીઓ અને શક્તિવાન શેઠીઆઓએ કરવી કેટલી જરૂર છે, એ વીશે કહી જણાવ્યું, અને પોતાની ઇચ્છા આવી મુસાફરી કરવાની ઘણીજ છે. પણ તે ક્યારે પુરી પડશે, એ વીશે તેણે ઘણી ઇનતેજારી જણાવી હતી.

સહવારનાં સાડાસાત કલાકે તડકો વધવા લાગ્યો. રાજા શીકાર કરવા જનાર હતો તેથી તેણે હમને સાથે લઈ જવાને ઇચ્છા જણાવી, પણ પુરતો વખત હમારા હાતમાં નહીં હોવાનાં સબબથી, હમને ના પાડવાની જરૂર થઈ. જતી વખતે હમે પુછયું કે તે સાનો શીકાર કરવાને જાએછે. જવાબ મળ્યો કે રાની મરઘાનો. આ પક્ષીનો રાજાને ઘણોજ શોખ હતો. તેણે બીજું એવું કહ્યું કે શીકાર જવાને તે તઈઆર થઈ રહેલો હતો, એવામાં હમારી મુલાકાત વીશે તેને સંદેસો પોહોંચ્યાથી, તેણે વીહાં જવાનું મુલતવી રાખ્યું હતું.

રાજાની હિંમત અને તેના કેટલાએક ખુલ્લા વીચારો હમારા હિંદુ ભાઈબંધોને ધ્યાન પોહોંચાડવા લાયક છે. જંગલ વચ્ચે એખલો, પોતે એવા વીચાર સાથે મુસ્તકીમ રહી, હિંદુ રૈયતને પસંદ પડતી રીતિ એ રાજા પોતાનો અંમલ ચલાવેછે, એજ હકીકત તેની કીરતી બોલવાને બસ છે. અગર એવી રીતિ આપણા કેટલાક નામાંકીત દેશી વિદ્વાનો, આવી હિંમતથી અને ખુલ્લાં દીલથી જો પોતાનાં મત પોતાના ભાઈબંધોને જાણીતાં કરે અને તે મુજબ પોતે ખુદ અમલ કરે તો, તેથી આપણા દેશના સુધારાનો પ્રસારો વધારે મુસ્તકીમ પાયા ઉપર અને જલદીથી થઈ શકે એમાં સંદેહ નથી. પણ બોલવું અને તે મુજબ કરવું નહીં, આ ચાલ એટલી તો મુંબઈમાં સુધારો કરનારાઓએ અખતીયાર કરી છે કે હમો નહી ધારતા કે આવી રીતિજ જો તેઓ ચાલેતો આવતી પા સદીમાં પણ કંઈ ખરેખરો સુધારો થાય.

રાજા પાસથી સહવારના ૭ા વાગે હમે રૂખસદ લીધી અને તીહાંથી ૧૦ વાગે વેંકટાપુર ગામડાં આગળ આવી પુગા. એ ઠેકાણે જરા લાંબો વખત વીસામો લીધો, કેમકે લાંબી લાગટ કરેલી મંજલથી થાક વધારે લાગ્યો હતો. રાત્રે ૧૦ વાગે હીંયાંથી આગળ કુચ કીધી, અને હવેતો મુસાફરી બંગલા નહીં મલી આવીયાથી, ગાડામાંજ હુંગાવું બેહતર જાણીયું હતું, અને એવી આસરંભ પણ પડી ગઈ હતી.

તા૦ ૯ મી જાનેવારીને દીને સહવારનાં પરોઢીયામાં ૪ વાગે કૃષ્ણા નદીને કીનારે આવી પુગા. આગળથી સ્વારો મોકલ્યા હતા કે નદી પાર ઉતરવાને સઘળા બંદોબસ્તો અને જોઈતી ચીજો તૈયાર કરી રખાવે, પણ આ સ્વારોની બેપરવાઈ અને સુસ્તીથી કંઈપણ ગોઠવણ થયલી નહીં હતી, તેથી નદી કીનારે જારે પાછલી રાત્રે ૪) વાગે આવી પુગા તારે કોઇ સ્વાર અથવા કોઈ કાળું કુતું પણ હાજર નહીં હતું. છેક સહવારનું અજવાળું પડે તીહાંસુધી હમને ખોટી થઈ રેહેવું પડયું હતું. પણ એવી રીતે ખોટી થતાં એક ફાયદો એ થયો હતો કે નદી ઉતરવાને જે જાતના મછવા એ લત્તા તરફ વપરાયછે તે જોવાને અને તપાસવાને, સહવારનાં અજવાળાંથી હમને બરોબર તક મલી શકી હતી. નદી ઉતરવાને ઘણેએક ઠેકાણે લાકડાંના નાહાનાં મોહોટા મછવા અથવા હોડીઓ હોયછે તેવું એ તરફ જોવામાં આવ્યું નહીં હતું. હોડીને ઠેકાણે એ તરફ મોહોટા ગોલ ટેપલા વાપરેછે. આ ટેપલા, મજબુત જાડા બાંબુના બનાવેછે, અને તેની આસપાસ ચાંમડું શીવી લીધેલું હોયછે. ટેપ-.લાનો આકાર લોહોડાંની મોહોટી કઢા અથવા ઉંડી જાપ જેવો હોયછે, અને તેમાં

માણસો બેસીને હલેસાંએ કરીને એ ટોપલાને ગોલ ફેરવતા ફેરવતા પાણીમાં તેરવેછે. એ ટોપલામાં બળદની ગાડી અને તેવોજ બીજો ભારી સામાન પણ એક પારથી બીજે પાર લેઈ જવાઈ શકાયછે. એકેક ટોપલામાં ૧૫ થી ૨૦ માણસો બેસીને પાર ઉતરી શકેછે. એવા ટોપલા જળમાર્ગે મુસાફરી કરવાને ઘણાજ જોખમ ભરેલા પેહેલવેહેલાં જોતાં માલુમ પડેછે. જારે હમારી નજર પેહેલ વેહેલી એવા ટોપલા ઉપર પડી ત્યારે હમોએ એકાએક એવું માન્યું નહીં હતું કે એમાં માણસો અથવા ગાડીઓ એક પારથી બીજે પાર જઇ શકશે, પણ જારે હમો તેમાં બેઠા ત્યારે હમારી ખાતરી થઈ કે એવા ટોપલા પણ હોડીને ઠેકાણે નદી ઉતરવાને વપરાઈ શકાયછે. પુછપરછ કરતાં એવું માલુમ પડ્યું કે એ લત્તા તરફ નદી નાળાંઓ ઉતરવાને એવીજ જાતના ટોપલા વપરાયછે અને હોડી અથવા મછવા જેવી ચીજ તેઓ વાપરતા નથી.

કૃષ્ણા નદીનું પાણી, પાહાડી જગાઓમાંથી એટલાં તો જોરથી વેહેછે કે તેના જોર આગળ લાકડાંની હોડી અથવા મછવાનો આસરો રહી શકતો નથી. નદીનો કીનારો એ તરફ જબરો ખડકવાળો છે, તેથી જેટલી ધાસ્તી હોડી અથવા મછવો ઘસડાઇ અને અફળાઈ ભાંગવાની છે તેટલી ધાસ્તી એ ટોપલાઓ વીશે નથી. આ અસ્લી ટોપલા, નદીના પાણી ઊપર ગોલ ચકર ફરતા, અજાએબ તરેથી તરતા રેહેછે. આ ટોપલા એણીગમથી પેલીગમ વાંકા ટીકા થતા, ઝોકા ખાતા, ધાંમટ કરતા, અને કોઈવાર કીનારાને અથડતા અથડતા પણ ઘણીજ ઝડપથી દોડતા, નદી તરી શકેછે. એઓની ભાર ખમવાની મજબુતી વીશે એવું જણાવવામાં આવ્યુંછે કે તોપખાનાનો સામન પણ પાર ઉતરવામાં તેમને ઉપયોગમાં લાવીયાછે, તેની સાથે બીજી સગવડ એ ટોપલાઓથી એ થાયછે કે નદીના જુદા જુદા પાટો પાર કરતાં, વચમાં જમીન આવી હોય તો તે ટોપલાને સેહેલાઇથી માથા ઊપર ઊંચકીને એક ઠેકાણેથી નદીના બીજા પાટ ઉપર લઇ જવાઈ શકાયછે. આવે ઠેકાણે જો હોડી અથવા મછવો હોયતો તેમ કરવાને મોટી અડચણ થઈ પડેછે. તુંગભદ્રા, પાનેર વીગરે નદીઓ કૃષ્ણા નદીને મળેછે, તે નદીઓ પાર ઊતરવાને સારૂ પણ એવાજ ટોપલા ઊપલાજ સબબોને લીધે વપરાયછે.

કૃષ્ણા નદીને પેલે પાર ઉતરયા બાદ પેાટરનું ગામડું કાંઠેજ આવેલું છે તે જોવાને ગયા. આ ગામડું ઉજડ હાલતમાં પડેલુંછે, પણ એની ઊજડ હાલતમાં જે જે

નીશાનો હમારી નજરે પડી હતી તે ઊપરથી એવું માલુમ પડયું હતું કે અસલનાં વખતમાં તે એક ઘણુંજ સુંદર અને મોહોટું ગામ હશે. હિંદુઓનાં દેહેરાં પુષ્કળ જોયામાં આવ્યાં હતાં, પણ તે સઘળાં ખીસમાર હાલતમાં હતાં. ઘણાંએક દેહેરાં ઉપર નકસી અને કોતરકામ ઘણુંજ સારૂં કરેલુ નજરે પડયું હતું. રામનું એક દેહેરૂં જોયામાં આવ્યું હતું, તેનાં દરવાજા ઉપર રામચંદ્રજીની સભાનો ચીતાર એક આખા પથરમાં દરવાજાની બરશાખઉપર કોતરેલો છે, તે સભાનો ચીતાર જાણે આજેજ કોતરેલો હોય એવી સહીસલામત હાલતમાં જોયામાં આવીયો હતો. તેના પથર ઊપરનાં નકસીકામને જરા પણ અલવાર પોંહોંચેલી નહી હતી. તે ઓછામાં ઓછી ૨૦૦થી ૨૫૦ વરસની જુની માલુમ પડી હતી. પોટર ગામડાંની મસજીદનાં ઓટલા ઊપરજ તુરત ઊતારો કીધો, કેમકે સહવારનાં નદી ઉતરતાં અને પેલા ટોપલાઓમાં સામાન, ગાડાં ઈત્યાદિ ચહડાવી પાછાં ઊતારતાં ભારી થાક લાગી હતી અને તેમજ વખત પણ થઇ ગયો હતો. ખાણું તઈયાર થાય તીહાંસુધી મસજીદનાં ખુલ્લા ઓટલા ઊપર બેસીને આસપાસનાં ઝાડો તથા જંગલની રચના જોતા હતા અને પેલા ટોપલા વીશે વાત કરતા હતા કે ખરેખર આ જાતની હોડી એક નમુના દાખલ ઇંગલંડ મોકલવા લાયક છે, તેવામાં દુરથી એક બે માણસ ૧૦થી ૧૫ ગધેડાં, પખાલ લાધીને લઈ જતાં માલુમ પડયાં. હમે સમજયા કે નદીએથી પાણી ભરીને ગામમાં પોંહોંચાડવા તે પખાલીઓ પાણી લઈ જતા હશે, અને તે ઊપરથી તેમની પાસે પાણી માંગ્યું, ત્યારે તેઓએ ઊત્તર વાળ્યો કે પખાલમાં પાણી નથી પણ "સીંદી છે." તાડીને આ લોક સીંદી કેહેછે, અને તે પખાલોમાં તાડી ભરીને, ગામનાં દારૂનાં ગુત્તાવાળા તે લઈજતા હના. તાડીની પખાલો ગધેડાંઊપર લાધીને ગામમાં એવી રીતે દીવસમાં બે ત્રણ ખેપ જાયછે, એવું સમજીને વાંચનાર વીચારમાં પડશે કે ગામડામાં અને તેની આસપાસની વસ્તીમાં તાડીનો કેટલો ખપ હશે. પુછપરછ કરતાં માલુમ પડયું કે એ લત્તા તરફ લોક, તાડી જબરાં પીનાર છે. સહવાર, સાંજ, બપોર અને વખત બેવખત, નાહાનાથી તે મોહોટાં સુધી, સઘળાં તાડીથી ભીનેલાં રહે-છે. એ બાબદમાં પારસી લોકનાં મોબેદોને એઓ શરમમાં નાખે, એટલાં તાડી પીનારાં છે. વળી આટલી તાડી પીને મારામારી કરનાર પણ તેટલાંજ જબરાં છે. જેટલો તાડીનો દારૂ પીવાયછે તેના કરતા ફકત તાડી (ખાટી અથવા મીઠીનો ફરક તો કોઈ રાખતું હોય એવું તો જાણીયામાં આવીયું નથી) દશગણી વધારે જબરી પીવાયછે.

મુસલમાન અને હિંદુલોકમાં એનું વ્યસન એ લણા તરફ અતીશય થઈ પડેલુંછે. તાડીની કેફથી લોકમાં મારામારી હેવી તો થાયછે કે તેમાં ખુન વટીક પણ ખાલી નથી. તાડી કંઈ ખજુરાંનીજ નરદમ હોતી નથી, એમાં બજરબટુની, માહાડની, તાડની એવી પંચભેળ હોયછે, અને તેમાં વળી વેચનારો બીજી કેફી વસ્તુ મીશ-રીત કરતા હશે તે જુદી. એ લત્તા તરફ મહુડાંનાં ઝાડ ઘણા નથી તેથી તેનો દારૂ તેમને મળી શકતો નથી. હમો ધારીએ છીએ કે મહુડાંનાં ઝાડ નહી હોયાથી ખરે-ખર તેમનાં ઉપર ઈશ્વરની એક મોટી કૃપા થઇ છે.

મસજીદમાં નાસ્તો લઈ રહ્યા પછી હમારી સાથે આવેલા નીજામનાં ઘોડસ્વારોને કહી જણાવ્યું કે તેઓએ નદી કીનારે આગળથી આવીને ટોપલા વીગેરેની ગોઠવણ નહી કરવામાં મોહોટી ભુલ કીધી હતી અને તેથી હમને ઘણી ખોટી થઈ હતી તથા કેટલીક અડચણો ખમવી પડી હતી માટે ફરીને એવી ગફલતી નહી થાય એટલા સારૂ ખુબ ચોકાશી રાખવી, અને હવે તે દીવસે "કરનુલ" ના મુસાફરી બંગલા-માં પોંહોંચતાં કદાચને રાત્ર પડે, માટે થોડાક સ્વારોએ આગળથી જઇને બંગલામાં ઉતારો કરવાની ગોઠવણ કરી રખાવવી, અને રસ્તો બરોબર દેખાડવાને કેટલાએક સ્વારોએ હમારી સાથે રેહેવું. કૃષ્ણા નદી પાર ઉતરીયા પછી, કરનુલ તરફ આગળ ચા-લતાં જમીન નીચી ઢલાવવાળી આવેછે અને રસ્તો બરોબર નથી; તથા તેમાં પુષ્કળ પથરા તથા ખાડા ખબોચીયા છે, તોએપણ જેટલો ખડક કૃષ્ણા નદી મુકયા પછી તુરત રસ્તામાં લાગેછે તેટલો કરનુલ તરફ વધતાં ઓછો થતો જાયછે. આટલું સર્વુ સમજાવીને કહ્યું તોપણ આ સ્વારોથી કંઈ બરોબર કામ થઈ શકયું નહી હતું; અને તેઓ કામ કરવામાં ઘણાજ બેદીલ માલુમ પડ્યા હતા. પુછપરછ કરતાં માલુમ પડયું કે હમારી સાથે મુસાફરી કરતાં નીજામ સરકારનાં ખરચથી ખાવાંને બદલે તેઓ પોતાનું ગાઠનું નાણું ખરચી ખાતાં હતા, અને ખાવા પીવાની તેઓ ઉપર જબરી વેહેલા પડતી હતી. ઘોડાઓઉપર પણ ઘાસ દાણાની એવીજ તંગી પડતી હતી, તેથી સ્વારો જલદી પાછા ફરવાની વધારે ઇંતેજારીમાં હતા. હમને આ વાતની ખબર પડી ત્યારે તે સ્વારોને ખાવા પીવાની અને ઘાસ દાણાની જોગવાઈ કરી અપાવી હતી; અને સઘળાને, કરનુલ પોંહોંચ્યા પછી પાછા રવાના કરવાનો વીચાર કરી મુકયો હતો.

પોટર ગામડામાંથી ૧૦॥ વાગે સહવારનાં નીકળ્યા હતા અને જો કે રસ્તો બરો-

ખર દેખડાવવાની આગળથી ચેતવણી આપી રાખેલી હતી તોએપણ તેમાં અંતે ભુલ થઈ. સાંજ સુધી સઘળું કામ બરોબર ચાલ્યું પણ જરા અંધારૂં થતાં, પેલા સ્વારો ઢાંચાબાંચા થવા લાગા. બે જણ દેખાય તો બે જણ નહી દેખાય, અને આપણે પુછીએ ત્યારે કેહે કે જરા પાણી પીવા ગયા છે, ફલાણો સ્વાર જરા ખુદરતી હાજતને લીધે પછવાડે રહયો છે. પણ મુખ્ય કારણ થોડી વારમાં એવું જણાવા લાગુ કે સાંજ પડતાં, પેલી પખાલીની ભેટ લેવાની તલબ આ સ્વારોને થતી હતી. ભુખ લાગવાથી જેટલું ખાતા નહી હશે તેટલું પીઇને ખીચારાઓ પોતાની ભુકને શાંત અથવા નરમ પાડતા હોએ એવું જણાતું હતું. સ્વારોની આવી ગફલતીથી ગાડીવાળાઓ રસ્તો ભુલ્યા, અને તેમનાથી આડ રસ્તો લેવાયો, જેનો ખુલાસો છેક રાત્રે ૧૧ાા વાગે થયો, તે એ પ્રમાણે કે "કરનુલ" ગામ પોંહોંચ્યા પછી મુસાફરી બંગલામાંજવાને બદલે, ગાડીવાનો, બે હડી માઇલ આડા, ગાંમમાં ગાડી ચલાવી ગયા. અગર હમારી સાથે એકુ પણ સ્વાર રહયો હતે તો આવું નહી બનતે. ગામમાં ગયા તારે તે વખતે એક પણ માણસ જાગતું નહી હતું, અને જો આ વખતે ચંદ્રની રોશની નીકળી નહી હતે તો તે રાત્રે ખચીત ઘણાજ હાડમાર થતે. કોઈ મળ્યું નહી, ત્યારે પુછપરછ કરવાનું પણ નહી બનીયું. હાંક મારી ઘરનાં બારણાં ઠોકીને પુછીએતો ઘરમાંથી પાછો જબાબ મળવો મુશકેલ હતો, અને કદી કોઈ ઉઠીને બાહેર આવ્યો તો તેનાં મોહોડામાંથી એવો જવાબ નીકળતો હતો કે "મહને કંઈ ખબર નથી." ગામડાનાં લોક તરફની બેપરવાઇ જોઇને અલબતાં કોઇને પણ ઘણો ગુસ્સો આવે તેમાં નવાઈ જેવું નથી, પણ બીજી તરફથી વીચાર કરતાં અને આગળ કહ્યું તેમ ગાંમડાંના લોકને વેઠે પકડીને તેમની પાસે જુલમથી કાંમ કરાવવાની અણઘટતી ચાલ અંદરનાં પ્રાંતોમાં કેટલાએક હલકા અને અણસમજુ અમલદારો ચલાવેછે, તેથી આવી તરેહની ઇજા અથવા સંકટ ઘણાએક મુસાફરોને ખમવી પડે એમાં પણ નવાઈ જેવું નહી જાણીને, એવી વખતે ભલી ભલાઇથી કામ લેવું ફાયદા ભરેલું સમજીયા હતા. એણીગમ પેલીગમ ઘણા રખડયા પછી, અંતે ઇનામની આશા આપીને તથા નરમાસ ભરેલી રીતે કહ્યાથી, ગામમાંથી એક જણ હમને મળી આવ્યો તેણે હમારી ભુલ ભાંજી કે મુસાફરી બંગલામાં જવાનો જે રસ્તો છે તે જુદોજ છે;

અને હમે નજદીક બે હડી માઈલ આડા ચાલી આવ્યા હતા, એવું કહીને તે પોતે હમારી સાથે ભોમીયા દાખલ આવ્યો અને હમને પાછા વાળીને બરોબર રસ્તાઉપર લઈ આવ્યો. હીયાંથી મુસાફ્રી બંગલામાં હમે રાત્રે સાડાબાર અથવા એક વાગે પુગા. તીહાં જઇને જોઈએ છીએ તો જે સ્વારોને આગળથી મોકલેલા હતા તેઓ તીહાં આવીને પોતાનાં ઘોડાઓને બાંધીને પોતે મજેથી ઉંઘમાં પડેલા હતા. તેઓએ હમારે સારૂ કંઈજ કીધું નહી હતું. બંગલાનાં મેસમેનને ખાણા પીણા વીરો, અથવા હમો આવવાનાં છીએ તે વીશેની તૈયારી રાખવાને એક શબ્દ વટીક પણ કહ્યો નહી હતો; અથવા બંગલો ઉઘડાવી એક કોચ મજાત તૈયાર કરાવ્યો નહી હતો. તેથી જારે હમે પુગા ત્યારે હમારે સારૂ એક કપ ચાહે અથવા એક કળસલી પાણીએ તૈયાર નહી હતું. એક તો આખા દીવસનાં ભુખ્યા, બીજું, આડ રસ્તે ભુલા પડયાથી હલાક થયલા, ત્રીજું, ભોમીયો સોધતાં નજદીક એક કલાક પગે રખડેલા, અને છેલ્લું મુસાફ્રી બંગલાનો ઓરડો આગળથી જઇને આપણા સ્વાધીનમાં લેઇ રાખવાને ખામુખા જે સીપાહી લોકને મોકલીયા હતા તેમની બેપરવાઈથી અંતે હમારી આગમચ કોઈ ઇંગ્રેજ આવીને તુરતનોજ ઉતરેલો હતો, તેથી હમારે સારૂ ઉતારાની જગા પણ બંગલામાં પુરતી નહી રહેલી, આ સઘળા કંટાળા ભરેલા બનાવોથી હમોને ભારી ગુસ્સો ચઢીયો હતો. અંતે એક નાહાના ઓરડામાં જેમ તેમ રાત્રનો બાકીનો વખત કાહાડતાં હમારી ધીરજની પરીક્શા સારીપેઠે થઈ હતી. જો આગળથી જઈ પુગેલા સ્વારોએ તેમને ફરમાવ્યા પ્રમાણે બંદોબસ્ત કીધો હોત તો આ સઘળી ખીકટ નહી ખમવી પડતે, અને તે પડી તો પડી, પણ આટલું તો ખચીત થતે કે હમારે સારૂ મુસાફ્રી બંગલાનો મોહોટો ઓરડો તો આસાએસ લેવાને હાથ લાગતે. પણ તેવું નહીજ થયું, હમારી ઉપર આ ખીકટ એકંદર આવી પડી તે સઘળી પેલા નીજામનાં આળશુ, બેપરવા સ્વારોથી થઈ હતી. ખેર, રાત્ર તો જેમ તેમ કરીને કાહાડી. ભુખનો આધાર સહવારનાં નાસ્તા ઉપર સઘળો હતો. બપોર તો રોજા ખોલવા વગર કાહાડી હતી, અને હવે રાત્રે ૧ વાગે માત્ર ચાહે અને બીસકોટ ઉપરજ શુકરાનાં કરવાની હમારી ફરજ થઈ પડી. સુવાની જગાનાં પણ વાખા હોવાથી, જે નાહાનો ઓરડો હમને કેટલી મેહેનતથી મળ્યો હતો તેમાં એક જણ અને બાકીનાં સઘળા ગાડીમાંજ સુતા હતા.

તા૰ ૧૦ મી જાનેવારી—એ દીને સહવારનાં કરનુલના ડેપ્યુટી કલેકટર તથા તેનો ભાઈ, આ બંધે ગૃહસ્થો તીહાનાં દેશી અમલદારો હતા તેમને ખબર પડ્યાથી, તેઓ હમારી મુલાકાત લેવાને આવ્યા, તેમની આગળ આગલી રાત્રે રસ્તામાં પડેલી અડચણો વીશે કહી જણાવીવું. વાતચીત કરતાં તેમનાં મત પ્રમાણે હમોએ જે વીચાર હેદરાબાદથી નીકળતી વખતે કીધો હતો કે કડાપા અને કરનુલને રસ્તે થઈ મદ્રાજ જઈશું તો જલદી જવારો, તે વીચારને આ ઠેકાણે, આ અમલદારોની મસલહતથી ટેકો મળીયો અને તેથી તે પાકો અને વધારે મજબુત થયો. આ ઠેકાણેથી, પેલા નકામાં અને બેદીલ સ્વારોને હેદરાબાદ પાછા રવાના થવાને ફરમાવ્યું. હેદરાબાદથી કરેલા ગાડાંવાળાઓને પણ આ ઠેકાણેથી, હમે રૂખસદ આપી. તેઓ કડાપાને રસ્તે મદ્રાજ જવા નાખુરા જણાયા, જેનું કારણ એ કે તેઓ એ રસ્તાથી તદન અજાણ્યા હતા, અને આગલી રાત્રે રસ્તો ભુલ્યાથી તેમની ઊપર જે સંકટ અને અડચણો ગુજરી હતી તેથી તેઓ ધરાઈ ગયા હતા! અને તદન નાહીંમત થઈ ગયા હતા.

કરનુલ રોહેર દેખાડવાને પાછલા પોહોરનાં ચાર વાગે ડેપ્યુટી કલેકટર તથા તેમના ભાઈ, એક શીગરામ લઈને ઠરાવ પ્રમાણે આવ્યા. રોહેરમાં હમો ફરવા ગયા. રોહેરનો દેખાવ જેમ ઘણો તવંગરી ભરેલો નહીં તેમ ઘણો ગરીબી ભરેલો પણ નહી દેખાયો હતો. લોક ચંચલ, ઉદ્યોગી તથા ઝડપવાળાં માલુમ પડયાં હતાં. ઉદ્યોગની નીશાનો, કપડ બજારમાં સારી નજરે પડી હતી. લોક કાનડી ભાષા ઘણું કરીને બોલેછે. બીજાં ગામો અથવા ગામડાં તથા રોહેરો કરતાં હીયાંના રસ્તા સારી હાલતમાં દેખાયા હતા, તેનું મુખ્ય કારણ એટલુજ હતું કે કરનુલ રોહેરમાં ઇંગ્રેજોની વસ્તી તથા બંગલા છે, તથા લશ્કરની તુકડીઓ વખતે વખત આવજાવ કરતાં આ ઠેકાણે થોડીવાર છાવણી કરેછે. ફકત રોહેરની વસ્તી ૨૫૦૦૦થી ૩૦૦૦૦ માણસની આસરે ગણાયલી છે.

નીજામ હેદરાબાદથી કરનુલ રોહેર ૧૩૦ માઈલની મુસાફરીને છેટે છે. કરનુલ રોહેર અને તેને લગતાં ગાંમો, બાલાઘાટ પ્રગણાંનો એક ભાગ છે. ઇસિવી સન ૧૮૦૦ નાં સાલમાં ઇંગ્રેજ અને નીજામ સરકાર વચ્ચે જે કરારનામું થયું હતું તેની સરતો મુજબ નીજામ સરકારે બાલાઘાટ પ્રગણાં ઇંગ્રેજ સરકારને સ્વાધીન કર્યાં હતાં. બાલાઘાટ પ્રગણાંની હદ કૃષ્ણા અને તુંગભદ્રા નદીઓની દક્ષીણ

દીશાએથી સીરૂ થાયછે, અને એ સઘળાં પ્રગણાં પાહાડી જગાને મથાળે આવેલાં છે તેથી તેમને બાલાઘાટનું નામ આપ્યામાં આવ્યું છે. "બાલાઘાટ" શબ્દનો અર્થ "ઘાટની ઉપરની જગા" એવો થાયછે અને તેનાથી ઉલટો શબ્દ "પેયનઘાટ" કરીને બોલાયછે, તેનો અર્થ "ઘાટની નીચેની અથવા પાયા આગળની જગા" એવો થાયછે.

આગલા દેશી રાજાઓનાં વખતમાં બાલાઘાટ પ્રાંત ઘણાં પ્રગણાંમાં વેંહેચાયલું હતું. તેમાં કરનુલ, કડાપા અને બેલારી વીગરે બીજાં દશ પ્રગણાં મુખ્ય હતાં. ઇંગ્રેજને સ્વાધીન થયા પછી, બાલાઘાટ પ્રાંતના બે ભાગ કરયામાં આવ્યા છે, એક ભાગને કડાપા જીલ્લામાં દાખલ કીધો છે અને બીજો બેલરી કલેકટરેટમાં છે.

તવારીખ અને દસ્તાવેજો ઉપરથી એવું માલુમ પડેલું છે કે આખો બાલાઘાટ પ્રાંત ઇંગ્રેજ સરકારને સ્વાધીન થયા આગમચ, જારે નીજામ સરકારનાં તાબામાં હતો ત્યારે તીહાંની રૈયતની અવસ્થા અતીશય માઠી અને તેમનો જીવ સટોસટ હાલતમાં હતો. જમીન તો ઘણીજ સારી અને ફલવંત છે. ઘણું કરીને કાળી મચેડીવાળી જમીન વીશે એવું અનુભવ ઊપરથી માલુમ પડેલું છે કે જો એવી જમીનને એક વખત સાફ કરીને હોલથી બરોબર ખેડી હોય તો પછી વીસ વરશ સુધી ફરીને તેને ખેડવાની કાંઈજ જરૂર પડતી નથી, માત્રે જમીનને ઉપર ઉપરથી ફેરવી નાખેલી બસ છે. કનેરા અને મલબાર પ્રાંત તરફની જમીન કરતાં આ પ્રાંતની જમીન વધારે ફળવાન છે. ફકત બે અથવા ત્રણ રાત્રનો વરસાદ એ જમીન ઉપર પડેલો કાનેરાની જમીનનાં વીસ્તાર સાથે સરખાવતાં વધારે પાક ઉપજાવી શકેછે; પણ તેની ખેડણી કરી તેમાંથી નીપજતી આએપત સહી સલાંમતીથી ખાવાની, રૈયત બીલકુલ આશા નહી રાખતી હતી. રૈયત હંમેશ લુટાતી હતી, અને તેમને લુટનાર કોણ હતા? નીજામ સરકાર તરફથી જે જમાબંદી કરનાર અમલદારો ઠરાવેલા તેજ! તથા જે કોઈ એવા અમલદારોને જમણપ્રસાદ આપી શકે એવા રૂશવત આપનારા સઘળાં લોક! નીજામનું લશ્કર જાથુક જમાબંધીનાં કામમાં લડાઈ કરવાને રોકાયલુંજ રહેતું હતું, અને ગામ ગામડાંવાળા હમેશ એકબીજા સાથે નબળા ઉપર જોરાવર ફાવવાને લડાઈ કરવામાં ગુંનાયલાજ રેહેતા હતા. દરેક ગામ ગામડાંના રોડીઆઓએ પોતાનું લશ્કર રાખેલું હતું, અને જમાબંધી કરનારા અમલદારો

સાથે તેમને હંમેશા લડાઈ અથવા જપાજપી થયાજ કરતી હતી. કેહેછે કે નીજામ સરકાર એવી લડાઇ કરતી કરતી બેજાર થઈ ગઈ હતી, અને આવી લડાઈ કરતાં તેને જમાબંધીની ઉપજ આવા મોહોટા પ્રાંતમાંથી કંઈ જુજવીજ થતી હતી.*

એક દાખલા પ્રમાણે આ ઠેકાણે હમે જણાવવાની જરૂર જોઇએ છીએ કે દેશની જમાબંધી જો બરોબર અને રૈયતનાં ખરાં સુખની મતલબ ધ્યાનમાં રાખીને કીધી હોયતો ખચીત તેની રૈયત અને સરકાર એ બંધેને ફાએદો થયા વીના રેહેનાર નથી, અને તેની સાથે દેશની જમીનની હાલત પણ બેહેતર થતી જવાની. ઇંગ્રેજ સરકારની જમાબંધી કરવાની રીત અને કાયદા ખરેખર ઘણાજ વાજબી અને રૈયતની તથા સરકારની અને જમીનની હાલત બેહેતર કરવાને લાયકનાજ છે, અને એની સાબેતી હિંદુસ્થાનમાં જીહાં જીહાં ઇંગ્રેજ સરકારની જમાબંધી ચાલુ થઈછે, તીહાં તીહાં રૈયતની હાલત તથા જમીન, બંધે બેહેતર થયલી માલુમ પડી છે; અને જીહાં જીહાં એ સરકારની રીત ચાલુ થઇ નથી, તીહાંની રૈયત, જમીન અને તે સરકાર પોતે સાથે ત્રણે જણો માઠી અવસ્થામાં ગોતાં ખાયાં કરેછે. આ ખરી બીના આપણે નજરે નજર જોઇએછ. જીહાં જમાંબંધી રીતો આવા બંદોબસ્તો નથી તીહાં વગર ખેડણીએ જમીન જંગલી હાલતમાં પડી રહેલી છે, રૈયત ગરીબ અને નાઉમેદીમાં જેમ તેમ પોતાના દીવસો ગુજારેછે, અને સરકાર પણ તેવીજ લાઈલાજ અને ગુંચવાડામાં પોતાનું કામ ચલાવ્યા કરેછે. કદાચ ઉપર જણાવેલી બાબદની વિરૂદ્ધ એવું કેહેવામાં આવે કે ઇંગ્રેજ સરકારની જમાબંધીમાં પણ રૈયત ઉપર જુલુમ ગુજરેછે, તેઓની હાલત બેહેતર થતી નથી, દુકાળ પડેછે, લોકમાં ભુખમરો ચાલેછે, અને એ વીગરે બીજી ફરીઆદો થાયછે, પણ એનો ખુલાસો તુરત થઈ શકે એવો છે. ઉપર કહેલી ફરીઆદ ઇંગ્રેજ સરકારની જમાબંધીની રીતો અથવા કાયદાને લાગુ પડતી નથી. તે રીતો અને કાયદા તો ઘણાજ હકવાજબી અને લાયક છે, પણ એવા કાયદા ચલાવવામાં અને તે ઉપર અંમલ કરવામાં કેટલાએક અણસમજુ અંમલદારો ભુલ કરેછે, કેટલાએક બીલકુલ લુચ્ચાઈ ચલાવેછે તેથી એવી ફરીઆદ ઉઠેછે. પણ જો અંમલદારો

*હામીલટન ગેજેટીયર, બીજી આવૃતી, વાલમ ૧, પાનું ૧૧૩-૧૧૭.

લાયક અને પ્રમાણિક હોયા તો એ સરકારની જમાબંધીની રીતો અને કાયદા ખરેખર રૈયતની હાલત બેહેતર કરે તેવાજ છે. તો જુઓ, આજે ગાયકવાડી જમીનની તથા બીજા દેશી રજવાડા હસ્તકની જમીનની શી હાલત છે? હવે જેટલો ભાગ ઇંગ્રેજ સરકારની જમાબંધી તળે આવેલો છે તેની હાલત સરખાવી જુઓ. હમે હીમતથી તથા વગર શકે બોલીએ છૈએ કે આ રાજની જમાબંધીની રીત અને કાયદા જો દેશી રાજાઓ તેવા લાયક અને હોશીયાર અંમલદારો રાખીને પોતાના હસ્તકનાં પ્રગણાંઓમાં દાખલ કરે તો આખાં હિંદુસ્તાનની હાલતમાં થોડાં વરસમાં ઘણોજ બેહેતર ફેરફાર થઈ જાય, એ નિશ્ચય જાણવું.

આ બાબદ વીશે લંબાણ તકરાર કરવાની જરૂર નથી. આપણી આંખ સાંમે દાખલા તઈયાર છે, જેમાં આપણને દેખાયછે કે જમાબંધી કરવા ઇંગ્રેજી સરકારના કાયદા કાનુનો ઘણાજ ઉપયોગી અને ફાયદા ભરેલા છે, અને તેમની ખુબી પીછાની તેમને દેશી રાજાઓએ પોતાની હકુમતમાં દાખલ કરીયા છે અને કરતા જાયછે. આવી રીતની જમાબંધીની ખુબી પીછાનવાનું પેહેલું માન નીજામના બાહોશ અને દુરઅંદેશી વજીર સર સાલારજંગને ઘટેછે. આ ચંચલ અને ભારી અનુભવ ધરાવનાર વજીરે એકદમ એ કાયદા પોતાની હકુમતમાં દાખલ કીધા અને તે સારી પેઠે અમલમાં લાવવાને અને તેના ફાયદા દેખડાવાને, લાયક અમલદારોને આ અગતનું કામ સોંપીયું. રાજદરબારી ખાતાંમાં સારીપેઠે પરોઠાયલાં વીકાજી તથા પેસ્તનજી મેહરજીના ખાનદાનમાંથી તેણે આ અગતના ઓધાઓ ઉપર, કેટલાક ગૃહસ્થોને ચુંટી કાહાડી તેમની નેમણુક કીધી, અને જે ઉમેદથી તેણે આ નેમણુકો કીધી, તે ઉમેદ આ ચંચલ અને હોશીયાર અમલદારોએ આછી રીતે પુરી પાડી છે. હવડાં આ અમલદારો, નીજામ સરકારના કામ કારભારમાં સારો ભાગ લીએછે અને એ સરકારની ઘણી તારીફ લાયક ચાકરી બજાવેછે. શેઠ બાપુજી વીકાજી મેહરજી દક્ષીણ હેદરાબાદની સઘળી તાલુકદારીનું કામ ચલાવે છે. શેઠ જીવણજી પેસ્તનજી, સર સાલારજંગની દરબારમાં એક મજલસી છે, જે દરજો કાઉનસીલના ઓહેદારને મળતો આવેછે. શેઠ બરજોરજી વીકાજી પણ તાલુકદારીનાં કાંમ ઉપર હતા, પણ એ બીચારાની ઉમર લાંબી ટકી નહી. એવણની જગા ઉપર શેઠ ખુરશેદજી બાપુજી વીકાજીની નેમણુક થયલી છે. શેઠ રૂસ્તમજી વીકાજી જેવણ આગળ રાએચુર જીલ્લામાં આસીસટંટ કમીશનરના ઓધા ઉપર હતા,

તેમને નીજામ સરકારે ત્રણ મોટા જીલ્લાની તાલુકદારીનું કામ સોંપીયું છે. શેઠ જીવણ રતનજી, તે શેઠ વીકાજીની છોકરીના છોકરા, એવણ હસ્તક પણ સાત તાલુકાનું કામ સોંપેલું છે. તેમજ આ ખાનદાનના શારી પેઠે જણાયલા બે ચાર ગૃહસ્થો મુંબઈમાં પણ સરકારી ખાતામાં અને વેપારી ખાતાંમાં ઘણી સારી આબરૂ ઇજતથી પોતાનો ઓધો ચલાવેછે, એ ઉપરથી શેઠ વીકાજી મેહરજીના ખાનદાન વીરો શું સરકારમાં કે શું ખાંનગી મંડલીમાં, સઘળી આબરૂ સાથે જોવામાં આવેછે, અને આથી આપણા પારશી ટોલાને મોટું માન છે. ઇંગ્રેજી સરકારની જમાંબધી કરવાના કાયદા કાનુનોથી નીપજતા ફાએદાનો એક બીજો દાખલો આપી એ બાબદ પુરી કરીએછ.

બાલાઘાટનાં પ્રગણાં ઇંગ્રેજ સરકારને સ્વાધીન ઇસિવી સન ૧૮૦૦ ના અકટોબર મહીનાની ૧૨મી તારીએ થયાં, ત્યારપછી એ પ્રગણાં કરનલ ટમસ મનરોને હસ્તક આપીયાં હતાં. એ કલેકટરે તુરત રૈયત ઉપરથી નીજામ સરકાર જે મેહેસુલ લેતી હતી તે ઓછી કરી નાખી, અને જેમ જેમ ખેડુતની આપવાની શકતી વધતી ગઈ તથા જમીનની હાલત બેહતર થતી ગઈ તેમ તેમ તે મેહેસુલમાં વધારો કરતો ગયો.

આ નામાંકીત અમલદારના હાથ તળે સાત વરસની મુદતમાં એ પ્રગણાંઓની એખલી જમીનની મેહેસુલ ૧૦,૦૬,૫૯૩ સ્ટાર પગોડાથી* વધીને ૧૫,૧૭,૨૭૨ પગોડા થઈ ગઈ હતી, અને તીહાંની રૈયત જે આગળ લુચ્ચી, લુટારૂઓની માફક બેકાયદાસર વીખરાએલી પડેલી હતી, તે સુધરીને કાયદાને માન આપનાર અને અમલદારોને તાબેદાર એટલી થઈ ગઈ હતી કે મદ્રાજ ઇલાકાનાં તાબા તળેની એક લાયક રૈયત જેવી આ પ્રગણાંઓની રૈયત ગણાવા લાગી. ઇસિવી સન ૧૮૧૭ નાં સાલમાં એટલે ઇંગ્રેજ સરકારને સ્વાધીન થયા પછી ૧૭ વરસે એ પ્રગણાઓની કુલ મેહેસુલ વધીને છેક ૧૭,૪૦,૩૦૪ સ્ટાર પગોડા થઈ હતી.†

એ પ્રગણાંઓમાં ગુળીનો પાક ઘણોજ થાયછે, અને તેની સાથે હલકી

---

*સ્ટાર પગોડા એક જાતનો સોનાનો શીકો છે જે કિંમતમાં રૂ. ૩-૧૨-૨, પૈ બરોબર છે.

† હામીલટન ગેજેટીઅર, બીજી આવૃતી, વાલમ ૧ લો, પાનું ૧૧૮.

જાતની ખાંડ તથા ગોળ પણ તીહાં બનાવેછે. રૂનો પાક પણ થાયછે, અને તે પેહેલાં પડતી હાલતમાં હતો, પણ હમણાં આ વેપારની એક અગતની જીનસનાં પાકમાં વધારો થતો જાયછે. સન ૧૮૬૩ નાં સાલની સરૂઆતમાં જારે હમારૂં તીહાં જવું થયું હતું ત્યારે તે સાલમાં હમારી પુછપરછ પ્રમાણે ફકત કરનુલને લગતાં પ્રગણાંમાંથી તે સાલના રૂના પાકની એક લાખ ગાંસડી ઉતરવાની ગણત્ર થયલી હતી.

એ તરફથી નીકળતો રૂ સઘળો મદ્રાજને માર્ગે થઈ બીજા દેશાવરોમાં જાયછે. કરનુલ લગા તરફથી માલ મદ્રાજ પુગતાં નજદીક એક માંસની મુદ્દત, બળદના ગાડાંની મુસાફરીથી થાયછે. એવી રીતે માલ પોહોંચાડતાં ઘણામાં ઘણો ખરચ ૩ કનટલમ રૂ પછવાડે (એટલે ૪૫ મણ રૂ પછવાડે રૂ ૪૦) થાયછે, અને દરેક કનટલમ (એટલે ૧૫ મણ) પછવાડે ગાંસડી બંધામણ અને રસ્તાની મંજલમાં ઠાર, ધુમસ અને તેવી બીજી નુકસાનીનાં કારણોથી બચાવ કરવાને રૂ ૪) નો બીજો ખરચ થાયછે. પણ હવે ઉપલી સઘળી અડચણો રેલવે થયાથી નીકળતી જાયછે, અને રૂ વધારે સારી હાલતમાં અને સસ્તે ભાવે ઠેકાંણાસર જઈ પોહોંચવાની દરરોજ ઉમેદ વધતી જાયછે.

કરનુલ શેહેરને "કમીર નગર" પણ કેહેછે. એની ઉપર અમલ કરનાર આગલા સુબાઓ અફગાની વંશના હતા. તેઓ દિલ્લીના આગલા બાદશાહ શાહા જીહાનના તાબા તળે અંમલદારી ચલાવતા હતા. ઔરંગજેબ પાદશાહે કરનુલ પ્રગણું ખીજરખાન નામના એક સુબાને ઇસવી સન ૧૬૫૧ નાં સાલમાં એક જાગીર દાખલ બક્ષીસ આપ્યું હતું. એની પછવાડે આવેલા સુબાઓ અને નવાબોમાં કોઈપણ લાયક રાજ ચલાવનારો નહી હતો. તેઓમાં કુટુંબ કલેશ જબરો ચાલ્યો હતો અને રાજકારભાર ચલાવવાની પુરી શકતી નહી હતી, તેથી કરનુલ પ્રગણાંની રૈયત ઉપર ભારી જુલમ ગુજરવા લાગો. છેક ૧૫૦ વરસ સુધી નવાબોએ હકુમત જબરીથી ચલાવી. ઉપર કહેલાં બાલાઘાટ પ્રગણાં, નીજામ તરફથી અંતે જારે ઇંગ્રેજ સરકારને સ્વાધીન થયાં ત્યારે કરનુલ તાલુકો પણ ઇંગ્રેજી અમલ તળે આવ્યો હતો. એ પછી નવાબોની બરદાસ્ત ઇંગ્રેજ સરકાર તરફથી થવા માંડી. ઇસવી સન ૧૮૧૫ નાં સાલમાં "અલીફખાન" નવાબનાં મરણ પછી "મુજ્જફરખાન" તેનો સઉથી નાહાનો છોકરો વગર હકે

ગાદી ઉપર ચઢી બેઠો, તે વેળા ઇંગ્રેજ સરકારને વચમાં પડવાની ફરજ થઈ હતી, અને પોતાનાં લશ્કરનાં બળથી મુજ્જફરખાનને ઉઠાડીને મનવરખાન ગાદીનો ખરો વારસ હતો તેને તખત ઉપર બેસાડયો હતો, ત્યારથી એ તાલુકા ઉપર ઇંગ્રેજી હકુમત ચાલેછે.

દખણી રાજનું પટન રાજ, કરનુલ અને કડાપા પ્રગણાંઓમાં ઘણાં વરસ સુધી ચાલેલું હતું, અને આજે એ લત્તા તરફ એ પટન રાજનાં જુના કુટુંબીઓ વસેલા છે તેમનાં મોહોડેથી હિંદુસ્થાની ભાષા હજુ ઘણીજ ચોખી અને સફાઈ ભરેલી બોલાયછે.

કરનુલ અને તેને લગતાં પ્રગણાંઓનાં તોલનું કોષ્ટક નીચે પ્રમાણેછે.

૩૪ તોલાનો	....	૧	સેર.
૪૮ સેરનો	....	૧	મણ.
૧૫ મણનો	....	૧	કનટલમ.
૨ કનટલમ	....	૧	ખાંડી.

કરનુલ શેહેરમાં ફરતાં તેનો દેખાવ અને હવા હમને પસંદ આવી હતી; આપણી મુંબઈમાં પરેલનાં અને ભાએખળાનાં બજાર તરફ આપણે ફરતા હોઇએ એવો દેખાવ અને રચનાં નજરે પડતી હતી. બળદની ગાડીમાં હમો ફરવા નીકળ્યા હતા, પણ રસ્તા સારા હોયાથી અને તેમજ આસપાસનો દેખાવ પણ દીલપસંદ હતો તેથી હમને કંટાળો ઉપજ્યો નહી હતો.

રસ્તામાં જતાં ઘણે ઠેકાણે હમે માણસનાં ટોળાં થઇને ઉભેલાં જોયાં, અને તે વીશે હમારી સાથે આવેલા મીત્રોને પુછ્યાથી એવું માલુમ પડયું કે તીહાંના લોક ગરીબ અને તવંગર સઘળા તાડી પીવાનો જબરો શોખ રાખેછે; તે શોખ એટલોતો છે કે જાહેર મકાનો ઉપર ઘણુંકરીને સાંજના ૪॥ અથવા ૫) વાગે દોસ્તોની નાહાની નાહાની ટોલી અથવા મંડળી થઈ, જે ઠેકાણે તાડીની દુકાનો માંડેલી હોય તીહાંથી તાડી વેચાતી લઇને પીએછે અને એક બીજાને જાહેર રીતે પાયછે. એવું તીહાં દરરોજ થાયછે, અને આ મોજ સાધારણ જે પ્રમાણે મુંબઈમાં દરરોજ મેદાન ઉપર સાંજના હવા ખાવાને લોક ફરવા જાયછે અને તીહાંથી લટાર મારી હોટેલોમાં આઈસ ક્રીમ ચાખવાની મોજ મારવાને કેટલાકો જાયછે, તે પ્રમાણે આ શેહેરમાં તેઓ તાડીની મોજ ભોગવેછે.

એ તરફની જમીન સારી અને ફળવંત તથા રૂના પાકને લાયકની કાળી મટોડી-વાળી છે, પણ પાણી પુરૂં નહી મળી આવ્યાના સબબથી તીહાં મનમાનતી રોપણી અથવા ખેતી થઈ શકતી નથી. આ ઉપરથી નેહેર બાંધીને તીહાંની નદીનું પાણી લાવી જમીન ખેડવાનું કામ ચલાવવા સારૂ ખાનગી કંપનીઓ ઊભી થઇ છે. તેઓએ થાપણ એકઠી કરી નેહેર બાંધવાનું કામ શીરૂ કર્યું હતું, તેને સારૂ પુલો બંધાતા હમારા જોયામાં આવ્યા હતા. નેહરની ખોદણીનું કામ તે વખત સુધીમાં ઘણું ચાલેલું હમારા સાંભળવામાં આવ્યું હતું. જે ખોદણી હમારા જોયામાં આવી હતી તે કરનુલ શેહેરની એક બાજુએથી ચાલેલી હતી. એવી બીજી ઘણી જગા હિંદુસ્થાનનાં પ્રાંતોમાં છે તીહાંની જમીનને જો પુરતું પાણી પોહોંચતું થાય તો તે જમીનમાંથી વરસનાં બે પાક ઉતરે તેવી તે જમીન છે, અને પાણી પોહોંચતું કરવાનો ઉપાય એજ છે કે નેહેરો બાંધીને પાણીને અંદર આવતું કરવું. પણ એ મહાભારત કામ ખાનગી કંપનીઓનું નથી. એ કામ સરકારનાં જાહેર કામોમાંનું એક અગતનું કામ છે, અને એ ઊપર સરકાર અગત કરીને ધ્યાન આપે તો તેથી ખચીત રૈયત તથા સરકાર, બંધેને ફાયદો થાય એમાં શખ નથી. નેહેરો બાંધ્યાથી ફાયદા થશે એ સાબેત કરવાની કંઈ જરૂર રહી નથી. ફકત એક નાહાનો કકડો એવી નેહેરનો, ગંગા નદીમાંથી વેહેતો કીધો છે જે GANGES CANAL "ગ્યાનજીસ કનાલ"ને નામે ઓળખાયછે, તે ચાલુ થયાથી, તેની આસપાસની ઉજડ જમીન બાગેબાગ જેવી થઈ ગઇ છે, એટલુંજ નહી પણ જેમ નદી કીનારે ગામડાંની વસ્તી શીરૂ થાયછે તેમ એ નેહેરની આસપાસ વસ્તી અને ખેતીવાડી થોડા વખતમાં જાણે ઉભરી નીકળેલી છે. જેમ જેમ નેહેર આગળ વધેછે, તેમ તેમ તેનાં પાણી સાથે વસ્તી અને ખેતી આગળ ચાલેછે, એ વીશે હમે આગળ ઘટતે ઠેકાણે વધારે બોલશું, પણ અત્રે ઇશારો માત્ર એટલોજ કરેલો બસ છે કે હિંદુસ્થાનના ઘણા પ્રાંતોની જમીનના ફળવંતપણાંમાં જે ગુપ્ત અને પુષ્કળ ધન દબાયલું છે, તેને મોકળું કરવાનો ઉપાય એજ છે કે નેહેરો અને રસ્તા બાંધી, પાણીની આવગ અને જગાને ખોલ્લી કરી આપવી. આથી જે દોલત ખુલી થઈ પડશે તેના ફાયદા ભોગવનાર ઇંગ્રેજ સરકાર પોતેજ છે. હિંદુસ્થાનની રૈયત જેવી તાબેદાર અને નીમકહલાલ રૈયત, પૃથ્વી ઉપર બીજાં થોડાંજ રાજ્યોની હશે. હિંદુસ્થાનની રૈયતને સુખ થયાથી તે રૈયત એકલપેટાપણાંથી એ સુખ ભોગવશે, એવું કવચીત બનવાનું નથી. રૈયતનાં સુખથી તેની

ઊપર રાજ કરનારાઓનું સુખ કાયમજ છે, માટે એવાં કામ ઊપર જો સરકાર મેહનત અને પુરતું ધીયાન આપે તો હિંદુસ્થાન, ઇંગ્રેજી રાજના ખજાનાનો એક અખુટ ભંડાર થાય એમાં કંઈ શક જેવું નથી.

હમને જે આગળ ખબર મળી હતી તેમુજબ કરનુલનાં ડેપ્યુટી કલેકટર તરફથી પણ આ ઠેકાણે એવીજ ખબર મળી કે મદ્રાજથી નીકળેલા રેલવેનાં રસ્તાની એક શાખા "ત્રીપટી" ગાંમડાં સુધી ચાલુ થયલી છે. માટે હમારે એ ગાંમડાં સુધીજ ગાડાંમાં જવું પડશે, અને તીહાંથી રેલવેની મારફતે મદ્રાજ જવાઈ શકાશે.

કરનુલથી જે નવાં ગાડાં કીધાં તે હેદરાબાદથી કરેલાં ગાડાં કરતાં વધારે સાંકડાં હતાં, અને તેમાં બે જણથી તો કદી પણ બેસી અથવા લાંબા થઇને સુવાઈ શકાયજ નહી. એવાં ગાડાંનું ચિત્ર પાસે આપેલું છે. એ ચિત્રમાં મુસાફરી બંગલાની પાસે એવાં ગાડાં છોડેલાં અને બળદોએ અસાએસ લીધેલી દેખાડાવેલી છે. ગાડાંની ઊપર ખપેડો બાંધી લીધેલો હોયછે, અને અંદરથી ઘાંસ સારીપેઠે પાંથરીને ઉપર ગોદડું મુકયું હોય તો બે ચાર દીવસ આંચકા ખાવાનો મહાવરો પડયા પછી એવી ગાડી લાંબી મુસાફરી કરવાને પસંદ અને સવલ પડેછે. બેસવાનો મહાવરો પડયા પછી ગમે તેવું ખાઇને એવી ગાડીમાં હમે બેઠા હતા પણ તેથી હમને કશી તરેહની અડચણ કે ઈજા થઈ નહી હતી; થોડી વારમાં ખાધેલું હજમ થઈ જતું હતું, ઉંઘ ઘણી સારીપેઠે આવતી હતી; અને સહવારનાં તંદરોસ્તી ભરેલા, સારી ભુક સાથે, જાણે આપણા પોતાનાં ઘરનાં ખીછાનાં ઉપરથી ઉઠીએ તેમ હમે સઘળા એ ગાડાંમાંથી ઊઠતા હતા. આગળ બે જણ વચ્ચે એક ગાડી હતી, તે હવે એક એક જણ વચ્ચે એકેક થતાં ગાડીની સંખ્યા વધી ગઈ હતી. જારે હમે કરનુલથી રાત્રે નીકળ્યા ત્યારે ૨૦ ગાડીની એક લાંબી હાર થઈ હતી, તે દેખાવ જાણે એક મોહોટાં લશ્કરી અથવા સોદાગરી કાફલાનાં જેવો દમામ ભરેલો લાગતો હતો. આ ગાડીવાળાઓ પણ કાનડી ભાષાજ બોલતા હતા, પણ તેઓ થોડું ઘણું હિંદુસ્થાની સમજતા હતા.

તા૦ ૧૧ મી જાનેવારી—કરનુલથી આગળી રાત્રે ૧૦॥ વાગે નીકળેલા એ દીને "કટવાના પાહાડ" અથવા જે ઠેકાણાંનું બીજું નામ "બગા" ગાંમ કરી કેહેછે તીહાંના મુસાફરી બંગલામાં જઈ પુગા. મુસાફરી બંગલો આ ઠેકાણે એક ટેકરીનાં મથાલે એક ઘણીજ સારી હવાની જગા ઉપર આવેલો છે. ટેકરીની હેઠળની

BULLOCK BANDIES FOR LONG TRAVELLING _MADRAS

૧. લાંબી મુસાફરીની બળદના ગાડી.

કોરેથી એક સુંદર નાળું વેહેછે. તેનું પાણી ઘણુંજ થડું ગાર જેવું અને લેહેજતદારછે. એ નાળું છેક નંદીયાલ ગામ સુધી જઈ પોહોંચેલું છે, તેનું છેટું છેક ૪૦ માઇલિ સુધી ગણાયછે. આ ઠેકાણે જુવાર, કુલથી, તુઅર, અને મગનો પાક સારો થાયછે. એ લત્તા તરફ ૬) ગાઉ ઉપર લોઢાંની ખાંણ લાગેલી છે એવું હમારા સાંભળવામાં આવીયું હતું. એ ખાંણમાંથી બનાવેલાં લોઢાંના કેટલાએક નમુના, એ જગાનો તેહેસીલદાર હમને મળવા આવ્યો હતો, તેણે હમુને દેખડાવીયા હતા. જો કે ગાળી કાહાડેલાં લોઢાંનાં નમુના સારા દેખાઇતા હતા, તોએપણ જમીનમાંથી ખોદી કાહાડેલો લોઢાંનો "ઓર"(મીટ્ટી સાથે મળેલું લોઢું) કંઈ ઘણીઉંચી અને ચોખી જાતનું નહી હતું. આ ગામડાંની પડોસમાં હીરાની ખાંણ લાગેલી સંભળાઈ હતી તેને ગોલકંડાની હીરાની ખાંણ કેહેતા હતા. ગોલકંડાની હીરાની ખાંણ વીશે એવું જણાયલું છે કે તે ખાંણ ખરેખરી ગોલકંડામાં નહી હતી, પણ તે આ ઠેકાણે હતી, અને એ સઘળા પ્રાંતો એકવાર નીજામનેજ તાબે હતાં, અને તે વખતે ગોલકંડા રોહેરનું નામ વખણાયલું હતું, તેથી આ ઠેકાણેથી મળતા હીરાને ગોલકંડાની ખાંણમાંથી નીકળતા હીરા કેહેતા હતા. બરોબર બોલીએતો ગોલકંડામાંથી હીરાની એકુ કગરસ વટીક મળી નથી, પણ આસપાસનાં પ્રગણાઓમાંથી જે હીરા હાત લાગતા હતા તેમને સાફ કરવાને તથા કાપીને રોનકદાર કરવાને ગોલકંડામાં લાવવા પડતા હતા, તે ઉપરથી તે હીરા જાણે ગોલકંડાની ખાણમાંથી મળી આવીયા હોય એવું કેહેવાતું હતું. ઉપર જણાવેલો તેહેસીલદાર જાતનો કાયત હિંદુ હતો, જેની વાતચીત ઉપરથી તે ચબરાક અને ખબર રાખનાર અમદાર માલુમ પડયો હતો. એનું નામ લાલા રામાનંદપ્રસાદ કરીને હતું. હમોએ માંગ્યા ઉપરથી એ અમલદારે લોઢાંની ખાંણમાંથી નીકળતા પથરો તથા હીરાની ખાંણની જગા ઉપરના કેટલાક પથરોનાં નમુનાં હમારા મિત્ર ડાકતર ભાઉ દાજીને આણી આપ્યા હતા, પણ તેમાં એકુ પણ હીરા સાથનો પથર નહી હતો, જો હતે તો હમો સઘળા ખચીત ઘણા ખુશી થતે, આ ઠેકાણેથી હમે પાછલા પોહોરનાં ૩ા વાગે નીકળ્યા. તેહેસીલદાર હમને થોડેક દુર સુધી મુકવાને આવ્યો હતો. રસ્તામાં હમને એક ફ્રેંચ મુસાફર મળ્યો, જે પાલખીથી મુસાફરી કરતો મદ્રાજ જતો હતો. ગાડાંએ મુસાફરી કરતાં પાલખીએ જલદી જવાઈ શકાયછે, પણ તેનો ખરચ એક માણસ પાછળ ઘણોજ વધારે થઈ પડેછે. ટપે ટપે હમાલો રાખવા પડેછે, અને એવી રીતે મુસાફરી કરતાં, આ-

સપાસ જોવા તપાસવાની અવકાશ પુરતી મળી શકતી નથી. ચાલુ પાલખી સાથે આઠ હમાલો હોયછે, એક હમાલ એક કાવડમાં ઉંચકાય એટલો મુસાફરનો બોજો ઉંચકીને સાથે દોડેછે, અને રાત્રે બે હમાલ મસાલો લઈ આગળ દોડેછે. આવી તરેહની મુસાફરી જે ધણીને ઉતાવળથી દોડી જવું હોય તેને સવલ પડેછે.

આ લત્તા ઉપર પાહાડી જગો આવીયાથી જેમ સાંજ પડતી ગઈ તેમ આસપાસનાં જંગલનો દેખાવ ઘણોજ થંડો અને પસંદ પડતો થવા માંડયો હતો. રસ્તો સીધો અને પોહોળો હતો, માત્ર ધુળ સફેદ રંગની પુષ્કળ હતી. આસપાસ, ઝાડોની ઘટા ઘણીજ સુંદર દેખાતી હતી; તરેહવાર જાતનાં પક્ષીઓ તથા ઝાડપાનો અને ફુલો નજરે પડતાં હતાં. ખરેખર ઝાડપાનના વિદ્યાર્થીને સારૂ તો આ ઠેકાણે એક મોહોટો ખજાનોજ હતો. પાહાડની કઢણે અને કોરે કોરે રસ્તો ગોલ ચકર જેવો ફરતો હતો, જંગલમાંથી સુગંધ ભરેલી લપટ એવી તો આવતી હતી કે હમને ગાડીમાંથી ઉતરીને ચાલવા ગમ્યું હતું, અને અંધારૂં થયું નહી હોત તો ખચીત લાંબા વખત સુધી હમને તીહાંની મઝા ભોગવવાને તથા તેનું બયાન કરવાને બની શકતે. હમો દિલગીર થયા કે આવી જોવાલાયક જગા એ હમારૂં રાત્રે આવવું થયું; અને વધારે દીલગીર એથી થયા કે પુરતો વખત હાતમાં નહી રેહાથી, આવો ખુરાનુમાં દેખાવ, અંધારામાં વગર જોવે વટાવી જવાની હમને ફરજ થઈ પડી હતી

તા૦ ૧૨ મી જાનેવારી— એ દીને સહવારનાં ૧૦ વાગે નંદીયાલ ગામમાં આવી પુગાં. આ ઠેકાણે મુસાફરી બંગલામાં ઉતરવાને બદલે ગામનાં તળાવનો બંધ ઉપર હમે ઉતારો કીધો, કેમકે એ ઠેકાણું ઘણુંજ હવાદાર અને ગામની નજદીક હતું, અને મુસાફરી બંગલો ગામથી ઘણો દુર હતો. એ તળાવમાં નદીનું પાણી આવતું કરીયું છે. તળાવનો ઘેરાવો ૨ થી ૩ માઇલનો કીધેલો છે તેથી જોનારને મોહોટી ખાડી અથવા દરીયા જેવો તે દેખાયછે. તળાવનું પાણી પીવામાં ઘણુંજ સારૂં છે. પણ તેને જરા ઠરવા દેવું અને ગાળવું પડેછે. જીહાંથી તળાવનું પાણી વહીને બાહાર જાયછે તીહાંજ માત્ર હીંદુ લોકો નાહેછે, તેથી પીવાનું પાણી ખરાબ થતું નથી. તળાવમાં નાહાવા ધોવાથી પાણી ખચીત બીગડેછે, એવીરો હમોએ, તીહાં આવનાર લોકને સારી પેઠે સમજ પાડી હતી. એ દિવસે હિંદુ લોકનો કંઈ તેહેવાર હતો તેથી પુષ્કળ પુરૂષો અને સ્ત્રીઓ તળાવ ઉપર નાહાવાને આવ્યાં હતાં. પવન ઘણોજ જોરમાં હતો તેથી તળાવનું પાણી દરીયાનાં મોજા મારે એમ

બંધના ઢોળાવ ઉપર અફળાતું હતું. આગળ મંજલ સારૂ ગામમાંથી ખોરાકી સાથે લેવાની હતી તેથી આ ઠેકાણે જરા વધારે વખત કાહાડવો પડયો. એ અરસામાં નંદીયાલ ગામના મોટા ગવઈયા હમારી મુલાકાતે આવીયા હતા, અને તેઓએ ગાયન ગાઈ સંભળાવાની ઇચ્છા દેખાડાવીયા ઉપરથી, તે હમોએ ખુશી સાથે કબુલ રાખી હતીઃ થોડા વખતમાં એક અચ્છી રચના બની ગઈ હતી. એક ગમથી તળાવનાં પાણીનો અફળાવાનો અવાજ, બીજી ગમથી પવનનો ઘોંઘાટ અને આ બંધે વચે તંબુરા, સારંગી, મૃદંગ, અને ડફ ઉપર પડતી થાપ અને ચાલતું બજાયન, તથા વળી એ સઘળામાં ગવૈયાઓએ ઉલટમાં આવી જે પંચમના સુરે તાંન અને અલાપ લીધી હતી તેથી થોડી વારમાં તળાવના કીનારા ઉપર બહુ અચ્છી રચના અને ધુમ મચી રહી હતી. તેમાં વળી ગામનાં લોક આવી હમારી નાહાની મજલીસમાં સામેલ થઈ ગયાથી, તે ઠેકાણે એક મોહોટી પંચભેળ મંડળી બની રહી હતી. ગાયન જો કે ઘણી ઉંચી કીસમનું નહી હતું તો પણ ગવૈયાઓએ તેમની શકતી મુજબ જે દીલભર રીતે ગાયું હતું તથા જે ગામડાંના તેઓ રેહેવાસી હતા તે ગામડાંની હાલત જોતાં, હમો ધારીયેછ કે ગાયન તે વખતસર ઘણુંજ સારૂં સાંભળ્યામાં આવ્યું હતું, અને સારાં ગાયનનું જે સાધારણ પરીણામ છે કે ગાયન કરનાર અને સાંભળનાર બંધે એક બીજાથી રાજી ખુશી થઈ ઊઠેછે, તેજ પરીણામ આ ગાયનથી નીપજ્યું હતું.

નંદીયાલથી એક મંજલ આગળ ગયાપછી, રસ્તો ઘણોજ ખગબ અને વાંકો-ટીકો આવશે એવા ખબર પડયાથી, આ ઠેકાણેથી ગાડીયાસાથે મસાલો લઈ જવાની ગોઠવણ કરી લીધી. સાંજના સાડાછ વાગે નંદીયાલથી કુચ કીધી.

તા૦ ૧૩ જાનેવારીને દીને સહવારનાં ૯ વાગે શીરવાલ ગામ આગળ આવી પોહોંચ્યા. તીહાં જમીને પાછલા પોહોરના ૩ા વાગે પાછી કુચ કીધી, કારણ જેમ દીવસનાં ઉજડમાં ભાંગેલા રસ્તાની મંજલ કપાય તેમ સારૂં. તે રસ્તો ઘણોજ ભાંગેલો હોવાથી, ગાડીયો વાંકીટીકી બહુ થતી હતી, તો પણ સાંજના સાડાસાત વાગ્યામાં એવા ખરાબ રસ્તાનો કેટલોક ભાગ પસાર કરી શકયા હતા, અને ત્યાર પછી રસ્તો જરા ઠીક હાલતમાં આવતો માલુમ પડવા લાગો, પણ મુસાફરી બંગલો હીયાંથી હજુ એટલો તો દુર હતો કે છેક મધ્યરાત્ર થાય તીહાં સુધી તે ઠેકાણાં

ઉપર પોહોંચી શકાય એવું નહી હતું. આ ઉપરથી રાત્રે સાડાઆઠ વાગે રસ્તામાં એક મોહોટાં ઝાડ તળે થોડીવાર ઉતારો કીધો, બળદોને ઘાંસ દાણો ખવડાવી, ગાડીવાનો જમી લીએ એટલામાં હમોએ પણ જરા ચાહા તથા બીસ્કોટ ખાઈ લીધી. હીયાંથી રાત્રે ૧૧ વાગે પાછી કુચ કીધી. ધાર્યા કરતાં મંજલ વધારે લાંબી માલુમ પડી હતી.

તા૦ ૧૪ જાનેવારીએ પરોઢીયાંમાં પાંચ વાગે "ચાંગલમેરી" નજદીક આવી પુગા. રાત્રે ફકત ચાહા બીસ્કોટ ઉપરજ ગનીમત કરી હતી તેથી ભુખ્યાં પેટે "નજદીક" શબ્દનો અરથ બરોબર જાણવાની તલાસ કીધી, કે "નજદીક" તે હવે બાકી કેટલુંક દુર? એવો સવાલ ગાડીવાળાને પુછીયો. એક ગાડીવાને થંડે પેટે જવાબ દીધો કે, હીયાંથી મુસાફરી બંગલે પોંહોંચતાં હવે ફકત છ કોસ એટલે ૧૨ માઈલની મંજલ બાકી રહી હશે! આ વાત સાંભળીને સઘળા જણનાં ભુખ્યાં પેટે દેખાઈતી તો ખામોશી પકડી પણ અંદરખાનેથી જબરો પોકાર મારીયો હતો. આ પુછપરછ તો છેક સહવારના થઈ હતી, પણ પરોઢીયાંમાં પાંચ વાગે એક ચમતકારીક બનાવ બનીયો હતો. "ચાંગલમેરી" ગામની હદ ઉપર હમો આવી પુગા હતા અને આસરે ૩ા વાગાનો પરોઢીયાંનો વખત થયલો હતો. તે વખતે ગાડીવાનો ગાડી હાંકતાં હાકતાં ઘણું કરીને ઉંઘી ગયલા હતાં. બળદો પોતાની મેળે ધરેડે ચાલતા હતા અને જીહાં સુધી રસ્તો સારો હોય તીહાં સુધી એવી રીતે બળદો પોતાની મેળે ચાલીયાથી કંઇ ફીકર જેવું નથી ગણાતું. પણ વાટ આડીઅવડી અને રસ્તો ખરાબ ભાંગેલો હોય તો તેવી વખતે અને ઠેકાણે ગાડીવાનોને સાવધ રાખવાની ઘણીજ અગત છે. આ રસ્તા ઉપર આવી અગત જાણીને પેહેલી ગાડી સઉથી સાઉચેત અને હોશીયાર ગાડીવાળાની રાખી હતી અને વડોલ કામાજી, આ રસ્તાની ચોકસાઈ તથા પોતાના દોસ્તોની પાસબાની કરવાના ઈરાદાથી પોતે તે ગાડીમાં બેઠા હતા. છેક રાત્રે ૩ વાગા સુધી સઘળી મંજલ સંભાળ અને સમાધાનીથી કપાઈ હતી. મસાલવાળા પણ બરોબર ચાલીયા હતા, પણ તે વખત પછી થોડા વારમાં ઠંડા પોહોરના પવનની લેહેકીએ મસાલચીઓની આંખોમાં ઉંઘ આણી હતી, તેથી તેઓ ઉંઘાતા ઉંઘાતા ચાલતા હતા; તેમને પોતાની મસાલોમાં તેલ પુરવાની સુધ ન રેહાથી તેમની મસાલો પણ વગર તેલે ઝુકવા માંડી. જારે મસાલચી અને મસાલ બંધે ઝુકવા લાગા, તારે

ગાડીવાળાઓની આંખો પણ ચીપચીપ મીચાવા લાગી, અને છેલ્લું શું થયું કે શેઠ ખુરશેદજીને પણ તેજ વખતે પવનની ઠંડી લેહેરી લાગાથી તેવણ પણ ઊંઘાઈ ગયા, અને બીજા સઘળા તો જબરી ઉંઘમાં પડેલા હતા તેમને વીશે તો બોલવાની કંઈજ જરૂર નથી. આવી હાલતમાં સઘળી ગાડીઓ ફક્ત અવાચક બળદોના આધાર ઉપર ચાલતી હતી. તેવામાં પેહેલી ગાડીની સાંમે એક ઉંચો ટેકરો આવીયો જેની ઉપર ગાડીનું ચાક ચઢી ગયાથી તે ગાડી આખીને આખી ગોલાંટ ખાઈ ઉંધી વળી ગઈ. ગાડું ઉંધું વળતાંજ અફળાવાનો જે અવાજ થયો તે બીજી ગાડીવાળાએ થોડો ઘણો સાંભળીયો, અને ઝપકીને આંખો ચોળતો બુમ પાડવા લાગો કે "અરરર, ગાડી ઉંધી વળી ગઈ." આ બુમ બેચાર બીજા ગાડીવાળાઓએ સાંભળી હતી પણ ઉંઘમાં પડેલા તેથી કોઈ તુરત મદદે દોડી નહી જઈ શકયું હતું. હવે જીહાં ખુદા રાખનાર હોયછે તીહાં ગમે તેવી કજા થાય તોપણ માણસના એક બાલ વટીકને પણ ઈજા પોંહાંચતી નથી, તેમ આ હોનારતમાં બનીયું હતું. જેવું ગાડું ઊંધું વળીને નીચે પડયું, એટલામાંજ બળદો જોતરમાંથી એકાએક છુટા થઈ એક કોરે જઈને ઉભા રેહા હતા; ગાડાંવાળો ઉંઘાયલોજ એકગમ સરી પડયો હતો, તે હળવેથી આંખો ચોળતો ઊઠયો હતો, અને શેઠ કામાજી પણ ગભરાયલા પણ મુગા મુગા હાથમાં સપાટ લઈ ગાડીની પછવાડેથી સરીને બાહેર આવ્યા હતા. એમાં કોઈના શરીરને જરાબી નુકસાન નહી પોંહોંચીયું હતું, ગાડાંનો એકુબી ભાગ ભાંગો તુટો નહી હતો, અને આ સઘળો જાણે હસવા સરખો બનાવ સહવારના પરોઢીયાંમાં બની ગયો હતો. જે ટેકરા ઉપર ગાડીનું ચાક ચઢી ગયું હતું તે એટલો ઉંચો હતો કે તે ઉપરથી ગાડી નીચે પડતાં જરાબી તે ભાંગીયા વગર રેહે નહી, પણ તેવું કંઈજ બનીયું નહી હતું. આ બનાવથી તે સાહેબની હમો સઘળા ઊપર જે બેહદ મેહરબાની થઈ હતી તેનો ઊપકાર માનવાને આ હોનારત હમારી સહવારની બંદગીમાં હમારૂં હઈયું પીગળાવવાને એક અચ્છું કારણ થઈ પડયું હતું. ટેકરા ઊપરથી ગગડી પડેલું ગાડું પાછું રસ્તા ઉપર લાવ્યા અને પાછી આગળ કુચ કીધી, તેથી સહવારના ૧૧ વાગે "ચાંગલમેરી" ગામમાં આવી પુગા. આ ઠેકાણા ઊપર એજ દીને વળી આગળના જેવીજ એક બીજી હોનારત બની હતી. ગામમાં પેસતા રસ્તો અતિશય ભાંગેલા હતા, તે માર્ગથી એક શિવાય સઘળી ગાડીઓ તજવીજથી પસાર થઈ શકી હતી. પણ સામાનની જે ભારી ગાડી હતી તેને એક આંચકો લાગાથી

તે ગાડું ઉંધું વળીયું હતું અને તેમાં બેઠેલા હમારાં એક નવલુ નામના માણસને માથામાં મજબુત જખમ લાગો હતો, જેથી લોહી પુસ્કળ નીકળ્યું હતું. પાંચ કલાક આગમચ થયલી હોનારતમાં ગાડું ઉંધું વળીયું તેમાં કોઇને જરા પણ ઇજા નહી પોંહોંચી હતી, અને તે બનાવ વળી અંધારામાં બનીયો હતો; પણ હવે તો દીવસનું અજવાળું થયલું હતું, બીજા ગાડીવાળા સઘળા જાગતા હતા, અને આવી સાવચેતી છતાં, જે બીજી ગાડી ઉંધી વળી તેમાં બેઠેલાં માંણસનાં માંથામાં સખત જખમ થયો અને લોહી વેહેતું થયું એ કેટલું તાજુબી ભરેલું છે! હોનારતોમાં ખુદાતાલાની તરફથી શું થાયછે એ સમજવાની કોણ માનવી શક્તિ ધરાવેછે? એવે પ્રસંગે જે બનાવો તે સાહેબની કુદરતથી બનેછે, તે જોઇને તેની સમજણ આપવાને આપણ અધુરાં માનવીઓએ ઠાલી ટકટક કર્યા કરતાં, તે સાહેબની ઇચ્છાને શરણ થઈ, પોતાના હોટ ઉપર આંગલી મુકી, ચુપકીદી અખતીઆર કરેલી વાજીબ છે.

નવલુનાં માથામાં જે જખમ થયો હતો, તે ધોઇને ડાકતર ભાઉદાજીએ મલમપટી લગાડી, અને તુરત તેને આરામએશ આપવાની જરૂર માલુમ પડતાંજ હમો સઘળાએ તેજ ગામડાંના તેજ ઠેકાણે એક હેવણ પડેલાં દેહેરાંના ચોક ઉપર ઉતારો કીધો. આ ઠેકાણેથી સરકારી મુસાફરી બંગલો હજુર એક માઇલ દુર હતો, પણ ઉપલા સબબને લીધે હમે બંગલે પોંહોંચીએ તીહાં સુધી ખોટી રેહેવું વાજબી નહી ધારીયું હતું. હીયાં પાણી ઘણુંજ ખરાબ હતું અને વળી તે ગદલું હતું, તોએ પણ રાત્રની જબર ભુખ લાગેલી હતી અને આવો બનાવ બનીયાથી, હીયાંજ ઉતારો કરી જેમ તેમ કરીને સારી પેઠે જમી તો લીધું. હીયાંથી સાંજે સવાપાંચ વાગે પાછી કુચ કીધી તે રાત્રે અગીયાર વાગે "દુઆર" ગામના મુસાફરી બંગલામાં જઇ પુગા. રસ્તો હજુર ભાંગેલોજ મળતો હતો, અને આંચકાથી ગાડીઓ જબરી ખખડી ગઈ હતી, તેમજ હમારા સઘળાંનાં શરીર પણ પછડાયાથી થાકી ઢીલાં થઈ પડયાં હતાં. "દુઆર" ગામમાં ખાધ ખોરાકીની તેવી સારી જીનસો મળતી નથી, અને તીહાં આવી પોંહોંચીયા, તે રાત્રે બેદાં શીવાએ ખાજું કંઇજ નહી મળી આવીયાથી તેજ ઉપર શુકર કરી, તથા તે ઉજડ જગા ઉપર કંઈ તેવું જોવા જાણવા લાયક નહી હોવાથી, જરા આરામએશ લઇ રાત્રે બે વાગે પાછી કુચ કીધી.

તા૦ ૧૫ જાનેવારીને દીને સવારના ૬ વાગે "મૈદાપુર" ગામમાં જઈ પોહોંચીયા. આ ઠેકાણે પણ લાંબો વખ્ત રેહેવાની જરૂર નહીજ જોયાથી, તીહાંથી પાછી કુચ કીધી. હજુર રસ્તો ભાંગેલોને ભાંગેલોજ આવીયો હતો. બપોરના સાડાત્રણ વાગે "રાજાપટ" ગામડામાં આવી લાગા. આ ઠેકાણેથી રસ્તો જગ જરા બેહતર હાલતમાં માલુમ પડવા લાગો. રસ્તાની બંધે બાજુએ, હારબંધ ઝાડો તુરતનાં રોપેલાં દેખાયાં હતાં, અને ખબર કાહાડતાં માલુમ પડયું કે હીયાંથી રસ્તો બાંધેલો છે અને તેની બરાબર વખ્તસરની મરામત કરી તેને સારી હાલતમાં રાખ્ખીયામાં આવેછે. આ ઠેકાણાં ઉપર રસ્તાનાં એનજીનીયરો અને ઉપરીઓને રેહેવાસારૂ નાહાની નાહાની બંગલીઓ હારબંધ બાંધેલી હમુને નજર પડી, તેથી હમો સમજીયા કે હીયાં ઉતારાની જગા હશે. પણ તીહાં પેલી નાહાની "કાટેજો" શીવાએ બીજો કોઈબી મકાન નહી હતો. ગાંમ દુર હતું, અને ખબર કાહાડતાં હમુને એવું જણાવામાં આવીયું હતું કે આ ઠેકાણે ખોટી થતાં, આગળ મંજલમાં "બાનાર" નદી આડ આવશે, તે પાર કરવાને મોડી રાત્ર થઈ જશે, અને રાત્રના ૭ વાગે ભરતી થવાનો વખ્ત તે દીવસે હતો, તેથી જો ભરતીની આગમજ તે નદી પસાર કરી તો બેહેતર, નહીં તો, નદી કીનારે જીહાં ઉતારાની જગા બીલકુલ છેજ નહીં, તેવી કફોરી જગા ઉપર સારી રાત્ર ખોટી થવું પડવાનું. આ ખબર ઉપરથી હમોએ "રાજાપટ" ગામમાંથી જલદી આગળ વધવાનું જરૂર જાણીયું. ગાડીઓ થોડુંક સુધી આગળ ચાલીયા પછી, એક ગાડીવાળાએ લુચ્ચાઇથી પછવાડે પડી, પોતાની ગાડીના સારા બળદ છોડીને તેમને પાણી પીવા લઈ જવાને બાહાને, એક મુરદાર બળદની જોડી લાવી હમારા સામાનની બળદની ગાડીમાં જોડી. થોડા વારમાં આ ગાડી હમારી ગાડીઓથી છેક એટલી પછવાડે પડી કે તે નજરથી દુર થઈ, અને આ ગાડીવીશે ચોકાશી કરતાં માલુમ પડીયું કે એના બળદો જલદી ચાલી શકે એવા નહી હતા. જારે તે ગાડી હજુ હજુ આવી લાગી તારે તેમાં બેઠેલાં હમારાં માણસે પેલા ગાડીવાળાની લુચ્ચાઈ વીશે ફરીયાદ કીધી, તારે ખુલ્લું માલુમ પડી આવીયું કે જે ઝડપથી હમોએ આગળ મંજલ કાપવાનો ઠરાવ કીધો હતો તે ઝડપ સાથે પેલા બળદીયા કંઇ ટકી શકે એવા નહી હતા, અને મંજલમાં તે ગાડી બચીત એખલી પાછળ પડે એની ધાસ્તી પડી હતી. પેલા ગાડીવાળાને તેની આવી ચાલનો સબબ પુછીઓ અને ખાત્રી ભરેલો જબાબ નહી મળી-

યાથી તેને થોડોક કોપરાંપાક જમાડીયાથી તે જઇને પેલાં સારા બળદ પાછા લાવીયો હતો. આવી રીતે બળદ બદલવાની શું મતલબ હશે તે ચોકસ કેહેવાઈ શકાતું નથી, પણ તે વખતે હમો સઘળાને એવો શખ ઊત્પંન થયો હતો કે સામાનની ગાડી ઉપર કેટલાક લોકની બદનજર થઈ હોય, અને તે રાત્રે લુટી લેવા સારૂ, તે ગાડી એખલી પાડવાને, આવા ખરાબ બળદો તેમાં જોડી આપીયા હોય. આ સઘળી ગડબડ પુરી થતાં સાંજ પડવા આવી હતી, અને પેલી નદી કીનારે પોંહોંચતાં છેક વખત ભરાઈ જાય એવું થઈ પડયું હતું. સંકટ હંમેશ બીજી સંકટોની સાથે જમાવ થઇને આવેછે, તે મુજબ ઉપલી ગાડીના અટકાવની બાબદ વીશે તકરાર કરતાં કોઈ તરેહની ગેરસમજુતી હમારા એકુ બે મીત્રોમાં થઈ પડયાથી તેઓ વચ્ચે એકાએક જે ઝગડો થઇ પડયો હતો, તેથી જેમ એક તરફ જરા રમુજ તેમ બીજી તરફ આગળની મંજલની ફીકરથી સઘળાના દીલ જગાવાર ખટમીઠાં થઈ પડીયાં હતાં. પણ પેલા કોપરાંપાકની લેહજતથી જારે ગાડીવાળાએ પેલા સારા બળદની જોડી પાછી લાવી આપી હતી તીઆરે સઘળાનાં જીવ પાછા ખુશાલ થયા હતા, અને તેથી પેલી સઘળી તકરાર, ગડબડ અને કોપરાંપાકની વાત તેજ જગામાં દાટીને સઘળા જણ ખુશ ખુશાલીથી આગળ ચાલીયા હતા. જો કે અસુર થયાથી ગાડી ઘણીજ ઊતાવળે દોડાવી હતી, તો પણ નદી કીનારે જઈ પોંહોંચતા અંતે રાત્રે ૮ાા સાડાઆઠ થઈ ગયા હતા. ચંદ્ર નીકલી ચુકેલો હતો, અને નદીમાં ભરતી શીરૂ થઈ ચુકેલી હતી. "પાનાર" નદી વીશે એવું હમોને કેહેવામાં આવીયું હતું કે જો કે તેનો પાટ ઘણો પોહોળો છે તો પણ તેમાં પાણી ઘણું ઊંડું થતું નથી, અને વળી પાણી પુરતું ભરાયલું નહી હતું તેથી એકદમ જલદીથી પાર નીકલી જવાને હમોએ ગાડીવાળાઓને હુકમ આપીયો હતો. "પાનર" નદીનો પાટ આ ઠેકાણે બેવડી વલાણ લઈ, બે જુદી જુદી પાટે ફરી વળેલો છે, તેથી નદીનો એક પાટ પાર કીધા પછી, થોડીક સુકી જમીન લાગેછે, અને તે પસાર કરીયા પછી જાણે વળી કોઇ બીજી નદી આડે આવી હોય એમ તેજ નદીનો ફરી વળેલો બીજો પાટ પાછો આડો આવેછે. સઘળી ગાડીઓ નદીમાં દાખલ થઈ, પેહેલા મોટા પાટમાંથી પસાર થઈ હતી, તેમાં હમારી ગાડીના બળદો જરા નબળા હોવાથી તેઓ બીજી ગાડીઓની સાથે નહી રેહી શકયા. ગાડી-વાળો વળી કોઈ નાદાન વગર અનુભવવાળો છોકરો હોવાથી તેનાથી બળદોને

પાણીમાં બરોબર હાંકી નહી શકાયું. તેથી બળદો અટકીને નદી વચ્ચે ઉભા રેહા. ગાડી ઉભી રેહેતાં, તેનાં પઈડાં નરમ રેતીમાં બેસવા લાગાં. તેમજ હમારેથી થોડીક દુર જે સામાનની ગાડી હતી તેનો હાલ પણ હમારી ગાડીના જેવોજ થઈ પડ્યો. હમારી સાથે હમારો જરમન મીત્ર મી૦ એડવર્ડ જે જબરો તરનાર હતો, તેની હીંમત હમુને ઘણી હતી. ગાડી કદાચને ડુબે એટલા ઉપરથી આગળ નીકલી ગયલા હમારા મીત્રોને બુમો મારીને કેહ્યું કે હમારી મદદે કોઈને મોકલો, પણ હમારી બુમો કોઈના સાંભળવામાં આવી નહીં શકી હતી, કારણ કે દરેક ગાડીવાળો પોતાના બળદોને ચાંપી રગડીને હાંકી જલદીથી નદી પાર કરી જવાની ઈનતેજારીમાં પડેલો હતો. સઘળા ગાડીવાળાઓની બુમથી નદીમાં ઘોંઘાટ થઈ રહ્યો હતો અને કોઈનો પોકાર કોઈ સાંભળી નહી શકતું હતું. હમોએ હમારા બળદોને આગળ ચલાવાને ઘણી મેહનત કીધી, તેમનાં પુછડાં પકડીને તાણીયાં, મરડીયાં, તેમને લાકડીઓ મારી, ગાડીવાળા ઉપર ગુસ્સે થઈ તેને પણ ધબા મારીયા પણ અંતે કંઈજ વળીઊં નહી, અને પાણી છેક ગાડીની અંદર આવા લાગું. હમો ભીનાવા લાગા તારે નદી ઉપર ટેપલા ફેરવનાર કોળીઓને બોલાવા પોકાર મારી તેમની મદદ માંગી, જેથી તેઓ થોડા વખતમાં હમારી નજદીક ટેપલા સાથે આવી પુગા. આ વખતે પાણી એટલું ગાડીમાં આવીલું હતું કે બીછાનું સઘળું ભીનાઈ ગયું હતું. તુરત ગાડીમાંથી હમારાં કપડાંનાં કોથલા લઈ હમો બંધે જણા ટેપલામાં કુદી પડ્યા હતા. આ ટેપલાવાળાઓએ જારે નદી ઉપર ઘણો ઘોંઘાટ સાંભળીયો તારે તેઓએ જોયું કે તેમની મદદની જરૂર થઈ પડી છે, આ ઉપરથી તેઓ તીહાં આવી પોહોંચીયા હતા. આ સઘળી ગડબડાટમાં ગાડીઓ એક બીજાથી છુટી પડી ગઈ હતી અને કોઈ એણીગમ અને કોઈ પેલીગમ નીકલી ગઈ હતી. નદીનો પેહેલો પાટ પસાર કરીયા પછી જારે સુકી જમીન ઉપર આવીયા તારે તીહાં સઘળી ગાડીઓ પાછી એકઠી મળી હતી. હમારી તથા સામાનની ગાડી જે અટકી પડી હતી તે કેટલેક વારે ઘણી સખ્ત મેહનત કરી ખેંચી કાહાડી હતી. નદીનો બીજો પાટ હમોએ ટેપલામાં પસાર કીધો હતો, કારણ હવે ગાડીમાં બેસીને નદી પસાર કરવી, સલામતી ભરેલું નહી જણાયું હતું. હમારી સાથે જે ભોમીયો લીધો હતો તેણે હમને એવું કેહ્યું કે તે સઘળી ગાડીઓને આ બીજા પાટમાંથી બરોબર પસાર કરી પેલે પાર લઈ આવશે, કારણ બીજા પાટમાં પાણી ઘણું નહી ભરાતું હતું. આ

ઉપરથી હમોઆગળથી પેલે પાર જઈ હમારા ગાડીવાળાઓની વાટ નચીંત જોતાં બેઠા. છેક રાત્રે સાડાઅગીયાર કલાકનો સુમાર થયો તોબી ગાડીવાળાઓ નહી આવી પુગાથી તરેહવાર વીચાર હમોને આવવા લાગા. એવામાં કોઈ માણસો એક બીજા સાથે જોસ્સા ભરેલી ભાંજગડ કરતા હોય એવો દુરનો અવાજ સાંભળીયાથી હમો સાંબા જઈ જોઈએછ તો સઘળા ગાડીવાળાઓ પેલા ભોમીયા સાથે ખુબ ગુસ્સામાં આવી ગયલા હતા. પેલો ભોમીઓ માત્રે નામનો ભોમીઓ હતો, અથવા તો રાત્રે ઘભરાઈ જઈ રસ્તો ચુકી ગયલો હતો, એ વાત હમો નથી જાણતાં, પણ એટલું માલુમ પડીયું કે નદીનો બીજો પાટ વટાવવાને તેણે રસ્તાની ભુલ કીધાથી, ગાડીવાળાઓને નજદીક અરધો કોસ દુર આડ વાટે લઈ ગયો હતો જેથી ગાડીવાળાઓનું એક તો નદીના પેહેલા પાટમાં મેહનત કીધાથી જે પાકી ગયલું હતું તે આ બીજા પાટની મેહનતથી ફુટી ગયું હતું અને તેવો સઘળાનો ગુસ્સો એબલા ભોમીઆ ઉપર જઈ પડીયો હતો. અંતે ગામમાં જવા સારૂ કીનારા ઉપર પડેલા ગાડીના ચાકની નીશાણો પકડીને છેક બાર વાગે ગામમાં દાખલ થયા હતા જે ગામનું નામ "ચીનોર" હતું. તીહાં પુછતાં માલુમ પડીયું કે ઉતારો કરવાની જગા છે નહી તેથી હમો સઘળાને ઘણીજ દીલગીરી લાગી, કારણ અરધી રાત્રે પાણી સાથે જે ખેલ રમવો પડયો હતો તેથી ઘણા થાકી ગયા હતા. અંતે એક કલાક આરાએશ લઈ તીહાંથી આગલ કુચ કરી હતી અને રાત્રે ચાંદરણી હતી અને હવેથી રસ્તો સારો લાગેલો હતો તેથી ગાડાંમાંજ સુઈ જવું બેહતર જાણીયું હતું.

તા૦ ૧૬ મી જાનેવારીની સહવારના ૬ વાગે કડાપાના મુસાફરી બંગલામાં જઈ પુગા. આ મથકઉપર આવતાં હમોએ હેદરાબાદથી ૨૫૩ માઈની મંજલ પુરી કીધી હતી અને હવે મધરાજ પોંહોંચવાને ૧૫૩ માઈલની મુશાફરી બાકી રહી હતી.

કડાપા, બાલાઘાટનાં પ્રગણાંઓનો બીજો મોહોટો ભાગ ગણાયછે. કડપાનાં લત્તાની જમીન ઘણી ખરી સપાટ છે, અને જેમ જેમ એ લત્તા તરફથી, કૃષ્ણા નદી તરફ જઇએ તેમ તેમ જમીન ચઢતી થતી જાયછે. એ લત્તા તરફ એપ્રિલ અને મે માંસમાં આસપાસનાં પાહાડો જબરા તપ્યાથી ગરમી ઘણી સખત લાગેછે. એ વખતમાં અહીયાંનું પાણી પણ જરા ખારાટ ભરેલું થાયછે, પણ ચોમાસામાં તે ઘણુંજ સારૂં અને લેહેજતદાર બની જાયછે. કેટલેક ઠેકાણે એ લત્તા ઉપર વળી બારે માસ પાણી ઘણું સારૂંજ રેહેછે. કડાપાના લત્તાની પૂર્વ દીશાયે આવેલી

ટેકરીઓમાં મટોડી સાથે લોઢાંનો ભાગ મળેલો છે, તેવી મટોડીમાંથી સોડાખાર પુષ્કળ પેદા થાયછે, અને એવી મટોડીમાં જે જે ઠેકાણે એ ખાર ઘણો પાકેછે, તે તે ઠેકાણાંનો દેખાવ વરસનો ઘણો ભાગ ઊજડ અને ભીનાસ અથવા ખબોચીયાં ભરેલા રહેછે, અને તીહાંની મટોડી સહવારની વખતે કાલા રંગની દેખાયછે. જારે એ મટોડી ઘણી સફાઈદાર થાયછે, ત્યારે તેને ગામનાં ધોબીયો કપડાં ધોવામાં સાબુને ઠેકાણે વાપરેછે, અને એ ઉપરથી એ મટોડીને ધોબીની મટોડી કેહેછે. બીજી જગાઓ ઉપર સોડાખારને ઠેકાણે નીમક પાકેછે. તલાવો ખોદનારા એવી તરેહ પાકતાં નીમકને મટોડીમાંથી છુટું પાડી ખાધ ખોરાકીમાં વાપરેછે. કડાપાનાં પ્રગણાંઓમાં ઘણે ઠેકાણે એવી રીતે પુષ્કળ મીઠું બનેછે, તેથી, એ તરફ બાહેરથી ઝાઝું મીઠું આવતું નથી, અથવા આવેછે તે ઘણુંજ જુજ. સુરાખારનો પણ એ લત્તા તરફ ઘણો પાક થાયછે, અને તે ઘણીજ સેહેલી રીતે મટોડીમાંથી છુટો પડી શકેછે. નાલીયરી તથા તાડ એ લત્તા તરફ ઘણાં થતાં નથી. હીયાંની જમીન અને હવા બંધે એ જાતનાં ઝાડોને માફક નથી. કરનુલની જમીન સાથે સરખાવતાં કડાપાની જમીન પાક ઉત્પંન કરવામાં ઉતરતી જણાવી.

કડાપા શેહેર પણ કરનુલની પેઠે પટનનાં નવાબોનાં તાબા તળે હતું. હીયાં વેપાર ઘણો તેજ ચાલી શકતો નથી. લોક ઘણું કરીને જંગલી તથા સુસ્તી છે. કડાપા શેહેરનું નામ કોઈવાર "કૃપા" એટલે મેહેરબાની અથવા દયા એવું પણ બોલાયછે. હીયાં વાણીયા તથા બીજી જાતનાં હીંદુ વેહેવારી વછીયાતોની પેહેડીયો છે, અને તેઓનો ધંધો ઘણું કરીને સરાફી છે. રૂ તથા અફીણ પણ એ ઠેકાણે પેદા થાયછે, પણ તે ઘણુંજ જુજ. ગુલીનો પાક એ ઠેકાણે ઘણો થાયછે.*

કડાપાથી ચાર વાગે પાછલા પોહોરનાં નીકળ્યા. હીયાંથી તો રસ્તો ઘણોજ સારો લાગેલો હતો.

તા૦ ૧૭ જાનેવારીએ પરોઢીયાંમાં "ઊન્ટામીટા" નાં મુસાફરી બંગલે જઈ પોહોંચ્યા. આ ઠેકાણે હમારો વીચાર ઊતરીને ફકત તાજું દુધ પીઇને આગળ જવાનો હતો, પણ ગાડીમાંથી ઊતરીને આસપાસ જોઈએછ, તેવામાં હમારા મીત્ર ડાકતર બાઊની નજરે દુરથી કંઈ મીનારા જેવું દેખાયું. તેથી તેમણે

---

* હામીલટન ગેજેટીયર, બીજી આવૃતી, વાલમ ૧ લો, પાનું ૪૫૮.

તે વીશે પુછપરછ કીધી, કેમકે એ ધુંધી અને ચંચલ મીત્રનું પેહેલું કામ એજ હતું કે જીહાં ઊભા તીહાં આગળ જણાવ્યા પ્રમાણે પેહેલી પુછપરછમાં એજ હતું કે "હીયાં કંઇ જુના દેહરાં અને લેખોછે?" જીહારે હમને ખબર પડી કે તે મીનારા જેવું જે અંધારામાં દેખાતું હતું તે "ઊન્ટામીઠા" ગામનું એક ઘણુંજ મોહોટું અને જુનું શીવનું દેહરૂં છે, તે શબ્દો સાંભળતાને વાર હમારા મીત્રનાં દીલમાં ખુસાલીનો જુસ્સો એકદમ ચઢી આવ્યો! તુરત મસાલ સલગાવીને ડાકતર તથા હમે બે ત્રણજણ તેમની સાથે તે દેહરાં તરફ દોડતાજ ગયા અને જેમજેમ નજદીક જતા હતા તેમ તેમ તે દેહરૂં ઘણુંજ મોહોટું દેખાતું હતું. હમારા મીત્રનાં મોહોડામાંથી ખુસાલીનો અવાજ નીકળતો હતો, કે આજે આ ઠેકાણેથી આપણને કંઈ પણ જુના શીલાલેખો મળસે. ખુશીમાં અને ખુશીમાં દેહરાં આગળ જઈ પુગા, પણ ઊપર ચઢવાની ઘણીજ પાયરીઓ હતી તેથી બીજી મસાલો સલગાવીને ઉપર ચઢયા. મુંબઈમાં મહાલક્ષમીમાં શેઠ ધાકજી દાદાજીનાં દેહરાં ઉપર જવાને જેવી પગથીઓ બાંધેલી છે, તેવીજ કીસમની આ ઠેકાણે પણ બાંધેલી હતી. ઉપર ચઢીને ડાબી બાજુએ આગળ ચાલ્યા તેવામાં દુરથી મસાલની રોશનીથી લેખનાં બે પથરા ઉભા ગોઠવી મુકેલા ડાકતરની નજરે પડયા, જેથી તેઓનાં મનમાં એટલો તો સંતોશ અને આનંદ ઉપજ્યો કે, મોહોટેથી હસીનેતે પથરા તરફ દોડી જઇ તેમને કોટી (આલિંગન) કીધી અને બોલ્યા કે, હા! આજે મને બહુ આનંદ આ મારા જુના મીત્રોને મળ્યાથી થયો છે! પછવાડેથી માલુમ પડયુંહતું કે તે લેખો ઘણા પુરાણા નહી હતા. તખ્તી ઉપર શાલીવાહાન ૧૪૮૦ નો સાલ વાંચીયો હતો. તખ્તી દેવનાગરી અક્ષરોમાં કોતરેલી હતી, જે ઉપલા સને પ્રમાણે માત્રે ૩૦૦) વરસ પુરાણી માલુમ પડી હતી. બીજું આસપાસ જોતાં ઘણું નકસી કામ દેવાલોઉપર અને બારણાં બારીયો ઉપર દેખાયું હતું, પણ તે અંધારાનાં સબબથી ખુલ્લું નજર નહી આવી શકયું હતું. આ ઠેકાણેથી બરોબર જોયા વગર પાછું જવાનું કોને ગમે? તેથી તુરત ઠરાવ કીધો કે "ઊન્ટામીઠા" નાં મુસાફરી બંગલામાં ઉતારો કરવો, અને સવારનાં એ દેહેરૂં બરાબર જોવું, તથા પેલા લેખોની નકલ છાપી લેવી. ડાકતર પાસે એવી રીતે નકલો છાપી લેવાનો સઘળો સરંજામ તૈયાર હતો. દેહેરાં ઉપરથી પાછા આવી ગાડીવાનોને ગાડી છોડવાનો હુકમ આપ્યો, તથા હમોયે હલકો જેવો નાસ્તો કીધો, અને પાછાં દેહરાં ઉપર ગયા. પેહેલું કામ પેલા લેખો ઉપરથી નકલ છાપી લેવાનું હતું.

લેખોના પથરા ઊપર પુશ્કળ ધુળ અને મેલ ચડેલા હતો, તે સઘળો પાણીથી ધોઇ નખાવ્યો, તેથી લેખ ઘણાજ ખુલ્લા નજરે આવવા લાગ્યા. તખ્તી ઉપરથી છાપ લેવાનું કામ સીરૂ કીધું પણ તેમાં તો વખતનું કામ હતું અને તે ઉતાવલે થાય એવું નહી હતું. જેમ જેમ કામ ચાલતું ગયું તેમ તેમ સહવારનાં દેહરાં ઉપર જે જે લોક આવતાં હતાં તેઓએ હમને જોઇને આખાં ગામમાં ખબર આપી કે કોઈ સાહેબ લોક આવેલા છે તેઓ દેહરાંમાંની મુર્તીઓ અને લેખોની નકલ કરી લીએછે. ગામનાં લોક હમને યુરોપીયન પાદરીઓ સમજ્યા હતા. ગમે હેવી તે લોકની ખાતરી કરવાને હમોયે કોશેશ કીધી કે હમે દેશી લોક છઈએ અને હમે મુંબઈના પારશીઓ છયે, હમારા સદ્રા કુસ્તીની નીસાણો બતલાવી, તથા હમારી સાથે હમારાં મીત્ર ડાકતર ભાઊનાં બ્રામણ ચાકરો હતા તેઓએ કહ્યુંકે, હમો પાદરી લોક નથી, તોયેપણ તેઓની મુતલક ખાતરી થઈ નહી હતી, અને હમારા બોલવા ઉપર તેમને ભરૂસો નહી આવ્યો હતો. ઘણો ખરો સખ હમારી સાથનાં મીત્ર મી૦ એડવર્ડ ઊપરથી તેમને ગયો હતો, કે જેવો આ યુરોપીઅન છે તેવાજ આ બીજાઓ પણ હશે. એવા શખ ઉપરથી તેઓએ દેહરાંની છેક અંદરની કોઠડી જીહાં પુજા અથવા દરશણની જગો હતી, તે મકાનનું બારણું ઢાંકેલું ને ઢાંકેલુંજ રાખ્યું, અને તેનો રખેવાલ બ્રાહ્મણ જેહેની પાસે બારણાંની કુંચીયો હતી તે બ્રાહ્મણ ગામ બાહાર ગયો છે, તેને આવતાં વાર લાગશે, એવાં એવાં બાહાના કાહાડીને અંતે તે ઓરડો હમને નહીજ દેખડાવીયો હતો. હમોએ ઘણાં કાલાવાલા અને સમજાવી પટાવીને કહ્યું પણ હમારૂં કંઈજ વળ્યું નહીં, તોએ પણ આ ઓરડા શીવાય બાકીનું આખું દેહરૂં સઘળી તરફથી બરોબર જોયામાં આવીયું હતું. એ દેહરૂં શીવનું છે, અને તે "Granite sandstone" જાતનાં પથરનું બાંધેલું છે. ઇંટનું કામ પણ અંદર પુશ્કળ ઠેકાણે કરેલું છે, અને દિવાલો ઉપર, સીલીંગ (એટલે છત) ઉપર અને થાંભલાંઓ ઉપર તરેહવાર નકસી કામ સાથે, દેવદેવીઓની મુર્તીઓ ચુના અને પથરની બનાવેલી અને કોતરેલી છે, તેમાં મોટમોહોટી સભાઓ પાડેલી છે, અને દેવતાઓની લડાઇનો દેખાવ પણ ઘણીજ મોહોટી રચનાં સાથે દેખડાવેલો છે. દેહરાંનાં મુખડાં આગળ ત્રણ મોહોટા પડઘેરાકી મીનારા બાંધેલા છે, તે સઘળામાં ઇંટરડીનું કાંમ ઘણું કરેલું છે. આ મીનારા ઉપર ત્રણ તબક કરેલા છે, પણ તેમના પેહેલા તબકાની પગથીયો ભાંગી ગયાથી ઉપર ચઢવાનો મારગજ અટકી પડેલો

હતો. દેહરાંની પગથીઓ ઉપર ચઢયા પછી આસપાસ ચોમેર ફરવા લાયક મોહોટો અને ખુલ્લો ચોક પથરની ફરસબંદીનો બનાવેલો છે. મુર્તીનો ઓરડો વચમાં રાખી આસપાસ ફરતી વરાંડા પથરની બનાવેલી છે. એ વરાંડાના આરકાં અને સ્થંભો ઉપર આગળ જણાવેલું સઘળું નકસી કામ કરેલું છે. પશ્ચીમ તરફની દેવાલો ઉપર ઘણી બેમુલાહજા ભરેલી મુર્તીઓ પાડેલી છે, પણ જોનારને તે એકાએક દેખાતી નથી, કેમ કે મુલાહજા ભરેલી અને બેમુલાહજા ભરેલી મુર્તીઓ ભેળસેળ પાડેલી છે. સ્ત્રીઓના સ્તંનો ઉપર દેવતાઓ હાથ મુકીને ઉભેલા તથા બેઠેલા આસનમાં પાડેલા છે. દેવતાઓનાં લીંગો ઉપર પુરૂષ તથા સ્ત્રીયો હાથ અને માંથાં મુકી તેમને નમસ્કાર કરેછે. લીંગોના દરશણ કરવાની બીજી ઘણી બેમુલાહજા ભરેલી રીતો દેખડાવેલી છે, તેમજ દેવતાઓ દેવીયો સાથે બગલગીરી કરી મોહોસાથે મોહો, માથાંસાથે માંથાં લગાડી ઉભેલાં છે. આ પુસ્તકનું માન જાલવવા આવા અઘટીત દેખાવ વીગે હીયાં બયાન કરવું હમો વાજબી નથી ધારતા, આટલુંજ કેહેવું બસ છે કે "ઉન્ટામીટા" નાં દેહરાં ઉપર જેવી નીર્લજ મુર્તીઓ જોઈ તેવી બીજે કોઈ ઠેકાણે હમારા જોવામાં ખુલ્લી આવી નથી. પણ ખોલ કાહાડતાં માલુમ પડયું છે કે એથી પણ વધારે નઠારી અને લાજ વગરની મુર્તીઓ એ લત્તા તરફના દેહરાંઓમાં ઘણે ઠેકાણે છે, પણ તે ખુલ્લી જગા ઉપર મુકેલી નથી, તેમને છેક અંદરની ઓલીઓમાં ઘણું કરીને મુકેલી હોયછે. આ દેહરાંની હેઠળ ઉતરતાં તેનાં દરવાજાની સામણે લાકડાનો એક મોહોટો રથ હમોએ જોયો. ઠરાવેલ દીવસોયે દેવની મુર્તીને તેમાં બેસાડી લોક તે રથને પોતે ખેંચી ગાંમમાં ફેરવેછે. આ લાકડાનાં રથ ઉપર પણ ઘણું નકશી કામ વળી એવું હતું કે દેહરાંની દેવાલો ઉપરની મુર્તીઓને એક કોરે બેસાડે. રાધા-કૃષ્ણના રાસની ક્રીડા આ રથ ઉપર કોતરેલી હતી પણ એટલું ઠીક હતું કે રથ જુનો થયલો હતો, અને તેની ઊપર કોત્રેલી મુર્તીઓ પણ જુની થઈ ધુળથી સઘળી ભરાઈ ગયલી હતી, તેથી કોઈને તે ઉપર શું પાડેલું છે તે એકાએક નજરે પડી નહી શકતું હતું. આ ઠેકાણે આવો દેખાવ જોઈ હમને ઘણીજ દીલગીરી લાગી હતી. દેહરાંમાં આવેલા કેટલાએક દેખઈતા સમજુ માણસોને એ બાબદસર હમોએ પુછયું ત્યારે તેઓ સઘળાના મોહોડામાંથી આવો જવાબ નીકળ્યો હતો કે, એ વાત હમે શું જાણીયે! દેવદેવીયોની આ વાત છે, તે આપણ માનવી જાત શું સમજીયે!

અને એ મુર્તીઓ કોણે અને શું કરવા આવી રીતની પાડી હશે એ પણ તેઓ જાણતા નહી હતા. હમો અને તેઓ વચ્ચે એ બાબત વીશે તકરાર ઘણી ચાલી હતી, પણ તેથી કંઇજ તેઓની ઉપર અસર થઈ નહી હતી. આ સઘળો ભગવાનનો ખેલ છે, અમાં માણસ શું કરી અથવા સમજી શકવાનું છે! આટલાજ વીચાર તેમનાં મનમાં એવા તો ઠરેલા માલુમ પડ્યા હતા કે તે ખીસાડવા મુસ્કેલ હતા. તકરાર કરતાં ભીડ ઘણી વધવા લાગી હતી, પણ હવે તીહાં જોવાનું કંઈ વધારે રહ્યું નહી હતું, તેથી હમોયે બપોરનાં ૧) વાગે તીહાંથી રૂખ્સદ લીધી. મુસાફરી બંગલામાં પાછલા પોહોરનાં ત્રણ વાગે જમીને પાછી કુચ કીધી અને આસરે એક કોસ મંજલ કાપ્યા પછી "મડકમપલ્લી" ગામ આગળ આવી પોહોંચતાં, આ ઠેકાણે મદ્રાસ તરફથી આવતા રેલવેનું કામ ચાલતું દેખાયું. તે વખતે રેલવેનાં રસ્તાની પુરણીનું કામ ચાલતું હતું, તથા લાકડાંની "સ્લીપરો" નો જમાવ તીહાં થતો હતો; ગાડીમાંથી ઉતરીને એ કામ જોયું, પણ સાંજનું અંધારૂં થતાં પાછા ગાડીમાં બેશીને રાત્રે સાત વાગે "નંદલુર"નાં મુસાફરી બંગલામાં જઈ પોહોંચ્યા હતા. "ઉન્ટામીટા"થી તે "નંદલુર" સુધી રસ્તો પાછો ઘણોજ ભાંગેલો અને ખરાબ હતો, અને ગાડીને ઘણી ઇજા પોહોંચાડે તેવો હતો, પણ મડકમપલ્લીથી રસ્તાનો જેટલો ભાગ નંદલુર તરફ જવાનો છે તે જરા સારો બાંધેલો રસ્તો હતો, નંદલુરના બંગલામાં જમીને રાત્રે ૧૧ વાગે રવાને થયા તે બીજે દીને,

તા૦ ૧૮ જાનેવારીને દીવસે સહવારના ૭) વાગે "પલંમપેટા"નાં મુસાફરી બંગલામાં આવી પુગ્યા. આ ઠેકાણે રેલવેનાં એક સરવેયર સાથે હમારી મુલાકત થઈ. એ શખ્સે હમારી બાકીની મુસાફરી ટુંકી કરવાને અને જલદીથી "ત્રીપટી"નાં રેલવેનાં સ્ટેશન ઉપર પોહોંચાડવાને સારૂ જો રસ્તામાં "લાગી" નામની હાથગાડી જે પાટા ઉપર ચલાવેછે, તે મળે તો તે હમુને આપવાને પોતાનાં એક મીત્ર ઉપર ભલામણ આપી હતી. આ ઠેકાણે હમારી મુલાકાત કરનલ આરથર કાટન સાથે થંઈ હતી. તે પોતાનાં ભાઇને મદ્રાસ મુકીને પાછો પોતાનાં કુટુંબ સાથે કરનુલ જતો હતો. કરનુલ તરફ જવાનું કારણ તીહાંની નેહેર બંધાતી હતી, તે જોવાનું હતું. મંજલ નજદીક પુરી થવા આવી હતી, તેથી ઠેકાણે ઠેકાણે હવે વધારે વાર ખોટી નહી થવાનો વીચાર રાખી, જમીને આ ઠેકાણેથી પોણાબાર વાગે આગળ ચાલ્યા, રસ્તામાં એક ઘણુંજ મોહોટું તલાવ બે તબકાનું જોયું. પેહેલા તબકા ઉપરથી

પાણી ઉતરીનેતે તબકાની આસપાસની જમીનની ખેડણીસારૂ કામે લગાડેલું હતું, અને તીહાંથી નીકલી બીજા તબકાઉપર પડતું હતું, અને તીહાંની જમીન ઉપરતે ફરી વળતું હતું. એ તલાવનુંનામ રઢીપલ્લીનો "લેક" એટલે સરોવર બોલાયછે. એ પાણીથી પુષ્કળ ધાન્યનો પાક થાયછે તથા નાળીયરની પણ આ ઠેકાણે પુષ્કળ ઉત્પત્તિ છે.જારે હમે બપોરનાં બે વાગે એઠેકાણેથી જતા હતા તારે તડકો સખ્ત હતો, તોયપણ આસપાસની હવા ઘણીજ ઠંડી લાગતી હતી, કારણ કે, પાણીનાં મોહોટા પ્રસારા ઉપર થઇને તે હવા આવતી હતી. તલાવની રચનાં એવી થયલી છે કે, રસ્તાનો કેટલોક ભાગ પેલા બે તબકાની વચમાંથી આવેલો છે, તેથી બંને બાજુયે પાણી અને લીલોત્રીથી ભરેલાં ખેતરો દેખાતાં હતાં, જેથી એઠેકાણેથી જતાં હમારાં દીલને ઘણુંજ ખુશ લાગતું હતું. "પલંમપેટા" થી "કોદુર" નાં મુસાફરી બંગલા તરફ જતાં એ તલાવનો મોટો ભાગ ડાવા હાથ ઉપર આવેછે. રાત્રે ૧૧) વાગે "કોદુર" ના મુસાફરી બંગલામાં જઈ પુગા હતા; તીહાં જમીને ગાડીમાંજ સુતા, અને ગાડીવાનોને હુકમ આપી મુકયો હતોકે હમુને ઉઠાડયા વગર ચાર વાગ્યામાં એકદમ કુચ કરવી. એમુજબ કુચ થયાથી,

તા૦ ૧૯ મી જાનેવારીને દીને બપોરના બે વાગે "બાલાપલ્લી" નાં મુસાફરી બંગલામાં આવી ઉતરયા. આ બંગલો હમારી મદ્રાજ લત્તા તરફની મંજલનો છેલ્લો મુસાફરી બંગલો હતો, હીયાંથી જરા આડ મારગે થઇને "ત્રીપટી" નાં રેલવેનાં સ્ટેશન ઉપર જવાનું હતું તેથી બપોરનાં જમીને સાંજે પાંચ વાગે કુચ કીધી તે રાત્રે બે વાગે "ત્રીપટી" રેલવે સ્ટેશન ઉપર આવી પુગ્યા હતા.

હૈદરાબાદથી તા૦ ૪ જાનેવારીને દીને રાત્રે ૧૨॥) વાગે નીકલ્યા હતા તે તા૦ ૧૯ જાનેવારીની રાત્રે બે વાગે હમારી એ લત્તા તરફની બળદના ગાડાંથી કરેલી મંજલ પુરી થઇ તેમાં આખ્ખા પંદર દીવસ ગુજર્યાં હતા અને હમે રાત દીવસ જો ઉપરાસાપરી મંજલ નહી કરી હોત તો, જેટલા દીવસ લાગ્યા તેથી બમણા દીવસો એ મુસાફરીમાં ગુજરતે. હૈદરાબાદથી "ત્રીપટી" સુધી સઘળો આડ રસ્તો ગણતાં નજદીક ૪૮૦) માઇલની મંજલ થઇ હતી.

ત્રીપટી આગળ કરનુલનાં ગાડીવાળાઓને સારી બખ્ખશીશ આપી હતી કેમકે તેઓ એ રસ્તાની મંજલ રાત અને દીવસનો ફેર ગણ્યા વગર જેમ હમોયે કહ્યું તે પ્રમાણે અને વળી કોઈ કોઈ વાર આડ રસ્તે કીધી હતી, તેથી તેઓ ખરેખર

Vincent Brooks, lith.

MADRAS RAILWAY TERMINUS (EXTERIOR)

૨. મધરાજ રેલવેના છેડાનું સ્ટેશન.

(બાહારનો દેખાવ.)

ઈનામ મેળવવા લાયક થયા હતા. સઘળાને ઠરાવેલાં ગાડીભાડાં કરતાં વધારે આપ્યું હતું તથા બક્ષીસની પણ એક સારી રકમ આપી હતી. તેની સાથે કોઈને વાસકુટ, કોઇને ગરમ કપડું, આપ્યું હતું, તેથી તેઓ ઘણાજ ખુશી થઇ ગયા હતા.

તા૦ ૨૦ જાનેવારીને દીને સહવારનાં ૬) વાગે "ત્રીપટી" થી આગગાડીમાં બેઠા તે સહવારનાં ૧૧) વાગે એટલે ૫) કલાકનાં અરસામાં નજદીક ૨૦૦) માઈલની મંજલ પુરી કીધી હતી. ૪૮૦ માઇલની મુસાફરી કરતાં અરધો માસ ગુજરયો હતો, હાલ બસેં માઈલની મુસાફરી ફકત પાંચ કલાકમાં થઈ ગઈ હતી; પણ આગળ જણાવ્યું તેમ હવે ગામેગાંમ જોવાનું નહી બની શકયું હતું, હવે તો દોડતી ગાડીયે જે જોઈ સકાય તેજ. "ત્રીપટી" અને "મદ્રાસ" વચ્ચે "આરકટ જંકશન" કરીને એક સ્ટેશન આવેછે. આ મથક આગળ, બેપુરથી આવેલો રેલવે મળેલો છે, માટે જેઓ મદ્રાજથી હૈદરાબાદ જવાના હોય તેઓ એ ઠેકાણેથી ગાડી બદલીને ત્રીપટી જનારી ગાડીમાં બેસેછે, અને જે બેપુર જવાનાં હોય તેઓ પાધરા તે તરફ જાયછે. બરોબર ૧૧ા વાગે સહવારના મદ્રાસનાં રેલવે સ્ટેશન ઉપર જઈ પુગા હતા. એ સ્ટેશન ઘણુંજ મોહોટું અને દબદબા ભરેલી બાંધણીનું છે, તેની ઉભરણી પણ ઘણીજ ઊંચી લીધેલી છે, જેહેનું ચીત્ર અત્રે આપ્યું છે.

સ્ટેશન ઊતરતાં શેઠ એદલજી દીનશાહાજી પાંડેનાયે તેમના મીત્ર શેઠ કાવસજી—દાવર નામનાં એક ગૃહસ્થને હમુને એસતેકબાલ લેવાને મોકલ્યા હતા, તેમની સાથે ગાડીમાં બેશીને હમો શેઠ એદલજી દીનશાહાજી પાંડેને ઘેર ગયા, જે મદ્રાસના "બ્લાક ટાઊન" એટલે જીહાં ઘણાં ખરાં દેશી લોકજ વસેછે, તીહાં છે. શેઠ એદલજીયે હમારે સારૂ પોતાનાંજ મુકામ ઊપર ઊતારો કરવાને ઘણીજ તજુમલથી સઘળી ગોઠવણ અને તઈયારી કરાવી રાખી હતી. હમારા મીત્ર ડાકતર ભાઊને સારૂ પણ એજ ઠેકાણે જુદો મકાંન તઈયાર કરાવી રાખ્યો હતો, પણ તે તેમને પસંદ નહી આવ્યાથી પોતાને સારૂ ત્રણ ચાર માઈલ દુર એક બીજોજ મકાન તેવણે લીધો હતો. હમુને પણ હીયાંથી થોડા વારમાં એ મકાંન છોડી શેઠ એદલજીના બીજાં દુરનાં મકાંન ઊપર જઇ રેહેવાની ફરજ થઈ પડી હતી. પેહેલું તો "બ્લાક ટાઊન"નું પાણી સારૂં લાગ્યું નહી હતું; બીજું, ગટરોનો વાસ જબરો મારતો હતો; ત્રીજું, હવા ખુશી નહી હતી. ઊતારો કીધા પછી હમારે સારૂ નાહાવાનું પાણી ગરમ કરીને મુકયું હતું, તે પાણીનો કોગલો કરવાને જેવો એક ઘોટ મોહડામાં લીધો તો તે તમામ

ખારૂં અગર જેવું અને પછવાડેથી કડવું લાગ્યું હતું. બદન ઊપર રેડતાં ચીકણું લાગ્યું હતું, તેથી હમને એટલો તો કંટાલો ઊપન્યો કે નાહાવાનું તુરત બંધ કરીને અમસથુ દીલ નુંછી કપડાં પેહેરી લીધાં. આ લત્તાનું પાણી એક અથવા બે જગો શીવાય સઘળી તરફ ખરાબ છે, પણ તેમ વળી એક બે જગાનાં પાણીની ઘણીજ તારીફ થાયછે. વાહાણવાળા ઘણું કરીને તે પાણી ઘણુંજ પસંદ કરેછે, કેમકે તે પાણી વાહાણમાં ખરાબ થયા વગર ઘણા દીવસ ટકી સકેછે. "બ્લાક ટાઊન"ની હવા તથા પાણી સારૂં નથી. તેનાં કારણો છે, તે અજબતાં જાણવાજોગ સમજીને તેવીરો વીસ્તારીને જણાવવું જરૂર છે. મદ્રાસ સેહેરનો અરધો ઉત્તર તરફનો અને અરધો દક્ષીણ તરફનો ભાગ મળીને "બ્લાક ટાઉન" થયલું છે. ઉત્તરના અર્ધા ભાગને તીહાંના લોક "પાંડુનાયક પેંટ" અને દક્ષીણનાં અર્ધાં ભાગને "મુથીયાળ પેંટ" કેહેછે. એ બંધે પેટને ઇંગ્રેજો "બ્લાક ટાઉન" કેહેછે. મદ્રાસ સેહેરનો સઉથી વસ્તીવાળો અને અગતનો ભાગ તથા વેપાર વણજનું મથક આ બંધે ભાગઉપર સમાયલાં છે. ઇંગ્રેજ લોક જારે મદ્રાસમાં આવી વસ્યા, ત્યારે એ "બ્લાક ટાઉન" નાં બચાવને સારૂ તેઓએ તેનાં ઉત્તર અને પશ્ચીમનાં મુખડાં ઉપર કોટ બાંધી લીધો હતો. હવે તો એ કોટનો કેટલોક ભાગ ભાંગી તુટી હાલતમાં આવી પડેલો છે, અને લોકની વસ્તી દાહાડે દાડાડે વધતી જાયછે, તેમ તેમની સગવડને માટે તે કોટનો કેટલો એક ભાગ ભાંગી નાખતા જાયછે. "બ્લાક ટાઉન" માંથી જે ધોરી રસ્તા બાંધવામાં આવ્યા છે તે મોહોટા, પોહોળા, અને વગર વલાણનાં એક બીજા સાથે કાટકોને સીધા ને સીધા ઘણાંજ સારી તરેહનાં બાંધેલા છે, પણ એ શીવાયે "બ્લાક ટાઉન" નાં બીજા રસ્તા સાંકડા, વાંકાટીકા, અને હવા જવા આવવાના મારગ વગરનાં છે. રસ્તાની બંધે બાજુયે આપણી મુંબઈમાં જેવી કેટલેક ઠેકાણે ઉંધાડી સાંકડી ગટરો છે તેવીજ છે, જેમાંથી સેહેરની ગલીચીનું પાણી જતું કરેલું છે. આ ગટરોમાંથી પોતાની મેળે અને તેમને સાફ કરતી વેળાયે જે બદબો નીકળેછે, તે કોઈવાર તાવનાં રોગને ઉત્પંન કરે એવી છે. સહવારસાંજ ઠેકાણે ઠેકાણે કીચડના દુરગંધ ભરેલા ઢગો ગટરોમાંથી કાહાડીને રસ્તા ઉપર ઘરો આગળ એકઠા કરી મુકેછે, તે કીચડનાં ગાડાંવાળાઓ હળવે હળવે આવી ઉપાડી લઈ જાયછે, તેથી એવી જગાઉપર હવા અને તનદુરસ્તી સારી પેઠે રેહેવી મુસ્કેલ છે.

આ લત્તા તરફ માતબર દેશીઓનાં ઘર ઘણું કરીને ચુનો ઇંટરડી અને પથરાનાં બાંધેલાં હોયછે, અને તે ઈમારતોની રચનાં ઘણું કરીને હેવી કર્યામાં આવી છે કે, ચોતરફ ફરતા હારદોર ઓરડા બાંધેલા હોયછે, અને વચમાં ચાર ખુણાંનો ચોક, રોશની અને ખુલી હવા આવજાવ થવાને સારૂ રાખ્યામાં આવેછે. ગરીબ લોકનાં રેહેવાનાં ઘરો નીચા છાપરાંનાં છે, અને તેમાં દેવાલો કાદવની બનાવેલી હોયછે; કોઈ કોઈ ઠેકાણે તો ફકત તેમનાં ઊપર વાંસનાં બનાવેલાં છાપરાં હોયછે. જેમ જેમ "બ્લાક ટાઉન" ના ભાગની ઉત્તર તરફ દુર જઇયે છૈયે તેમ તેમ વસ્તી ઓછી થતી જાયછે, અને ઘણાંજ ગરીબ લોક છુટાં છુટાં એતરફ વસેછે. આ લત્તાને "તોંડીયાર પેંટ" કેહેછે. આ તરફ નાલીયરીની તાડી ઘણીજ મીઠી અને લેહેજત-દાર મળેછે, અને હીયાં ઘણું કરીને હીંદુ લોકની ગાંમ બાહેરની વસ્તીનું રેહેઠાણ છે. આ ઠેકાણાં ઉપર ગાંમઠીઓનાં રેહેવાનાં કોઇ કોઈ ઘર સારી તરેહની બાંધણીનાં છે, બાકીનાં ભાગઉપર મછીમારોના કાદવથી બાંધેલાં ઝુંપડાં આવેલાં છે. હીયાંથી જરા દક્ષીણ તરફ ફરતાં "રાયપુરાંમ" નો લત્તો આવેછે, તીહાં મદ્રાસ રેલવેના છેડાનું મથક આવેલું છે. તેને લગતી ઈમારતો ઘણીજ સુંદર બાંધણીની બનાવેલી છે, જેવી મદ્રાસ સેહેરમાં થોડીજ હસે. રાયપુરાંમ લત્તાતરફ "મોનીગર ચોલટરી" અને "લીપર હાસપીટલ" તથા "ફાઉંડલીંગ અસાઇલમ" ની ઈમારતો જોવાની છે. એ ઈમારતોમાંની પેહેલી બે ઈમારતોમાં મદ્રાસનાં લાચાર ગરીબ લોકને ઓસડપાણી અને ખાવા પીવાનું મળેછે. ઇસવી સન ૧૮૦૮ નાં વરસમાં એક દુકાળ પડયો હતો તે સબબથી જે ઉઘરાણું થયું હતું તેમાંથી આ ખાતાં ઉભાં થયાં છે. લોક તરફની મદદથી અને સરકાર તરફની વારશીક બક્ષીશથી હાલ આ ખાતાંઓનો ખરચ ચાલેછે. "ફાઉંડલીંગ અસાઇલમ" એટલે છુપી રીતે મુકી ગયલાં છીનાલીનાં બાલકોની બરદાસ્ત કરવાનું મકાન શી રીતે અને કોના ખરચથી ચાલેછે તે વીસે કંઈ જણાયલું નથી.

"બ્લાક ટાઉન" ના દક્ષીણ ભાગ ઉપર વચલે વાઘેના યુરોપિયન અને યુરેશીયન લોકની વસ્તી છે, તેઓમાં ઘણાં ખરા સરકારી ખાતાંનાં અને વેપારીઓની પેહેડીનાં લખનારા "કલાર્કો" વીગેરે વસેછે. એ લોકોનાં ઘર સારાં બાંધેલાં છે, તેમનાં ઉપર નળીયાનાં છાંપરાં છે, અને તેઓ દેખાવમાં પણ રોનકદાર છે. ઘરોની આસપાસ સફાઈ પણ તેઓ સારી પેઠે રાખેછે.

મદ્રાજમાં વસનારા યુરેશિયન રેહેવાશીઓ વીશે એવું સાંભળવામાં આવ્યું છે, (તેનાં ખરાપણા વીશે હમે ચોકસ કહી શકતા નથી,) કે એઓની વસ્તી ઘણી અચ્છી રીતે વધતી જાયછે! અને તેનું કારણ એવું ધાર્યામાં આવેછે કે, તેઓ દેશી સ્ત્રીયો સાથે લગન કરીને અથવા કેટલાકો તેવી બીજી રીતે વશીને કુટંબ કબીલાવાળા થઇ પડયા છે, અને આ જગાએ આવા કબીલાઓના રેહેઠાણ થયાથી તેમની વસ્તી મદ્રાસમાં વધી પડેલી ખુલ્લી જણાયલી છે.

"બ્લાક ટાઉન" નો જે ભાગ દરીયા કીનારા તરફ અને જે મદ્રાસનાં બારાની સાંમણે આવેલો છે, તે સારી હવાનું અને સફાઈ ભરેલું ઠેકાણું છે. આ લત્તા ઊપરની ઈમારતો હારેદોર બાંધેલી છે, તેમની બાંધણી સારી રોનકદાર અને મજબુત છે, તેથી તેમની હારનો દમામ ઘણોજ ભપકાદાર દુરથી દેખાયછે. વાહાણવાળાવોને તો તે દેખાવ ઘણોજ દબદબા ભરેલો બારામાંથી નજરે પડેછે. આ ઈમારતોમાં કસ્ટમ હાઊસ, મદ્રાસની હાઇકોર્ટ, અને મુખ્ય યુરોપિયન વેપારીયોની હાફીસો અને વખારો આવેલી છે. આ ઈમારતોની સામણેજ દરીયામાં બાંધેલો મદ્રાસનો લોઢાંનો ધક્કો (પીયર) આવેલો છે, જેહેનું બયાન ઘટતી જગાએ કરેલું છે. મદ્રાસમાં યુરોપિયન વેપારીયોની હાફીસો ઉપર વાવટાકાઠી અને વાવટો મુકેલો હોયછે. જીઆરે યુરોપિયન વેપારીઓ તેમનાં દરરોજનાં કામ કારભાર સર હાફીસમાં હાજર થાયછે, ત્યારે હાફીસનાં છાપરાં ઉપરની વાવટાકાઠી ઊપર વાવટો ચડાવેછે, જીઆરે વાવટો ચહડેલો નહી હોય ત્યારે જાણવું કે ધણી હાફીસમાં હાજર નથી થયલો.

મદ્રાસની દેવાની અને ફોજદારી જેલ, ટંકશાળ, માંબાપ વગરનાં છોકરાંઓની બરદાસ્ત કરવાનું મકાન, જનરલ હાસપીટલ, જેમાં યુરોપીયન વાહાણવટી અને લસ્કરનાં માણસોની તથા લાચાર યુરોપીયન દરદીઓ અને અકસમાત બનાવોથી બીમાર થયલા દેશીયોની બરદાસ્ત થાયછે; "મેમોરીયલ હાલ" જે ઈ. સન ૧૮૫૭ ના બલવાની યાદગારી સારૂ બાંધ્યામાં આવ્યો છે, રોમન કયાથલીકનું દેવલ, અરમાનીયોનું દેવલ, આ સઘળી ઈમારતો "બ્લાક ટાઉન" માંજ આવેલી છે.

મદ્રાસનાં બાગ બગીચાવાળો અને ખેતરોની જમીનવાળો ભાગ "કોમ" નદીની ઉત્તર તરફ અને "કાકરેન કનાલ" ની પશ્ચીમ તરફ આવેલો છે. એ લત્તાનું નામ "વીસરામ વાડી" કરીને તીહાંનાં લોક કેહેછે. આ ઠેકાણાં ઉપરના વીસ-

રામવાડીનાં મોહોટાં તળાવનાં પાણી કેટલીક એતી વાડીને પણ પુરા પડી શકેછે. "કોમ" નદી જે મદ્રાસ સેહેરમાં ફરી વળેલી છે, તે મદ્રાસના "ફોર્ટ સેન્ટ જાર્જ" નામનાં કીલ્લા આગળ સમુદ્રને મળેછે, અને માળ્યા આગમચ તેનાં બે ફાંટા થઈ ગયલા છે. તે ફાંટાં પાછાં એક બીજાને માળ્યાથી તેમની વચમાં નજદીક પોણો માઇલ લાંબો અને અર્ધો માઇલ પોહોળો જમીનનો કકડો પાણીથી ઘેરાયલો છે, તેહેનો એક ટાપુ બનેલો છે. એ ટાપુ મદ્રાસ સેહેરથી છુટું નથી, પણ પુલોથી જોડાયલું છે, જેમ મુંબઈની સરહદમાં કુલાબા ગણાયછે તેમ તે ટાપુ મદ્રાસની સરહદમાં ગણાયછે. આ ટાપુની વચોવચમાં રસ્તા ઉપર સર ટામસ મનરોનું કાંસાનું બાવલું ઊભું કરવામાં આવીયું છે. નદી એટલી સાંકડી અને છાલકી છે, કે તેમાં થોડેક છેટે સીવાય બીજીગમ એક નાહાનો મછવો વટીક પણ તરી શકતો નથી. મદ્રાસના જોવા લાયક મકાંનોની એક ટીપ હેઠળ આપી છે, અને તેમનું બયાન ઠેકાણાં સર જેમ જેમ હમે જોતાં ગયા તેમ તેમ કીધેલું છે, અને તેમને લગતી કેટલીક બીજી બાબદો ઊતાવળનાં સબબથી હમારા જોવામાં આવી નહી હતી, તે વીશે પછવાડેથી પુછપરછ કરતાં અને તેવીરો બીજે ઠેકાણેથી ખોળ કરીને વાંચતાં જે માલુમ પડ્યું છે, તે વાંચનારાઓને સારૂ આ ઠેકાણે જાહેર કર્યું છે.

૧ "બ્લાક ટાઉન." "ફોર્ટ સેન્ટ જાર્જ" (કીલ્લો). લોઢાંનો બાંધેલો "પીયર" (ધક્કો.)	૧૦ જનરલ નીલનું બાવલું.
૨ પીપલ્સ પાર્ક.	૧૧ શીનો ટાફ (યાદગારીનો ગુંબજ.)
૩ આગ્રી હાર્ટીકલચરલ ગારડન.	૧૨ આબસરવેટરી (વેધશાળા.)
૪ મ્યુઝીયમ (સંગ્રહસ્થાન).	૧૩ ટંકશાળ.
૫ નીઉ ટાઉન, એસપ્લેનેડ, દરીયા કીનારાનો રસ્તો, અને બેંન્ડ સ્ટાન્ડ.	૧૪ ગન કયારીયેજ માન્યુફાકટરી (તોપનાં ગાડાંનું કારખાનું.)
૬ વીદ્યા હુનર શાળા.	૧૫ ગીંડીમાં ગવર્નરનો બાગ (મકાન મેહેલ.)
૭ દીવાદાંડી.	૧૬ સોનોરનું સરોવર, (મહાબલીપુરંમ) મોહોટા બળીનું અથવા સાત દેહરાંનું સેહેર).
૮ લાર્ડ કારનવાલેસનું બાવલું.	૧૭ પ્રેસીડેન્સી કાલેજ.
૯ સર ટામસ મનરોનું બાવલું.	૧૮ મેડીકલ કાલેજ.

૧૯ શીવીલ ઇંજીનીયરીંગ કાલેજ.

૨૦ પાચ્ચાપા (સ્કુલ.)

૨૧ ફ્રેંડ ઇન્ નીડ સોસાઇટી અને તેને લગતાં કારખાંનાં. ગરીબ સ્ત્રીયોની હાસપીટલ. સુવાવડખાનું. મેગડેલન અસાઇલિમ.

૨૨ સેન્ટ જાર્જનું દેવલ.

૨૩ બાંકયુએટીંગ હાલ.

૨૪ વેપરી ઠેકાણાં ઉપરનું દેવલ.

૨૫ કલબ હાઉસ તથા તીહાંનાં હમામખાનાં.

૨૬ યુરોપીયન હાસપીટલ.

૨૭ ફ્રીમેસનનોની લાડજ.

૨૮ ઓકની કંપનીની (યુરોપ શાપ) તરેહવાર જીનસોની દુકાન.

૨૯ મારકીટ (શેહેરનું મોટું બજાર).

૩૦ ગુજર બજાર (સાંજનું બજાર), ચોર બજાર.

૩૧ મદ્રાસનું રેલવે સ્ટેશન.

૩૨ ખેતીનું શીપણું કરવાને કુવાઓમાંથી પાણી કાહાડવાની દેશી રીત.

૩૩ મદ્રાસની ભાડુતી ગાડી (શીગ્રંપો), ઝટકો તથા હાથગાડી.

પેહેલા દીવસનાં પાછલા પોહોરનાં ચાર વાગે સેઠ કાવસજી દાવરને સાથે લઇને "પીપલ્સ પાર્ક", જે રઇયતનાં ઉપયોગ અને તેમને ફરવા હરવા અને સેલગાહ કરવા માટે બનાવેલો એક બાગ છે તે જોવાને હમો ગયા હતા. આ બાગનું મંડાણ મદ્રાસનાં ગવરનર સર ચાર્લસ ત્રીવેલીયનની સુચનાં ઉપરથી તેનાં વખતમાં શીરૂ થયું હતું. રસ્તામાં જતાં ગુજર બજાર જોઈ. આ બજાર મદ્રાસમાં રોજ સાંજ સાંજનાં ભરાયછે, અને વેચનારો તરેહવાર જીનસો રસ્તાની બંધે કોરે જમીન ઉપર પાથરીને મુકેછે. આ બજારમાં મોહોટી ભીડ રોજ થાયછે. તેમાં ઘણું કરીને ગરીબ લોક પુશ્કળ આવેછે. આ બજારનો દેખાવ આપણાં મુંબઈનાં કાસમ બજારને મળતો આવેછે. આ ઠેકાણે ઘણું કરીને ચપડાવેલી જીનસો સસતી મળી શકેછે, તેથી એ બજારને ચોર બજાર પણ કોઈ કોઈ વાર કેહેછે, પણ તેહેનું ખરૂં નામ ગુજર બજાર અથવા સાંજનું બજાર કરીને કેહેછે. એમાં ગરીબ માણસોને સામાન તથા માલમતા લેવા વેચવાને દરરોજ ઘણુંજ સવલ પડેછે.

જે વખતે હમે "પીપલ્સ પાર્ક" માં ગયા હતા તે વખતે તેમાં ઝાડપાન અને તેવી બીજી ગોઠવણો કરવાનું કામ ચાલતું હતું, તથા થોડા ઘણાં ઝાડપાન પણ સારાં થયલાં હતાં. આ ઠેકાણે પોહોંચતાં અશુર થઈ ગયું હતું, તેથી તે ઠેકાણાં ઉપર જે જોવાનું હતું તે સઘળું જોવાઈ શકાયું નહી હતું. આ મકાન ઉપર ફરીને વખત-

સર આવી બરોબર જોવાનું કોઈ બીજા દીવસ ઉપર મુલતવી રાખવું પડયું હતું, જે વીરોની બાકીની વીગત તા૦ ૨૫ મી જાનેવારીનાં અહેવાલમાં જુવો.

હીયાંથી નીકળ્યા તે મદ્રાસનાં મેદાનમાં જીહાં ઘણું કરીને અઠવાડીયામાં રવીવાર શીવાય દરરોજ (બેંડ) વાજું વાગેછે, અને ગૃહસ્થ સ્ત્રી પુરૂષોનો સારો મેળાવડો થાયછે, તીહાં ફરવા ગયા. આ ફરવાનું ઠેકાણું મદ્રાસનાં કીલ્લાની દક્ષીણ બાજુએ આવેલું છે, અને તીહાં દરીયાનો કિનારો પણ આવેલો છે, તેથી તે ઠેકાણે હવા ઘણી સારી અને તનદુરસ્તી ઉપજાવે એવી છે. મદ્રાસના શોખીલાં અને માતબર લોક ગાડી ઘોડે અને પગે રોજ સાંજનાં હીયાં હવા ખાવાને આવેછે. તીહાં થોડાવાર ગુજારતાં વાજાંના મધુર અવાજથી તથા દરીયા ઉપરથી આવતી થંડા પવનની લેહેરીથી, ફરવા આવનારનું દીલ ઘણુંજ ખુશ અને તાજું થઈ શકેછે. આ જગોએ કીનારે લગતો લાંબોને લાંબો એક રસ્તો સેલગાહ કરવાને સારૂ મરનાર લાર્ડ એલફીનસ્ટન જીઆરે મદ્રાસનો ગવરનર હતો તીઆરે તેણે બંધાવ્યો છે. આ રસ્તાને એજ ગવરનરનું નામ આપ્યામાં આવ્યું છે. આવા લાંબા ટપ્પાનો અને સીધો, કીનારેથી બાંધેલો રસ્તો જો સરખાવીયે તો તે મુંબઈની મહાલક્ષ્મી અથવા ખંભાલાનાં તથા વરલીનાં પુલ સાથે મળતો આવશે, તથા બેકબે ઉપર છેક મેદાન ઊપરથી તે વાલકેશ્વર સુધી જે રસ્તો બંધાયલો છે તેને ઘણોજ મળતો આવશે. આ ઠેકાણેથી પાછા "બ્લાક ટાઉન"માં શેઠ એદલજી પાંડેનાં મકાન ઉપર આવ્યા. તાજી હવા જે ખુલ્લી જગા ઊપર ખાઈ આવ્યા હતા તેથી જીવ ખુશાલ થયો હતો, પણ જેહેવા મોહોલામાં આવ્યા કે પેલી ગટરોનાં વાસ સાથે તુરત પાછી મુલાકાત થઈ પડી હતી. રાત્રે ટેબલ ઉપર જમતી વખતે શેઠ એદલજી સાથે અને તેવણના સાહેબજાદા ભાઈ કાવસજી જેવણ એક ઘણાજ ચંચલ ગૃહસ્થ જણાયા હતા તેવણ સાથે વાતચીત કરતાં મદ્રાસના પાણી તથા હવાની વધારે ખબર મળી હતી, તથા બીજે દીને "બ્લાક ટાઊન" માંથી નીકલીને શેઠ એદલજીનું બીજું મકાંન વધારે સારી હવાની જગા ઉપર ગીંડી તરફ હતું, તીહાં જઈ રેહેવાની ગોઠવણ આ સેઠે મેહેરબાનીની રાહેની કરી હતી.

મદ્રાસનાં પાણી વીશે એવું જણાવામાં આવ્યું હતું કે, "બ્લાક ટાઉન"માં કેટલીક જગા ઉપર તથા "ફીલ પાર્ક" અને "અગમોર"નાં લત્તા ઉપર ઘણુંજ સારૂ અને પુરતું પાણી ૨૦) થી ૩૦) ઉંડા કુવાઓમાંથી મળી શકેછે. મદ્રાસનાં બાકીનાં ઘણાં ખરા ભાગમાં જે પાણી મળેછે, તે ખારાટ ભરેલું અને ખાવા-

પીવામાં વાપરવાને નાલાયક છે. "બ્લાક ટાઉન"નાં ઉત્તર તરફનાં કોટની દેવાલ આગળ એક ઠેકાણાં ઉપર "સાત બાવડી"નું પાણી મળેછે, તે પાણી ઘણુંજ સાફ અને ચોખ્ખું ગણાયછે. વાહાણવટી લોકનું આ પાણીવીશે એહેવું મત છે કે, વાહાણમાં બગડ્યા અથવા વાસ માર્યા વગર, આગળ હમોયે જણાવ્યું છે, તેમ લાંબી મુદત સુધી તે સફાઇ ભરેલું રહી શકેછે. એ પાણીનાં ઝરા Quartz "ક્વાર્ટ્ઝ" નામની ચકમક જાતની રેતીની જમીન અંદરથી નીકળેલા કેહેછે, પણ એ રેતીનાં પડની હેઠળ જે પાણીનાં ઝરા લાગેલા છે, તેનું પાણી હલકી જાતનું છે. પાણીને કુઆઓમાંથી ખેંચીને મોહોટ મોટી ઉંચી ચડાલેલી ટાંકીઓમાં ભરેછે, તીહાંથી નળની વાટે કીલ્લામાં અને મદ્રાસનાં બીજા ભાગોમાં લઈ જવામાં આવ્યું છે. ફકત બેજ કુવા હાલ કામે લાગેલા છે, બાકીનાં કાદવ વીગરેથી પુરાઈ ગયા છે. દરરોજ એ કુવાઓમાંથી ૩,૦૦,૦૦૦) ત્રણ લાખ ગ્યાલન પાણી સેહેરમાં પોંહોંચતું થાયછે. એ સીવાય કેટલાક મોહોટાં તળાવોનું પાણી પણ પીવાનાં ઉપયોગમાં આવેછે, જે પાણી પણ સારૂં ગણાયછે, પણ આગળ જણાવેલાં પાણીનાં જેવું તે નથી. વીસરવાડી, પેરામબોર, નંગંમ બાકમનાં તળાવોનું પાણી સારૂં કેહેછે, પણ તેમાં ઘણું કરીને વરસાદનુંજ પાણી પડેલું સારૂં રેહેછે, પછવાડેથી તે તળાવોના ઝરા બીગડેછે. આ તળાવોમાંથી કેટલીક ખેતીવાડીને પણ પાણી પુગેછે. કેટલાંક તળાવોની માવજત નહી બરાબર હોવાથી તેઓ આસ્તે આસ્તે પુરાતાં જાયછે. રાત્રે ૧૦ા વાગે સુવાગયા પણ વાસથી અને તેની સાથે મચ્છરથી ઊંઘ મુતલક આવી નહી હતી.

તા૦ ૨૧ જાનેવારી—આગલી રાત્રે ગોઠવણ કીધા પ્રમાણે આ દીને સહવારનાં વેહેલા ઉઠી "ગીંડી" જે બ્લાક ટાઉનથી આસરે ૫) માઇલ દુર છે તે ઠેકાણાં ઉપર ગયા. ગીંડી, હવાવાળી અને બાગ બગીચા ભરેલી જગા છે, જીહાં ઘણુંકરીને પરેલ, નાયગામ, મટુંગા અને છાસ્ટીની કેટલીક જગાનાં જેવો દેખાવ છે, તથા આબોહવા પણ તેવીજ બલકે તેનાં કરતાં સરસ છે. મદ્રાસનાં ગવરનરનો આ ઠેકાણાં ઉપર એક મોહોટો મુકામ છે, અને તેની આસપાસ અચ્છો સરકારી બાગ બનાવેલો છે. ગીંડીમાં કેટલેક ઠેકાણે નાહાનાં નાહાનાં છુટા છવાયા બંગલા છે, તેમનો દેખાવ તથા તેમાંની સગવડ કંઈ ઘણી પસંદ કરવા જોગ નથી, ઘણું કરીને તે આપણાં મુંબઈના છાસ્ટી ગાંમમાં અથવા મેહેમ અને વાંદરે જેવી નાહાની નાહાની બંગલી અને બંગલા આપણે જોઈએછ તેવાં મકાંનો છે. જે મકાંન ઉપર હમો ગયા હતા તીહાં રોઠ અદલજી પાંડેના ઘણીયાણી તેમની તનદુરસ્તીને સારૂ હવા ફેરબદલ કરવાને જઈ

રહેલાં હતાં, તે બંગલો એકુએ જણુની સગવડ લાયકનો હોવાથી અને આસપાસનાં બંગલામાંથી કોઈબી બીજો સગવડ ભરેલો નહી મળી આવ્યાથી તે દીવસે તો, સેઠ એદલજીનાજ બંગલામાં ઉતારો કરવાની ફરજ થઈ પડી હતી. સહવારનો નાસ્તો ખાઈ પાછાં સેહેરમાં ફરવાને ગયા. શેઠ એદલજીએ હમારી બરદાસ્ત કરવાને સારૂ પોતાનાં કુટંબ વટીકને જરા અડચણ ભોગવાવી હતી, આ ઉપરથી તેવણનો અમારી ઉપર મોટો અભાર થયો હતો તેની હમો આ ઠેકાણે ખુશીથી નોંધ કરવાનું વાજબી ધારીએછ.

ગીંડીથી સેહેર તરફ પાછાં ફરતાં "માઉન્ટ રોડ" નામનો રસ્તો વચમાં આવેછે, અને હીયાંથી થોડુંક આગળ જતાં "કોમ" નદી ઉપરનો પુલ આવેછે, તે પસાર કરતાં આ નદીનાં બે કાંઠાથી જે ખુદરતી ટાપુ થયલું છે તે દેખાયછે (જેવીરો આગળ બયાન કરેલું છે,) ટાપુનું મંડાણ અથવા શીરૂવાત પુલ આગળથી થયલી ગણાયછે. હીયાંથી જરા આગળ વધતાં રસ્તાની વચમાં કાંસાનું એક મોહોટું બાવલું જોનારની નજરે પડેછે. આ બાવલું બ્રીગીડીયર જનરલ નીલનું છે જેહેની યાદગારી માટે તે તીહાં ઉભું કરવામાં આવ્યું છે. ઈ૦ સ૦ ૧૮૫૭ નાં સાલનો આ દેશનો લશકરી બલવો બેસાડી દેવાને પોતાની ચુનંદી લશકરી ટુકડીને, દુશમન ઉપર હોમલો કરવાને હુકમ આપતી વેલાની ઢપમાં આ સુરા સરદારનું બાવલું ઉભું કરેલું છે. જે પથરની બેઠક ઉપર બાવલાને ચઢાવી મુકયું છે તે પથર ઉપર નીચે જણાવ્યા પ્રમાણે લેખ કોતરેલા છે :—

જેમ્સ જાર્જ સ્મીથ નીલ, સી. બી.

રાણીનો એડીકાંગ.

મદ્રાસ ફયુજીલીયર લશકરનો લેફટેનંટ કરનલ.

હિંદુસ્થાનમાં બ્રીગીડીયર જનરલ.

જંગી બાહાદુર, દેલાવર અને આપ તવકુલ સીપાહ.

બંગાલમાં બલવાના જોસ્સાને અટકાવામાં

સઘળાઓએ કબુલ રાએલા પેહેલા આગેવાન.

૨૫ મી સપ્ટેંબર ૧૮૫૯ ઈસવીને રોજ

૪૭) વરસની ઉમરે

લખ્નૌનો છુટકારો કરતાં

તમામ બાહાદુરી ભરેલી રીતે માર્યો ગયો છે.

લશકરની ટુકડીના જે સરદારો અને માણસો માર્યાં ગયાં છે, તેમનાં નાંમ બેઠકની બંધે બાજુયે કોતરેલાં છે, અને તેની હેઠળ લખનૌમાં આલમબાગ ઉપર જે ધસારો કીધેા હતો, જેમાં આ બાહાદુર જનરલ માર્યો ગયેા હતો, તે હમલાનું ચીત્ર કાંસા ઉપર "બાસરીલીફ"માં એટલે સપાટીની ઉપર ઉપસાઈ આવેલા ચીત્રનાં આકારમાં પાડેલું છે.

આગળ જણાવેલાં ટાપુનાં મધ્ય ભાગમાં જે બાવલું રસ્તામાં ખુલ્લું મુકેલું છે, તે "સર ટામસ મનરો"નું છે. આ બાવલું, મદ્રાસની રઇયતની આ ગવર્નર ઉપર અતી ઘણી પ્રીતિ હતી માટે જાહેર ઊઘરાણું કરીને બનાવ્યામાં આવ્યું છે. "સર ટામસ મનરો"નું બાવલું, ઘોડેસ્વાર આસનમાં, કાંસાનું બનાવેલું છે, એની ઉંચાઈ આસરે ૩૦) થી ૩૫) ફુટની દેખાયછે. એનું ચીત્ર અત્રે આપ્યું છે. ઘેાડો બનાવામાં બનાવનારે કોઈ એકુ ઘોડાની નકલ નથી કરી, પણ પોતાના હુંનરની સઘળી કારીગીરી અને હોશીયારી બતલાવવાને, ઉમદામાં ઉમદા હેવાં જાનવરમાં જે જે ખુબીયેા સમાયલી છે તે સઘળી અને સંપૂર્ણ આ બાવલામાં કરી બતલાવી છે, તથા તેની ઉપર જે નામદારે સ્વારી કરી છે તેને જોકે બનાવનારે નજરે તો જોયેાજ નહી હતો, તો પણ તેહેની સબી ઉપરથી તેહેનું પુતળું આબેહુબ તેહેનાં ચેહરાને મળતુંજ બનાવ્યું છે, હેવું લોકોનું મત છે. સર ફ્રાન્સીસ ચાનટ્રે નામનાં વખણાયલા પુતલાં બનાવનારે પોતાને હાથે આ આખું બાવલું બનાવ્યું છે, અને એ ઉપર આસરે સવાલાખ રૂપૈયાનો ખરચ થયલો જણાયછે. સર ટામસ મનરો, મદ્રાસનો ગવરનર, કોલારાનાં રોગથી તા૦ ૯ જુલાઈ સને ૧૮૨૭ ને દીને, પેટીકાન્ડા નામની જગા ઉપર મરણ પામ્યેા હતો.

સેહેરમાં જતાં તડકો સખત લાગવા માંડયેા હતો, માટે એક ઠેકાણે આઇસક્રીમવાળાની દુકાન નજરે પડ્યાથી તીહાં ઊતરી જરા ઠંડા થયા હતા, અને રાત્રે પણ ગરમી ખમવાની ધાસ્તીથી બરફ તથા આઇસક્રીમ હમારાં રેહેવાનાં મકાંન ઊપર મોકલવાને આ ઠેકાણે હુકમ આપ્યો હતો. હીયાંથી નીકલીને ફરાંક કંપનીવાળાઓનું લીલાંઊખાનું અને કમીશન એજંટની દુકાન જોવા ગયા, એટલીજ મતલબથી કે જોઈએ મદ્રાજનાં લીલાંઊખાનાં, યુરોપશાપ, અને કમીશન એજંટની દુકાનો અને આપીસો મુંબઈનાં આવાં ખાતાં સાથે સરખાવતાં કેવી પ્રકારની છે. મદ્રાજમાં સાધારણ ધંધા રોજગારવાળા અને પરચુરણ જીનસોની દુકાનવાળાઓમાં, ત્રણ ભાગઉપર, યુરોપીયનોની દુકાનો છે, અને દેશીઓની

Vincent Brooks lith.

SIR THOMAS MUNRO. MADRAS
(BRONZE STATUE)

૩. સર ટામસ મનરો.—મદ્રાસ.
(કાંસાનું બાવલું.)

તો કંઈ જુજવીજ છે. યુરોપીયનોની દુકાનો નાહાની અથવા મોહોટી બંધે ઘણીજ સારી રીતે અને કાયદાસર રચેલી છે, જેથી તેમનો દેખાવ જોવા લાયક અને પસંદ પડતો લાગેછે. વળી એ બાબદમાં, મદ્રાજની દુકાનોની રચના કરતાં કલકત્તાની દુકાનોની રચના આથી પણ વધારે બેહેતર છે, જેનું બયાન ઘટતે ઠેકાણે વાંચીયામાં આવશે. આ બંધે જગા ઉપરની દુકાનોની રચના, સગવડ અને સફાઈ ભરેલી જોઈ હમો ઘણાજ ખુશી થયા હતા, પણ તુરત તેનીસાથે દિલગીરી એટલા સબબથી પેદા થઈ હતી કે તેમની સાથે આપણાં મુંબઈ શેહેરની એવી કીસમની દુકાનોની સરખામણી કરતાં તેમની આગળ આપણી બેચાર યુરોપરાપ સીવાય બાકીની સઘળી દેશી દુકાનોની રચના પોઈસ થઈ શકે એવી જણાઈ હતી. કલકત્તાની યુરોપીયન દુકાનો સાથે તો અત્રેની દુકાનોનો મુકાબલો કરવોજ નહી જોઇએ. તેઓ તો યુરોપ ખંડની મોટી દુકાનો સાથે હરીફાઈ કરી શકે એવી છે. આપણાં દેશી લોક દુકાનોમાં સામાન રચવાના કાયદા કાનુનોથી ઘણુંકરીને તદન અણજાણ્યા છે. તેઓ સામાન એવો તો બેકાયદાથી ભરી મુકેછે કે તેમની દુકાનને સામાનની વખારનું નામ આપીયે તો તે ચાલી શકે એવું છે. હીયાં ઘણે ઠેકાણે સઉથી સરસ માલ અને વળી તે મોટી કીમતનો એકઠો કરેલો હોયછે, પણ તેને એવી તો કફોરી રીતે રચેલો હોયછે કે એક સરસ જીનસની પાસેજ એક રદ બાતલ થયલી જીનસ પડેલી હોયછે. બીજી કસુર એ હોયછે કે તેથી એક જીનસને બાહેર કાહાડતાં દસ જીનસોને ખીસાડવી પડેછે, અને તે ખીસાડેલી જીનસોને પાછી તેમની જગા ઉપર મુકવાની તો કોઇને બચગીથીજ ટેવ નહી, જાણે તે જીનસો પોતાની મેળે ચાલીને પાછી પોતાનાં ઠેકાણાં ઉપર જઈ બેસશે, એવું દુકાનવાળા સમજેછે! વળી કાંચનાં સામાનસાથે લાકડાંના અને ધાતુના સામાનનો ભેળાભેળ કરી નાખેલો હોયછે. જીહાં ખુણે ખાંચલે જે જીનસ સમાઈ શકી તેને તીહાં ઓસી દીધેલી, અને જારે કામ પડતાં બાહેર કાહાડીને કોઈ બીજે ઠેકાણે મુકી તો તે વળી તીહાંજ ખુણામાં પડી રેહેલી. આવી રીતે ઘણીક જીનસો આખ્ખાં દુકાને થોડા વખતમાં ફરીવળેછે, અને તેવામાં ઘણીવાર એવું બનેછે કે કોઈ ચીજ જોઇએ તારે તે હાથ લાગતી નથી, પછી તેહેને શેાધવાને જોઈએ એટલાં ફાંફાં મારાયજ કરો. આવી ખામીઓથી ઘણીવાર ભારી કીમતી દુકાનવાળાઓનો મુંબઈમાં કોઈ ભાવ પુછતું નથી, અને એવી દુકાનો ઉપર કોઇને જવાં પણ ગમતું નથી. દુકાન છોડી આપણાં દેશીયોની

પેહેડી અને આફીસો અંદરની રચનાં તપાસીયે તો તીહાંપણ એવીજ તરેહનો ગોંદલ જોઈ લેવો. થોડેજ ઠેકાણે આપણે જોઈશું કે વેપાર વણજનાં કામકાજ સારૂ, લખવા, વાંચવા, અને હીસાબ ગણવાની જુદી એલાહેદી જગા કરી રાખેલી હશે જીહાં બીજું કંઈજ કામ થતું નહી હોય. થોડેજ ઠેકાણે એવું હશે કે જીહાં સેઠ અને તેનાં માણસો કાયદાસર પોત પોતાને દરજ્જે બેસી કામ કારભાર કરતા હશે. હમો અતરેના માતબર હીંદુ, વાણીયા તથા ભાઠીયા વીગેરેની પેહેડીયોની અંદરની રચના વીશે બોલીયેછ. આ વીશે આપણાં કેટલાક પારશીઓને તો હમારા વીચાર પ્રમાણે જરા ભલાઈ છે, જો કે તેઓ કેટલાક પણ આવી ખામીથી ખાલી નથી. વાણીયા, ભાઠીયા શેઠીઆઓની પેહેડીમાં જઈ જુઓ, જે જગાઉપર મોહોટા સેઠ મોહોડાંમાં પાનનો ડુચો ઘાલી ચાવતા બેઠેલા હશે તેમનીજ પાસે જરા દુરથી તેમનાં વડા કારભારી અથવા મેહેતા પાનની બીડીની પચકડી દેવાલ ઉપર મારતા બેઠેલા હશે; પચકડીના રેલાથી દેવાલ સઘળી લાલ અને પીળી બની રહી હશે, જે કોઈની આંખમાં નઠારી અથવા નજીસાઈ ભરેલી નથીજ દીસવાની! મેહેતાની જોડે પેહેડીનાં ઉઘરાણી કરનાર માણસો તેમનાં ખરડાયલા જોડા કાહાડી પોતાની સામણે તે જાણે દરશાને મુકી બેઠેલાં હશે. ચોકી કરવા રાખેલો કોઈ શીપાઈ હોયો તો તે વળી સેઠની સાંમણેજ, ખુણે બેશી કોપરાં જોખતો હશે; પેહેડીની ગાદી ઉપર પાન તંબાકુનો ભુકો અને એલચી સોપારી બાંધવાનાં પાત્રાં તથા વાખ, પગેપગ અટવાતાં પડેલાં હશે! મોહોટા શેઠે પેહેડીની ગાદી ઉપર બેશીને સોખથી સહવારનાં પોતાને હાથે વાલપાપડી સમારી, વાલ કાહાડી, છલટાં પેહેડીની ગાદી ઉપરજ નાખેલાં, તે તીહાંજ પડી રહેલાં દેખાશે, જે વારી લેવાને, વલ્લભ રસોઈયાને પાંચવાર કહેલું, પણ વલ્લભનાં ભેજામાં સફાઈ સું ચીજ છે, તેનો વિચાર બરોબર જઈ શકેલોજ નહી, તેથી વલ્લભને બોલવતાં તે ચારવાર આવી ગયલો ખરો, પણ પોતાનાં પગની ઠોકરે પેલાં પાત્રાંઓને એકગ-મથી ઝાટકી બીજીગમ ઉરાડી મેળેલાં, પણ પોતાની કંમર મરડી, વાંકુ વળીને કચરો કાહાડી; જગા સાફ કરવી, આ વિચાર તેનાં ઘી ખાધેલાં મગજમાં નહીંજ આવેલો. આવી કંટાલા ભરેલી અને બીન કાયદાસર રીતથી આજ મોહોટ મોટા વેપારીયોની પેહેડીનાં કામ ચાલ્યાં તો જાયછે, પણ અંતે તેનાં પરીણામ માઠાંજ નીપજેલાં હશે, અને તેથી તેમને કેટલી અણજાણતાં નુકસાની થઈ હશે અને હજુર પણ થતી હશે, આ વીશે તેમને કશી ખબર છેજ નહી. કાયદો ઇશ્વરી ગુણ છે અને તે

દરેક માણસ જાતમાં હોવો જોઈએ. કોઈબી કામ અથવા ધંધો કરવામાં, પછી તે ગમે એવું કઠણ અથવા સેહેલું હોય તોએપણ તેમાં ચોકસ કાયદા અને રીત તે હોવીજ જોઇએ.

જેનું કામ તે તેણેજ કરવું, જે વખતે જે કામ કરવું ઘટતું હોય તેજ વખતે તે કામ કરવું, જે રીતે તે થવું જોઈએ તેજ રીત પ્રમાણે તે કરવું, તોજ તે કામ બરોબર થવાનું. આપણા દેશી દુકાનદારો અને વેપારીયો જબરી મેહેનત કરનારા છે, પણ તે સઘળી બીન કાયદે અને બીન રીતે કરવાથી, યુરોપિયન દુકાનદારો અને વેપારીયોની બરોબરી તેઓ કરી શકતા નથી. આપણા દેશી ધંધાદારીઓ પોતાનું કામકાજ, જેમ તેમ, વખત ઉપર બની આવ્યું તેમ કાયદે અથવા બેકાયદે કર્યા જાયછે, તેમ યુરોપીયન નથી કરતા અથવા કરનાર. આપણો દેશી ધંધાદારી રાત્રે બારવાગા સુધી બેસી, કસરનાં ઝુંકતા દીવા આગળ, હીસાબનાં ચોપડાં લખાવાનો, અને બીન રીતે કામ કરતો કરતો તે રોકાયલોને રોકાયલોજ રેહેવાનો, તેનાં કામનો છેડોજ નથી આવવાનો, તેની જીંદગી, ઘસાઇને તે જલદી બુઢો થઈ ડાચા હીલાવતો, તકીયે લાગીને અશક્ત થઈ બેસવાનો, પણ યુરોપીયન ધંધાદારી આવું ગધેડા વહીતરૂં કદી નથી કરનાર. તે આવી બીન કાયદાની રીતને, આપઘાત કરવા જેટલી તકસીર સમજેછે. તેથી પોતાનું કામ બજાવવાને તેણે પોતાના કાયદા અને રીત બાંધી તેજ મુજબ તે ચાલેછે. તે ઠેરવેલ વખતેજ પોતાનું કામ હાથમાં લીયેછે, અને તે લીધું કે તે બજાવવાને તેની પાછળ મંડેલોજ રેહેછે. પણ જે વખત તેણે આસાએસનો ઠરાવેલો હશે, તે વખતે સઘળું કામ પડતું મેલીને તે પોતાનાં શરીરને સુખ અને આસાએસ તો આપવાનોજ. તેનું મગજ કંટાલીયું તો તે પાંચ પચીસ રૂપીયાનાં ખરચની દરકાર કર્યા વગરે, તે આસાએસ લેવાને, ૧૦૦ ગાઉ દુર ટેકરી ઉપર, અથવા બાગ બગીચામાં દોડી જવાનો, અને આસાએસ મેળવી પાછો પોતાનાં કામ ઉપર નવાં કઊઅતથી લાગવાનો. આ ટુંક બાબત આપણા દેશીઓ સારૂ વીચાર કરવા જોગ જાણી અત્રે મુકી છે. મુંબઈમાં હવે ઘણાં યુરોપીયનોનું આવવું થયું છે અને તેમની રીતભાંત મુજબ ચાલવાની ટેવ આપણાં કેટલાક બુંધી અને ચાલાક દેશીયોમાં પડતી જાયછ. કેળવણીનો તેમ પ્રસારો પણ થતો જાયછ, તેથી ઉમેદ છે કે ધંધા વેપારને લગતી આ અગતની બાબત ઉપર આપણા દેશીઓ ધીયાન પોહોચાડશે. ધંધા રોજગાર કાયદાસર અને કેવી રીતે કરવો આ અ-

ગતની બાબત ઉપર દેશીઓ, યુરોપિયન લોકની આવી બાબદમાં જે રીતભાંત છે તેની નકલ કરે તો તેથી દેશીઓને બચીત મોટો ફાયદો થશે. તેમના પોશાક અને ખાવાપીવાની નકલ કરવા કરતાં આ અગતની બાબદની નકલ કરવાને હમો હમારા ભાઈ બંધુઓને વધારે તાકીદની ભલામણ કરીએછ.

મદ્રાસની દુકાનો જોઇને સાંજનાં ૪ વાગે "બ્લાક ટાઉન" માં થઈ પાછા ગીંડી ગયા. સાંજનાં રસ્તામાં આસપાસનો દેખાવ જાણે આપણે પરેલ, મોટ, નાંયગાંવ, અને મટુંગાના રસ્તા ઊપરથી જતાં હોઈએ તેવો ઝાડોની ઘટાથી રળીઆમણો લાગતો હતો. રાત્રે ગીંડીમાંજ આરામ કીધો, કેમકે મદ્રાસની એ મોસમની સરત બીજે દીને સવારનાં થનાર હતી, તે જોવાનો ઇરાદો હમે રાખ્યો હતો. મદ્રાસની સરત ઘણું કરીને સહવારનાં પોહોરમાં ઘણો તડકો નહી પડે એવા તાજા અને ઠંડકનાં વખતમાં થાયછે, અને તે જોવાને દુરવેરથી ઘણાં લોકની ઠઠ મળેછે.

તા૦ ૨૨ જાનેવારીને દીવશે પાછલી રાત્રથી ગાડી ઘોડા અને લોકની હીલચાલની ગડબડાટ સાંભળવામાં આવી હતી. જાણે કેવું એક અગતનું કામ હોય તેમ લોક પરોઢીયાંમાંથી દોડ ધામમાં પડ્યાં હતાં. સરવે કોઈ સરત જોવાને જગો મેળવવાની હોંસથી, સરતનાં રસ્તાની બાજુ ઊપર છેક પાછલી રાત્રથી અંધારામાં આવીને જગો ઘેરી ઊભાં રહ્યાં હતાં. ઘોડદોડની જગા મદ્રાસના "બ્લાક ટાઉન" થી આસરે ચાર માઇલ દુર છે, તોયેપણ એટલે દુર સુધી પુશ્કળ લોક આવ્યાં હતાં. મદ્રાસનાં લોક ઘણાં ખરાં ભારી મોજીલાં અને સોખીલાં છે. સરતના બંગલાની સાંમે ગૃહસ્થ લોકને સગવડથી બશીને ઘોડદોડ જોવાને બની આવવા સારૂ કામ ચાલુ માંડવ બાંધીને તેમાં ખુરશી તથા બાંકની બેઠક કરેછે, અને તેની ટીકીટો જાહેર વેચ્યામાં આવેછે. હમે ગયા હતા તે વખતે દરમાણસ દીઠ ટીકીટનો રૂપીયા ૧) લેતો કીધો હતો. આવી બેઠક કરવાનું કામ સરતની આગમચ કંત્રાકટરો પોતાને માથે લીયેછે, અને તેમાંથી સારી રકમ તેઓ કમાયછે; આવી બેઠકનો લાભ સારાં સારાં માણસો પોતાના કુટંબ કબીલા સાથે લીયેછે.

મદ્રાસની સરત જોવા આવનાર તમાસગીર લોકમાંથી ભાયગે સોયે દસ માણસ ખાધા પીધા અથવા મોજ કર્યાં વગર પાછાં જતાં હશે, હેવું હમને જણાવવામાં આવ્યું છે, તથા તેવું હમોએ જોયું પણ છે. સરવેકોઈ કંઈ ખાવાની વસ્તુ

SHIGRAMPO, HORSE HACKERY.—MADRAS.

૮. શીગરાંમ પેા. ભાડુતી ઘેાડાની ગાડી.—મધરાજ.

પોતાની સાથે ભાતીપું બાંધી લાવેછે, અથવા રસ્તામાં તેવી દુકાનો મંડાયછે તેમાંથી તો એ દીને સઘળા જણ ઘણીજ તલબદુ ભુખે સહવારનો નાસ્તો કરેછે. નાસ્તા સાથે તીહાં કાફી, ચાહે અને દુધ પણ મળેછે, પણ તે દીવસે ચાહા કાફી વપરાવમાં પડી, તેની ઉપર તાડીની ચડુડતી ઘણીજ થાયછે. તાડીનો ખપ તે દીવસે એટલો તો થાયછે કે સરત થઈ રેહા પછી રસ્તામાં દેશીયો તાડીખાં ઇંજીનીયરો બનીને, જમીન માપતા તથા જગા લેટ કરતાં, છેક સહવારનાં નીકળેલા સાંજે પોતાને ઘેર ઘણું કરીને સહી સલામત પુગેછે, અને કેટલા એકોને તો સંભાળ સાથે પોહોંચાડવામાં આવેછે!

એ દીને મદ્રાસની ભાડુતી ગાડીયોનો ખપ પણ ઘણો પડેછે. મદ્રાસની ભાડુતી ગાડીનું ચીત્ર આ ઠેકાણે આપ્યું છે, તે જોયાથી માલુમ પડશે કે તે બે પઈડાંની નાહાંની સીગરામ છે. એનું નામ મદ્રાસના લોક "સીપ્રંમપો" બોલેછે, જે શબ્દોનો અર્થ "જલદી જા," એહવો થાયછે. ચારજણ આ ગાડીમાં, બબે સાંમાસાંમી બેસેછે. પછવાડે બારણું ઊઘાડવાવાળો ઉભો રેહેછે, અને આગળ "કોચ બાકસ" ઊપર કોચમેન હાંકવા બેસેછે, તેહેને મદ્રાસમાં "સાઈસ" બોલેછે. ચાર ઊતારૂઓ કરતાં કોઈવાર વધારે માણસો, છ વટીકપણ, ભચડાઈ સંકડાઇને બેસેછે. એ ગાડીનો દેખાવ જેવો ચીતાર પાડનારે સારો પાડયો છે તેવો સઘળી સીપ્રંપોનો નહી સમજવો. ઘોડાનું "હારનીસ" સુતળી, દોરડી અને કાથાથી ઘણુંકરીને બાંધેલું હોયછે, અને શીપ્રંપોનું લાકડકાંમ પણ ઘણીજ તકલીદી બનાવટનું અને ભાંગીતુટી હાલતનું હોયછે. જીહારે હેવી ગાડીયો એકબીજા સાથે સામાસામી જોસથી અથડેછે, તીઆરે તેહેનો દેખાવ ઘણું કરીને જોવાલાયક થઈ પડેછે. ગાડીનું ખોખું, ચક્કર અને પુલથી ભાંગી છુટું પડી જાયછે, તેનાં પાનેયો ભાંગીને જુદાં પડેછે, અને તેમાં બેસનારો પોતાનાં કપડાં ખંખેરતાં અને ધુળ પખોડતાં ગાડીનાં ભાંગેલા પીંજરામાંથી બાહેર નીકળેછે. ગાડી એટલી તો નાહાની અને નીચી હોયછે કે, તે ભાંગાથી બેસનારને ઘણું કરીને વાગવા જેવું કંઇજ બનતું નથી. થોડા વખતમાં સઘળો સરંજામ, ભાંગી, તુટી, ફાટી, અને વેરાઈ એવો તો છુટો થઈ પડેછે, કે તે થયાથી સઘળું થઈ ચુકું જાણવું. ગાડી ભાંગાથી ઘોડાને મોકળો કરવા હારનીસ કાપવાની કંઈ જરૂર પડતીજ નથી, તેના પટેપટા પોતાની મેળે કાંચા સુતરની મોઆફક તુટી જાયછે. હાંકનાર ઘણું કરીને જેવો ચોટ અને બોચડ તેવોજ તેહેનો

ઘોડા પણ થંડા અને મુરદાર હોયછે, તેથી મસ્તીની અથવા ઉથલપાથલ થવાની જરાપ્પી ધાસ્તી રેહેતી નથી. આ ગાડીનું નામ "શીઘ્રપો" એટલે "જલદી "જા" કરીને તો બોલાયછે, પણ ઠુસુક ઠુસુક કરતાં અલબતાં અર્ધે કલાકે માઇ-લકની મુસાફરી એવી ભાડુતી ગાડીયો જો કરે તો બેસનારનાં સારાં ભાયેગ જાણવાં.

એક બીજી તરેહની ભાડુતી ગાડી મદ્રાસમાં વપરાયછે, તેહેનું નામ "ઝટકો" બોલેછે. એનું ચીત્ર આપેલું છે, તે જોયાથી માલુમ પડશે કે આ ગાડી, બેાલી અને રેહેકલા જેવી છે, અને તેમાં એક બળદ જોડેછે. હાંકનાર આગળ બેસેછે અને તેની પાછળ ઉતારૂ બેસેછે. એ ગાડીનું નામ "ઝટકો" કરીને છે તેહેની મતલબ એવી છે કે કોઈ ઠેકાણે જલદીથી ઝપાટામાં જવું હોય તો એવી ગાડીમાં એક ઝટકામાં જવાયછે. ખરેખર એ ગાડીને જે નામ આપ્યું છે તે ખરેખરૂંજ આપેલું છે, કેમકે જીઆરે બળદ જોરમાં આવી દોડેછે, તીઆરે આપણી નજર તે દોડતી ગાડી ઉપર ઠરી શકતી નથી, એટલી જોરમાં તે નીકળી જાયછે, પણ બેસનારે ખુબ સારી પેઠે પગ ઠસાવીને બેશવું જોઈએછ, નહી તો દોડતી ગાડીયે જરા આંચકો લાગતાં તે ખચીત ઊડી પડયા વગર નથી રહેવાનો. ઝટકો પણ સીગ્રમપોની માફક અથવા તેથી પણ વધારે તકલદી ગાડી છે, અને જીઆરે ઝટકો અથડીને ભાગેછે તીઆરે તો જેમ ખુરદાની એક કોથળી પડીગયાથી તેહમાંનાં દોહોડીયાં વેરાઇને ગગડી જાયછે, તેમ એ ગાડીના ભાગો ખુરદો થઈને આસપાસ ગગડી વીખરાઈ જઈ પડેછે.

આવી ભાડુતી ગાડીયો શીવાએ બીજી ઘણી સારી ભાડુતી ગાડીયોનાં પણ તબેલાં મદ્રાસમાં ઇંગ્રેજ લોકે અને દેશીઓએ રાખેલા છે, અને આપણે હુકમ મોકલીયે તે પ્રમાણે બે ઘોડાની અથવા એક ઘોડાની, જેહેવી માગીયે તેહેવી ગાડી, ભાડે મળી શકેછે. પણ એ ગાડીઓનાં કોચમેનો વીશે ખુબ શંભાળ રાખવી જોઈએછ, કેમકે તેઓ ઘણાજ બેપરવા અને મુરખ હોયછે. મદ્રાસમાં ગાડી પછવાડે ઘોડાવાળા ઘણું કરીને બેસતાં નથી, પણ ચાલતી ગાડી સાથે દોડેછે. તેઓ કોઈજ વાર અથવા કદાચજ પછવાડે બેસેછે, પણ વસ્તીનો ભાગ આવ્યો એટલે તીહાંથી ઉતરીને સાથે દોડતાંજ રહેછે, પછી ગમે એટલું લાંબે દોડવું પડે, તેની તેઓ દરકાર કરતાં નથી. મદ્રાસમાં રસ્તે ચાલનારાઓને "બોઈસ" "બાજુ થા" એવા શબ્દો ઘોડાવાળા પોકારીને નથી કેહેતા, પણ આ, ઈ, ઊ, એવા

૫. બહેલ. ભાડુતી બળદની ગાડી.—મદ્રાસ.

ફક્ત સ્વરોનાં આવાજ મોંહોડેથી કાહાડીને વચમાં ચાલનારાઓને બાજુયે જવાની ચેતવણી આપેછે. કોઈજ વખતે "બાજુ" શબ્દનો પોકાર સાંભળ્યામાં આવેછે.

મદ્રાસની સરત જોયાપછી ગીંડીના બંગલામાં પાછાં ગયા, અને નાહીને નાસ્તો કરીને ૧૦) વાગે મદ્રાસનો ફોર્ટ સેન્ટ જાર્જ નામનો કીલ્લો જોવા ગયા.

મદ્રાસનો કીલ્લો હાલ જે જોવામાં આવેછે, તેમાં અને અસલના જુના કીલ્લાના આકાર અને બાંધણીમાં ઘણોજ ફેર પડી ગયો છે. અસલ કીલ્લાની આસપાસની દેવાલ અથવા કોટ ઘણોજ તકલદી અને નાકુઅત હતો અને લડાઈનાં હીંગામમાં બચાવ કરવાનાં કામને નાલાયક હતો. હાલનો બાંધેલો કીલ્લો નિમગોલ આકારનો છે, તેની સીધી સપાટ બાજુ ઉત્તરથી દક્ષીણ, દરીયા તરફથી આવેલી છે. દરીયાનું પાણી છેક કોટની દેવાળ નજદીક આવેછે,પણ મોજા અને ભરતીનું પાણી દેવાળને અથડે નહી અથવા ભાંજે નહી એ માટે પથરનાં બાંધકામની આડ કરી લીધેલી છે. તેની સાથે લોઢાંનાં થાંભલાં હવડાં દરીયામાં દાટીને પાણીનો વધારે અટકાવ કરેલો છે અને એથી પાણી થોડું ઘણું દુર હઠેલું પણ છે. જમીનની બાજુએથી કીલ્લાનો બચાવ બેવડી દેવાળનો નીમગોલ કોટ બાંધીને કીધેલો છે. કોટના વાયવ્ય તરફનાં છેડા આગળ બે મજલાની બરાએો બાંધેલી છે, તેમાં હેઠળ લશ્કરનાં માણુસોને અને માલા ઊપર અમલદારોને રેહેવાની જગા કરી આપેલી છે. બરાખની જોડેજ એક બજાર છે, તેમાંથી લશ્કરનાં માણુસોને ખોરાકી મળી શકેછે. કીલ્લાની અંદરની ઘણી ખરી ઈમારતો જુદાં જુદાં સરકારી ખાતાંઓની આફીસોને સારૂ વપરાયછે. કીલ્લામાં જોવા લાયક ઈમારત સેંન્ટ મેરીનું દેવળ છે, જે નજદીક ૧૦૦) વરસ પુરાણું છે, અને તેમાં સારી સારી યાદગારીઓની નીશાનો છે. આખા મદ્રાસ શેહેરમાં જુનાંમાં જુનું આ દેવળ ગણાયછે. "આરસીનલ" એટલે તોપખાનું અને લડાઇનો સરંજામ રાખવાની જગા પણ કીલ્લામાંજ છે, અને તે એવું તો સારી પેઠે રચેલું છે કે સાધારણ જોનારનાં મન ઊપર તીહાંની રચના જબરી અસર કરેછે. અંદર જતાંજ દરવાજા આગળ, ટીપુની પાસેથી જીતી લીધેલી બે તોપો શીણગાર દાખલ મુકેલી છે; એ તોપનાં મોહોડાં ઊપર વાઘનાં માથાંની સીકલ કોતરેલી છે. લાર્ડ કાર્નવાલીસનું પુતળું પણ કીલ્લામાંજ ઉભું કરેલું છે. આ સુરા સરદારને ગ્રાનાઈટ પથરનાં ઘુંબજ વચ્ચે ઊભો રાખેલો છે, અને જે બેઠક ઉપર તેહેને ઉભો રાખેલો છે તેહેની એક બાજુ

ઉપર ઈસવી સન ૧૭૯૨ના સાલમાં ટીપુ સાથે જે કોલકરાર થયા હતા તેપ્રમાણે ચાલવાની જામીનગીરીમાં, તેહેનાં બે છોકરા ઇંગ્રેજ સરકારને શરણ કર્યામાં આવ્યા હતા, તે ફતેહની યાદગારીનો દેખાવ કોતરેલા છે. આ પુતળું ઈસવી સન ૧૮૦૦) નાં સાલમાં ઊભું કર્યામાં આવ્યું હતું.

એજ સરદારનું એક બીજું પુતળું "માઉંટ રોડ" ઉપર પણ ઉભું કરેલું છે, અને તેહેની ઉપર એક ઘુંબજ બાંધી તેની આસપાસ લોઢાંનાં કટેરા ભરી લીધેલા છે. કટેરા વીશે એવું જણાયલું છે કે ઈસવી સન ૧૭૯૯ નાં વરસમાં ઇંગ્રેજી લશ્કરે શ્રીરંગપટણ ઉપર ઘેરો ઘાલ્યો તારે લાર્ડ કાર્નવાલીસનાં હાથમાં જે તોપો જીતમાં આવી હતી તે તોપોને પીગળાવી તેનાં લોઢાનાં આ કટેરા બનાવેલા છે. ઘુંબજની બેઠકની ચારે બાજુ ઉપર લાર્ડ કાર્નવાલીસનું નામ ઇંગ્રેજી, તેલંગી, હિંદુસ્થાની અને તામીળ ભાષામાં કોતરેલું છે. એવોજ ઘુંબજ અથવા એને નજદીક મળતો આવે એવો ઘુંબજ આગળ મુંબઈનાં કોટનાં ગ્રીનચોકમાં હતો, તેમાં પણ લાર્ડ કાર્નવાલીસનુંજ પુતળું ઉભું કરેલું હતું.

મદ્રાસનો હાલનો કીલ્લો દેખાવમાં અને રોનકમાં ઘણોજ સુંદર દીસેછે, અને લડાઈના વખતમાં બચાવ કરવાને પણ તે ઘણોજ લાયક, મજબુત અને કાયદાસર બાંધેલો છે, એવું લશ્કરી અમલદારોનું મત છે. કીલ્લામાંના રસ્તા શેહેરના રસ્તા કરતાં ઘણાંજ સાફ સફાઈ ભરેલા જોયામાં આવ્યા હતા.

કીલ્લામાંથી નીકળ્યા તેવાજ પાધરા મદ્રાસની દીવાદાંડી જોવાને ગયા. કીલ્લાની ઉત્તરે ખુલાં મેદાનમાં આ દીવાદાંડી ગ્રાનાઈટ પથરની મજબુત બાંધેલી છે; જેની ઉંચાઈ જમીનની સપાટીથી ૧૨૫) ફુટ છે, તેહેનાં પાયાના પુસ્તા સુધાં પોહેળાઈ ૫૫) ફુટ છે. દાંડીનાં મથાળાં ઉપર જવાને મીનારાની અંદરથી ગોલ ફરતો દાદર બનાવેલો છે, તેનાં ફાંગીયાંનો આધાર અથવા ટેકાવ મીનારાની પથરની ભીતના બાંધકામમાં આડી લોઢાંની જાડી ગરાદો ચીણી લઈ તે ઉપર કીધેલો છે, અને બીજીગમથી ફરતા લોઢાંના કટેરા મુકેલા છે. આ ગોલ દાદર ઊપર છેક મથાળે સુધી ચઢ્યા પછી જો ઊપરથી નીચે જોયું હોય તો આ દાદરનાં ફરતાં ગોલ ફાંગીયાંનાં પેચોની ઊઢણ અથવા ચક્કર ઘણુંજ વીચીત્ર નજરે પડેછે, પણ સઉથી જોવા લાયક તો આ પેચોની વચમાં જે ખુલો, ખાલી, ઊંડો, ઉપરથી પોહોળો અને નીચેથી સાંકડો બીંદુ જેવો ઓઘો જે ઊધાપડાના આકારમાં દેખાયછે તે

જોવાથી મનઊપર ઘણી અસર થાયછે. દાંડી ઊપરથી મદ્રાસ શેહેરનો આસપાસનો દેખાવ તેમાં મુખ્ય કરીને બ્લાક ટઉનનો દેખાવ ઘણોજ જોવા લાયક છે. આવા એક દેખાવનું ચીત્ર હીયાં આપ્યું છે.

જે દીવાની રોશની વાહાણવાળાઓને સારૂ દાંડી ઊપર મુકવામાં આવી છે તેની ઉંચાઈ દરીયાની સપાટીથી ૧૨૮) ફુટ છે અને એ રોશની વાહાણવાળો દરીયામાં ૨૦) માઈલ દુરથી વાહાણનાં તુતક ઊપરથી જોઈ શકેછે. સાંચાની મદતથી આ રોશનીને ફરતી રાખી છે, જેથી રોશનાનો પ્રકાશ પડ્યા પછી તે પાછી અંધારી થઈ જાય તે વખતમાં અને વળી તેનો પ્રકાશ પાછો પડે એ અંતરમાં ૨) મીનીટ અને ૧॥) મીનીટનો ફેર રેહેછે; એટલે બે મીનીટ શુધી જો રોશનીનું અજવાળું દેખાય તો ૧॥) મીનીટ સુધી અંધારૂં રેહેછે. વખતનો આ રીતનો ફેર, જોનારને જેટલો તે કીનારાથી દુર હોય તેટલો તેને તે ફેરબદલ થતો માલુમ પડેછે. આખી દાંડી ઉપર ૭૫૦૦૦ પંચોતેર હજાર રૂપીઆનો ખરચ થયો છે તેમાં ૧૫૦૦૦) પંદર હજાર રૂપીયા ફકત દીવાબતી અને પ્રકાશ પાડવાની આરશીયો તથા તેને ફેરવવાનાં સાંચા પછવાડે લાગા છે.

દાંડી જોયા પછી મદ્રાસનાં બારાં ઊપર બાંધેલો લાઢાંનો ધક્કો જોયો. મદ્રાસનું બારૂં ખુદરતી એવું તો કફોરૂં આવેલું છે કે કીનારેથી વાહાણ ઊપર અને વાહાણ ઊપરથી પાછા કીનારે આવતાં, વચમાં જેટલો દરીયાનો ભાગ આવેલો છે તેહેનાં મોજાનું જોર હમેશ ઘણુંજ જબરૂં રેહેછે. ઘણું કરીને એટલા ખટકામાં એવા તો જોરાવર ત્રણ મોજાં વટાવવાં પડેછે કે, તે સહી સલામત પસાર કરવાને હમેશ મોહોટું સંકટ ભોગવવું પડેછે. પાણી એટલું તો એ ઠેકાણાં ઉપર ઊછાળો કરેછે કે મછવો, પડાઉ, અથવા બોટોનો તેહેનાં છોળ આગળ ટકાવ રહી શકતોજ નથી. મોજાં એક વાર એટલાં તો ઊંચે ચઢેછે કે તેહેની ઉપર આવેલા મછવા, અથવા પડાઉને પણ સાથે છેક ઉંચે શુધી ચઢાવેછે, પણ તે મોજો ધીમે ધીમે નીચે ઉતરવાને બદલે એટલો તો જલદી ભાંગી જાયછ કે, તે ઠેકાણે પાંણીનો, મોહોટો ઉંડો ખોલ પડી જાયછે, જેહેમાં પેલો ઉછલેલો મછવો એકાએક આવી ગયાથી તે ઊંધો વળીયા વગર કોઈજ વાર બચી શકેછે. એવા સંકટની સાંભે થવાને મદ્રાસનાં બારામાં જે મછવા અને પડાઉઓ રાખેલા છે તે સઘળા જોડી અથવા કલાસીબંધ કરેલાં પાટીયાનાં બનાવેલાં નથી, પણ તેઓ મજબુત વણેલી દોર-

ડીથી બાંધી અથવા સીવી લીધેલાં પાટીયાંના બનાવેલા હોયછે; અને પાટીયાં એણીગમ પેલીગમ વળી શકે તેહેવાં રમતાં રાખેલાં હોયછે. એવાં ઢીલાં પાટીયાં ઉપર પાણી અફળાયાથી પાટીયાં વળી જઈ સાંધાવાટે પાણીને રસ્તો કરી આપેછે જેથી મછવાની ઉપર પાણીના ઝપાટાનું આખું જોર લાગુ પડી શકતું નથી. કીનારેથી બારામાં આવેલાં વાહાણો ઉપર તુરત જવું પડે તો એક એક અથવા બે માણસ "કાટમારૂન" કરીને લાંકડાનાં બાંધી લીધેલાં કકડાઓનાં નાહાના કોટીયામાં જાયછે. આ "કાટમારૂન" પેલા ત્રણ મોજાં વટાવતી વખતે તરેવાર રીતે પાણીમાં ગોતલીયાં ખાતી, તરતી, ડુબતી જાયછે તે દેખાવ જોવા જેવો છે. જેઓ અનુભવ ધરાવનાર અને કસાયલા કોળી હોયછ તેઓજ માત્ર કાટમારૂનમાં જઈ શકેછે, અને જ્યારે તોફાન હોયછે ત્યારે તો એ "કાટમારૂન" ને પણ પેહેલાં ત્રણ મોજા વટાવી વાહાણ ઉપર પોંહોંચવાને ઘણીજ મુશ્કેલી પડેછે. "કાટમારૂન" ની મારફતે ફકત કાગળ અથવા તેવું નાહાનું બંડલ લઈ જવાઈ શકાયછે. આવાં બંડલને મીણકપડમાં વીટાળી તેને વળી સાદડીના એક પડમાં મુકી, લઈ જનાર કોળી પોતાનાં માથાં ઊપર તે બંડલને મજબુત બાંધી રાખેછે; કારણ "કાટમારૂન" સાથે કોળીને ઘણીવાર પાણીમાં ઉપર નીચે બચકોળાં ખાવા પડેછે, તેથી જો કોઈબી જીનસને અલગ અથવા છુટી રાખી તો તે સરી પડચા વગર રેહેનાર નથી. ઉપર કહી જણાવેલી સઘળી અડચણો ટાળવાને આગળ કહેલો લોઢાંનો ધક્કો બાંધ્યો છે. આ ધક્કો બાંધવાનું મુખ્ય કારણ એટલુંજ કે, આ ધક્કાની છેક નજદીક વાહાણ આવી શકે અને તેમાંનો માલ તથા ઉતારૂઓ સહીસલામત ઉતરી શકે. આ ધક્કો એટલો તો લાંબો બાંધેયો છે કે પેલા ત્રણ મોજાં વટાવીને પણ તેમની પેલીમેર લઇગયા છે. તોયપણ બાંધનાર ઇંજનીઅરો તેમની ઊમેદમાં નીરાફળ થયા છે. ધક્કા આગળ પણ મોજાંનું જોર એટલું તો થાયછે કે પવનની વખતે તો બંદરબોટથી ધક્કાની સેહેડી આગળ એક અર્ધો અથવા પા મીનીટ પણ અટકી થમ ઊભું રહી શકાતું નથી. તે એટલા તો જોરથી ધક્કાની સેહેડી સાથે અથડેછે કે બોટ ભાંગી કકડે કકડા થઈ જાયછે. સાધારણ સમેમાં આ ધક્કો ઘણું કરીને ઉપયોગી થઈ પડે એવો છે.

આ ધક્કો ઈસવી સન ૧૮૬૨ ના સાલમાં પેહેલ વેહેલો વાપરવામાં આવ્યો છે. હમોયે જે વખતે જોયો તે વખતે આ ધક્કાને વધારવાનું અને કેટલીક તરફથી

મરામત કરવાનું કામ ચાલતું હતું. આ ધક્કાની આખી લંબાઈ ૧૦૦૦) ફુટ છે, અને પોહોળાઈ ૪૦) ફુટ છે, અને તેહેનો છેડો દરીયામાં ગયો છે તે (T) ટી ઇંગ્રેજી અક્ષરના આકારનો લંબાઇમાં ૧૬૦) ફુટ અને પોહોળાઈમાં ૪૦) ફુટનો રાખ્યો છે. મોટાંમાં મોટાં જુઆલનાં પાણીની સપાટીથી ૧૫) ફુટ ઊંચો તે રાખ્યો છે, અને તેની ઊપર ચાર ગાડી આવજાવ કરે એટલી લોઢાંની રેલ ગોઠવેલી છે. રેલની બંધે બાજુયે આસપાસ માણસોને ચાલવા સારૂ ખુલી પગથી રાખી છે. ધક્કાનાં છેડા અથવા મુખડાં ઊપર માલ ઊતારવા ચઢાવા સારૂ ૬) છ "ક્રેન" (યારી) મુકી છે, જેથી ૩) થી ૧૦) ટન એટલે ૨૪૦) થી ૮૦૦) મણ સુધી, ભારી દાગીનો ઊચકી શકાયછે.

એની પાસે વળી બીજી આઠ "ક્રેન" એવી મુકેલી છે જે એકગમથી બીજીગમ બીરાડી શકાય એવી છે, અને દરેકથી ૩૦) હેંડ્રેડવેટ એટલે ૧૨૦) મણ બોજો ઉપાડી શકાયછે. "મીચલ્સ પેટંટ સ્ક્રુ પાઈલો" (લોઢાંના નળા) જે દસ દસ ફુટને છેટે દરીયામાં છેક નીચે જમીનમાં ગાડેલા છે, તે ઉપર ધક્કાનો ટેકાવ કરેલો છે. આ ઈસકરૂ પાઇલોને આડા અવલા લોઢાંનાં જાડા પાટાઓથી મજબુતજ જકડી બાંધી લીધેલા છે. તેની સાથે વળી લાંકડાનાં થામલા પણ દાટીને તેમને ઈસકરૂ પાઇલો સાથે લોઢાંનાં પાટાથી બાંધી લીધેલા છે. ધક્કા ઉપર ચાલવાની અને રેલ ગોઠવવાની જગાયે સાગલી લાકડાંનાં પાટીયાં ૬) ઇંચ પોહોળાં અને ૪) ઇંચ જાડાં, એક એક ઇંચનો ગાલો રાખી જડી લીધાં છે, જે વાટે નીચે દરીયાનું પાણી દેખાયછે. આ ધક્કાની બાંધણીનો આકાર બગેડા અને સેંટ્રલ ઇંડીયા રેલવે કંપનીના સાલસેટમાં વસઈનાં દરીયા ઉપરનાં પુલને મળતો આવેછે, પણ તેનાં કરતાં, હીયાંની બાંધણી વધારે પોહોળી અને મજબુતાઈ ભલીરે છે. ધક્કો બાંધવાનો સઘળો ખરચ પાઊંડ ૧૧,૦૦૦૦૦) અગીયાર લાખ પાઊંડ, એટલે રૂ. ૧,૧૦,૦૦૦૦૦) એક કરોડ ને દસ લાખ રૂપીયાનો ગણ્યામાં આવ્યો છે.

જ્યારે હમે એ ધક્કો જોયો ત્યારે તેનું કામ આગળ ચાલતું હતું, અને તેહેનાં લાંકડકામ ઉપર કાલુ વળગી ગયાથી તે કેટલું એક સડી ગયલું હતું, તે કાહાડી નાખીને બીજું નવું લાંકડું ઘાલતા હતા, તેહેની સાથે ઓટની વખતે લાંકડાંનાં નવા થાંભલા કુરીને દાટી ધક્કાની પોહોળાઈ વધારવાની ગોઠવણ ચાલતી હતી.

ધક્કા જોતાં જોતાં અને તેવીશે પુછપરછ કરતાં છેક ૪) ચાર વાગી ગયા હતા. હીયાંથી પાછું ગીંડી સુધી દુર જતાં અને તીહાંથી રોજ પાછું સહવારનાં શેહેર તરફ આવતાં ઘણી અડચણ પડવા લાગી હતી, તેથી આ વખતે એવોજ ઠરાવ કીધો કે એક બે દીવસને સારૂ બેહેતર કે "બ્લાક ટાઉન" માં સેઠ એદલજીનાં ઘરમાંજ પાછો મુકામ કરવો.

તા૦ ૨૩ મી જાનેવારીને દીવસે પરોઢીયાંમાં ઊઠી મદ્રાસની મોટી બજાર જોવાને ગયા. યુરોપીયન અને માતબર લોક ઘણું કરીને આ બજારમાંથી ખાધ ખોરાકીની જીનસો લેછે તેથી તીહાં ઘણાં ખરાં ગરીબ લોક પોતાનું બજાર લેવાને નથી આવતાં. તેઓ શેહેરની અંદરની બીજી બજારોમાંથી પોત પોતાની ખાધ ખોરાકી જેમ જેને સવલ પડે તેમ લેછે. યુરોપીયન તથા માતબર લોકનું બજાર જે હમો જોવાને ગયા હતા તે "બ્લાક ટાઉન" માં ઇંટરડી અને ચુના કામથી બાંધેલું છે, અને તેહેની જમીન ગ્રાનાઇટ પથરની ફરસબંધીની બનાવેલી છે. જુદી જુદી જાતની જીનસો વેચવાને એલાહેદા દુકાનો કીધાં છે, તેથી બજાર કરનારને જે ચીજો જોઈએ તે તુરત મળી શકેછે. દુકાનો માંડવાનો હક વરશો વરશ હરરાજી કરીને આપ્યામાં આવેછે. આ ઠેકાણે હમારા જોવામાં હમા ચીજો આવી હતી, અને તે વળી ઘણીજ સોજી તથા તાજી હતી. બજાર અંદરથી ઘણીજ સફાઈ ભરેલી હાલતમાં જોઈ હતી અને તેવીજ સફાઇ ભરેલી હાલતમાં તીહાંની દુકાનો પણ દેખાઈ હતી. હીયાં ઠેકાણે ઠેકાણે બજારમાં મટોડીની ટોપલીઓ ખુણાંમાં મુક્યામાં આવેછે, જેમાં લોક પાનસોપારીની પચકડી થુંકેછે, એમ કરવાનું કારણ એ છે જે મદ્રાસી લોક જબરા પાનસોપારી અને તંબાકુ ખાનારા છે, તેથી તેમની પાનસોપારીની પચકડી નાખવાની જો આવી તદબીર નહી રાખી હોય તો, આખી બજાર થોડી વારમાં લાલ પાણીથી ખરડાઈ લચડાઈ જયાવગર રેહે નહી. આપણી મુંબઇમાંની તે વખતની બજારો વીશે હમને તીહાં યાદ આવી હતી તેથી હમને મોહોટી સરમીંદગી લાગી હતી તથા એ વીશે અદેખાઈ ઉત્પંન થઇ હતી કે આવી સફાઈ અને સગવડ ભરેલી રચનાંવાળી બજાર આપણાં શેહેરમાં કીહારે થશે. તોપણ હવે તેહેના કરતાં વધારે સરસ, સોભઈતી, અને સોજી બજારો મુંબઈ શેહેરમાં આજે થઇ છે એ જણાવાને ઘણી ખુશી ઉત્પંન થાયછે. મી૦ આરથર ક્રાફર્ડ માર-કીટની ઇમારતોની શોભા અને રચનાં આગળ મદ્રાસ, કલકત્તા, અને આખી

દુનીયાની મારકીટો, માત્રે જરમન દેશમાંની એક સીવાય, સઘળી પોઇસ થઈ પડીછે. એમ કેહેછે કે એક માતબર સ્રીયે જરમનીમાં એક બજાર બંધાવેલી છે જેની ઈમારત, સગવડ અને રોનક આગળ યુરોપખંડની કોઈબી બજારની ઈમારત બરોબરી કરી નથી શકતી. પણ મુંબઇ શેહેરમાં આપણા ધુંધી, સાહાસિક અને ઉંચા દરજાની મનશકિત ધરાવનાર મ્યુનીસીપલ કમીશનરે મારકીટ સારૂ જે ઇમારતો બનાવી છે અને જેને ઘટતી રીતે આમ લોક તરફથી "આરથર ક્રાફર્ડ મારકીટ"નું નામ આપ્યું છે, તેની ઇમારતો, તેની સગવડ અને રોનક, ઉપર જણાવેલી મારકીટની બરોબરી કરી શકે એવી બનેલી છે. કોઇબી શેહેરમાં જો સારી સફાઇ ભરેલી બજાર હોય તો તીહાં જવાની ઉલટ ચડતાં ઉતરતાં સઘળા વર્ગનાં સ્રી પુરૂષોને પણ થાય, જેથી ખુદ પોતાની નજરે જોઈ પોતાને મનગમતી ખાધ ખોરાકીની જીનસો લેવાને તેમનાથી બની આવે. એટલુંજ નહીં પણ ઘણીવાર ચાકર નફરોનાં વિશ્વાસ અને ઇચ્છા ઉપર આપણને ઘણુંકરીને બજારના ભાવ અને ખાવાની જીનસો વીશે જે આધાર રાખવો પડેછે, અને જે કંઈ મોંઘું સોંઘું, તથા કાચું પાકું તેઓ બજારમાંથી લઈ આવીને રાંધી ખવડાવે તે ખાવું પડેછે, આ મોહોટી અડચણ અને કંટાળો સોજી બજારો થવાથી નીકળી ગયો છે. બીજો એક મોટો ફાયદો એ થયો છે કે, સોજી બજારથી ખાધ ખોરાકીની જીનસો પણ સફાઈ ભરેલી હાલતમાં રેહી શકેછે. આવી જીનસો ખોરાક તરીકે વપરાતાં, તનદુરસ્તીને બીલકુલ ઇજા નહી પોંહોંચાડે એવી હાલતમાં તે ઘણુંકરીને હમેશ મળી શકવાની ઉમેદ થાયછે. મદ્રાસની બજારમાં ઘણાં આબરૂવાળા દેશી ગૃહસ્થો અને ઇંગ્રેજો, સોખથી, પોતાનાં કુટુંબની સાથે, પોતાનાં માણસો લઇને આવેછે, અને આખી બજારમાં ધીરજથી ફરીને જે કંઈ પોતાને મનગમતી જીનસો નજરે પડેછે, તે માણસો પાસે ખરીદ કરાવેછે. કલકત્તામાં પણ એવોજ સ્વઇયો છે, માત્રે મુંબઈમાંજ આગળ એવું જોવામાં આવતું નહી હતું, અને તેનું મુખ્ય કારણ એજ હતું કે મુંબઈની બજાર ઘણીજ ગલીચ હાલતમાં રેહેતી હતી, અને તેઓ એવી તો કફોરી ગોઠવણની બાંધેલી હતી કે કોઈ પણ ગૃહસ્થને તીહાં જવાને સુગ લાગતી હતી. પણ હવે આગળ જણાવ્યું તેમ મુંબઈની મ્યુનીસીપાલીટીએ બજાર વીશે જે સગવડ અને સુખ કરી આપી છે તેથી મુંબઈની વસ્તી ઉપર આ ખાતાંનો મોટે ઉપકાર થયો છે. આજે મુંબઈનાં બજારો યુરોપખંડનાં પેહેલે દરજ્જેનાં શેહેરોની આ બાબદમાં અચ્છી

બરોબરી કરી શકે એવાં થઈ પડયાં છે. આથી આપણને થોડી ખુશી નથી ઉપજવાની, અને તેમજ તેનાથી ફાયદા પણ કંઈ થોડાજ નથી ઉપજવાના.

મદ્રાસના દેશી લોકની બજાર "કોટવાલ બજાર"ને નામે જણાયલી છે, જે શેહેરની અંદર વસ્તીમાં આવેલી છે અને તેમાં દુકાંનો ખુણે ખાંચે માંડેલી છે, તેનો દેખાવ ઘણુંકરીને આપણાં, ગાંમ ગાંમડાંની સાધારણ બજારના જેવો દેખાયછે. ચોમાસાંની રૂતમાં એવી બજારો પાણી અને કાદવથી ભરાઈને ગલીચ હાલતમાં રેહેછે. બીજી નાંહાંની નાંહાંની બજારો જેમ બીજાં ગામોમાં ઠેકાણે ઠેકાણે હોયછે તેમ મદ્રાસમાં પણ ઠેકાણે ઠેકાણે વેંહેંચાયલી છે.

મદ્રાસની બજારમાં અને બીજી જગોએ, દુકાનો ઉપર ઘણું કરીને વેચવા સાટવા, પુરૂષના કરતાં સ્રીયો વધારે બેસેછે. આ ચાલ ધાર્યા પ્રમાણે એક રવૈયા દાખલ તીહાં ચાલી આવેલી હોય એવું માલુમ પડેછે. અલબતાં સ્રી વેચનાર જો દુકાન ઉપર વેચવાને બેઠી હોય, અને તે જો ખુદરતી સ્વરૂપવાળી અથવા ચલકતી બનીને બેઠી હોય તો તેની દુકાન ઉપર જેટલો વધારે વકરો થવાની વકી રાખીયે તેટલી વકી પુરૂષ વેચનારની દુકાન ઉપર નથી રાખી શકાવાની. યુરોપખંડમાં તો એવી રીત ઘણેક ઠેકાણે ચાલુજ છે, અને એવી દુકાનો ઉપરનાં વેચાણો સેહેલથી થઇને તેમનાં માલિકોને મોટો ફાયદો થાયછે, તેમાં કંઈજ શખ નથી. મદ્રાસના લોકોએ આ ચાલ અથવા રીત અખત્યાર કરવામાં, માણસ જાતના ખુદરતી સ્વભાવની વલાણ તરફ વધારે ધ્યાન પોંહોંચાડેલું દીસેછે.

બજારમાંથી પાછા ફર્યાં અને ઘર આવી નાસ્તો કીધો. ત્યારપછી પાચાપાની સ્કુલ જોવાને ગયા. પાચાપા મુદલીયાર નામનો મદ્રાસનો એક દેશી ગૃહસ્થ નાણાંની એક મોહોટી રકમ પોતાની પછવાડે નીશાળ સ્થાપવાને મુકી ગયો, તેનાં નામની યાદગારીમાં આ નીશાળ સ્થાપીયામાં આવી છે. એ નીશાળ મોહોટી છે અને એમાં ઘણું કરીને હીંદુનાજ આસરે ૬૦૦ છોકરા કેળવણી લેછે, એવું હમોને જણાવ્યામાં તે વખતે આવ્યું હતું. આ નીશાળમાં "પ્રેસીડેન્સી કાલેજ" ની રીતી પ્રમાણે કેળવણી આપ્યામાં આવેછે. આ શેહેરમાંની બીજી નીશાળો કરતાં, પાચાપા સ્કુલ ઘણે દરજે ચઢતી પદ્દવીવાળી અને સારા પાયા ઉપર મંડાયલી છે. એનો કારભાર ટ્રસ્ટીઓની મારફતે ચાલેછે. જ્યારે હમે જોવાને ગયા ત્યારે પાચાપાની નીશાળનાં ફંડમાં હરકોઈ દેશી અથવા પારકા દેશનાં ગૃહસ્થને બખ-

ગેરા તરીકે નાણાંની રકમ ભરવાની છુટ હતી. નીશાળના છોકરાઓની હોશીયારી અને ચંચલાઈ જોઈ હમો ખુશી થયા હતા તે ઉપરથી છોકરાઓને ઈનામ આપવાને સારૂ સેઠ ખુરશેદજી નુસરવાનજી કામાજીયે એક સારી રકમ ભરી આપી હતી. આ નીશાળનો પ્રિન્સિપાલ એક યુરોપીયન ગૃહસ્થ હતો; બાકીના શીક્ષકો દેશી વીદ્યાર્થીઓ હતા.

મદ્રાસની નીશાળો ઘણું કરીને બે તરેની છે. પેહેલા વર્ગની નીશાળોમાં ઇંગ્રેજી ભાશાનું સારૂં ગ્નાન આપવામાં આવેછે, તેહેની સાથે એકુ દેશી ભાશાનું ગ્નાન તથા જુગોલ, ઈતીહાસ, અંકગણીત, ભુમીતી, બીજગણીત, અને એવી બીજી વીદ્યા તથા કોઈવાર "લાટીન" અથવા "ગ્રીક" ભાશા શીખાડવામાં આવેછે. બીજા વર્ગની નીશાળોમાં માત્ર વાંચવા લખવાના મુળતત્વો, અંકગણીતની સેહેલી રીતો, જુગોલ, અને ઈતીહાસની સીરૂવાત વીગેરે સાધારણ ગ્નાન શીખાડવામાં આવેછે. ઘણી ખરી સઘળી આવી નીશાળો, ખાનગી ગૃહસ્થો, અથવા શેહેરની લોક મંડળીનાં આસરાથી સ્થાપ્યામાં આવી છે, અને એવીજ રીતે તેઓનો કારભાર પણ ચાલુ છે. આવી નીશાળોમાં ધર્મને લગતી બાબતો મુતલગ શીખવવામાં આવતીજ નથી. પાદ્રીઓની નીશાળોમાંજ ધર્મ અને તેને લગતી બાબદો શીખવેછે. મદ્રાસનાં દેશીયો હળવે હળવે કેળવણીનાં ફાયદા જાણવા લાગ્યા છે, તેથી તેઓએ એ બાબદ ઉપર દીલથી ધ્યાન પોહોંચાડવા માંડ્યું છે. તેઓએ દેશી ભાશા શીખવવાની નીશાળો, ઇંગ્રેજી નીશાળોનાં કાયદા કાનુનો પ્રમાણે સ્થાપવા માંડી છે; હજુ તેમાંની કોઈ નીશાળ ચઢતે દરજે પુગી નથી, તોપણ તેમનું કામ સારી ઉમેદ ભરેલી રીતે ચાલ્યું જાયછે.

ઉપલી નીશાળ જોયા પછી આગળ ચાલતાં,

Friend in Need Society, The Ladies' Workshop, and the Lying-in Hospital,—"ફ્રેન્ડ ઈન્ નીડ સોસાઈટી" "લેડીસ વર્કશાપ" અને "ધી લાઈંગ ઈનુ હાસપીટલ" એવે નામનાં ત્રણ ધરમખાતાં જોવાને ગયા હતા.

"ફ્રેન્ડ ઈન્ નીડ સોસાઈટી" તથા "લેડીસ વર્કશાપ" એ બંને ખાતાં સન ૧૭૮૭ અને ૧૭૮૮ માં યુરોપીયન લશ્કરી સીપાઈયોનાં માંબાપ વગરનાં છોકરાંઓને કેળવણી આપવા તથા તેમની બરદાસ્ત કરવાની મતલબથી સ્થાપ્યામાં આવ્યા હતાં; બચ્ચાંઓને એ ખાતાંમાં સારા દરજાની કેળવણી મળેછે, અને જારે છોકરાઓ

પુખ્તી ઊમરે પોંહોંચેછે તારે સાંભો પગાર આપીને તરેવાર ધંધો પેશો, શીખવેછે, અને તેઓ પોતાનું ગુજરાણ પોતાની મેળે કરી શકે એટલા સારૂ હર કોઇ રસ્તે તેમને કામે લગાડી દેછે. "ફ્રેન્ડ ઇન્ નીડ સોસાઇટી" નો ખરચ તથા કારભાર જાહેર ઊઘરાણું અથવા બક્ષીસ ઊપર તથા એ ખાતાં સાથે જે નાહાની સરખી એક વર્કશાપ એટલે કેટલી એક જાતનો સામાન બનાવવાનું કારખાનું છે, તેમાં જે જીનસો બને તેના વેચાણથી ઉપજતી કમાઈ ઉપર ચાલી શકેછે.

આ ખાતાં સ્થાપવાની મુળ મતલબ એટલીજ છે કે જેઓ લાચાર હોય તેવા માણસોમાંથી જેવો કામ કરવાને શકતીવાન અને ખુશી હોયતેમને પોતાનું ગુજરાણ ચલાવવાને આ ખાતાં તરફથી મદદ આપવી. હીયાં આવતાં માણસોને દોરડાં, સાદડી, ટોપલી અને તેહેવી બીજી જીનસો બનાવવાનો હુંનર શીખવેછે તથા શીખનાર પોતાનાં કામમાં હોશીયાર થાય એટલે તેની શક્તી પ્રમાણે તેનો પગાર કરેછે. એજ રીતે સ્ત્રીલોક પાસે પણ તેમની શક્તી પ્રમાણેનું કામ લેછે, તેઓ તરેવાર જાતનાં જાડાં પાતળાં કપડાં સીવેછે, જેવાં કે ઘોડાવાળાના ડગલા, વાસકુટ, પાટલુન, કમરબંદ, પીછોડી, નાહાનાં છોકરાંના ઇસ્ટાકીન (પગના મોજાં), ટુવાલ અને એવીગેરે બીજાં કામ જોગ ઘરમાં વપરાતાં તરેવાર કપડાં. શીવવાનું કપડું તથા સોય દોરા વીગેરે, જરૂરીયાત સર સરંજામ, આ ખાતાંનાં ફંડમાંથી આપ્યામાં આવેછે. મરદનાં ખાતાં ઉપર મદ્રાસના કેટલા એક મરદ ગૃહસ્થોની એક કમેટી ઉપરીપણું ચલાવેછે, અને સ્ત્રીલોકનાં ખાતાં ઉપર, એક બે આબરૂવાળી મદ્રાસનાં લશ્કરી અમલદારોની બાનુઓ, પોતાની ખુશીથી ઊપરીપણું ચલાવી, સઘળી બાબદની નીગેબાની રાખેછે. સ્ત્રીલોકનાં ખાતાંમાં, સીવવા, સાંધવાનાં ધંધા સાથે નાહનાં બચ્ચાંઓને વાંચવા લખવાની પણ કેળવણી આપ્યામાં આવેછે.

"ફ્રેંડ ઇન્ નીડ સોસાયટી"માં અને તેને લગતાં કારખાનામાં પેહેરવાનાં સુતરાઊ તથા ઉનનાં તરેવાર કપડાં શીવાયછે, તેમાંની ઘણી જીનસો હમોયે આ ખાતાંને એક ઊત્તેજન આપવા દાખલ ખરીદ કીધો હતી, અને એ બંધે ખાતાંનાં ફંડમાં એક સારી રકમની બખશીસ શેઠ ખુરશેદજી નુસરવાનજી કામાજીયે આપી હતી.

"ધી લાઇંગ ઇન્ હાસપીટલ"નું ધરમખાતું ઇસિવી સન ૧૮૪૪ ના સાલમાં દરદી સ્ત્રીયો અને બચ્ચાંઓની બરદાસ્ત કરવાસારૂ સ્થાપવામાં આવ્યું હતું. આ ધરમખાતું, "કોમ"નદીના કીનારા ઉપર "સેંટ આંદ્રુસ ચર્ચ"ની પડોસમાંના એક

મકાનમાં છે. સઘળી જાતની અને સઘળા ધર્મની સ્ત્રીયોને, આ હાસપીટલમાં દાખલ થવાની છુટ છે, અને જીહાંસુધી તેઓ હાસપીટલમાં રેહેછે, તીહાંસુધી સરકારી ખરચે તેમની બરદાસ્ત અને માવજત થાયછે. આ ધર્મખાતાંને લગતો સ્ત્રીયોનો એક વર્ગ ઉભો કર્યામાં આવ્યો છે, તેમાં સુવાવડની તજવીજ અને વેવાડવાનું કામ શી રીતે કરવું, એ તેમને શીખવવામાં આવેછે.

આગળ ચાલતાં "ક્રીલપાર્ક" નામનાં લતા ઉપર "મેગડેલેન અસાઇલિમ" કરીને એક બીજું ધરમખાતું સ્થાપેલું છે. આ ખાતાંની મતલબ ઘણીજ નેક અને પરમાર્થ છે. યુરોપીયન અથવા ઇંડોબ્રીટન ખાંનદાન અથવા જાતની જે સ્ત્રીયો નીતી છોડી અનીતીનો માર્ગ પકડીને બીગડી હોય, તેઓની ઈછા, આ ભુંડો માર્ગ છોડી, પાછો નીતીમાર્ગ પકડવાની થઈ હોય તો, તેવી સ્ત્રીયોને એ ખાતાંમાં લઈ આશરો આપીને સુમાર્ગ ઉપર પાછી આણવાને, તેમને સઘળા પ્રકારની મદદ આપ્યામાં આવેછે. તેમની પાસે તેમની શક્તી જોગ ઉદ્યોગ કરાવેછે, અને તે ઉદ્યોગની ઉપજનો કેટલાએક ભાગ આ ખાતાંનો ખરચ ચલાવવાસારૂ બાદ કરી, બાકીનો આજ ખાતાંની કેટલી એક સ્ત્રીઓને ખુદ તેમના અંગ ખરચ સારૂ આપવામાં આવેછે. આ ખાતાંનો સઘળો ખરચ, કામ આમ લોક પાસેથી એકઠાં કરેલાં જાહેર ઉઘરાણાંમાંથી થાયછે.

અફસોસ છે, મુંબઈ જેવાં માતબર અને ધરમખાતાંઓ ઊભાં કરવામાં પ્રખ્યાત થયલાં શેહેરમાં આવું એકું પણ ખાતું હજુ સુધી થયું નથી. હીયાં ઘણાંએ ધરમખાતાં છે, પણ આ છેલ્લાં ખાતાં જેવું હજુ લગી એકુ પણ ખાતું આપણા કોઈબી સખી શેઠીઆએ ઉઠાવી ઉભું કીધું નથી. પણ આવીશે હવે ધ્યાન પોહોંચાડવાની આ શેહેરના લોકની ફરજ છે. તેની સાથે, જનાકારીથી જે છોકરાં પેદા થાયછે અને જે નીર્દોશ બાલકોનો જીવ જનાકારીનો ઘુના છુપાવવાની મતલબે બરબાદ જાયછે, તેનો અટકાવ કરવાને પણ આવાં એક ખાતાંની ઘણીજ અત્રે અગત છે. આવા ખાતાં કાહાડવામાં કેટલા એક જણ એવું ધારેછે કે એથી તો છીનાલાને મદદ કીધા બરોબર છે. પણ લાંબો વીચાર કરશું તો એવું નથી ઠરવાનું. વ્યભિચારથી ઉત્પંન થયલાં નીર્દોશ બાલકોનાં કુમળા જીવની ઘાત થયાથી, છીનાલાંનાં એક પાપસાથે લગોલગ વળી જે ખુન કરવાનું બીજું પાપ થાયછે, તે મહા પાપનો અટકાવ, એવાં ખાતાંથી જો થાય, અને દર વરશે

જેટલા જીવની આવી રીતે ધાત થાયછે, તેમાં ઘટાડો થાય, તો ખરેખર આવાં ધરમખાતાં જેવાં નેક ખાતાં અને એનાથી નીપજતાં પુનનાં કામો જેવાં નેક બીજાં થોડાંજ ગણાશે.

ચેપી રોગના ફેલાવાનો અટકાવ કરવાને, જો સરકાર તરફથી ધારા બાંધીયામાં આવીયા, અને રઇએત પાસેથી કર ઉઘરાવેલાં નાણાંમાંથી વેશીયા અને વ્યભીચારી લોકના ફાયદા સારૂ "લાક હાસપીટલ" અને તેને લગતું ખાતું ઉભું કરી ચલાવાનું વાજબી ગણાયું તો, શું વ્યભીચાર અથવા જનાકારીથી જે સ્ત્રીઓ પોતાની લાજ રાખવાને તેમના નીરદોશ બાલકોનો જીવ લીએછે અને ખુન કરવાનાં પાપને આધીન થાયછે, તેમના ફાએદાને સારૂ અને નીરદોશ બાલકોના જીવના બચાવને શારૂ શું આપણે કંઈજ ઉપાય નહી કરીએ વારૂ? લાંબો વીચાર કરતાં એવું ધારીયામાં આવેછે કે, આવું પરમાર્થ ખાતું જો ઊઘડીયું તો તેનો ખરચ પુરો પાડવાને પેહેલાં જેટલું ભારી લાગશે તેટલું પછવાડેથી નથી લાગવાનું. માણસ જાતનો ખુદરતી સ્વભાવ સમજવાનો અનુભવ ધરાવનારો ઊપર જણાવેલું મત બાંધી શકશે. સરકાર તરફથી વેશીયાઓની હાલ જે બરદાસ્ત, જો કે જબરદસ્તીના કાયદાથી થાયછે, તો પણ થોડા વખતમાં એ વીશે વેશીયાઓને સમજ પડશે કે આ કાયદા અને ગોઠવણો તો તેમના પોતાના ફાયદાને સારૂ થયલી છે. આ ઉપરથી, અગર સરકાર તરફથી સાંભણો કોઇ તરેનો તેઓ ઉપર કર લાગુ પાડીયો તો તે કર વટીક તે લોક મોટી ખુશી સાથે આપશે એમાં કંઈજ નવાઈ અથવા શાખ નથી. આ વીચાર ૧૮૭૦ના જુલાઈ મહીનામાં આ પુસ્તક લખનારને થયલો છે, અને તેનું ખરાપણું ભવીશ કાળ સાબેત કરી આપશે એવું ધારીયામાં આવેછે. હમો ધારીએછ કે આવું જો થયું તો તે વાજબી ગણાશે, કારણ હાલ રઈએત પાશેથી લેતા કીવેલા કરમાંથી આ ખાતાંનો જે ખરચ ચલાવીયામાં આવેછે તેમાં એક તરેનો ગેરઇનસાફ રઈએતનાં નેક અને ભલાં માણસો ઊપર ગુજરેછે.. નેક અને ગૃહસ્થ લોક પાશેથી પઈસા લઈ છીનાલવા લોકનો બુરો શોખ પુરો પાડવો, અને તે વળી સઘળી સંભાળ ભરેલી રીતે પુરો પડી શકે એવા ઉપાયો કરવામાં વાપરવો, એ ખરેખરજ ગેરવાજબીપણું છે. એમ થવુંજ નહી જોઈએ. પણ હાલ જે શીરૂઆત થઈ છે તે જાણે માત્રે એવા ભુડા લોકને એક ચેતવણી તરીકે થઇ છે, એ મતલબે કે જો તેઓને તેમનો બુરો હવસ સંભાળ

ભરેલી રીતે પુરો પાડવો હોય તો આવું એક ખાતું શેહેરમાં હોવું જોઇએ, અને તે ખાતાંનો ખરચ આ ટોળીનાજ લોકોએ પુરો પાડવો જોઇએછ. જે છીનાલ સ્ત્રી પોતાની તનદુરસ્તી જાળવવાને સરકારને આ ખાતાં સંબંધી ઠરાવેલો કર આપશે તે નાણું તેજ સ્ત્રી પોતાની સાથે વેહેવાર કરનાર પુરૂશ પાસેથી પાછું કદાચ વીયાજ સાથે સેહેલાઇથી લેઈ શકશે, અને અંતે વાજબી ઈનસાફ એવોજ થશે કે આવાં બદકાંમ કરનાર સ્ત્રી પુરૂષોને માંથેજ આવાં ખાતાંનો ખરચ જઈ પડવાનો, અને આવીજ ગોઠવણ થયલી વાજબી ગણાવાની.

ઉપલીજ તકરારના આધાર ઉપરથી એવું પણ તારે વીચારીયામાં આવી શકેછે, કે છીનાલાથી ઊત્પંન થયલાં બાલકોનો બચાવ કરવાને જે ખાતું સ્થાપીયામાં આવે તેનો ખરચ પણ પુરો પાડવાને આવાં કર્મો કરનાર પોતેજ વાજબી વીચારશે. તે ખરચ શી રીતે તેઓ પુરો પાડવાને તજવીજ કરશે તે ધારવું શેહેલ છે. જેબી કોઈ હરામનું છોકરૂં એવાં ખાતાંમાં છુપી રીતે મુકવાને જશે અથવા મુકવાને મોકલશે તેઓ તે બાલકની સાથે થોડા ઘણા પઈસા મોકલશે, એવું સમજીને કે તે નાણાંથી તે બાલકના પોશાણ થવામાં થોડી ઘણી મદદ થઈ પડે. બચ્ચાં ઊપર પીયાર થવો એ તો ખુદરતીજ ગુણ છે. જેવો પીયાર ગૃહસ્થ સ્ત્રીનો તેનાં બચ્ચા ઊપર થાયછે, તેવોજ પીયાર છીનાલ સ્ત્રીનોબી થયાવના નથી રેહેવાનો. માટે આજે આવાં ખાતાં વગર જે બાલહતીયાનું પાપ થાયછે, તે આવું ખાતું ઊઘાડતાં બંધ થઈ બાલકોના જીવની સલામતીનું તે ઘર થઈ પડશે; અને તેમાં, છીનાલીનાં બચ્ચાં મુકનારો ખચીત નાણાંની રકમ મુકીયા વગર નથી રેહેનાર. આ વાત તો છીનાલો વીશે થઈ. પણ હવે જે ગૃહસ્થ સ્ત્રી પુરૂશો એવાં બુરાં કામ કરેછે, અને તેમનાથી જે બાલકો પેદા થાયછે, તેવાં બાલકોના જીવનો પણ નાશ થવાને બદલે તેવાં બાલકો આવાં ખાતાંમાં આવતાં થયાથી નાણાંની મોટી રકમ સાથે લેતાં આવશે. નીરદોશ બાલકનો જીવ લેવાને કોઇને ખુદરતી રાહે ગમતું નથી, પણ પોતાની લાજ આબરૂ જાળવવાને ખુન જેવું દુષ્ટ કામ તેઓ કરેછે, અને તેવું કરવાને હજારો રૂપીયા દાઈઓ તથા કુટણી કુટણાઓને આપેછે. પણ આવું ખાતું ઊભું થતાં, તેવાં નીરદોશ બાલકોનું ખુન કરવાને કોઇને જરાપણ વીચાર નથી આવવાનો. જેવું છોકરૂં પેદા થયું એટલે તેની સાથે રૂપીયાની કોથલી આપી આ ખાતામાં બાલકોને તેવા લોક બેધડક મોકલી આપશે, અને એવું થયાથી કેટલા નીરદોશ

જીવોનો દર વરસે ભોગ થતો બચવાનો! આપણા દેશમાં આવું નેક કામ કોણ ઉઠાવી લેવામાં પેહેલ કરેછે, તેને ધન્ય હોજો! ઇંગ્લંડ અને યુરોપ ખંડમાં આજે આવાં ખાતાં ચાલુ છે, જેમનો ખરચ, જાહેર ઉઘરાણાંમાંથી સખી અને પરમાર્થ લોકની બક્ષિસથી અને એજ ખાતાંમાં છુપી રીતે મુકી ગયલાં બાલકો સાથે આવતી મોટી રકમોમાંથી સારી રીતે પુરો પડી શકેછે. એવાં ખાતાંમાંથી ઉછરી નીકળેલાં ઘણા સ્ત્રી પુરૂષો આજે મંડળીમાં ભેગાં થઈ પડ્યાં છે, અને તેમાંના ઘણાં લોક સારી કેળવણી પામી આબરૂદાર ગૃહસ્થો તરીકે પોતાનો સંસાર ગુજારેછે, જો કે તેમને ખબર નથી કે તેઓ કોણ માય અને કોણ બાપનાં છોકરાં છે!

હીયાંથી નીકળ્યા તેવા મદ્રાસની ઉદ્યોગ તથા કળા હુંનર શીખવવાની શાળા જોવાને ગયા હતા. આ શાળા "પુનામાલી" નામનાં રસ્તા ઊપર અને આગળ જણાવેલાં સેન્ટ આંદ્રુસનાં દેવલની સાંભેનાં રસ્તા ઉપર છે. આ શાળાનું મંડાણ ડાકતર અલેકઝાંડર હંટર નામનાં સરકારી ખાતાંનાં એક ડાકતરે ઇસિવી સન ૧૮૫૦ના સાલમાં પોતે શીરૂ કર્યું હતું. નીશાળીયાઓ હુંનર શીખવાને આવતા હતા તેમની પાસેથી લેવા માંડેલા લવાજમમાંથી, છોકરાઓએ પાડેલાં ચીત્રો તથા બીજી બનાવેલી જીનસોનાં વેચાણમાંથી, આમ લોક તરફથી જે બક્ષિસો મળતી હતી તેમાંથી અને આ લાયકીવાળા ડાકતરની ખાનગી કમાઈમાંથી આ ખાતાંનો ખરચ સન ૧૮૫૫ના સાલ સુધી ચલાવામાં આવ્યો હતો. ત્યારપછી સરકારે પોતે આ ખાતું લઈ લીધું અને એની ઉપર એક ઉપરી, ઈગ્લંડની ઉદ્યોગ તથા કળા હુંનરની શાળામાંથી બોલાવીને રાખ્યો હતો. આ શાળામાં ચીત્ર પાડવાનો હુંનર, લાંકડાં અને ત્રાંબા ઉપર કોતરકામ કરવાનો હુંનર, "પ્લાસ્ટર આફ પેરીસ" નામની મટોડીનાં પુતળાં અને તરેવાર વાસણો બનાવવાનો હુંનર તથા તમામ સઘળી જાતનાં મટોડીનાં વાસણો અને ઘર બાંધવાની જીનસો બનાવવાનો હુંનર શીખવવામાં આવેછે. મટોડીનાં તરેવાર વાસણો, ફુલોનાં અને ઝાડોનાં તરેવાર રંગીન ચીત્રો, પ્રાચીન યુનાન અને રોમ શેહેરનાં પુતલાંઓની નકલ, "પ્લાસ્ટર આફ પેરીસ" નામની મટોડીનાં પુતલાંઓમાં આબેહુબ કીધેલી ઘણીજ સુંદર અને જોવા લાયક બનેલી હમારા જોવામાં આવી હતી.

બારણાં આગળ ચોક પુરવાનાં નમુનાં જેટલા મેળવી શકાયા તેટલા કલકત્તા અને

મદ્રાસમાંથી મંગાવી ડાકતર હંટરે એક મોટો સંગ્રહ કીધેલો હતો તે હમને દેખડાવ્યો હતો. નજદીક ૧૦૦૦) નમુના તેણે એકઠા કરેલા હતા, અને હમને કહ્યું હતું કે મુંબઈનાં લોક પાસે એવા ચોક પુરવાના બીજા નમુનાં હોય તો તે તેને પોંહોંચતા કરી આપવા. આ ઊપરથી હમારા મીત્ર ડાકતર ભાઉ દાજીયે કબુલાત આપી હતી કે મુંબઈ જઇને આ વીશે ધ્યાન પોંહોંચાડવામાં આવશે.

આ શાળામાં ફોટોગ્રાફીનો હુંનર પણ શીખવ્યામાં આવેછે. ડાકતર હંટરે મદ્રાસ અને તેહેની આસપાસની જગોનાં ઘણાં ફોટોગ્રાફ આ ખાતાં તરફથી લીધેલા નમુને દેખડાવ્યા હતા.

"પ્લાસ્ટર આફ પેરીસ" નામની મટોડી યુરપ ખંડથી અત્રે આવેછે, અને પુતળાં બનાવવાને અતીશય ઊપયોગી પડેછે, એવી જાતની અથવા એને મળતી આવે તેવી મટોડી ડાકતર હંટરે મદ્રાસ શેહેરની નજદીકીમાંથી શોધી કાહાડી છે, પણ આ મટોડીનાં બનાવેલાં પુતળાં અને બીજી જીનસો સુકાયા પછી "પ્લાસ્ટર આફ પેરીસ"નાં જેવી સુફેદ રંગની અને ચીકણી રેહેતી નથી, પણ તેમાં તડ પડેછે અથવા સુફેદી ઝાંખી થઈ જાયછે, એમ ડાકતરે જણાવ્યું હતું, પણ તેને ઉમેદ હતી કે એ અડચણ કેટલી એક મેળવણીથી તે કાહાડી શકશે.

આ ઉદ્યોગશાળા સ્થાપીયા પછી તેમાં નજદીક ૨૦૦૦) માણસો શીખવાને દાખલ થયાં છે, અને તેમાંથી ઘણાં ખરાં તરેવાર હુંનરની કેળવણી લઈ બાહેર પડ્યાં છે અને સારી કમાઈ ભરેલા રોજગાર તેમને મળ્યા છે, અને કેટલાકોને ઘણી સારી ફાયદા ભરેલી ચાકરી પણ લાગી છે.

ડાકતર હંટરની સાથે જે થોડો વખત હમોયે ગુજાર્યો હતો, તે વખતમાં તેણે જે મેહેનત લઇને હમને પોતાનાં આખાં કારખાનાંમાં ફેરવ્યા હતા તથા તરેવાર બાબત વીશે હમે જે સવાલો પુછ્યા હતા તેનાં જવાબો તેણે સેહેલાઇથી અને ખુશીથી આપ્યા હતા તેથી હમને જે જ્ઞાન થોડી વારમાં મુફત મળ્યું હતું તેની કીમત હમારાથી થઈ શકતી નથી; હમને તે વખતે મુંબઈના ડાકતર બ્યુસ્ટની યાદ આવી હતી, કારણ એ કે તેનાં જેવો ધુંધી, ઉદ્યોગી, ખુસીથી શીખવનાર અને ઉદ્યોગશાળા અને કળા હુંનરોનો ફેલાવો થયલો જોનાર આજ સુધી મુંબઈમાં કોઈ દેખાયો નથી. જે દીલભર મેહેનતથી ડાકતર બ્યુસ્ટને હમોયે મુંબઈમાં કળા હુંનરનો ફેલાવો કરવા પછવાડે મશગુલ થયલો જોયો હતો તેવીજ દીલભર મેહેન-

તથી કળા હુંનરનો ફેલાવો કરવા પછવાડે ડાકતર હંટરને હમોયે મદ્રાસમાં મશગુલ થયલો જોયો હતો.

હુંનરશાળા જોઇને મદ્રાસનું મ્યુઝીઅમ એટલે ખુદરતી ચાજોનું સંગ્રહસ્થાન જોવાને ગયા.

આ સંગ્રહસ્થાન મદ્રાસ સરકારે ઇસિવી સન ૧૮૫૧ નાં વરસમાં ઊભું કીધું છે, અને "પાનથીયન" નામની એક મોહોટી અને ફોસાદ ઇમારત જે મદ્રાસમાં "પાનથીયન રોડ" ઊપર આવેલી છે, તે મકાનમાં આ સંગ્રહસ્થાનની જગા કીધેલી છે. હમો જ્યારે તે જોવાને ગયા હતા ત્યારે કપતાન મીચલ તેનો ઉપરી અને રખેવાલ હતો. એ અમલદારની મુલાકાત લેતાં અને સંગ્રહસ્થાન જોવાની પરવાનગી માગતાં, એવું માલુમ પડ્યું કે નાતાલનાં તેહેવારના સબબને લીધે આ ખાતું બંધ રાખ્યામાં આવેલું હતું; અને જે શખ્સને સ્વાધીન તે મકાનની ચાવીઓ હતી તે એક બે દીવસની રજા લઇને બાહેર સેહેલગા કરવાને ગયલો હતો, તેથી હમારા જોવામાં અટકાવ થઈ પડયો હતો. આ બનાવથી કપતાન મીચલે પોતાની ઘણીજ દીલગીરી જણાવી હતી, અને હમો મદ્રાસથી મેલને ટાંકણે કલકત્તે ઉપડી જનાર હતા તેથી લાંબો વખત મદ્રાસમાં હમારાથી રેહેવાને પણ બની શકતું નહી હતું તેથી તે વધારે દીલગીર થયો હતો. તોયપણ તેણે હમને ઉમેદ આપી હતી કે, મેલ આવી પુગવાની આગમચ મ્યુઝીયમ ખચીત ઊઘડશે, અને જે દીવશે તે ઊઘડસે તે દીવસે તે હમને લખી જણાવશે, તથા તેણે હમારી ઉપર મેહેરબાની કરવાને ધારી એવું પણ કેહું કે, "હું સહવારનાં પોહોરમાં મોહોટી ખુસીથી પોતે તીહાં હાજર રહીને આ સંગ્રહસ્થાન તમને દેખડાવીશ, અને જેખી કંઈ તમુને જાણવું, પુછવું અથવા તીહાંથી લેવું હોય તે હું મોટી ખુશીથી બજા લાવશ."

હીયાંથી રૂખસદ લઇને મદ્રાસની "આગ્રી હાર્ટીકલચરલ ગારડન" જોવાને ગયા. આ સરકારી બાગ "મૌંટ રોડ" ઊપરૂ આવેલો છે અને તેમાં નજદીક ૨૪) ચોવીસ એકર જમીન રોકાઈ છે. આ બાગ પેહલાં ઇસવી સન ૧૮૩૫ નાં સાલમાં મદ્રાસ લશ્કરના એક સર્જન નામે ડાકતર રાઇટની મેહેનતથી ઉભો થયો હતો. આ બાગની રચનાં ઘણીજ સોભા ભરેલી રીતે કીધેલી છે, અને તેહેમાં સુંદર ફુલવાળાં અથવા જે સંસાર વેહેવારનાં કામમાં ઉપયોગી પડે તેવા દર એક દેશનાં ઝાડ પાનોનાં રોપ કરેલાં છે. જે ફુલો પાણીમાં થાયછે તેવાંને ઉગાડવાને એક મોહોટું તળાવ

Vincent Brooks, lith.

VEPERY CHURCH, MADRAS

બનાવ્યામાં આવ્યું છે, અને બીજા સોભઈતા રોનકદાર ફુવ્વારા, ટાંકીયો, અને તરેવાર પક્ષીયોને રાખવાનાં ઘર, પાંજરાં અને તેમને લાયકનાં માલા બનાવાનું કામ હમો જોવાને ગયા તારે તીહાં ચાલતું હતું. એ ગોઠવણ પુરી થયા પછી બાગની રચનાં ઘણીજ રોભાયમાંન થસે એમાં કાંઈ રાક નથી. એ બાગનાં એક ખાતાંમાં તરે તરેનાં રોપાં ઉગાડવા તથા તેમની તપાસ રાખવા અને માવજત કરવાને એક એલાહેદી જગા કરી મુકેલી છે, તીહાં ઘણી જાતનાં રોપાંઓને કુંડીયોમાં માવજતથી રાખેલા છે. જે શખ્સો એ બાગનાં ફંડમાં લાગટ લવાજમ ભરેછે તેવા મેમબરોને ઝાડ પાનની કલમો, બીજ, વીગરે આ કુંડીઓમાંથી, મુફત આપ્યામાં આવેછે, બીજાઓને ઠેરવેલ ભાવે વેચાતાં આપેછે. આ બાગમાં લોકની ગમત તથા ચેનને સારૂ દર મંગળવારે સાંજનાં બેંડ વાગેછે, અને ફરવા આવનાર લોકના સુખ સગવડને સારૂ ઠેકાણે ઠેકાણે બેઠકો કરેલી છે.

દર વરસની શીરૂઆતે આ બાગમાં તરેવાર જાતનાં ફુલ, ફલ, તરકારી, અને બીજાં કામનાં ઝાડ પાનનો એક મોહોટો મેલો ભરીયામાં આવેછે, અને તેમાં સઉથી સરસ જીનસો લાવનારાઓને ઈનામો આપ્યામાં આવેછે. આ ઠેકાણે અંધારૂં થઈ ગયાથી વધારે ફરી શકાયું નહી હતું.

તા૦ ૨૪ જાનેવારીને દીવસે મદ્રાસ રોહેરનાં એક બે ખ્રીસ્તી ધરમનાં દેવલો, ફ્રીમેરાનનોની લાડજો, અને કલબ હાઉસ વીગરે ઈમારતો જોવાનો ઠરાવ કીધેલો હતો તે મુજબ તે જોવાને નીકળ્યા હતા.

મદ્રાસ રોહેરમાં ખ્રીસ્તી ધરમને લગતાં મોહોટાં અને નાહાંના દેવલો જુદા જુદા પંથવાળાઓનાં ઘણાં છે. એમાંનાં ઘણાં એક દેવલો ઊંચી કીસમની બાંધણી તરીકે ગણાયછે, જેમાં કેટલી એક ઇમારતો એવી તો રોનકદાર છે, કે તેમનું બાંધકામ અને દેખાવ ઇંજીનીયરીંગ વીદ્યા અને હુંનરનાં ઘણાં ઊંચા નમુના ગણાયછે. આવી ઊંચી જાતની રોનકદાર બાંધણીમાં સેંટ જાર્જનું દેવલ, સેંટ આંદ્રુસ, સેંટ પાલ, અને સેંટ મથાયસનાં દેવલો છે.

પાસે આપેલું ચીત્ર સેંટ મથાયસનાં દેવલનું છે, તે વેપરી નામના લતા ઉપર છે તેથી તેહેનું નામ "વેપરી ચર્ચ" પડેલું છે. આ દેવલની અંદરની રચનાં એવી તો રોનક ભરેલી છે કે તે જોનારને પેહેલ વેહેલાં ખાલી સાદા દેખાવવાળી નજરે પડેછે, પણ જેમ જેમ જોનાર ધીરજથી આસપાસ જોતો જાયછે તેમ તેમ તે ખાલી

દેખાવ બદલાઈ, ખરો મોહોટો, દબદબા ભરેલો, અને ગંભીર નજરે પડવા માંડેછે. અંદરની બેઠકોની વચ્ચે જે કબરો આવેલી છે તેની ઉપરના સંગેમરમરના પથરો જડેલા છે તે ઉપર જોનારનું ધ્યાન લાગેછે, અને તે પથરો ઉપર જે શીખામણનાં વાકયો કોતરેલાં છે તે વાંચ્યાથી રૂએ રૂઆં ઉભાં થાયછે. કાચની બારીઓ અને દેવાલો ઉપર જે નકસી અને ચીતાર કામ કરેલું છે તેહેમાંની સખીયો જોયાથી, આપણ મનુષ્ય જાતને કેટલી નમનતાઇથી અને દયા ભરેલાં દીલથી આ દુની-યામાં પોતાનાં ભાઈ બંધુઓ સાથે ચાલવું અને વસવું જોઈએછ તેવીરો જોનારનાં મનમાં ચુપ અને મુગો ઉપદેશ થાયછે અને તેનું દીલ અંદરથી બોલેછે, અરે! આજ શુધી કેટલી ભુલો આપણથી થઈ ચુકી છે! આ મુગાં ચીત્રો આ ભુલો વીશે આપણને કેવી નસીએત દેછે! શું એ નસીએતો ઉપર આપણે વધારે વાર આં-ખવીચામણી કરીએ વારૂ! એમ નફકરાપણે કીહાં સુધી આપણે ચાલીઆ કરશું! દેરો દેશની એવી જાતની ઈમારતોને તો ખાસુખા મુસાફરોયે અગત કરીને જો-વીજ જોઇયે, કેમકે એવી ઇમારતોની બાહારની અને અંદરની રચના બરોબર ધ્યાન પોહોંચાડીને જોયાથી, દેરો દેશનાં રેહેવાસીયોનાં ધરમ સંબંધી આચરણો, રવૈયા, સંસારી રીત ભાંત અને કેટલીક બાબદમાં તેમની નીતીની હાલત વીશેનું સારૂં ગ્નાન પ્રાપ્ત થઇ શકેછે.

આ બાબદ બોલતાં હમુને એક ખીના ઈયાદ આવી છે, તે એ જે, આ પુસ્તકમાં આપેલાં ચીત્રોનાં નમુના જારે હમારા હાતમાં પેહલ વેહેલા આવીયા અને તે એક હમારા મીત્રના જોવામાં આવીયા તે જોઇને તે મીત્રે પોતાનું મત એવું જાહેર કીધું હતું કે તે પોતે હમારી જગા ઉપર હતે તો આવાં ચીત્રો નહી પસંદ કરતે. તેવણે કહ્યું કે મોહોટ મોટી ઈમારતો, પાહાડો, સરોવર અને નદીઓના અને હેવા બીજા દેખાવો હમારે પસંદ કરવા હતા, તેને ઠેકાણે હમોએ તો માત્રે સઘળી મસીદ અને દેવલ દેહેરાંજ પસંદ કીધાં હતાં. એવાં ચીત્રો તે મીત્રને નાપસંદ પડીયાંહતાં. હવે આ વાત તો ખરીજ છે કે ખુદરતી દેખાવોનાં ચીત્રો અલબતાં ઘણાંજ જરૂરનાં છે, પણ તેવાં દેખાવોનાં ચીત્રો હમારે હાથ તે વખતે નહી લાગી શકયાં તેથી તેવાં ચીત્રો આ પુસ્તકમાં આપી નથી શકયા. પણ હમોએ જે ચીત્રો પસંદ કીધાં છે તે સઘળીજ મસીદો છે, અને દેવલ દેહેરાંજ છે, આ વીચારમાં ભુલ છે અને આવો વીચાર કદાચ બીજાઓને આવે તેથી તે વીશે આગમજથી ખુલાસો કરેલો નકામો

નથી ગણાવાનો. હમોએ અત્રે જે ચીત્રો આપીયાં છે તે આપણા દેશની આગલી ફીરતી અને જાહોજલાલી દેખાડવાના ચુનંદી ઇમારતો નમુના માત્રે છે, જે જોયાથી, માલુમ પડશે કે હીંદુસ્થાનમાં આગલા વખતમાં કેવી તરેની કારીગીરીનાં કામો થયલાં છે. આ પુસ્તકમાં આપેલાં ચીત્રોમાં ગુંબજ અથવા મીનારા જેખી ઈમારતો ઊપર દેખાય તેવી સઘળી ઈમારતોને મસજીદ નહી સમજવી. હીંદુ-સ્થાનની પ્રાચીન ઈમારતોમાંની સઉથી સરસ ઈમારતો, જેની બાંધણીની કંઈ જુજવી નીશાનો હાલ થોડી ઘણી રેહેલી છે, તે સઘળીને તપાસી જોતાં એવુંજ માલુમ પડેછે કે દરેક બાંધણી ઊપર તે વખતના ફીસખી મીસ્ત્રીઓ અને કારી-ગરોએ પોતાના હુંનર અને મનરાકતીનું બળ મોહોટ મોહોટા ઉંચા મીનારા અને ગુંબજો તથા સ્થંભો અને તેવાંજ જબરાં ચોડાં અને ઝુલતાં આરકાં બાંધી દેખડાવેલું છે, જેમાં કેટલાંક કામો એવી તો ચંચલાઈ અને કારીગરીથી કરેલાં છે કે તેવાં કામો આજ યુરોપ ખંડમાં પણ એક નમુના તરીકે થઇ પડે એવાં છે. જે રોનક હીંદુસ્થાનની બાંધણીઓમાં પ્રાચીન કાળે વાપરેલી છે, તેવીજ અથવા તેને મળતી આજે યુરોપ ખંડમાં પણ ચાલેછે. તીહાંપણ આજે મોહોટ મોહોટી ઇમા-રતોને સુંદર શોભાયમાન કરવા તેમની ઊપર મીનારા અને આરકાં અને ગુંબજો ઉઠાવેછે. જેખી દેશીઓએ ઇંગ્લંડમાં મુસાફરી કરી છે, તેઓએ જોયું હશે કે આખા યુરપ ખંડની આવી સઘળી ગુંબજ અને મીનારાવાળી ઈમારતો, દેવલ, દેહેરાં અને મસજીદ નથી પણ તેઓ જુદી જુદી મતલબના બાંધેલા સુંદર મકાનો છે!

મદ્રાસનો "બ્યાનકુએટીંગ હાલ" (એટલે મેજબાનીનો મકાન) "બ્લાક ટાઊન" આગળ છે. આ ઇમારત ચઢતે દરજાના ઇંગ્રેજોના મોહોટાં ખાણાંપાણી અથવા નાચ રંગ રાગ અને એવી જાતની મીજલસો સારૂ વાપરવામાં આવેછે. આ ઈમારત ઘણીજ મોહોટી અને દેખાવમાં સોહામણી અને મજબુત બાંધેલી છે, પણ તેમાં બરાબર વગ સગવડ નથી, અને જે કારણ સારૂ તે બાંધવામાં આવી છે અને હાલ વપરાયછે, તેને તે મુતલક લાયક નથી. એની પડોસમાંજ, મદ્રાસના ગવરનરનો આગળો રેહેવાનો મકાન છે, જેમાં હાલ મેહેસુલ ખાતાંની કેટલીએક સરકારી આફીસો ફીઘેલી છે, તેહેને લગતો તીહાં એક મોહોટો બાગ આ-વેલો છે, જે બાગનાજ કંપાઉંડમાં ઊપર જણાવેલો મેજબાની આપવાનો મકાન પણ બનાવેલો છે. આ ઈમારતનું ચીત્ર હીયાં આપેલું છે. આ ઈમારતની બાંધણી

ઘણીજ સાદી છે, જેમાં જમવાનો હાલ વચ્ચોવચમાં કરેલો છે. અને આસપાસ ઊંચી "ગ્યાલરી"ની બેઠક બનાવી છે, પણ તે એટલી તો ઊંચી અને કફોરી બાંધેલી છે કે તીહાં બેસી જોનારને હાલમાં જમવા બેઠેલી મજલીસ બરોબર દેખાઈ શકતી નથી, તથા ટેબલ ઉપર જમીયા પછી જે ભાશણો થાય તે પણ આ ગ્યાલરી ઊપર બેસનારાઓને બરોબર સંભળાઈ નહી શકાય એવી કઢંગી ગોઠવણથી તે બાંધેલી છે. મેજબાનીનાં દીવાનખાનાંમાં ઘણી જોવા લાયક ચીજો છેજ નહી, માત્રે કુટ, કારનવાલીસ, મેંડોસ, સર ટામસ મનરો અને તેની બાનુ, તથા બીજા થોડાક શુર વીરો જેઓએ હીંદુસ્થાનને ઇંગ્રેજોના તાબામાં લાવી મુકયું છે, તેમની શબીઓ તીહાં અચ્છી રીતે બીરાજેછે.

ઉપલો મકાન જોયા પછી મદ્રાસનો "કલબ હાઉસ" જે માઉન્ટ રોડ ઉપર છે તે જોવા ગયા. સરકારી સીવીલ, મીલીટરી અને મેડીકલ અમલદારો અને જેઓ જાહેર મંડળીમાં "ગૃહસ્થોની" પદવી લાયક પુરષો ગણાયછે તેવાજ શખ્સોને માત્ર આ "કલબ"નાં મકાનમાં રેહેવાની અને જવા આવવાની પરવાનગી છે, અને તેને લગતા કાયદા કાનુનો બાંધેલા છે તે મુજબ એવા ગૃહસ્થોને સભાસદ કરેછે તથા કલબને લગતા બીજા હક આપીયામાં આવેછે. કલબનો મકાન ઘણીજ હવાની અને એકાંત બાગબગીચા ભરેલી જગા ઉપર બાંધેલો છે અને તેમાં સઘળી પ્રકારની એટલી તો સગવડ કરી રાખેલી છે કે કોઈ જુદું, છુટું ઘર માંડીને એટલી સગવડ અથવા સુખ નથી ભોગવી શકવાનું. શરીરને અને મનને બંનેને ગમત આપવાની સઘળી ગોઠવણ અત્રે કરીયામાં આવી છે. તેવાજ લાયક "બીલીઅર્ડ રૂમ," (રાકેટ કોર્ટ) દડા રમવાની જગા, પુસ્તકખાનું, હમામખાનું, તરવાની હોજો, વીગરે બીજાં ઘણાં ઉપયોગી ખાતાં આ "કલબ હાઉસ" માં કરેલાં છે. મુંબઈના ઇંગ્રેજી "ભાયખલા કલબ હાઉસ" કરતાં ઘણે દરજે સરસ મદ્રાસનું "કલબ હાઉસ" ગણાયછે. હમામખાનાંને સારૂ તો એક એલાહેદોજ મકાન બાંધેલો છે, તેમાં નાહાવા, તરવા અને ડુબકી મારવાને સાફ સોજાં પાણીની એક મોટી હોજ બાંધેલી છે. હોજને તળીએ ચઢતા ઊતરતા તબક્કા બાંધેલા છે, જેથી તરનારની ઇચ્છા અથવા શકિત પ્રમાણે જેટલાં ઊંડાં પાણીમાં તે જવા ચાહે તેટલું પાણી તેને જુદા જુદા તબક્કા ઉપર મળી શકેછે. હોજનો ઉંડામાં ઉંડો તબક્કો વીસ ફુટ પાણીનો

રાખેલા છે, જે ઉંડાઈ કંઇ થોડી નહી જાણવી. ઈસવી સન ૧૮૩૨ થી આ "ક્લબ" ચાલુ થયલો છે.

નાહાવાનાં જાહેર મકાનો હીંદુસ્થાનનાં ઘણાંખરાં મોહોટ મોહોટાં શેહેરોમાં ઠેકાણે ઠેકાણે બાંધેલાં છે, એવાં મકાનો બનારસ (કાશી) દીલ્લી, આગરા, લખનૌ વીગરે શેહેરોમાં હમારા જોયામાં આવ્યાં છે. તેમનું વીગતવાર બયાન ઘટતે ઠેકાણે કરેલું છે, તે વાંચ્યાથી એવા મકાનોની અંદરની રચનાં અને ગોઠવણ તથા એવાં મકાનો શેહેરમાં હોયાથી શેહેરના લોકની તનદુરૂસ્તી સાથે તેઓ કેટલો સંબંધ રાખેછે તેહેની સમજ પડશે. યુરપ ખંડમાં અને બીજા સુધરેલા દેશોમાંતો નાહાવાનાં જાહેર મકાનો ઠેકાણે ઠેકાણે બાંધેલાં હોયછે, તેનો લાભ તીહાંનાં રેહેવાસીઓ ઘણો લેછે. જેમને પોતાનાં ઘરમાં નાહાવાને પુરતું પાણી મળતું નહી હોય અને શરીર બરાબર સાફ કરવાની સગવડ પણ નહી મળી શકતી હોય તેવા લોકને આવાં જાહેર હમામખાનાંથી ઘણોજ ફાયદો થાયછે; કંઈ જુજ નાહાની સરખી રકમ આપતાં જેટલું જોઈએ તેટલું પાણી શરીર ઉપરનો મેલ સાફ કરવાને તેમને મળી શકેછે, તેથી જેમ જેને ફાવે તેમ કોઈ રોજ, કોઈ અઠવાડીયામાં બે વાર, કોઈ ત્રણ વાર, કોઈ પખવાડીયે એક વાર, એવાં જાહેર મકાનો ઉપર નાહાવાને જાયછે, અને તીહાં સારી પેઠે નાહીને આવેછે. માણસોને સારી પેઠે નાહીને પોતાનાં શરીરની સફાઈ રાખવાની જોગવાઈ મળ્યાથી તેમની તનદુરૂસ્તી સારી રેહેછે એ વાતની સચ્ચાઈ સાબેત કરવાની તો કાંઇ જરૂર નથી. સર્વ કોઈ આ વાત તો કબુલજ રાખશે કે જેટલી શરીરની સફાઈ તેટલી તનદુરૂસ્તીનો બચાવ અને જેટલું શરીર મેલું અને ગંદું તેટલો તનદુરૂસ્તીનો બીગાડો થાયછે. માટે શેહેરની તનદુરૂસ્તી અને સુઘરાઈ વીશે જેઓ ધ્યાન પોહોંચાડતા હોય તેમની એક આઇનિ ફરજ છે કે શેહેરના લોકને નાહાવા સારૂ પુરતી ગોઠવણો કરી રાખે. આપણું મુંબઈ શેહેર એક મોટું શેહેર ગણાયછે, પણ તેમાં આવાં જાહેર હમામખાનાં છેજ નહીં. તો પણ આપણી હાપુના ધુંધી કમીશનરનું ધીયાન આ અગતની બાબદ ઉપર લાગેલું છે, અને થોડા વખતમાં મારકીટો વીશે જેવું સુખ આ ચંચલ અને શાહાશીક અમલદાર તરફથી આપણને મળતું થયું છે તેજ મુજબ ગરીબ લોકને નાહાવા ધોવાની લાયક જગા અને શોખી લોકને સારૂ લાયક હમામખાનાં મળવાની પણ ઉમેદ થઈ છે. આ ખાતાંની અગત આપણા મ્યુનીસીપલ કમી-

શનરે સારી પેઠે જોઈ છે, અને જો નાણાં સંબંધી સગવડ થઈ તો પેહેલાં આ સુખની વધારે ગરજ જે ગરીબ લોકને સારૂ છે, તે લોકની ગરજ પુરી પાડવાને કમીશનર કધી પણ પછાત નથી પડવાનો એવું હમો ધારીએછ. મુંબઈની આટલી બોહોલી વસ્તીમાં ગરીબ લોકને આ અગતનું સુખ આપવાની ફરજ અગર કોઈ સખી દીલના શેઠીઆઓ ઉઠાવી લીએ, તો તેઓ અને મુંબઈની મ્યુનીસીપાલીટી બંન્ને મળીને આ કામ ઘણુંજ ફતેમંદી ભરેલી રીતે પાર પાડી શકશે. જેમ બીમાર ગરીબોને દવા દારૂ આપવા અને તેમની તનદુરૂસ્તીની જાળવણી કરવાને હાસ્પીટલો બાંધી આપવાનાં કામો મહાભારત ગણાયાં છે, તેમજ ગરીબ લોકને સારી પેઠે નાહાવા ધોવા અને તેમનાં શરીર સાફ અને સાજાં રાખવાને અને તેથી તેમની તનદુરૂસ્તી જાળવી રાખવાને જાહેર હમામખાનાં બંધાવી આપવાં આ પણ મહાભારત અને પુનનાંજ કામો થયલાં ગણાવાનાં.

મદ્રાસ "કલબ" વીશે બોલતાં, આપણી મુંબઈના આટલા સંધા સુધરેલા દેશીઓમાં એવી એક પણ આબરૂ ભરેલી "દેશી મડળી" થયલી નથી, આ વીશે થોડાક શબ્દો બોલવાની જરૂર લાગેછે. અત્રે આવો એકુ પણ "કલબ" નથી, કે જેમાં ગૃહસ્થની પદ્વિ ધરાવનારાઓનો જમાવ અથવા મંડળી થયલી હોય, અને જે "કલબ" સુધરેલી મંડળીના ઠરાવેલા કાયદા કાનુનો મુજબ ચાલતો હોય, અથવા દેશી મંડળીમાં તે કોઈબી તરેની આગેવાની ભોગવતો હોય. આપણા દેશીઓમાં આવો જરૂરનો બંધાણ હજુર સુધી થયલો નથી એ ઉપરથી દેશી મંડળીની બાંધણીમાં કોઈ તરેની મોટી ખામીની હસ્તી છે એવું બેશખ સાબેત થઈ શકેછે. આવી મંડળી નહી હોયાથી દેશી આગેવાનો અને શીકેલા દેશી ગૃહસ્થો એક બીજાથી જુદા, દુર, અને જાણે વીખરાયલા પડેલા છે. હાલ આપણી કોમની મંડળીમાં ફરતાં જોઈએછ તો દરેક શખસ જેમ જેની નજરે નેક અને સારૂં લાગેછે તેમ તે બેધડક ચાલેછે. બીજાઓની નજરમાં કોઈ ચાલ ચલગત જો ગેરવાજબી લાગી તો તે વીશે તેઓ એક બીજાની જરા પણ દરકાર કરતા નથી. સુધરેલી મંડળીના કાયદા કાનુનો અને રેવાજો, જે દરેક વીચારવાળો શખસ પોતાની ઉપર એક આંકોસ તરીકે સમજેછે, અને પોતે આડાઆવળા અને બેઅંદાજેથી ચાલવામાં અટકાવ કરવાના તેમને

સાધનો ગણેછે તેવાં સાધનો આ મંડળીના બંધાણમાં મુતલક દેખાતાંજ નથી. સુધરેલી મંડળીના કાયદા કાનુનો મુજબ આજે થોડાજ જણ ચાલતા હશે અથવા તેવા કાયદાની તેઓ દરકાર કરતા હશે. જારે સુધરેલા અને તેથી વીચારવાળા દેશીઓમાં આવો એકુ "કલબ" હજુરસુધી બની નથી શકયો તારે તેમની તરફેણમાં આપણે શું બોલી શકશું? હમો ઘણાજ દીલગીર છઈએ કે આ બાબદ ઉપર બોલતાં હમો એક ઘણીજ નાજુક બીના ઉપર આવી પડ્યા છઈએ. આ વીશે બોલતાં હમારા કેટલાક હમશરીકો વીશે, તેમના ગુણ દોષ દેખડાવી બોલવાની હમારી ઉપર ફરજ આવી પડી છે, જે બજાવતાં હમોએ કોઇનોબી જીવ દુખવવાની મતલબ રાખી નથી, તે વીશે સઘળા વાંચનારાએ સત કરી જાણવું.

હમો સઘળી નમનતાઇથી સવાલ કરીએછ કે આટલા બધા કેળવણી પામેલા આપણા દેશીઓ હોવા છતાં, (પછી શું પારશી કે શું હીંદુઓ) માં આજે શું એટલી શકિત અને સંપ નથી કે આવો એક "કલબ" તેઓ બનાવી શકે કે જેમાં પોતાની પદ્વિનાજ તમામ ગૃહસ્થો, એક દીલીથી મળી ભેટીને ચાલે? એક ઠરાવેલી જગાએ તેમનો વખતે વખત મેલાવડો થાય, જીહાં એક બીજાના વીચાર એક બીજા સાથે આવજે માવજો કરીયામાં આવે, જીહાં દોસ્ત આરાનાઓ સાથે દીલ ખુશ કરનારી વાતચીત થાય, જીહાં એક બીજાની સંસારી હાલત વીશે મેહરબાની ભરેલી પુછપરછ થાય, જેમાં જે મીત્રો, મદદ લેવા જોગ હાલતમાં આવી પડેલા માલુમ પડે તેમને જે મીત્રો મદદ કરવા જોગ હાલતમાં હોય તેઓ પોતાનો જમણો હાત આપી ઉઠાવી લીએ, જીહાં ભેગા થતા સઘળા મીત્રો એક દીલીથી, એક બીજાની ઈમાનદારી અને વિશ્વાસ ઉપર સાબેત અને મુસ્તકીમ રેહી પોત પોતાનાં ધંધા રોજગારનું કામ, ઈજત અને આબરૂથી બજાવતા રેહે, અને જરૂરની વખતે તેઓ સઘળા એક આવાજે બાહેર પડી શકે, અને મંડળી સંબંધી અથવા હરકોઈ અગતની જાહેર બાબદ સંબંધી સવાલ ઉઠતાં, આ "કલબ"નું શું મત છે તે જાણવાને સઘળા જણ ઈનતેજાર રેહે, એટલો વીશ્વાસ અને માન, લોક તરફથી આ મંડળીએ મેળવીયું હોય, પછી ગમે એવા વચલી પદ્વિવાળા ગૃહસ્થોનો એ "કલબ" બનેલો હોય તો શું મુજાકો છે? આ સવાલ હમો ફરીને પુછીએછ કે આવો "કલબ" આપણા દેશીઓમાં બની શકે અથવા નહી?

23

હવે જારે આવી મતલબની મંડળી કેળવણી પામેલા આપણા દેશી ગૃહસ્થોમાં હજુર સુધી નથી બની શકી તારે તેના અટકાવનાં જે કારણો, હમારા આધીન વીચારમાં આવેછે, તે ખોલ્લાં કરી જણાવવાં જોઈએછ, અને એમ કરીયાથી કેળવણીના પવિત્ર નામને તેઓ દોષ લગાડનારાં થઈ પડેછે, એથી હમો ખચીત ઘણાં દીલગીર છઈએ.

મુંબઈમાં સુધારાવીરો જે મોહોટ મોટા પોકારો અને બરાડા વારે ઘડીએ ઘણાક દેશી વર્તમાન પત્રોમાં અને જાહેર મંડળીઓમાં સંભળાયછે, તે ખરા અને સંગીન સુધારાના નહી જાણવા, પણ પોળાં ખાલી ઘરોમાંથી નીકળતા ખોટા અને ભંપાળ આવાજો બરોબર જાણવા. સુધારો બોલી દેખડાવવો અને સુધારો કરી દેખડાવવો, આ બંધે જાણે જુદીજ વાત હોય આવી રીતે સુધારાના આવાજો નીકળતા આવીયા છે. આજેબી કેટલાક આવા શખસો છે જેઓ લોકને શીખામણ દેવામાંજ, ડાહપણ અને માન સમજેછે, પણ તે મુજબ પોતે ચાલવું કેટલું જરૂરનું છે આ વીરો તેઓ કશી પણ દરકાર કરતા નથી. કલમ, સીહાઈ અને કાગજ ઉપર પોકળ વીચારો લખીને તેમને ડીબાંમાં ગોઠવી સુધારાના વાવટા તરીકે જાહેર પાડવામાંજ, સઘળો સુધારો થઈ ગયલો તેઓ સમજેછે. ખરો સંગીન સુધારો જોવા જઈએછ તો તે કોઈ જુજ ઠેકાણે અને તેબી કોઈ એકમારગી લોક જેઓના મોહોડાંમાંથી એક હરફ વટીક પણ સુધારાના પોકાર તરીકે નીકળેલો નથી અને નીકળવાનો પણ નથી, તેવે ઠેકાણે માત્રે જોવામાં આવેછે. બાકી આપણા લોકમાં બીજીગમ જીહાં જોઈએછ તીહાં સુધારાવીરો બાર મણ તેલે અંધારૂં નજરે દેખાયછે અને તે અંધારામાંથી સુધારાવીરો ફકત ઢંઢાર આવાજો માત્રે સંભળાયછે. તો જુઓ અકલમંદ વાંચનારો, આજે કેળવણી પામેલા દેશી ગૃહસ્થોમાં કેટલો ઓછો સંપ અને કેટલી થોડી એખલાસી છે! શું એને શુધારો કહીએ વારૂ! શીખેલાઓમાં જો સંપ અને એખલાસી નહીં હોય તો પછી બીજા કોણ લોકમાં હોય વારૂ? આવી હાલતમાં આપણ પોતે હોઇને પછી બીજાઓને શીખામણ દેવા બાહેર પડીએ તો એ ચાલ વાજબી ગણાશે વારૂ? 'ચારણી કડવડાને હીણે' આ કેહેવત વીચાર કરવા જોગ છે, અને તે આ ઠેકાણે લાગુ પડી શકેછે તેથી તે અત્રે ટાંકી છે, વાસ્તે માફ કરવી! આવી હાલત શીખેલાઓની આજે થઈ પડેલી છે. તેઓ વચ્ચે એખલાસી અને સંપ છે અથવા નહી આ વીરો જે

કોઈ સવાલ પુછે તેને જવાબ આપવાનું કઠણ કામ હમારી ઉપર આવીયું છે. જવાબ તો ટુંકો છે પણ તે જબર કડવો છે. તે બોલતાંજ સાંભી ગમથી લપડાક ખાવાની હાલતમાં હમો આવી પડીએછ! પણ હવે કરીએ શું? તે લપડાક ખાયા વગર છુટકોજ નથી, કારણ ખરો જવાબ જે છે તે આપીયા વગર પણ છુટકોજ નથી. તો લેઓ તે જવાબ એટલોજ છે કે હા, ઘણાં ખરા શીખેલાઓમાં સંપ અને એખલાસી તો નથીજ, પણ વળી તેઓ એક બીજા તરફ અદેખાઈની નજરથી જુએછે! આ બીના હમારી તરફથી બોલાતી સાંભળીને હમારા કેટલાક હમશરીકો, હમારી ઉપર ખચીત ખફા ભરેલી નજરથી જોશે. એકવાર કદાચ તેઓ એમ પણ બોલશે કે, હમારો વીચાર તદન ખોટો છે, તો હમો તે વીશે વધારે ભાંજગડ નથી કરવાના. હમો દીલાજાનથી ચાહીએછ કે ખોદા કરેને હમારૂં આ મત ખોટું હોય; પણ હમારૂં દીલ તે કબુલ રાખી શકતું નથી. હમોને તો ઉલટું એવું લાગેછે કે જેઓ હમારી ઉપર ગુસે થતા હશે, તેઓ પોતાનાં મનમાં તો એવુંજ સમજતા હશે કે ગમે એવો ઠપકો આ પુસ્તક લખનારને આપણે આપીએ, પણ આ લખાણમાં પરદો ઉઘાડી જે હકીકત જાહેર કરી છે તે વાત તો સોળે સોળ આના ખરી છે, એમાં તો કંઈ શખ છેજ નહી.

શીખેલાઓમાં આજ ઘણા જણ એવા છે જેઓ એક બીજાને પોત પોતાની પદ્વિ બરોબર અથવા તેથી વધતા ચઢેલા જોવાને ઇચ્છતા નથી અને એવી રીતે કોઈ ચઢતું હોય તો તેઓ એક બીજાને તોડી પાડવા સારૂ વચમાં પથરા નાખવાને પણ ચુકતા નથી! કેટલાકો વળી એખલપેટાની પેઠે પોતે એખલાજ પોતાનું ભલું કરીયા જાયછે, અને પોતાની સફવાળાઓને પોતાના બારણની જગામાં પગ પેસારો વટીક કરવા દેતા નથી. સારી અને સુખી હાલતવાળા જેટલા શીખેલાઓ આજે છે તેઓમાંના કોણ કોણે પોતાની સફવાળા (પણ તેમના જેટલા ભાયગશાલી નહી) ઓને બોલાવીને તેમની હાલત વીશે પુછપરછ કરી છે? કે "મીત્રો તમારી હાલત હાલ કેવી છે, કોઈબી રીતે જો હમારાથી તમારે સારૂ કંઈ થઈ શકતું હોય તો તે સુખેથી ફરમાવવું, તે કરવાને હમો ઘણાંજ ખુશી છઈએ?" હમો ધારીએછ કે આવા કોઈ નહી હશે અથવા હશે તો કોઈ જુજ એવા પરોપકારી ગૃહસ્થો હશે. નહી શીખેલાઓ આવી દયા ભરેલી ફરજો જો નહી બજાવે તો

તેમાં તેમની તકસીર આપણે જાજી કાહાડી નથી શકવાના; પણ શીખેલાઓએ તો આવા પરોપકાર વીરો પુષ્કળ ગ્નાન મેળવેલું છે, તેઓ જો આવી અગતની ફરજો વીશે પોતાનું હઈયું કઠણ અને એખલપેટું રાખે તો તેઓ ભારી ઠપકાને લાયકના છે. વળી કેટલાક શીખેલાઓએ પોતાની ખાનગી મતલબને સારૂ તરેવાર રીતે પોતાની ચાલ ચલણમાં ફેરફાર કરીયો છે. જેમ એક અટકી પડેલું વાહાણ એરીયાં બારીયાં કરી પવન ઉપર પોતાની જગાની ફેરબદલી કરીયા કરેછે તેમ કેટલાક શીખેલાઓએ પોતાની ચાલ દેશી શેઠીઆઓ તરફ ચલાવી છે. આજે શેઠીઆઓની તરફેણમાં રેહી બોલવું, બીજી વખતે તેમની વીરૂધ થઈજવું. વળી કોઈ સંજોગ થઈ પડતાં પાછા પોતાની પેહેલી બાજુ પકડવી અને વળી વાત ફરતાં પાછા તેમની સાંભણે થવું. આવી રીતે ડામાડોલ ચાલ ચલાવી કેટલાક શીખેલાઓ પોતાનો મોભો અને ઈજત ખોઈ બેઠા છે, એટલુંજ નહી પણ આવી ડામાડોલ ચાલથી પોતાની સફવાળાઓ તરફ પણ આંગલી થાય એવું કામ કીધું છે. વળી કેટલાક શીખેલાઓએ જબરો ઈતરાઠ, અભીમાન અને નહી તામોસ થઈ શકે એવી આપખુદી કરી બતલાવી છે. આવા ખાલી દમામથી સાંભા લોકના મનમાં તેઓએ આવો ભય ભરેલો વીચાર ઉત્પંન કરયો છે કે જેથી તેઓનાં મોહોડાંમાંથી આવા શબ્દો નીકળતા થયા છે કે "બાપરે આવા શીખેલાઓથી ખોદા પનાહમાં રાખે!" જે નમનતાઈ, ગંભીરપણું, ધીરજ, દુરંદેશો, અને પોતાના માંબાપ અને વડીલો તરફ સઘળી તાએબેદારી અને આદરમાનની રાહે જોવું અને ચાલવું જરૂર છે (પછી ગમે તેવા તે વડીલોના વીચાર એકવાર કસુર ભરેલા હોયા તો શું થયું) આવા સદગુણો ઉંચે દરજેની ખરી કેળવણી પામેલા ગૃહસ્થોમાં હોવા જોઈએ તેવા સદગુણો જારે આવા શીખેલાઓમાં નહી માલુમ પડીયા, અને તેમને બદલે ઈતરાઠ, આપફજુલી, ગરદનકશી અને આપખુદી નજર આવી તારે નહી શીખેલાઓએ એકદમ એવું મત બાંધી દીધું કે "જેટલા શીખેલા તેટલા બધા ગયલા." આવું મત બાંધવામાં જો કે તેઓએ ઘણી ઉતાવળ કરી છે, અને અલબતાં લાંબો વીચાર ફરીને કરતાં, એ મત અલબતે ફેરવાય એવું છે, તોયપણ શીખેલાઓ તરફથી ઉપર જણાવેલા દોષ ભરેલા દાખલાઓ દમપર દમ મળી આવીયાથી, આવું મત બંધાવાનાં કારણો આપણા દેશીઓને મળી આવીયાં છે, આ વાત કોઈથી ના નથી પાડી શકાવાની.

આવા સબબથી શીખેલાઓમાં અને દેશીઓ અને દેશી આગેવાનોમાં મોટો અંતર થઈ પડ્યો છે. આ અંતર પાડવાનો દોષ જો કે પુરેપુરો, સઘળા કેળવણી પામેલાઓ ઉપર નથી લાગુ પડી શકતો, તોએ પણ કેટલાકો પર લાગુ પડી શકેછે. માટે સમજુ અને દુરંદેશી શીખેલા ગૃહસ્થો હવે જો ખુલો અને પુખ્ત વીચાર કરશે તો તેમને એવું માલુમ પડશે કે આ અંતર કાહાડી નાખવાની ફરજ તેમનાજ ઉપર આવી પડેલી છે અને તેઓજ પોતાની હવેપછીની નમનતાઈ ભરેલી તેમજ ઓજ અને મોભા ભરેલી અને એકજ ઠરાવેલા કાયદાસર રાખેલી ચાલ ચલગતથી આ અંતર કાહાડી શકશે, અથવા બીજા શબ્દોમાં બોલીએ તો તેઓ સલુખાઇ અને ઓજ ભરેલી રીતે વરતીયાથી દેશી આગેવાનોને પોતાની તરફેણમાં સેહેલાઈથી ખેંચી શકશે.

હવે શેઠીઆઓ જેઓ દેશી આગેવાનો કેહેવાયછે તેમના વીશે પણ આ બાબદમાં બોલવાની હમારી ફરજ છે, જે બજાવામાં પણ સઘળી વાત ખુલી કરીને બોલવી પડશે.

ઘણા શેઠીઆઓ, આજે શીકેલા દેશી ગૃહસ્થોથી જુદાં અને અલગા રહેલા છે, આ વીશે હમો સઘળી નમનતાઈથી બોલવાની રજા લેઉંએછ કે આવું કરવામાં એ સાહેબોની એક મોટી ભુલ છે. તેઓમાંના કેટલાક સાહેબોનો આવો વીચાર સાંભળવામાં આવીયો છે કે શીકેલાઓને અગર ઉંચે દરજે ચઢવા દેશું તો તેઓ શેઠીઆઓનાં માંથાં ઊપર ચઢી બેસવાની કોશીશ કરશે! હમો જાણવા માગીએછ કે એ મુજબ આજસુધીમાં કોણ અને કેટલા તેમની ઉપરવાર થઈ બેઠાં છે. હમો ખચીતાઈથી બોલીએછ કે ખરી કેળવણી પામેલા બુનીયાદ ગૃહસ્થોથી તો આવું હલકું કામ કદી પણ થઈ નથી શકનાર. આ વીશે આપણા આગેવાન સાહેબોએ બેફીકીર રેહેવું. હવે જેઓ ખરા બુનીયાદ નહીં હશે તેઓથી આવી બેઅદબી કદાચને થાય અને આવું થાય તેમાં નવાઈ સાની? એવાઓથી કીહાં ભલાં અને નેક કામો નીપજવાની આપણે ઉમેદ રાખીએ તે કોઈ જાણતું નથી. ગમે એવી ચઢતે દરજેની કેળવણી તેઓએ લીધી હશે તોએ પણ જો બુનીયાદી નહીં ધરાવતા હશે તો કેળવણીથી શું તેમના જીગર ઉપર અસર થવાની છે? શેખ શાદીએ કહ્યું છે કે 'વરૂનું બચ્ચું વરૂજ થવાનું,' પછી ગમે એવી સારી સંગતમાં અને તરબીએતથી તેને ઉધારો તો શું થવાનું છે? પણ જેઓ ખરા બુનીયાદ કેળ-

વણી પામેલા ગૃહસ્થો છે, પછી ગમે એવા ગરીબ માબાપોનાં તેઓ ફરજંદ હોય તો શું મુજાકો છે, તો તેવા ગૃહસ્થો ચઢતી પદ્વિએ જઈ પોતાના વડીલોને અથવા પોતાની કોમના આગેવાનોને કદી પણ અપમાન નથી આપવાના અથવા તેમના ઉપર સરસાઈ ભોગવવાનો વીચાર પણ કદી નથીજ કરવાના. હમારૂં આધીન મત એવું છે કે ખરી કેળવણી પામેલા અસરાફ ગૃહસ્થો સાથે દેશી આગેવાનોએ હજુર સુધી લાંબા વખતની ઓળખ, અને મીત્રાચારી, તથા પીછાન અને મેળ-ભેટ અથવા ગરોબો રાખીયોજ નથી. તેઓએ એક બીજાને કસીને, ત-પાસી જોયા નથી. સંકટ અને સુખમાં એક બીજાની જે પરીક્ષા થાયછે એવા પ્રસંગ આ બંધે બાજુવાળાઓ વચ્ચે પડયોજ નથી, તેથી અલબતાં એક બીજા-ની ખરી પીછાન એક બીજાથી થઈ શકી નથી. પણ આજ સુધીમાં કોઈવાર કેટલાક શેઠીઆઓએ લાંબો વીચાર કરીયા વગરે અને ખરી પીછાન મેળવીયા શીવાએ, કોઈ તેવા ખોટા દમામ અને ખાલી ધડપચં દેખડાવનારોને મોટી કેળ-વણી પામેલા ગૃહસ્થો સમજીને પોતાની સોડે બેસાડીયા હોય, અને તેવા અધુરા શખસોથી પછવાડે તે શેઠીઆઓને અપમાન પોંહોચીયું હોય અથવા નુકસાન ખ-મવું પડીયું હોય અથવા તેવા શખસો છકી ગયલા ઈતરો જેવા તેમને માલુમ પડીયા હોય, તો એવા થોડા દાખલા ઉપરથી શેઠીઆઓ ઉતાવળા પડી એકદમ સઘળા કેળવણી પામેલા દેશી ગૃહસ્થો ઉપર દોષ નાખે અને તેઓથી દુર રેહેવાને પોતાના બીજા હમશરીક શેઠીઆઓને ભલામણ કરે તો ખરેખર કેળવણી પામે-લા ગૃહસ્થોના વર્ગ તરફ એક મોટી ગેરવાજબી ચાલ ચલાવેલી અને તેથી આગેવાનો તરફથી એક મોટી ગેર ઈનસાફી થયલી કેહેવાએ એમાં શક નથી. આ અગતની બાબત ઉપર હમો સઘળા દેશી આગેવાનોને ધ્યાન પોંહોંચાડવાની ભલામણ કરીએછ. સર્પનો ડંખ ખાઈ પછી સઘળાં દોરડાંને સર્પ ગણવાં આ વીચાર કેટલો ભુલ ભરેલો છે તે જાણવું સેહેલ છે. તેમજ બેચાર અધુરી કેળવ-ણી પામેલા શખસોની ચાલ ચલગત ઉપરથી કેળવણી પામેલા આખા વર્ગ વીશે આવો હલકો વીચાર બાંધવો, તે દેશી આગેવાનો જેવા દુરંદેશી અને કસાયલા ગૃહસ્થોને સજાવાર નથી. દેશી આગેવાનો સારી પેઠે સમજતા હશે કે પાંચ આંગલીઓ આપણી સરખી નથી, તેમજ સઘળા શીખેલાઓ પણ સરખા નથી. તેમજ વળી આગેવાન સાહેબોખી જાણતા હશે કે તેમની

સફ્રમાં પણ સઘળા સરખી ખુબી ધરાવનારા ફરેસ્તા નથી. દેશી આગેવાન સાહેબો તો તેમના મોટા કસાએલા અનુભવથી પુરતા વાકેફ હશે કે સુધરેલી કોમના આગેવાનો પોતે મોટી કેળવણી પામેલા શખ્સો હોયછે, અને તેમજ તેઓ પોતાની સફ્રમાં પણ તેવાજ શીખેલા અને મોટા વિદ્વાન શખ્સોને અગત કરીને સામેલ રાખતા આવીયા છે. પોતાનો બોજ, વગ, અને માન જાળવેલું રાખવાને તેઓ હંમેશ પોતાથી ઉતરતી પદ્વિવાળાઓ સાથે મેહેરબાની ભરેલાં દીલથી પોતાની પારો આવજાવ કરવાની છુટ આપેછે, અને તેમની સાથે પોતે મેળમેટ રાખી તેમની હાલત વીશે, સારી રીતે પુછપરછ કરતા રેહી તેમનો પ્યાર મેળવેલો રાખેછે. સઘળું હમોજ કરીએ અને જે હમો કરીએ તે બીજા સઘળાંઓએ કબુલ રાખવું જોઈએ આવો વીચાર આપણા દેશી આગેવાનો ગ્રખેછે આવી ફરીયાદ ઘણેક ઠેકાણેથી સંભળાયછે, (હમો નથી માનતા કે સઘળા આગેવાનો આવો વીચાર ધરાવતા હોય), તો આ નાપાયાદાર વીચાર ઉપર લાંબા વખત સુધી કોઈથી અમલ કરી શકાવાનો નથી, અને આજસુધી કોઈ કરી પણ શકયું નથી. તવારીખમાં બનેલા પુશ્કળ આવા દાખલા આશકારા થયલા છે જેમાં એવું જણાયલું છે કે પ્રજાના આગેવાનોએ જારે ઉપર જણાવીયા જેવી આપખુદી કરવા માંડી હતી, ત્યારે પ્રજા પોતે તેમની સાંભણે ઉલટી, આગેવાનોને બીસાડી મેળીયા હતા. આપણા દેશી આગેવાનો સારીપેઠે વાકેફ છે કે જો બોજ, વગ, અને માન ભરેલી આગેવાની ચલાવવી હોય તો તેમની મંડળીમાં બોજ, વગ, અને માન ભરેલાંજ શખ્સો સામેલ હોવા જોઈએ. આવી મંડળીમાં પદ્વિ અને ઓધાવાળા ગૃહસ્થો હોવા જોઈએછ, દુરંદેશી અને કસાયલા દેશીઓ હોવા જોઈએછ, દેશને લગતી જુદી જુદી બાબદો વીશે અચ્છી માહીતગારી રાખનારા, સરકાર દરબારમાં અને પોતાના દેશી લોકમાં જાણીતા અને મોભા ભરેલી રીતે વગ ચલાવી શકનારા, ઈનસાફ અને દરબારના કાયદા કાનુનોથી સારી પેઠે વાકેફગાર, વેપાર વણજની ગણત્રી રાખનારા અને તેમાં જોઈતી ધીરજ, સંભાળ, અને ચોકસાઈ ભરેલા અને છેલ્લું સારી કેળવણી અને મજબુત મનશકિત ધરાવનારા, તથા પ્રમાણીક અને નીતીવાળા ગૃહસ્થો હોવા જોઈએછ. આટલા સંઘા ગુણો જે મંડળી ધરાવી શકે તેજ મંડળી ખરેખર બોજ, વગ, અને માન ધરાવનારી થઈ શકશે. લાગવગથી બનાવેલી મંડળી કોઈબી તરેનો બોજ

ધરાવી શકશે એમાં મોટા શખ છે. પણ ઉપલી કીશમની મંડળી જાહેર રીતે બનાવાને દેશી આગેવાનો પુરતા લાયક છે એમાં તો કંઈજ શખ નથી.

હવે આપણા આગેવાન સાહેબોની ખાસ સંગતમાં, અને તેમની સાથે મીત્રાચારીનો ગરોબો રાખનાર કેવી પ્રકારના ગૃહસ્થોનો જમાવ હાલના વખતમાં થયલો છે, તેમની ખાનગી મસલહત અને વીચાર કરવાની મજલીસમાં સામેલ થનારા કોણ કોણ ગૃહસ્થો છે, તેમના દરરોજના વેપાર વહીવટને લગતાં કામ કારભાર ચલાવનારા, કોણ કોણ અને કેવા શખસો છે, આ બાબત જાણવી ઘણીજ અગતની છે. તપાસી જોતાં આવું માલુમ પડેછે કે દેશી શેઠીઆઓની સંગત મસલહતમાં ઘણું કરીને સારી કેળવણી પામેલા કંઈ જુજ શખસોજ જોયામાં આવેછે. તેઓ પોતાનો સઘળો બોહોળો વહીવટ સાધારણ કેળવણી પામેલા માણસોની મારફતથી બજાવતા આવીયા છે, તોયપણ તેમની સાથે સારી સલાહ અને વીચાર આપવાને તેવા લાયક ગૃહસ્થો હોય એવું નથી દેખાતું, આ ખચીત દીલગીરી ભરેલી વાત છે. તેઓ જાણે બની આવે તેમ કેળવણી પામેલા વર્ગથી દુરના દુર રહેલા છે, એ મોટી તાજુબી લાગેછે. તારે ઉંચે દરજ્જેની કેળવણીવાળાઓમાં શું એવું હશે કે તેમની પસંદગી આ ઠેકાણે થતી નથી. આ અંતર શું સબબથી થઈ પડ્યો છે તે ચોકસાઈથી કેહેવાઈ શકાતું નથી. આ વીશે લોક તરેવાર અટકલ કરેછે, અને તે અટકલ જેમ જેની નજરમાં આવેછે તેમ કરેછે. પણ તે અટકલો વીચાર કરવા જોગ છે, અને તેમાંથી એક અગતનો સાર આપણે વીચારશક્તિથી કાહાડી શકીએછ. આ જુદાઇના સબબો જે અટકલવામાં આવેછે તેમાં પેહેલો સબબ એવો કહેછે કે કેળવણી પામેલામાંના કેટલાકો આગેવાનોની બધી વાતોમાં હાંજી હા કરવાને નાદુરસ્ત વીચારેછે તેથી તેઓ નાપસંદ થઈ પડ્યા છે. વળી કેટલાકોએ આપખુદી અને સુખન પરવરી દેખડાવી છે, અથવા તો કોઈવાર આગેવાનોની સાધારણ ભુલચુક ઉપરથી તેમની સાથે પોતાના ઉછલતાં લોહીના જુસામાં આવી ઘણી બેઅદબી અને નાસજાવાર ચાલ ચલાવી છે, આટલા કારણોથી કેળવણી પામેલા ગૃહસ્થો શેઠીઆઓને અણગમતા થઈ પડયા છે. ત્રીજું કારણ એવું કેહેવામાં આવેછે કે, કેળવણી પામેલાઓમાંના કેટલાકોએ, તેમના મગજમાં અભીમાનનો ધુમાડો ઉપજાવી એવાજ વીચાર રાખ્યાયા છે કે હમો વીદ્યા હુંનર

અને લખવા ભણવામાં ઉંચે દરજેની કેળવણી પામેલા ગૃહસ્થો છઈએ, અને દેશી આગેવાનોમાં કોઈ તેવા ભણેલા ગૃહસ્થો નથી, તેઓ માત્રે માલિમુસ્તાક અને પોતાની બાપીકી દોલત ઉપર તવંગરી અને તાજારી ભોગવેછે અને ખાલી આપણી ઉપર હુકમ ચલાવા માગેછે તે કેમ બની શકે? એઓ એમને ઘેર અને હમો હમારે ઘેર! હવે આપણે આ સઘળાં સબબોને વીચારના તરાજુમાં તોલીએ અને આગેવાન સાહેબોની સાંભણેની તકશીર તથા કેળવણી પામેલા સાહેબોની સાંભણેની તકસીર સરખાવી જોઈએછ તો જે બાજુએ અભીમાનનો બોજો વધારે પડેલા છે તે બાજુએ ઠપકો જવો જોઈએછ, અને એ બાજુવાળા સાહેબોએ આ ઠપકામાંથી મોકળા થવાના ઉપાયો કરવાને દરીઆફત કરવી જોઈએછ. આ કેહેવત તો મશાહુર છે, કે ભણેલા તકોબરો કરતાં અજ્ઞાની અસીલો વધારે પસંદ કરવા અને માન આપવા જોગ છે, તેમજ તવંગર તકોબરો કરતાં અસીલ મુફલીસો પણ વધારે પસંદ કરવા અને માન આપવા જોગ છે.

ખેર, હવે જુદાઈનાં કારણો વીશે ખોલાસા ભરેલી રીતે બોલીયા પછી, આ જુદાઈ ટાળી, મેલાપ પાછો કેમ થાય આ વીશે થોડાજ શબ્દોમાં કેહી જણાવીએછ. સઘળી બાબદની ગઈ ગુજરી કરી નાખી, દેશી આગેવાનોએ કેળવણી પામેલા ગૃહસ્થો સાથે વધારે મેળભેટ, વધારે મીત્રાચારી, અને તેમના ઉપર વધારે વિશ્વાસ રાખવો જોઈએછ. તેમજ કેળવણી પામેલા ગૃહસ્થોએ વડીલો સાથે ઘટતા આદરમાનથી ચાલી, પોતાના દરજાને જાળવી જેમ બની આવે તેમ આપણા આગેવાનોની ખાત્રી કરી આપવી જોઈએછ કે તેમના ઉપર મુકાયલા વિશ્વાસ તેમનાથી નથી થવાનો, અને આગેવાનોની તરફથી કદાચને કંઈ ખામી થાય તો ખરી કેળવણીવાળા તે કેટલે દરજે નમનતાઈ અને સમજુતીથી દરગુજર કરી શકનાર છે, તેમજ કેળવણી પામેલાઓ પોતાથી કંઈ ખામી થતાં તે એકરાર કરવાને અને સુધારવાને તેઓ કેટલા આતુર અને કેટલા ખુલાં દીલવાળા છે આવું તેઓએ બતલાવી આપવું. એકવાર જો આવો સંજોગ બન્યો તો પછવાડેથી શેઠીઆઓ અને કેળવણી પામેલા ગૃહસ્થો વચ્ચે દોસ્તીનો અને પ્રીતીનો મજબુત જુગ બંધાવાનો. એકવાર આવો જુગ બંધાયો તો તેની મદદથી આપણા સંસાર વેહેવારની કઠણ બાજુમાં જે જે સંકટો અને નડાની સાટકીયો વારંવાર આપણી આડે આવી પડેછે તેમને આ જુગના બાંધનારો પોતાનાં એખલાસી ભરેલાં મતની જબરી કલ્લ્જલ નાખી

સેહેલાઈથી મારી હટાવશે અને આ અંએર સંસારની બાજીમાં તેઓ સઘળા જીતેલા અને જીતેલાજ રેહેશે.

ઉપલું લખાણ આવું ખુલી રીતે હમોએ બંધે બાજુવાળાઓ વીશે કરયું છે, જેમાં અરધો બાંધો અને અરધાનો ખુરદો, આ નાજુક બાબદ ઉપર બાંધે તરફથી કરી આપીયો છે, આથી હમો ખરેખર દીલગીર છઈએ. પણ આગળ કહી જણાવીયું તેમ આવું કરવામાં હમોએ કોઈનોખી જીવ દુખવવાની મતલબ રાખી નથી. આ નાજુક બાબદ ઉપર બોલતાં શેકસપીયર કવીના શબ્દો ધીયાનમાં રાખી, બંધે બાજુ સરખી રીતે દેખડાવી આપી છે. માંણસ જાતની પુરી ખુબી પીછાનનાર આ સાઅેરે એક બાબદ વીશે જીકર કરતાં કેહી જણાવીયું છે કે "આ ચીત્ર ઉપર પણ જુઓ અને પેલાં ચીત્ર ઉપર પણ જુઓ," તેમજ આ અગતની બાબત ઉપર વીસ્તારીને બોલતાં, હમોએ ખી એવુંજ કરીયું છે કે "શીખેલા અને સુધારા કરનારાઓની ચાલ ચલગત ઉપર પણ જોઓ અને નહી શીખેલા અને જુને મારગે ચાલનારાઓની ચાલ ચલગત ઉપર પણ જુઓ." હવે આ બંધે બાજુમાં કહી બાજુએ વધારે ખામી છે તે દરેક વીચારવાળો વાંચનાર જાણવાને શક્તિવાન છે.

મદ્રાસ "કલબ" ને લગતી બાબદ ઉપર બોલતાં હમોએ વાંચનારનું ધીયાન, મુંબઈની દેશી મંડળીને લગતી કેટલીક બાબદ ઉપર ખેંચીયું છે. આ બાબદ પુરી કરતાં, પાછા હમે મદ્રાસ શેહેરના બયાન ઉપર જઈએછ.

તા૦ ૨૫ જાનેવારીને દીને, મદ્રાસમાં જે મકાન ઉપર હમારા મીત્ર ડાકતર ભાઉ દાજીએ ઉતારો કરીયો હતો, તે જોવાને ગયા. આ ઠેકાણું "બ્લાક ટાઉન"થી આસરે ચાર પાંચ માઇલ દુર હતું, જેને ધોબી પેંઠને નામે તીહાંના લોક બોલેછે. મદ્રાસના ગારૂડી લોક પણ પોતાના હુંનરને લગતી હાતચાલાકીની જબરી કસરત કરી બતલાવનારા છે. એવો એક ગારૂડી ડાકતરને તીહાં કસરત દેખડાવાને આવીયો હતો. તેની હાતચાલાકી ઘણાજ ચઢતા દરજેના હુંનરવાળાઓના જેવી હતી, એટલુંજ નહી પણ તેણે એક તલવાર આખી મુઠ સુધી ગળી જવાની જે કઠણ કસરત કરી બતલાવી હતી તે ખરેખર જેવી જોવાને તાજુબી ભરેલી લાગી હતી તેવીજતે જોખમ અને ભય ભરેલી હતી. આ કસરત કરવામાં તે શખ્સ પેહેલાં જમીન ઉપર પલાંઠી વાળીને બેઠો હતો. પછી એક

ચકચકીત તલવાર, બે અથવા ત્રણ ફુટ લાંબી કાહાડીને તેહેની અણીનો છેડો પોતાનાં મોહોડાંમાં લીધો અને બે હાથે ધીરજથી તે પોતાના ગળામાં ઊતાર્યો. ત્યારપછી હળવે હળવે, તે ગળાની અંદર ઊતારતો ગયો, તે છેક બેથી ત્રણ ફુટ સુધી અંદર ઊતાર્યા પછી બાકીનો તલવારનો જે ભાગ મુઠ આગળનો બાહાર રહ્યો તેહેની ઊપર એક ગોલ ચક્કર મુક્યું, અને તે ચક્કરની અંદર બંદુકનો દારૂ ભરીને જેમ આતસબાજી ફુટતાં ચક્કરો ફરેછે તેમ તે મુઠ ઊપર આતસબાજીનું ચક્કર મુકી તેને સળગાવ્યાથી, તે ચક્કર જોસભર પેલી તલવારની મુઠ ઊપર ફરવા લાગ્યું હતું, અને તેમાંથી ફટાકા વીગરે આતશબાજી ફુટવા લાગી હતી. જીહાં સુધી તે આતશબાજી સઘળી ફુટી રહી તીહાં સુધી તે ગારૂડી ઉંચું મોહું રાખીને પેલી ગળેલી તલવારની મુઠ ઊપર જોયા કરતો હતો અને ફટાકાના ફુટવાથી અને ચક્કરના ફરવાથી જે આંચકા લાગતા હતા તે વગર દુખે ખમ્યા કરતો હતો! આખરે સઘળું થઈ રેહા પછી તેણે તલવારને જેમ હળવે હળવે ગળી હતી તેમ પાછી કાહાડી અને તે હમોએ જોઈ ત્યારે કેટલેક ઠેકાણે તે ઊપર લોહીની છાંટ લાગેલી હતી. તલવાર ગળવાની કસરત જે મદ્રાસનાં કેટલાએક ગારૂડીયો કરી દેખાડેછે તે ખરીજ કસરત છે. પુછપરછ કરતાં માલુમ પડ્યું કે એવી કસરત કરવાને બાલપણથી તેઓ બાંબુની પાતળી ચીપો ગળામાં ઉતારવાની અને પાછી કાહાડવાની ટેવ પાડેછે. આ ચીપો ગળતાં તેમનાં ગળાનો રસ્તો ઘસાઇને મોકળો તથા સુણો થઈ રેહેછે. બાંબુની ચીપો ગળ્યા પછી પાતળી લોઢાંની અથવા તીખાંની બુઠી ચીપો ગળવાની ટેવ પાડેછે, અને ત્યારપછી છરી, તલવાર, વીગરે એવાં હથીયારો ગળામાં ઉતારેછે. છરી અથવા તલવારો જે ગળામાં ઉતારેછે તે ઘણું કરીને વાંકી વળી શકે અથવા મરડાઈ શકે એવી હોયછે.

આ ગારૂડીની સાથે એક બીજો ખેલાડી હતો, તે જુદી જુદી જાતનાં પક્ષીયોનાં જેવો આવાજ કાહાડી શકતો હતો, તેમાં કેટલાક પક્ષીયોનાં આવાજની તો ઘણીજ બરાબર નકલ કરી શકતો હતો. આપણાં દેશમાં ઠેકાણે ઠેકાણે જુદી જુદી જાતની કસરતો કરનાર ખેલાડીયો વીખરાયલા છે, તેમાંનાં કેટલાક ઘણીજ હેરત ભરેલા અને નવાઈ જેવા ખેલો કરી શકેછે. પણ આ લોક જે કફોરી રીત ભાંતથી ખેલો કરી બતલાવેછે તથા પોતાનાં ધંધામાં દીલ લગાડીને તેમાં વધારો કરતા નથી, અને બેપરવા જેમના તેમ એકજ તરેની કસરત કરતા કરતા એણીગમ પેલીગમ રખડતા

ફરતા ફરેછે, તેથી એ લોકનો ભાવ આજે કોઈ પુછતું નથી. જે પેશાથી પશ્ચીમ દેશનાં ખેલાડીઓ આજ ઘણીજ સારી કમાઇ કરી પોતાની જીંદગી ગુજારેછે એવા પેશાથી આપણાં દેશીયો, લાચાર અને ઘણીજ કંગાલ હાલતે પોતાનું ગુજરાણ કરતા પડેલા છે. આ વીશે જેવો દોષ આપણાં દેશી ખેલાડીઓની બેપરવાઈ અને આળસાઈ ઉપર મુકાયછે, તેવોજ દોષ આવા ખેલનાં જોનારા દેશી ગૃહસ્થો ઉપર પણ લાગુ પડી શકેછે. એવા ખેલ કરનારાઓને પોતાના ધંધા પેશામાં વધારે ઉલટ ભરેલા રાખવાનો તેમની પાસે વારંવાર ખેલો કરાવી, દેશીઓએ તેમને ઉત્તેજન આપવું જોઇયેછ. વારંવાર તેમની પાસે નવા નવા ખેલો જોવાની ઇચ્છા દેશીઓયે બતલાવવી જોઇયેછ, અને જારે નવા નવા ખેલો કરી બતલાવે તે વખતે તેમને સારી કમાણી થાય એવી તકો તથા ગોઠવણો કરી આપવી જોઇયેછ. જેમ દેશીયો તરફથી, તેમજ દેશી રાજવંશીઓ તરફથી પણ દેશી તમાસગીરોને મદદ તથા ઉલટ મળવી જોઇયેછ. નાટકશાળાઓ અને તેવા લાયક ગમતનાં મકાંનો દેશી ખેલાડીઓને સારૂ બંધાવા જોઇએછ, તોજ દેશી ખેલાડીઓને જોઇયે તેટલી ઊલટ મળશે. જે દેશમાં ખેલાડીયો ઘણાં હોય અને નાટકશાળા તથા તમાસાનાં મકાનો પણ તેટલાંજ હોય અને તીહાં દરરોજ તેવા લાયક ખેલો, વીદ્યા સંબંધી અખ્તરા કરી દેખાડવાની મજલીસો અને બીજા તેવા તરેવાર, દીલપસંદ, તેમ દીલને ચાનાક આપનારા નાટકો, હાતચાલાકીના અને કસરતના મેલાવડા, તથા ઉંચી કીસમના તમાસા, ગાયનો થતાં હોય, તો ખરેખર તે દેશની હાલત ચઢતે દરજેની જાણવી.

આ બાબદ ઊપર થયલાં ઊપલાં લખાણ વીશે ગેરસમજુતી નહીં થાય, એટલા ઉપરથી હમો ખુલ્લી રીતે હીયાં જણાવાની જરૂર જોઇયેછ કે વારંવાર નાટકો અને તમાસા થવા વીશે જે અત્રે ભલામણ કરીયામાં આવી છે, તે ખરેખર સારાજ નાટકો વીશે કરીયામાં આવી છે. તે નાટકો એવા કે જેથી નાટક જોનારો અને કરી બતલાવનારો બધાના જીવને થોડાવાર આનંદ ઊપજે, તેની સાથે તેમનાં મનમાં સારાં વીચાર ઊત્પન્ન થાય, તેમના સંસાર વેહેવારમાં કામજોગ થઈ પડે એવી કેટલીક નસીએતો તેમને મળે, અને ઈનસાન જાતના સારા નરસા ગુણોની તરેવાર અસરો ખુલ્લી રીતે તેમની સાંભે જાહેર થાય, આવી કીસમનાં નાટકો વારંવાર થવાની અને તે જોવા જવાની હમોએ ભલામણ કરી છે.

મુંબઈમાં હાલના વખતમાં જે નાટકો થાયછે, એ વીશે હમો લંબાણથી લખવાની જરૂર જોતાં નથી. પણ એકુ બે ચેતવણી હમો હમારા દેશીઓના ભલાને સારૂ આપીએછ, તે જો તેમની નજરમાં વાજબી લાગે તો સઘળા માબાપોએ અને જેમને લાગે વળગેછે તેઓએ એ બાબદ ઉપર સારી પેઠે ધીયાન આપી અમલ કરવો જોઇએછ.

નાટક કરવાનું કામ નાદાન બચ્ચાં અને નાહાની ઊંમરના કાચા અનુભવવાળા છોકરાઓનું નથી. તેઓ એવાં કામ કરવાને તદન નાલાયક છે. માટે વીસ વરશની અંદરના જેબી જુવાન છોકરાઓ આવી બાબદમાં રોકાયા છે, તેમનાં ભલાં માટે તેમને ચેતવણી અને એક સારી મસલહત આપીએછ કે એવાં કામમાંથી તેઓએ તુરત હાથ ઉઠાવવો અને તેમની ઊંમરનો આ કીમતી વખત જે નીશાળમાં જઇ કઠણ અભ્યાસ કરવાનો છે, તે મુજબ લખવા પહડવાનું અને વીદ્યા હુંનર તથા ધંધો પેશો શીકવામાં કામે લગાડવો, અને પોતાના માબાપોનું અને પોતાનું ગુજરાણ કરવાને પેહેલાં શક્તિવાન થવું. તારપછી પાંચ પઇશા મેળવતા થઇ, અને પુખ્ત ઊંમરે પોંહોંચીયા પછી તેવણની મનશકિતની વલાણ એવાં કામોમાં સામેલ થવાને અંદરખાનેથી તેમને ઊલટ આપતી હોય, અને તેઓએ મેળવેલી કેળવણી એવી બાબદમાં આગળ વધવાને તેમને મદદ આપી શક્તી હોય તો તેઓએ પોતાનો ફુરસદનો વખત (તેબી થોડો એક, સઘળો એકદમ નહી) એવાં કામ પાછળ રોકીયો હોય તો તે વીશે તેમને કોઈ ઠપકો વાજબી રાહે નથી આપી શકવાનું. પણ આજે તો ઘણા જુવાન છોકરાઓને એક જાતનું ઘેલાપણું લાગેલું છે, કે શીકવા ભણવાનું એક કોરે મુકી, નાટક કરવાનાં કામમાં તેઓ જઇ પડેલા છે, અને ખરેખર બોલીએ તો, ફસી પડેલા છે. આ નાદાન નાકકાન જેવા છોકરાઓ નાટક તે સું છે, તે કરવામાં કેટલી અક્કલ, હોશ, અને દુનીયાના અનુભવની જરૂર છે, તે ફરી બતલાવનારાઓમાં ઉંચે દરજેની કેળવણી કેટલી હોવી જોઇએછ, આ વીશે તેઓ તદન નાવાકેફ અને બેહોશ છે. નાટક કરવામાં તેઓ બીચારા એટલુંજ સમજેછે કે, ચકચકીત પોશાકો પેહેરવા, માથાં ઉપર યુરોપીયન લોકના જેવા બાલ રાખવા અને ખોટી દાહાડી મુછ બાંધવી! નાટક કરવામાં તેઓ એટલુંજ સમજેછે કે, વગર અદબ આદાબે જેમ જેની નજરમાં આવે તેવો બેકાયદે પોશાક પેહેરી, ઢાલ, તલવાર અને

લાકડીઓ બાંધી, ચેહેરા ઉપર રંગ લગાડી રાતા સુરણ જેવા બનીને, નાટકના તખતા ઉપર મોહોટ મોટી બુમ, શોહોર પાડવી અને ઘાટું પડે એટલા જોરના આવાજથી બોલીને, દોડધામ, મારામારી અને અફડાતફડી કરવી! જીહાં તીહાંથી લોકને ખુબ હસાવવાની મતલબે, થોડોવાર દીવાના લોક જેવા થઈ પડવું એટલે સઉથી સરસ નાટક તેઓએ કીધો, એટલુંજ નાટક વીશે તે છોકરાઓ સમજેછે! વારૂ આ બીના તો એક કોરે રહી. પણ જે જુવાન કુમલીવયના બચ્ચાં અને છોકરાઓ આવા નાટકોમાં સામેલ થાયછે, જે કુમલી લસણ જેવાઓનાં કુમલાં ભેજાંમાં હુજુર તો આ દુનીયાદારીના કામ કારભાર વીશે એક રતીભાર પણ વીચાર ઉત્પન્ન નહી થયો હશે, તેવા નીર્દોષ બચ્ચાંઓ નાટકમાં સામેલ થઈ સ્ત્રી જાતનો વેશ લઈ, સઘળી રીતે ઓરતોની મોઆફક દેખાવાની કોશેશ અને મેહનત કરેછે, ઉઠવામાં, બેસવામાં, ચાલવામાં, વાતચીતમાં અને સઘળી બીજી પ્રકારે સ્ત્રી જાત જેવા બની જવા માંગેછે, તેમના માંબાપોને એક ચેતવણી તરીકે જણાવાની હમો ફરજ સમજીએછ કે આવી તરેની તાલીમ તેમનાં કુમલી વયનાં બાલકોએ લીધાથી, તે બચ્ચાંઓ મરદના ગુણો ખોઇને સ્ત્રીની ખાસીએત પકડવાના. બીજા દીલગીરી ઉપજાવનારા શબ્દોમાં બોલીએ તો તેમના છોકરાઓ નામરદ અને આસીબાએલા જેવાં થઈ પડવાના, આ વીશે તેઓએ ખુબ સંભાળ રાખવી. નાટકનું કામ આવાં બચ્ચાંઓને મુતલક લાયક છેજ નહી. યુરોપ અને અમેરીકા ખંડમાં મોહોટ મોટા નાટકો થાયછે, જીહાં નાટકની પુરતી ખુબી તેઓ સમજેલા છે, તીહાં વટીક સ્ત્રી તરફથી જેબી બોલવા ચાલવાનું હોયછે તે સ્ત્રી જાતને પોતાને સામેલ કરીને તેની પાસે નાટકનો તે ભાગ બોલાવેછે અને કોઇખી ચોકસ કારણ શીવાય ઓરત જાતનું કામ મરદને કભીપણ બજાવાને આપતા નથી, તેમજ મરદની વીતી તેનો ભાગ ઓરત બજાવતી નથી. પણ હીયાં મુંબઈમાં તો આપણા દેશી નાટક કરનારોએ જે વલાણ પકડી છે તે ખચીત ઘણીજ સુખન નાખવા જોગ અને પાછળથી ભય ભરેલાં પરીણામ ઊત્પન્ન કરે એવી લાગેછે!

આવા જુવાન શખસોના જનમ સુધીના ફાયદા તરફ ધીયાન પોંહોંચાડી હમો દીલોજાનથી તેમને ભલામણ કરીએછ કે આવાં કામમાં તેઓએ આવી કુમલી વયથી કધી નહી પડવું જોઈએ. એમાં તેમની આકેબત ખરાબી થવાની છે તે સત જાણવું. બીજી અગતની ચેતવણી એ આપવાની છે કે આવા જુવાન

કુમલી વયના છોકરાઓએ નાટકમાં સામેલ થઈ, એશકની બાબદો ઉપર ધીયાન પોંહોંચાડવું, એબી તેમને નાસજાવાર છે. તેઓએ સારી પેઠે યાદ રાખવી કે કુમલી વય તે નશીયત અને સારી કેળવણી લેવાનો વખત છે. જેમ કુમલા બાંબુને વાળીએ તેમ તે વળી શકેછે, પણ તે મોટો અને પુખ્ત થયો એટલે તે કધી મરડાઈ શકાવાનો નથી, અને જોર કરી મરડસું તો તે ભાંગી જવાનો. તે મુજબ આવી કુમલી અને નાહાની વયમાં મનશકિતને તથા શરીર શકિતને જેવી વલણ આપીએ તેવી તે પકડી શકશે. તેથી જો બાલપણુથીજ ઇશક, આરામ, અને લુચ્ચાઈ લફંગાઈના વીચારો ઉપર મન લગાડયું અને તે બાબદનો અભ્યાસ કીધો તો મોટી વયે પોંહોંચતાં આવીજ બાબદની વલણ ઉપર મન લાગેલું રેહેવાનું. પછવાડેથી તેને બીજી બાબદ ઉપર ફેરવી લગાડવું મુશ્કેલ થઈ પડશે. હમોને ઘણીજ ચીંતા લાગેછે કે નાટકનાં કામકાજમાં જે કુમલી વયના છોકરાઓ પડેછે અથવા પડ્યા છે, જેમના માંબાપો પોતાના આવી નાંધલી વયના છોકરાઓને એવાં કામમાં પડવાની રજા આપેછે, તેમને પછવાડેથી ઘણો પસ્તાવો ખમવો પડશે. કસાએલી નાટક ટોળીના ઉમરે પોંહોંચેલા શખસો, જેઓએ નાટક વીશે થોડી ઘણી સારી માહીતગારી મેળવી છે, તેમને હમો ભલામણ કરીએછ કે તેઓએ પોતાની મંડળીમાં જેટલા ૨૦) વીસ વરસની અંદરના નીશાળે કેળવણી લેવા લાયક છોકરાઓ હોય, તેમને દુર કરવા, અને હવે પછી એવાઓને કધી ફરીને સામેલ નહી કરવાં. હમો ભલામણ કરીએછ કે આપણા દેશીઓ આ વીશે ચોકસાઈ અને સંભાળ રાખી પોતાનાં ઊધરતાં બચ્ચાંઓને એવાં કામમાં સામેલ નહી થવા દેશે. છેલી હમો અરજ ગુજારીએછ કે આવા ચુલબુલીયા કેટલાક જુવાનો, જેઓ પોતાના માંબાપની નાફરમાની કરી, પોતાના વડીલોના હુકમ તોડી, પોતાના મીત્રોની શીકામણની વીરૂધ ચાલી, ઢોંગ ભરેલા નાટકો કરેછે, અને મોહોટ મોહોટી જાહેર ખબરો છપાવી, તેમાં લોકને એવું જાહેર કરેછે કે આજે તો "એક નવી અફલાતુન નાટક ટોળી પોતાનો પેહેલી વારનો ખેલ કરી બતલાવનાર છે," કાલે વળી કોઈ બીજીજ ટોળી "જુની આદરગોશાશસ્પ નાટક મંડળી નામે જાહેરખબર છપાવેછે," અને પરમદીને કોઈ ઢોંગી ટોળી "નામદાર જીહાં બખસની નાટક ટોળીનું નામ ધારણ કરીને લોકને ઠગાવા બાહેર પડેછે,"

તેમના નાટકો જોવાને આપણાં બીચારા, આખર કરે પણ પોતાના નીયાગાઓનાં નામ સાંભળીને સેહેલાઈથી ઉસકેરાઈ શકાય એવા ખરા બુનીયાદ પારશીઓ દીલાજાનથી પોતાનો સકમાઇનો પઇશો ખરચી સામેલ થાયછે, તેમ તેઓએ નહી કરવું જોઈએછ. હમો સઘળા વીચારવંત આપણા દેશીઓને અરજ કરી જણાવીએછ કે તેવા ઢોંગીઓના નાટકોમાં તેઓએ કદીપણ જવું નહી, અને આવા નાદાનોને ઉત્તેજન આપવું નહી. આપણાં દેશીઓમાં હાલ ફકોરા નાટકનું જે એક નવું દરદ દાખલ થતું જાયછે, તેને પેવસ થતાંજ ડાંભવું જોઇએછ, અને તેમ થશે તોજ તેનો અટકાવ થશે.

ડાકતર ભાઉ દાજીનાં ઉપર જણાવેલાં મદ્રાસમાં મકાન ઉપર હમો ગયા હતા તે દીવશે, મદ્રાસની લેજીસલેટીવ કૌનસીલના તે વખતના દેશી મેમબર, મસ્નાર ધી હાનરેબલ સાધા ગોપા ચારલુ, મુલાકાત લેવાને આવીયા હતા, તેમની સાથે હમો સઘળાની ઓળખાણ થઈ.

હીયાંથી નીકળ્યા તે મદ્રાસની મેડીકલ કાલેજ જોવાને ગયા. રવીવારનો દીવસ હતો તેથી એ મકાન ઉપર કોઈ પ્રોફેસર અથવા વીદ્યાર્થી હાજર નહી હતા. મદ્રાસથી હમને રૂખસદ લેવાનો દીવસ પણ ઘણોજ નજદીક આવેલો હતો, અને ફરીને આ મકાન જોવા આવવાની હમને ઊમેદ નહી હતી, તેથી તીહાંનાં રખેવાળની સાથે આ મકાનમાં ફરીવળીને જે કંઈ નજરે પડ્યું તે જોયું હતું. ઈમારતની બાંધણી, આપણી મુંબઈની મેડીકલ કાલેજ જેવી લાયક કોશાદ અને સગવડ ભરેલી હમારા જોયામાં નહી આવી હતી, તોયપણ આ ઈમારતની ગોઠવણમાં વૈદ્યકશાસ્ત્રને લગતી જુદી જુદી બાબદો શીખવવાને, જુદા જુદા વર્ગોને સારૂ, કેટલીક સગવડ, તથા જોઇતો સરસરંજામ, સુંદર નકસા, તથા પુસ્તકોના સંગ્રહસાથે, શરીરનાં જુદા જુદા ભાગનું જ્ઞાન આપવાને બનાવેલા મીણની મેળવણીનાં નમુનાં, વીગરે બીજો ઘણો સામાન સારી રીતે પુરો પાડેલા હતા.

હીંયાંથી નીકળીને યુરોપીયન હાસપીટલ જોઇ, અને સર ચાર્લસ ત્રીવલીયનનો "પીપલ્સ પાર્ક" જે આગળ અધુરી રીતે જોવામાં આવીયો હતો તે ફરીને બરોબર સારીપેઠે જોવાને પાછા તીહાં ગયા હતા. મદ્રાસના લોકને સેલાગહ, ફરવા હરવા અને મોજ જોગ કરવાને બની આવવાસારૂ "બ્લાક ટાઊન" ની પશ્ચીમ દીશાયે આ પાર્કને સારૂ જમીનનો મોહોટો ભાગ રોકયામાં આવ્યો છે, જેનું નામ "નવા શેહેરનું

મેદાન" કરીને પાડ્યું છે. આ બાગમાં પાણીના નાહાનાં મોહોટાં તલાવો અને સરોવરો આવેલાં છે, તેહેમાંનાં બે સરોવરની વચમાં એક નાહાનો જમીનનો કડકો ઘેરાયલો છે, તે એક બેટ અથવા ટાપુ જેવો થઈ પડ્યો છે. આ ટાપુ ઉપર લોક બોટમાં બેસીને ફરવા જાયછે, લોકની ગમતને સારૂ તરેવાર જાતનાં જનાવરો, પશુ અને પક્ષીયોનો પણ એક મોહોટો સંગ્રહ હીયાં કરી રાખવાની ગોઠવણ થઈ છે. હમે જીયારે તીહાં ગયા હતા, તીયારે કેટલાંએક જનાવરો એકઠાં કરેલાં હતાં અને બીજાં આવનાર હતાં. સરકારી મ્યુઝીયમમાં એકઠાં કરેલાં સઘળાં જાનવરોને પણ એજ ઠેકાણે રાખવાનો વીચાર થયલો હતો. બચ્ચાંઓને રમવા અને મોહોટાં માણસોને કસરત કરવા અને તાલીમ ખેલવાની સગવડ અને લાયક જગા આ ઠેકાણે કરી આપવાની પણ ગોઠવણ થવાની છે એવું હમુને તે વખતે જણાવીયામાં આવીયું હતું. આ પાર્ક હમોએ જોયો તે વખતે પુરી હાલતમાં આવેલો નહી હતો, પણ જારે એની અંદર કરવા ધારેલી સઘળી ગોઠવણો અને રચના પુરી થશે તીયારે મદ્રાસ શેહેરમાં એ "પીપલ્સ પાર્ક" એક મનોરંજક અને સઘળાને આનંદ અને ગમત આપનારી ફરવા હરવાની જગા થઈ પડશે, એમાં કંઈ શક નથી.

"પીપલ્સ પાર્ક" જોયાપછી, હમારા મીત્ર ડાકતર ભાઉએ મદ્રાસની "આગ્રી હાર્ટીકલચરલ ગારડન" જોઈ નહી હતી, તે દેખાડવાને તીહાં ગયા, પણ પાછી સાંજ પડી ગયાથી આ ઠેકાણાં ઉપર વધારે વાર થોભી નહી શકાયું હતું.

આવીશે થોડીક વીગત તા૦ ૨૩ જાનેવારીના અહેવાલમાં આપી છે. હીયાંથી નીકળીને લાર્ડ એલફીનસ્ટનનાં વખતમાં કીનારાની બાજુયેથી જે નવો રસ્તો બનાવ્યામાં આવ્યો છે તેવીશે હમોયે તા૦ ૨૦ મી જાનેવારીના અહેવાલમાં વીગત આપી છે, તીહાં ફરીને પાછા "બ્લાક ટાઉન" માં આવ્યા હતા.

મદ્રાસથી ૩૫) માઈલ દુર, મહાબલીપુરમ કરીને એક ગામ છે, તીહાં હીંદુઓનાં પુરાનાં દેવળ દેહરાં અને પથરમાં મોટું કોતરકામ ઘણી તરેનું છે તે જોવાની ઇચ્છા ડાકતરને, મદ્રાસ શેહેર જોવાનાં કરતાં વધારે થયાથી, જેવા હમે સઘળા મદ્રાસ શેહેરમાં આવી પુગા કે લાગલે બીજેજ દીવસે ડાકતર એબલાજ તેતરફ કુચ કરી ગયા હતા. મદ્રાસ શેહેરમાં હમારૂં રેહવું ઘણાજ થોડા દાહાડા થયું હતું, અને "મેલ સ્ટીમર" આવવાની વખ્ત ઘણીજ નજદીક હતી, તેથી હમારાથી મહાબલીપુરમ જવાઈ શકાયું નહી હતું.

મહાબલીપુરમને ઇંગ્રેજ લોક "ધી સેવન પગોડાસ" એટલે સાત દેહરાંને નામે ઓળખેછે. હીંદુ લોકની કથા પ્રમાણે આ ગામ આગળા વખતમાં એક ઘણુંજ મોહોટું શેહેર હતું, પણ હાલ દરીયા ફરીવળ્યાથી તે શેહેરનો ઘણોક ભાગ ગરક થઈ ગયલો છે. મદ્રાસની "અદીયાર" નદી આગળથી નીકલતાં કનાલને મારગે ઘણીજ સેહેલાઈ અને આસાનીથી થોડાક કલાકની બોટની મુસાફરીથી તીહાં જવાઈ શકાયછે. જેઓને પુરાણી ઈમારતો અને કોતરકામો જોવાનો શોખ હોય તેઓએ મંહાબલીપુરમનાં જુનાં દેહરાં જરૂર કરીને જોવાં જોઇયેછ, તેથી તેમનો ફેરો ફોકટ જશે નહી, આવું હમોને ડાકતરે પણ કેહું હતું, અને આવું ઘણાં જણનું મત છે. ડાકતર ભાઉએ આ ઠેકાણે કંઈ નવું જોયું નહી હતું, તોયપણ ૩૫) માઇલની મુસાફરીનો બદલો તેમનાં વીચાર પ્રમાણે તીહાંની પુરાણી ઈમારતો અને પથરનાં કોતરકામો જોવાથી વળી રહ્યો હતો.

મદ્રાસની ટંકશાળ પણ એક જોવા લાયક મકાન છે, જેઓએ મુંબઈની ટંકશાળ જોઈ હશે તેમને આ ખાતું જોવાની નવાઈ નથી. મદ્રાસમાં આ ખાતું ઇસિવી સન ૧૮૦૭ માં ચાલુ થયું તેની આગમચ શિક્કા પાડવાનું "કંત્રાકટ દેશીયોને આપ્યામાં આવતું હતું, અને શિક્કા બરોબર પાડવાને "કંત્રાકટરો" ઉપર સરકારની તરફથી "મીંટ માસ્તર" અને "આસે માસ્તર" ઉપરીપણું ચલાવતા હતા. હાલ એ ખાતું સરકાર પોતેજ ચલાવેછે. આ ખાતું સાંચા વગેરે સઘળી બાબતમાં સંપૂર્ણ છે. "બ્લાક ટાઉન" માં "સાત બાઉડી" એટલે સાત કુવા નામની જગા છે તેની પડોસમાંજ મદ્રાસની ટંકશાળનું ખાતું છે.

મદ્રાસના ખરાબ દરીયા અને મોજાને લીધે બોટમાં બેસીને સેલગાહ કરી મજાહ ભોગવવાને નજદીકીમાં તેવી સારી જગો તીહાંના લોકને નહી મળી આવીયાથી, "એનોર" કરીને મદ્રાસથી નવ દસ માઇલ દુર એક ઠેકાણું છે, તીહાં ખારા પાણીનાં સરોવરો છે તેમાં બોટોમાં બેસીને સેલગાહ કરવાને યુરોપીયન લોક ઘણુંકરીને જાયછે, તેહેની સાથે માછલી અને કાલું ખાનાર શોખીયોને જેટલો જોઇયે તેટલો ખોરાક આ ઠેકાણે મળી શકેછે, એટલા ઉપરથી એ ઠેકાણે ઘણાં ઇંગ્રેજો તેહેવારનાં અને ગરમીનાં દીવસો ઉપર કાલું ખાવાની મોજમારવાને જાયછે. આ ઠેકાણે મીઠાંનો પણ ઘણો પાક થાયછે.

મદ્રાસની "આબસરવેટરી" વેધશાળા ઘણી પુરાણી બાંધેલી ઇમારત છે. આ

ખાતું, ઈસવી સન ૧૭૯૩ ના સાલમાં કોરટ આફ ડેરેકટરો જીઆરે હીંદુસ્થાન ઉપર અમલ ચલાવતા હતા તે વખતથી ચાલુ થયલું છે. હાલ તેમાં તારા જોવાના અને હવામાં થતી લોહોચુંબકી અસરો નોંધવાના ઘણા ઉપયોગી યંત્રો ગોઠવેલાં છે. આ ખાતું મુંબઈની "આબસરવેટરી" ના જેવુંજ છે.

મદ્રાસમાં માંબાપ વગરનાં લાચાર છોકરાંઓની બરદાસ્ત કરવાનાં ઘણાં ખાતાં છે, તેમાં અગત કરીને લશ્કરી ખાતાંને લગતાં પુરૂષ અને સ્ત્રીને લગતાં બે જુદાં જુદાં ખાતાં છે. પેહેલું ઈસવી સન ૧૭૮૮ માં અને બીજું સન ૧૭૮૬ માં ઉભું થયલું છે. આ ખાતાંઓનું કામ ઘણીજ સારી રીતે ચાલેછે, અને કેહેછે કે પુરૂષોનાં ખાતાંમાંથી નજદીક ૩૩૦૦ છોકરાઓ ખાવાપીવાની સઘળી જરૂરની ચીજ મેળવતાં, સારી કેળવણી લઈ બાહાર પડ્યા છે. તેમાંનાં આજે ઘણાં જણ સરકારી ચાકરીમાં રહેલા છે, કેટલાક વેપારીઓ બનીયા છે, કેટલા એક જુદા જુદા ધંધા રોજગારી થઈ પડ્યા છે, અને કેટલા એક મીશનરીઓ તરીકે કામે લાગેલા છે. જેઓનાં માંબાપ અથવા બેમાંથી એક પણ મરણ પામ્યું હોય, તેમનાં છોકરાંઓને બીજાઓ કરતાં પેહેલાં આ ખાતાંમાં લેવાનો કાયદો રાખીયો છે, આપછી જેઓનાં માંબાપ હોનારત અને અકસમાત કારણથી અશકત થઈ ગયાં હોય, તેમાંનાં બચ્ચાંઓને લેછે; અને માત્ર થોડાંજ છોકરાંઓને, તેમની પાસથી ખાવાપીવાનાં અને શીખવાનાં ખરચનો લવાજમ લઈ દાખલ કરવામાં આવેછે.

માબાપ વગરની છોકરીઓનાં ખાતાંમાં સરકાર અને લોક તરફથી પૈસાની વાર્શીક મદદ થાયછે. એની અંદર છોકરીયોને ઘરસંસારનું કામકાજ, સીવવા સાંધવાનું, કપડાં ધોવાનું અને આજારી માણસોની બરદાસ્ત કેમ કરવી, આવી બાબદો શીખવવામાં આવેછે. જે છોકરીયોમાં, ઘણીજ ચંચળ અને હોશીયાર નીવડવાનાં લક્ષણો આગમચથીજ દેખાયછે, તેવી છોકરીયોને શીક્ષકનું કામ કેમ ચલાવવું તે વીરો કેળવણી આપવામાં આવેછે. આ ખાતાંનું કામ કેટલાએક સરકારી અમલદારોની પરોપકારી બાયડીયો ચલાવેછે તેથી કેળવણી તથા બીજી તરેની તરબીયત આપવા પછવાડે આ ખાતાંમાં ઘણી સારી તપાસ રેહેછે, જેથી આ ખાતાંનો કારભાર ઘણોજ મનમાનતી અને ફાયદા ભરેલી રીતે ચાલેછે.

હમો દીલોજાનથી ઉમેદ રાખીએછ કે જેમ કેટલીક ભલી યુરોપીયન બાનુઓ આવા ઉપયોગી ખાતાં પછવાડે તેમનાં દીલ લગાડી પરોપકારી કામો કરેછે, તે

મુજબ આપણી ભલી દેશી સ્ત્રીઓ પણ કરશે. આવી આગેવાની આપણી કોમની પેહેલા દરજાવાળી ગૃહસ્થ સ્ત્રીઓથી થવી જોઈએછ, કારણ આવાજ દરજાવાળી બાનુઓ આ કામને લાયકની છે. ઘણીક બાબદમાં દરજો જાળવવાની મોટી જરૂર છે.

દરજો ખુદરતી હદ છે, તે હદમાં રેહી હરેક કામ કરવું એમાંજ ડાપણ છે. આ ઉપરથી એક સવાલ ઉઠશે કે પેહેલા વર્ગની સ્ત્રીઓ કેળવણી પામેલી નથી તારે તેઓથી આવાં કામમાં આગેવાની કેમ કરી શકાશે? આ સવાલનો જવાબ સેહેલ છે. મોટાં કામમાં આગેવાની કરવાસારૂ જો કેળવણી સાથે દરજાવાળા શખ્સો સામેલ નહી હોયા તો તે એક મોટી ખુટ ગણાવાની. મુંબઈ શેહેરમાં આજે આ એક અગતના સવાલ વીશે અજાએબ તરેની ભુલ ચાલી જાયછે. ઘણા જુવાન કેળવણી પામેલા પુરૂશો આવું ધારેછે કે બોજવાળા સાહેબોની મદદ વગર, ઉતરતી પદ્વિવાળાઓ એખલાજ કોઈબી મોટું કામ માથે ઉઠાવી તે ફતેમંદીથી પુરૂં બજાવી શકશે. હમારૂં મત એઓથી તદન ઉલટુંજ છે. તો જુઓ મેહરબાન વાંચનારો, સ્ત્રીકેળવણી જેવું અગતનું કામ, જો કે વચલી પદ્વિવાળા શીખેલાઓએ ઉઠી તો ઉભું કીધું, પણ તેને ફતેમંદીથી અનજામ પોહોંચાડવાને, માતબર અને દરજાવાળા શેઠીઆઓની મદદ લેવી પડી હતી કે નહી? આવી મદદ માંગવાની જરૂર પડી હતી કે નહી? ત્રણ શેઠીઆઓએ આગેવાની કરી, શીખેલાઓનો હાત પકડી તેમને આગળ પાડયા હતા કે નહી? શેઠ ફરામજી નુશરવાનજી પટેલ, શેઠ ખુરશેદજી નુશરવાનજી કામાજી, શેઠ ધનજીભાઈ નુશરવાનજી કામાજી, જેવા દેશી આગેવાનોએ છુપી અથવા જાહેર મદદ કીધી હતી કે નહી? આ વીશે કોઇને અણજાણ્યું નથી. એઓની મદદ નહી મળી હતે તો સ્ત્રીકેળવણીનું કામ હમો કહીએછ કે કદાચ નહી પારપડી શકતે. એજ પ્રમાણે પારસી લોકને તેમના વારસા હીસા અને લગન તથા તલાક સંબંધી સરકાર તરફથી જે ધારા મળીયા છે તે પણ શેઠીઆઓનીજ આગેવાનીથી મળીયા છે કે નહીં? આવા બીજા ઘણા દાખલા આપવા માગીએ તો મોજુદ છે. માટે ઘણાં માહાભારત કામો જે આજસુધી થયાં છે તે સઘળાં કેળવણીજ પામેલાઓની એખલાની આગેવાનીથી નથી થયલાં, પણ તે સઘળા કાંમોમાં કેળવણી પામેલાઓને દેશી આગેવાનોએ પોતાના બોજ અને દરજાથી અચ્છી રીતે ટેકો

આવીયો છે તેથી બન્યાં છે. આવીજ રીતે બંધે તરફથી ઘટતી સમજુતી અને સંપ થયાથીજ મોહોટ મોટાં કામો પાર પડયાં છે અને બીજા મોહોટ મોટાં કામો પાર પડવાની ઉમેદ છે.

તા૦ ૨૬ મી જાનેવારી. તા૦ ૨૫ જાનેવારીની સાંજના કપતાન મીચલે પોતાની કબુલાત મુજબ હમને ખબર આપી કે બીજે દીને એટલે તા૦ ૨૬ મીએ સહવારના પોહોરમાં "મ્યુઝીયમ" જોવાને આવવું. આ દીને કલકત્તા તરફ જતી "ઇંગ્લંડની મેલ સ્ટીમર" ની આવી પોંહોંચવાની વકી થઈ રહેલી હતી, તેથી તાકીદેથી સહવારના સકારેથી "મ્યુઝીયમ" જોવાને ગયા હતા, અને તે ઠેકાણે કપતાન મીચલ પણ પોતાની કબુલાત મુજબ સકારેથી આવી હાજર થયલો હતો.

મદ્રાસનું સંગ્રહસ્થાન ઘણુંજ મોહોટું અને ઘણી એક બાબદોમાં સંપૂર્ણ છે. મુંબઈનું મ્યુઝીયમ તેની આગળ કુચ બીસાતમાં નથી. ખુદરતની હમા જીનસોનો એક અચ્છો પસંદ પડતો જમાવ આ ઠેકાણાં ઉપર કરી રાખેલો છે, જેમાં એકુ બે કલાક ફકત અમસ્થા ફરીવળીયા હોઈએ તો તેથી આ દુનીયાના જુદા જુદા ભાગોમાં કેવી કેવી વસ્તુઓ ઉત્પંન થાયછે, એવીરો પુશ્કળ જ્ઞાન મળી શકેછે. કપતાન મીચલે આ સઘળી જીનસોને જુદા જુદા વર્ગોમાં ઘણી ચોકસાઈ ભરેલી રીતે ગોઠવી છે. પૃથ્વીમાં જણાયલી કોમનાં જુદા જુદા પોશાક, તેમની તરેવાર રીતભાંત અને સંસાર વેહવારમાં વપરાતી તરેવાર જીનસો, વાસણ અને કારીગીરીની વસ્તુઓનો એક મોહોટો જમાવ કરી તે સઘળો એક એલાહેદા ઓરડામાં ગોઠવી રાખેલો છે. મદ્રાસ શેહેરની સરહદમાં જુદી જુદી જાતની જે માછલીઓ મળી શકેછે તે દરેક જાતના નમુનાનો એક મોહોટો સંગ્રહ કરેલો છે અને તેમાં નવી નવી જાતની માછલીઓના નમુના ઉમેરાતા જાયછે. હમોએ જે વખતે આ સંગ્રહ જોયો તારે તેમાં ૫૦૦) પાનસો જુદી જુદી જાતની માછલીના નમુના એકઠા કરેલા હતા. માછલીને ચીરી તેના પેટાખાનાંમાંની જીનસો કાહાડી લઈ તે ઠેકાણે દવાની મેળવણીથી બનાવેલો રૂ ભરીને પેટ પાછું સીવી લીધું હતું. આવી રીતે તજુમલથી બનાવેલા માછલીના નમુના આપણને જાણે તાજી હવડાંજ પકડેલી માછલી હોય, એવા નજરે દેખાયછે અને તેમના તરેવાર રંગો આબેહુબ રહેલા છે. એક મોહોટો સંગ્રહ જુના પુરાણા અને હાલના ચલની સીક્કાઓનો કરેલો છે, તે જોવા લાયક છે. સીક્કાનાં નાંમ, તે કહે ઠેકાણે અને

શેહેરમાં વપરાયછે, તે કહયા વખતમાં આગળ વપરાતા હતા, કોણ પાદશાહાના તે સીક્કા હતા, તેનો સને અને એ ઉપરથી તવારીખને લગતી કેટલીક નોંધ, સીક્કાઓ સાથે કરીને રાખી છે, જે જોનારને ઘણીજ ઉપયોગી અને જ્ઞાન આપનાર છે. આખી પૃથ્વી ઉપરના દેશોમાં મળતી સઘળી પ્રકારની ધાતુ અને ખાણીજ વસ્તુઓનો એક ઘણોજ અમુંલ્ય જથો હીયાં જમાવેલો છે, અને તેની રચના પણ કાયદાસર કરેલી છે, જેથી ખંડેખંડની જુદી જુદી જીનસો સેહેલાઇથી માલુમ પડી શકેછે.

આ સંગ્રહસ્થાનને લગતો એક મોટો બાગ કરેલો છે, તેમાં જીવતાં જાનવરોનો પણ એક નાહાનો સરખો જમાવ કરેલો છે. આ જમાવની હજુ તો માત્ર શીરૂઆત થયલી હતી. હમો જોવાને ગયા તે વખતે બાગમાં તરેવાર જાતના પક્ષીયો, વાંદરા, હરણ, જંગલી ડુકર, ગેંડો, રીછ, ચીત્તો, વાઘ, અને આવાં બીજાં જાનવરો એકઠાં કરેલાં હતાં. આ સઘળાં જાનવરોને આ મ્યુઝીયમના બાગમાંથી કાહાડીને મદ્રાસના "પીપલ્સ પાર્ક" નાંમના મોહોટા બાગમાં રાખવાની ગોઠવણ થવાની છે એવું તે વખતે હમારા સાંભળવામાં આવીયું હતું.

મ્યુઝીયમ સાથે એક મોટું પુસ્તકખાનું અને વાંચવા સારૂ એક મોહોટું દીવાનખાનું પણ જોડેલું છે. હીયાં ખુદરતી વીદ્યાને લગતી બાબદો ઉપર સત્તા ભરેલાં પુસ્તકો, તથા બીજી તરેવાર બાબદોને લગતી ચોપડીઓ, ચોપાનીયાં, વીગેરેનો જમાવ કરેલો છે. માત્ર આબરૂવાળા ગૃહસ્થોનેજ આ મકાનમાં દાખલ થવાની રજા આપીયામાં આવેછે.

કપતાન મીચલે થોડી વારમાં હમને મ્યુઝીયમનો ઘણો ખરો ભાગ ઘણી મેહેરબાનીથી ભરેલી રાહે દેખડાવીયો હતો, અને જેટલીવાર એની સાથે હમો ફરીયા હતા, તેટલી વારમાં પુષ્કળ જાણવાજોગ બાબદો વીશે જ્ઞાન હમને તેનાથી મળ્યું હતું. આ લશ્કરી અમલદાર ઘણોજ મીલનસાર હતો અને ખુદરતી વીદ્યાના જ્ઞાનનો તો જાણે એક મોહોટો ભંડાર હોય એવો તેની વાતચીત ઉપરથી તે હમને જણાયો હતો. જો હમને વધારે વખત મળીયો હતે તો આવા જ્ઞાની પુરૂષની સંગતમાં હમોએ "મ્યુઝીયમ" જોવાને ખચીત રોકયા હતે, પણ સહવારનાં ૧૧) વાગામાં "મેલ સ્ટીમર" આવી પુગવાની ખબર તોપની મારફતથી સાંભળવામાં આવી તેથી આ ઠેકાણેથી કપતાન મીચલનો ઉપકાર માની તુરત રૂખશદ લેવી

પડી, અને તાબડતોબ પી. એંડ ઓ. કંપનીની આફીસમાં જઈ કલકત્તે જવાના ઉતારૂ તરીકેની "પાસીજ"ની ટીકીટો લઈ લીધી, અને તેજ આફીસના કારભારી-ઓમાંથી એક જણે, હમારો સઘળો સામન સ્ટીમર ઉપર પોહોંચાડવાનું કામ ઉપાડ લેવાની ઇચ્છા જણાવીયાથી, હમોએ તે તુરત તેને સોંપી દીધું, કારણ હમારા હાતમાં વખત હવે પુરતો નહી રહેલો હતો.

સહવારથી આ દીવસે જરા વાદળ થઈ આવીયું હતું, પણ બે વાગામાં તે વધી પડયું હતું. વરસાદની ઝીણી ઝીણી છાંટી આવવા માંડી હતી. જરા રહી વરસાદ વધ્યો હતો, અને પવન જોરમાં ફુકવા માંડયો હતો, અને તે થોડી વારમાં ઘણોજ જોસ ભરેલો થઈ પડયો હતો. એવામાં ખબર પડી કે એક સ્ટીમર બારામાં આવતી મોજાનાં જોરથી, ખરાબા ઉપર ચઢી ગઈ છે. આથી ઘભરાટ વધી પડયો, સ્ટીમર ઉપર જવાને બોટો મળી નહી, કેમકે પી. એંડ ઓ. કંપની-નો કેટલોક સામન સ્ટીમર ઉપર લઈ જવાને કેટલી એક બોટો આગળથી રોકાયલી હતી. તેમ વળી બીજી બોટવાળાઓ તોફાનનાં સબબથી નાહીમત થઈ પડ્યા હતા. ચાર વાગામાં દરીયો પુષ્કળ જોરમાં આવી ગયો હતો. જેમ તેમ સમજાવતાં એક બોટવાળો હાથમાં આવ્યો. તેની બોટમાં હમે છ જણાં લાગલાજ બેસી ગયા. કીનારા ઉપરથી બોટમાં ચઢતાંજ પેહેલી મોહોટી અડચણ નડી હતી. બોટ ભાગ્યેજ ચાર સેકંડ સુધી પણ સીધી ઊભી રહી શકતી હતી, જો કે છેક કીનારા ઉપરનાં પાણીમાં તે તરતી હતી તોયપણ મોજાનાં જોરથી તે જબરી ઊથલ પાથલ થયા કરતી હતી. અંતે ખુદાનું નામ લઈ, હલેસાં મારી આગળ વધ્યા પણ પેલા ત્રણ મોજા જે મદ્રાસના બારાનું એક મોહોટું સંકટ અને જીવનો કાળ ગણ્યામાં આવેછે, તે વટાવતાં નજદીક પોણો કલાક સુધી, જીવ ખોવા જેટલાં ફાંફાં મારવાં પડ્યાં હતાં. જેટલી મેહેનત કરીને આગળ જઇયે તે સઘળી મેહેનત એક મીનીટની અંદર મોજાનાં સાંભા ઘસારા બંધ અને ઘસડી લઈ જનાર જોરથી વ્યર્થ જતી હતી, અને મોજો બોટને કીનારા તરફ એક પલવારમાં પાછી ખેંચી લાવતો હતો. કીનારેથી જરા આગળ પાણીમાં વધીયા પછી હમોને એક આફત જેવો દેખાવ જોવા પડયો હતો. મોજો કોઈવાર બોટને એટલી તો ઉંચે ચઢાવી દેતો હતો કે હમો જાણે આકાશમાં અને દરીયો નીચે છેક ઊંડો થઈ ગયલો નજર આવતો હતો, અને વળી બીજી વખતે મોજો એખલો એટલો તો ઊંચો ચઢી જતો

હતો કે, હમારી બોટ જાણે પાણીમાં ઓઓ ગરક થઈ જશે એટલી ઊંડાણમાં હમો આવી પડતા હતા : અને આવો જબરદસ્ત ઊંચે ચઢેલો મોજો પછી જાણે એકદમ તોપો છુટી હોય એવા ભયંકર આવાજે આવીને બોટઉપર અફળાઈ પડતો હતો. તેહેનો આંચકો અને આવાજ અંદર બેડેલાઓને ધભરાવી અને બેહેરા કરી નાખતો હતો. મોજાનું પાણી બોટઉપર રહીને ચાલ્યાયું જતું હતું અને અંદર બેડેલા ભીનાઈતરબોર થઇ ગયા હતા, તથા સામાન ઉપર તથા હમારાં મોહોડાં ઉપર વારંવાર પાણીની છોડ જબરી લાગતી હતી. તેમજ મછવામાં ધામટ પણ એટલું વધારે થઈ પડયું હતું કે કોળીઓ સખત મેહેનતથી તે પાછું બાહેર કાહાડી શકતા હતા. મોજાના આવા સખત આંચકા ખમવાને મદ્રાસની સીવી લીધેલાં પાટીયાંનીજ બોટ ટકી શકે એવી છે. જો આવા આંચકા આપણી કલાસીબંધ જડી લીધેલાં પાટીયાંની બોટને લાગે તો હમો ધારીએછ કે આરધા કલાકમાં તેના ફાડચે ફાડચાં થઈ જાય એમાં કંઈજ શખ નથી. બોટ ઊપર બાર હલેસાં મારનાર મદ્રાસનાં મજબુત કોળીયો હતા. તેઓએ સખત મેહેનતથી અને ભારે બુમો પાડીને જેટલું જોર થઈ શકે તેટલું મોજાની સાંમે કીધું હતું, તોયપણ ધણીએક વારે અતીશય મેહેનત કરતાં, માત્ર બે મોજા વટાવ્યા હતાં, અને હજુ તો ત્રીજો જીવ લેનાર મોજો, વટાવવાને બાકી હતો, તેટલામાં તેઓ સઘળા થાકી ગયા હતા !

સઘળાની હીમતની આ વખતે અચ્છી તપાસ થઈ હતી. હમારા સઘળાનાં મોહોડાં રૂની પુણી જેવાં સુફેદ થઇ ગયાં હતાં ! હમારા જનમમાં મદ્રાસનાં બારાનું સંકટ જોયું નહી હતું, અને જે શાભળ્યું હતું તે નજર આગળ આવી એકદમ ઊભું રહ્યું હતું તોયપણ આ પુસ્તક લખનારનાં સફરવીશે કાચા અનુભવ પ્રમાણે તે વખતે તેને તે સંકટનું પુરેપુરૂં ગ્નાન થયલું નહી હતું. તેથી જારે બોટ વાંકી વળતી હતી અને અંદરનાં લોક બુમો પાડતા હતા, ત્યારે સઘળાનો જીવ કેટલો જોખમમાં પડતો હતો એ વીશે સઘળા દીલગીર થતા હતા, પણ હમોને પેલા શેાર અને પોકારથી હસવું આવતું હતું. પણ જારે ત્રીજો મોજો પસાર કરવાનો વખત આવ્યો; જે વખતે એક જબરો મોજો બોટ ઉપર અફળાઇને ખીજીગમ નીકળી ગયો તે વખતે જે ભયંકર આવાજ થયો હતો તથા જે જોસાથી પાણી હમને વાગું હતું, અને જેથી હમો ગરદા પેચ થઇ પડયા હતા, તથા બોટ વાંકી થઈ ગઈ હતી, અને તેની અંદરનો સઘળો સામાંન એક બાજુયે ગગડી પડયો હતો, તથા સઘળા કોળીઓએ એક

મોહોટી ચીચીયારી પાડી હતી, તે વખતે જે ઘભરાટ થયો હતો તે સાંભળીને અને આસપાસ કંઈજ નહી પણ બંધે બાજુએથી ઊંડેલા દરીઆવ અને હમે વચમાં ગરક થઈજતા હોઇયે, એવો મામલો જોવામાં આવ્યો ત્યારે હમારી છાતી જબરી ધડકવા લાગી હતી, અને હોસ આવી હતી કે, ખરેખર ભારી સંકટ તે હવે ખચીત આવી પડ્યું છે. જે ચીચીયારી પેલા કોળીઓએ પાડી હતી તે આ ઘણાંજ ઊંડાણમાં આવી પડયાથી પાડી હતી, અને હવે પછી જે ત્રીજો ભયંકર મોજો આવનાર હતો તે રખેને બોટ ઉપર ફ્રીવળે તેની ધાસ્તીથી પાડી હતી, તથા એ આવતા મોજાની હેઠળ જવાને બદલે તેની ઉપર બોટને હલેસાંના જોરથી ચઢાવી દેવા એક જોરથી કોરોસ કરવાને તેઓએ ચીચીયારી પાડી હતી, તે ચીચારી સમેતની કોરોસમાં ખુદાતાલાની મેહરબાની થયાથી, હમારી બોટ આ ત્રીજા મોજાની હેઠળ ગરક થઈ જવાને બદલે અંતે ફતેમંદીથી તે મોજા ઉપર થઈ પસાર થઈ શકી હતી. જેવો ત્રીજો મોજો વટાવ્યો કે સઘળા કોળીઓએ ફરીને એક મોહોટો પોકાર મારીયા હતો, જેમાં તેઓ, હે સ્વામી ? હે સ્વામી ? હે સ્વામી ? આવા શબ્દો જોસા ભરેલી રીતે બોલીયા હતા, જેનો અર્થ એવો હમને સમજાવીયામાં આવીયો હતો કે અરે ખુદા ! અરે ખુદા ! અરે ખુદા ! આવું બોલવાની મતલબ એ હતી કે જારે બોટ મોજા ઉપર થઈ પાર પડી તારે તેની ખુશાલીમાં તેઓએ ખુદાતાલાને યાદ કીધો હતો, કે આવી ભારી સંકટમાંથી તે કીરતારે સઘળાને છોડવીયા હતા !

પણ હજુ સઘળાં સંકટનો અંત આવ્યો નહી હતો. સ્ટીમર આગળ સાડા-પાંચ વાગે બોટ જઈ પુગી હતી, પણ તેહેમાંથી ઊતરીને સ્ટીમરનાં દાદર ઊપર પગ મુકવાની એક જગા પણ જોગવાઈ ગુસ્સામાં આવેલો દરીયો આપતો નહીં હતો. બોટ, સ્ટીમરનાં દાદર આગળ ૫) સેકંડ સુધી સીધી અથવા થંભ ઊભી રહી શકતી નહી હતી એટલું જોર પાણીમાં આવેલું હતું. જેઓ બોટમાંથી ઊતરતા હતા તેઓ બોટ જેટલી નજદીક લઇ જવાય એટલી સ્ટીમરનાં દાદર પાસે લઈ જઇને કુદકો મારીને દાદર ઉપર ચઢી જતા હતા, એહેવી હાલતમાં, ઊતરવું ખરેખર ઘણુંજ જોખમ ભરેલું હતું, પણ જીહાં બીજો ઊપાય રેહોજ નહી તારે અંતે સંકટમાં માથું ઘાલ્યા વગર છુટકોજ નહી હતો. હમારા મીત્રોમાંથી હમો દરેક જણ એકક પછી કેટલેક વારે કુદીને સલામતીથી સ્ટીમર ઉપર જઈ શકયા હતા, પણ મી. ખુરશેદજી

રૂસ્તમજી કામાજી એવી રીતે કુદકો મારીને ઊતરતા હતા એવામાં મોજાનાં જોરથી બોટ એકાએક જોસ્સાબંધ ખસી ગયાથી મીત્ર ખુરસેદજીનો પગ સ્ટીમરનાં દાદર ઉપર પોંહોંચી નહી રાકયો જેથી એક મોહોટી હોનારતમાં તેઓ આ પ્રસંગે આવી પડ્યા હતા! પણ તેવણની સમયસુચકતા સારી રહ્યાથી તેવણે તુરત દાદરનાં દોરડાંનો છેડો પકડી લઈ તેને ટંગાઈ રહ્યા હતા, અને પાણીમાં પડવાથી ઘણીજ હીમત ભરેલી રીતે તેવણે પોતાનો બચાવ કીધો હતો! બીજી બે બોટોમાં હમારો સામાન તથા માણસો પછવાડેથી આવ્યાં હતાં, તે વખતે દરીયો નરમ પડેલો હતો, જો કે પાણીની છોળથી તેઓ સઘળા તમામ ભીનાઈ ગયા હતા, તથા હમારા સામાનના પણ હાલહવાલ થઇ ગયા હતા. છ અથવા સાડાછ વાગે સાંજના સ્ટીમરે લંગર ઉચકીયું હતું. હમોને આગળ વધતાં એવી ઉમેદ થઇ હતી કે તોફાન નરમ પડી જશે, પણ હમને તે બે દીવસ લાગટ લાગ્યું હતું અને ત્રીજે દીવસે તે નરમ પડ્યું હતું. અવીશે એહવાલ આગળ વાંચવામાં આવશે.

આ ઠેકાણે મદ્રાસ શેહેરનો એહવાલ પુરો કર્યા આગમચ તે જગા ઉપરની ખાવાપીવાની કેટલીક જીનસો વીશે, તથા તીહાંનાં સ્ત્રીપુરૂષોનાં પોશાક વીશે, અને ખેતીવાડી કરવાની રીતભાંત વીશે, થોડીક બાબદ જે હમારા જોવામાં આવી હતી તે જાણવા જોગ ધરીને અત્રે દાખલ કરી છે.

મદ્રાસનાં પાંઊ ઘણાંજ સોજાં અને લેહજતદાર હોયછે, તથા તેમનો રંગ ઘણોજ સુફેદ રેહેછે, તથા આ પાંઊ જલદી વાસી થઈ જતાં નથી. એ ગુણ તીહાંની તાડી ઊપર તથા આટાની સફાઈ અને ચોખાઈ ઊપર આધાર રાખેછે. પાંઊ તરેવાર આકાર અને રોનકનાં બનાવેછે, તેથી જેમ સ્વાદમાં જીભને તેમ આંખને પણ જોવામાં સારાં લાગેછે. પાંઊ પછી "ઓપમ" કરીને ચોખાની બનાવટની એક ખાવાની જીનસ મદ્રાસમાં સાધારણ વપરાયછે. "ઓપમ"નો આકાર અનેસ્વાદ નકરો આપણાં મુકતાદના તેહેવારોમાં બનાવેલાં સાંધણાંને મળતો આવેછે, અને જો બરાબર બોલીયે તો સાંધણાંનીજ મેળવણી પ્રમાણે ઘણું કરીને તે દરરોજ હીયાં બનાવ્યામાં આવેછે. મદ્રાસના ઘણા લોક સહવારના નાસ્તાની સાથે અથવા નાસ્તો કર્યા પછી "ઓપમ" ખાયછે. સારી તાડીનાં સબબથી ખમીર ઘણું ચઢેછે તેથી "ઓપમ"નો સ્વાદ ઘણોજ લેહજતદાર થાયછે, અને એ સાંધાણું કદમાં ખીળેલું પણ વધારે રેહેછે. દુધ, દહી, છાસ, સહવારનાં ખાવાનો

CULTIVATOR & HIS WIFE _ MADRAS

૭. કુણબી અને તેની બાઈડી.—મધરાજ.

સાધારણ રવૈયો છે, અને ગરીબ માણસો તો આવી જીનસો રોજ ખાયછે. સહવારનાં ચાહેને ઠેકાણે તેઓ તાડી પીયેછે. વળી એક ત્રીજી જીનસ ખાવાની છે તે આપણી સુતરફેણીને મળતી આવેછે. તે એક જાતના હીયાંની દેશી મીઠાઈ છે. પાન, સોપારી, ચુનો અને કાથો, આ તો દેશી લોકની આખા દીવસની સાધારણ ચાવવાની અથવા વગોળવાની જીનસો છે.

સહવારનાં પોહેરમાં અને સાંજ મળી બેવાર દેશી લોક પોતાનાં ઘરનાં ઊંબરો આગળ હમેશ ચોક પુરેછે, તેમાં તરેવાર આકારો તેઓ પાડેછે. આપણા લોક ચોક પુરવામાં માત્રે થોડીક સાધારણ આકૃતિ શીવાય બીજા ઘણા આકાર કાહાડી શકતા નથી, પણ હીયાંના લોકપાસે હજારો આકાર છે જે તેઓ સેહેલાઈથી પોતાનાં બારણાં આગળ પાડી શકેછે. મદ્રાસના દેશી લોક કાળા રંગના છે, તોયપણ તેમનાં શરીર તથા ચેહેરા ઘણાજ સારા આકારવાળા અને સોહામણાં છે. હિંદુ દેશી ગૃહસ્થ સ્ત્રીયો પોતાના પોશાકમાં ફકત એક સાડી પેહેરેછે તથા હાથમાં ચીતલ તથા ઘરેણું ઘાલેછે, તેઓ ચોલી તથા જોડા મુતલક પેહેરતાં નથી. ચોલી માત્રે વેશીયાઓજ પેહેરેછે, અને તેથી ચોલીવાળી સ્ત્રી મદ્રાસમાં નજર આવી તો તેને ગૃહસ્થ સ્ત્રી નહી જાણવી. આ પોશાકવીશે આવો રવૈયો આજસુધી ચાલુજ રહેલો છે, અને તે લાંબી મુદતથી ચાલતો આવેલો છે. આસ્તે આસ્તે સુધરેલા ચઢતી પદ્વિના લોકોએ હાલ વાસ્કુટ પેહેરવા માંડ્યાં છે, પણ તેવાં લોક હજુર ઘણાંજ થોડાં છે. પાસે આપેલું ચીત્ર મદ્રાસનાં એક ખેડુત અને તેહેની બાયડીનું છે. ખેડુત ખેડણીનાં હથીયારો લઈ ઉભો છે, તથા બાયડી મેવાની ટોપલી લઈ માથે સાડીની ઉઢણી કરીને બેઠેલી છે. એ ચીત્ર ફોટોગ્રાફ પાડનારે ખામુખા એવી રીતે પુરૂષને ઉભો રાખીને તથા સ્ત્રીને બેસાડીને પાડેલું છે, એ ઉપરથી જોનારને હીયાંનાં મરદ ઓરતોના પોશાક અથવા પેહેરણનો વીચાર થોડો ઘણો બરાબર આવી શકસે. મરદનાં શરીર ઉપર જે ટીલાં, બાજુ, છાતી અને કપાળઉપર પાડેલાં દેખાયછે, તે મદ્રાસનાં હીંદુઓની જુદી જુદી જાતની નીશાનો જણાવેછે.

મદ્રાસનાં હીંદુઓ તેમાં ઘણું કરીને તેમનાં બ્રાહ્મણો ઘણાં સાંકડા વીચારવાળા છે, તેઓ પર ગ્નાતનાં હીંદુઓને અંદરખાનેથી અતીશય ધીકારેછે, તે એટલા સુધી કે બની આવે તો તેમનું ખુન વટીક કરવાને અચકાય નહી, એવા મુસલમાનોના જેવા ધરમજનુની છે.

મદ્રાસનાં હીંદુ રેહેવાસીવોનો ઘણો ખરો ભાગ ખાધાપીધામાં માસ (ગોશ્ત) અને દારૂ છુટથી વાપરેછે.

મદ્રાસ તરફનાં બ્રાહ્મણો વીશે અથવા તો હીંદુસ્થાનની દક્ષીણ દીશાયે કૃષ્ણા નદીની હેઠળથી તે છેક કેપ કન્યા કુમારી સુધીનાં પ્રંતોમાં, રામાનુજાચાર્ય નામના બ્રાહ્મણોનો એક પંથ વસેલો છે, તેમના વીશે થોડીક બીના વીસ્તારીને જણાવાની આ ઠેકાણે જરૂરની જાણીયેછ, કેમકે આ ટોળાનાં બ્રાહ્મણોનાં સ્વભાવ, વીચાર અને ચાલ ચલગતમાં કપટ, નીર્દયપણું, અભિમાન તથા તોછડાઈ બીજા બ્રાહ્મણો કરતાં અતીશય વધારે છે. મુખ્ય મતલબ આ ઠેકાણે એવીશે જણાવાની એટલીજ છે કે એકજ ધર્મનાં ધર્મ ગુરૂઓમાં, ધર્મ વીચાર સંબંધી મતોમાં કંઈ જુજ ફેર પડવાથી તેઓ એક બીજાથી એવાં અને એટલાં તો છુટા પડી ગયાછ કે, એક બીજાનાં લોહીનાં તરસ્યા થઈ પડયા છે. મનુષ્ય જાતની કમ અક્કલની આ એક મોહોટી ખાંમી આખી દુનીયામાં સઘળી કોમ અને જાતમાં જણાતી આવી છે. જંગલી અથવા સુધરેલી કોમમાં ધર્મ ગુરૂઓનાં મત એક બીજાની વીરૂધ થયાથી તેમની અને તેમનાં પંથનાં લોકોની હાલતમાં મોહોટો ફેરફાર થવાનાં કારણો આ કમ અક્કલ ધર્મગુરૂઓજ થઈ પડયા છે.

આ બ્રાહ્મણો વીષ્ણુના ભકતો છે. આખા હીંદુસ્થાનમાં બ્રહ્મા, વીષ્ણુ, અને રૂદ્ર અથવા શીવ, આ ત્રણેને સરખે આદરમાને અને સરખી પદ્વિનાં ઘણાં ખરા હીંદુઓ ગણેછે, અને તેમની પુજા કરેછે, તોયપણ આ વૈષ્ણવ બ્રાહ્મણો વીષ્ણુને બ્રહ્મા તથા શીવ કરતાં વધારે ચઢતી પદ્વિનો ગણીને તેહેની ભકિત તથા પુંજા વધારે આદરમાનથી કરેછે, તેથી બ્રહ્મા અને શીવને માનનારા તપોધન અને વૈષ્ણવોનાં પુજારીઓમાં તડાં પડી તેઓ એક બીજાને અણગમતા થઈ પડેલા છે.

વૈષ્ણવ બ્રાહ્મણો પોતાને બીજાઓથી ઓળખાવા સારૂ પોતાનાં કપાળ ઉપર ત્રણ લાંબી રેખા પાડેછે, તેમાં વચમાંની રેખ લાલ અથવા પીલા રંગની અને દરેક બાજુની એક જાતની ધોળી મટોડી જેને આ લોક "નામ" કરીને કેહેછે તેની પાડેછે. આ ત્રણ રેખોને હેઠળનાં છેડા આગળથી જોડેછે એટલે કપાળ ઉપર આ નીસાન ત્રણદંતી ⋃|⋃ આવા આકારની આપણાં જોયામાં આવછે. ઉપર કહેલી ધોળી મટોડી "મેગનીસીયમ કલે" જાતની એક મટોડી છે, એ મટોડીને "ગોપીચંદન" પણ કેહેછે. એવું કેહેછે કે દ્વારકાથી આ માતી પુષ્કળ આવેછે.

ગોપીચંદન આ શબ્દનો અર્થ, કૃષ્ણની ગોવાલણોનું ચંદન (સુખડ) એવો થાય-છે. શ્રીકૃશ્ણનાં મરણની ખબર સાંભળીને તેહેની લાડકી ગોપીઓએ દ્વારકા શેહેર-માંનાં એક તળાવમાં ડુબીને તેમનો જીવ પોતાનાં વાહાલા શ્રીકૃષ્ણજીને અર્પણ કરી દીધો હતો, એવું કેહેવામાં આવ્યું છે, તે ઉપરથી ઊપસી માતીનું નામ "ગોપીચંદન" પડયું છે. ત્રણદંતી તીલક, વૈષ્ણવોનાં બ્રાહ્મણ સીવાય બીજી ઊતરતી જ્ઞાતીનાં શુદ્ર લોક પણ તેમને કપાળે અને શરીર ઉપર કરેછે તેથી તેઓ પણ વૈષ્ણવમાર્ગી ગણાયછે.

વૈષ્ણવ બ્રાહ્મણોનો સ્વભાવ ઘણોજ આકરો છે. એવું થવાનું કારણ એટલુંજ કે તેઓ પોતાનાં મનમાં એવો અભિમાન રાખેછે કે બીજા સઘળા પંથનાં બ્રાહ્મણો કરતાં તેઓ સઊથી ચઢતી પદ્વિનાં છે, એવા અહંકારથી તેઓ એટલા તો ફુલી ગયા છે કે બીજી જાતનાં બ્રાહ્મણો સાથે તેઓ ખાવા પીવા અને કોઈ પણ તરેની સગાઈ અથવા વેહેવાર, મેલાપ ભેટ કરવાથી અલગા રેહેછે. પણ વાસ્ત-વીક બોલતાં તો એવું માલુમ પડયું છે કે આ પંથનાં બ્રાહ્મણો પોતેજ ઘણાં હલકી પદ્વિનાં છે, તેથી તેમની જોડે ખાવા પીવાનો અને બીજો વેહેવાર રાખવાને, બીજા પંથનાં બ્રાહ્મણો બીલકુલ નારાજી અને નાખુશ છે.

વૈષ્ણવ બ્રાહ્મણોનાં અભિમાન અને કપટપણાનાં દાખલા જે હમે મદ્રાસ શેહેરમાં જોયા છે, તે ઉપરથી હમે દીલગીરી સાથે જણાવીયે છૈયે કે આ ત્રણદંતી તીલક કરનારોના આશ્રય તળે અથવા તેમનાં ઘરબારનાં ઓટલા અથવા આંગણાં ઊપર બીજી જાતનાં હીંદુ મુસાફરોયે ખુબ સાઊચેતી રાખી ઊતારો કરવો લાજીમ છે. એવાઓને તીહાં પેહેલા તો ઊતારો મળવોજ મુશ્કેલ છે, પણ એકાદ વાર મળ્યો તો, પુરેપુરા ભરોસાથી આવે ઠેકાણે રેહેવું મુશ્કેલ છે. આ પંથવાળા બીજા પંથવાળાઓનાં લોહીનાં એવા તો તરસ્યા છે કે, તક મળતાં તેઓ પોતાને ઘેર આવેલા પરોણા અથવા વાટસરૂનું ખુન પણ કરવાને ચુકે તેવા નથી. એવાં પાતકી કર્મો થયલાં છે આ વીશે તવારીખમાં લખેલું છે, અને આવું વેર હજુ સુધી તેઓમાંથી મટયું નથી. તે વંશપરંપરા ઊતરતુંજ ચાલી આવ્યું છે. જે વખતે હમે મદ્રાસમાં હતા તે વખતે એવો એક પ્રસંગ બન્યો હતો, કે કેટલાએક હીંદુઓ આગગાડીએ મદ્રાસમાં આવી પોહોંચીયા હતા, તેમને તે ઠેકાણે ઓળખાણ નહી હતી તેથી ભોગજોગે આ ત્રણદંતી તીલકવાળાનાં ઘર આગળ તેઓ આવી

લાગા. તેઓનાં મનમાં એવું કે બ્રાહ્મણ જેવાને ઘેર ઉતારો કરવાને કેહેશું તો કોઈ કદી ના કેહેશે નહી. તેથી તેઓએ તીહાં ઉતારો કરવાને વીનંતી કરી પણ તે વીનંતી પુરી થઇ નહી, તેટલામાંથી ઘરનાં ધણીયે કહ્યું કે બાહાર ઉભા રહીને બોલો, હીયાં કોઇને ઉતારો આપવાની જગા છેજ નહી. જગા પુષ્કળ હતી અને ઘરમાં જુજ માણસ સીવાય બીજું કોઈ નહી હતું. પેલા હીંદુઓએ કહ્યું કે, હમને માત્ર જુજ જગા જોઈએછે, અને તે વળી કંઈ ઘણાં દીવસ જોઈતી નથી. એકાદ બે દીવસમાં હમો હીયાંથી જનાર છઇયે. તેઓએ બીજી વાત એ કહી કે હમે પણ જાતનાં બ્રાહ્મણ છઇયે, અને હીંદુ ધર્મની ક્રીયા રસમને માન આપી તે મુજબ ચાલનારા છૈયે. "હમે બ્રાહ્મણ છૈયે," આ શબ્દો સાંભળતાને વાર ત્રણ તીલકી દૈષ્ણુવ બ્રાહ્મણનો મીજાજ હાથથી ગયો. તેણે સાફ ના કહી કે આ મારૂં ઘર છે, હું હીયાં તમને નથીજ ઉતરવા દેવાનો, તમે સું કહોછો? તમે હીયાંથી હવડાંને હવડાં જાઓ, એવું કહી બુમો પાડવા માંડી! પેલા હીંદુ મુસાફરોયે કહ્યું કે, બસ ભાઈ, એટલી બધી ગડબડ કરવાની કંઈ જરૂર નથી, હમો હીયાંથી જઈએછ, પણ વારૂં, ઉતારો કરવાની બીજી જગા વીશે કંઈ ખબર અથવા ઠેકાણું જણાવવાની તમે તસદી લેશો તો તમારો ઉપકાર માન્યામાં આવશે. એ સાંભળીને વળી તેણે બુમ પાડીને કહ્યું કે, "હું કોઈના ઉતારાની જગા જાણતો નથી, અથવા કેહેતો પણ નથી, તમે જઈ શોધી કાહાડો, અને બસ હવે તમે વધારે ના બોલો, અને હીયાંથી જાઓ!" પેલા મુસાફરોયે આ સખત દીલનાં બ્રાહ્મણને બે ત્રણ દીવસ રેહેવાને રૂ. ૨૦) થી ૨૫) સુધી ભાડાંનાં આપવાને કેહયું, તોયપણ તેહેનું દીલ જરા પણ કુંળું નહી! આ વાતચીત અને તકરાર ઘણીવાર લગી ચાલી હતી, એટલામાં પેલો બ્રાહ્મણ પોતાનાં પડોશીને ગુપચુપ પોતાનાં માણસોથી ચેતવણી આપી ચુક્યો હતો, તેથી જેહને તીહાં પેલા હીંદુઓ અથવા તેનાં માણસો ઉતારાની જગા વીશે પુછવા ગયાં હતાં તેમને સઘળી તરફથી એકજ જવાબ મળ્યો હતો, "હમારે તીહાં જગા નથી, કીહાં ઉતરવું તે આગળ જઇને પુછો, હમે નથી જાણતા!" આવી નીર્દય ચાલ જોઇને હમને ઘણીજ તાજુબી લાગી હતી. પેલા હીંદુ ગૃહસ્થોને જગા મળી કે નહી તેની હમને ઘણીજ ચીન્તા ઉત્પંન થઈ હતી, તેથી ખબર કાહાડતાં માલુમ પડયું કે અંતે તે બીચારાઓને રોહેરથી ત્રણ ચાર માઇલ દુર કોઇનું નાહાનું સરખું ખાલી ઘર મળ્યું તે ભાડે લઈ રેહેવું પડયું હતું. બીજી

દીલગીરી ભરેલી વાત એ બની હતી કે, છેક, બપોરનાં ૧) વાગે તે હીંદુ મુસાફરોને પાણીની ઘણીજ તરસ લાગ્યાથી તેઓએ પીવાનું પાણી માગ્યું હતું, તે પણ પેલા બ્રાહ્મણે અને તેનાં પડોસીઓએ આપવાને ના પાડી હતી, અને એ મુસાફરો પણ જાતે પોતે બ્રાહ્મણ હતા તેથી કોઇ બીજા શુદ્રને તીહાંનું પાણી તો પીવાય નહી, તેથી બીચારાઓને ભુખે અને તરસે બહુ ટોકાવું પડ્યું હતું. વૈષ્ણવપંથના અને બીજા પંથનાં બ્રાહ્મણો વચ્ચે ધરમ સંબંધી જેજે બુનરેજીઓ થઈ છે તેહેનું વીગતવાર બયાન, ફારબસ ઇંડીયા, એશીયાટીક રીસરચીસ અને એવા બીજા સત્તા ભરેલાં પુસ્તકોમાં કરેલું છે, અને તેમાં જે બનાવો જણાવેલા છે તેમની સાથે સરખાવતાં તો ઉપર જણાવેલો દાખલો કુચ્ચ બીશાદમાં નથી.

આ પંથનાં બીજા કેટલાએક બ્રાહ્મણો મથુરા અને વૃંદાવનમાં હમને મળ્યા હતાં. મદ્રાસમાં બનેલી હકીકત ઉપર ત્રણદંતી તીલકવાળા બ્રાહ્મણો વીરો હમોયે હમારૂં મત બાંધ્યું હતું તે મત વાજબી છે એ વીશે વૃંદાવન શેહેરમાં હમારી ખાતરી થઇ હતી. એની સવીસ્તર વીગત આ જગાએ આપતા નથી. મથુરા અને વૃંદાવન શેહેરોનાં બયાનમાં તે જણાવી છે. હીયાં માત્ર આટલુંજ કેહેવું બસ છે કે, જે દેહેરૂં હમે વૃંદાવનમાં જોવા ગયા હતા તે દેહેરૂં કંઇ ઘણું જોવા લાયક નહી હતું, તોયપણ તે હમોયે સારીપેડે જોયું હતે, અને તીહાંના રખેવાળો બીજી જાતનાં બ્રાહ્મણો હતા તેઓએ પણ દેખડાવ્યું હતે. દેહેરાં જેવી ઇમારતો જેવામાં હમને કોઈ પણ ઠેકાણે હીંદુઓની તરફથી ઘણો અટકાવ થયો નહી હતો, પણ આ ઠેકાણે તો જે બે ચાર ત્રણદંતી તીલકવાળા વૈષ્ણવપંથીયો હતા તેથી હમને તથા હમારી સાથેનાં સઘળા જણાને અંદર જવાની અથવા દેહેરાંની પાસે ઊભા પણ નહી રેહેવાની એટલે સુધી મનાઇ કરી હતી કે, હમો પારશી તથા હમારો યુરોપીયન મીત્ર એકવાર કદાચ ઊભા રેહે તો તે આ બ્રાહ્મણો દેખી શકે, પણ હમારી સાથે જે હીંદુ મીત્રો હતા તેમાં કેટલાએક તો મથુરાનાં હીંદુ વેપારીઓ અને વળી, તીહાંનાજ રેહેવાશીઓ વીગેરે હતા, પણ તેઓ બીજા પંથનાં હતા તેથી તેમના ઉપર તો પેલા બુનીઓએ એટલા તો વેર ભાવથી જોયું હતું કે થોડી વારમાં, છીટાં શોધી એટલી ગડબડાટ કરી નાખી કે, આ કઠોર દીલનાં બ્રાહ્મણોમાંના એકે તો હાથમાં સોટો પણ પકડ્યો હતો, અને જો વધારે બોલાચાલી થતે તો તીહાં સોટાબાજીનો ભોગ ભોગવવો પડતે! હમે આ પંથવીશે જે સાંભળ્યું હતું તે નજરે નજર

જોયું હતું, તેથી આ ઠેકાણેથી શેતાન ડાવા કરીને તીહાં વધારે વાર ખોટી નહી થવું બેહેતર જાણી, ખામોશી અખ્તિયાર કરી, મુગામુગા આગળ ચાલતી પકડી હતી.

આ વૈષ્ણવો રામાનુજ નામનાં એક હીંદુ આચાર્યનાં સેવકો છે. રામાનુજ ઈસવી સન ૧૨૦૦ ના વર્ષમાં હીંદુસ્થાનનાં દક્ષણ ભાગમાં પ્રખ્યાત થઈ ગયો છે. કાનજીવરમ (કાંચી) શેહેરમાં એણે આ પંથના ધર્મનો પ્રસારો કીધો હતો. તે ઘણું કરીને ત્રીચીનાપોલી શેહેરની નજદીકમાં રેહેતો હતો. હીયાંથી એણે હીંદુસ્થાનનાં જુદા જુદા ભાગમાં ઘણીવાર આવજાવ કરી હતી. જીહાં જીહાં એ ગયો હતો તીહાં તીહાં બીજા પંથવાળાઓ સાથે ધર્મવીરો વાદવીવાદ કરીને તેમનું ખંડણ કરતો હતો, અને વીષ્ણુની પુજાની સ્થાપના કરતો હતો. ફકત માણુસોનેજ એક પંથમાંથી કાહાડીને પોતાનાં પંથમાં ખેંચતો હતો એટલુંજ નહી પણ ઘણાં દેવલો અને દેહેરાં બીજા પંથવાળાઓના હાથમાંથી છીનવી લઈ અથવા છોડાવીને તેમાંના દેવતાને બીસાડી, વીષ્ણુની મુરતી તેઓમાં બેસાડતો ગયો, અને તે દેવલા અથવા દેહેરાં પોતાનાં પંથવાળાઓને સ્વાધીન કરતો ગયો. આવી રીતે હાથ કરી લીધેલાં દેહેરાંઓમાંનું સઊથી મોહોટું અને સુશોભીત તથા જોવાલાયક રચના ભરેલું દેહેરૂં ત્રીપટી આગળ છે.

મદ્રાસમાં બોજો ઊચકનારા મરદો બોજો પોતાનાં માથાં ઊપર ચઢાવતા નથી પણ ખાંધઊપર અથવા પીઠ (વાંસા) ઉપર મુકેછે, અથવા માલને હાથગાડીમાં મુકીને એક ઠેકાણેથી બીજે ઠેકાણે એક અથવા બેજણ મળી ખેંચી લઈ જાયછે. બળદનાં ગાડાં અથવા ગાડી સામાન ઉચકી લઇજવાને હીયાં વપરાતી નથી.

મદ્રાસ શેહેરમાં ખેતીવાડી, કુઆના અને તળાવોનાં પાણીથી, ઘણું કરીને કરેછે. નદીનું પાણી પણ જે જે ઠેકાણે મળી આવેછે તીહાં વાપરેછે. મદ્રાસનાં કુવા ઘણા ઊંડા નથી, તેથી તેમાંથી પાણી કાહાડવાની એક ઘણીજ સેહેલી પણ અસલી રીત હજુ ચાલુજ છે. કુવા અથવા તળાવનાં વરા આગળ લાંકડાનો એક ઊભો ખુંટો દાટેછે, અને તેના મથાળાં ઊપર આડું એક લાંબું પાટીયું, એવી રીતે બાંધેછે કે તે પાટીયાંનો એક છેડો વધારે લાંબો અને બીજો છેડો ટુંકો રેહેછે, અને તે પાટીયું ત્રાજુની માફક, ઉપર નીચે, ઊચકાઈ તથા પડી શકેછે. પાટીયાંના લાંબા છેડાને નાકે દોરડાં સાથે, ચામડાંની એક ડોલ બાંધેછે. જીઆરે કુવામાંથી પાણી કાહાડવાનું હોય તીઆરે એક માણસ પેલા ખુંટાને મથાળે જઈ

ઊભો રેહેછે, અને એક બીજો માણસ કુઆના વરા આગળ ઉભો રેહેછે. હવે પાટીયાંનો લાંબો છેડો ભારી હોવાથી હમેશા નીચે પડેલા રેહેછે, તેને ઉંચકવાને સારૂ ખુંટાને મથાળે ચઢી ઉભેલું માણસ પાટીયાંના ટુકા છેડા ઉપર ચાલી જાયછે, જેથી તે છેડા ઉપર ભાર પડવાથી, પાંટીયાનો લાંબો છેડો ઊંચકાયછે, તેની સાથે બાંધેલી ડોલ પાણી ભરાયલી ઊંચકાઇને ઊપર આવેછે. જેવી ડોલ ઉપર આવી કે વરા આગળ ઊભેલું માણસ તેને ખાલી કરી નાખેછે તેવામાં પેલું ઉપર ચઢેલું માણસ પાટીયાંના ટુકા છેડા ઉપરથી એક બાજુએ નીચે ઉતરી પડેછે તેથી લાંબો છેડો ડોલ સાથે પોતાના ભારથીજ પાછો કુઆમાં પોતાની મેળે પડેછે. વળી ડોલ ભરાઈ, એટલે પેલા ઉપરવાળો, પાછો પાટીયાંઊપર ચાલી જાયછે એટલે બીજીવાર ડોલ ઉપર આવેછે. એ પ્રમાણે પાણી કુવામાંથી બેજણ મળીને કાહાડેછે, અને તે પાણી પેલા બેજણ રોજના માહાવરાથી એટલી તો ઝડપથી કાહાડેછે કે આપણી નજર ઠરી શકતી નથી. હમે ધારીયે છઇયે કે એક મીનીટમાં પંદરથી વીસ ડોલ પાણી તેઓ કાહાડી શકતા હશે. ઊપલી ગોઠવણ ઘણાં ઊંડા કુઆઓમાંથી પાણી કાહાડવાને હમે ધારીયે છૈયે કે સવલ પડે એવી નથી. આ માત્ર થોડી ઊંડાઇનાંજ કુઆઓને લાગુ પડી શકે તેવી છે. નદી કીનારે પણ એવી ગોઠવણો કરેલી હમારા જોયામાં આવી હતી.

મદ્રાસ ઈલાકામાં નાળીયરી, તાડ અને ખજુરાં, અતીશય છે. જારે આગગાડી મુંબઈથી ઠેઠ મદ્રાસસુધી ચાલુ થશે તે વખતે હમે હમારા મોબેદ સાહેબોને ભલામણ કરીયે છૈયે કે નીજામ હેદરાબાદની અને મદ્રાસ ઈલાકા તરફની તાડીની પરીક્ષા તેઓએ જરૂર કરીને કરવી ! હમારૂં મત આ લતા તરફની તાડી વીશે તો હલકું છે, તોયપણ જેઓ તાડીનાં ખાં છે તેમનું મત આવી બાબદમાં લીધેલું વધારે વજનદાર ગણાસે!

આગળ જણાવીઉં છે તેમ તા૰ ૨૬ મી જાનેવારીની સાંજના મદ્રાસથી "મેલ સ્ટીમર" માં ઉપડીયા હતા. તોફાન જબરૂં લાગું હતું અને રાત્રે તેની સાથે જબરો વરસાદ પણ પડીયો હતો. સ્ટીમર ઉપડીને ચાલવા માંડી કે હમારા મીત્રોને એકક પછી વાહાણ લાગવા માડયું. થોડી વખતમાં નાહાના અને વડા કામાજી બંધેજણ બેચેન થઈ પડયા, તેવણની પાછળ ડાકતર ભાઊ સાહેબ પણ સીક થઈ ગયા. તેવણના હીંદુ માણસોને પણ દરીયો લાગો. હમુને પણ જરા જરા બોર

આવતી હતી પણ જરા સોડાવાટર અને બરાંડી પાણી લેઈ, કેબીનમાં રેહેવાને બદલે બાહેર તુતક ઉપરજ રેહા હતા. પણ થોડાવાર પછી વરસાદ ઘણો થયાથી તુતક ઉપર નહી રેહેવાઈ શકાયું હતું તેથી નીચે ઉતરી જમવાની ટેબલ આગળજ ફરીયા કીધું હતું. કેબીનમાં જતાંજ જીવ પાછો ઉકળતો હતો. એક કલાક સુધી હમોને જરા બેચેની રેહી હતી, પણ આઈસ અને બરાંડી પાણી જરા જરા વારે ટપકાવીયા કીધું હતું તેથી સઘળી સમાધાની થઈ ગઈ હતી. હમો સારી પેઠે રેહાથી હમારા મીત્રોની બરદાસ્ત લેવાને, તેમને કાંજી વીગેરે પુછવાને હમારેથી બની શકયું હતું. જેથી હમારા મીત્રોની હમોએ બરદાસ્ત કીધી હતી તેમજ હમોએ હમારી પોતાની બરદાસ્ત પણ અચ્છી કીધી હતી. જમરી ભુખે, દીવસમાં ત્રણ વાર, કેબીનની પાસેનીજ ટેબલ ઉપર એખલા બેસીને શુકરાના કરી એવું તો સેરવી આપીયું હતું કે તેની યાદ નીકળી નથી શકવાની! રોસ્ટ અને બાફેલા પપેટા અને અમેરીકન માખણની બરણીની ખબર ઘણીજ સારી રીતે રોજ લેયા કીધી હતી. હમારા મીત્રોએ બે દીવસ બેચેની ભોગવી હતી અને બીચારાઓએ કાંજી ઉપર આધાર રાખીયો હતો, પણ ત્રીજે દીવસથી તે સાહેબોએ ટેબલ ઉપર જે સપાટા મારીયા હતા તેમાં પેહેલા બે દીવસના ઉપવાસનો બદલો તેઓએ સારીપેઠે વાળી લીધો હતો. જેને વાંહાંણ સદીયું તો તે ખરેખરજ તનદુરસ્તી ભોગવાનો પણ જેને વાંહાંણ લાગતું હોય તે બીચારાનો હાલ ખરેખરજ દયા ઉપજાવા જોગ થઈ પડેછે.

તા૦ ૨૭ મી અને **તા૦ ૨૮ મી** જાનેવારીના બે દીવસ વરસાદ લાગો હતો પણ તા૦ ૨૮ મીની સાંજના તે નરમ પડી ઉઘાડ થયો હતો, અને કેબીનોની બારીઓ જે વરસાદનાં સબબથી ઢાંકી રાખી હતી તે ઉઘાડીયામાં આવી હતી. સ્ટીમરની તુતક સઘળી સાફ સફાઈ બરેલી કરી હતી અને ઉતારૂઓ ઉપર આવી એક બીજાની બેરે આફીયત પુછવા લાગા હતા. દેખાવ ઘણોજ ખુશનુમા થઈ પડયો હતો. સેત્રંજનો દાવ ડાકતર ભાઉ સાહેબે સ્ટીમરના ડાકતર સાથે ચલાવીયો હતો, જેમાં સઘળા રમી જાણનાર યુરોપીયન ઉતારૂઓ એક બાજુએ થઈ આપણા ડાકતરને હરાવાની તજવીજ કીધી હતી તોયપણ અંતે આપણા ડાકતરની જીત થઈ હતી અને સાંભાઓની માહાત થઈ હતી. ડાકતર ભાઉ, બચગીથીજ સેત્રંજની રમત ઘણીજ ચાલાકીથી રમવામાં પ્રખ્યાત થયલા છે.

તા૦ ૨૯ મી જાનેવારીની રાત્રે આસરે સાડાનવ વાગે, હમો તુતક ઉપર પસાર

કરતા હતા એવામાં સ્ટીમર ઉપર એક આવાજ ઉઠીયો કે કલકત્તાની ખાડી આગળ આપણે આવી પુગા. આ ઉપરથી થોડા વારમાં તુતક ઉપર દોડધામ થઈ રેહી હતી. સઘળા ઉતારૂઓ ઉપર આવીને, સલામત આવી પોહોંચવાની એક બીજાને મુબારકબાદી આપવા લાગા. દુરથી એક દીવો દરીયામાં દેખાતો હતો, તે દીવો આસ્તે આસ્તે હમારી સ્ટીમરની પાસે આવતો માલુમ પડ્યો હતો. આ દીવો પાઈલટની બોટનો હતો. પી. એંડ ઓ. કંપનીની "મેલ સ્ટીમર"ના દરીયાવરદી કાયદા કાનુનો મુજબ હમારી સ્ટીમર ઉપરથી બે બાણુ અને બે "બ્લુ લાઇટ" એટલે બપોરીયા સળગાવી, નીશાન કરી દેખડાવી હતી. થોડા વારમાં પાઈલટ સ્ટીમરની બોરડુએ આવી પુગો હતો. તેણે ઉપર આવી સ્ટીમરને આગળ ચલાવા સારૂ પોતાને સ્વાધીન સઘળો અખ્તિયાર લઈ લીધો હતો. પાઈલટની સાથે, પાણી માપનાર એક શીખાઉ અમલદાર પણ આવેછે, જેનું કામ એજ હોયછે કે ખાડીનું પાણી માપતો રેહે અને કીઆ માર્ગથી પાઈલટ સ્ટીમરને ચલાવેછે તે માર્ગ ધીયાનમાં રાખે. આટલું જણાવાની તો કંઈજ અગત નથી કે પાઈલટના સ્ટીમર ઉપર આવીયા પછી તે બારકસને આગળ ચલાવાનો સઘળો અખ્તિયાર તથા જોખમ તેના ઉપર રેહેછે.

જે ઠેકાણાં ઉપરથી પાઈલટ સ્ટીમર ઉપર આવેછે તેને *Sandshead of Calcutta* એટલે કલકત્તાનું રેતીનું મથક કરીને કેહેછે. આ ઠેકાણાં ઉપર જો દીવસના આવી પુગા હોઈએ તો ઉતારૂઓને દરીયાનાં પાણીનો રંગ બદલાયલો નજરે પડેછે. ભર દરીયાનાં પાણીનો રંગ ઘણો ખરો નીરમળ પણ કાળો અથવા ઘેરો આસમાની રેહેછે; પણ આ ઠેકાણાં ઉપર "હુગ્લી" નદીનાં પાણીનો ચીકલ, રેતી, મટોડી વીગરે જે બીજો કચરો ખેંચાઈ આવી દરીયાનાં પાણી સાથે ભેળાયછે તેથી, પાણીનો રંગ, ગદલો અને ભુરો થઈ ગયલો હોયછે. "હુગ્લી" નદી જે ગંગા નદીની એક શાખા છે, તે બંને નદીઓ વરસાદની મોસમમાં, એટલે માસ જુન, જુલાઈ, આગસ્ટ અને સપટેમબરમાં બંગાલાના આખાતમાં આસરે ૬,૦૮,૨૦,૪૧,૬૦૦) છ અબજ કયુબીક ફીટ અથવા ૩૩,૯૮,૧૩,૭૬૦) તેત્રીસ કરોડ ટન ચીકલ લાવી નાખેછે, એવું ગણત્રીથી માલુમ પડયું છે. આ હીસાબે આ નદીના મુખ આગળ દરીયામાં કેટલો ચીકલ એકઠો થતો હશે

અને તેથી વાંહાંણવાળાઓના માર્ગને કેટલો અટકાવ થઈ પડતો હશે આ વાત સેહેલાઈથી વીચારમાં આવી શકેછે. આ મથકનું નામ "સાંડસહેડ" પડયું છે તે ઉપલાંજ સબબથી, કે ગંગા અને હુગ્લી નદીયો, આ ઠેકાણાં ઉપર પુશકળ રેતી, ચીકણ અને કચરો લાવીને મહાસાગરમાં નાખેછે. આ વેરાન જેવાં ઠેકાણાં ઉપર તરતી રાખેલી નીશાનો વાંહાંણવટીઓને આવી ચેતવણી આપેછે કે હીંદુસ્થાનનું પાયાતખ્ત કલકત્તા હજુર હીયાંથી ૧૦૦ માઈલ દુર છે, અને તે પોહોંચવાની આગમચ "હુગ્લી" નદીની કઠણ વલાણો અને પેચ ભરેલી વાટ ખુબ સંભાળથી વટાવવી પડશે.

જો પાઈલટ બોલકણો, મીલનસાર અને ખુશ મીજાજી હોયો તો કલકત્તાની થોડી ઘણી તાજી ખબર તેનાં મોહોડાંથી ઉતારૂઓને મળી શકેછે, અથવા તે પોતાની સાથે છેક નજદીકની તારીખના વર્તમાનપત્રો લઈ આવેછે તે ઉતારૂઓને વાંચવાને આપેછે, જેથી કલકત્તે પોહોંચાયાં આગમચ કેટલીક અગતની ખબરો મળી શકેછે. પણ પાઈલટ જો બરતું છાગ્યું હોયું તો તેનાં મુગામંતરથી ઉતારૂઓને તેવી ખબર મળી શકતી નથી.

પાઈલટ આવીયા પછી સ્ટીમર આગળ ચાલવા માંડેછે, તોયપણ બંગાલાનો કીનારો એકદમ નથી નજરે પડતો. કેટલુંક સુધી આગળ વધીયા પછી અને તરતા રાખેલાં લાલ અને સુફેદ રંગના કેટલાક બોહીયાં પસાર કરીયા પછી કીનારાની નીશાનો રફતે રફતે નજરે પડવા માંડેછે. જો દીવસ હોયો તો આકાશના કાંઠા આગળથી હળવે હળવે ઝાડોના મથાલાં દેખાવા માંડેછે, જે દેખાવ હમારી નજરે હમોએ જોયો હતો કારણ હમારૂં દીવસના વખતમાં તીહાં જઈ પોહોંચવું થયું હતું. પણ રાત્રે કીનારાનો દેખાવ નહી નજરે પડી શકયાથી, આવે વખતે દીવાદાંડી ઉપરથી જે ફરતી રોશની ઝટદઈને ચમકતી દેખાયછે અને આસ્તે આસ્તે ઝાંખી થતી જાયછે, તે જોયાથી કહી શકાયછે કે સ્ટીમર ઉપરથી હવે કીનારો દેખાવા માંડીયો છે. જે ઝાડો અને રોશની પેહેલી દેખાયછે, તે સાગર નામના ટાપુઓ ઉપરની જાણવી. આ ટાપુઓ કલકત્તાથી ૮૩) માઈલ દુર છે. "સાગર" ટાપુઓ, માત્રે આગળા વખતમાં જંગલ અને વેરાન જમીન હતી અને આજે પણ કેટલોક ભાગ હજુર તેવીજ હાલતમાં છે. તીહાં વાઘોની જબરી વસ્તી છે, અને તે ઠેકાણાંની આબો હવા પણ ઘણીજ અસુખાકારી ભરેલી છે.

એક વખત આ ટાપુઓ ઉપર હીંદુ લોકની એક ઘણીજ કમકમાટ ઉપજાવનાર ધરમ સંબંધી ક્રીયા દર વર્ષ થતી હતી, અને તે વખતે તીહાં એક જાત્રા અથવા મેલો ભરાતો હતો. આ ક્રીયામાં હીંદુ લોકની સ્ત્રીઓ માનતાં પાલવાને પોતાનાં કુમલાં જીવતાં એકક બાલકને પોતાને હાતે "શાર્ક" એટલે સાસવાટ જાતની માછલીનાં મોહોડાંમાં ભોગ આપતાં હતાં! આ અજ્ઞાની સ્ત્રીઓ એવું માનતી હતી કે આવી ખુન ભરેલી ક્રીયાથી ઇશ્વરની કૃપા તેમની ઉપર અને તેમના બાકીજીવતાં રેહેલાં છોકરાંઓ ઉપર થશે! સાસવાટ માછલીને તેઓ પોતાનો દેવ સમજીને આવાં નીરદય કર્મ તેઓ અજ્ઞાનપણાથી કરતાં હતાં, અને આથી હજારો કુમલાં નીરદોશ બાલકોના જીવનો ઘાત દરવરશે આ ટાપુઓ ઉપર હીંદુ માતાઓને હાતે જાહેર રીતે થતો હતો! પણ ધન્ય છે ઇંગ્રેજ સરકારને અને યુરોપીયન મીશનરીઓને કે તેઓએ આ અનર્થનું ઘાતકીપણું દેશી લોકને ખાત્રી ભરેલી રીતે સમજાવીયું અને સરકારે અદલ ઇનસાફની રાહે આવા ખુનરેજી ભરેલાં કામોનો ફતેમંદી ભરેલી રીતે અટકાવ કીધો છે. સાગર ટાપુઓનો દેખાવ કોઈ પણ રીતે ઘણો જોવા લાયક નથી, તોયપણ કલકત્તા તરફ જનારા મુસાફરોને ઘણાં દીવસ સુધી લાગટ પાણી અને આકાશ શીવાએ બીજું વાંહાંણ ઉપરથી કંઈજ દેખાઈ શકાતું નથી, તેમની નજરે જારે જમીન પેહેલ વેહેલી દેખાયછે તારે અલબતાં ગમે એવી ઉજડ જગા પણ તેમની આંખોને પસંદ પડતી થઇ પડેછે.

સાગર ટાપુ આગળ પેહેલ વેહેલાં આપણી સાંભણે ખરાં બંગાલી લોક, પણ ઉતરતી જાતનાં, દેખાવા માડેછે. તેઓ જાતના મચ્છીમારો છે. તેમને જોયાથી બંગાલી લોક વીશે ખરેખર ઘણોજ હલકો વીચાર આપણાં મનમાં આવીયા વગર નથી રેહેવાનો, પણ આટલું જાણવું જોઈએછ કે તેઓ સઉથી હલકી જાતના બંગાલી લોક છે. બરોબર બોલીએ તો આ મચ્છીમારોમાં જાતીભેદ જેવું કંઈ પણ છે નહી. મુંબઈના કોળીઓ અને મચ્છીમારો સાથે બંગાલાના કોળી અને મચ્છીમારોની સરખામણી કરવાને હમો વાજબી જોતા નથી, કારણ એમ નહી સમજવું કે હમો હમારાં મુંબઈ શેહેરની અથવા હમારા આ શેહેરી ભાઈ બંધુઓની તારીફ કરીએછ, પણ આવી સરખામણી કરવાથી જાણે શેહેરી પુરૂષો સાથે જંગલીઓને સરખાવવા બરોબર છે! મુંબઈના મચ્છીમાર અને કોળીઓ ગમે એવા ઉતરતી પદવીના છે તોયપણ તેમનાં શરીરનો બાંધો

મારો, શોભતો અને ઘાટમદાર છે, ચેહેરા ઉપર ચંચલાઈ અને ઉદ્યોગ તથા કઠણ મેહનત આપણે જોઈ શકીએછ. આ ઉપરથી માલુમ પડેછે કે આ જાતમાં કંઈ પણ અંદરખાનેથી મનશકિતનું બળ છે. પણ કલકત્તાનો કોળી અથવા મચ્છીમાર તો, રૂઢી પ્રમાણે બોલતાં, ખરોજ નકરો કાળો કોળી, ચેહેરા ઉપરથી દેખાતો છે, તેની સાથે સુસ્તી અને મુર્ખ, જેવો નજર આવેછે, તથા તેના શરીરના બાંધાનું બયાન કરવાને સારૂ તો હમારી પાસ લાયક શબ્દો નથી મળી આવતા. તેઓ ઘણું કરીને પતલા, મુરદાર સાટકા જેવા નજરે પડયા હતા, બળવાન અને હોશીયાર તો ઘણાજ થોડા જણ હમારાં જોવામાં આવીયા હતા. મચ્છીમાર અને કોળીઓની જાત તેમની સખ્ત દરીયાઈ મેહનત પ્રમાણે તો ઘણી મજબુત અને શરીરે દંડ ભરેલી હોવી જોઈએછ, જેવા કે આપણી મુંબઈનાં ઘણા ખરા કોળીઓ અને ગામ ગાંમડાંના કોળીયો હોયછે તેમ. પણ કલકત્તાના કોળીયોમાં તો લાંબાં ચેહેરાવાળા, ચીમડાયલા ગાલવાળા અને કંતાયલા શરીરનાં પાંજરાવાળા માણસો ઘણાં જોયામાં આવીયાં હતાં. તેમની બોટ અથવા મછવા પણ તેમનાજ જેવા નાજુક, પાતલા, ઓએ પવનના એક ઝપાટાથી ઉંધા વળી જાય એવા દેખાયછે, તોયપણ આવાં નાજુક બારકસો અજાએબ રીતે પાણી ઉપર મજબુતાઈથી અને મખમ રેહી શકેછે. કલકત્તા તરફ જતાં વાંહાંણોને સારૂ પાઈલિટની સાથે હમેશા આવા એકુ બે મછવા રેહેછે, અને તેમનું કામ આજ ઠરાવેલું હોય છે કે વાંહાંણની બંને બોરદુ તરફનું પાણી માપતા રેહેવું અને પાઈલિટને આ વીશે સારી પેઠે જાણીતો રાખવો. આ કામમાં કેળવાયલા કેટલાક કોળીઓ ઘણા ચપલ રેહેછે અને પાણીનું માપ ભરોસો રાખવા જોગ રીતે ઘણીજ ઝડપથી અને ચોકસાઈથી કરી શકેછે. જેમ આપણી તરફના મછવાઓ બંને બોરદુએથી સાંકડા અને બંને છેડેથી અણીદાર અથવા અણીયારા હોયછે તેમ કલકત્તાના મછવા નથી. તેઓ ઘણા ખરા એક છેડે સાંકડા પણ બીજે છેડે ઘણાજ પોહોળા છે.

જરા આગળ ચાલતાં, "કેડગીરી" થી નીકળેલી "ડાક બોટ" ટપાલના કાગળો લાવંતી સાંભણે મળેછે. મેલ સ્ટીમરના ઉતારૂઓને સારૂ, તેમના કલકત્તાનાં મીત્રોએ જે કાગળો મોકલીયાં હોયછે તે આ બોટમાંથી ઉતારૂઓને મળી શકેછે. આ કાગળો મળીયાથી કલકત્તાની બીજી તાજી ખબર અને ઉતારૂઓને ખુદ પોતપોતાની ખાનગી બાબદો વીશે ખબર પડીયાથી કોઇને ખુસાલી

અને કોઇને ગમી ભરેલા સમાચારો મળેછે, જેથી થોડીવાર મેલ સ્ટીમર ઉપર તરેવાર દેખાવો થઈ પડેછે. કોઈ ખુસાલીથી ગીત ગાવા માંડેછે, કોઇ દીલગીર થાયછે અને કોઈ વમાસનમાં પડેછે. આ મથકથી કલકત્તા પોહોંચવાને જો સારો પવન હોયો અને સંજોગ બનીયો તો એક દીવસમાં પોહોંચી શકાયછે અને એ મુજબ હમો જઈ પુગા હતા. આવું પણ કોઈવાર બનેછે કે પાણીનો સાંમો જોર અને મોહોડાં ઉપરનો પવન હોયો તો કલકત્તે જઈ પોહોચતાં આખું એક અઠવાડીયું પણ ભાગેછે.

આગળ વધતાં, નદીની બંને બાજુના કીનારા હવે ખુલ્લા નજરે દેખાવા માંડેછે. પશ્ચીમ તરફનાં કીનારા ઉપર "કાઉકાલી"ની દીવાદાંડી દેખાયછે, જે કલકત્તાથી ૭૪ માઇલ દુર છે. જરા આગળ વધતાં "કેડગીરી"નું મથક આવેછે. થોડાં વરસોની વાત ઉપર મોહોટ મોટાં "ઇનિડયામેનો" એટલે યુરપ ખંડ તરફથી વેપારના કારણસર આવતાં મોહોટાં વાંહાણો, આ ઠેકાણાં ઉપર લંગરવાર થતાં હતાં. હાલના વખતમાં "કેડગીરી" માત્રે એક પોસ્ટ આફીસ અને તારથી સંદેસા મોકલવાનું મથક છે. નદીની પોહોળાઈ હીયાં સાતથી આઠ માઇલ સુધીની છે. ઉગમણ તરફનો કીનારો હજુર ઉજડ અને વેરાન દેખાયછે, પણ આથમણના કીનારાની જમીન ઉપર "કેડગીરી" આગળથી સારી લીલોત્રી અને ખેડણી કરેલી માલુમ પડેછે. "કેડગીરી" આગળથી કલકત્તા હવે ૬૮) અડસેઠ માઇલ દુર છે.

આ મથકથી આગળ વધતાં "મડ પાઇન્ટ" એટલે કીચલનું મથક એવે નામનું ઠેકાણું આવેછે. હીયાં હારબંધ ઊંચા "Cassurina" જેને આપણા કેટલાક લોક ભુલથી જંગલી સરોવરના ઝાડ કેહેછે, તેવાં ઝાડોની ઘટા અચ્છી લાગેલી દેખાયછે. આ ઠેકાણે આગલા વખતની મોહોટી પણ હાલ પાયામાલ થઈ ગયલી ઇમારતોની નીશાનો હજુર જોવામાં આવેછે. એમ કેહેછે કે ઈ૦ સ૦ ૧૮૩૩ના સાલમાં એક જબરૂં તોફાન હીયાં થયું હતું, જેથી નદીનાં પાણીના જોરથી આ જગા સઘળી ધોવાઈ ગઈ હતી. આગળ વધતાં, "સુંદરબંદ" ની જમીન દેખાયછે. "સુંદરબંદ" શબ્દોના અર્થ ઉપરથી વાંચનારના વીચારમાં આવું આવશે કે આ જમીન ઘણીજ રળીયામણી અને સુંદર હશે. પણ તે માત્ર જંગલ, ખબોચીયાં અને ચીકલની જગા છે. આ જગાના નાહાના મોહોટાં તરેવાર આકારવાળાં ટાપુઓ બનેલાં છે.

આ ટાપુઓ ઉપર એવું કેહેછે કે આગળ મોહોટી અને સારી વસ્તી અને ઘણી ઈમારતો હતી, પણ નદીનાં પાણીનો બરોબર અટકાવ નહી કીધાથી વારંવારની રેલે, આ ટાપુઓનો નાશ કરી નાખ્યો છે. આવી જગાઉપર હજુર કેટલીક વસ્તી છે અને તીહાં ભાતની ઉપજ પુશકળ છે. મુંબઈ શેહેરના સટ્ટાના દીવાનાપણામાં કલકત્તાના દેશીઓએ સામેલ થઈ, આવી જગો ખેડીને તેને ફળવંત કરવા સારૂ એક કંપની ઉભી કીધીહતી જેનું નામ "પોર્ટ કયાનીંગ" કંપનીને નામે કફોરી રીતે મશહુર થઈ પડેલું છે. આ કંપનીનો કારભાર ફેરફાર કરીને પાછો ચલાવીયો છે, અને ઉમેદ છે કે તેથી ફાયદો થઈ શકશે, કારણ કારભારીઓ ઘણા સારા હોશીયાર અને પ્રમાણીક ગ્રૃહસ્થો મળેલા છે. "સુંદરબંદ"ની પાયામાલ થયલી મીલકતોની નીશાનો હમણા આપણા જોયામાં આવેછે અને કોઇ તો આવુંબી કેહેછે કે તે વખતની દોલત વટીક પણ હજુર તીહાં દટાયલી મોજુદ છે. પણ તેને કાહાડે કોણ? તીહાં વાઘો, ઝેરી સાંપ અને રોગી પવન એવા તો જબરો ફુકેછે કે થોડા જણ તે મથક ઉપર ગયલા પાછા સલામત આવી શકયા છે. તીહાં દોલત દટાયલી પડેલી છે, આ વાત વીશે તો હમારેથી કંઈ કેહેવાઈ શકાતું નથી, પણ સુંદરબંદની બદ હવા જે ઘણીજ ઝેહેરી અને રોગી કેહેવાયછે, તથા વાઘ અને સાંપની તીહાં મોટી વસ્તી છે આ વાત તો ખરેખરી અને સત્તા ભરેલી છે. જીવનો વીમો ઉતારનાર કંપનીવાળાઓએ તો તેમની "પાલીસી" એટલે વીમાના લખતની સરતોમાં ખુલ્લું સાફ લખી જણાવેલું છે કે ફલાણી ફલાણી જગા ઉપર જીવનો વીમો ઊતરાવનાર શખસોએ કભી પણ જવું નહી, એમાં "સુંદરબંદ" ટાપુઓનું નામ મુકેલું છે, અને તેવી જગા ઉપર ગયાથી જો તે શખસનું મરણ નીપજીયું તો વીમાવાળાઓ તેના જીવની નુકશાનીના જવાબદાર નથી ગણવાના એવી ચોકસ સરત લખેલી છે.

નદીમાં આગળ જતાં "રંગા ફુલા" નામનું એક મોહોટું ગીચ જંગલ નજર આવેછે. આ જંગલમાં પણ વાઘની ઘણી વસ્તી કેહેછે. હમારી નજરે તો કોઈ પણ જાનવર તે વખતે નહી દેખાયું હતું પણ આવું સાંભળીયામાં આવીયું છે કે આ ઠેકાણા ઉપર વાંહાણવાળાઓને કોઈ કોઈ વાર દુરથી જંગલમાં ફરતો વાઘ નજર પડીયો છે, અને એક વાર તો તે ઠેકાણાં ઉપર કેટલાક કોળીયા હીમત કરીને માછલી મારવાને ગયા હતા, તેમનામાંના

એક જણને વાઘ આવી ઊંચકી લઈ જતો વાંહાંણવાળાઓએ નજરે નજર જોયો હતો, એવું લખાયલું છે. વળી આગળ ચાલતાં, વાંહાંણવાળાઓએ પોતાનો રસ્તો પીછાની રાખવાને એક ઠેકાણાં ઉપર એક નોંધી રાખવા જોગ ઝાડને નીશાન તરીકે નજરમાં રાખી મુકયું છે અને તેનું નામ તેમના રમુજી મીજાજ અથવા તોરમાં "રૂપાનાં ઝાડનો મીનારો" કરી રાખીયું છે. જરે આ ઝાડ આગળ આવી પુગા એટલે કલકત્તા ૫૭) માઈલ દુર છે એવું વાંહાંણવાળા જાણેછે.

આ ઠેકાણેથી પસાર થતાં આગળ નદીના ઉગમણ કીનારા ઉપર વસેલું ગામડું પેહેલ વેહેલું નજરે પડેછે. આ ગામડાંનું નામ "કલ્પી" કરીને કેહેછે, જેમાં એક પુરાણું હીંદુનું દેહેરૂં છે અને થોડાંક ઝાડોનો ઝુખ્ખડો માત્રે દેખાયછે.

હવે હીયાંથી બંગાલાની વેરાન અને જંગલ જેવી જમીનનો છેડો આવી માણસ જાતની વસ્તી લાયક જગા આપરૂી નજરે પડતી જાયછે. હમોએ આ ઠેકાણે સ્ટીમર ઉપરથી ઉતરીને નજરે નજર કંઈબી જોયું નથી, પણ વાંહાંણના તુતક ઉપરથી જે કંઇ દેખાઈ શકતું હતું તે ઉપરથી એવું કેહેવાને બની આવેછે કે આ વસ્તીની જગા ઉપર ખેતીવાડી થયલી હોય એવું હમુને અછડતું નજરે પડીયું હતું. આ ગામડાનું નામ "કલ્પી" કેહેછે અને હીયાંથી કલકત્તા ૪૮) માઈલ દુર છે.

"હુગલી" નદીની કફોરી વલાણ અને પેચ ભરેલો માર્ગ હવે હીયાંથી શીરૂ થાયછે. જે વલાણ ઉપર "ડાયમંડ હારબર" નામનું મથક છે, તીહાં આગળ એક વાર ઈસ્ટ ઇંડીયા કંપની સરકારનાં વાંહાંણો આવી લંગરવાર થતાં હતાં. હાલ આ મથક ઉપર પોસ્ટ આફીસ, તારની આફીસ અને માંડવી ખાતું છે. આ છેલાં ખાતાંમાંથી એક અમલદાર આ મથક ઉપરથી સ્ટીમર ઉપર આવેછે અને જીહાંસુધી આપણે કલકત્તે પોંહોંચીએ તીહાંસુધી સ્ટીમર અંદરનાં સરવે સામાન ઉપર જકાતની બાબદ વીરો તે ચોકાસી રાખેછે. બરોબર બોલીએ તો આ અમલદાર સરકાર તરફથી સ્ટીમર ઉપર આવેછે, અને તેમાં આવેલો જકાત લાયક માલ, તેવા સાહુકાર ઉતારૂઓ વીસરભોમાં અથવા ભુલથી વગર જગાત આપવે પોતાની સાથે લેઈ ચાલતી નહી પકડે, આ વીરો તે સંભાળ રાખેછે!

જરા આગળ વધીયા કે નદીના હવે ઘણાજ ધાસ્તી ભરેલા ભાગ ઉપર આવી પોંહોંચીએછ, જીહાંથી પસાર થતાં વાંહાંણવાળા ઘણીજ સંભાળ રાખેછે. આ ઠેકાણાંને "જેમ્સ એન્ડ મેરી" નું નામ આપેલું છે. હીયાં રેતીનો એક જબરો

મોટો ઢગ થયલો છે. "હુગ્લી" નદીની સાથે બે બીજી નાહાની નદીઓ "રૂપનારન" અને "દમુદા" મળીયાથી આ બંધે નદીનાં પાણીસાથે ઘસડાઈ આવતી રેતી, મટોડું, કચરા વીગેરેના જમાવ થયાથી આ ઢગ અથવા ટેકરો બનેલો છે. આ ઠેકાણાંનું નામ ઇંગ્રેજ લોકના કાનમાં હંમેશા ઘણીજ ધાસ્તી ઉપજાવનારૂં છે, કારણ એ કે આ જગાએ કેટલાંક કમબખ્તી ભરેલાં વાંહાંણો કંઈ મુદત ઉપર ભાગામાં આવીયાં હતાં. રૂપનારન અને હુગ્લીના દોઆબના ઉત્તર કીનારે "ફોર્ટ મારનીંગટન" નામનો કીલ્લો અથવા બતેરી આગલા વખતમાં ઉભી કરેલી હતી, અને આ મથક, કલકત્તા તરફ જતાં, પેહેલી ચોકી તરીકે ગણાતું હતું. એની સાંભણેના કીનારાનું નામ "હુગ્લી પાઇંટ" આપેલું છે, જે વટાવી આગળ જતાં, જમીનનો દેખાવ વધારે અને વધારે રળીઆમણો નજર પડતો જાયછે. "હુગ્લી પાઇંટ" આગળથી કલકત્તા ૩૩) માઇલ દુર છે. ગામ ગામડાંનાં ઝુપડાં નજરે પડેછે તેમનો દેખાવ ગોલ અને અણીદાર ઘાંસની ગંજીઓના જેવો દેખાયછે. સઘળાં ઝુપડાંનાં છાપરાં એક તરેના ઘાંસનાંજ બનાવેલાં હોયછે. ગામડાંઓની વસ્તી મોહોટી કેહેછે. બંગાલ પ્રાંતની જમીન, કીનારા આગળ સું કે અંદર જમીન ઉપર સું, બંધે ઠેકાણે નીચી અને સપાટ છે. કોઈબી ઠેકાણે એકુ પણ ટેકરી અથવા ડુંગરી જેવું કંઈ નજરે પડતું નથી. સ્ટીમર ઉપરથી ગામડાંનાં ઝુપડાં જાણે નીચાણમાં પડેલાં હોય એમ દેખાયછે. નદીનાં પાણીને, બંધ બાંધીને તજવીજથી અટકાવી રાખેલાં છે. આ બંધ જો નહી હોય તો મોહોટા ઉધાનનાં પાણી આખી જમીન ઊપર ફરી વળે એટલી જમીનની સપાટી નીચી છે.

"હુગ્લી પાઇંટ" છોડી સાત અથવા આઠ માઇલ આગળ ચાલતાં, "દમુદા" નદીનું મુખ ડાવા હાત ઉપર આવેછે, જે ઠેકાણાં ઉપર "ફૂલટા" નામનું એક ગામડું છે, જીહાં વલંદા વેપારીઓએ વેપારનું પેહેલ વેહેલું મથક કરીયું હતું. ઈ૦ સ૦ ૧૭૫૬ ના સાલમાં, ઇંગ્રેજ લોક કલકત્તાથી નાહાસી આવી, આ મથક ઉપર વાંહાંણોમાં અને તંબુઓ મારી ખીચોખીચ ભરાઇ સંતાઈ બેઠા હતા. પણ જેવા બુરા હાલ કલકત્તામાં સપડાયલા ઇંગ્રેજોના "બ્લાક હોલ" નામના પ્રખ્યાત કેદખાનાંમાં સુજાઉદ દોલાને હાતે થયા હતા, તેવાજ બુરા હાલ આ ઠેકાણાં ઉપર પણ નાહાસી આવી ભરાઈ રેહેલા ઇંગ્રેજોના, મરકીથી અને ખીચોખીચ વસીયાથી થયા હતા, જેમાં ઘણા જીવની ઘાત થઇ હતી. "ફૂલટા" ગામડાંથી કલકત્તા ૨૭) માઇલ દુર છે.

હીવાંથી આગળ ચાલતાં નદીમાં, હવે ઠેકાણે ઠેકાણે ગામઠી હોડીયો, મછવા, પડાઉ મળેછે, જેમનો તરેવાર દેખાવ પેહેલવેહેલા જોનારને ખુશનુમા લાગેછે. મછવા તથા પડાઉના સડો જે મોહોટા અને લાંબા બાંબુઓ સાથે બાંધેલા હોય-છે અને જેઓ ભારથી વાંકા વળી ગયલા અથવા મરડાઈ ગયલા દેખાયછે, તે જોઇને આપણાથી ટીકા કરયા શીવાય રેહેવાતું નથીઃ પણ તે સડ વળી ફાટી ગયલા, થીંગર થાંગર કરેલા, કોઈ કોઈમાં તો મોહોટાં ગાબડાં અને બગાડાં પડેલાં જોઇને તો, કલકત્તાના પડાઉ અથવા હોડીઓ અને હોડીવાળાઓની આળસાઈ અને બેપરવાઈ ઉપર હસવું આવીયા વગર રેહેવાનુંજ નથી. કોઈ કોઈ જગા ઉપર નદીમાં હવે એક વાંહાંણ પણ લંગરવાર થયલું નજરે પડવા માંડેછે અથવા કોઈ સ્ટીમર ધુમતી અને આવાજ કરતી આપણી સ્ટીમરની બોરદુએથી ઝડપમાં નીકળી જતી પણ દેખાયછે.

આગળ જતાં "મોયાપુર" નામનું કલકત્તાથી ૧૮ માઇલ દુર, એક મથક આવેછે, જીહાં સરકારી બારૂત રાખવાનાં મકાનો બાંધેલાં છે. કલકત્તા તરફ જતાં સઘળાં બારકસોની પાસે તેમનાં કામ જોગ કરતાં વધારે દારૂ ગોળો તેમની પાસે હોયો તો તેવાં સઘળાં બારકસોને આ ઠેકાણાં ઉપર તે દારૂ ખાલી કરવો પડેછે. આજ ઠેકાણાં ઉપર ઈ૦ સ૦ ૧૭૫૬ ના સાલમાં, હીંદુસ્થાન ફતે કરનાર "કલાઇવ" પોતાના સીપાઇઓ લેઇને, કલકત્તા પાછું જીતી લેવાને ઉતરીયા હતો, અને આજ ઠેકાણે ફ્રેંચ લોકોએ તેમનાં વેપારનું એક વેળા મથક કરયું હતું. "મોયાપુર" આગળ થોડાક વખતની વાત ઉપર, વાંહાંણના આવવા જવાની કલકત્તે ખબર આપવાને, એક વાવટાકાઠી હતી, પણ જીઆરથી તારની મારફતથી સંદેસા મોકલવાનું કામ જારી થયું છે, તીયારથી "મોયાપુર" આગળની વાવટાકાઠી કાહાડી નાખીને એક માઇલ આગળ "આટચીપોર" નામની જગા ઉપર તે ઉભી કરવામાં આવી છે.

આગળ વધતાં "ફોર્ટ ગ્લાસ્ટર" નામનું મથક આવેછે. આ મથકને જો કે "ફોર્ટ" એટલે કીલ્લાનું નામ આપીવું છે તે છતાં પણ તીહાં માત્રે એક મોહોટી રૂની ગીરણી સીવાએ બીજું કંઇજ નથી એવું જાણવામાં આવ્યું છે. આ કીલ્લા આગળથી કલકત્તા ૧૨॥ સાડાબાર માઇલ દુર છે. "ફોર્ટ ગ્લાસ્ટર"ની સાંબણેના કીનારા ઉપર "બજબજ" નામનો એક બીજો કીલ્લો છે, જે

જમીન ઉપર ઘણેા અંદરથી છે તેથી સ્ટીમર ઉપરથી દેખાઈ શકતેા નથી. પણ આ કીલ્લા વીશે તવારીખમાં એક રમુજી બીના લખાયલી છે તે જાણવા જોગ સમજી અત્રે આપી છે. કેહેછે કે ઈ૰ સ૰ ૧૭૫૬ ના સાલમાં જારે કલકત્તા પાછું જીતવાને ઇંગ્રેજી લશ્કર આ ઠેકાણાં ઉપર આવી પોંહોંચીયું, તારે ૨૯ મી ડીસેંબરને દીવસે, દરીઆઈ લશ્કરનાં આડમીરલ વાટસનનું "કેન્ટ" નામનું એક વાંહાંણુ, આ ઠેકાણાં ઉપર લડાઇને સારૂ લંગરવાર થયલું હતું. વાંહાંણુ ઉપરથી કીલ્લા ઉપર તેાપગેા મારો ચલાવેલા હતા અને તેથી કીલ્લાના કેાટમાં બગાડાં પડીયાં હતાં, તેાયપણ તે કીલ્લેા ઇંગ્રેજોના હાતમાં હજુ તુલીક આવેલેા નહી હતેા. તા૰ ૨૯ મી ડીસેંબરની રાત્રે, છાવણીમાં સઘળી સમાધાની હતી, અને લડાઈ બંધ હતી. તેવા વખતમાં "કેન્ટ" વાંહાંણુ ઉપરનેા એક ઇંગ્રેજી સેલર (ખલાસી), જેનું નામ સ્ટ્રેહન હતું તે સેલરને દારૂ પીવાનેા પુષ્કળ મળી આવીયાથી, તેને સુગું પડી રેહેવા નહી ગમીયુંહતું. તે પેાતાની જગા ઉપરથી પીધેલાની બાહારમાં બાહેર નીકળ્યેા. કેાઈએ તેને જોયેા નહી તેથી તે રખડતેા છેક કીલ્લાની નજદીક જઈ પુગેા. તે કીલ્લાની એટલેા નજદીક જઈ પુગેા કે, તેનાં માથાંમાં એવેાજ પવન આવીયેા કે તેાપથી પડેલાં બગાડાં વાટે કીલ્લામાં દાખલ થવું! તુરત તે બગાડાં વાટે અંદર ધુસી ગયેા, અને જોએછે તેા કેટલાક મુસલમાન સીપાઈઓ તીહાં બેઠેલા હતા. તેણે તુરત પેાતાની પાસે વાંહાંણુની "કટલાસ" કુરાડી હતી તે કાહાડીને તેમની ઉપર ઘસારો કીધેા, અને પેાતાની પાસે ભરેલી એક પીસ્તેાલ હતી તે પણ સીપાઇઓ ઉપર ઝાડી, અને "હુર્રે" ના ત્રણ મોહોટા પેાકાર મારીને બોલીયેા કે "કીલ્લેા મારા હાતમાં આવીયેા!" મુસલમીન સીપાઈઓ તેવાજ તેની ઉપર તુટી પડ્યા, પણ પેલા સેલરે એખલે હાતે તેમની સાંભણે ઘણીજ દીલાવરીથી અને તાજુબી ઊપજાવે એવી બાહાદુરીથી પેાતાનેા બચાવ કીધેા હતેા. સાંભાં સાંભી લડતાં અંતે તે સેલરના હાતમાંની કુરાડી એક સીપાઇએ મારેલા ઝટકાથી કપાઈ બે કકડા થઇ પડી હતી, જે થયાથી સેલરનેા જીવ હવે ભારી જોખમની અણી ઉપર આવી પડ્યેા હતેા! એવામાં બીજા બે સેલરેા આવીજ રીતે રખડતા રખડતા કીલ્લા આગળ આવી પોંહોંચેલા હતા, તેમના કાન ઉપર પેલી "હુર્રે" નેા પેાકાર પડ્યાથી તેઓ લાગલાજ અંદર ધુસીગયા હતા અને જે વખતે પેલાની કુરાડીના બે કકડા

થયા હતા, તેજ પ્રસંગે આ નવા બે ત્રણ સેલરો અંદર ધુસી ગયાથી તથા ધુસતા વારજ તે સેલરોએ પણ "હુર્રે" નો પોકાર જોરથી મારીયાથી, આખી ઇંગ્રેજી છાવણીમાં, શોહોર અને પોકાર થઈ રેહ્યો હતો. પેલા મુસલમીન સીપાઈઓ આવો બનાવ જોઇ, ખરેખર ધભરાટથી બેસાવધ થઈ ગયા હતા. છાવણીમાં પોકાર થતાંજ, ઇંગ્રેજી લશ્કર એકદમ ઉઠીને, જો કે તેમને કોઇએ હુકમ નહી આપીયો હતો, તોયપણ પડતું ખડતું એકદમ દોડી ધસારો કરીને કીલ્લા ઉપર ચઢી ગયું હતું. આ રાત્રની વખતે સઘળો ગડબડાટ અને હુમલો બીન કવાયદે જેમ તેમ થયલો હતો, તોયપણ તેમાં એક અકસમાત સીવાએ બીજી કંઈ નુકસાની નહી થઈ હતી. માત્રે એક નામીચો સરદાર "ડયુગલ કાંપબેલ" નામનો કપતાન પોતાનાંજ લશ્કરનાં માણસની બંદુકની ગોળી લાગાથી મરણ પામીયો હતો. કપતાન કુટે તુરત રાતોરાત્ર કીલ્લા પોતાના હસ્તકમાં કરી લીધો હતો અને સહવારના દીવસ ઉગતેજ કીલ્લા ઉપરથી તોપો છોડી આડમીરલ વાટસનની મનવારને સલામતીનું માન આપીયું હતું! ખરી સેલરી બાહાદુરીનો આ એક અચ્છો દાખલો છે, અને ખરા મરદની દીલાવરી તે એનેજ કેહેવી જોઇએછ, જો કે છાટાં પાણીના બાહારમાં આ બનાવ બનીયો હતો એટલીજ ખામી એમાં થઈ હતી. સેલર સ્ટ્રેહનને જારે સહવારના ધમકી આપીને કેહેવામાં આવીયું હતું કે તેણે લશ્કરી કવાયદના કાયદા કાનુનો તોડીયા હતા, અને દારૂ પીને આવું તોફાન ઉઠાવીયું હતું, આવો અન્યાય તેની ઉપર મેલીયામાં આવીયો છે, તે ઉપરથી એવું કેહેછે કે પેલા સેલરે મનમાં બડબડીને જવાબ આપીયો કે "——" ફલાણાના મહને કસમ છે કે જીહાં સુધી હું જીવતો છું તીહાંસુધી ફરીને હું કોઇબી બીજો કીલ્લો મારી મેજે એખલો કદી પણ જીતી નથી લેવાનો"!

આ ઠેકાણાં ઉપર નદી ધણીજ સાંકડી થયલી છે, અને બંધે બાજુના કીનારા ઉપર પુષ્કળ ગાંમડાં, વસ્તી તથા ખેતીવાડી નજરે પડેછે. હીયાંથી હમા ચીજો મછવાઓમાં કલકત્તા તરફ ભરાઇને જતી આપણા જોવામાં આવેછે. મેવો, તરકારી, બાળવાના લાંકડાં, ધાંસ, પેંડા, કોડીકામ, કાચકામ, ઇંતરડી, ધર બાંધવાની બીજી ચીજો, અને હજારો જાતની બીજી જીનસો હીયાંથી કલકત્તા તરફ જતી દેખાયછે. આટલા ઉપરથી જોનારની નજરે હવે એવું દેખાવા માંડેછે, કે તે કોઈ મોહોટાં વેપારનાં શેહેર અથવા મથકની નજદીકીમાં આવી પોંહોચેલા

છે. હીયાંથી જરા આગળ વધતાં "મેલનકલી પાઇંટ" નું મથક આવેછે. આ ઇંગ્રેજી શબ્દનો અર્થ દુઃખ અથવા દીલગીરીનું મથક એવો થાયછે, પણ તેવું કંઈ તીહાં છે નહી. આ ઠેકાણાંનું અસલ હીંદુસ્થાની નામ "મલીકહલ" કરીને હતું. પણ ઇંગ્રેજોથી આવો ઉચ્ચાર બરોબર નહી બોલી શકાયાથી, તેઓ "મલીકહલને" ઠેકાણે એક કફોરો બોલ "મેલનકલી" લગાડી દીધો હતો, અને તે આજ સુધી બોલીયામાં આવેછે. આ ઠેકાણાં ઉપર બીજું જાણવાજોગ કંઈ નથી, તોયપણ એક બીના તવારીખને લગતી હીયાં બનેલી છે, જેમાં એવું જણાયલું છે કે ઈ૦ સ૦ ૧૭૫૮ ના સાલમાં, તા૦ ૨૪ મી નવેમબરને દીવસે, ત્રણ ઇંગ્રેજી વેપારીના નાહાનાં વાંહાંણોએ મળીને વલંદાનાં સાત લશ્કરી વાંહાંણો સાથે આ ઠેકાણાં ઉપર લડાઈ કરી હતી અને બે કલાક કહણ મારો ચલાવીયા પછી વલંદાઓને તદન અને પુરા હરાવી નાખીયા હતા, અને સાત વાંહાંણોમાંનાં છ વાંહાંણ ઇંગ્રેજોએ પકડી પોતાના તાબામાં લીધાં હતાં. સાતમું વાંહાંણ હીયાંથી નાહાઠું હતું, તે આગળ જણાવેલાં "કલ્પી" નામનાં મથક આગળ બીજાં ઇંગ્રેજી વાંહાંણવાળાઓના હાતમાં સપડાયું હતું. આ ઠેકાણું કંઈ દરીયાઈ લડાઈ કરવા જોગ મથક નહીં હતું, તોયપણ હીયાં લડાઇ તો થઈજ હતી એમાં તો કંઈ શખ છેજ નહીં. આ મથકના ઉગમણ કીનારા ઉપર "અકરા" નામનું ગામ આવેલું છે, જીહાંથી કલકત્તાના ઘણાં ખરા ભાગ ઉપર અને તીહાંથી જતાં વાંહાંણવાળાઓને મીઠું દીધેલા ખોરાકની જીનસો થોડાક વખતની વાત ઉપર પોંહોંચાડીયામાં આવતી હતી. "અકરા" ગામથી કલકત્તા સાડાસાત માઇલ દુર છે. હીયાંથી "સંક્રલ સાન્ડ" નામનાં મથક ઉપર થઇ, રાજગંજ ગાંમડું છોડી તથા "થાણા" અને "આલીગડ" નામના કીલ્લા જે "ક્લાઇવ" અને "શારનાક" સરદારોએ સેહેલાઇથી ફતે કીધા હતા, તે કીલ્લાની હેવણ પડેલી જગા વચ્ચવી આગળ વધતાં, "ગારડનરીચ" નામના એક રળીયામણા અને બાગોબાહાર જેવાં મથક ઉપર આપણ આવી પોંહોંચીએછે, જે મથકની ખુરાનુમાઈ ઉપર આખું કલકત્તા ખુરબાન અને મગરૂર છે. દરીયા ઉપર સફર કરનારા ઘેરાયલા ઉતારૂઓ, જેમને લાંબા વખત સુધી દરીયો અને આકારા શીવાય જાજું બીજું કંઈજ નહી નજરે પડેલું, તથા "હુગલી" નદીમાં આવીયા પછી પણ જે કંઈ દેખાવ જોયલો તે સઘળો વેરાન, ઉજડ અને જંગલી હાલત જેવો જોવામાં આવેલો, તેમની

આંખો જારે આવા ખુશનુમા "ગારડનરીચ" નામનાં મથક ઉપર પડેછે, ત્યારે તે જોયાથી જે દીલમાં આનંદ ઉત્પન્ન થાયછે તે આનંદ ભોગવીયા શીવાય, ફકત વાંચીયાથી નથી હાંસલ થઈ શકવાનો. એક હાત ઉપર નદીનું પાણી સ્થીર પંથરાયલું છે, જાણે પાણીની નકરી એક મોહોટી થાળી ભરાયલી છે, તેની એક કોર આગળ ફુલવાડીના રળીઆમણા બાગોનાં સુંદર ઝાડોનો પ્રતીબીંબ પાણીની સપાટી ઉપર, જાણે આરસીમાં દેખાતો હોય તેમ દેખાયછે; બીજી કોરે ઊંચાં, ઉભા કદનાં, કદાવર ઝાડોની દબદબા ભરેલી હાર લાગેલી છે; તેમનો આબેહુબ જોડો પાણીની સપાટી ઉપર, તમામ બારીકી ભરેલો દેખાયછે, અને આ સઘળાની અંદર એક મોહોટી સુંદર ઈમારત, જેનો ઉઠાવ તબકા ઉપર તબકા બાંધીને કરેલો છે, તે નજરે પડેછે; આ દેખાવ કંઇ જેવો તેવો નહી સમજવો! પેલાં ઊંચા કદાવર દબદબા ભરેલાં ઝાડોની જે હાર દેખાયછે, તે ઝાડો કલકત્તાના સરકારી બાગનાં ઝાડો છે, જે બાગમાં પૃથ્વિના ઘણા ખરા દેશોના ઝાડ પાન અને વનસ્પતીનો એક ઘણોજ કીમતી અને જોવા લાયક જમાવ, છુટે હાતે ખરચ કરીને સરકાર તરફથી બનાવીયામાં અને ચાલુ રાખીયામાં આવીયો છે. આ બાગનો દેખાવ નદી ઉપરથીજ જોનારનાં મનને પોતાની તરફ ખેંચી લીએછે. હીયાંથી જોનાર તેની ઉપર જાણે મોહીત પડી તે અંદરથી કેવો ખુશનુમા હશે તે જોવાની ઈનતેજારીમાં પડેછે. કલકત્તે જઈ આવેલા જેખા કોઇએ આ બાગ નહી જોયો હશે, તેમને હમો ખરેખર એક લેખે ખુદરતી મોજ ભોગવનારોમાં ખરાજ કમનસીબ ગણશું. પેલી તબકા ઉપર તબકાવાળી જે ઈમારત દેખાયછે તે "બીશપ કાલેજ" છે. હીયાં ઇંગ્રેજી કેળવણી આપવાનું એક મોહોટું ખાતું છે, જે કલકત્તાના વડા બીશપની કોશેસથી સ્થાપવામાં આવીયું છે.

બીશપ કાલેજની સાંભણી બાજુએ અને ગારડનરીચની પડોસમાંજ પી. એંડ ઓ. કંપનીની સ્ટીમરો લંગરવાર થાયછે. હીયાંથી ઉતારુઓ સ્ટીમરમાંથી ઉતરેછે અથવા ચઢેછે. આ ઠેકાણાં ઉપર સ્ટીમરમાંથી ઉતરતાં જો ભરતીનો વખત હોયછે તો સ્ટીમર છેક ડંકાની જમીનની નજદીક શુધી જઈ શકેછે. આ ઠેકાણાં ઉપર ઉતરતાં કલકત્તાનું શેહેર હીયાંથી નજદીક ત્રણ માઈલ દુર છે, જીહાં પોંહોંચવાને ગાડીમાં જવું હોય તો ભાડેની ગાડીઓ અથવા બીજી રીતે લાવ લઈ જવાને પાલકી, ઘોડા તઈયાર મળી શકેછે.

ગારડનરીચ આગળ આવી પોહોંચતાં, હજુર કલકત્તાના શેહેરનો દબદબો બરોબર નજરે પડી શકતો નથી. જે કંઈ તે ઠેકાણાં ઉપર દેખાયછે તે માત્રે ગોદીઓ, અને તેમને લગતાં કારખાનાં, ઝાડોની ઘટા અને ઈમારતો માત્રે દેખાયછે. એક ગમથી ખુલ્લું સપાટ મેદાન દેખાયછે, જીહાં મેંઢાં અને બકરાં ચરેછે. બીજી ગમથી સેંટપાલ નામના ક્રીસચીયન લોકના દેવલનો મીનારો અને ચૌરંગી લતા ઉપરની સુફેદ રંગની ઈમારતો પેલી ઝાડોની ઘટામાંથી છુટી છવાઈ નજરે પડેછે. શેહેરનો ઘણો ખરો ભાગ તો, કોટની દીવાલ અને ફોર્ટ ઊલીયમ નામના કલકત્તાના કીલ્લાથી ઢંકાયલો રેહેછે. તેમાંથી માત્રે વાવટા કાઠીનો ઉપરનો ભાગ અને દેવલનો મીનારો માત્રે દેખાયછે.

તા૦ ૩૦ જાનેવારીને દીને સાંજના ૪ા કલાકે મેલ સ્ટીમર તેના ઉતારાની જગા આગળ આવી પુગી હતી અને તેની થોડો વખત આગમચ, સ્ટીમરના માણસોએ ઉતારૂઓનો સર સામાન, પેટી, પેટારા, વાંહાંણના હોલમાંથી કાહાડીને સ્ટીમરની તુતક ઊપર હારબંધ ગોઠવી દીધા હતા. એમાંથી નામ વાંચીને જેનો જે સામાન હતો તે ઉતારૂઓ ચપોચપ પોતે ઉઠાવી લેતા હતા. આ વખતે કલકત્તા તરફથી ઉતારૂઓના સગાવાહાલા, દોસ્ત આશનાઓ, કીનારા ઊપર આવી ઊભા હતા, તે વખતે એક જોવા જેવી રચના, જેવી આપણા પાલવાના બંદર ઊપર આવા ટાંકણાસર થાયછે તેવી તીહાં થઈ રહી હતી. તેમાં એક મોહોટો ફેર એ હતો કે આપણી મુંબઇના પાલવાના ડંકા ઉપર તો બંદર બોટમાં ઊતારૂઓ સ્ટીમર ઊપરથી ઊતરીને આવેછે, પણ હીયાં કલકત્તામાં તો મોહોટી સ્ટીમર છેક ડંકાની બોરદુએ જઈ શકેછે, અને કીનારા ઊપર ઉભા રહેલાં માણસો સ્ટીમર ઊપરના માણસોને જોઈ શકેછે અને એકમેક સાથે વાત કરી શકેછે એટલા નજદીક બંધે તરફવાળા આવી જાયછે, જેથી દેખાવ વધારે જોવા લાયક થઈ પડેછે.

જેમ બીજાઓને તેમ હમને લેવાને હમારા કેટલાક મીત્રો તથા કામાજીની પેહેડીના મીત્રો આવીયા હતા. સ્ટીમર ઉપરથી ઊતરીને કેટલાક ઓળખીતાઓ સાથે અને કેટલીક નવી ઓળખો સાથે મેલભેટ કીધી. હમારે સારૂ જે ગાડી અમારા મીત્રો લાવીયા હતા તેમાં બેસવાની જગા જો કે ચાર જણની હતી તોએપણ તેમાં પાંચમા હમારા એક મીત્ર, જેવણ કલકત્તાના રેહેવાશી હતા તેમને જબરદસ્તીથી હમારી સાથે બેસાડીયા હતા,

આવી મતલબથી કે જેથી કંઈ હમોને જાણવું હોય તે તેવણને પુછી હમો વાકેફ થઈ શકીએ. પાંચ જણ એક ખુલ્લી ગાડીમાં ભચડાઇને બેસવા તથા આવી રીતે રસ્તા ઊપરથી ખુલ્લી ગાંડીમાં શેહેરમાં ફરવાને હમો ખચીત મુંબઈમાં હતે તો જરા આંચકો ખાતે, પણ આ વખતે તો કલકત્તા શેહેર જોવાની ઉલટ એટલી તો થઇ હતી, અને પરદેશમાં જાજી ઓળખાણ પીછાન નહી હોવાના સબબથી હમને જરા વધારે છુટથી ફરવાની હીમત થઈ હતી, તેથી આવી રીતે ભચડાઈ કચડાઇને બેસી ફરવાને તે વખતે કંઈ અણઘટતું નહી લાગું હતું. ગાડીમાં બેસ્તાંજ સાંભેથી એક જણ ટોપલીમાં કોઈ તરેના ફલો મુકીને હમારી આગળ વેચવાને લાવીયો હતો. હમોને ખબર નહી હતી કે તે ફળ સું હતાં. પણ જારે હમારા જાણવામાં આવીલું કે તે ફળ કલકત્તાનાં બોર હતાં, તારે હમને તેનાં કદ વીશે ઘણીજ તાજુબી લાગી હતી, કારણ હમોએ આ તરફનાં બોર આગળ જોયલાં નહી હતાં. હાલ તો મુંબઇમાં રેલવે દાખલ થયાથી એક ગમથી છેક સુરત, ભરૂચ, અમદાવાદ, અને વડોદરા અને બીજી તરફથી છેક નાગપોર સુધીથી બોર અને બીજો સારો મેવો આવવા લાગો છે, પણ તે વખતે આવું કંઈ આવતું નહી હતું. કલકત્તાનું બોર મોહોટાં કદનું છે. તે વચલા કદનાં પેર જેટલું મોહોટું થાયછે, આવી જો મીસલ આપીએ તો તે સહરાવીને નહી બોલેલું કેહેવાશે. કલકત્તાનું બોર મોહોટાં કદનું છે એટલુંજ નહી, પણ તે સ્વાદમાં પણ ઘણુંજ મીઠું અને પુશ્કળ માવાદાર છે, અને તેનાં કદ પ્રમાણે તેનો ઠડીયો ઘણોજ નાહાનો છે. તેનાં કદ વીશે બીજી રીતે બોલીએ તો આવું કેહેવાઈ શકાશે કે જો એક આખું બોર મોહોડાંમાં મુકીએ તો તે સેહેલાઇથી ચાવી નથી શકાવાનું, એટલું મોહોટું છે. તેની એક બીજી ખુબી એ કેહેવાની છે કે જાનેવારી મહીનાની થંડી, તેના મીઠાસ સાથે ભેળાવાથી, બોરની લેહેજતમાં વધારો થાયછે. આ ફળ હમોએ એક તો નવું જોયું હતું, બીજું તો તે લેહેજતમાં, મુંબઈનાં બોરને વટાવમાં નાખે એવું હતું, ત્રીજું, બજારમાં તે લેવા જયા વગરે, તે હમારી નજર સાંભણે પુછતું આવીયું હતું, અને ચોથું, તે સસ્તું, રેલછેલ થતું હતું. આ ચાર સબબોથી હમો સઘળાઓ ગાડીની અંદરજ, અને લોક જુએ એવી રીતે તે ખાવા મંડી ગયા હતા, અને એક આખી નાહાની ટોપલી ભરીને તે ખાધાં હતાં, અને તે ખાતી વખતે એક બીજાના ઉપસાયલા ગાલો જોઇને હમુને ઘણીજ રમુજ થઇ

પડી હતી. આવી રીતે ખાવાને હમો મુંબઈ શેહેરમાં એકાએક હીમત નહીં ચલાવી શકતે! આ સ્વાદનો છેડો જલદીથી આવી ગયો હતો. ગાડીમાં જેટલા બોર ખવાયાં તેનો અરધો ભાગ પછવાડેથી બીજે અથવા ત્રીજે દીને નહીં ખાવા ગમ્યો હતો, અને પછી રફતે રફતે તે એટલો તો ઓછો થઈ ગયો હતો કે તે ફળ વીશે વીચાર વટીક પણ નહીં આવતો હતો. કલકત્તામાં બોરનો ઊપયોગ અચાર ભરવામાં પણ ઘણો થાયછે.

ગાડીમાં બેસી પસાર થતાં આસપાસ જે મોહોટ મોટી ઇમારતો નજરે પડતી હતી તેમની બાંધણી અને દબદબા ઉપરથી પેહેલ વેહેલા જોનારનાં મન ઊપર કલકત્તા શેહેરની ખુબસુરતી અને દમામ વીશે સારી અસર થયા વગર નથી રેહેવાની. જેમ જેમ ગાડી આગળ વધતી જાયછે તેમ સુંદર દેખાવ અને બાંધણીવાળી ઇમારતો એક પછી એક નજર સાંભણે આવતીજ જાયછે, તે જોઇને કલકત્તાને "સીટી આફ પાલસીસ" એટલે મેહેલોનું શેહેર કરીને જે નામ અપીયામાં આવીયું છે તે ખરેખરૂંજ આપીયું છે, એવું ધારવાને ખરા સબબો મળી આવેછે. પણ આવો દેખાવ લાંબા વખત સુધી નથી રેહેતો. થોડા વખતમાં આ દમામ ભરેલી રચનાનો છેડો આવી જાયછે. કલકત્તાની દેશી વસ્તીના લતા ઉપર આવી પુગા કે ઇમારતોનો આગલો દબદબા ભરેલો દેખાવ બદલાઈ કલકત્તાના નામને ઝાંખ લગાડનાર દેખાવ જોવામાં આવેછે. મેહેલોનાં શેહેરનો ભપકો હીયાં નરમ પડી ગયલો દેખાયછે. દેશીઓનાં ઘર એવાં તો બેડોલ નજરે પડવાં માંડેછે કે આપણને તાજુબી લાગીયા વગર નથી રેહેતી કે શું બસ આટલાંમાંજ મેહેલોનાં શેહેરનો છેડો આવી ગયો અને કોઇ બીજુંજ શેહેર નજર આગળ આવીયું કે? તેની સાથે રસ્તા એવા તો વાંકી વલાણના અને ગલીચ હાલતમાં હમારા જોવામાં આવીયા હતા કે તેમની સરખામણી જો આપણે કરવા જઈએ તો આપણી મુંબઇના ભુસારી અને રંગારી મોહોલા તથા ચીચબંદરના લતા તરફના મોહોલા જેવા તેઓ દેખાતા હતા. આ ઠેકાણાં ઉપરનો વાસ, હવા અને સગવડ તરફ નજર કરતાં, આપણી મુંબઈના ઉપર જણાવેલાં ઠેકાણાં, હાલની હાલતમાં ઘણેક દરજે કલકત્તા કરતાં વધારે બેહેતર હાલતમાં જાણવાં. કલકત્તા શેહેરનો દેખાવ નદીમાંથી અને ગારડનરીચ આગળથી જેવો દીલપસંદ દેખાયો તે ઉપરથી જોનારે જે મત બાંધીયું હશે તે મત આ દેશી વસ્તીના લતા ઉપર આવી પોહોંચવા પછી

તેને ફેરવવાની ફરજ પડશે. આ સઘળું થવાનો સબબ એટલોજ છે કે કલકત્તાની ભપકા ભરેલી અને મેહેલ જેવી ઈમારતો વીગરે જે ખુબસુરતી ભરેલો દેખાવ છે તે એક ચોકસ હદમાં અને લતા તરફજ માત્રે આવી રેહેલો છે. જીહાં યુરોપીયન અને જુજ દેશી વેપારીયો તથા સરકારી ચાકરીવાળા ઘણા ખરા અમલદારોનો તમામ વહીવટ ચાલુ થઈ રેહેલો છે તે લતા તરફ ઘણીજ મોહોટી હારબંધ ઈમારતો બંધાયલી છે, મોહોટ મોટા પોહોળા રસ્તા, ફરવા હરવાની જગા, મેદાન, વીગરે સઘળી બાબદની સગવડ અને સફાઈ રાખવામાં આવી છે. પણ હીયાંથી આગળ જતાં દેશી વસ્તીમાં કંઈ તેવું જોવામાં આવતું નથી.

વેપાર વણજની ધુમધામનો કલકત્તાનો ભાગ, ચંદપાલઘાટ અને કલકત્તાની નવી ટંકસાળ, જે બંધે ઠેકાણાં નદીની ઉગમણ દીશાએ આવેલાં છે, તીહાંથી તે બડા બજાર અને કાસીતોલ્લાના મોહોલા સુધી અને કાસીતોલ્લાના મોહોલા આગળ જે બે રસ્તાનાં નાંકાં આવેલાં છે, એક ધરમતોલ્લાનો રસ્તો અને બીજો ચવરંગીનો રસ્તો, આ હદ સુધીમાં છે. ચવરંગીના રસ્તા ઉપર ઘણાં ખરા યુરોપીયન માતબર લોકની વસ્તી છે, અને દેશીઓમાં માત્રે આપણાં માન પામેલા શેઠ રૂસ્તમજી કાવસજી બનાજીના સાહેબજાદા શેઠ માણેકજી રૂસ્તમજી કાવસજી બનાજીનો એકલાનોજ રેહેવાનો મકાન છે. ચવરંગી લતા ઉપરની કેટલીક ઈમારતોનો દેખાવ ઇંગ્લંડની ઈમારતોની રોનકદારીની બરોબરી કરી શકે એવો છે, એવું જેઓ ઇંગ્લંડ જોઈ આવીયા છે તેમનું મત છે. આપણી મુંબઈના એલફીનસ્ટન સરકલનો દેખાવ અને હાલ મી. ત્રીચરની કંપની, ફ્રેંચ બેંક અને ઓરીએંટલ બેંક વીગરે બીજી જે ઈમારતો મેદાન ઉપર બંધાયછે, જેમાંના બેચાર ચીત્ર અત્રે આપીયાં છે તેમની સાથે, ચવરંગીની ઈમારતોના દેખાવનો મોકાબલો કરી શકાય એવું છે, પણ જારે આપણી મુંબઈની મેદાન ઊપર બંધાતી સઘળી ઇમારતો પુરી બંધાઈ તઈયાર થશે, તે વખતે હમો ધારીએછ કે મુંબઇનો આ લતા ઉપરનો દેખાવ ચોરંગીને ટકર મારે એવો થઈ પડશે. ચોરંગીમાં જીહાં યુરોપીયન લોક વસેછે તીહાંના કેટલાક રસ્તા ઘણાજ મોહોટા અને કોશાદ છે, લંબાઈમાં આસરે બે માઈલ લાબાં અને સરાસરી એંસી ફુટ પોહોળા, અને તેમની ઉપર ગ્યાસ લાઈટ મુકીયામાં આવી છે. હમો જીઆરે તીહાં હતા તે વખતે ગ્યાસ લાઈટ તુરતનીજ દાખલ કરીયામાં આવી હતી. શેહેરના દેશી ભાગમાં તો ભોયસીંગનાં તેલના

દીવા ઝુકતા દેખાતા હતા. હાલ તો અલબતાં મ્યુનીસીપાલીટીએ તીહાં ફેરફાર કરી નાખીયો છે, અને ઉમેદ રાખીયેછ કે નીચે બયાન કરેલા ધરમતોલ્લાના મોહોલામાં જીહાં આપણા ચંચલ પારશી ભાઈ બંધુઓ વસેછે તે જગા ઉપરનું મચ્છરખાનું નીકળી ગયું હશે!

દેશી વેપારીઓની પેહેડીઓ અને રેહેવાનાં મકાન ધરમતોલ્લાના મોહોલામાં છે, જેનો દેખાવ ખચીત ઘણોજ રેજધાન અને નાપસંદ છે. હમો જારે મી. ખુરશેદજી નુસરવાનજી કામાજીની કલકત્તાની પેહેડી ઉપર જઈ પુગા તારે જાણીયું કે આપણા મેહરબાન પારશી વેપારીઓ કલકત્તામાં કેવી જગા ઉપર વસતા હતા. તીહાં ગયા આગમચ હમારાં મનમાં એવો વીચાર હતો કે આ સાહેબો ઘણીજ પસંદ અને હવાવાળી જગા ઉપર વસ્તા હશે, પણ આ હમારો વીચાર ખોટો પડયો હતો. જે મોહોલામાં આપણા પારશી વેપારીઓની પેહેડીઓ જોઇ તે ઠેકાણું આપણી મુંબઇનો વાણીયાવાડ જેવું હતું. ગલીચી અને દુરગંધી જબરી લાગતી હતી, અને તેની સાથે તે ખરેખરજ એક મચ્છરખાનું હતું. કારણ પુછીયું કે આવી જગા ઉપર પેહેડી રાખવાની સું મતલબ હતી, તારે હમોએ જાણીયું કે સઘળી પેહેડીયો એક બીજાની નજદીકીમાં હોયાથી વેપારનાં અને બીજાં કામ કાજમાં સેહેલાઈ પડતી હતી. બીજું કારણ એવું કેહેવામાં આવીયું હતું કે જીહાં સુધી સઘળી પેહેડીવાળા સાહેબો આ મકાન બદલી કોઈ બીજી જગા ઉપર જાય તોજ સઘળાઓથી આ મચ્છરખાનું છોડી શકાય! ત્રીજું કારણ એવું જણાવીયું હતું કે આતશ આદરીયાન આ મોહોલામાં નજદીક હોવાથી, પારશીઓને તેમના ધરમ સંસારની કેટલીક બાબદો જાલવવાને પણ આ મચ્છરખાનાંવાળા મોહોલામાં રેહેવું જરૂરનું, ફાયદા ભરેલું અને સવલ પડતું હતું! આપણા ધુંધી અને દુરંદેશી પારશી પરદેશી વેપારીયોનો આવો વીચાર સાંભળી હમોને થોડોવાર ભારી અંદેશો થઈ પડયો હતો પણ પછવાડેથી માલુમ પડયું કે "જુનું તે સુનું" આ કેહેવત પ્રમાણે તેઓ જીહાં લાબાં દીવસસુધી વસ્તા આવીયા તીહાંજ વસવું ઠીક છે, એવું સમજી આ ઠેકાણાંને તેઓ વળગી રેહ્યા હતા! પણ આવી જગાને હવે પછીના તીહાંના જુવાન અને કળી ફુટતા વેપારીયો લાંબા વખત સુધી વળગી રેહેશે, એ શખ ભરેલું લાગેછે. કામાજીની પેહેડી ઉપર એક કલાક ખોટી થયા હતા, તેટલા વખતમાં ધરમતોલ્લાના મોહોલાની ખુબી સારી પેઠે હમો

સઘળાઓએ જાણી લીધી હતી. વાત કરતાં મસ્છરનું ભણભણતું ટોલું મોહોડાંમાં પેસી જતું હતું, જેનો અટકાવ કરવાને રૂમાલથી અથવા પંખાથી ઝાટક ઝુટક કરવી પડતી હતી. મોહોલાની ગટરોનો પમરાટ નાકને ગુંગરાવી નાખતો હતો, અને જો કે ફેબરવારી મહીનાની શીરૂઆત હતી તેથી થંડીનો હીંગામ હતો, તોએપણ આ ઠેકાણાં ઉપર ગરમીથી પસીનો જબરો પડતો હતો. હમારા ઉતારાને સારૂ મી. કામાજીની પેહેડીએ દુર એલાહેદો એક મકાન કાશીપોરમાં કરાવી રાખીયો હતો, તીહાં એકદમ જવું હમોએ બેહેતર ધારીને ધરમતોલ્લાના મોહોલામાંથી રૂખસદ લીધી હતી. કાસીપોર, ધરમતોલ્લાથી આસરે ૪) અથવા ૫) માઈલ દુર છે, જીહાં નદીના કીનારા ઊપર કેટલાક રેહેવાનાં મકાનો નીરાંત જગા ઉપર બાંધેલાં છે. કલકત્તાના દેશી અને પારશી વેપારીયો દર શનીવાર અને રવીવારે અથવા તેહેવારના દીવસો ઉપર સેહેલગાહ કરવાને અથવા બાગ વાડીએ મોજ જોગ કરવાને આ ઠેકાણાં ઉપર જાયછે. કાશીપોરમાં હીંદુસ્થાનના આગલા કોર્ટ આફ ડાયરેકટરોના વખતમાં બંધાયલું લશ્કરી કામસર પીતળ કામ ઓતવાનું એક મોહોટું કારખાનું નદીના કીનારા ઉપર બાંધેલું છે.

ધરમતોલ્લાથી કાસીપોર જવા નીકળ્યા તે વખતે જેજે મોહોલાઓમાંથી તથા વસ્તીમાંથી હમારી ગાડી પસાર થઈ, તે વખતે જે દેખાવ જોયામાં આવીઓ તે ઊપરથી એવું માલુમ પડીયું હતું કે કલકત્તાની દેશી વસ્તી ઘણીજ ગીચ વસેછે. પણ ખબર કાહાડતાં એવું જાણીયામાં આવીયું છે, કે કલકત્તાની વસ્તી કેટલાકોનાં મત પ્રમાણે પાંચથી છ લાખ માણસની ગણાયછે, પણ એમાંથી માત્ર ત્રણ લાખ માંણસોજ ખુદ કલકત્તાના જાથુકના રેહેવાશીયો છે, અને બાકીની વસ્તી આવ જાવ કરતી અથવા જેને ફરતી વસ્તીને નામે બોલેછે, તેવી છે.

કલકત્તાના દેશી લોકની વેહેંચણી, તેમના ધંધા પેશા મુજબ નીચે જણાવીયા પ્રમાણે થયલી છે. આખી મુસલમાન લોકની અને હલકી જાતનાં હીંદુઓની વસ્તીનો બરોબર અરધો અરધ ભાગ, યુરોપીયન લોકની નોકરીમાં છે, અને આ અરધા ભાગનો ઘણો ખરો ભાગ યુરોપીયનોનાં ઘર સંસારને લગતાં કામ કાજમાં ચાકરીએ લાગેલા છે, અને બાકીનો સરકારી ખાતાંઓમાં અને વેપારીઓની પેહેડીનાં કામ કાજમાં ચાકરીએ લાગેલા છે. ઉપલી વસ્તીનો બાકીનો અરધો ભાગ, જમીન ઉપરથી નદી ઉપર અને નદી ઊપરથી જમીન ઉપર માલ

ચઢાવા ઉતારવાની મજુરી કરનારી, પાલખી ઊંચકનાર હમાલો, હેલકરીઓ, અને "ટીકા" એટલે ભાડુતી ગાડીઓના કોચમેન તરીકે ધંધો કરી પોતાનું ગુજરાણ કરનારી વસ્તી છે. આ બે ભાગ બાદ કરતાં બાકીની વસ્તી, ખલાસીઓ, કણીયા, તલી, કાપડીયા, રોજીંદું કામ કરનારા, ખાધ ખોરાકીની પરચુરણ જીનસો વેચનારા છે.

કલકત્તાનું જે મોહોટું નામ "સીટી આફ પાલસીસ" મેહેલાનું શેહેર કરીને પડીયું છે, તે ઉપરથી વાંચનાર વીચારશે કે આ બુલંદ શેહેરમાં મોહોટ મોટી જાહેર સુંદર ઈમારતો, અને ઘરો ઘણાં હશે. પણ તીહાં ખરેખર આવી ઈમારતો કંઈ ઘણી નથી. માત્રે થોડીક સુંદર ખાનગી બાંધણીઓ ઉપર, કલકત્તાના મોહોટાં નામની કીર્તીનો આધાર રેહેલો છે. પણ આસરે પચાસ વરસ થયાંજ કલકત્તાના રેહેવાશીઓને આ વીશે સમજ પડી છે, કે જુદાં જુદાં જાહેર કારણો સારૂ, જુદી જુદી જાહેર ઈમારતો બાંધવી આ તેમની અને સરકારની એક ફરજ છે. જેને જાહેર ઈમારતનું નામ આપી શકીએ, અને જેનો ઉપયોગ જાહેર પ્રજાનાં કામસરજ કરવાની મતલબથી તે બાંધીયામાં આવી હોય, એવી બાંધણીયો આજ સુધી કલકત્તામાં આસરે અઢાર અથવા વીસ છે, જેમાંના કેટલીકોનાં નામ નીચે આપીયાં છે :—

ગવરમેંટ હાઉસ (સરકારી મેહેલ.)
ટાઉન હાલ.
મેટકાફ હાલ.
ફીવર હાસપીટલ.
પ્રેસીડેનસી કાલેજ.
બીશાપ કાલેજ.
ધી મદરેશા.
મહમદન કાલેજ.
} જેમાં હીંદુસ્થાની, ફારસી અને અરબી ભાશા શીખવે છે.
જનરલ આસેમબ્લી ઈનસ્ટીટયુશન.
મેડીકલ કાલેજ.
આરફન સ્કુલ.
જનરલ હાસપીટલ.

આઈસ હાઉસ.
મારટીનીયર.
ધી મીંટ (ટંકસાળ.)
એશીયાટીક સોસાઈટીનું મ્યુઝીયમ તથા લાઈબ્રેરી.
બેથીયુન છોકરીઓની નીશાળ.
બેંગાલ બેંક.
પ્રીનસેપ્સ ઘાટ.
મોહોટી જેલ.
ફોર્ટ ઉલીયમનો કીલ્લો.
કાસીપોરમાં સરકારી પીતળનું ઓતકામનું કારખાનું.

BANK OF BENGAL, CALCUTTA

૨. બંગાળાની બેંક.

ધરમતોલ્લાથી સાંજના ૬) વાગે નીકળેલા આસરે રાત્રે ૭) વાગે કાસીપોર જઈ પુગા હતા. આગળ કેહવું તેમ રસ્તાનો દેખાવ કંઈ ઘણો જોવા જોગ નહી નજર આવીયો હતો. વસ્તી ઘણી ગીચ દેખાઈ હતી, જેનો દેખાવ આપણી મુંબઈના મુંબાદેવીના કનસારા વાડ જેવો હતો. જે ગાડીમાં હમો બેશી ગયા હતા તે ગાડીના કોચમેન તથા પાછળ ઉભા રેહેનાર બે ઘોડાવાળા રસ્તા ઉપર ચાલનારા લોકને એક એાર તરેથી બાજુએ ખીસી જવાને પોકારતા હતા. તેઓ "ચાલરે બાજુ," "પોઈસ," આવા શબ્દોથી પોકાર નહી મારતા હતા, પણ "બાં દીકે," "ડાંઇનિ દીકે," "દરી કારો," "સરે જા," "બચાવ," આવા શબ્દો પોકારીને બોલતા સંભળાયા હતા, જે શબ્દોનો અર્થ પુછવાથી હમુને એમ સમજ મળી હતી કે "ડાવી બાજુ," "જમણી બાજુ," "ઉભો રેહે," "ખીસી જા," "સંભાળજે," એ મુજબ તેઓ રસ્તે ચાલનારાઓને પોકાર મારી કેહેતા હતા. પોઇસ, ચાલરે, બાજુના કરતાં આ શબ્દોથી તો પગે ચાલનારને સારી પેઠે, અને સાઉચેતી ભરેલી ચેતવણી આપીયામાં આવેછે કે તેણે રસ્તાની કહી બાજુએ સલામતી સારૂ ખીસી જવું, આ રીતનો પોકાર "ચાલરે બાજુ"ના કરતાં વધારે ચોકસાઈ ભરેલો છે એમાંતો કંઇજિ શખ નથી.

હાલ આપણી મુંબઈમાં જે નવા રસ્તા બંધાયછે તેમની બંધે બાજુએ ચાલવાને સારૂ જે ઉંચી પગથી બનાવાનું મંડાણ આપણા ચંચલ મ્યુનીસીપાલ કમીશનરે કરીયું છે, તે પગથીઓ રસ્તામાં ચાલનારા લોકને ઘણી ફાયદાકારક થઈ પડવાની છે. હવે આ પગથી ઉપરથીજ ચાલવાને પોલીસની અથવા કાયદાની રૂએ, જો લોકને ફરજ પાડે તો, આપણી ગ્રપુમાં દર વરસે ગાડી ઘોડા તળે અકસમાત ચંપાઇને જેટલા જીવોની ઘાત થાયછે, તેમાં કેટલો ઘટારો થઈ પડે, આ બાબદ સત્તાવાળાઓને ધીયાન પોંહોંચાડવા જોગ છે. હમો ધારીએછ કે આ સારી ટેવ આપણાં લોકમાં પાડવાને જો આપણી પોલીસ માથે લીએ, અને થોડા વખત સુધી ચાંપ રાખીને રસ્તા ઉપર જવા આવવાની ડાવી અને જમણી બોરદ મુકરર કરી રાખે, અને તે મુજબ પગે ચાલનારાઓને ચાલવાની જબરીથી ફરજ પાડે, અથવા આ હુકમને તાબે નહી થનારને સેજસાજ દંડની સજા કરીયામાં આવે, તો ખચીત થોડા વખતમાં આ સારી ચાલ લોક અખ્તિયાર કરી રાકરો, અને હાલ જેમ ગાડી ઘોડા વીરો ડાવી અને જમણીબાજુ ઉપર હાંકવાની

ચોકસાઈ અને કાયદો રાખીયામાં આવેછે તેમજ ચાલવાની બાબદમાં પણ એવીજ ચોકસાઈ અને કાયદો રાખીયામાં આવશે. ઇંગ્લંડમાં તો આ વીશે ધારાની રૂએ બંદોબસ્ત કરીયામાં આવીયો છે અને કોઈબી માણસ ભુલથી ડાવી બાજુ ઉપર ચાલવાને બદલે જો જમણી બાજુ ઉપર ચાલતો હોય તો કાનસ્ટેબલ તેને મોટેથી પોકારીને ચેતવણી આપેછે કે સાહેબ તમે તમારી ઘટતી બોરદુએથી ચાલો! આવો કાયદો હીયાં પણ લાગુ પાડવો જોઈએછ.

કાસીપોર પોંહોંચતાં રાત્રે સાત વાગાનો અમલ થયો હતો. જે બંગલામાં હમો ઉતરીયા હતા તે નદીને કીનારે, હવાવાળી અને એકાંત જગા ઉપર હોવાથી હમો સઘળાને તે ઘણોજ પસંદ પડ્યો હતો. અંધારૂં થઈ ગયલું હતું તેથી આસપાસનો દેખાવ તો કંઇ નજરે નહી પડી શકયો હતો. માત્ર નદીનાં પાણી જે કીનારા ઉપર ધીમાં ધીમાં અફળાયાં કરતાં હતાં, તેનો નરમ અને ગંભીર આવાજ દીલને ઘણીજ આરાએસ આપતો હતો. તા૦ ૨૬ મી જાનેવારીની રાત્રથી તે તા૦ ૨૯ મીની રાત્ર સુધી, લાગટ ચાર દીવસ અને રાત્ર, સાંચાનો ધપકારો અને ઘોંઘાટ સાંભળવામાંજ સ્ટીમરમાં ગુજારી હતી, જેથી કાન એવા તો થઈ ગયા હતા કે ઉંઘમાં પણ સાંચાના ધપકારાનો આવાજ આવીયાજ કરતો હતો. કાશીપોરમાં આવીયા પછી આ ઘોંઘાટનો છેડો આવીયો હતો અને આજ રાત્રે નીરાંતથી ઉંઘાઈશું એવી જે ખાત્રી જીવને મળી હતી તેથી મનમાં ઘણોજ આનંદ ઉપજીઓ હતો. રાત્રે જમીને આગાસી ઉપર જરા અરેટાયલા હતા, નદીનું પાણી સાંભે દેખાતું હતું, થંડા સીતળ પવનની ધીમી ધીમી લેહેકી આવતી હતી, નદી ઊપરથી કોઈ છુટો છવાયો મછવો ચુપાચુપ ચાલી જતો હતો, જે તેના ઝાંખા, અને પાણી ઉપરથી સરીને ચાલી જતા દીવાથી દેખાતો હતો, જેનાં એકું હલેસાંનો પાણી સાથે છપકોરાવાનો નરમ આવાજ કાન ઉપર આવતો હતો, તથા દરેક છપકોરે પાણીમાંની ઝીણી માંછલીઓનો ચળકાટ દેખાતો હતો, તેમાં વળી કોઇ શોખીલા કોળીનો ગાયન કરતો દુરનો સાદ સંભાળાતો હતો, તથા કીનારા ઉપરનું કોઈ માણસ હોડીવાળા સાથે અથવાં હોડીવાળાઓ પોતપોતામાં ધીમે ધીમે આવાજે અને થોડે થોડે વારને અંતરે એક બીજા સાથે વાતચીત કરતા હતા, આ સઘળો નીરાંતી ભરેલો દેખાવ જોયા અને ભોગવીયાથી જીવને ભારી ચેન અને આત્માનંદ થઈ પડયું હતું! આવે વખતે હમને હમારી નીશાળમાં શીખેલાં, કવી "બાઈરન" નાં કેટલાંક દીલખુશ,

નીચે જણાવેલાં કાવ્યો યાદ આવીયાં હતાં. આ કાવ્યોની ખુબી તથા મતલબ, નીશાળે શીખતી વેળા તો પુરેપુરી શું, પણ થોડી ઘણીબી નહી સમજી અથવા હાંસલ કરી શક્યા હતા, પણ તે કાવ્યની પુરી મતલબ અને ખુબી આ ઠેકાણે હમો અચ્છી રીતે સમજી અને પામી શક્યા હતા.

All is gentle : nought
Stirs rudely ; but, congenial with the night,
Whatever walks is gliding like a spirit.
The tinklings of some soft guitars ;—the dash
Phosphoric of the oar, or rapid twinkle
Of the far lights of skimming gondolas,
And the responsive voices of the choir
Of boatmen answering back with verse for verse ;

* * * * * *

How sweet and soothing is this hour of calm !

ઉપલી કવીતાનો તરજુમો કરવાની હમો જરૂર જોતાં નથી, કારણ કાસીપોર નદીના દેખાવ વીશે જે ઉપર બયાન કરયું છે તેમાં આ કવીતાની સઘળી મતલબ આવી ચુકી છે. ઉપલા દેખાવનીજ ઝુમમાં નીંદ આવીગઈ હતી, જેનો છેડો સહવારના ઊઠીયા તીયારે આવીયો હતો. કેહેવત પ્રમાણે, સઘળા જણ તે રાત્રે સારી પેઠે પેટ ભરીને ઉંઘાયા હતા.

તા૦ ૩૧ જાનેવારી. સહવારના સકારેથી ઊઠી, તે દીવશે "ફલાવર શો" એટલે ફુલપાન અને મેવા તરકારીનો વારશીક મેળો કલકત્તામાં ભરાવાનો દીવસ હતો તે જોવાને ગયા હતા. આ મેળો જે હમો ચુકતા નહી હોઇએ તો ચોરંગીના લતા ઊપર મોહોટાં મેદાનમાં ભરાયલો હતો. આ ઠેકાણે ફુલપાન અને મેવાનો એક અચ્છો જમાવ થયલો જોયામાં આવીયો હતો, જેમાં દેશી માલીઓએ કળા, હુંનર અને માવજતથી ઘણીક જાતનાં રોપ અને ફુલો સારીપેઠે ઉગાડેલાંના નમુના હાજર કરયા હતા, તેથી એઓમાંના ઘણા જણે ઇનામ મેળવીયુ હતું. આ ઠેકાણે રાસબેરી પુશ્કળ દેખાતી હતી અને તે થંડીની મોસમથી શ્વાદમાં ઘણીજ લેહેજતદાર લાગતી હતી. બોરના નમુના પણ ઘણાજ મોટા છેક મોટાં પેર જેટલા જોયામાં આવીયા હતા. તેમજ કાલીફલાવર, ચેરી, બીટરૂટ, કોબી, સલગમ, નોલકોલના પણ ઘણાજ તોફો નંગ ઇનામ મેળવવા લાયક, નજર આવીયાં હતાં.

બીટરૂટની રતાસ તો ઘણીજ દીલખુશ નજર આવતી હતી, નકરાં જાણે લાલ લોહી જેવાં ચલકતાં માણેકના કકડા! આ મેળો સહવારના સાડાઆઠ વાગામાં ખલાસ થઈ ચુકો હતો. હીયાં ઘણા યુરોપીયનો તેમનાં કુટંબ સાથે અને દેશીઓ ઘણું કરીને એ ખલા તમાસો જોવાને આવીયા હતા.

આ ઠેકાણાં ઉપર હમારી મોલાકાત કલકત્તાવાળા જાણીતા શેઠ માણેકજી રૂસ્તમજી કાવસજી બનાજી સાથે થઇ હતી. તેવણની ઇચ્છા ઉપરથી તેવણની આફીસમાં હમો ગયા હતા. દસ વાગામાં જબરી ગરમી પડવા લાગી હતી. આ ઠેકાણાં ઉપર જરા વીસામો લઈ, વીચાર કીધો કે હીયાંથી કાસીપોર સુધી છેક લાંબે જઇને શેહેરમાં પાછું આવીયા કરતાં, હીયાંથી નીકળીને જે કંઈ રસ્તામાં જોવાલાયક મકાન અથવા જગા મળે તે જોઇ લેવી અને તીહાંથી પાધરાજ પાછા કાસીપોર જવું. આ વીચાર સઘળાની મરજી મુજબનો થયાથી, શેઠ માણેકજીની આફીસમાંથી હમોએ રૂખસદ લીધી હતી. આ વખતે આ મેહેરબાની ભરેલાં દીલવાળા શેઠે હમો સઘળાને એવું કહી જણાવીયું કે કલકત્તા શેહેર જો બરોબર જોવું હોય તો શેહેરમાંજ હમોને રેહેવું જોઈએછ અને છેક કાસીપોર સુધી દુર નહી રેહેવું જોઇએછ. એટલા ઉપરથી તેવણે પોતાના ચોરંગીના રેહેવાનાં મકાનમાં હમોને સાથે રાખવાની ઇચ્છા કહી જણાવી હતી. હમોએ તેમનો ઉપકાર માની કેહ્યું હતું કે જો હમુને એક બે દીવસ ફરતાં અડચણ લાગશે તો તેવણની મેહેરબાની ભરેલી ઇચ્છા હમો મોહોટી ખુશીથી કબુલ રાખશું.

હીયાંથી નીકલીયા તેવા ચોરંગીના "પાર્ક સ્ત્રીટ" નામના રસ્તા ઉપર જીહાં કલકત્તાની "મ્યુઝીયમ" અને એશીયાટીક સોસાઈટીનું મોહોટું પુસ્તકખાનું છે, તે જોવાને ગયા. બંગાલાની એશીયાટીક સોસાઈટીની સ્થાપના ઈ૦ સ૦ ૧૭૮૪ ના સાલમાં સર ઉલીયમ જોન્સ નામના પ્રખ્યાત ન્યાયાધીશને હાતે થયલી છે. આ ખાતાંને લગતાં સંગ્રહસ્થાનમાં ખુદરતી તવારીખને લગતી ઘણીજ જોવાલાયક સુંદર જીનસો છે. તરેવાર જાનવરોનાં શરીરનાં પાંજરાં ઘણી માવજતથી અને કારીગીરીથી બનાવી રાખેલાં છે; તેમજ કેટલીક જાતનાં પક્ષીનાં પેટ ચીરી, તેમાં દવાની મેળવણીથી બનાવેલી જીનસો ભરી, તરેવાર પક્ષીઓનો એવો તો એક સંગ્રહ કરેલો છે કે એક નજરે હજારો પક્ષી આપણી સાંભણે જોવાને મળી શકેછે. ધાતુ, ખાણીજ વસ્તુ અને ઝાડ પાન તથા જાનવરના હાડકાં તથા ઝાડપાન, લાંબી

મુદતે બદલાઈ પથર થઈ ગયલાં (જેને ઇંગ્રેજીમાં Fossils કરીને કેહેછે) એના ઘણાજ કીમતી નમુના આ ઠેકાણે એકઠાં કરેલા છે. હીંદુધર્મને લગતા ઇમારતે ઉપરનાં કોતર અને નકસી કામના પથરના કકડા હીંદુસ્થાનમાંથી જુદે જુદે જમાને મળી આવેલાને એક મોટો જથો એકઠો કરેલો છે. અસલ બ્રહ્મધર્મને લગતા, પછીના બુદ્ધધર્મને લગતા, અને હાલના હીંદુધર્મને લગતા, એવા ત્રણ વર્ગોમાં આ પથરોને વેંહેચેલા છે. આ ખાતાંના ઉપલા ભાગમાં હીંદુસ્થાનનાં જુદા જુદા પ્રાંતોમાં રેહેનારાં લોકના વાપરવામાં આવતાં તમામ જાતના હથીયારોનો સંગ્રહ કરેલો છે, તેનીજ પાસે "સાઉથ સી આઇલિંડ્સ" એટલે અમેરીકાની દક્ષીણ તરફના ટાપુઓમાં જે દેશીઓ વસેછે તેમના વાપરવામાં આવતાં હથીયારો એકઠાં કરેલાં છે. આ સોસાઈટીના મહાભારી પુસ્તકખાનાં વીશે જેટલું બયાન કરીએ તેટલું થોડું છે. છાપેલાં અને હાતના લખેલાં ઉગમણ પ્રાંતની બાબદોને લગતાં કંઇ હજારો પુસ્તકો અને કાગજો છે. થીબેટ ભાશાના, ચીનાઈ ભાશાના, બ્રહ્મી ભાશાના હાતના લખેલાં હજારો દસ્તાવેજોનો સંગ્રહ હીયાં કરેલો છે. સોસાઈટીના હાલમાં જે નામાંકીત પુરૂષોની સબીઓ બીરાજેછે તેમના જેવા લડાયક અને મહા વિદ્વાન પંડીતોની મંડળી કોઈબી જગા ઉપર તેઓ જીયારે જીવતા હશે તીયારે આવી સાથે એકઠી નહી થઈ શકી હશે. આ વિદ્વાનોની ચુપ અને મુગી મંડળીમાં નીચે જણાવેલા પ્રખ્યાત અને નિપુણ ગૃહસ્થોની સબીયો અને બાવલાં જોવામાં આવીયાં હતાં:—

સર એડવર્ડ રાયન.
મી. આર. હોમ.
કલનલ જેમ્સ ગ્રાંટ ડફ.
સર જાર્જ એચ. બારલો.
ગીલબર્ટ અરલ આફ મીંટો.
રીચર્ડ મારકયુસ વેલેસલી.
ચારલસ અરલ કારનવાલીસ.
સર ઉલીયમ જોન્સ.
એચ. એચ. ઉઇલસન.
ડબલ્યુ. ડબલ્યુ. બર્ડ.

એચ. ટી. પ્રીનસેપ.
ડાકતર જે. આદમ.
જનરલ જોન્સ.
એચ. ટી. કોલબ્રુકનું બાવલું.
સર ઉલીયમ જોન્સ. ,,
એચ. એચ. ઉઇલસન. ,,
ડાકતર ડબલ્યુ. એચ. મીલ ,,
જેમ્સ પ્રીનસેપ. ,,
બી. એચ. હાડજસન. ,,

આ ખુદરતના ખજાનાના મેહેલમાંથી નીકલીને કલકત્તાના એક મોહોટા જહવેરીની દુકાન જોવાને ગયા હતા. કાચની કબાટોમાં જે યુકતી અને કળા વાપરીને તમામ જવાહેર અને કીમતી જીનસોની ગોઠવણ કરેલી હતી તેનો દેખાવ એવો તો ભપકા ભરેલો અને દીલપસંત થયલો હતો કે તે દુકાન અથવા બરોબર બોલીએ તો જવાહેરખાનાંમાં પેસતાંજ જોનારની આંખો ચમકી પડતી હતી. તમામ દાગીના ખુલા દેખાઈતા મુકેલા હતા, તોએપણ તેઓ એવી તો બંદોબસ્તીમાં મુકેલા હતા કે કોઈ એકાએક ઉઠાવી લેઈ જવા પામી નહી શકે. મોટા કાચોની બંધ કબાટોમાં તેમને તજવીજથી રચેલા હતા એવા કે તેમની સઘળી બાજુ ખુલી જોવામાં આવી શકતી હતી. કોઇબી દાગીનો જોવાને હાત લગાડવાની જરૂરજ નહીં પડતી હતી. તેની કીંમત પણ તેનીજ સાથે જોડેલી હતી કે લેનારને વીચાર કરવાને બની આવે અને વેચનારને ઘડી ઘડી પુછવું નહી પડે. આ જવાહેરના સંગ્રહમાં કહયું કીમતી નંગ નહી હતું એ હમારાથી કેહેવાઈ શકાતું નથી, એટલું તે સંપૂર્ણ હતું. કેહેછે કે લંડનમાં જહવેરાતની જે મોટી દુકાનો કેહેવાયછે તે વર્ગની આ દુકાન હતી. એની સાથે આપણી મુંબઈની કોઈબી દુકાન આપણે સરખાવી નથી શકવાના. હીયાંની સઉથી સરસ આ કીસમની દુકાન કલકત્તાની હામીલટન જહવેરીઓની દુકાન આગળ, હમો બીહીને કેહીજીએચ કે ૧૫) આના વટાવમાં છે.

આ ઠેકાણેથી નીકલીને પાધરા કાસોપોર ગયા. આખા દીવસની રઝડથી આવું લાગું હતું કે કલકત્તા શેહેરમાંજ રેહેવાથી તે શેહેર જોવાને વધારે સગવડ ભરેલું થઇ પડવાનું, કારણ ફકત ઉપલાં બેજ ઠેકાણાં જોઈ પાછાં ફરતાં બપોરે બે વાગી ગયા હતા. બપોરના જમતી વેળા ટેબલ ઉપર દેખાવમાં ઘણીજ તોફો માંછલી મુકેલી હતી. આવીશે પુછપરછ કરતાં એવું માલુમ પડયું કે તે નદીની માછલી હતી. કલકત્તામાં નદીની માંછલી પુશ્કળ મળેછે, તેમાં "મેંગો ફીશ" નામની માછલીની અતીશય તારીફ થાયછે. હમુને બરોબર યાદ નથી કે એ માંછલી દરીયાની છે અથવા નદીની, પણ આટલું જાણીએછ કે એની લેહજત અને ખુબસુરતી વીશે ઇંગ્રેજોમાં અને દેશીઓમાં ભારી વખાણ થાયછે. આ માંછલીને "મેંગો ફીશ" ને નામે બોલેછે તેનું કારણ એવું જણાવામાં આવીયું છે કે આપણા દેશની કેરીની મોસમ ઊપર એ ઘણું કરીને મળી આવેછે. દેશી

લોક એ માંછલીને "તપસ્વી" કરીને કેહેછે, એટલે "તપ કરનાર" માંછલી. કેટલાક યુરોપીયનોથી આ કઠણ શબ્દ "તપસ્વી" બરોબર નહી બોલી શકાયાથી તેમની એક સાધારણ ટેવને લગતો "ટીપસી" શબ્દ "તપસ્વી" ને ઠેકાણે લાગુ પાડી કેટલાકો આ માંછલીને "ટીપસી" માછલી બોલવા લાગા. હમોએ આ માછલી જોઈ નથી, પણ જેઓએ જોઇ છે તેઓ એવું કેહેછે કે તે હંમેશ પોતાનું માંથું નીચું રાખેછે, જે કોઈની નજરમાં તપ કરતું અને કોઈની નજરમાં "ટીપસી" એટલે છાકટાની પેઠે ઝુલતું દેખાયછે.

કલકત્તામાં આવી એક માઠી રસમ ચાલતી આવી છે કે તીહાંના દેશી લોકનો ઘણો ખરો ભાગ તેમના મરણ પામેલાં માણસોનાં મુડદાંને નદીના પાણીમાં હોમી દીએછે. તીહાંનાં કેટલાક હીંદુ લોક મુડદાંને બાળેછે આ વાત ખરી છે, પણ ઘણા ગરીબ અને હલકી પદ્ધિનાં લોક જેઓની ગુંજાસ બાળવાનો ખર્ચ પુરો પાડી શકવાની નથી તેઓ બીચારા મુડદાંને નદીનાં પાણી ઉપર તરતાં છોડી દીએછે. શક્તિવાળા લોક પણ મુડદાંને પુરેપુરૂં બળવા નથી દેતા. પોણો ભાગ બળી રેહું કે બાકીનું નદીનાં પાણીમાં હોમાવી દીએછે. આવી રીતે નદીમાંનાખેલાં મુડદાં પાણી ઉપર ઘમડાયછે, અને તીહાંની માંછલીઓ આ મુડદાંનો ભક્ષ કરેછે. નદી ઉપર સરકાર તરફથી મછવા ફરતા રેહેછે અને જેબ્બી મુડદાં તરતાં હાત લાગેછે તેમને પથર બાંધી પાણીમાં ગરક કરી નાખેછે. આ રસમ ઘણી સુખ્યન નાખવા જોગ છે, પણ ચાલતી આવેલી રસમથી લોકના દીલમાં આવીશે કંઈ ઘણું નથી લાગતું. જેમ આપણા પારસીઓના રવાનોને પક્ષીઓ ચાસણી કરી જાયછે અને તે વીશે ઘણા ખરા પારશીઓને કંઈ વીચાર આવતો નથી, તેજ પ્રમાણે આ દેશના હીંદુઓને પણ નદીનાં પાણીમાં પોતાનાં મુડદાંઓને હોમાવી દેવામાં કંઇ જજો વીચાર આવતો નથી, જો કે પરકાઓને એ વીશે ઘણુંજ કમકમાટ ભરેલું લાગેછે. આ બાબદ ઉપર કલકત્તાના બાલીયા ઘાટ એટલે દેશી લોકના મુડદાં બાળવાનો ઘાટ, આ વીશે બયાન કરતાં, વધારે ખુલાસાથી બોલશું.

ટેબલ ઉપર જમતી વેળા મોટી માંછલી જોઈ એકજણ ટકોર કરી બોલીયો કે, આ માંછલીએ કોણ જાણે કલકત્તાના કેટલા દેશીઓનો ભક્ષ કરીયો હશે! આવામાં કોઈ બોલીયું કે, જુઓ પેલી માંછલીનાં મોહોડાંમાંથી કોઈના હાતની એક આંગલી દેખાયછે! આ વાત સાંભળીને ટેબલ ઉપર જમવા બેડેલા હમારામાંના કેટલાકોનો

દેખાવ અજાએબ તરેહનો થઈ પડ્યો હતો. કોઈ માંછલી તરફ ચોકસાઈ ભરેલી નજરથી જોવા લાગ્યું, કોઈ પોતાનો બુક ચાવતાં ચાવતાં અટકી પડ્યું હતું અને કોઇએ પોતાનાં મોહોડાંમાં મુકવાને તઈયાર કરેલો બુક હાતમાંજ રાખી મેલીયો હતો! ટેબલ ઉપર આવેલી માંછલી જો કે પાછી તો નહીજ ગઈ હતી, તોએપણ થોડીવાર એક રમુજી દેખાવ થઈ પડયો હતો. એકુ બે જણને જરા સુગ લાગાથી તેઓએ તે માંછલી ખાધી નહી હતી. બીજે દીવસે, એટલે તા૦ ૧ લી ફેબરવારીએ કહી કહી જગા જોવાને જવું આ વીરો રાત્રે ઠરાવ કરી રાખીયો હતો તે મુજબ,

તા૦ ૧ લી ફેબરવારીને દીવસે કલકત્તાના એક માતબર કુટંબવાળા બાબુ નામે બાબુ સામચરન મલીકનો એક મોટો બગીચો કલકત્તામાં મશહુર થયલો છે તે જોવાને ગયા. આ બગીચાનું નામ "સેવન ટાંકસ" એટલે સાત તલાવનો બગીચો એવું જાહેર થયલું છે. આજ ઠેકાણાં ઉપર, આ માતબર કુટંબવાળા બાબુઓએ કલકત્તાના દેશીઓ તરફની જીયાફત આપણી મહારાણીના શાહાજાદા ડયુક આફ એડીનબરોને જીયારે તે કલકત્તે પધારીયા હતા તીહાંરે આપી હતી. મલીકનું ખાનદાન કલકત્તાના બાબુઓમાં ઘણું મોટું ગણાયછે અને આ કુટંબના શખસો ખુદરતી ચીજો અને વીદ્યા તથા એલમ હુંનરના ભારી શોખી છે. તેઓમાંના કેટલાકોએ ઇંગ્રેજી ભાશાનો ઘણોજ સારો અભ્યાસ કરયો છે, અને કલકત્તાના દેશી આગેવાનોમાં આ ખાનદાને સારી પદ્વિ રાખી છે. સેવન ટાંકસનો બગીચો એક જબરો મોહોટો બાગ છે. એની સરખામણી કરવાને મુંબઈમાંની કોઈબી તેવી ચોગાન જગાનું નામ હમો દેઈ શકતા નથી. હમો ખાહીને બોલીએ તો એટલું કહી શકીએછ કે આપણી મુંબઈના ગવરનરના પરેલના રેહેવાના બાગ જેવા ૫) બાગ જેટલી મોટી જગા તો તે ખચીત હશે. આથી વધારે મોહોટી પણ ઓછી તો નહીજ હશે. આ ઠેકાણાં ઉપર ખુદરતનો દેખાવ, ઝાડ પાનની લીલાતરી અને તજ્રુમલથી રચેલા બાગનો દેખાવ ઘણોજ દીલપસંદ હમને લાગો હતો. જે મેહેલ જેવી એક ઇમારત હીયાં બાંધેલી છે, તેની અંદર આ અમીરી શોખ ધરાવનાર બાબુએ કાચ ઉપર, કપડાં ઉપર, અને કાગજ ઉપર પાડેલી સબીઓનો જે એક મોટો જમાવ કરેલો છે તે ઉપરથી આ બાબુનો ચીત્ર વીદ્યા જે ઉંચે દરજેનો શોખ છે તે સારીપેઠે જણાઈ આવેછે. ઘણો વખત, હમોએ આ ઠેકાણે ગુજારીયો હતો, અને જુદી જુદી છાપેલી અને હાતની પાડેલી સબીયો જોતાં જોતાં હમો

થાકી ગયા હતા; પણ તે સખીયોની સંખીયાનો અંત નહી આવીયો હતો. હમારી પાસે આ સખીયોની એક તપસીલવાર ટીપ છે તેમાં નજદીક ૩૦૦ સખીના નામ છે, પણ હમો ધારીએછ કે એ ઉપરાંત બીજી ઘણી જોવા લાયક સખીયો અને જીનસો હતી. આ સખીયોમાં, યુરપખંડ અને પૃથ્વિને લગતી તવારીખ, તથા લડાઈઓ, નામાંકીત પુરૂશ અને સ્ત્રીઓ તથા તરેવાર ખુદરતી દેખાવોનો સંગ્રહ હતો, અને તેમાં કેટલીક સખીયો મોટા કીસબી અને નામાંકિત સખી પાડનારોના હાતના નમુના હતા, જેવા આજે સઘળે ઠેકાણે મળવા મુશ્કેલ છે. આ સઘળો દેખાવ જોતાં જોતાં હમો થાકી ગયા હતા અને તેથી પાણીની તરસ ઘણી લાગી હતી. આ ઉપરથી પાણી માંગતાં, હમારી સાથે જે બાબુ મીત્રો આ મકાન દેખાડવાને આવીયા હતા તેઓમાંના બેત્રણ જણે હમોને "એક ગ્લાસ બીર લેશો" એવી પોતાની ખાયશ જણાવી હતી. બાબુને મોહોડેથી આવી પુછપરછ સાંભળી તે વખતે હમુને જરા રમુજ થઇ પડી હતી! પણ બાબુ લોક વીશે હમોએ એવું સાંભળીયું હતું કે કેટલાક સુધરેલા બાબુઓ બીર, વાઈન, બ્રાંડી વગેરે સારી પેઠે વાપરવાને શીખેલા છે! અને વળી તેમાંના કેટલાક તો જાહેર મોહોટે વાઘેની હોટેલોમાં નીરાંતથી તે ઠેકાણાં ઉપર બનાવેલાં પકવાનો અને સઘળી તરેની પીવાની જીનસોની લેહજત લેતાં કલાકના કલાક સુધી તીહાં અચ્છી રીતે બેસી વાતચીત કરેછે, અને એવું કરવાને તેઓ તીહાંના કાયમ ઘરાક થઇ પડેલાં છે, તેથી, આવી રીતે બીર પુછીઓ એમાં કંઈ નવાઈ નહી હતી! કલકત્તાના બાબુઓ કેળવણીમાં મુંબઈ કરતાં ઘણાજ આગળ વધેલા છે. તેમની મનશક્તિ પણ વધારે મજબુત છે. એવા ગૃહસ્થાને હમારેથી શીકામણ દેવાઇ શકાતી નથી, પરંતુ આટલું હમારૂં આધીનમત તેમની આગળ રજુ કરવાની અને તે ઉપર વીચાર કરવાની સઘળી નમનતાઈથી તેમને અરજ ગુજારીએછ, કે કેળવણી અને સુધારાનો ફેલાવો, યુરોપીયન લોકની અતીશય દારૂ પીવાની અને ખાવાની ટેવ અખતીયાર કીધાથી નથી થવાનો, પણ એ લોકની બાઈબિલમાં જણાવેલાં ચોખ્ખાં નીતી અને સચાઈના તત્વો છે તે મેળવીયાથી થઈ શકશે. જો ફકત ખાવાપીવાનીજ છુટ અખતીયાર કીધાથી સુધારો ગણાતો હોય તો એવો સુધારો અખતીયાર કરવાને હમો આગેવાની કરવાને નાખુશ છઇએ. આટલું પણ જણાવવાની જરૂર છે કે ઘણી ઉંચી કેળવણી અને પદ્વિ ધરાવનાર બાબુઓ છે,

જેમાંના કેટલાક સરકારી અમલદારો છે તેઓની સુધારાની વલાણ ખાણાં પીણાં તરફ નથી, પણ ખરી મન કેળવણી અને શરીર કેળવણી વધારવા તરફ તેઓએ પોતાની કોશેસ અને ધીયાન ચલાવેલું છે. કેટલાક કેળવણી પામેલાં મુંબઈના હીંદુઓ પણ એવીજ વલાણ ઉપર ફરતા અથવા ફરેલા દેખાયછે, જો કે અત્રે પણ ઘણા વિદ્વાન શીખેલા અને ઉંચી પદ્વિ ધરાવનાર હીંદુ ગૃહસ્થોએ ખાણાં પીણાં વીશે એવી છુટ લીધીજ નથી અને તેઓ લેવા ધારતા પણ નથી. ખાવાપીવાની છુટ સુધારા સાથે કંઈ ઘણી અગતની નીસબત નથી રાખતી એવું તેઓનું મત છે, અને હમો તે વાજબી સમજીને પુરેપુરૂં સ્વીકારીએછ. આવીશે આગળ ઠેકાણાસર વધારે ખુલાસાથી બોલવાની ઉમેદ રાખીએછ.

આ ઠેકાણાં ઉપરથી નીકલીને બાબુ રાજેંદ્રલાલ મલીકના રેહેવાના મકાન ઉપર ગયા. આ મલીક ખાનદાનના ગૃહસ્થો ખુદરતના ખરાજ શોખી અને મોજી છે એવું આગળ કેહું છે, આ તેમની ખુબી તેમના મકાન ઉપર જે તરેની આરાસ્તગી કરી રાખેલી છે તે ઉપરથી ખુલ્લી માલુમ પડી આવેછે. બાબુ સામચરન મલીકના સાત તલાવના બગીચામાં તરેવાર તરેની આરસી અને સબીઓનો એક ગંજાવર જથો જોયો હતો, તેને બદલે આ તેજ ખાનદાનના બીજા ગૃહસ્થના મકાનમાં જઈ જોઈએછ તો તેના બાગ અને બગીચામાં તરેવાર તરેનાં જીવતાં પક્ષીઓ, અને કેટલાંક ચોપગાં જાનવરોની એક નાહાની જેવી દુનીયા જોઈ હતી. બાબુ મલીક પોતે જાતે ઝાડ પાન અને જાનવરની બાબદોનો એક અચ્છો વીદ્યાર્થી છે. આ બાબદને લગતી શોધો અને વધારા જે યુરપખંડમાં થતા જાયછે તેવીશે તે સારી ખબર વાંચવા લખવાથી રાખેછે, અને આ બાબદ વીશે દેશી જ્ઞાન પણ પુષ્કળ સંપાદન કરીયું છે, તેથી ફલાણાં પક્ષીને ફલાણી જાતનો ખોરાક મોઆફક આવશે, ફલાણાં જાનવરને આવી રીતિ અથવા આવી તજુમલથી રાખીયું તો તે પલાઈ શકાશે, એ પ્રમાણે તેણે પોતાના બાગમાં ઘણાં જાનવરોને તેમને લાયકની જગા અથવા માળા બનાવી આપી રાખેલાં હમોએ જોયાં હતાં. બાબુએ પોતે તસદી લઈ, હમોને પોતાની સાથે બાગમાં ફેરવીયા હતા, અને તરેવાર પક્ષીઓ દેખડાવી તેમનાં નામ અને તેમની કેટલીક ખાસીઅતો હમોને કહી જણાવી હતી. કેટલાંક રૂ ભરેલાં પક્ષીઓ પણ તેના મકાન ઉપર કબાટોમાં ગોઠવેલાં હતાં, તેજ પ્રમાણે સંગેમરમરના અને પ્લાસ્ટર આફ પારીસનાં ઘણીજ ઊંચી કારીગીરીથી

બનાવેલાં પુતલાંનો પણ એક સારો, પસંદ અને ચુંટી કાહાડેલો સંગ્રહ તીહાં કરેલો હતો, અને એ સઘળાંને જેમ તેમ નહી ગોઠવેલાં હતાં, પણ તવારીખના કાયદાસર તેમને રચેલાં હતાં, અને તેમને સાફ રાખવાને તજવીજ ભરેલાં માંણસો ઉપરી રાખેલાં હતાં. આ મકાન અને સંગ્રહ જો કે પોતાના શોખ સારૂ કરેલો હતો, તોએપણ મોટાં દીલવાળા બાબુ મલીકે તે લોકને જોવા સારૂ ખુલ્લો પણ રાખેલો હતો, અને જેબી લોક શોખથી જોવાં જાય તેમને પરવાનગીથી અંદર ફરવા હરવાની છુટ આપેલી હતી, તથા તેવાં સારાં માણસો જોવાને આવીયાં તો મલીક પોતે જાતે તેમની સાથે ફરી વળતા હતા. જો કે મલીક પોતે મોટો માતબર ગૃહસ્થ છે, તો-એપણ તે સાદો, મીલનસાર તથા ભલો છે. આખાં કલકત્તા શેહેરમાં મલીકનું ખાનદાન એલમ વીદ્યા, હુંનર અને ખુદરતના શોખીઓમાં મશાહુર થયલું છે.

કલકત્તામાં માન પામેલા આપણા દેશી શેઠ માણેકજી રૂસ્તમજી કાવશાજી બનાજીએ આ દીવસે રાત્રે પોતાની સાથે જમવાનું નોત્રું હમને કરેલું હતું તેથી રાજેંદ્રલાલ મલીકના મકાનમાંથી તે ભલા બાબુનો ભારી ઊપકાર માનીને રૂખસત લેઈ પાધરાજ શેઠ માણેકજીનો મકાન જે ચોરંગીમાં છે તીહાં ગયા હતા. હીયાં આવીયા પછી શેઠ માણેકજીએ ફરીને પેહેલાં દીવસની પોતાની ઇચ્છા કેહી બતલાવી હતી અને પુછીયું હતું કે કાસીપોરસુધી દુર જઇને રેહેવું અને તીહાંથી કલકત્તા શેહેર જોવા, આવજાવ કરવાને આ બે દીવ-સમાં હમને કેવું લાગું હતું. હમો સઘળાનો જવાબ એવોજ હતો કે અલબતાં દુરથી આવ્યા જવામાં વખત ઘણો ફોકટ નીકલી જતો હતો તેમ જરા શરીરને પણ અડચણ લાગતી હતી. આ ઉપરથી શેઠ માણેકજીએ દીલોજાની ભરેલી મેહર-બાનીથી કેહું કે તેવણનો આખો મકાન હમારે સારૂ તઈઆર છે, અને તેવણ-નું કુટુંબ તે વખતે મુંબઈમાં હતું, એટલા ઉપરથી તેવણની સાથે તેમના મકાન ઉપર રેહેવાથી તેવણને જરા પણ અડચણ કે અગવડ નથી પડવાની, બલકે હમારી સંગત મળવાથી તેવણને વધારે ખુશી અને ગમત મળશે. શેઠ માણેકજીનું દીલ ખુદરતી ઉપકાર ભરેલું અને મીલનસાર છે, તેથી હમોએ તેવ-ણનો સુખન કબુલ રાખી તીહાંજ રેહેવાનો ઠેરાવ કીધો. હમો આસરે દસ દીવસ શેઠ માણેકજીનાં મકાનમાં રેહા હતા તે વખતમાં આ મીલનસાર અને મોટાં દીલ-વાળા સેઠે હમારી જેવી રીતે પરોણાગત અને બરદાસ્ત કરી હતી તેના ઉપકારની

યાદદાસ્ત હમારાં મનમાંથી કદી નથી નીકલી જવાની. આ શેઠનો સ્વભાવ એક ખરાજ ખાનદાની ગૃહસ્થના જેવો છે. પોતાનો દરજો જાલવતાં, બચ્ચાંની સાથે બચ્ચાં જેવા ખુશ મીજાજી થઈ શકેછે, તેમજ મોટાની સાથે તેવીજ લાયકી ભરેલી રીતે વરતનારા શખ્સ છે. પોતાના કામકાજમાં સારી પેઠે રોકાયલા રેહેતાં આ શેઠ બીજાં સારા અનેજાહેર કામોમાં ધીઆન આપવાને સામેલ થયલા રેહેછે, અને દેશી લોકમાં જેવા ગમતા અને માનવંતા છે તેવાજ યુરોપીયન વેપારી અને રાજ દરબારીઓમાં પણ એવણને સારો વગ અને જાણ પીછાન છે તથા તેમનું સારૂં મત આ શેઠ ધરાવેછે. દસ દીવસ હમોએ એવણના મકાનમાં એવણની સાથે ગુજારીયા તે વખતમાં જાણે હમો હમારાં પોતાનાં ઘરમાં રહેલા હોઈએ એવી આસાએશ અને છુટથી હમો તીહાં રેહી શકયા હતા. શેઠ માણેકજીએ આવી મેહેરબાની ભરેલી મેહમાનદારી ફકત હમારીજ કરી નથી, પણ જેબી ભાયગસાલી મુસાફર આપણી જાતવાળો કે કોઈ બીજો એવણને તીહાં ગયો હશે તે તીહાંથી સારૂં મત બાંધીઆ વગરે પાછો ફરેલો હમારા સાંભળવામાં નથી આવીયો. આટલી સંધી એવણે હમારી ઉપર મેહેરબાની કીધી અને જે મોહોબત એવણે હમો સઘળા તરફ બતલાવી હતી તેનો ઉપકાર આ ઠેકાણે જાહેર રીતે માનવાની હમો એક ફરજ સમજી તેની નોંધ મોટી ખુશી સાથે કરીએછ.

એજ દીને સાંજના કલકત્તાના એક મોહોટા વેપારી અને જુના રેહેવાશી મી. આપકારની મોલાકાત કરવાને શેઠ માણેકજીની સાથે તેમનાં ઘર મધે ગયા હતા. આ વખતે કલકત્તામાં તુરત ગ્યાસ લાઈટ દાખલ થયલી હતી અને તે મી. આપકારે તે પોતાનાં ઘરમાં લીધેલી હતી અને જે સલગાવી જોવાનો દીવસ તેજ પેહલ વેહેલો હતો. ગ્યાસનો ઉજાસ ઘણોજ સારો હતો અને મીણબતીની રોશની તેની આગળ વટાવમાં પડી હતી. મુંબઈમાં ગ્યાસ હવે દાખલ થઈ ચુકી છે તેથી આ બાબદ વીશે વધારે હીંયા બોલવાની કંઈ જરૂર જોતા નથી. આરમીનીયન ટોલાના ઘણાં માતબર કુટુંબો કલકત્તામાં આગળ વસ્તાં હતાં, પણ હાલ તેઓમાં મી. આપકાર અને કેટલાક થોડા આબરૂવાળાં કુટુંબ સીવાએ કોઈ જાજા આરમીનીયનો તીહાં નજર નથી આવતા. આ કોમના ઘણાં વેપારીઓ પડતી દશામાં આવીઆથી આ દેશ છોડી ગયા છે, લીયાં થોડાંજ લોક

વરશેછે. આ જુના ભલા રેહેવાશી કુટંબ સાથે વાતચીત કરીયા પછી અને તેમની ઇચ્છાથી તેમનીસાથે એક ગ્લાસ વાઇન પીને તીહાંથી રૂખસત લીધી હતી.

આ દીવસની રાત્રે શેઠ માણેકજીએ કલકત્તાના સઘળા પારસી વેપારીઓને હમારી સાથે જમવાને ઇજન કીધું હતું તે મુજબ તે સઘળા સાહેબોની સાથે હમને મુલાકાત તથા ઓલખાણ પીછાન કરવાની એક સારી જોગવાઈ મળી આવી હતી. આપણા પારસી વેપારીઓને હમોએ તે વખતે સારી હાલતમાં જોયા હતા, અને પરદેશમાં રેહાથી જે હીંમત અને આપભરોસો માણસમાં ઉત્પન્ન થાયછે તે ગુણો તેઓમાં નજર આવીયા હતા. કલકત્તાના આપણા પારસી વેપારીઓની મંડળીમાં જો કે ઘણું કરીને જુવાન ગૃહસ્થોની સંખ્યા વધારે હતી, તોએપણ દુનીયાદારીનું કામકાજ જે તેમને માથે પડેલું હતું અને જેથી તડકો છાંયડો તેઓએ ભોગવેલો હતો, જેથી આ જુવાનોના કપાળ ઉપર હોશ, અક્કલ અને સારો અનુભવની નીશાનો પડેલી હમો જોઈ શકયા હતા. આ તેમના સદગુણો જોઇ હમો ઘણાં ખુશી થયા હતા. ટેબલ ઉપર જમીયા પછી કલકત્તાના પારસી વેપારી અને રેહેવાશીઓની સલામતી લેતી વખતે આ બાબદવીશે ખુલું કહી જણાવીયામાં આવીયું હતું કે પારસીઓ પરદેશી વેપારી તરીકે જેવા ઉદ્યોગી, સાહાસીક અને આપતવકલ બનેછે, તેવા તેઓ મુંબઈમાં મુતલક નજર નથી આવતા. એટલા ઉપરથી પારસીઓને લાયકછે કે મુંબઇમાંજ ભરાઈ બેશી, બેઠા ખાવાની ટેવ જલદીથી છોડી દેવી જોઇએછ. તેમને દેશો દેશ ફ્રીવળી તેવાં સારાં વેપાર વણજને લાયકના શેહેરોમાં પેહેડી માંડવી જોઈએછ અને આબરૂ ઇજત જાળવી પોતાની હાલત બેહેતર કરવી જોઇએછ. બીજું, પરદેશમાં એકલા રેહીને પોતાના વેપાર વણજનાં કામમાં ધીયાન આપતાં, પોતાનાં ખાનગી ઘરબારવીશે પણ ધીયાન આપવાની તેમનાઉપર બેવડી ફરજ આવી પડેછે, તે ટાલવાને ઊપાય કરવા જોઇએછ, અને આ વીશે તેમને આવી સુચના કરવામાં આવી હતી, કે તેઓ જો પોતાનાં કુટુંબને બોલાવી પરદેશમાં સાથે રાખે તો જેટલો વખત તેઓનો પોતાના ખાનગી કામકાજમાં રોકાયછે તેટલો પોતાના ધંધા રોજગાર સર વાપરવાને તેઓ સેહેલાઇથી બંચાવી શકશે. તેની સાથે તેમનાં ઘર સંસારનું કામ પણ તેમનાં કુટુંબને હાથે ઘણુંજ કરકસરથી બેહેતર અને ફાયદા ભરેલી રીતે ચાલી શકશે. આ સુચના જો કે કેટલાકોને પસંદ પડતી થઇ હતી,

અને તે અમલમાં લાવી દેખડાવાનું કામ પણ તે સાહેબોના હાતમાં હતું હવડાંના વખતમાં કલકત્તે જવાને વાહાંણની તો કંઈ જરૂર લાગતી નથી. આગગાડીથી સઘળી વાતની સગવડ થઇ પડી છે, તેથી ધારવામાં આવે છે કે કલકત્તે રેહેનારા પારસી સાહેબો પોતાનાં કુટુંબોને રફતે રફતે હવે તીહાં બોલાવીને સાથે રાખી શકશે. છડા અથવા એકલા રેહેવામાં પણ એક તરેનો ફાયદો છે, અને તેવી હાલતનું સુખ અને થોડી ઘણી મોજ મજાહ જેઓએ ભોગવી છે તેમને આપણે હીયાં લખી જણાવીએ તેના કરતાં તેઓ પોતે તે વધારે સારી પેઠે સમજી શકેછે! પણ લાંબા વખતે જોતાં એકલી હાલતના કરતાં કુટુંબ સાથે રેહેવાની હાલત, પછી શું દેશમાં કે શું પરદેશમાં, બંધે ઠેકાણે, ખરેખરજ વધારે ફાયદા ભરેલી છે. કલકત્તામાં વેપારી તરીકે પોતાનાં કુટુંબસાથે લેઈ વસવાનું માન પારસીઓમાં શેઠ રૂસ્તમજી કાવશાજી બનાજી અને તેવણની પાછળ તેવણના સાહેબજાદા શેઠ માણેકજી રૂસ્તમજીને ઘટે છે. શેઠ માણેકજી વીશે હમો એક શબ્દ વધારે બોલવા માંગીએછ જે વીશે હમે માગી લીજીએછ કે તે શેઠ માફ કરશે. આ ગૃહસ્થની વિચારશક્તિ અને હોશીઆરી એવી કીસમની છે કે હાલના કલકત્તાના દેશી જુવાન કેળવણી પામેલાઓ જેવા એવણના મીત્રો થઈ પડયા છે, તેવાજ જુના વીચારવાળા ગૃહસ્થોભી એવણના ઘણાજ સારા મીત્રો છે. બંધે તરફવાળાઓને આ ચતુર શખ્સે પોતાના દોસ્તો કરી રાખેલા છે આ ખુબી કંઇ જેવી તેવી નહી જાણવી. આ ખુબી નકલ કરવા જોગ છે.

તા૦ ૨ જી ફેબરવારીનો દીવસ મેશર્સ લીપેજ અને થાકર ઍંડ સ્પીંક તથા આસલર ઍંડ જેનીંગ્સની દુકાનો જોવામાં રોકીયો હતો. આ દુકાનો, જનરલ એજેનસીની દુકાનો છે, અને હીયાં સઘળી બાબદને લગતાં પુસ્તકો મળી આવી શકેછે. આ પેહેડીવાળા કલકત્તામાં મોટાં પુસ્તકો વેચનારા અને પ્રગટ કરનારા ગૃહસ્થો છે.

આ દીવસે કલકત્તાના ભાડુતી ગાડીવાળાઓ વીશે હમને થોડો ઘણો અનુભવ મળી શકયો હતો. મદ્રાસની ભાડુતી ગાડીવાળાઓને અને નીઝામ હેદરાબાદમાં ત્રીમલગીરીના ભાડુતી ગાડીવાળાઓને કલકત્તાના ગાડીવાળાઓ વીસરાવે એવા બુબખો તેઓ નજર આવીયા હતા. હમોને હમારા એક મીત્રને કલકત્તામાં મળવા જવું હતું તેથી બપોરના બે વાગે એક ભાડેની

શીગરાંમ હમોએ મંગાવી હતી. આ મીત્ર કીહાં રેહેતો હતો તેવીશે હમને ખબર નહી હતી. હમોએ શેઠ કામાજીની પેહેડી ઉપરના એક માણસથી એવીશે વાકેફ થઈ તે ઠેકાણું હમારી શીગરાંમના કોચમેનને જણાવા કેહું હતું. થોડા વાર રેહી હમો તઇઆર થઈ નીચે ઉતરીયા. ગાડી આગળ જતાંજ કોચમેને ભપકામાં અને જડફથી ગાડીનું બારણું ઉઘાડ્યું હતું. જેવા હમે અંદર બેઠા કે બારણું બંધ કરી કોચમેન લાગલો કોચબાક્ષ ઉપર ચઢી બેઠો હતો અને શીગરાંમ એકદમ ચલાવી દીધી હતી. આ કોચમેને હમને પુછીયું નહી કે કીહાં જવાનું છે, તે ઉપરથી હમોએ વીચારીયું કે એવીશે હમારા કેહા પ્રમાણે તેને આગમજથી ચેતાવેલું હશે. આ બુબખ કોચમેને હમોને એક મોહોલામાંથી બીજા મોહોલામાં અને બીજામાંથી ત્રીજામાં એવી રીતે કોઈ સાતથી આઠ મોહોલામાં નજદીક એક કલાક સુધી ફેરવીયા કીધા હતાં! આ મોહોલાનાં નામ રસ્તાનાં પાટીયાં ઉપરથી વાંચતાં વાંચતાં હમોને કંટાલો આવીયો હતો, અને હમારો મીત્ર કેટલો દુર રેહેછે તેને વીશે હમુને વીચાર ઉપર વીચાર પડતો હતો. અંતે પેલા બુબખને તડકું જબર લાગાથી તેની સુધ જરા ઠેકાણે આવી હતી, તેથી તેણે ગાડી ઉભી રાખી. હમો સમજીયા કે હમારા મીત્રના ઘર આગળ હમો હવે આવી પુગા હશું. પણ પેલા કોચમેને થંડે પેટે હમુને પુછીયું કે "સાહેબ તુમારેકુ કીદર જાના હએ!" આ સવાલ સાંભળતાંજ હમોને એક તરફથી ગુસો અને બીજી તરફથી બેઅખ્તીયાર હસવું આવીયું હતું! ધરમતોલ્લાના મુરખ કોચમેનને હવે હમે સું કહીએ! હમોએ તેને પુછીયું "કે તુને આફીસમાંથી કેહું હતું કે નહી કે કીહાં જવું છે?" તેણે જવાબ આપીયો કે, નહી. તારે હમોએ પુછીયું કે એક કલાક સુધી શાસારૂ હમુને ફેરવીયા કીધા, પેહેલથીજ કાંય નહી પુછીયું? કોચમેન બોલીયો કે કીહાં જવું છે તે ઠેકાણાં ઉપર તમે મહને ગાડી ઉભી રાખવાને કેહેરો તેથી જીહાં ગમે તેમ મેં ગાડી હાંક્યા કીધી! આ સઘળું તે ઠંડે પેટે બોલીયો હતો જે ઉપરથી એવું જણાયું હતું કે તે ખરેખરજ બુબખ હતો. હવે તેને હમોએ હમારા મીત્રનું નામ દેઈ કેહું કે મી. લાલ બેહારી ડે ને તીહાં હમને લઈજા. તારે તેણે જવાબ દીધો કે હું એ ઠેકાણું જાણતો નથી. વાંચનાર હવે વીચાર કરશે કે આ કોચમેન એક લપડાક ખાવાને લાયક થયો હતો કે નહી! હમને ગુસ્સો તો ઘણો આવીયો હતો, પણ બુબખ કોચમેનોના નમુના હમોએ

આગળ જોયા હતા તેમાં માત્રે આ એક વધારે નોંધી રાખવા જોગ નમુનો હમને મળીઓ હતો એવું સમજી હમોએ દરગુજર કરી હતી. કલકત્તાના સઘળા દેશી બાબુઓ હીંદુસ્થાની ભાષા નથી બોલી શકતા તેથી કેટલીક મુસ્કેલીએ પુછતાં પુછતાં બાબુ લાલ બેહારી ડે નું રેહેવાનું ઠેકાણું શોધી કાહાડીયું, અને તે જોઈએછ તો ગાડીમાં જતાં નજદીકીમાંજ હતું. કામાજીની આફીસમાં જઇ આ બાબદ વીશે પુછપરછ કીધી તારે તીહાંથી ખબર એવી મળી કે કલકત્તાના ભાડુતી ગાડીના કોચમેનો કંઇ જુજ શીવાએ સઘળા હેમક ખીન ઉલ્લુ અને બુબખના ભાઈઓ છે! આ દીવસની સાંજે કલકત્તાના ફ્રીમેસનોની એક લાડજ નામે "હયુમીલીટી અને ફાટીટયુડ" ની મોલાકાત કરવાને ગયા હતા અને તીહાં વખતસર અને ઠેકાણાસર પોંહોચવાને હમોએ કોચમેનની સાથે એક માણસને બેસાડયું હતું. આ મંડલી વીશે હમો કંઈ હીયાં વધારે બોલી શકતા નથી. આટલુંજ કહેલું બસ છે કે મેહેલાના શેહેરમાં અને જીહાં યુરોપીયન લોક ઘણું કરીને ચઢતે દરજેની હાલતમાંજ વસેલા છે તે લોકની રીતભાંત અને શોખ સાથે કલકત્તાના ફ્રીમેસનોની લાડજ સઘળા જોઇતા અને ઘટતા સીણગાર સાથે ઘણીજ સંપૂર્ણ હાલતમાં હમોને લાગી હતી. મુંબઈમાં ફ્રીમેસનોનું એવું સીણગાર ભરેલું એક પણ મકાન હજુર સુધી નથી બનેલું તેથી હમો દીલગીર છઇએ.

તા૦ ૩ જી ફેબરવારીને દીવસે પ્રેસીડન્સી કાલેજ જોવાને ગયા હતાં. આ ખાતાંને હીંદુ કાલેજનાં નામથી પણ બોલેછે. આ મદરેશા ૧૮૧૫ ના સાલમાં સ્થાપીયામાં આવી હતી, અને એની સ્થાપના એક દેશીઓનું ભલું ઇચ્છનાર અને દેશીઓને ઉંચે દરજેની કેળવણી આપવાની જબરી હીમાએતી કરનાર મી. ડેવીડ હેર નામના શખસથી થયલી છે. કલકત્તામાં બીજી જીયાફત હમને શેઠ બરજોરજી ફરામજી મોદીની કંપનીની આફીસ અને રેહેવાના મકાનમાં કલકત્તાના પારસી વેપારીઓ તરફથી મળી હતી, જે વખતે તીહાં ભેગા થયલા ઘણા બીજા સાહેબો સાથે હમને ઓળખ પીછાન થયાથી હમો ઘણા ખુશી થયા હતા. આ મેહમાનદારીમાં જારે સઘળા જણ સરખા દીલ ભરીયા સામેલ થયા હતા તારે એમાંથી કોણને વીશે તારીફમાં બોલીએ તે કેહેવાઈ શકાતું નથી. હમો ધારીએછ કે આ જીયાફતની મોલાકાતમાં સઘળા સાહેબોએ ઘણીજ લાયકી અને અચ્છી મેહમાનદારી બતલાવી હતી અને આથી હમારા

દોસ્ત આરાના અને નવી ઓળખાણ પીછાનવાળાઓનો જે ઉપકાર હમારી ઉપર થયો હતો તે હમોએ તે વખતે માનીયો હતો પણ ફરીને આ જોગવાઈએ જાહેર રીતે હમો તેની એક નોંધ અત્રે ખુશી સાથે કરીએછ.

ખાણાંની મીજલસથી ફારગ થયા પછી, કલકત્તાનો દેશી નાચ જોવાની અને તીહાંનું ગાયન બજાયન સંભળાવાની આ ઠેકાણાં ઉપર હમને હમારા મેજબાનોએ એક સારી તક આપી હતી. નાંચનારી સ્ત્રીઓ વીશે તો અત્રે કેહેવાનું કંઈ નવું નથી. હીયાંની સઘળી રીતભાત આ બાબદમાં આપણા શેહેરના જેવીજ છે, પણ કલકત્તાની દેશી ગાનારીઓનો ઘટમ તથા ગાયન બંધે હમને ઘણીજ ઉતરતી કીસમના નજર આવીયાં હતાં. આપણુ તરફની હીંદુ ગાનારીઓની ખુબસુરતી અને ઘટમ સાથ સરખામણી કરતાં, સ્ત્રી જાતની રૂઢી પ્રમાણે બોલીએ તો કલકત્તાવાળીઓ મુંબઈવાળી આગળ પાણી ભરવા લાયક છે, આવું હમોએ જોયું હતું. ગાયનમાં પણ કંઈ ઘણો દમ જોયો નહી હતો, જો કે સાદી ઠુમરી ટપા તેઓએ ઠીક ગાયા હતા. એક ગવઈઓ તીહાં વધારે સારી અલાપથી ગાતો હમોએ સાંભળીયો હતો, અને તેનું દેશી ભાશાનું ગાયન એક નવાઈ તરીકે પેહેલું સંભળાયલું હમને ઠીક લાગું હતું. હમારી ઈચ્છા મુજબ કલકત્તાનું દેશી ભાશાનું ગાયન બરોબર સાંભળવાને હમને તક નહી મળી હતી તેથી હમો ખચીત દીલગીર છઈએ. કલકત્તાનાં ગાયનવીશે તથા લખનૌ દીલ્લી અને લાહોરનાં ગાયનવીશે ઘણી તારીફમાં બોલાયછે. આ મુસાફરીમાં એકુ બે ઠેકાણે હમોએ ઘણું સારૂં ગાયન સાંભળેલું છે, જેનું બયાન તે તરફના અહેવાલમાં આપીયું છે. ગાયન જે એક અગતની વીદ્યા અને હુંનર છે, તેને પાદશાહો અને અમીર ઊમરાઓ તરફથી હીંદુસ્થાનમાં આગળ જેવું ઊત્તેજન મળતું હતું તે હાલ નહી મળીયાથી, આપણા દેશનું ગાયન પડતી હાલતમાં આવી પડીયું છે, અને તે દરરોજ વધારે પડતું જાયછે. આ મહાભારત વીદ્યા હુંનરને જો પાછો જાગતો અને તેના પુરતા દરજા ઊપર ચઢાવવો હોય અને તેમાં જીવ અને આતમાને પવીત્ર આનંદ આપનાર જે ચોખો રસ છે તે રસ પીવો અથવા ચાખવો હોય તો આજે ગાયન શાસ્ત્રીઓને આપણા દેશી માતબર અને શક્તિવાળાઓથી સારી મદદ થવી જોઈએછ. સારૂં ગાયન કરનાર સ્ત્રીઓને લાયક ઉત્તેજન આપવા જોઈએછ અને તેમને ઈજત તથા

આબરૂદાર મંડળીમાં સામેલ કરવી જોઈએછ અને તેઓ પોતાનો દરજજો, લાજ, અને નીતી જાળવનારાં થાય એવા ઉપાય, પુરૂષોએ પોતે પોતાનો દરજ્જો, લાજ તથા નીતી જાળવીને કરવા જોઈએછ. હમો એવું માનીએછ કે ગાયનનો પેશો કરનાર સ્ત્રીઓને ફુસલાવી નઠારા માર્ગ ઉપર લઇ જવાનો દોશ પુરૂષ ઊપર છે. ઘણાં જણ એવું સાધારણ રીતે બોલછે કે સ્ત્રી પુરૂષને ફસાવેછે, પણ હમો તેથી ઉલટુંજ માનીએછ કે પેહેલ વેહેલાં પુરૂષે સ્ત્રીને ફસાવી હશે. સ્ત્રીઓને આડે મારગે ચલાવનાર તે પુરૂષ જાત છે, તે પેહેલ કરેછે, અને સ્ત્રી તેની પાછળ બીજી થાયછે. તે બીચારી નીરદોશ સ્ત્રી પેહેલાં ફસેછે, પણ તે ફસ્યા પછી એવી તો પક્કી અને લુચ્ચી થઈ પડેછે કે ઘણા નીરદોશ પુરૂષોહવે તેના જબરા પંજામાં શીકાર થઈ પડેછે. ગાયન કરનાર સ્ત્રીઓના વર્ગનો દરજજો ઊંચો કરવો હોય તો, તેનો ઈલાજ એજ છે કે તેવી સ્ત્રીઓ તરફ પુરૂષોએ માન અને નીતીના વીચારથી જોવું જોઇએછ. એમ જો થયું તો તે સ્ત્રી જાત કદી પણ ઊલટી નજરે પુરૂષ ઉપર નથી જોવાની. આ હમારા વીચાર સાથે જો કે જુજ લોક શીવાએ ઘણાજણ તો મળતા નથીજ થવાના, તોએપણ હમને એવી આશા છે કે આ હમારૂં મત ખરૂં અથવા ખોટું છે એ ઉપર ઘણાજણ ધીયાન દઈ વીચાર કરશે.

તા૦ ૪ થી ફેબરવારીને દીવસે કલકત્તાની લેજીસલેટીવ કાઊનસીલની મીજલસ જોવાને, આગમજથી ઘટતી પરવાનગી મંગાવી સરકારી મેહેલમાં ગયા હતા. કલકત્તાના સરકારી મેહેલની ઈમારત, જેના એક દરવાજાનું ચીત્ર અત્રે આપેલું છે, તે ખરેખરજ પાદશાહી મેહેલને લાયકનોજ મકાન છે. આ મેહેલની બાંધણીમાં, તેના દેખાવમાં, અને તેની સઘળી રચનામાં, જે શોભ અને દબદબો, ખુલ્લા નજરે દેખાતો થઈ પડયો છે, તેમાં એના બનાવનારની મનશક્તિ તથા તેણે સંપાદન કરેલી વીદ્યા હુંનર, કેટલું બળ ધરાવી શકેછે તેનો આ સરકારી મેહેલ એક અચ્છો જોવા જોગ નમુનો બની રહેલો છે. આ મેહેલનું આખું ચીત્ર આપી શકાયું નથી તેથી ખચીત દીલગીર છઈએ, તોએપણ તેના એક દરવાજાનું ચીત્ર તથા એ દરવાજા આગળથી દુરથી દેખાતી સરકારી મેહેલની રચના, જેટલી ચીત્રમાં માઈ શકે તેટલી અત્રે એક બીજાં ચીત્રમાં દેખડાવી છે. હીંદુસ્થાનના ગવરનર જનરલ મારકયુસ આફ વેલસ્લીની કારકીર્દીમાં, ઈ૦ સ૦ ૧૮૦૪ ના સાલમાં આ મેહેલ બાંધવામાં આવીયો હતો. એની પછવાડે આસરે

VIEW OF FORT WILLIAM, CALCUTTA

Vincent Brooks, lith.

GATEWAY GOVERNMENT HOUSE _ CALCUTTA

૪. સરકારી મેહેલનો દરવાજો.—કલકતા.

રૂપીયા ૧૩,૦૦,૦૦૦ થી ૧૫,૦૦,૦૦૦ તેર લાખથી પંદર લાખ સુધીનો ખરચ તે વખતમાં થયલો કેહેછે. આ મહાભારત બાંધણીમાં એક ખામી માત્રે એટલી કેહેવામાં આવેછે કે તેના દબદબા અને રોનક પ્રમાણે તેટલી તે મેહેલની પુરતી ઉભરણી અથવા ઉંચાઈ નથી બનાવેલી, તથા તેની બારીઓ નજદીક નજદીક પુશ્કળ મુકી છે. આ ખામી કંઈ હમારી નજરે તો દેખાઈ નહી હતી. હમારી ઉપર તો તેના દબદબાએ અને બાહેરના દેખાવે જબરી અસર કરી હતી. કલકત્તાને મેહેલોનું શેહેર જે બોલવામાં આવેછે, તે નામ, આ સરકારી મેહેલ જોયાથી બરોબર બેસ્તું અને વાજબી આપેલું ગણાયછે. આ ઠેકાણેથી જોતાં સઘળી તરફ ભપકાદાર અને મસ મોહોટી ઇમારતો અને પોહોળા રસ્તા અને મેદાન અને શોભઈતા મકાનો કટારબંધ ઉભેલા, જોનારની આંખો ઉપર એવો તો ધસારો કરેછે કે તે જોતાંજ એક પલવારમાં આપણા મોહોડાંમાંથી "વાહ વાહા" નો સંતોશ ભરેલો આવાજ નીકળ્યા વગર નથી રેહેવાનો. આ મેહેલ આગળ મુંબઈની એકબી સરકારી અથવા ખાનગી ઇમારત બરોબરી નથી કરી શકવાની.

સરકારી મેહેલના બુલંદ દરવાજા ઉપર એક જબરા સીંહનું બાવલું મુકેલું છે. સીંહ પોતાની પુછડી સાધારણ પડેલી રાખીને, અને તેના એક આગલા પગતળે ફતેમંદીની નીશાનનો ગોળો ઝાલીને નીરાંત અને નચીંત ઉભેલો છે. આ સીંહ આપણને એવું કેહેછે કે "હું તે ઇંગ્રેજી સીંહ છઉં કે જે આજે ગ્રેટબ્રીટન" "અને હીંદુસ્થાન ઉપર રાજ ચલાઉંછું. હું શાંત, અદલ અને ખુશાલ ઊભો છઉં," "અને તેમજ શાંત, અદલ અને ખુશાલ મારી રઈએતને જોવા ચાહુંછું. પણ "મહને કોઈએ ગેરવાજબી છેડીયો તો પછી મહને જોજો કે હું કેહેવો છું." ઇંગ્રેજી રાજની ખુબી અને નીતી, સુલેહ સંપજ, અદલાઇ, અને આબાદાનીમાં સમાયલી છે. આ રાજ લડાઈ કરવાને મુતલક ચાહાતું નથી, પણ કોઈ આ રાજને ગેરવાજબી સતાવે તો તેની સાંભણે પુરતાં જોર અને હીમતથી તે લડવાને, સીંહની મોઆફક હંમેશા તઈયાર છે. આ સીંહના બાવલાંમાં જે યોજના કરેલી છે તે દેશીઓનાં મન ઉપર ઇંગ્રેજ સરકારની ખુબી, નીતી અને મજબુત પાયાદારી વીશે અરછી રીતે અસર કરે એવી છે. દરવાજા અને મેહેલ ઉપરના નકસી કામ વીશે અત્રે વીસ્તારીને જણાવાની જરૂર જોતા નથી. તેમજ તેની અંદરના સંગેમરમરનાં

દીવાનખાનાં, તેમાં જવાની કટારબંધ સીહીડીઓ, દાદરો, તીહાંના ઓરડા, અગાસી, સીલીંગ, સાગનાં લાંકડાંની વારનીસથી ચકચકતી સફાઇદાર સપાટ જમીન, સીલીંગમાંથી લટકતાં ઝુમરો, બારીઓ વચ્ચે ભીતઉપર જડેલી આરશીઓ અને એ વીગરે બીજી હજારો ચીજોનું બયાન કરવાની કોશેશ કરેલી હમો ધારીએછ કે ફોકટ છે; કારણ તેનું બયાન પુરતી રીતે કોઇબી શબ્દોથી થઈ નથી શકાવાનું, તે સમજવાને તે મેહેલ નજરે નજર જોવો જોઇએછ. મેહેલ ઉપરનાં દીવાનખાનાં, અને ઓરડા રાજ દરબારી મજલસીઓ સારૂ, જીઆફત, અથવા બાલ અને નાચ રંગ સારૂ, વારંવાર વાપરવામાં આવેછે. કલકત્તાનો ગવરનર જનરલ આ મેહેલના એક ભાગમાં તદન એલાહેદો પોતાના રેસાલા સાથે રેહેછે. ગવરનર જનરલના મકાન વીશે આવી તો ગોઠવણ કરી છે કે તેની રેહેવાની જગાઉપર, મેહેલના બીજા ભાગોમાં વસનારાઓને પોતપોતના કામ કાજસર જતાં આવતાં, એક બીજા સાથે આમણ સામણ થવાની જરૂર નહી પડે, એવો તે મકાન એલાહેદો રાખેલો છે. ગવરનર જનરલની લેજીસલેટીવ કાઉનસીલમાં હમો હાજર થયા હતા, પણ તીહાં તે વખતે બયાન કરવા જોગ દેખાવ નહી જોવામાં આવીયો હતો, તેથી તે વીશે હીયાં કેહેવાનું કંઈ વધારે નથી.

આ ઠેકાણાં ઉપર હમને કાઉનસીલના દેશી મેમબર રાજા સર દેવ નારણસીંગ કે. સી. એસ. આઇ. સાથે મોલાકાત અને ઓળખ થઈ હતી. આ રાજા બનારસનો એક મોટો જમીનદાર તથા ઇંગ્રેજી રાજનો મોહોટો ખેરખા અને ખરો દોસ્ત થઈ ગયો છે. આ રાજા મોહોટો સદગુણી, અક્કલ અને હોશીયારી બરેલો તથા પોતાનાં દેશીઓનું ભલું કરવાની ઇચ્છાથી ઇંગ્રેજ સરકાર અને દેશીઓ વચ્ચે દોસ્તી રખાવાને એક ઘણોજ લાયક રાજદરબારી મજલસી હતો. તેના આવા સદગુણોની તારીફ આ પુસ્તકમાં નોંધીને આ રાજાને મુબારકબાદી આપવાની હમોએ ઉમેદ રાખી હતી, પણ માઠાં ભાગ્યેગે આ રાજાના અણચીંતા મરણથી, હમો તેનાં મોટાં કુટુંબ અને દોસ્ત આસનાઓ સાથે ગમગીનીમાં સામેલ થઇએછ અને ઘણીજ દીલગીરી સાથે આ ઠેકાણે આ પરોપકારી રાજાના દુઃખ ભરેલાં મરણની નોંધ કરીએછ. આ રાજાના મરણથી ખરેખર ઇંગ્રેજ સરકારે પોતાનો એક ખરો મીત્ર અને મસલતીયો ખોયો છે, અને આપણ દેશીઓએ આપણો એક ભલું ચાહનારો, દયાળુ અને સ્વદેશહિતેચ્છુ રાજા ખોયો છે.

LORD HARDINGES MONUMENT.—CALCUTTA

૩. લારડ હાર્ડીંગનું પાવળું.—કલકતા.

બલવાના વખતમાં રાજા સર દેવ નારણસીંગ તરફથી ઇંગ્રેજ સરકારને તે વખતને લાયકની મસલહત તથા મદદ ઘણી સારી મળી શકી હતી. આ રાજાની સાથે જો કે હમારી પેહેલ વેહેલીજ ઓળખ થઈ હતી, તોએપણ તે પારશી લોક વીશે ઘણી મોહોબત અને સારૂં મત ધરાવતો હતો, અને હમો જો ચુકતા નહી હોઈએ તો હેવું ધારીએછ કે અકસર કરીને કલકત્તામાં શેઠ માણેકજી રૂસ્તમજી બનાજીની સાથે આ રાજાને ઘણી મીત્રાચારી હતી, તેમની સાથે રાજા સાહેબને વાકેફકારી પડયાથી અને શેઠ માણેકજીની લાયકી જોયાથી, પારશીઓ વીશે કદાચને આ રાજાએ સારૂં મત બાંધીયું હોય. થોડા વખતની વાતચીતમાં રાજા સાહેબે હમારી મુસાફરીની મકસદ જાણી લીધી હતી, અને તે તેમને ઘણી પસંદ પડી હતી. હમો બનારસ (કાશી) શેહેર જોવા જનાર છઈએ, એવું જાણીને આ અહેસાનમંદ રાજાએ હમને પોતાના મેહેલમાં ઉતારો કરવાની પોતાની ખાયશ કહી જણાવી અને કેહું કે, બનારસ શેહેરમાં જઈ કોઈબી બીજે ઠેકાણે હમોએ ઊતારો કરવો નહી. રાજાએ તેજ વખતે પોતાના માણસોને હુકમ કીધો કે બનારસમાં તેમના કારભારીઓને લખી જણાવે કે આગગાડીના ઠેઠ મથકથી તે છેક શેહેરમાં મેહેલસુધી હમો સઘળાઓને લઈ જવા અને પાછા પોહોંચાડવાની તજુમલ કરી રાખવી, અને જેટલા દીવસ હમો બનારસમાં રહીએ તેટલા દીવસ આખો મેહેલ હમને ખુલો કરી આપવો, અને શેહેરમાં ફરવાહરવાને રાજાસાહેબના પોતાના હાથીઓ અને ગાડીઘોડા હાજર રાખવા, અને સઘળી બાબદમાં હમારી બરોબર બરદાસ્ત રાજાસાહેબ તરફથી કરવી. આ રાજાએ પોતાનાં મોટાં દીલથી ખરા આભારનો એક જબરો કોટ જેવો કોટ હમારી ઉપર એકદમ ગગડાવી દીધો હતો જે અહેસાનમાં હમો ગર્ક થઈ ગયા હતા. હમો સઘળાએ રાજા સાહેબનો આ વીશે અતીશય આભાર માનીયો હતો, અને તે વખતે હમારેથી એટલુંજ બોલાઈ શકાયું હતું કે રાજા સાહેબનાં મોટાં દીલવીશે તથા દેશીઓ તરફ તેમની પરોપકારી નજર વીશે હમોએ ઘણી સારી વાતો સાંભળેલી છે, પણ હમારી ઉપર જે આટલી સંધી મેહેરબાની રાજા તરફથી એકદમ થઈ છે, આવીશે હમોએ આટલી બધી ઉમેદ નહી રાખી હતી, પણ તે જારે થઈ પડી છે તારે તેનો પુરતો ઉપકાર માનવાને હમારી પાસે લાયક શબ્દો નહી હતા. રાજા જો કે મોટો માતબર જાગીરદાર હતો, તોએપણ કલકત્તામાં તેના રેહેવાનાં

ઘરની સાદાઈ અને રાજાની વાતચીતમાં મીલનસારી, નરમાસ, અને લાયકી ભરેલા સુખનો વાપરવાની તબે અને તેનું સાફ દીલ જોઈ, હમારાં મન ઉપર એવી અસર થઈ હતી કે ખરી મોહોટાઈ તે ઊપલાજ ગુણોમાં છે.

આ દીવસે કલકત્તાની ટંકશાળ જોઈ હતી, તથા દેશી વેપારીયોની પેહેડી ઉપર જઈ કેટલાક ઓળખીતાઓની મોલાકાત લીધી હતી. કલકત્તાની ટંકશાળ ઈ૦ સ૦ ૧૮૨૪ ના સાલમાં સ્થાપવામાં આવી હતી. આ ખાતાંના સાંચા કામની ગોઠવણ અને શકિત એવી અને એટલી તો છે કે એક દીવસે સાત કલાક કામ ચાલતાં આ ટંકશાળમાંથી આસરે રૂ ૩,૦૦,૦૦૦ ત્રણ લાખના શીક્કા છપાઈ તયાર થઈ શકેછે. આ ખાતાંની ઈમારત પછવાડે આસરે રૂ ૧૩,૦૦,૦૦૦ તેર લાખ અને સાંચા કામ પછવાડે આસરે રૂ ૧૧,૦૦,૦૦૦ અગીયાર લાખનો ખરચ થયલો કેહેવાયછે.

બપોરના ચાર વાગે કલકત્તાનું ચીના બજાર જોવાને ગયા હતા. આ બજારમાં છુટક કપડ, કપડાં, ઘરશીનગારનો પરચુરણ સામાન, ખાવાપીવાની તમામ જીનસો, કાચકામ, કોડીકામ, લોખંડી કામ, તરેવાર જાતનો દારૂ, પણ ઉતરતી જાતનો, અને બીજી હમા ચીજો મળી શકેછે. આ બજારનો દેખાવ ઘણું કરીને આપણી મુંબઈના કાસમબજાર અને કોટના હોરાબજારને મળતો આવે હેવો છે. હમો આ ઠેકાણે આવી સાધારણ બજારની નોંધ કરવાની કંઈ જરૂર જાણતે નહી, પણ આ બજારમાં ફરવા જનારને જે જોવા લાયક બીજા દેખાવો અને જીનસો મળેછે તેટલા સાંરૂ આ ચીના બજારનું બયાન અત્રે આપીયું છે. હમોને એવું જણાવામાં આવીયું હતું કે આ ચીના બજારમાં જે માણસોની ભીડ અને જમાવ થાયછે તેમાં જો તપાસીને જોઈએ તો આવું બોલવાને બની શકશે કે આ ઠેકાણાં ઉપર, આ પૃથ્વિનાં માત્રે અતીશય જંગલી અને અતીશય થંડીના દેશના રેહેવાશીઓ શીવાય, સઘળા જણાયલા દેશમાંના ઘણાક લોકના નમુના આપણને મળીયા વગર નથી રેહેવાના. આ ઠેકાણે તીબેટ—લાસાના રેહેવાશીઓ, પેહેલવેહેલા હમોને હમારા ભોમીયાએ દેખડાવીયા હતા. તેમના ચેહેરાનો આકાર અથવા ઘટમ ઘણું કરીને ચીનાઓને મળતો હતો, જો કે તેઓની કાઠી કદાવર હતી, અને ચામડી કેટલાકોની સફેદ અને કેટલાકોની ઘઊંલા રંગની હતી. તેમની પાસે કેટલીક જાતનાં જાનવરોના રૂવાં સાથના સુકવેલાં

ચામડાં, વેચવાનાં હતાં. તેઓ રખડતી અને ભમતી જાતના ગ્રેલાના લોક હતા, જેઓનો પેશો એવી જાતની જીનસો વેચવાનો હતો. દરેક જણની બાજુ ઉપર અને ગળામાં, તાવીજ પેહેરેલાં હતાં અને તે એટલી તો સંભાળથી રાખેલાં હતાં કે તેમને દાબડી અથવા કોથલીમાં બંધ રાખેલાં હતાં. આ તાવીજો જોયાથી હમોએ તેમને ઈશારતથી પુછીયું કે તેમાં શું છે, જે ઉપરથી તેઓએ ઈશારતથી આકાશ તરફ હાત કરી જવાબ આપીયો કે તેમાં તેઓનો ખોદા છે. હમોએ જારે તે જોવા માંગીયા તારે તેઓએ ઈશારતથી કેહું કે, તે કદીબી દેખડાવી શકાય નહી. હમોએ પૈસાની લાલચ જણાવી પણ તેઓમાંના એક જણે કેહું કે "હજાર રૂપીઆ" આપો તોબી તેઓ દેખાડી નથી શકવાના. એઓના ગળામાંના તાવીજો જોતાં મદ્રાસના લીંગાઈત લોક પોતાના ગળામાં માહાદેવના લીંગની નીશાન પેહેરે- છે, તેમની યાદ હમને આવી હતી, તથા તેમની દાબડી અથવા કોથલીનો આકાર પણ લીંગની દાબડી જેવોજ હતો. આવાં તાવીજો બાંધવાનું કારણ પુછતાં, તેઓએ કેહું કે આ તાવીજોની ખુબીથી તેમના ઉપર કોઈની નજર નથી લાગી શકવાની!

તા० ૫ મી ફેબ્રુઆરી.—આ દીવશે કેટલાક દેશી વેપારીઓની પેહેડી ઉપર તેમને મળવા ગયા હતા, જે વખતે મદ્રાસ શેહેર કરતાં આ શેહેરની દેશી પેહેડીઓની અંદરની ગોઠવણ વધારે બેહેતર હાલતમાં જોવામાં આવી હતી, તેમાં અગત કરીને આપણા પારશી વેપારીઓની પેહેડીમાં, સારો બંદોબસ્ત દેખાયો હતો.

હીયાંથી ફારગ થઈ કલકત્તાના આંડ ઉપર ફરવાને હમો ગયા હતા. કલકત્તામાં "આંડ", ફરવા હરવા અને હવા ખાવાનું એક મોહોટું મેદાન છે. આ મેદાન આપણી મુંબઈના બૅંડસ્ટાંડના મેદાન કરતાં વીસ્તારમાં ઘણુંજ મોહોટું છે. હીયાં કલકત્તાના ઘણા ખરા યુરોપીયન રેહેવાશીયો ગાડી ઘોડે અથવા પગે ચાલતાં ફરવા આવેલા હમોએ જોયા હતા. જે ઠેકાણા ઉપર બૅંડ વાગેછે તીહાં શેહેરનાં યુરો- પીયન અને દેશી બંડે લોકનો એક અચ્છો મેલાવડો થાયછે. હીયાં ઘણા દેશી લોક હવા ખાવાને આવેલા નજરે પડયા હતા અને તેમાં કલકત્તાના જુવાન કેળવણી પામેલા બાબુઓ પણ તેમની ચોકસ ધપમાં હમારી નજરે પડયા હતા. આ ઉપરથી હમને તે વખતે આપણી મુંબઈના બૅંડસ્ટાંડ વીશે અને તે ઠેકાણાં ઉપર આપણા

દેશી જુઆનો, દરરોજ સાંજના બરોબર ચોકસ વખતે હારબંધ થઈ હાજર રેહે-છે, જેવા તેઓ પોતાના વખતમાં પોતાની નીશાળે ચોકસ વખતસર જઈ હાજર નહી થયલા હશે, તેમની ખુશ યાદ આવી હતી! તેની સાથે કેટલાક બાબુઓનાં પાટલુન, બુટ તથા ડગલા સાથનો પોશાક જોઇને હમને આપણી મુંબઈના કેટલાક જુવાન ગબરૂઓની રંગ બેરંગી ઈજાર અથવા પાટલુન, ડગલા, તેમના હાતમાં રમતી લાકડી, તેમનો આઈગ્લાસ, અને તેમની લટકતી ચાલની પણ યાદ આવી હતી; અને આ સઘળાની સાથે, તેમની કેળવણીનું ભંડોલ, કલકત્તાના જુવાન કેળવણી પામેલાં બાબુઓની આવી શકિત સાથે સરખાવાની અછી તક મળી હતી. મુંબઈના દેશી કેળવણી પામેલાં જુવાનો કરતાં કલકત્તાના દેશી કેળવણી પામેલા બાબુઓ ઘણે દરજે ચઢતા છે. તેઓ આ ઉપલી પોશાકની ફીશીયારીમાં જો કે પછાત પડેલા માલુમ પડયા છે, તોપણ આ બાબી હમો તેમના હકમાં બેહતર ધારીએછ. તેમજ એક બીજી અગતની બાબદ વીશે અત્રે નોંધ કરવાની જરૂર જાણીએછ તે એ જે, કલકત્તાના જુવાન બાબુઓએ હજુરસુધી તેમની સ્ત્રીઓને પુરૂશોની જાહેર મંડળીમાં આમેજ નથી કીધી. આવી રીતના તેમના જનાની રેવાજ સાથે જો કે હમો તદન એકમળતા નથી થતા, તોએપણ આટલી વાત તો હમો કબુલ રાખીએછ કે સ્ત્રી પુરૂશો વચે યુરોપીયન લોકના રેવાજ મુજબની સઘળી છુટ આપણા દેશીઓમાં નહી દાખલ થવાની તરફેણમાં હમારૂં મત છે. આપણા પારસી ટોલાના જુવાન સાહેબોએ પોતાની સ્ત્રીઓને પુરૂશોની મજલીસમાં બીરાજવાને અને પોત પોતાના ધણી અને કુટંબીઓ સાથે જાહેરમાં જવા આવવાનો રેવાજ દાખલ કરીયો છે તે જેટલે દરજે અતીયાર સુધી દાખલ થઈ ચુકો છે તે ઘણોજ થયલો સમજવો અને હવે બસ કરવી સજાવાર છે. એથી વધારે તો હવે નહીજ જવું જોઈએ, બલકે આ સઘળી લીધેલી છુટને બની આવે તેમ ઘણા અંદાજથી અને ખુબ વીચારથી વાપરી તો તેથીજ ફાયદો છે. એમાં જેટલો અંદાજે રેહેશે તે ઘણો નથી બોલાવાનો. મુંબઈના હીંદુઓ અને પારશીઓ, કલકત્તાના બાબુઓના જેટલા જનાની રેવાજમાં બંધ પડેલા નથી, તેટલા હજુર તેઓ યુરોપીયન લોકના રેવાજની સઘળી પાંતીની છુટ ભોગવતા થયા નથી, માટે જે સમતોલ હાલત તેઓ હાલ ભોગવેછે તેની આગળ વધવાને જેબી ડગલું હવે પછી ભરાશે તે આપણી દેશી સંસારી હાલતની ખચીત ખરાબીનું બી રોપાયલું ગણાશે.

આ વીશે હમારેથી કંઇબી કઠણ બોલાઈ શકાતું નથી. આટલોજ ઈશારો બસ છે, કે આ ઘણીજ અગતની અને નાજુક બાબદ ઉપર આપણા દેશીઓ દુરંદેશા બરેલું ધીયાન પોંહોંચાડી અમલ કરતા રેહેશે.

કલકત્તાના આંડ ઉપર ફરીને રાત્રે સાતવાગે શેઠ માણેકજીના મકાન ઉપર પાછા આવીયા. રાત્રે જમતી વેળા ઠરાવ કીધો કે બીજે દીને સહવારના મરહુમ શેઠ રૂસ્તમજી કાવસજી બનાજીનો અસલ રેહેવાનો મકાન જે ચોરંગીથી આસરે ચાર અથવા પાંચ માઈલ ઉપર છે તે જોવા જવું, તેનીસાથે કલકત્તાની સહવારની પોહોરની રચના કેહેવી છે તેબી જોઇ લેવી.

તા૦ ૬ ઠી ફેબ્રુઆરી. આગળા દીવસના ઠરાવ પ્રમાણે સહવારના પોહોરમાં ઉઠીને શેઠ માણેકજીની સાથે એવણના મુરબીનો અસલ મકાન જોવાને નીકલીયા. જે જે રસ્તાઓ ઉપરથી હમારૂં જવું થયું હતું તેમનો દેખાવ જાણે આપણે પુણાના ભવાની પેટના રસ્તા ઉપરથી પસાર થતા હોઇએ એવો દેખાવ નજર આવીયો હતો. સહવારની થંડી સારી લાગી હતી. રસ્તાઉપર તે વખતે કંઈ ઘણી વસતી નહી દેખાઈ હતી આટલા ઉપરથી એવું જણાયું હતું કે કલકત્તાના દેશીલોક મુંબઇના દેશી લોકની પેઠે પરોઢીયાંમાં નથી ઊઠતા અને સહવારના સકારેથી પોત પોતાના ધંધા રોજગાર સર કામે નથી લાગી જતા. કલકત્તાનું દેશી લોક મુંબઇના જેટલું ચપળ અને ઊદીયોગી નથી જણાતું, આ બાબદ તીહાંનો સહવારનો દેખાવ સારી રીતે સાબેત કરી શકેછે.

શેઠ રૂસ્તમજી કાવશજી બનાજીનો જુનો મકાન એકાંત અને હવાવાળી જગા ઉપર છે પણ શેહેરથી ઘણોજ દુર છે. આ જુનો પુરાણો મકાન અને તેની આસપાસનો બાગ જોયાથી હમોને મુંબઇના મેહેમની આગલી પટેલની વાડી અને ટેકા પર ટેકા આપેલા બંગલા, તથા વાંદરાની કેટલીક વાડીયોનીયાદ આવી હતી.

તીયાંથી પાછા ફરતાં રસ્તામાં તરેવાર કીસમના દુકાનો અને તેમની ઉપર લટકાવેલાં નામ અને ધંધો રોજગાર જણાવાનાં પાટીયાં જોવામાં આવીયાં હતાં. આ પાટીયાં વાંચતા વાંચતા હમો એક ફોટોગ્રાફરની દુકાન આગળ આવી પોંહોંચીયા. આ સબી પાડનાર વીશે હમને સારી ભલામણ થયાથી હમો સઘળાઓએ ઠરાવ કીધો કે એકંદર થઈ સઘળાની એક સબી પડાવવી. આ પુસ્તકમાં જે ચીત્ર આપીહું છે તે તે વખતે થયલા વીચારને તુરંત અમલમાં

મુકેલાનું પરીણામ છે, જો કે તે વખતે હમારા કોઈના સ્વપનામાંબી નહી હતું કે આવું ચીત્ર આ પુસ્તકમાં આવશે.

આસરે અગીયાર વાગે પાછા ચૌરંગીના મુકામપર આવી પુગા. બપોરનું ખાણું લેઇને, કલકત્તા શેહેરની મોલાકાતના રવૈયા પ્રમાણે કેટલાક સરકારી યુરોપીયન અમલદારો જેઓની ઊપર હમે મુંબઈથી ભલામણ અને ઓળખાણના કાગજ પત્રો લીધાં હતાં, તેમની મુલાકાતને ગયા હતા. કલકત્તામાં અથવા તીહાંથી છેક લાહોર અને પેશાવર સુધી જીહાં જઈએ તીહાં, આવી એક માઠી રસમ ચાલુ છે, કે કોઇબી સરકારી અમલદાર, અથવા શેઠ સાહુકારની મુલાકાત કરવાને તેમના ઘરમાં ગયા હોઈએ તો તીહાં દરેક ઠેકાણે બખશીસ નામના એક કંટાળો આપનાર રવૈયાને તાબે થઈ ચાલવું પડેછે, જેથી જેની મુલાકાતે જઈએ તેનાં ઘરના દરબાનને, કંઈબી રકમ, બખશીસ તરીકે, પાછા ફરતી વેળા આપવાને વારંવાર એક ફરજ થઈ પડેછે. આ દરબાન એવું સમજેછે કે મોલાકત કરવા આવનારનો ફકત પેગામ લઈ જઈ પોતાના શેઠને પોંહોંચાડીયો અને તેથી જો મુલાકાત થઈ તો દરબાનનો "લવાજમ" અથવા "હક" લાગુ પડી ચુકો. આપણે મુલાકાત કરી પાછા ફરીયા કે દરબાન દરવાજા આગળ આપણી સાંભણે આવી, સઘળી તાજીમ તવાજોથી સલામ કરીને બોલેછે, "ગરીબપરવર, હુજુર, કુછ બખશીસ." હમો આવી માંગણીથી પેહેલ વેહેલાં તાજુબ થયા હતા, પણ પાછળથી પુછતાં માલુમ પડચું હતું કે આ રેવાજ તો, કલકત્તાથી છેક હીંદુસ્થાનની હદ સુધી, દેશી નોકરોનો જાણે એક હક થઈ પડેલો છે. "ખુદાવદ બખશીસ," "જીહાં પનાહ બખશીસ," "ગરીબપરવર બખશીસ" આવા ચીકાસ ભરેલા શબ્દો ઠેકાણે ઠેકાણે સાંભળવામાં આવેછે, પછી જેવી જે પ્રાંતની માખણીયાં જબાન. આ "બખશીસ" જબરદસ્તીથી કોઈ નથી માંગતું, એ તો આપનારની ખુશીનો સોદો છે, પણ આટલું ઘણું કરીને થાયછે કે "બખશીસ" આપીયાથી જેવી જલદીથી મુલાકાત થઈ શકેછે, તેવી નહી આપીયાથી મોલાકાત કરવા જનાર શખસને ઘરના બારણા આગળ અછી રીતે તપી રેહેવું પડેછે, જેથી તેની સબુરીની ઘણીવાર જબરી તપાસ થાયછે.

તા૦ ૭ મી ફેબ્રુઆરી. આ દીવશે કલકત્તાની જેલ જોવાને ગયા હતા. જેલની જગા ઘણા મોહોટા વીસ્તારવાળી છે. કેહેછે કે લગભગ તેમાં ૧૪) એકર જમીન

Vincent Brooks lith

OCHTERLONY MONUMENT.—CALCUTTA

૮. આક્ટરલોનીની માન્યુમેંટ, કલકતાની દીવાદાંડી.

રોકાયલી છે. જેલની અંદર ફોજદારી મુકરદમાને લગતા બંધવાઓમાંના ઘણા ખરાના ફોટોગરાફ લીએછે, અને તેમાં એવી એક ગોઠવણ કરેલી છે કે જે બંધવાની મરજી પોતાની સખી નહી પડાવા દેવાની હોય તોપી તે નહી જાણે એવી રીતે તેની સખી છુપી રીતે લઈલિવાની યુક્તિ કરી રાખેલી છે. જેલની ઈમારતની ભોંય સઘળી સલગ ઇંટની બનાવેલી છે. ઇંટ કોરવંકી મુકીયામાં આવી છે, અને તેનાં બાંધકામમાં જે ચુનો વાપરેલો છે તે ઘણીજ સારી જાતનો ચીકાસવાળો છે. કલકત્તાની ઇંટ પણ ઘણીજ પાકી અને મજબુત છે, આપણી મુંબઈની ઇંટ તેમની આગળ વટાવમાં જાણવી. જેલનો ગવરનર આ મકાન દેખાડવાને હમારી સાથે ફરીયો હતો. ત્યાર પછી કલકત્તાનો એક્સચેંજ હાલ જેમાં અફીમનું સરકારી લીલાંઊ વખતે વખત થાયછે તે જોવાને આ દીવસે ગયા હતા. આ ઠેકાણે, એટલાં તો માંણસોની થટ મળેછે, અને તીહાં એટલોતો ઘોંઘાટ થાયછે કે એક જણનું બોલવું પાસેવાળો બીજો સાંભળી શકતો નથી. લીલાંઊ કરનારા શું ભાવ બોલેછે તે કોઈથી બરોબર સંભળાતો નથી, તેથી જે ભાવ બોલાયછે તે ભાવનો આંકડો એક પાટીયાં ઉપર મોટા અક્ષરે લખીને તે એક લાંકડી ઉપર ઉંચકી આખી ભીડમાં સઘળાને દેખડાવેછે. હમોને આ ભીડમાં એટલી તો ગરમી લાગી હતી કે જો કે પવન નાખવાને પંખા ચાલતા હતા તોએપણ હમારેથી અરધો કલાક તીહાં ઉભું રેહી શકાયું નહી હતું. આટલી ભીડ, ઘોંઘાટ અને ગરદીમાં થતી આંચકા ઊંચકીની ગડબડમાં પણ લીલાંઉ કરવાને અંદર બેઠેલા કેટલાક કામદારો, મહાવરાથી પોતાનું કામ મુગા મુગા ઠંડે પેટે જાણે પોતાની પેહેડી ઉપર બેઠેલા હોય તેમ ચલાવતા હતા. આ લીલાંઉમાં લખો રૂપીયાનું અફીમ સરકાર તરફથી વેચાઈ દેશી વેપારીઓના હાતમાં આવેછે. વખતે વખતનો પાટીયાં ઉપર બોલાતો ભાવ બજારમાં ખબર પાડવાને કેટલાક દલાલો પાટીયું જોતાને વાર તીહાંથી દોડી જાયછે અને આ દોડાદોડીમાં, ગપાગપી પણ જબરી થઈ પડેછે, અને કેટલાક તમાસગીરોને તેમની અચકચારી ચાલને લીધે, પોલીસને હાતે સારી પેઠે મેથી જમવી પડેછે અને તે ખાધા બાદ યા તો સહી સલામત પોતાને ઘર અથવા તો ચોકીમાં પણ જવું પડેછે.

હમો લીલાંઉથી ફારગ થયા પછી, સરકારી મેહેલની સાંભણે મેદાનમાં "Ochterlony Monument," આક્ટરલોની માન્યુમેંટ નામનો એક મોટો

મીનારો છે તે જોવાને ગયા. આ મીનારો, મેજર જનરલ સર ડેવીડ આક્ટરલોની નામના એક લશકરી સરદારની, લડાઈમાં અને રાજ દરબારી કામ કાજમાં, મેળવેલી કીર્તિની જાહેર યાદગારી રાખવાને ઊભો કરવામાં આવીયો છે. આ સુરા સરદારનું મત હીંદુસ્થાનના ઈસલામી લોક તરફ વધારે માન ભરેલું હોવાથી, આ મીનારાની બાંધણી, આ લોકની આગલી જાહોજલાલીના વખતના તરીકા મુજબની કરીયામાં આવી છે, જેથી તેની રોનક દીલ્લીના કુતબ મીનારને ઘણું કરીને મળતી આવેછે. અગત કરીને આ મીનારાને મથાલે જે બે તબક્કા કરેલા છે તે કુતબ મીનાર સાથે વધારે એકસરખા માલુમ પડેછે. આ બંધે મીનારાનાં ચીત્રો જોયાથી ઉપલી હકીકત બરોબર ધીયાનમાં આવી શકશે. આક્ટરલોનીનો મીનારો ૧૬૦ એક સો સાઠ ફુટ ઊંચો છે, એનો પાયો અથવા બેઠક, મીસર દેશની બાંધણીની રોનકની કરેલી છે. આ આખી બાંધણી પાછળ રૂ ૩૫૦૦૦, લાગા છે. જેબી શખ્સ જરા તસદી લેઇને આ મીનારાના ગોલ ચકરીદાર દાદરો ઉપર ચઢી, મીનારાને મથાલે પોહોંચી જે દેખાવ આસપાસ જોશે તેની મેહનતનો બદલો સારીપેઠે વળી શકશે, એવું હમો માનીએછ. આ ઊંચાણપરથી કલકત્તાનું આખું શેહેર અને તેને લગતાં મીઠાંના સરોવરો છેક દુર સુધી ખુલા નજરે પડી શકેછે, જે દેખાવ ખરેખર જોવા લાયક છે.

એજ દીને મહમદન કાલેજ અથવા જેને મદરેસા નામથી પણ બોલેછે તે જોઈ હતી. વેલસ્લી સ્કોયર નામના રસ્તા ઉપર આ ખાતાંની ઈમારત છે, જે ઈ. સ. ૧૭૮૦ ના સાલમાં નામદાર વારન હેસટીંગે, મહમદન લોકને આરબી જબાનની પુરતી માહીતગારી આપવાને સ્થાપી હતી. એ સ્થાપવામાં હીંદુસ્થાનના આ પેહેલ વેહેલા ગવરનર જનરલની એક ભલી નેમ એ હતી કે આબરૂદાર અને ઊંચ કુટંબના ગૃહસ્થોને મહમદન કાયદા કાનુનોથી સારીપેઠે વાકેફગાર કરવા, જેથી તેઓ ઈનસાફની દરબારમાં લાયક જાહેર અમલદારોની પદવી ઉપર ચઢી શકે અને પોતાના દેશનો કારભાર પોતે ચલાવાને શકતીવાન થાય.

સાંજના પાછા ફરતી વખતે હમોને ખબર પડી કે કલકત્તાના કેટલાક સુધારકોએ બ્રહમો સમાજ નામનો એક નવો પંથ ઉભો કરીઓ છે તે પંથવાળાઓની એક જાહેર સભા તે દીવસે મળનાર છે. આ નવાઈ જેવા પંથની સભા તથા તેમાં ઇંગ્રેજી વાજીંત્ર "હારમોનીયમ" સાથે થતી બંદગી અને બાકુ લોકની દેશી

ભારામાં થતું ભાશણ કેવું હશે, એ જાણવાની ઇછાથી હમો તે રાત્રે બ્રહમો સમાજની સભામાં ગયા હતા.

બ્રહમો સમાજ પંથનો વીગતવાર એહવાલ આ ઠેકાણે હમો આપવાની જરૂર જોતા નથી. આ સમાજ વીશે માત્ર એટલુંજ જણાવેલું બસ છે કે કેટલાક બાબુઓને મુરતીપુજા અને એકથી વધારે ઇશ્વર માનવાનું ખોટું લાગાથી તેઓએ આ વીચાર છોડીને ફકત એકજ ઇશ્વરને માનવાનું વાજબી ધારીયું. રાજારામ મોહનરાય આ વીચારનો ફેલાવો કરવામાં પેહલ વેહેલો દેશી બાબુ આગેવાન થયો હતો અને આ બ્રહમો સમાજ પંથ ઉભો કરવાનું માન એ રાજાને મળીયું છે. આ રાજાનું ધર્મસંબંધી મત ઘણુંકરીને યુનીટેરીયન ક્રીસચીયન પંથવાળાઓના મત સાથે મળતું હતું.

જે સભામાં હમો ગયા હતા તીહાંની સઘળી રીતભાંત, બંદગી, ધર્મોપદેશ કરવાની રીત યુરોપીયન દેવલમાં ચાલતી રીતભાંત સાથે મળતી આવતી હતી. સમાજવાળાઓએ તે સભામાં એક બે અભંગ ઇશ્વર કીરતીનાં ગાયા હતા તેની જોડની, ઇંગ્રેજી રાગની જોડની ઉપર રચેલી હોવાથી અને "હારમોનીયમ" સાથે ગાયાથી "યુરોપીયન દેવલમાં જેમ "હીમ" ગવાયછે તે ગાયનને આબેહુબ મળતો હતો. જો હમે બાહેર રસ્તા ઉપરથી સાંભળતે તો એમજ સમજતે કે આ ઠેકાણે કોઈ યુરોપીયનના દેવલમાં બંદગીનું ગાયન થાયછે. ગાઈ રેહા પછી, વખણાયલા બાબુ કેસબ ચંદ્ર સેને દેશી બંગાલી ભારામાં ભાશણ કરી સંભળાવીયું અને કેટલાક શ્લોક ભણી સંભળાવીયા. આ શ્લોક જો કે હમો મુતલક સમજી નહી શકયા હતા તોએ પણ તેના પદોનો આવાજ, આપણા પારશી મોબેદો ઘેહે સારતી વખતે કેટલાક હા ભણેછે, તે પદોના આવાજને ઘણો ખરો મળતો આવતો હતો.

હાલ જમાનાના સઘળા ધર્મોમાંથી જે કઈ સારાં તત્વો છે, તે ચુંટી કાહાડીને બ્રહમો સમાજવાળાઓએ પોતાનો એક નવો ધર્મ ઉત્પંન કરીયો છે. હવે એક નવો ધર્મ અથવા ફીરકો ઉભો કરી આ પૃથ્વી ઉપરના ધર્મોમાં એક નવી સંપ્રીઆ ઉભેરવાના કરતાં, હમો ધારીએછ કે બ્રહમો સમાજ એકદમ એક ડગલું મજબુતાઈથી આગળ મુકીને "યુનીટેરીયન ક્રીસચીયન" ટોલાના મત સાથે મળી જાય તો, બ્રહમો સમાજ એકદમ મુસ્તકીમ પાયા ઉપર આવી શકશે.

અને હજુર સુધી તેઓ હીંદુ વેદને ધરી રાખી તેમાં જણાવેલા હીંદુ ધર્મના કેટલાક તત્વોનો પોતાનાં પંથની મતલબને મળતો અર્થ કરવાને જે કલ્પના તેમને કરવી પડેછે, તે કરવાની જરૂર નથી પડવાની. હમો બ્રહમો સમાજના કોઈબી પંથીનું દીલ દુખવવા ચાહાતા નથી, પણ જે વલણ પેહેલાંથી આ ચંચલ પંથવાળાઓથી લેવાઈ છે, તે વલણ આખેરીએ ક્રીસચીયન ધર્મમાં આમેજ થયાવીના નથી રેહેવાની, આવું હમારૂં આધીન મત છે. આજસુધી માત્રે એટલુંજ થયું છે કે તે વલણ ઘણી ધીમી આગલ ચાલી છે. આ પંથવાળા બ્રહ્મો થઇને હીંદુ રેહેવાના જે દેખાવો કરેછે, અને જાણે તેઓજ ખરા અસલ હીંદુ છે અને બાકીના હીંદુઓ આડે રસ્તે ચાલેછે, એવો દેખાવ દેખાડવાને બદલે, જો બ્રહમો પંથવાળા એમજ ખુલે ખુલું કહે કે હમો હીંદુ નથી, હમો યુનીટેરીયન ક્રીસચીયન છઇએ તો આ ખરેખરૂં બોલવું તેમને વધારે માન ભરેલું થઈ પડશે. પણ બ્રહ્મો થઇને, જાતીભેદ કાહાડી નાખીને, માંસ તથા દારૂ પીવાની છુટ લેઇને, અને પર ન્યાતની સ્ત્રીઓ સાથે લગ્નનો પવીત્ર ગાંઠ બાંધવાની છુટ લેઇને, પછી વળી એમ બોલે કે હમો ખરાજ સન્માર્ગી હીંદુ ધર્મ માનનારા છઇએ, અથવા હમો હીંદુ છઇએ અને વેદને માત્ર માનીએછ, તો આવું બોલવું અથવા માનવું આખા સન્માર્ગી હીંદુ ટોલાની મશ્કરી અથવા તેમને અપમાન કરવા જોગ છે. આવું લખીયાથી એમ નહી સમજવું કે આ પંથવાળાઓની નીતીવીશે હમો કંઇબી વીરૂધ બોલીએછ. બાબુ કેસબ ચંદ્ર સેન ઉપર અને તેના ધર્મવીચાર વીશે અને તેની જાતી વર્તણુક વીશે હમો અતીશય માનથી જોઈએછ, અને જે કોશેશ તેણે પોતાના દેશીઓને સુધારવાને અને બેહતર કરવાને કરી છે અને કરેછે તેમાં તેને હમો માનસાથે સઘળી ફતેમંદી ચાહીએછ. એક ખરા ઈશ્વરને માનવાનો વીચાર અલબતાં જારે આખાં હીંદુસ્થાનમાંના હીંદુઓ પકડશે તારે એમજ જાણવું કે તેઓએ સુધારાના મેદાનમાં એક ઘણુંજ મોહોટું અને અગતનું ડગલું ભરીયું અને આથી આખાં હીંદુસ્થાનને મોટો ફાયદો થવાનો, એમાં તો કંઈજ શક નથી.

તા૦ ૮ મી ફેબ્રુઆરી ને દીને રવીવાર હતો અને તેથી નીરાંતથી કલકત્તાની ‘‘બોટાનીકલ ગારડન’’ જે નદીને પેલે પાર છે તે જોવાનો ઠરાવ કીધો. આ દીવશે કલકત્તાના લાબાં વખતના એક પારસી સેઠીયા નામે શેઠ ફરામજી રતનજી ખીસની જેવણ શેઠ માણેકજી બનાજીને તીહાં પરોણા તરીકે આવી રહેલા હતા,

તેવણની પીઠ ઉપર લાંબા વખતની એક મોટી વસુડી થયલી હતી, જેથી તેમને સુવા બેસવાને ઘણી ઈજા ખમવી પડતી હતી, તે વસુડી આપણા ચંચલ ડાકટર બાઉ દાજીએ, સહવારના પોહોરમાં ચીરી કાહાડી હતી. આ વસુડીનું કદ એક નાહાના પેર જેટલું હતું. આ વસુડી એટલી તો ચપળાઈથી કાપી કાહાડી હતી કે દરદીને દવાથી બેસુધ કરવાની પણ જરૂર પડી નહી હતી.

કલકત્તાની "બોટાનીકલ ગારડન" જોવા જતાં, કીલ્લામાં થઈને પણ નદી કીનારે જવાનો રસ્તો હતો, તેથી એક ફેરામાં કીલ્લો અને બાગ જોવાને સાથે બની આવવા સારૂ, પેહેલાં હમોએ હમારી ગાડીં કીલ્લા તરફ લઈજવાનો હુકમ આપીયો હતો. હમારો ભોમીયો અણજાણો હોવાથી કીલ્લાની અંદર દાખલ થવાના દરવાજા વાટે જવાને બદલે કીલ્લાની અંદરથી બાહેર નીકળવાના દરવાજા વાટે હમારી ગાડીઓ અંદર દાખલ કીધી હતી, જે થોડુંક આગળ ચાલતાં પેહેરો ભરનાર સીપાઈએ અટકાવી હતી અને સીધે દરવાજે કીલ્લામાં જવાને કેહું હતું, જે ઉપરથી હમોને હમારી ગાડીયો ફેરવી સીધે દરવાજે દાખલ થવું પડયું હતું.

કલકત્તાના કીલ્લા વીશે વીગતવાર બયાન વાચવું હોય તો હામીલટન ગેજેટીયરની બીજી આવૃત્તીના વાલમ પેહેલાના સફે ૩૧૭ થી ૩૧૯ સુધીમાં તે આપેલું છે. હમો અત્રે કેટલીક અગતની બાબદો જે ઉપર હમારૂં ધીયાન તે વખતે પોહોંચાયું હતું, તે આ ઠેકાણે લખી જણાવીએછ. પેહેલી બીના જેની ઉપર હમારૂં મન લાગું, તે એ હતી કે જેવા કીલ્લામાં હમો દાખલ થયા કે તીહાંના રસ્તા એવા તો તજુમલથી બનાવેલા અને સફાઇદાર માલુમ પડ્યા હતા કે હમારા સઘળા જણના મોહોડામાંથી એકજ આવાજ નીકલીયા કે જુઓ, કલકત્તાના શેહેરના રસ્તા કેવા ગલીચ અને જુઓ જીહાં ઈંગ્રેજી લશ્કર વશેછે તીહાંની જગા અને તેની સફાઈ કેટલી સરસ છે. કીલ્લામાં ઘણું ખરૂં લશકર યુરોપીયન લોકનું છે, અને દેશી લશકરના કેટલાક સીપાઇઓને માત્રે વારી પ્રમાણે ફેરબદલ કરતા રાખેલા છે. કીલ્લામાં નજદીક ૧૫૦૦૦ પંદર હજાર માણસ રેહી શકે એટલી જગા છે. અંદરની જગા ખુલી અને લીલોત્રી બરેલી છે, તેમાં ફરવા હરવાની પગતીઓ બનાવેલી છે. અને થંડક છાંયડા સારૂ કટારબંધ ઝાડો ઉગાડેલા છે, અને ઠેકાણે ઠેકાણે તોપના નાહાના મોહોટા ગોળાઓને એવા તો તરેવાર આકારમાં રચી ગોઠવેલા છે કે તેમના ઢગો જોયાથી જેવી એક તરફથી દેહેશત તેવી બીજી તરફથી ખુશાલી ઉત્પન થાયછે.

કીલ્લામાં દાખલ થવાને ત્રણ દરવાજા વટાવા પડેછે અને જેમ આપણી મુંબઇમાં આગળ કોટની આસપાસ ચર હતી તે મુઆફક દરેક દરવાજાની હદે કીલ્લાને ફરતી ચર છે, જેમાંની કોઈ સુકી અને કોઈમાં પાણી હતું. આવો ફરતો કોટ, આઠ ખુણાનો બાંધેલો છે, જે કોટ, પ્લાસીની લડાઈ ઇંગ્રેજ લોક જીતીયા પછી ઈ૦ સ૦ ૧૭૫૭ ના સાલમાં લાર્ડ કલાઇવે બંધાવાને શીરૂ કીધો હતો. એવું કેહેછે કે, આખા હીંદુસ્થાન વચે આ કીલ્લો ઘણોજ મજબુત છે, અને લડાઈની વખતે સારીપેઠે બંચાવ કરવાના કાયદા કાનુનો મુજબ તે બાંધેલો છે. કીલ્લાનો થોડો ભાગ નદી તરફ આવેલો છે જે બાજુ તોપોની ગોઠવણથી ઘણીજ મજબુત કરી રાખેલી છે, અને જમીન તરફથી તો આ કીલ્લા ઉપર ધસારો થવાની કંઇજ ધાસ્તી રાખવામાં આવતીજ નથી. કીલ્લામાં, કેટલાક પીવાના પાણીના કુઆ નદીના પાણીથી છેક ૧૫૦૦ ફુટ દુર છે તેમાંનું પાણી ગરમીની રૂતુમાં ખારૂં થઇ પીવાને નાલાયક થઇ પડેછે તેથી સરકારે વરસાદનું પાણી ભરી રાખવાને મોહોટ મોહોટી ટાંકીયો બંધાવી છે.

કલકત્તા શેહેરમાં પીવાનું પાણી ઘણું કરીને લોક નદીનું વાપરેછે અથવા જેબી કુઆ છે તેમાં ઘણા ખરા નદીનાજ પાણીના ઝરા લાગેલા હોયછે. આ કુઆઓમાં કેટલાકનાં પાણી થોડી મુદત સુધી સારી હાલતમાં રેહી શકેછે, પણ જેમ જેમ ગરમીના દીવસ નજદીક આવતા જાયછે તેમ તેમ તે પાણી મોરચાં અને પછવાડેથી ઘણા ખારાં થઈ પડેછે. કેટલેક ઠેકાણે, કલકત્તામાં વરસાદનું પાણી જાથુક પીવાને, ટાંકાની પેઠે મોહોટી બરણીઓ અથવા ઝાલાઓમાં ભરી રાખેછે. આ બરણીઓમાં વરસાદના દીવસ ઉપર પાણી ભરી લીએછે, અને દરેક બરણીની અંદર લાલ તપાવેલાં લોહોડાંનો એક સળીયો ટાંગી મુકેછે અને પછી બરણીનું મોહોડું તજુ-મલથી ઢાંકી બંધ રાખેછે. આ લોહોડાંનાં સળીયાથી, લાંબી મુદત સુધી પાણી સફાઇ ભરેલું રેહી શકેછે અને તેમાં જીવ નથી પડતા. આવી રીતે રાખેલું પાણી પીવામાં ટાંકાંના પાણી જેવો સ્વાદ આપેછે, જો કે એના કરતાં કેટલેટ ઠેકાણે કુઆનાં પાણી મોરચાં લાગેછે, તોએ પણ તે વધારે હજમીએત છે.

કીલ્લામાંથી પાછા બાહેર નીકળતાં, પ્રીનસેપ્સ ઘાટ આગળ આવી પુગા હતા. આ ઘાટનું ચીત્ર આપેલું છે. ઘાટ શબ્દનો અર્થ આ લત્તા ઉપર અને આખા હીંદુસ્થાનમાં "દરવાજો" અથવા "જવા આવવાનો રસ્તો" કરીને થાયછે. જમીન

PRINCEP'S GHAUT, CALCUTTA

૧. પ્રીન્સેપ્સ ઘાટ.—કલકત્તા.

ઉપર થઈ નદી ઉપર જવું હોય અથવા નદી ઉપરથી ઉતરી જમીન ઉપર આવવું હોય તો જે ઠેકાણેથી અથવા માર્ગેથી વાહાણ ઉપર જઈએ અથવા તીહાંથી ઉતરીએ તે રસ્તાને બંગાલ પ્રાંતમાં ઘાટ કરીને બોલેછે. "પ્રીનસેપ્સ ઘાટ" નામનો હુગલી નદી ઉપર જવાનો એક રસ્તો છે, તે રસ્તાઉપર એક ઘણીજ સુંદર ઈમારત બાંધેલી છે અને તે ઈમારતનું નામ, "પ્રીનસેપ્સ ઘાટ" કરીને કલકત્તાના દેશીઓએ આપીયું છે. મી. જેમ્સ પ્રીનસેપ્સ, ઉગમણ પ્રાંતની ભાશા અને તેને લગતી બાબદોનું પુશ્કળ ગ્નાન ધરાવનાર એક નામાંકીત વીદ્યાર્થી થઈ ગયો છે. આ વીદ્વાન પુરૂશે ઉગમણ પ્રાંતના એલમના અભીયાસનો વધારો કરવાને અને આ તરફની પુરાણી બાબદો ઉપર અજવાલું પાડવાને ઘણીજ મેહનત કરી છે, તેની યાદગારી કાયમ રાખ્યવાને કલકત્તાના શેહેરી રેહેવાશીઓએ આ "પ્રીનસેપ્સ ઘાટ" ની સુંદર ઈમારત બંધાવી છે.

નદી કીનારે આવી પોહોંચીયા પછી, બોટાનીકલ ગારડનમાં જવા સારૂ, બોટમાં બેસીને નદી પાર કરી હતી. કીનારા આગળ પુશ્કળ કીચલ હોવાથી હમો દરેક જણને ચાર હાથાવાળા એક પાટીયાં ઉપર બેસાડીને, ચાર ખલાસીઓ પાલકી ઉંચકે તેમ ઉંચકીને બોટમાં લઈગયા હતા. બોટ, નદીની સાંમી બાજુના કીનારા ઉપર જઈ પુગા પછી, હમને એક લાંબડી સીડીવાળા ભાગ ઉપર ઉતારીયા હતા, જે ઉપર થઈ "બોટાનીકલ ગારડનમાં જવાનો રસ્તો હતો.

કલકત્તાના આ મોહોટા સરકારી બાગનું બયાન આ ઠેકાણે કરવું હમારી શકતીથી દુર છે. જે બાગનો નજદીક ત્રણથી ચાર માઈલ વીસ્તાર છે અને જેમાં, સહરાવીને નથી બોલતા પણ, ઘણું કરીને આખી પૃથ્વીની વનસ્પતી અને ઝાડો અને રોપા અને ફુલ પાનના નમુનાનો એક રાખશસી જમાવ કરેલો છે, જેમાં ફરી વળવાને અને જોવાને નજદીક એક આખાં અઠવાડીયાનો વખત પણ પુરતો નથી ગણાવાનો, તે બાગ હમો બેચાર કલાકમાં જોઈ વળીયા, તારે હમોએ કેટલું થોડું જોયું હશે, તે વાચનારે સમજી લેવું. તોએબી આટલા થોડા વખતમાં હમારો સાથે તીહાંનો એક યુરોપીયન રખેવાલ આવીને, બાગનો જે જોવાલાયક ભાગ હતો, તે તેણે દેખડાવીયો હતો. હમારા વીદ્વાન મીત્ર ડાકટર ભાઉ દાજીની સાથે ફરતાં પણ બાગનો બીજો કેટલોક ભાગ હમો સારી પેઠે જોઈ તથા પીછાની શકયા હતા. બાગમાં ફરીને ફકત જોવું, અને જોઈને તે પીછાનવું, આ બે વાતમાં ઘણોજ ફેર

છે. વીદ્વાન લોકની સાથે ફરવામાં એક મોહોટો ફાયદો એ છે કે જેબી આપણી સાંભણે નજરે પડેછે તે સું છે, તેનો ઉપયોગ સું, તેમાં કહયા કહયા ગુણો છે, આ સઘળી બાબદની આપણને સમજણ મળી શકેછે. હમને હમારા ઈંગ્રેજ ભોમીયાએ નજદીક ૯૦) નેવું જુદી જુદી તરાના ગોલાબ દેખડાવીયા હતા. હમારો ભોમીયો બાગાયતની બાબદમાં અછો માહીતગાર હતો. તેણે, નાળીઅરીની તાડ, ખજુરી અને કેડની નજદીક ૧૦) દસ જુદી જુદી જાત બતલાવી હતી, જેમાંની કેટલીક અમેરીકાથી લાવીયા હતા, કેટલીક આફ્રીકા અને કેટલીક મીસર દેશમાંથી લાવેલી પેદાસ હતી. સાગુ ચોખાના ઝાડો જે એજ જાતની અંદર છે, તે ઘણાંજ સુંદર ખીલી રેહેલાં હતાં. લાંકડાનાં ઝાડોમાં, આપણું સાગ, ઈંગ્રેજી ઓક, મહાગની, દેવદાર, ફર, ફણસી, સીસમ, અબનુસ વગેરે બીજી ઘણી જાત હતી. તેમજ મેવા અને ફુલોના ઝાડો પણ ઘણાજ હતાં, તે સઘળાનું તો બયાન આ ટુંક જગામાં થઈ શકતુંજ નથી. માટે આટલુંજ જણાવેલું બસ છે કે આ બાગોમાં યુરોપખંડ અને થંડીના મુલકના તરેવાર ઝાડપાનો, જેમાં નીપાલદેશ અને હીમાલયા પરવત આગળની જમીન ઉપરના કેટલાંક ઝાડો; જાવા, સુમાત્રા, મલાકા, પીનાંગ અને આ લતા તરફના મેવા તથા મસાલાના ઝાડો, આફ્રીકાખંડના, કેપ આગળના સંસ્થાનનાં, તથા અમેરીકા ખંડ અને બ્રેઝીલ દેશના ઝાડોનો એક પસંદ અને જોવાલાયક સંગ્રહ, આ કલકત્તાના બોટાનીકલ બાગમાં હમારા જોવામાં આવીયો હતો. થંડીના દેશવાળા કેટલાંક રોપાને તજુમલથી કાચના ઘરમાં ઉગાડીયામાં આવેલા હતા, અને તેમની જોઈતી બરદાસ્ત કરવાની ગોઠવણો કરેલી હતી, પણ એવા રોપ માત્રે થોડાજ નમુના તરીકેના હતા. આ બાગમાં ફરતાં જે થોડા વારમાં હમોને ઝાડપાન વીરો કેટલુંક ગ્નાન મળીયું હતું, તેટલું આ દેશના કોઈ બીજાં ઠેકાણા ઉપર નહી મળી શકયું હતું.

આ બાગમાં બેચાર ઠેકાણે બેસવા ઉઠવાના અને આરાએશ તથા નાશ્તો પાણી લેવાના કેટલાક મકાનો બાંધેલા છે. કેટલાક મકાનોમાં કાચના મોહોટ મોહોટાં ઓરડા બનાવેલા છે, જેમાં થંડ દેશના ઝાડપાનોને સઘળી તજુમલથી ઉગાડીયામાં આવેછે. બાગમાં કેટલીક જગો ઊપર કેટલાક નામીચા પુરશોના બાવલાં પણ મુકેલાં છે, તે સઘળાનું બયાન અત્રે આપી શકતા નથી. આ મોહોટા બાગની સઘળી જમીન લોકઉપયોગ સારૂ બાગ બનાવાને, જનરલ કીડે મુફત બખશીશ

REFRESHMENT ROOMS, EDEN GARDENS, CALCUTTA.

૭. ઈડન બાગમાં આસાએશ લેવાનાં મકાન-કલકતા.

PAGODA, EDEN GARDENS _ CALCUTTA

૨. ચીનાઈ ચૈનકનું દેહેરૂં, ઈડન બાગમાં.—કલકતા.

દાખલ આપી હતી, જેના બદલામાં આ સખી ગૃહસ્થનું બાવલું આ બાગમાં મુકીયામાં આવીયું છે, એવું હમોને હમારા ભોમીયાએ કેહું હતું. જનરલ કીડને આ જગા, બંગાલાના તે વખતના સુબેદારને હાતથી બખ્ખેશ તરીકે મળી હતી. બીજું બાવલું પ્રખ્યાત થયલા Roxburgh નું જોયું હતું, જે શખ્સ ઝાડપાનને લગતાં શાસ્ત્રમાં એક વખણાયલો વીદ્વાન થઇ ગયો છે. આ બાવલાંની ઊપર જે લેખ કોતરેલો છે તે લાટીન ભાશામાં જોડેલો છે, પણ તેનો તરજુમો ઇંગ્રેજીમાં નીચે મુજબ કરીયો છે:—

"Whoever thou art present here; if the amenity of the place imbues thy mind with suavity, or admonishes thee to feel piously of God,

Honour thou

Roxburgh

the Superintendent of these Gardens, a man distinguished for his knowledge of Botany, and a great adept at rural amenities.

His country preserves his ashes
His genius flourishes here
Be thou favourable and persevere.

B. M. P. C. [Erected by his] surviving Friends. A. D. 1821.

ઉપલી ઇંગ્રેજીનો નીચે મુજબ તરજુમો ગુજરાતીમાં કરીયો છે:—

"હીયાં હાજર થયલા શખ્સ, જેવી કોઈ તું હોય, જો આ જગાની ખુશનુમાઇથી તારૂં મન ખુશ ખુશાલ થતું હોય અથવા ખુદા તરફ પવીત્રાઈ ભરેલું કરવાને તુંને તે અંદરથી બોધ કરતું હોય તો,

માન આપજે તું

રાકસબરગને

જે આ બાગોનો ઉપરી થઈ ગયો છે અને જે પુરૂષ ઝાડપાનની વીદ્યાનું જ્ઞાન ધરાવામાં વખણાઈ ગયો છે અને જે બાગ બગીચાને લગતી મેહમાનદારી અને રમુજેમાં એક મશહુર દોસ્ત થઈ ગયો છે.

એના દેશે એની મીટી જાળવી રાખી છે,
એના મગજની ખુબી હીયાં ખીલી રેહી છે.
તું મેહેરબાન અને ઉદ્યોગી રેહેજે.

બી. એમ. પી. સી.* એની પાછળના એના દોસ્તોએ ઉભું કીધું છે.

ઈ. સ. ૧૮૨૧.

---

* આ અક્ષરોની સમજ પડતી નથી.—ગ્રંથકર્તા.

બાગમાં ફરતાં ફરતાં છેક થાકી ગયા હતા, તથા હમારામાંથી એકુ બે જણ એક બીજાથી છુટા પડવાથી ભુલા પડીયા હતા અને તેમને પાછા આવી મળતાં ઘણીજ અસુર થઈ પડી હતી. હમારી સાથે લીધેલું ભાતીયું એક મકાનમાં બેસીને, સારીપેઠે જમીયા અને સુરજ આથમીયા પછી, બાગમાંથી નીકળ્યા હતા. ભરતી પણ પુર ચહેડેલી હતી તેથી નદીનાં પાણી છેક સીડી સુધી આવી પુગાં હતાં, જેથી જમીન ઉપરથી એકદમ બોટમાં બેશી શકયા હતા, અને આગળની પેઠે પેલાં પાટીયાં ઉપર બેસીને બોટમાં જવાની જરૂર નહી પડી હતી. સાંજની વખતે નદી પસાર કરતાં હમારી આસપાસ હજારો વાંહાંણો અને દેશી મછવાની ગીચ હોવાથી, તેમની વચેથી હમારી બોટ પસાર થતી હતી, તે દેખાવ ઘણોજ ખુબસુરત લાગતો હતો. હમોએ હમારી બોટને હલેસાં મારનાર દેશી ખલાસીઓને તેમનું ગાયન ગાવાને ફરમાસ કરી હતી, પણ તે વીરો હમારી ઇછા પુરી નહી પડી હતી, કારણ એકુ બે જણે ગાવાનું શીરૂ કીધું તેમને બીજાઓએ ઊંચકી નહી આપીયાથી તે કોશેશ પડી ભાગી હતી. દેશે દેશના ખલાસીઓના તથા ગાડીવાનોના અને મેહનતુ મજુર લોકના રાગ અને ગાયન ઉપર તે લોકના કેટલાક વીચાર, તેમના ધંધા પેશાની ઝડપ, તેમનો જાતી શોખ, તેમના નીતી વીચાર વીગેરે ઘણી બીજી સંસારી બાબદો આપણને માલુમ પડી શકેછે, માટે ખુદરતના શોખીઓએ કોઈબી દેશના એવા લોકનું ગાયન અગત કરીને સાંભળવું જોઇએછ.

તા૦ ૯ મી ફેબ્રુઆરી. આ દીને કલકત્તાની "બેથ્યુન ફીમેલ સ્કુલ" જોવાને ગયા હતા. નામદાર બેથ્યુન જેનું નામ કલકત્તાના રેહેવાશીઓના મોહોડામાં રમી રેહેલું છે, જેની ઉલટ દેશી લોકને કેળવણીમાં વધેલા જોવાની મશહુર થયલી છે અને તેમાં અગત કરીને સ્ત્રીકેળવણી દાખલ કરવામાં આ નામદારે કલકત્તા શેહેરમાં જે આગેવાની કરી છે, તેની યાદગારી રાખવાને દેશીઓએ આ નામદારને સારૂ એક જાહેર ઉઘરાણું કરીયું હતું, જે રકમમાં આ દેશી લોકના ખરા હેતાળુ મીત્રે બીજી પોતાની તરફની રકમ ઉમેરીતે સઘળી રકમ દેશી સ્ત્રીકેળવણી પછવાડે ખરચવાને એક કમીટીને સ્વાધીન કીધી હતી. આ રકમમાંથી બેથ્યુનના નામની, સ્ત્રીકેળવણીની એક નીશાળ સ્થાપવામાં આવી હતી અને આ નીશાળને માટે એક સારી શોભઈતી અને કીમતી ઈમારત કલકત્તામાં બાંધેલી છે. આ ઈમારતમાં છોકરીઓને લાયકની સગવડ સારી પેઠે કરેલી છે.

જે દીવશે હમો આ નીશાળ જોવાને ગયા હતા તે દીવશે તીહાં નજદીક ૧૦૪) દેશી છોકરીઓ હાજર હતી. દર રોજ ૭૦) છોકરીઓ કેળવણી લેવાને સરાસરી, હાજર રેહેતી હતી એવું હમોને નીશાળની યુરોપીયન સ્ત્રીશીક્ષક અને ઉપરીએ જણાવીયું હતું. છોકરીઓને દેશીભાશા વાંચવા, લખવા અને સાધારણ સાદા પણ ઉપયોગી હીસાબ શીકવવામાં આવતા હતા. સંસાર ઉપયોગી પરચુરણ બાબદોનું ગ્નાન અને સીવા સાંધવાનું કામ પણ સીખાડવામાં આવતું હતું. ગાવાનું અથવા વાજીંત્ર વગાડવાનું હીયાં નહી શીકવવામાં આવતું હતું. ૬ વરશની ઉપરની અને આસરે ૮ વરસની અંદરની નાહાની છોકરીઓનાં કુમલાં મનની અને શરીરની ચપલાઈ ખીલવવાને તેમની પાસે દીવસમાં એક કલાક કસરત કરવાનો એક વરગ બનાવીયા હતા,.તે વરગની તપાસ હમારી સાંભણે કરી દેખડાવી હતી, જે જોયાથી હમો ખુશી થયા હતા કે કલકત્તાની નાહાની છોકરીઓ જો લાયક કેળવણી લીએ અથવા વધારે ચોકસાઇથી બોલીએ તો, જો તેમને લાયક કેળવણી વખતસરની આપીયામાં આવે તો તે છોકરીઓ આપણી પારસી છોકરીઓ જેવીજ ચબરાક બલકે કોઈ કોઈ વધારે સરસ નીવડી શકે, એવું હમારૂં મત છે.

કલકત્તાની સ્ત્રીકેળવણી જો કે મુંબઈ ઈલાકાની સ્ત્રીકેળવણીથી ઓછી દેખાયછે, પણ તે ઉપર આપણા મુંબઈવાળા દેશીઓએ ભુલાવો નહી ખાવો જોઈએછ. મુંબઈવાળા સ્ત્રીકેળવણીમાં જે ધણા વખણાઈ ગયા છે, તે માત્રે તેમના બાહેરના ભપકા ભરેલા દેખાવથી અને જબરો મોહોટો ઘોંઘાટ કીધાથી થયા છે! હીંદુઓ કરતાં પારસીઓએ કેળવણી આપવામાં વધારે ઉલટ દેખડવી છે આવીશે તો કોઈથી ના નહી કેહેવાશે. પણ આ સઘળા ભપકાનું પરિણામ આપણે તપાસોએ તો એટલુંજ નીકળેછે કે દસ વરસ થયા કેળવણી દાખલ થયાં છતાં આજ સુધી કોઈબી દેશી છોકરી કેળવણી આપવાને અથવા નીશાળ ચલાવાને લાયક થયલી જણાઈ નથી. કોઈબી દેશી સ્ત્રીએ પોતે નીશાળ સ્થાપવાની અથવા તેવી એકુ ચલાવાની હીકમત કરી નથી. નીશાળમાં જતી છોકરી દસ અથવા અગીઆર વરસની થવા આવી એટલે તે નીશાળ છોડી જવાની તઈઆરીમાં હોયછે અથવા તેને છોડાવાની સઘળી તરફથી તજવીજો થાયછે. કોઈબી એક સ્ત્રીએ પોતાની દેશી ભાશામાં એકુ નાહાની ચોપડી

અથવા ચોપાનીયું નથી લખીયું અથવા ઇબારત બંધી ભરેલો એકુ રીશાળો વટીક હજુર સુધી કોઈ પારસી અથવા અત્રેની હીંદુ સ્ત્રીને હાતનો ચોખો લખાયલો જાહેર અથવા બાતીનમાં માલુમ નથી પડીયો. તારે આજ દસ વરસની લાંબી મુદતમાં સ્ત્રીકેળવણી ખાતાંઓથી જે પરીણામ અત્રે નીપજ્યાં છે તે ખાલી દેખાવ ઉપર આપણ સઘળાઓએ સારી પેટે વીચાર કરવો જોઇએછ, અને ખરેખરો સુધારો દાખલ કરવાની, આ અગતની બાબદમાં સારી કોરોસ કરવી જરૂર છે, અને અમસ્થો ખાલી દમામ દેખડાવી પોતાને અને બીજાઓને ભુલાવામાં નહી નાખવા જોઈએછ કે મુંબઈમાં સ્ત્રીકેળવણી સંપૂર્ણ થઈ પડી છે!

હમો જો ભુલાવો નહી ખાતા હોઈએ તો હમારૂં આધીન મત એવું છે કે જો કે કલકત્તાના બાબુઓમાં સ્ત્રીકેળવણીએ આપણા જેટલો પસારો નથી કીધેલો એવું આપણને બાહેરથી જણાયછે, તો પણ તેઓમાં છુપી સ્ત્રીકેળવણી ઘણીજ સારી રીતે ચાલેછે. જેને "Zanana education" "જનાના એજ્યુકેશન" કરીને કેહેછે. તેવી રીતે હમો ધારીએછ કે કલકત્તાના ઘણા ખરાં કુટંબોમાં ખાનગી કેળવણી અને તે વળી સારા પાયા ઉપર ચાલેછે. આ હમારા વીચારને વખણાયલા બાબુ કેસબ ચંદ્રના જાહેર મતથી ટેકો મળેછે. આ બાબુએ પણ એવું જાહેર કીધું છે કે જોકે કલકત્તામાં મુંબઈની પેઠે જાહેર સ્ત્રીકેળવણીની નીશાળો ઉઘડેલી નથી તોએપણ ઘણાક કુટંબમાં ખાનગી કેળવણી આપવાની ચાલ જારી થયલી છે, જેમાં યુરોપીયન સ્ત્રીઓ મુગે મોહોડે પણ ખરાં દીલથી કેળવણીના આશીર-વાદ અછી રીતે નાખતી રેહેલી છે. થોડા વખતમાં માલુમ પડશે કે સ્ત્રીકેળવણી કયા પ્રાંતોમાં કેવી જાતના ફળ ઉતપન્ન કરેછે અને આથી દેશી સંસારી હાલતમાં કેટલો સુધારો દાખલ થઈ શકેછે. મુંબઈએ સ્ત્રીકેળવણીમાં જાહેર આગેવાની અને પેહેલ કરી છે, તેની સાથે જબરદસ્ત દમામ પણ કરી જણાવીયો છે, પણ કલકત્તાએ પોતાના જનાની રેવાજને વળગી રેહી આ આગતના સુધારામાં છુપી રીતે વધવાને આગળ પગલું મુકયું છે, તેમાં હવે માત્ર જોવાનું રેહ્યું છે, કે કોણ સંસારની સુખાકારી વધારવામાં વધારે અને ખરી ફતેમંદી મેળવેછે. કલકત્તાની દેશી સ્ત્રીઓમાંથી એકથી વધારે નામ આજ સુધીમાં તો સંભળાઈ ચુકાં છે કે તેઓમાંની કોઈ ગ્રંથકર્તી છે, કોઇ સંસ્કૃત ભાષાની અછી માહીતગારી ધરાવનાર છે; કોઈ કવીતા જોડનાર કવીણ છે; પણ મુંબઈની દેશી સ્ત્રીઓમાંથી, (પછી સુ

પારશીની કે શું હીંદુઓની) આજ સુધી કોઈનું નામ આવી ખુબી ધરાવતું નથી સંભળાયું. માત્રે જે સાંભળવામાં અને જોવામાં આવીયું છે, તે એટલુંજ છે કે મુંબઈની હીંદુ તથા પારસી સ્ત્રીઓમાંની કેટલીકોએ બુટ, ઇસ્ટાકીન, કસબી ટોપી પેહેરી પોતાના બદનને સુશોભીત કરવામાં અને યુરોપીયન લોકની રસમ મુજબ કેટલીક છુટ લેઈ બાહેર ફરવા હરવા અને મરદોની મીજલસમાં આમેજ થવાનો સુધારો કરવામાં હીમત બતલાવી છે. આ બાબદમાં કલકત્તાની દેશી સ્ત્રીઓને મુંબઈવાળીઓએ ખચીત હરાવી છે, એમાં તો કંઈજ શક નથી; પણ હમો હમારી મુંબઈની દેશી બેહેનોને આબ્રુ, નમનતાઈ અને ખરાં દીલથી ભલામણ કરીએછે કે ઉપર જણાવેલા તકલીદી શીણગારની સાથે ખરી કેળવણી તથા ધર્મશાસ્ત્રની બાબદનો અભીયાસ કરી તેથી પોતાની મનશક્તિને શીણગારવાને વધારે ધીયાન પોંહોચાડશે તો તેમાં તેઓને વધારે લાભ છે, આ વાત તેઓએ સત્ય જાણવી. ફકત શરીર શોભા ઉપરજ સઘણું ધ્યાન આપવું અને તેનેજ માત્ર કેળવણી અથવા સુધારો ગણવો, એમાં મોહોટી ભુલ છે.

હીયાંથી નીકલીયાં તેવા કલકત્તાના અને આખી હીંદુસ્થાનમાં વખણાયલા સ્કાટલંડની ફ્રીચર્ચ અસેમબ્લીના મીશનરી, રેવરેંડ ડાકટર ડફને ઘર તેની મોલાકાત લેવાને ગયા હતા. આ ચંચલ મનશક્તિવાળા અને હીંદુસ્થાનના દેશીઓનું ભલું ચાહાનાર અને તેમની રીતભાંતથી સારી પેઠે માહીતગારી ધરાવનાર બુજરગ મીશીનરી સાથે એક કલાકની મોલાકાતમાં, કલકત્તાના બાબુઓ વીશે, તેમના ખીલતા જુવાનોના વીચાર અને મનની વલણ વીશે, તીહાંની સ્ત્રીકેળવણી વીશે, હીંદુઓની સંસારી રીતભાંત વીશે, અને બીજી ઘણીક પરચુરણ બાબદો વીશે વાતચીત થઈ હતી અને તે બુજરગ પાદરીના મોહોડામાંથી હીંદુસ્થાનનાં ભવીષ વીશે મોટી ઉમેદ ભરેલા વચનો સાંભળીયા હતા, પણ તે સઘળી ઉમેદનો પાયો તે ભલા મીશનરીએ કેળવણીના ફેલાવા ઉપર બાંધેલો હતો. તે એમ બોલીયો હતો કે, જેમ જેમ કેળવણી છેક ઉતરતા લોકમાં પસરતી જશે તેમ તેમ હીંદુસ્થાનનાં લોકની હાલત બેહેતર થતી જશે, અને જો કે તેઓ એકદમ સઘળા ક્રીસચીયન તો નથી થવાના પણ મુરતીપુજા ઉપરથી તેમનો વીચાર આસ્તે આસ્તે ઉઠતો જાય તો તેમાં તેમને કોઈ અટકાવી નથી શકવાનું. કલકત્તાના બાબુઓની મનશક્તિ વીશે બોલતાં ડાકટર ડફનું મત ઘણું ઉચું જણાયું હતું. ગણીતશાસ્ત્રમાં અને ન્યાયની

બાબદમાં અને વૈદકશાસ્ત્રમાં તેમનું મગજ ઉંચે દરજેની મનશક્તિ ધરાવનારૂં છે, અને વીદ્યાભ્યાસ કરવામાં, તેઓ કઠણ અને મેહનતુ વીદ્યાર્થી માલુમ પડ્યા છે, એવું ડાકટર માનતા હતા. બાબુઓની, ધર્મ સંબંધી વીચારની વલણ સારી તંદરોસ્ત હાલતમાં નહી હોય એવું ડાકટરને જણાતું હતું. કેટલાકોની વલણ ખાણાપીણાની અને શરીર સુખ સંબંધી છુટ લેવાને જબરી ફરેલી જણાઈ હતી; તેમાં પીવાની છુટમાં ઇંગ્રેજી દારૂની તરફ તેમનું દીલ ખેંચાવા લાગાથી તેમની ભવીશ હાલતનો વીચાર ડાકટરનાં મનમાં તમામ દીલગીરી ભરેલો લાગતો હતો. બ્રહ્મો સમાજ વીશે વાત કરતાં, આ જઇફ ડાકટરે કેહું કે તેની પોતાની નજર સાંભણે તેના ત્રણ રૂપ એકેક પછી ફેરવાતાં તેણે જોયાં હતાં, અને જોકે બ્રહ્મો પંથવાળાઓનાં મત સાથે આ સજન પુરૂષનું મત એકમળતું નહી હતું, તોએપણ આ સમાજની એક ચોખી મતલબ, કે મુરતીપુજા છોડી, એક નીરાકાર ઈશ્વરની ભકિત કરવી, આ વીચારને તે ઘણોજ પસંદ કરતો હતો. બાબુ કેસબ ચંદ્ર સેન વીશે આ ડાકટરનું મત ઘણુંજ સારૂં અને ઉંચું હતું. આ બાબુ, હમો જો ભુલતા નહી હોઈએ તો ડાકટર ડફનો શાગીરદ અથવા ચેલો છે. ભાષણ કરવાની રીતભાંતમાં, બોલતી વેલા વીચારોને અલંકારી રૂપોમાં ફેરવવામાં, અને બોલવાની બીજી ઢપછપમાં, આ પ્રખ્યાત મનોહારી ભાષણકર્તાએ ડાકટર ડફને પોતાના ઉસ્તાદ તરીકે નકલ કરવાને, નજર સાંભણે રાખ્યાંયો હોય એવું લાગેછે.

આપણી મુંબઈના કેટલાક કેળવણી પામેલા હીંદુઓએ પણ કલકત્તાના કેટલાક બાબુઓની પેઠે બાટલીની મોજ ભોગવવાની છુટ લેવાના ચીન્હો બતલાવીયાં છે.તેમને ઉપર જણાવેલો ઈશારો બસ છે, અથવા ડાકટર ડફના શબ્દોમાં બોલીએ તો "એવાઓની ભવીશ હાલતનો વીચાર તમામ દીલગીરી ભરેલો છે," અને હમો ધારીએછ કે સઘળા વીચારવાળાઓને પણ તે તેવોજ લાગશે. આ વાત થયા પછી ડાકટરને હમોએ કહી જણાવીયું કે હમો કલકત્તાનો "બાલીયા ઘાટ," તે દીવસની સાંજે જોવાજનાર હતા. આ શબ્દ સાંભળતાંને વાર ડાકટરે અફસોસ ખાઇને કેહું કે આહ! કલકત્તામાં આટલી કેળવણી લીધેલા બાબુઓ છે, તેઓએ તેનો કંઇજ અટકાવ હજુરસુધી કીધો નથી, આ એક અતીશય દુઃખ ભરેલી બાબદ છે! (આ વીશે આગળ વાંચવામાં આવશે.) ડાકટર સાથની મોલાકાતથી ફારગ થયા પછી, પાછા ચૌરંગીનાં મકાન ઉપર ગયા હતા, અને બપોરનું

જમીને પાછલા પોહોરના ત્રણવાગે પાછા ફરવાને નીકળીયા હતા, કારણ તે દીવશે બે ત્રણ ઠેકાણાં જે જોવાનાં હતાં તે છેક ૪ થી ૫ માઇલની મંજલ ઉપર જઇને પાછું ફરવાનાં હતાં.

પેહેલાં તો કલકત્તાના પારસી લોકનાં આદરીયાનમાં સેજદો કરવાને ગયા હતા. આ મકાન, ધરમતોલાના મોહોલ્લામાં છે, જે જીલ્લો જબરો ગંધાતો છે, તોપણ લાંબી મુદત તીહાં વસવાથી તે આપણાં પારસી સાહેબોને વાહાલો થઈ પડેલો છે, તેથી તીહાંથી કોઈ ખીસવા માગતું નથી, અને આદરીયાનનો મકાન તીહાં હોવાથી તેમને તે વધારે મનગમતો થઈ પડેલો છે. આ આદરીયાન સેઠ રૂસ્તમજી કાવસજી બનાજીનું બંધાવેલું છે. આ પાકીજે મકાનને નીજામ હેદરાબાદના આદરીયાન સાથે સરખાવતાં હેદરાબાદનાં આદરીયાનની જગા ઘણીજ લાયક અને ખુશનુમા છે. કલકત્તાના પારશી વેપારીયો, અથવા એના માલિક શેઠ જો ચાહે તો એખલા અથવા સઘળા મળીનિ આવા પાકીજે મકાનને તેવી લાએક આરાસ્તગી ભરેલી જગામાં ગએ અથવા જીહાં હાલ મકાન છે તેની આસપાસ લાયક આરાસ્તગી બનાવે તો તેમાં કંઈજ મુશકેલ જેવું નથી. આટલો ઈસારો હમોએ ખામુખા નાખ્યોયો છે તે વીશે આ મકાનના માલિકે અને કલકત્તાના સેઠીઆઓએ હમોને માફ કરવી.

આદરીયાનથી રૂખસદ લેઈ, કલકત્તાના "બાલીયાઘાટ" ઉપર ગયા હતા. બાલીયા ઘાટ" હીંદુલોકના મુરદાં બાળવાની અથવા તેમને નદીનાં પાણીમાં હોમવાનું એક મથક છે જે નદીને કીનારે કરેલું છે. આ મથકને સરખાવીએ તો તે મુંબઈના સોનાપુર અથવા હીંદુલોકના મુરદાં બાળવાની જગાને મળતું આવે છે. પણ મુંબઈમાં હીંદુઓના મુરદાં બાળવાની રીત અને કલકત્તાના હીંદુઓની રીતમાં આસમાન જમીન જેટલો ફેર છે. અરે! અરે! આ ઘાતકી રીતમાં તો હમો હમારા મુંબઈવાળા હીંદુ ભાઈ બંધોને હજારો ભલાઈ આપીએછ! કલકત્તાના સનમાર્ગી હીંદુઓમાં એવી એક માઠી રસમ છે કે કોઈબી માણસ આજારી પડ્યું અને તેના કોઇ ડાકટરે એવું મત આપીયું કે આજારીની હવે બચવાની ઉમેદ નથી, તો તેજ વખતે તે જાણે મરીગયો હોય તેમ તે આજારીને જીવતો ને જીવતો એક ખાટલા ઉપર મુકીને જો રાત હોય તો રાત્રેજ, સખત ઠંડી અથવા વરસાદમાં, અથવા દીવસ હોય તો દીવસના, સખત તડકાની પણ દરકાર કરીયા

વગેરે, આ બાલીયાઘાટ ઉપર, નદી કીનારે, જીહાં એક બે કંગાલ ઝુંપડાંઓ છે. તેમાં લાવીને મુકી રાખેછે. હીયાં લાવીયા પછી પેલો આજારી જો જલદીથી મરણ નહી પામીયો તો તેનો કોઈ પણ ઈલાજ કરતું નથી, ફકત તેને ગંગા નદીનું પાણી જરા જરા પાયા કરેછે. અને અંતે તે બીચારો આજારી ભુખે અને વગર ઈલાજે રીબી રીબીને મરણ પામેછે! તેમાં વળી જો તેનો પ્રાણ અંત ઉપર આવીયો હોય પણ તે મરણ નહી પામતો હોય તો તેવાને જીવતો ને જીવતો ખાટલા સમેત ઉંચકીને નદીમાં સ્નાન કરાવાને બોળી કાહાડેછે, જેથી તે બીચારાનો ચાર કલાક વધારે જીવવાનો વખત હોય તેને બદલે પાણીથી ગુંગલાઈને જલદીથી તેનો નીકાલ આવી જાયછે. આવાં ઘાતકીપણાથી, અને મોહોત આવીયા આગમજ, કલકત્તાના બાલીયાઘાટ ઉપર અરેરે દર વરસે હજારો અને લખો માણસોના જીવનો નાસ થાયછે, આ વાતની કોઈબી દરકાર કરતું નથી! સુધારકો મોહોટ મોહોટી વાતો કરેછે પણ આ એક અગતની, જીવ બચાવાની વાત વીસે બેભાન અને સુને કાને, કઠણ છાતી કરી, કેળવણીવાળા હીંદુઓ આજ સુધી સુગા બેઠેલા છે! આ ઘાતકી કામનો અટકાવ કરવાને સરકારને વચમાં પડવાની ઘણીજ જરૂર છે. જો સતીની ઘાતકી કીરીયા સરકારે અટકાવી તો, આ ક્રીયા તેથી વધારે ઘાતકી છે. આ ક્રીયામાં હજારો માણસો પોતાની રાજીખુશીથી જાણે પોતે અપઘાત કરેછે, અને તે કરવામાં હજારો બીજા માણસો તેમને મદદ કરે-છે; અને આ સઘળો અનર્થ અંગ્રેજ સરકારના અદલ ઈનસાફની રૂબરૂ ધોરે દીવસે થાયછે, તેને કોઈ કાયદો અટકાવી શકતો નથી. નદી કીનારે જઈને મરવા સુવામાં હીંદુઓ એક મોહોટું પુન્ય અથવા સવાબ સમજેછે. તેઓના પુરાણમાં એવું લખેલું કેહેછે કે જે મનુષ્યના હાડકાં મુવા પછી પવીત્ર ગંગા નદીમાં પડ્યાં તો તે મનુષ્યને બચીત સ્વર્ગ એટલે બેહસ્ત મળવાનુંજ; પણ જે કોઈ મનુષ્ય પવીત્ર ગંગા નદીને કીનારે આવીને મરણ પામીયો, (પછી ગમે એવી બેશુદ્ધ હાલતમાં તેને તીહાં લાવીયા હોય) તો તે મનુષ્યને સ્વર્ગમાં મોહોટી પદ્વી મળવાની; પણ હેવો કોઈ ભાયગસાલી મનુષ્ય જેને આજારી હાલતમાં ગંગા નદીને કીનારે લઈ ગયા હોય અને તે પોતાની અકલ હોશીયારીમાં તે ઠેકાણાં ઉપર પોતાનો પ્રાણ છોડે તેને તો મોહોટામાં મોહોટું સુખ, જે ઈશ્વરથી આપી શકાયછે અને જે માનવી જાતથી મેળવી શકાયછે, તે સુખ મળી શકેછે, તે સુખ તે કહયું? તો તે એ જે માનવીનો

આત્મા અને ઇશ્વર આ બંને એક બીજામાં ભેળાઈ એકજ થઈ જાયછે તે સુખ. નરમદ કવી તો ઇશ્વિરી તત્વ સાથે પોતાના આત્માને જ્ઞાનના પ્રકાશથી ભેળી નાખવાનો બોધ કરેછે "મેતો નુરમાં નુર પોયું રે, જ્ઞાન પ્રકારો," આવી રીતે તે ગાયછે. તે કવી વળી ગંગા નદીમાં હોમાવા નથી માંગતો, પણ "નદી નીતિમાં" એટલે નીતીગુણની અલંકારીક નદીમાં પોતાનાં આત્માને હોમાવા ચાહેછે, અને તીયાર પછી ઇશ્વિર સાથે એક થઈ જવાની ઇછા બતલાવેછે. આ વીચાર પણ પુરાણીક છે. કવીએ પુરાણ વાંચીયા છે, પણ તેમના વીચાર "બાલીયા ઘાટ" ઉપર, મોહોત આવીયા આગમજ જઇને પડવાનો અને જીવતાં જીવત નદીનાં પાણીમાં હોમાઇ જવાનો નથી. આવા જે ફકરા પુરાણમાં લખાયલા હોય, તેમના ખરેખરા અને માણસની અકલ કબુલ રાખે એવા અર્થ કરી સમજાવનારા શું કલકત્તાવાળા હીંદુ બાબુઓને કોઈ પંડીતો મળી નથી શકતા વારૂ? આજારી માણસોને નદીકીનારે લઈ જઇને રાખવાં એમાં તો ખચીત ફાયદેજ છે, પણ એવી જગા ઉપર લઈ જઈને, તે આજારીઓની બરદાસ્ત કરવી, તેમની તબીએત લાયકનો સારો ખોરાક તથા દવાપાણી આપવું, આજ મનુષ્ય જાતનો ખરો ધર્મ અને સ્વર્ગમાં જવાનો સીધો રસ્તો છે. આટલી સંધી બરદાસ્ત કરયા પછી, ઇશ્વિર ઇછાથી તે આજારીનું મરણ નીપજીયું તો તેમાં કોઇને દોશ તરીકે કસું બોલવાનું છે નહી. પરંતુ જાણીબુજીને નદીકીનારે જઈ રીબવું, અથવા રીબાવવું, અને આજારીના આયુષ્યની દોરી ખામુખા તોડવી, આ માહા પાપનું કર્મ છે. જારે હમો બાલીયા ઘાટ ઉપર ગયા હતા તીયારે આસરે ૬૦) વરસના એક હીંદુને, તીહાં એક ઝુંપડાંમાં ખાટલા ઉપર પડેલો જોયો હતો. હમારા ચંચલ મીત્ર ડાકટર ભાઉએ કેટલીક બોહોંસ કરીને તે બીમારની નાડ જોઈ હતી, અને ડાકટર ભાઉનું મત એવું હતું કે તે બીચારો બુઢો, વગર ખોરાકે અને વગર ઓશડે, અતીશય નાકઉતીથી માત્ર રીબતો હતો, પણ બીજું દરદ તેને કંઈ નહી હતું. પુછપરછ કરતાં એવું માલુમ પડયું કે તે ઘરડં પુરૂષને તીહાં લાવી નાખીયાને ૪) આખા દીવસ થઈ ગયા હતા, અને તે હજુર સુધી મરણ નહી પામીયો હતો, તેથી કંટાળો ખાઇને તેના અતલગના સગાં વાહાલાં તેને છોડીને પોતાને ઘર પાછાં જઈ રેહાં હતાં અને એકાદ મનુષ્યને તીહાં રાખીયો હતો જે પેલા ઘરડાને કંઈજ નહી પણ ગંગાનદીનું જલ પાતો હતો! ડાકટરે ઘણી બોહોંસ કીધી અને તે બુઢાને

કેહું કે તું જો દવા લેશે તો થોડા વખતમાં સારો થઈ જશે, પણ તે બીચારાએ પોતાની આશા પોતાના ધર્મ વીચાર પ્રમાણે છોડેલી, અને વળી આસપાસ કોઈબી એવું નહી કે તેને સારી મસલહત આપે, તેથી તેણે દવા લેવાને ના પાડી. એવામાં તેના એકુ બે મીત્રો તીહાં આવી પુગા હતા, જેમને આ વાત કેહાથી તેઓ થંડે પેટે બોલીયા હતા કે "એ શું હવે જીવે"? જેઓ મરવાને સારૂ નદી કાંઠે આવી પુગેલા, તેઓમાંથી કોઇ પાછા ઘર ગયા નથી, ત્યારે એ કેમ જઈ શકશે! તમારી દવા કંઈ હવે કામ લાગવાની નથી! આટલું બોલીને બેદરકારપણે તેઓ ચાલતા થયા હતા. કલકત્તાના હીંદુઓની બાલીયાઘાટ ઉપરની આવી ઘાતકી રસમ હજુર તીહાં ચાલુ છે. આ વીશે જો કેળવણી પામેલા બાબુઓ આગળ પડી તેનો અટકાવ નહી કરે તો સરકારને લાજમ છે કે પોતે વચમાં પડી એ ઘાતકી રસમનો અટકાવ કરે. આ અટકાવ કરવામાં હીંદુ ધર્મની વીરૂધ જવાની અથવા લોકનાં મન ઉસકેરાય એવું થવાની કંઈજ ધાસ્તી નથી. આટલુંજ થવું જોઈએછ કે કોઈબી જીવતા આજારીને તે ઘાટ ઉપર લાવી ઝુફડાંમાં નાખી નહી મેલે અને કોઇબી જીવતા આજારીને લાવીયા તો તેને લાયકનાં મકાન ઉપર રાખીને, દવા દારૂ અને ખાણા પીણાથી તેની બરોબર માવજત કરે, અને જેમ હાલ ફકત ચમચા પાણી ઉપર રીબવા દેછે તેમ કભી નહી કરવાદે. આહા! સું કલકત્તામાં એવો કોઈ સખી દીલવાલો ભલો બાબુ નથી કે જે બાલીયાઘાટ ઉપર એક મોહોટી હાસપીટલ બંધાવીને જેઓ નદીકીનારે આવીને પોતાના ધર્મમાર્ગે પોતાના હોશ હોશીયારીમાં મરવાની ઇછા રાખતા હોય તેમને છેલી ઘડી સુધી દવાપાણી પોહોંચાડી તેમની બરદાસ્ત કરાવે! જેબી કોઈ ધર્માતમાએ આવું મકાન બંધાવીયું અને તે મકાનમાં આવી પડતા બીમાર હીંદુઓની છેલી ઘડી સુધી બરોબર બરદાસ્ત થવાના ઉપાય કરાવીયા તો આ જેવું માહા પુન બીજું કોઈ નથી ગણાવાનું. આવી હાસપીટલ બંધાવનાર શખસનો આતમા ખરેખર, હીંદુ પુરાણીક ફીલસુફી પ્રમાણે બોલતાં, ઇશ્વર સાથે જઈ મલવાનો. જે કોઈ આવું પુન કરવાને પોતાની દોલત વાપરે તેને ધન્ય!

બાલીયાઘાટ ઉપરથી રૂખસદ લઈ કલકત્તાનું પારસી લોકનું દખમું જોવાને ગયા, જે ખરેખર વસ્તીથી ઘણુંજ દુર છે અને પારસીના રવાનોને આટલે દુર લઈ જવાને વારવાર ભારી અડચણ પડતી સાંભળીયામાં આવી હતી, તે વીશે હમારી

ખાત્રી થઈ હતી. આ અગતની અડચણ ટાળવાને પણ કલકત્તાના પારસી સાહેબો શકતીવાન છે. દખમું ઘણી સારી હવાવાળી અને એકાંત જગા ઉપર છે, એ મકાન ઉપર જે પથરની તકતી મુકેલી છે, અને તેમાં જે વીગત જેમ લખી જણાવી છે તે આ દખમા વીરો અને તેના બાંધનાર વીરો અત્રે જાહેર કરેલી બસ છે.

"રોજ ૨૭ માહા ૪ ચીર ૧૧૯૧ ઈ. ૧૮૭૬ ના માહા સુદ ૪ સોમવાર"
"તા. ૨૮ જાનેવારી ૧૮૨૨ ઇંગ્રેજી શ્રી જરતુશ પેગંમબરની ભલી દીનના"
"પારશી લોકોને સારૂ હમોએ હમારી જાત મેહેનતથી અને પરવરદેગારની"
"મદદથી એ નેક બેહેશત મુકામની જગો બનાવી છે કે આપણી ભલી"
"દીનના સાહેબો હોય તેનાને લાજમ છે કે એ જગોના દખમાની હમેશ"
"ખબરદારી કરે."

લા. કમતરીન પારસી નવરોજી બીન શોહોરાબજી ઉમરીગરના.

આ ઠેકાણેથી પાછા ફરતાં ઇસ્ટર્ન બેંગાલ રેલવેના એક સ્ટેશન ઉપર થઇને જતાં, તીહાં જરા ખોટી થયા હતા, કારણ તે સ્ટેશન ઉપર, પેહેલીજ વારની ગ્યાસ-લાઇટ થવાની હતી જે હમારા જોવામાં નવી હતી. ગ્યાસલાઇટ થવાના વખત સુધી, સ્ટેશન ઉપર ખોટી થયા હતા, અને તેટલા વખતમાં હમો દરેક જણ તોલાયા હતા. હમો સઘળાનું તોલ નીચેની વીગતે થયું હતું:—

મી. મનચેરજી મેહરવાનજી નારીએલવાળા.	૮	મણ	૨૨	રતલ બંગાલી.
મી. ખુરશેદજી નુશરવાનજી કામાજી....	૪	,,	૯૦	,, ,,
મી. રૂસ્તમજી ફકીરજી કોપર........	૪	,,	૫૪	,, ,,
મી. એડવરડ રીહાસટીક............	૪	,,	૪૬	,, ,,
મી. અરદેસર ફરામજી મુસ..........	૪	,,	૩૪	,, ,,
મી. ખુરશેદજી રૂસ્તમજી કામા........	૪	,,	૧૪	,, ,,

આ તોલની વીગત આપવાની એટલીજ મતલબ છે કે ઉપર જણાવેલા દોસ્તોનો વજન હાલ એટલો હશે અથવા નહી આ બાબદની ચોકસાઈ કરવાને તેમનાથી બની આવે, અને તેમાંથી જેઓ વજનમાં વધીયા હોય તેઓ ખોદાના શુકર કરે અને જો ઘટીયા હોય તો, આટલોજ વીચાર કરી સંતોશ પામે કે તેઓ એક વખત એટલા વજનદાર થયલા હતા.

તા૦ ૧૦ મી ફેબ્રુઆરી. રેવરેંડ ડાકટર ડફ સાથે આગલા દીવસ ઉપર મોલાકાત

થઈ હતી તે વખતે એવો ઠરાવ થયો હતો કે કલકત્તામાં ફ્રીચર્ચ અસેમબ્લીના મીશનરીઓની સ્કુલ જોવાને હમોએ જવું, જે નીશાળનો આ ડાકટર તે વખતે પ્રાનસીપાલ હતો. આ નીશાળની મોલાકાત લેવાને ગયા તારે ડાકટર ડફ તીહાં હાજર હતો અને હમો સઘળાને સાથે લઈ આખી નીશાળમાં ફેરવીયા હતા. આ નીશાળમાં ત્રણ ભાગથી વધારે દેશી છોકરાઓની સંખીયા હતી, અને એક ભાગ ઓછો, ઇંડો બ્રીટન અથવા પોરટુગીસના છોકરાઓ હતા. મીશનરીઓની નીશાળના કાયદા મુજબ આ ટેકાણે સઘળા છોકરાઓને ખ્રીસ્તી ધરમની કેળવણી સાથે ઇંગ્રેજી ભાશા શીખવવામાં આવતી હતી. સ્કુલની ઇમારત ઘણીજ મોહોટી અને સઘળી વાતે સંપૂર્ણ છે. જુદા જુદા વર્ગોને બેસવાસારૂ એલાહેદા ઓરડા અને ચહડતી ઉતરતી બેઠકો જીહાં જોઇએ તીહાં કીધેલી છે. હમારી સાંભળે ચહડતા વર્ગના છોકરાઓને પરીક્ષા આપવા બોલાવીયા હતા, જે વખતે ઇતીહાસ અને ભુગોળ તથા ઇંગ્રેજી કવીઓનાં લખાણમાં તેઓએ સારી માહીતગારી મેળવેલી, સવાલના જવાબો ઉપરથી માલુમ પડી હતી. પણ એના કરતાં બાઇબલની બાબદોનો અભીયાસ તેઓએ સરસ કીધેલો જણાયો હતો. જેટલા તેઓ પોતાના જાતી ધરમના ગ્નાનથી અણજાણ હતા તેટલી આ ધરમની માહીતગારી તેઓ વધારે ધરાવતા હતા, પણ જેખી તેઓ જાણતા હતા તે સઘલું તેઓ પોતે માનતા હોય એવું તેમના જવાબ ઉપરથી નજર નહી આવતું હતું. આ બાબત નીશાળમાં શીખવેછે તેથીજ માત્રે તેઓ શીખીયા હતા. તેમના મગજ ઉપર આ ધર્મવીશે અથવા તેમાંથી જાણેતી બાબદોવીશે કંઈબી અસર થઈ હોય એવું દેખાતું નહી હતું. આ વાત જો કે ખોલી હતી, તોએપણ ડાકટર ડફ તેવીશે એવો ખુલાસો કીધો હતો કે જો કે આ નીશાળમાં શીખવા આવનાર સઘળા છોકરાઓને ધર્મ સાથની કેળવણી આપીયામાં આવેછે, તેથી આવાં પરીણામની તઓ ઉમેદ નહી રાખતા હતા કે સઘળાનાં મન ઉપર ધર્મ વીશે સરખી અસર થશે. ફળવંત જગામાં બીજ નાખીએછ તે સઘળાં અને દરેક નથી ઉગી નીકળતાં, તેમાંથી ઘણા બરબાદ જાયછે, તોએ પણ ઉમેદ રેહેછે કે કેટલાંક તેમાંથી ઉગી નીકળશે, અને તેમ થાયછે. આજ પ્રમાણે નીશાળના સઘળા છોકરાઓને આ અગતની બાબદની કેળવણી આપીયામાં આવેછે, આ વાવેલાં બીજમાંથી ઝાડનું ઉગવું અથવા ઉગાડવું આપણા પેદા કરનારના

હાતમાં છે. ડાકટર ડફનાં મત સાથે હમો તદન મલતા છઈએ. આ નીશાળમાં જેમ મનશક્તિને સારી કેળવણી આપીયામાં આવેછે, તેવીજ સારી રીતે શરીરશક્તિને પણ ખીલવવા સારૂ કસરતની તાલીમ પણ છોકરાઓને આપીયામાં આવેછે. સઘળી રીતે જોતાં અને તપાસતાં આ મોહોટી નીશાળ કલકત્તામાં પેહેલાં વર્ગની ગણાયછે.

આ ઠેકાણેથી નીકળીયા તેવા "મેટકાફ હાલ" જોવાને ગયા હતા. સર ચારલસ મેટકાફ થોડાક વખત સુધી હીંદુસ્થાનનો ગવરનર જનરલ થઈ ગયો છે. તેણે પોતાની ટુંક હકુમતમાં ઘણું ડાહપણ અને નરમાસ આપણા દેશીઓ તરફ દેખાડાવી હતી અને દેશીઓ ઉપર તે ઘણીજ મેહરબાની અને સખાવત ભરેલો તથા મોહોટાં દીલવાળો થઈ ગયો છે. એના હાતથી આ દેશને લગતાં રાજદરબારી ઘણાં કામો દેશના લાભમાં થયાં છે. પણ એના હાતથી એક છેલું અને ઘણીજ અગતનું કામ જે બનીયું છે તે એ જે હીંદુસ્થાનનાં છાપાખાનાને એનાથી છુટા-પણું મળીયું છે અથવા એણે મેળવી આપીયું છે, તેથી એનું નામ જાવેદાન સુધી, સઘળા માન સાથે આ દેશના દેશી રેહેવાશીઓ અને પરદેશી રેહેવાશીઓ બંધે સરખી રીતે યાદ કરતા રેહેલા છે. આવા પ્રમાણીક ગવરનર જનરલની યાદ આપણાં દેશમાં કાયમ રાખવાને કલકત્તાના દેશીઓએ જારે આ અમલદાર આ દેશ છોડી પોતાને વતન પાછો ગયો તારે એક મોહોટી રકમ નાણાંની ઉઘરા-વીને એના મુબારક નામની એક ઈમારત કલકત્તામાં બાંધવાનો ઠરાવ કીધો હતો. આ ઈમારત પણ તે નામદારની જાહેર ખુબી પ્રમાણે પ્રજા ઉપયોગી કામ સારૂ વાપરમાં રાખી છે, અને તેમાં આજે કલકત્તાનું એક મોહોટું જાહેર પુસ્તક-ખાનું છે. બાગાયત અને જીરાયતના ખાતાંને લગતી મંડળીની મોલાકાત હીયાંજ થવાને એક મોહોટો હાલ આ ઈમારતના બીજા માળ ઉપર કરી રાખીયો છે, અને તેમાં ઝાડપાનમાંથી ઉપજતી તરેવાર ઉપયોગી જીનસોના નમુના એકઠા કરીને મુકેલા છે, જેમાં ઘણી જાતનાં બીજો, સાખા—વાખ, મુલીયાં, છાલ, અને એ વીગેરે વેપારના કામ જોગની ઘણી જીનસો છે. આ સંગ્રહની મુખીય મતલબ એટલીજ છે કે આ દેશની ખેતીવાડી અને જમીનની પેદાશ વધારવાને ખેડુ-તોને અને જમીનદારોને દેખાડવવું કે ફલાણી ફલાણી જીનસો તેઓએ ખેડણીમાં ઉત્પન્ન કરવી જોઈએછ, અને તેવી ખેડણી સારી પેઠે કરવાસારૂ કેવાં કેવાં હથીયારો વાપરવાં જોઈએ અને બીજી સું સું તજવીજ કરવી જોઈએછ તે સઘળી

આ ખાતામાં પુછપરછ કરવાથી તેમને મળી શકશે. ઉપલા સંગ્રહની સાથે જમીનમાંથી ખોદી કાહાડેલી ધાતુ અને તરેવાર બીજી જીનસોનો એક જુદોજ જમાવ કરેલો છે, જે જોવા અને અભીયાસ કરવા લાયક છે. હીયાં આગળ વખતની કેટલીક જીનસો નમુના તરીકે જાળવી રાખી છે તેમાં બાબીલન શેહેરની પુરાતન ઇંતરડીઓ છે, ગોલકંડા શેહેરના મકબરા ઉપર કરેલા ચીની મીના કામના કકડા છે. (જુઓ આવાં નકસી કામનો નમુનો અકબરની કબર ઉપરના ગુંબજના ચીત્રમાં) ચીન દેશના નાનકીનના મોહોટા બુરજ અથવા મીનારામાંથી લાવેલી શોભાઈતી ચીની કામની ઇંતરડી, સુનેરી મીના કામમાં મઢેલા અરબી ભાશાના કેટલાક લેખો, હીંદુસ્થાનના જુદાં જુદાં ઠેકાણાં ઉપરથી મળી આવેલા લોહોચુંબકના અને આકાશમાંથી પડેલા પથરો, પુરાતન જાનવરોનાં માથાંની તુમડી, દાંત, હાડકાં, સીંગડાં, આગલા જમાનાના ઝાડો અને પાત્રાંના પડેલા આકાર જે ઘણું કરીને જમીનમાંથી ખોદી કાહાડેલા કોળશા ઉપર જોયામાં આવેછે.

આ ઈમારતની વચમાંના હાલમાં સર ચારલસ મેટકાફનું બાવલું મુકેલું છે, જેની ઉપર તેની ખુબી અને તેના હાથથી થયલાં કામોની યાદગારીનો લેખ કોત્રેલો છે.

સાંજે ફરવા જતાં, કલકત્તાની માહાકાલીનું દેહેરૂં જોવાને હમો ગયા હતા. આ દેહેરૂં કલકત્તામાં સઉથી પેહેલી પદ્વી ધરાવેછે, અને હીયાં એના તેવાર ઉપર લખો રૂપીયાનો ખરચ થાયછે અને લોક જાત્રાને માટે આવેછે. આ દેહેરાંમાં પર ગ્નાતવાળાઓને છેક અંદર સુધી જવા દીએછે, પણ જીહાં મુરતી મુકેલી છે તીહાં હીંદુ શીવાએ બીજા સઘળાં લોકને અંદર જવાની મનાઈ છે. હીયાં ઇંગ્રેજ લોક વારંવાર આવેછે. દેહેરાંની સાંભણે બેઠક સાથનો ખોલો ઓટલા જેવો રોનકદાર મકાન બનાવેલો છે, તીહાં જઈ પારકી ગ્નાતવાળા તમાસો જોવાને બેશેછે. હમો જીયારે તીહાં જઈ પુગા તારે પેહેલાં તો હમુને જરા અટકાવીયા હતા, અને જોડા કાહાડીને ઓટલા ઉપર જવા કેહું હતું, પણ હમોએ એ વીશે તુરત ના પાડી અને પાછું ફરવાની ઇછા દેખાડવતાં, કેટલાક લોકોએ દેહેરાંના વડા બ્રાહ્મણને ખબર પોહોંચાડી જેથી તુરત ચાર પાંચ જણ અંદરથી દોડી આવી હમુને માન આપીને જોડા સાથે ઓટલા ઉપર જઈ બેસવાને અરજ કીધી હતી. હમો પારસી લોક હતા, તેથી તેમની આશા આશેાદાદ વીશે જાગી હતી, અને હમારા મીત્ર ડાકટર

ભાઉ દાજી અને તેવણુની સાથના બે હીંદુઓને જોઇને પણ તેમને દક્ષણા મળવાની ઉસકેરણી થઈ હતી. જીહાં જોઇશું તીહાં સુ મોબેદો કે સું બ્રાહ્મણો બંધે એકજ મતલબવાળા અને એકસરખા લોભી મળવાના. દેહેરાંની અંદરથી એક જબરો, જાડો, ઘી અને લાડુ ખાઇને મોહોટાં પેટવાળો તથા ડુલડુલ થયલો બ્રાહ્મણ નીકળી આવીયો, અને હમોને અટકાવનાર માણસોને થંડે પેટે અને તેમાંનું પાણી નહી હલે એવી રીતે ધમકાવીયા, અને હમુને આદર સત્કાર કરીને બેસવા કેહું અને તીહાં ટાંગેલા ઘંટ જેટલા હતા તેટલા બધા વારાફરતા વગાડીયા, જે વગાડવું, એ એક માન આપવાની રીત છે. ઘંટ વગાડી રેહા પછી તેણે નરમાસથી હમને કેહી જણાવીયું કે સારાં માણસોને આ ઓટલા ઉપર આવવાની મનાઈ છેજ નહી. જારે હમોને પેહેલાં અટકાવીયા હતા, તે વખતે દેહેરાંની આસપાસથી કેટલીક જુવાન સ્ત્રીઓ હમારી આગળ દોડી આવી હતી, અને તેઓ હમુને કેહેવા લાગી કે અંદર જવાની કસી મનાઈ નથી, અને તેમાંનો કેટલીકોએ હમુને જાણે ઓળખતી હોય તેમ પેલા ઓટલા ઊપર લઇજવાને ઇછા જણાવી હતી. આ સ્ત્રીઓને પેહેલાં હમોએ ઓળખી નહી હતી કે તેઓ કોણ છે. પાછળથી જારે હમો ઓટલા ઉપર જઈ બેઠા, તારે આ સ્ત્રીઓ હમારી પાસે આવીને હમોને ફુલ આપવા લાગી, અને બીજા જે ચાળા કરી દેખડાવીયા તે ઉપરથી માલુમ પડીયું કે તેઓ દેહેરાંને અરપણ કરેલી સ્ત્રીઓ હતી, જેમને સઘળાની સાથે છુટ લેવાનો હક દેવી તરફથી જાણે મળેલો હતો! તેઓ આપણી તરફના ખંડોબાની મુરલી જેવી હતી. તેઓએ હમારી પાસે પઇસા માંગીયાં, જે વીશે હમોએ પુછીઉં કે, તમે પઈસાનું શું કરશો, તારે તેઓએ હસીને જવાબ આપીયો કે, સારૂં સારૂં ખાસું અને પીસું. હમોએ પુછીયું, શું ખાશો અને પીશો. તેઓએ જવાબ આપીયો કે જો ઘણા પઈસા આપશો તો હમે બકરાંનું ગોશ ખાશું અને દારૂ પી મોજ કરશું. આવી સ્ત્રીઓ આ દેહેરાંમાં પુશ્કળ છે અને હીયાંજ તેમનું ગુજરાણ થાયછે. હજારો લોક દરશણ કરવાને આવેછે તેમાંના કેટલાકો આ સ્ત્રીઓ સાથે સઘળી પ્રકારના અનીતી ભરેલાં કર્મો કરેછે અને તે સઘળાં આ માહાકાલીના દેહેરાંમાં અને તેની આસપાસની જગા ઉપર ધોરે દીવસે અને રાત્રે ધર્મને ચોખે બાહાને થાયછે! હીયાં છાકટપણું થાયછે! હીયાં ચોરી, છીનાલું, ઠગાઈ, મારામારી, લુટફાંટ, અને સઘળી તરેના અઘટીત કર્મો થાયછે.

પેલા મોહોટા પેટવાળા ખાઉ ભટજીએ આપણા ડાકટર સાહેબને દેહેરાંની અંદર લઇ જઈ દરશણ કરાવી તેમના પારોથી દક્ષણા કહડાવાની જબરી બોહોંસ કીધી. અંતે ભલા ડાકટરે તેની સાથે જઇને માહાકાલીની મુરતી જોઇને પેલા ભટજીને દક્ષણા આપી હતી, જેથી તે બહુ ખુશ ખુશ થઇ ગયો હતો. હમારી પાસથી પણ તે ભટજીએ મીઠી મીઠી વાતો કરી કંઈ થોડાક પઇસા લીધા હતા, અને તેના અવેજમાં હમને ફુલ આપીયાં હતાં. જારે ડાકટર એખલા દેહેરાંમાં ગયા હતા તારે હમો સઘળાને ઘણી ધાસ્તી લાગી હતી કે રખેને અંદર કોઠડીમાં લઈ જઇને ડાકટર સાહેબને, પઈસા કહડાવા, સારી પેઠે ચાંપી નાખે, આ ધાસ્તી ભરેલો વીચાર જીહાં સુધી ડાકટર એખલા સહીસલામત પાછા આવીયા તીહાં સુધી હમારા મનમાં રેહેલો હતો. દેહેરાંની આસપાસ દારૂના પીઠાં, ભઠીયારાના દુકાનો, અને કલેજી બુક્કા ભુંજાવાનો વાસ, અને બીજી તરેની વેસનવાળી જીનસો વેચવાની દુકાનો હારેહાર લાગેલી હતી, તેમાં તરેવાર જાતની મીઠાઈની પણ દુકાનો હતી. દેહેરાંમાં જે વેશીયાઓ દરશને આવતી હતી તેઓ દેવીની આસપાસ નાચી, ગાઇને ખુશી ખુસાલી ભોગવી પાછી જતી હતી. અત્રે બેમરયાનો એક નાચ થાયછે તે વીશે હમો બયાન કરવાને વાજબી નથી જોતા. માહાકાલીની મુરતી જે સોનાની બનાવેલી કેહેછે અને જેની આખમાં માંણેક જડેલાં છે, અને આખાં આંગઉપર ભારી ઝવેરાતનો શીનગાર કરેલો છે, તે મુરતી તો હમોએ જોઈનથી, પણ હમારા જોવામાં તેનું ચીત્ર આવીયું છે, તેમાં આ દેવીનું મોહોડું કાલું પાડેલું છે, આંગઉપર પુશ્કળ જવેરાત પેહેરાવેલું છે, અને આખ લાલ ખુની અથવા દારૂ પીને મસ્ત થયલાં માણસના જેવી પાડેલી છે. તેના ગળાની અંદર માણસના મસ્તકની તુમડીઓનો હાર કરી પેહેરાવેલો છે, અને સઘળો દેખાવ દારૂ પીને ખુન ઉપર અને મસ્તીમાં આવેલી સ્ત્રી જાતનો દેખડાવેલો છે. માસ ખાવાની અને દારૂ પીવાની પુર છુટ આ દેવીના ભક્તો લીએછે, એવું હમારા સાંભળવામાં આવીયું છે, અને તેઓ ખાઈપીને પાલીયા બની રહેલા છે. ઉત્તેજક ખાણું ખાઈ તથા દારૂ પીને તેની મસ્તીમાં આવી, સઘળી તરેના અનીતી ભોગ બોગવવાની પણ તેમને અથવા કોઈ પણ શખસને કાલીના દરશણે જતાં, છુટ છે, આવું પણ હમોએ સાંભળીયું છે. ખરેખર આ એહવાલ હીંદુના ધર્મને મોટી હીણપસતી લગાડનારો છે, અને આ ઉપર લખી જણાવેલી વાત જો ખરી હોય તો હમો ધારીએછ

કે આવા કર્મોમાં કોઈબી આબરૂવાળા હીંદુઓ તો ખચીત સામેલ નહીજ થતા હશે પણ માત્ર હલકી વરણના લોક આવાં કર્મો કરતાં હશે.

કાલી દેહેરાં ઉપરથી કલકત્તા શેહેરનું નામ ઉત્પન્ન થયું છે. ઈ. સ. ૧૭૦૦ ની સદીની આખરીએ ઇસ્ટ ઇનિડીયા કંપનીવાળાઓએ, દીલ્લીના શાહાનશાહ ઔરંગજેબ પાસેથી કેટલાંક વીખરાઈ પડેલાં ગામડાં, જીહાં હાલ કલકત્તા છે, તે માંગી લીધાં હતાં. તે ગામડાંઓમાંનાં એક ગામનું નામ "કલકાટ્ટ" કરીને હતું, કારણ તે ગામમાં કાલી દેવીનું દેહેરૂં હતું. "કલ" શબ્દનો અર્થ "કાલી" અને "કાટ્ટ" શબ્દનો અર્થ "દેહેરૂં" એવો બંગાલી ભાશામાં થાયછે, તે ઉપરથી આ ઠેકાણે જે શેહેર વસાવીયું તેનું નામ, આ દેહેરાં ઉપરથી, કલકત્તા કરીને રાખી-આમાં આવીયું હતું.

તા૦ ૧૧ મી ફેબ્રુઆરી. તા૦ ૯ મી અને ૧૦ મીની બે રાત્ર અને દીવસ વાદળ થયા પછી તા૦ ૧૦ મીની રાત્રે એકદમ વરસાદ પડીયો હતો જેથી તા૦ ૧૧ મીની સહ-વારે હવામાં થંડી પેદા થઈ હતી. સહવારના સઘળા રસ્તા ઉપર ચોમાસાની રૂતુમાં જેમ કાદવ અને કીચલ થાયછે તેમ થઇ પડયું હતું. આવો બનાવ બનીયાથી ચોમાસાની રૂતુમાં કલકત્તાનો કેવો દેખાવ થઈ પડેછે તે જોવાની હમુને સારી તક મળી આવી હતી. રસ્તામાં કીચલ એટલો તો પાતલો થઇ પડેલો હતો કે ગાડી ઘોડાની આવજાવથી રસ્તે ચાલતાં લોક જો સંભાળ નહી રાખે તો છંટાઇ જતાં હતાં. આપણા મુંબઈના રસ્તાની જેવી હાલત ચોમાસામાં થાયછે તેના કરતાં વધારે નબેહેતર હાલત હીયાંના રસ્તાની હમોએ જોઈ હતી. કલકત્તામાં વરસાદ કવખતે પડવાની નવાઇ નથી લાગતી, કારણ તીહાં હંમેશ કોઇ કોઈ વાર વખત બે વખતે તે પડતોજ રેહેછે, પણ જેટલો વરસાદ મોસમસર મુંબઇમાં પડેછે તેના કરતાં કલ-કત્તાનો આખો વરસાદ ઓછો છે. હીયાંના ઘણાં ખરાં ઘરો ઉપર લોહોડાંની શીકો મુકેલી હોયછે કારણ જેટલી વીજલી આ શેહેરમાં વધારે પડેછે તેટલી કોઇ બીજે ઠેકાણે નથી પડતી. સહવારના દસ વાગે પાછો વરસાદ શીરૂ થયો હતો તેથી આ દીવસે બાહેર ફરવા જવાને બની નહી શકયું હતું. માત્ર એક બે દુકાનો ઊપર ફરીને પાછા ઘર આવીયા હતા, અને આ દીવસ તો કેહવત મુજબ, ખીચડી ખાઈ ઘરમાંજ ગુજારવો પડયો હતો.

તા૦ ૧૨મી ફેબ્રુઆરી આ દીવસે, વરસાદ ઉગડી ગીયાથી સહવારના પોહોરમાં,

કલકત્તાની મારકીટ અથવા મોહોટું બજાર જોવાને ગયા હતા. આ બજારની ગોઠવણ ફક્ત એક મોહોટી છાપરાંની સલગ ઇમારતમાં કરેલી હમારા જોવામાં આવી હતી. એની ગોઠવણ મદ્રાસની મારકીટ જેવી નહી હતી, અને તેમાં ગલીચાઈ વધારે નજર આવતી હતી. તોએ પણ તે વખતની આપણી મુંબઈ શેહેરની મારકીટ અને બજાર કરતાં હજારે દરજે સરસ હતી. ગોશ્ત, માછલી અને તરકારીનાં ત્રણ ખાતાં જુદાં કરેલાં હતાં અને આ શીવાએ બીજી ગોઠવણ કોઇજ નહી હતી. જમીન ઉપર ઇંતરડીની ફરસબંદી કરેલી હતી, તોએ પણ તે સાફ નહી હતી, અને વરસાદ પડ્યાથી તીહાં પણ કીચલ થઇ પડેલો હતો. ખાટકીઓની દુકાનો ઉપર હમોએ કોડીયામાં સલગાવેલા મોહોટા કાકડા બળતા જોયા હતા, અને એનું કારણ પુછતાં હમુને એવી સમજણ મળી હતી કે એક જાતની માંખ ગોશ્ત ઉપર આવી બેસેછે જેથી ગોશ્તની ખરાબી થાયછે, તે માંખનો અટકાવ કરવાને આવી રીતે બત્તી, ખાટકીની દુકાન ઉપર મુકેછે. આ બત્તી આખો દીવસ સુધી રાખીયામાં આવેછે કે સહવારના પોહોરમાંજ રાખેછે આ વીશે હમુને ખરેખર ખબર મળી નથી. કલકત્તાની બજાર જોકે મદ્રાસ કરતાં દેખાવ અને ગોઠવણમાં ઊતરતી હતી, તોએ પણ તેની અંદર જે માલ વેચાવાને આવેલો હતો તે ઘણીજ સરસ જાતનો અને ભરપુર હતો. મેવા અને તરકારીની દુકાનો ઊપર થંડીના દેશની કેટલીક તરકારી ઘણીજ તોફા હતી, તેમજ કેટલોક મેવો પણ હતો. કાલીફલાવર, બીટરૂટ, સલગમ, કોબી અને નોલકોલ તો દેખાવમાં એવા તો સુંદર હતા કે ફક્ત નજર પડતાંજ કાચા ને કાચા ખાઇ જવા ગમતા હતા. બોરની મોસમ હોવાથી, તે ફળની રેલ થઇ પડતી હતી. અનેનાસની લેહજત વીશે તારીફ નથી થઈ શકતી, ગોશ્તબી ઘણુંજ ફરબા અને તલબદું હતું, પણ માછલીમાં કલકત્તાનું બજાર પછાત પડેલું હતું. નદીની માછલી ઘણું કરીને દેખાતી હતી, દરીયાની માછલી થોડીજ હતી. માછલી વેચવામાં ઘણું કરીને પુરૂષને ઠેકાણે સ્ત્રીઓજ હતી, પણ તેમનો દેખાવ આપણી મુંબઇની એ જાતની સ્ત્રીઓ જેઓ સોહામણો નહી હતો, જો કે બુમ પાડવા અને તગાદો કરવામાં તેઓ જબરી બાંગડ જણાતી હતી. તેઓની ગાલ અથવા ઝગડો સાંભળવાની હમુને કોઇ તક મળી નહી હતી તેથી હમો નાઉમેદ થયા હતા. ફુલપાનમાં પણ કલકત્તાનું બજાર ઘણુંજ સુંદર હતું. ટુંકામાં બોલીએ તો મેહેલાના શેહેરનું બજાર તેની

કીર્તી જાળવવાને લાયક હતું. હીયાં આબરૂવાળા યુરોપીયન લોક તેમના કુટુંબને લઈ બજાર કરવાને સાથે આવેછે અને આખા બજારે ફ્રીવળેછે. તેમજ દેશી માતબર લોક પણ આવેછે, પણ હમોએ કોઈબી એકુ બાબુની સ્ત્રી બજારમાં આવેલી નહી જોઈ હતી. ગોસ્તની દુકાન પાસે બીજી જીનસો હોવાથી તે વીરો કલકત્તાના દેશીઓમાં મુતલગ છીત છેજ નહી, અને જેમ મુંબઈવાળા કેટલાક અતીપવીત્ર બ્રાહ્મણો વાંધો લીએછે કે ગોસ્તની દુકાન ઉપરનો પવન વટીક જો આવીને બીજી જીનસને લાગે તો તે અપવીત્ર થાયછે, એટલા સંધા નાજુક વીચારવાળા બાબુ લોક નથી. કલકત્તામાં આવીયાને હમોને નજદીક ૧૨) દીવસ થઈ ગયા હતા, અને હમારી મુસાફરી હજુર તેા ઘણી લાંબી મંજલની બાકી રેહી હતી, તેની સાથે ગરમીની મોસમ સાંબી ચઢતી આવતી હતી તેથી વધારે દીવસ હીયાં ખોટી થવાને નાદુરસ્ત જાણી બીજે દીને સહવારના એટલે તા૦ ૧૩ ફેબ્રુઆરીને દીને કલકત્તાથી આગળ કુચ કરવાનો હમો સઘળાઓએ ઠરાવ કીધો. આગલની મંજલ સારૂ તૈયારી કરવામાં બાકીનો દીવસ હમો રોકાયા હતા, અને એ દીને રાત્રે બેથ્થુન સોસાઈટીમાં પ્રોફેસર કોવેલ એક જાહેર ભાશણ આપવાનો હતો તીહાં હાજર થવાને ડાકટર ડફે હમુને પોતાની ઈછા જણાવી હતી, તેને માન આપવાને હમો તીહાં રાત્રે સાતવાગે હાજર થયા હતા.

આ સભામાં કેળવણી પામેલા જુવાન બાબુઓનો એક અછો મેલાવડો થયો હતો, અને તે ઠેકાણાં ઉપર હમુને પ્રખ્યાત બાબુ કેસબ ચંદ્રસેન સાથે, બાબુ રેવરેંડ લાલ બેહારી ડે અને બીજા બાબુઓ સાથે, પેહેલ વેહેલી ઓળખ થઈ હતી. આ સભામાં સંસ્કૃત કાલેજના પ્રોફેસર કોવેલે એક અગતની બાબદ ઉપર પોતાનું લખાણ વાચીયું હતું. કાહાણી જેવા ઈતીહાસની અને ખરા ઈતીહાસની હદ તથા તેની ખુબી, આવી બાબદ ઉપર અછી રીતે અભીયાસ કરીને બનાવેલું એક સારૂં ભાશણ વાંચી સંભળાવીયું હતું. ભાશણકર્તાએ જબરી ગોલ કરેલી હતી જે તેના લખાણમાં માલુમ પડતી હતી, અને લખાણની એબારતબંદીમાં પણ અછું ધીયાન પોહોચાડેલું હતું. હમો આ નીબંધ વીશે આટલું બારીકીથી બોલીએછ તેનું કારણ એટલુંજ છે કે મુંબઈના હાલના વખતમાં કેટલાક લોકનાં મનમાં એવો વીચાર પેઠેલો છેકે કોઈબી સભાની સાંભણે ભાશણ આપવું એમાં શું મોટી બીસાત છે. થોડીક બાબદો એણીગમ પેલીગમથી જેમ જેને મળી આવે તેમ તેણે એકઠી

કરીને, સભાની સાંભણે પોતાની વીચારશક્તિ જેમ ફરમાવે તેમ તે બોલી અથવા વાંચી જવી, અને આવી રીતે સભાનો વખ્ત અરધો કલાક અથવા કલાક એક રોકીયો, એટલે એમ સમજવું કે તેઓએ ભાશણ કીધું, અને તે ભાશણ વળી મોહોડેથી બોલી જઈ તેઓએ કીધું! અને તે વળી એટલી બધી તો જોરાવર મનશક્તિથી કે કાગજ ઉપર લખીયા અથવા જોયા વગરે કીધું! શાબાશ! અવે બાકી શું રેહું! મુંબઈમાં જારે ઘણી ખરી બાબદો વીશે "ઢમઢોલ અને માંહે પોળ"ની કેહેવત મુજબ, ઠગબાજી રમાઈ રેહેલી છે, તારે આવી રીતે કેળવણીના મેદાનમાં પણ ઠગાઈ રમાએ એમાં નવાઈ નથી.

પ્રોફેસર કોવલનું ભાશણ પુરૂં થયા પછી તેને લગતી કેટલીક બાબદ વીશે સભાના શરનશીન ડાકટર ડફે વધારે ખુલાસો કરી સંભળાવીયો હતો અને તીયાર પછી સભા આગળ હમારી મોલાકાત વીશે કહી સંભળાવીયું અને એવી ઇછા કહી જણાવી કે કલકત્તામાં હમો મુસાફર તરીકે આવીયા તે જોઇને તેઓ ઘણા ખુશી થયા હતા અને હમોએ કલકત્તા વીશે, તીહાંનાં દેશી લોક વીશે, તેમની કેળવણી, રીતભાંત વીશે કેવો વીચાર બાંધીયો હતો આ વીશે જો હમો થોડું ઘણું કહી સંભળાવીએ તો સભા તે મોટી ખુશી સાથે સાંભળશે. આ ઉપરથી પેહેલાં હમારા મીત્ર ડાકટર ભાઊ દાજીએ કેટલાક વીચાર કહી સંભળાવીયા, તીયાર પછી આ ગ્રંથકર્ત્તાએ સ્ત્રીકેળવણીવીશે બાબુઓની પછાત જોઈ તે વીશે થોડાક વીચાર કહી સંભળાવીયા હતા, અને હમારી પાછળ શેઠ ખુરશેદજી રૂસ્તમજી કામાજીએ હીંદુઓની અને પારસીઓની કેટલીક પુરાતમ બાબદો મળતી આવેછે તે વીશે કહી સંભળાવીયું હતું. હમો સઘળા બોલી રેહા પાછળ સભાના સરનશીને હમારો ઉપકાર માનતા કલકત્તાના બાબુઓને એક જબરો ફટકો લગાવીયા હતો કે તેઓ હરેક બાબદ ઉપર બોલી જાણેછે અને વારંવાર માત્રે બોલેછે, પણ કરતાં કંઈ નથી, તેથી તેણે ત્રણ નાહાના વાકયો જબરી અસરકારક રીતે બોલી તેનું ભાશણ બંધ કીધું હતું. ડાકટર ડફે જે છેલા વચનો ઉચ્ચારીયા હતા તે આ હતા, "મીત્રો! હવે શબ્દો નથી જોઇતા, હવે કામ જોઇએછ! શબ્દો નહી, કામ! બોલવું નહી, કામ! વચનો નહી, કામ જોઈએછ." આ શબ્દોમાં કહી સંભળાવેલી નસીઅત અત્રેના મુંબઇ-વાળા સાહેબોએ પણ સારી પેઠે પોતાની નજર સાંભણે રાખવી જોઇએછ. આ સભાનો વીગતવાર એહવાલ કલકત્તાના ઇનિડીયન મીરરના ચંચલ અને ખુંધી

અધીપતી રેવરેંડ લાલ બીહારી ડેએ તા૦—૧૮૬૪ના વર્તમાન પત્રમાં છાપી જાહેર કરીયો છે. રાત્રે ૧૧ા વાગે હમો સઘળા પાછા ઘર આવી પુગા હતા, અને સહવારના પોહોરમાં હમો કલકત્તેથી રવાના થવાના હતા તેથી જલદીથી જમીને બીછાના ઉપર ગયા હતા.

આ ઠેકાણે કલકત્તાના સુવાનાં બીછાના વીશે કેહેવાનું એ છે કે તીહાં મછર એટલાં તો જબરાં છે કે ઘણું કરી સઘળા જણ કુરતની વગર રાત્રે સુઈ શકતા નથી. મછર કરડેચ તો કરડેચ પણ કરડીને વલગી રેહેછ, અને જલદીથી પાછું ઉડી જતું નથી, એટલું તે જબરૂં છે. જો કોઇ દોસ્તને રાત્રે કંટાળો આપવો હોય તો તેનાં બીછાંનાની કુરતની ઉઘાડી નાખી એટલે આખી રાત્ર તેને મછરથી જબરો કંટાળો ખમવો પડવાનો. આ ઠેકાણે કલકત્તાને લગતી કેટલીક બાબદો મુકીદેઈ હમને આગળ ચાલવાની ફરજ પડેછે.

તા૦ ૨૩ મી ફેબ્રુઆરી. કલકત્તાથી સહવારના સાત વાગે સઘળા દોસ્તોને મળી ભેટીને નીકલ્યા અને નદી પારકરી હોરાના સ્ટેશન ઉપર ૧૧) વાગે જઈ પુગા હતા. આ મથક ઉપરથી રેલવેના બે ભાગ થયા છે, એક લાઇન હીયાંથી નીકલેલી દીલ્લી તરફ ચાલેલી છે, અને બીજી લાઈન દક્ષીણ તરફ જબલપોર સુધી ચાલી છે, જીહાં, મુંબઈની જી. આઈ. પી. રેલવેની લાઈન, ઉપલી જબલપોરની લાઈન સાથે મળેછે. કલકત્તામાંથી રેલવેની ત્રીજી લાઈન ઊગમણ તરફ "આસામ" પ્રાંત તરફ જાયછે, જેનું મથક કલકત્તા શેહેરમાંજ છે.

હમોએ હોરાના સ્ટેશન ઉપરથી પેહેલાં રાણીગંજ જવાની ટીકીટો લીધી, કારણ રાણીગંજ આગળ કોળસાની એક મોહોટી ખાણ છે, જેમાંથી બંગાલના રેલવેને ઘણો ખરો કોળસો મળી શકેછે, તે જોવાની ખાએશ થઈ હતી. આગગાડી બરોબર ૧૧) વાગે ઉપડી હતી અને થોડુંક આગળ ચાલતાં હોરાનું ગામ હમારી નજરે પડયું હતું. આ ઠેકાણાં ઉપર નાળીએરી, તાડ, કેડ, ખજુરાંનાં ઝાડોની ગીચ ઘટા નજરે પડી હતી, તથા ભાતના અને બીજી ખેતી વાડીવાળાં ખેતરો પણ પુશ્કલ દેખાયાં હતાં. આસપાસની જમીન સઘળી સાફ સપાટ હતી, એક પણ ટેકરી અથવા ડુંગર અથવા ખડક નજર નહી પડતો હતો અને જમીન તમામ જાણે બાગ બગીચાવાળી હોય એવી તાજી અને લીલોત્રીથી ભરપુર નજર આવતી હતી. જે કોઇ મુસાફર પેહેલ વેહેલો હીંદુસ્થાનમાં દરીયાને માર્ગે કલકત્તે

આવે અને હીયાંથી આ દેશની જમીનની હાલત તપાસવાને બાહેર નીકલે, તો તે મુસાફરને જેમ કલકત્તામાં પેહેલ વેહેલું પગલું મુકતાંજ તે શેહેર જાણે મેહેલોનું શેહેર હોય એવું તેની નજર સાંભણે પડેછે, તેમજ હોરાથી આગળ ચાલતાં હીંદુસ્થાનની જમીન પેહેલ વેહેલી તેની સાંભણે તમામ ખેતીવાડી ભરેલી અને જાણે બાગ બગીચાથી ભરપુર હોય એવી થોડેક ઠેકાણે નજરે પડેછે, જેથી મુસાફરના મન ઉપર પેહેલીજ અસર એવી તો થઈ પડવાનીજ કે હીંદુસ્થાન ખરેખરજ ફુલવાડી અને બાગો બાહારની જમીન છે. હીયાંથી એકુ બે સ્ટેશન મુકીને આગળ વધતાં, સીરાંમપોરના સ્ટેશન આગળ આગ ગાડીએ પાંચ મીનીટનો વીસામો લીધો હતો. "સીરાંમપોર" શેહેરમાં જવાની હમને જોગવાઈ નહી મળી હતી. આ શેહેરમાં કલકત્તાનું એક વખણાયલું ઇંગેજી વર્તમાન પત્ર નામે "ફ્રેંડ આફ ઇનડીયા" છપાયછે. જો કે આ પત્રનું નામ "હીંદુસ્થાનનો દોસ્ત" કરીને રાખેલું છે, તોએબી હીંદુસ્થાનના દેશીઓના દોસ્તને બદલે હીંદુસ્થાનમાં આવેલા ઇંગ્રેજ લોકના દોસ્ત તરીકે એ પત્રે સારી સેવા બજાવી છે. જો આ પેહેલાં પુસ્તકમાં જગા વધારે મળી હતે તો કલકત્તાના વર્તમાન પત્રો અને મુંબઇના વર્ત્તમાન પત્રોનો મુકાબલો કરવાને હમને સારી જોગવાઈ હતી, પણ હાલ આ અગતની બાબદ વીશે હમારેથી કંઈ લખાઈ શકાતું નથી. વર્તમાન પત્રો વીશે હમારી મુસાફરીમાં કેટલીક બાબદો હમોને મળી છે તે હવે પછીના પુસ્તકમાં લખી જણાવાની ઉમેદ રાખીએછ, અને જે ઠેકાણાં ઉપર એ અગતની બાબદ વીશે બોલવાનું છે તે હવે પછીના મુસાફરીના એક અગતના ભાગમાં આવેછે તીહાં આ બાબદ વીશે વીસ્તારીને બોલશું.

હીયાંથી આગળ વધતાં "ચંદરનગર" નું સ્ટેશન આવેછે, જે શેહેર ફ્રેંચ સત્તાવાળાઓનું છે. બે અથવા ચાર સ્ટેશન બીજાં છોડીયાં પછી, "બરદ્વાન" શેહેર આગળ એક મોહોટું સ્ટેશન આવેછે, જીહાં આગગાડી નજદીક એક કલાક સુધી ખોટી થાયછે. હીયાંથી આગગાડીની એક લાઈનને જુદી પાડીને "રાણીગંજ" નાં કોળસાની ખાણ તરફ લઈ જવામાં આવી છે, તેથી "બરદ્વાન" સ્ટેશન આગળથી રાણીગંજ જવાને ઉતારૂઓને પેહેલી ગાડીમાંથી ઉતરી બીજી આગગાડીમાં બેસવું પડેછે. બરદ્વાનથી બપોરના બે વાગે નીકલીયા. હજુર જમીન સાફ સપાટ જોવામાં આવતી હતી, અને લીલોત્રી પણ તેમજ ખટકે ખટકે નજરે

પડયા કરતી હતી. પાનાઘર સ્ટેશન આગળ આવી પોહોંચતાં, ટેકરીઓ અને નાહાની ડુંગરીઓ નજરે પડવા માંડી, અને હીયાંથી જમીનનો દેખાવ લીલોત્રી ભરેલો દેખાવાને બદલે, વેરાન અને ખડક જેવો નજરે પડવા લાગો. પાછલા પોહોરના સવાચાર વાગે રાણીગંજના સ્ટેશન ઉપર આવી પુગા. આસપાસનો દેખાવ હવે ડુંગર, પાહાડ, અને બીયાબાન જંગલ જેવો હતો. જમીન પણ તેવીજ વાંકીટીકી અને એણીગમ પેલીગમ પાણીના ખબોચીયાવાળી હતી. સ્ટેશન ઉપર ઉતરીને રાત્રે રેહેવાસારૂ, તેવો લાયક મકાન મેળવવાની ખબર કાહાડતાં, માલુમ પડયું કે બંગલા જેવો કોઈબી મકાન તીહાં નહી હતો. એકાદ બે ઝાવલીના છાપરાં હતાં, જે હાટેલ તરીકે વપરાતાં હતાં. તેમાં જઈ રેહેવાને સગવડ જેવું નહી માલુમ પડીઆથી, રાત્ર તો, આગગાડીના સ્ટેશન ઉપરના ઉતારૂઓને આસરો લેવાના ઓરડામાંજ, ગુજારવાનો ઠરાવ કીધો. આ ઠેકાણાં ઉપર ખાવા પીવાની જીનસો સારી અને પુરતી નહી મળી આવવાની ખબર સાંભળીને સઘળાઓએ ઠરાવ કીધો, કે સહવારના પોહોરમાં કોળસાની ખાણ જોઈ બીજે દીને રાત્રે રાણીગંજથી રૂખસદ લઈ પાછા "બરદ્વાન" જવું. જે ઠેકાણે હમો ઉતરીયા હતા તીહાંથી કોળસાની ખાણ નજદીક બેથી ત્રણ માઈલ દુર હતી, માટે એ ખાણના ઉપરી મી. લાડની રજા, સાંજના લઈ રાખી, સહવારના પોહોરમાં થંડેપોરે તે જોઈ લેવી, એવો બંદોબસ્ત કરવાને હમારામાંથી બે ત્રણ જણ તેજ સાંજના કોળસાની ખાણના ઉપરીને તેને બંગલે મળવાને ગયા હતા. હમોએ ભાડુતી ગાડી માંગી જે ઉપરથી હમારે સારૂ એક ઘોડાની ભાડુતી ગાડી જેને તીહાંનાં લોક "એક્કા" કરીને બોલેછે, તે લાવી હાજર કીધી હતી. આ ગાડીમાં માત્રે બે જણ બેસી શકે એવી ગોઠવણ કરેલી છે. એક હાંકનાર આગળ બેસેછે અને તેની પાછળ એકજ ઉતારૂ બેસી શકે એટલીજ જગા હોયછે. એક્કાના ઘોડાનું હરનીસ, તથા ગાડી એવી તો જાસ્લાપોરી હાલતમાં હતાં કે ઢેકાંઢરીયાં અને ડુંગરની જગા ઉપર આવી ગાડીમાં બેસીને જવું હમોએ સલામતી ભરેલું નહી ગણીયું હતું, અને વધારે ધાસ્તી ભરેલું એ હતું કે ઘોડો ઉંચો અને ગાડીમાં બેસવાની જગો નીચી હતી, તેથી જો ઘોડો ચમકીને લાત ઝાડે તો હાંકનાર અને ઉતારૂ બંઘેના કોઠાં ગેપ થાય એવી કફોરી તે ગાડી હતી, અને જે વળી હમોએ પેહેલવેહેલી જોઈ હતી, તેથી તેમાં બેસવાને હમોએ નાપાડી. આ ઠેકાણે ભાડેની

પાલકી પણ મળી શકેછે, જે ઉપરથી હમોએ પાલકીઓ મંગાવી, કોળસાની ખાણના ઉપરીના બંગલે જવાને તેમાં બેઠા. થોડાક ઠેકાણાં સુધી રસ્તો સફાઈ ભરેલો હતો તેથી હમાલો મુગા મુગા ચાલીયા હતા, પણ જરા આગળ વધતાં, આગળના બંને હમાલોએ, તેમની બોલીમાં એક તરેનું ગાયન ગાવાનું સીરૂ કીધું. આ ગાયનની મતલબ હમો પેહેલાં સમજી નહી શકીયા હતા, પણ પુછવાથી ખોલાસો થયો હતો કે આગળના બે હમાલો ચાલતાં પોતાના પગતળે આવતી જમીનનું બયાન, રાગના અવાજે બોલી, પાછળના બે હમાલોને ચેતવણી આપતા હતા, કે જે તરેની જમીન પગેતળે આવેછે, તે જમીન કાંકરાની છે કે ખડકની છે, આડા ખબોચીયાની છે કે સપાટ છે, ચઢણનો ટેકરો આવીયો છે કે ઉતરણ આવી છે, એવી તરેનું બયાન ગાઇને બોલતા હતા. આગળના બે હમાલોના બોલવાને પાછલના બે હમાલો, હાં—હાં બોલી જવાબ આપતા રેહેતા હતા. આગળ પાછળના હમાલો ગાતા હતા, તેઓ આવી રીતે ગાતા હતા. સંભાળજે, ડાવીગમ કંકર (પથર)—પાછળના હમાલો,—હાં હાં.-સંભાળજે, જમણીગમ ખાડો. હાં, હાં, સંભાળજે, ડાવીગમ કાંટા,—હાં—હાં—. સંભાળજે, જમણીગમ પાણી,—હાં—હાં. સંભાળજે, ચઢણ આવી છે,—હાં—હાં. આ પ્રમાણે આગળના હમાલો, પાછળના હમાલોને ચોકસાઇથી ચાલવાને જે સુચના કરતા હતા, તેનો રાગ સાંભળવાને પસંદ પડતો હતો. આ ઠેકાણાં ઉપરના હમાલો કાહાર જાતીના બંગાલીઓ છે, જેમાંના ઘણુંકરીને કલકત્તામાં પાલકીજ ઉંચકવાંનો ધંધો કરેછે. તેઓ કાળા સીહા રંગના છે, અને તેમના ચેહેરાનો અથવા શરીરનો ઘટમ દીલપસંદ નથી. કોળસાની ખાણના ઉપરીને મળતાં છેક રાત્રે સાત વાગા હતા, અને ખાણમાં જવાસારૂ તેની પરવાનગી મેળવતાં તથા તેને લગતી બીજી વાતચીત કરતાં રાત્રે છેક આઠ વાગા હતા, અને રેલવે સ્ટેશન ઉપર પાછું આવતાં નજદીક રાત્રે નવથી દસ વાગાનો સુમાર થયલો હતો. થાક જબરી લાગી હતી, પાલકી હોવા છતાં પણ પગે જબરૂ રખડવું પડીયું હતું, થંડી બહુ પડતી હતી માટે આવતાંને વાર ગલાસ ભરીને પેલો ઉત્તેજક પદાર્થ ચઢાવી, જમવા બેસી ગયા હતા.

તા૦ ૧૪ મી ફેબ્રુઆરી. કોળસાની ખાણ જોવાને સહવારના નાસ્તો લેઇને નીકલીયા હતા. ખાણનાં ઉપરી મી. લાડે કેહેલું હતું કે સહવારના ૧૦) વાગા સુધી ખાણમાં કામ કરનારાં લોક આવતાં નથી, તેથી આ વખતની આગમચ જોવા

જવાને સવલ નથી પડવાનું. રાણીગંજની કોળસાની ખાણ ૧૮૫૨-૫૩ થી જણાયલી છે, અને તેમાંથી કોળસો ખણી કાહાડવાને "બૅંગાલ કોલ કંપની લીમીટિડ" નામની ભાગીદારોની એક કંપની થઇ છે, જેવાએ આજ સુધી સારી કમાઇથી કામ ચલાવેલું છે. બંગાલ પ્રાંતના રેલવે ઉપર ઘણું કરીને હીયાંનો કોળસો વપરાયછે, અને સુએજને મારગે કલકત્તે આવતી આગબોટોમાં પણ હવડાં એ કોળસો વપરાવા લાગો છે. કેહેછે કે આ કંપનીએ સેકડે ૧૦ ટકાથી ૧૬ ટકાનું વીયાજ આપીયું છે. રાણીગંજ અને તેની આસપાસની જગા ઉપર કોળસાની ખાણ મોટી લાગેલી છે, જો કે જે ખાણ હમારા જોવામાં આવી હતી તે ઘણીજ નાહાની હતી. તે આસરે વીસ્તારમાં બે માઈલ હતી. ખાણમાં ઉતરવાનો માર્ગ જમીનની સપાટી ઉપરથી અંદર ઉતરતો કરેલો છે. નવથી દસ ફુટ પોહોળો રસ્તો સેહેડીની માફક ઉતરતો બનાવેલો છે. જમીનની થોડીક ઉંડાણમાં આવે રસ્તે ઊતરીયા પછી, કોળસાનાં થર નજરે પડવા માંડુછે. એ પડોમાં ખોદણી કરીને "બોરઘાટ" ના જેવા ટનલો કોતરેલા છે. આ ટનલોમાંથી મસાલની રોશનીથી આગળ ચાલતાં, જે જગા ઉપર કોળસાની ખોદણી ચાલેછે તીહાં આવી પુગીએછ. આ ઠેકાણે સઘલું અંધારૂં અને હવા ઘણી ગરમ લાગેછે. સાફ ખોલી અને થંડી હવા તથા ઉજાસ આવવાને જમીનની સપાટી ઉપરથી બગાડાં પડેલાં છે. આવાં બગાડ આગળ આવીને જો આપણે ઉભા હોઈએ તો તીહાં થંડો પવન આપણને લાગેછે. આખી ખાણની અંદર ૨૫ થી ૩૦ બગાડાં ઠેકાણે ઠેકાણે પાડેલાં છે. કોળસાની ખોદણીનો આકાર મસાલની રોશનીથી જોતાં, આબેહુબ ઘારાપોરીના અથવા એવાંજ બીજાં પાહાડની અંદરનાં કોતરકામને મળતો આવેછે. જેમ જેમ કોળસો ખોદીને આગળ વધતા જાયછે તેમ તેમ ડાવી અને જમણી બોરદુએ કોળસાનાજ થામલા ટેકાવ સારૂ રાખીને આસપાસથી ખોદતા જાયછે. ખોદેલા કોળસાને ટોપલામાં ભરીને એક ઠેકાણે લાવી એકઠો કરેછે અને તીહાંથી લોહેડાંની રેલ ઊપર ચાલતી ગાડીઓમાં ભરીને માણસો કોળસાની ખાણના મોહોડાં આગળ લાવેછે અને જીહાંથી જમીન ઉપર કપીથી ખેંચી લીએછે. કોળસાના પડોમાંથી વરસાદની મોઆફક પાણીના ઝરા વરશેછે, જે પાણી બુંબાની મારફતે બાહેર ખેંચી કાહાડેછે. આએ ખાણની અંદર મસાલ લઈ જવામાં કંઈ ધાસ્તી જેવું નથી, તેનું કારણ એ જે એ ખાણ કંઈ ઘણી ઊંડી નથી, તેની

સાથે જોઈએ તે કરતાં વધારે તાજી હવા દાખલ કરવાને જમીનની સપાટી ઉપરથી બગાડાં પાડેલાં છે, તેથી અંદર ગુંગળાઈ જવા જેવી ધાસ્તી મુતલક છેજ નહી. જ્યારે હમો જોવાને ગયા તારે સઘળી મળીને ૩૦૦ ફુટ ઊંડી ખાણ ખોદાયલી હતી. કામ કરનારા મજુર લોકોની સંખીયા તે વખતે આસરે ૧૮૦૦ થી ૨૦૦૦ માણસોની હતી. તેમાં તરેવાર જાતનાં સ્ત્રી અને પુરૂશ લોક હતાં. સંથાલ જે મઉથી જંગલી જાત અને ઘણીજ ખુની જાત કેહેવાયછે, અને જે જાતના લોકોએ ઇંગ્રેજ સરકાર સાંભણે વારંવાર ફીસાદ ઉઠાવીયો છે, તે જાતનાં લોક આ ઠેકાણે ઘણાજ દીલાજાનથી ધંધે રોજગારે લાગી ગયલાં માલુમ પડયાં હતાં. બીજી જાતમાં કાહાર જાત (હમાલ લોક) બરાથીન, બૌરી, અને કોલી જાત હતી. સંથાલ લોકનું નાંમ સાંભળીને હમોને તે જાતના પુરૂશ, અને સ્ત્રીઓને જોવાની ઘણી ઇછા થઈ હતી. હમારી સાંભણે કેટલાકને લાવી ઉભાં રાખીયાં હતાં, જેમને જોયાથી, આ લોકના જંગલીપણાની અથવા ખુની ખસલતની નીશાનો તેમના ચેહેરા ઉપર મુતલક નજર નહી આવી હતી, બલકે ઉલટું એવું દેખાયું હતું કે આવા જંગલી લોકમાં તેઓના ચેહેરાનો ઘાટમ સારો સોભઇતો અને રાંક દેખતો હતો. તેમની ચામડીનો રંગ કાળો સીહાઈ જેવો પણ ચકચકીત હતો. સ્ત્રીલોક અંધારામાં જબરી સખત મેહનત કરતી હતી. કોળસો ખોદવાને પાહારાઈ અને પીકાંઉ મારવાનુ કામ મરદોને સોંપેલું હતું, અને કોળસો ટોપલીમાં ભરીને ઠેકાણાં સર લેઈજવાને સ્ત્રીઓને કામે લગાડેલી હતી. સહવારના ૧૦ વાગેથી તે સાંજના ૪ વાગાસુધી લોક કામઉપર રેહેછે અને રાત્રે સઉ કોઈ પોતાને ઘેર જાયછે.

ખાણમાં ઊતરવાને જરાબી ધાસ્તી જેવું નથી. હમો પેહેલાં એવું ધારતા હતા કે કપી અથવા ચારીથી હમુને નીચે જમીનમાં ઉતારશે. પણ આ ઠેકાણે ઊંડાણ ઘણી નહી હોવાથી ફકત સીડીડી જેવા રસ્તો હીયાં કીધેલા હતો, જો કે હમુને એવું કેહેવામાં આવીયું હતું કે બીજી જગા ઉપરની ખાણો વધારે ઊંડી ગયાથી, તીહાં કપીથી ઉતરવાના માર્ગો કરેલા છે.

ખાણમાંથી હમો પાછા ઊપર આવીયા અને અંદર કાહડેલા કોળસાનો ઢગ જાતા હતા એવામાં હમારી આસપાસ કેટલાક મજુર લોક આવી એકઠા થયા હતા. તેઓમાંના એક સંથાલ છોકરાને આપણા ચંચલ મીત્ર ડાકટર ભાઉ દાજીએ તેની દેશી ભારામાં ગાયણ ગાવાને કેહું. પેહેલાં તો તે છોકરો સરમાયો, અને

આનાકાની કીધી, પણ જારે પઈસા ઉપર તેની નજર પડી, એટલે તેને હીમત આવી. આ છોકરાએ જે રાગ ગાયો તેના શબ્દોનો અર્થ તો હમો સમજી શક્યા નહી, પણ તેના રાગની ધપ ઊપરથી અને બેચાર શબ્દો તેના મોહોડાંથી સંભળાયા તે ઉપરથી હમો સઘળા સમજીયા હતા કે તે છોકરાએ સંથાલ લોકની હોલીનો રાગ ગાયો હતો. આવા જંગલી લોકમાં પણ રાગની લેહજત અને રાગનું ગ્નાન છે, એ જોઈ હમોને ખુસી સાથની તાજુબી ઉત્પન્ન થઈ હતી. તાજુબી એટલા સારૂ કે આવા જંગલી લોકમાં પણ પેલા અવતારી કૃષ્ણનું નામ મશહુર થયલું છે, અને તે એકજ રીતે અને એકજ મતલબે આખ્ખા હીંદુસ્થાનમાં,શેહેરે શેહેર, અને ગામે ગામ અને હમો વધારીને બોલીએછ, કે જંગલે જંગલ વટીક જાહેર થઈ પડેલું છે. મથુરા શેહેરમાં જન્મ પામેલા શ્રી કૃષ્ણ, વિષ્ણુનો આઠમો અવતાર, નંદ ગોવાળીયાનો ચેલો, ગોકુળની હજારો ગોપીઓનો મનોહારી ગોપાલ,બીજકો બાંકોબાસી, શ્યામલ ગીરધારી, કાહાન અથવા જગપ્રસિદ્ધ કનૈયો અને તેની મધુર, મનમોહન મુરલી અથવા બાંસરી વીશે હીંદુસ્થાનમાં નાહાનાથી મોહોટાં અને જંગલીથી સુધરેલા તમામ લોક જાણીતાં થયલાં છે. પેલા સંથાલ છોકરાના મોહોડામાંથી આ શબ્દો નીકળતાંને વાર હમો પામી ગયા હતા કે "કાહાના બાંસરી બજાઈ" એ મતલબનું ગાયન તે કરેછે. ગાયનની બાબદ ઉપર હમો વધારે વીગતથી મથુરા, બીંદ્રાબન, ગોકુલ અને બીજ શેહેરો તથા દીલ્લી, ગોવાલીયર અને ઈનદોર વીશે બયાન કરતી વેલા બોલવાની ઉમેદ રાખીએછ. ગાયનનો રસ હજુર હીંદુસ્થાનના એ શેહેરોમાં કેવો અને કેટલો બાકી રહેલો છે તે હમો સારીપેઠે દેખડાવી શકશું.

સંથાલ લોક ઘણું કરીને કમરથી માથાસુધી નાગા રેહેછે, પણ આ ઠેકાણાં ઉપર કામે લાગેલા મજુરોએ આખ્ખાં શરીર ઉપર મુલાહજા ભરેલો પોશાક પેહેરેલો હતો, તે ખાણના ઉપરી યુરોપીયનના સમજાવીયા ઉપરથી, પેહેરેલા હતો, અને એકવાર તેમને ટેવ પડીયાથી તેવા પોશાક વગર તેમને ગમતું નહી હતું. આ લોક જબરા દારૂ પીનારાં છે, પોતાની કમાઇનો ઘણોખરો ભાગ દારૂ પીવામાં ખરચી નાખેછે, એવું હમને જણાવામાં આવીયું હતું.

હમો બાકીનો અહેવાલ આ પુસ્તકમાં વધારે આગલ ચલાવી નથી શકતા તેથી ખચીત દીલગીર છઈએ. જો આપણા દેશીઓ તરફથી આ અહેવાલના પેહેલાં પુસ્તકને પુરતો આસરો મળીઓ તો હમો આ મુસાફરીનો બાકીનો ભાગ

જે ઘણોજ વધારે જાણવાજોગ અને દીલપસંદ છે તે આપવાને આમ લોકની સેવા બજાવાને દીલોજાનથી હાજર થઈશું. પણ અગર એવું નહી બનીયું અને એની કદર નહીં બુજાઈ તો બીજું પુસ્તક લખવાને હમારી હીમત ચાલી નથી શકવાની. આ પુસ્તકને છેડે આપેલાં કીમતી ચીત્રો કેહેશે કે હજુર કેટલી અગતની બાબદો જાણવાની બાકી છે, પણ વગરમદદે આવું કીધાથી હમારી ઉપર નાણાં સંબંધી જે બોજો પડે તે ખમવાને, હમો હમારૂં અશક્તપણું છુપાવા નથી ચાહતા.

મુંબઈ, તા. ૩૦ એપરેલ, ૧૮૭૧.

પુસ્તક પેહેલું સમાપ્ત.

DILKHOOSHA — LUCKNOW

૧. દીલખુશા — લખનૌ.

MARTINIE

LUCKNOW

VIEW OF THE RIVER GOOMTEE.—LUCKNOW.

૩. ગોમટી નદીનો દેખાવ.—લખનૌ.

RIVER FACE OF CHATTAR MANZIL, LUCKNOW.

૪. છતરમંઝીલનો નદી ઉપરથી દેખાવ.—લખનૌ

CHATTAR MANZIL FROM WEST — LUCKNOW

૫. છતરમંજીલનો દેખાવ પસચીમ તરફથી-લખનૌ

CHATTAR MANZIL _ LUCKNOW

KHOORSHED MANZIL.—LUCKNOW

૭. ખુરશેદ મંઝલ.—લખનૌ.

GATE OF KAISERBAG, LUCKNOW.

૮. કૈસરબાગનો દરવાજો.—લખનૌ.

BAILEY GUARD GATE, LUCKNOW

૯. બેલીગાર્ડનો દરવાજો.—લખનૌ.

RESIDENCY, LUCKNOW

૧૦. રેસીડેનસી.—લખનૌ.

RESIDENCY LUCKNOW

૧૧. રેસીડેનસી.—લખનૌ.

GATE OF GREAT IMAMBARA, LUCKNOW

૧૨. મોટા ઇમામબારાનો દરવાજો.—લખનૌ.

GATE OF HOSEENABAD _ LUCKNOW.

૧૩. હુસેનાબાદનો દરવાજો.—લખનૌ.

TOMB AT HOS

૧૪. હુસેનાબાદ

... LUCKNOW

-લખનૌ.

FORT OF AGRA FROM THE RIVER.

૧. નદીપરથી દેખાતો આગરાનો કીલ્લો.

PALACE IN FORT _ AGRA

૨. આગરાના કીલ્લામાંનો મેહેલ.

JEHANGIREE MAHAL AGRA

૪. જહાનગીરી મેહલ.—આગરા.

૪. મોતી મસજીદ.—આગ્રા.

FRONT VIEW OF TAJ — AGRA

૫. તાજનો સાંમો દેખાવ.—આગરા.

TAJ FROM THE RIVER, AGRA.

૬. નદીપરથી દેખાવ.—આગ્રા.

TAJ FROM RIVER SIDE AGRA

૭. નદીની બાજુએથી દેખાતો તાજ.— આગરા.

TAJ FROM RUINED PALACE AGRA

૮. વેરાન મેહલપરથી દેખાતો તાજ.—આગરા.

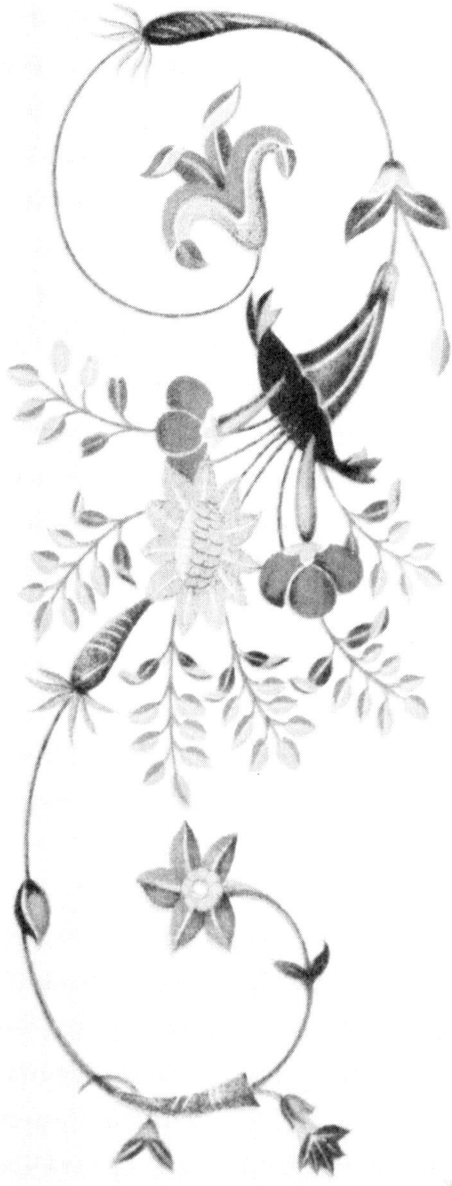

ORNAMENT ON THE TOMB.—AGRA.

૧૦. કબર ઉપરના મીનાકાર જવાહેરનાં ફુલો.-આગરા

PLANT ON THE TOMB, AGRA

૧૧. કબર ઉપરનું મીનાકાર જવાહિરનું ઝાડ.-આગરા.

THE TAJ MAHAL _ AGRA

૧૨. તાજમિહેલ.— આગરા.

GATEWAY OF THE TA. AGRA.

૧૬. તાજમેહેલનો દરવાજો.— આગરા.

Vincent Brooks lith.

SIDE VIEW OF THE GATE _ AGRA

૧૪. તાજના દરવાજાનો બાજુનો દેખાવ.—આગરા.

TOMB OF EMPEROR AKBAR AT SECUNDRA.

૨૫. સેકિંદરા આગળ શાહાનશાહ અકબરની કબરઘા.—
આગરા.

Vincent Brooks lith

INTERIOR OF THE TOMB OF AKBAR AT SECUNDRA

૩૯. સીકંદરા આગરા અકબરની કબરમાંની અંદરનો

GATEWAY AT FUTTEHPORE SECREE.—AGRA

૧૭. ફતેપુર સીકરી આગળનો દરવાજો.—આગરા.

GATEWAY TO THE TOMB OF THE SAINT SALEEM AT FUTTEHPORE SECREE.

૨૭. ફતેપુર સિક્રી મકબરાનો દરવાજો.—આગ્રા.

TOMB OF ITMADOOD DOWLA—AGRA

૧૮. ઇતિમાદુદ દૌલાની કબરગાહ.—આગરા.

LAHORE GATE PALACE DELHI

CASHMERE GATE DELHI

૨. કાશ્મીર દરવાજો.—દીલ્હી.

SELIMGAD AND PALACE DELHI

૩. સેલીમ ઘડ અને મેહેલ.—દીલ્હી.

JUMMA MASJID __ DELHI

૪. જુમ્મા મસજીદ.—દિલ્લી.

TOMB OF MAHOMED TOGLUCK, DELHI

૫. મહમદ તુગલખની કબરથા.—દીલ્હી.

FEROZASHAH'S LAT. DELHI

૯. ફીરોઝશાહની લાટ.—દીલી.

KOOTAB MINAR _ DELHI.

કુતબ મીનાર.—દીલ્હી.

GATE AND IRON PILLAR, DELHI

૮. દરવાજો તથા લોખંડી સ્તંભ.—દીલ્હી.

Vincent Brooks lith.

TOMB OF SUFDARJANG, DELHI.

૬. સફદર જંગની કબરસ્થા.—દીલ્હી.

Vincent Brooks Day & Son, lith.

THE LATE EMPEROR OF DELHI.

૧૦. દીલ્લીનો માજી શાહાનશાહ.

AKBAR SHAH 1836.

૧. અકબરશાહ.

SHAMSHOODIN.

HUNG FOR THE MURDER OF Mr FRASER.

૨. શમશુદીન. જે મી૰ ફ્રેસરના ખુન સારૂ ફાંસી ગયો.

MAUSOLEUM OF THE POET KHUSROO

૩. ખુશરો સાયરની કબરસ્થા.

TOMB OF THE SAINT SALEEM AT FUTTEHPORE SECREE.

૪. ફતેપોર સીકરી આગળ, પીરસાહેબ સલીમની કબરસ્થા.

MIRZA SALEEM, THE EMPEROR'S SON.

૫. બાદશાહ શાહાનશાહનો છોકરો. મીરઝાં સલીમ.

BEGAM SOMBRE

૬. બેગમ સોમબેર.

MAUSOLEUM OF MAZMOODIN OULEEA

૭. મજમુદીન ઓલીયાની કબરસ્થા.

TOMB OF HOOMAYUN.

૮. હુમાયુનની કબરસ્થા.